Management Studies

PEARSON
Custom
Publishing

We work with leading authors to develop the strongest educational materials bringing cutting-edge thinking and best learning practice to a global market.

Under a range of well-known imprints, including Financial Times/Prentice Hall, Addison Wesley and Longman, we craft high quality print and electronic publications which help readers to understand and apply their content, whether studying or at work.

Pearson Custom Publishing enables our customers to access a wide and expanding range of market-leading content from world-renowned authors and develop their own tailor-made book. You choose the content that meets your needs and Pearson Custom Publishing produces a high-quality printed book.

To find out more about custom publishing, visit
www.pearsoncustom.co.uk

A Pearson Custom Publication

Management Studies

Compiled from:

Management: An Introduction
Fouth Edition
by David Boddy

Corporate Governance
Third Edition
by Kenneth A. Kim, John R. Nofsinger and Derek J. Mohr

*Work Psychology: Understanding
Human Behavior in the Workplace*
Fifth Edition
by John Arnold and Ray Randall

Management and Organisational Behaviour
Ninth Edition
by Laurie J. Mullins

PEARSON
Custom
Publishing

Pearson Education Limited
Edinburgh Gate
Harlow
Essex CM20 2JE

And associated companies throughout the world

Visit us on the World Wide Web at:
www.pearsoned.co.uk

First published 2011

This Custom Book Edition © 2011 Published by Pearson Education Limited

Compiled from:

Management: An Introduction
Fouth Edition
by David Boddy
ISBN 978 0 273 71106 3
Copyright © Prentice Hall Europe 1998
Copyright © Pearson Education Limited 2002. 2008

Corporate Governance
Third Edition
by Kenneth A. Kim, John R. Nofsinger and Derek J. Mohr
ISBN 978 0 13 510158 2
Copyright © 2010, 2007, 2004 by Pearson Education, Inc., publishing as Prentice Hall

Work Psychology: Understanding Human Behavior in the Workplace
Fifth Edition
by John Arnold and Ray Randall
ISBN 978 0 273 71121 6
Copyright © Financial Times Professional Limited 1998
Copyright © Pearson Education Limited 1991, 1995, 2005, 2010

Management and Organisational Behaviour
Ninth Edition
by Laurie J. Mullins
ISBN 978 0 273 72408 7
Copyright © Laurie J. Mullins 1985, 1989. 1993, 1996, 1999, 2002, 2005, 2007, 2010

ISBN 978 0 85776 227 6

Printed and bound in Great Britain by 4edge, Hockley, www.4edge.co.uk "FSC Certified"

Contents

Chapter 1

Managing in organisations

Aim

To introduce the tasks, processes and context of managerial work in organisations.

Objectives

By the end of your work on this chapter you should be able to outline the concepts below in your own terms and:

1 Summarise the functions of organisations and how management affects their performance

2 Give examples to show how management is both a universal human activity and a distinct role

3 Compare the roles of general, functional, line, staff and project managers

4 Explain how managers influence others to add value to resources through:

   a. the process of managing (Stewart, Mintzberg and Luthans)

   b. the tasks (or content) of managing and

   c. shaping the contexts within which they and others work

5 Evaluate a manager's approach to the role by analysing how they influence others

6 Explain the elements of critical thinking and use some techniques to develop this skill.

Key terms

This chapter introduces the following ideas:

entrepreneur

innovation

organisation

value

management as a universal human activity

manager

management

management as a distinct role

role

general manager

functional manager

line manager

staff manager

project manager

stakeholders

management task

critical thinking

Each is a term defined within the text, as well as in the Glossary at the end of the book.

Ryanair   www.ryanair.com

In 2007 Ryanair, based in Dublin, was Europe's leading low-cost airline. It was created in 1985 to offer services between Dublin and London, in competition with the established national carrier, Aer Lingus. In the early years the airline changed its business several times – initially a conventional, though slightly cheaper, competitor for Aer Lingus, then a charter company, at times offering a cargo service. The Gulf War in 1990 discouraged people from travelling by air, and caused financial problems for the company. In 1991 senior managers decided to focus the airline as a 'no-frills' operator, in which many traditional features of air travel (free food, drink, newspapers and allocated seats) were no longer available. It aimed to serve a group of flyers who wanted a functional and efficient service rather than luxury.

In 1997 changes in European Union regulations enabled new airlines to enter markets previously dominated by established national carriers such as Air France and British Airways. Ryanair quickly took advantage of this, opening new routes between Dublin and continental Europe. Managers were quick to spot the potential of the Internet, and in 2000 opened Ryanair.com, a booking site: within a year it was selling 75 per cent of seats online, and now sells almost all seats this way. It also made a long-term deal with Boeing to purchase 150 new aircraft over the next eight years.

Several factors enable Ryanair to offer fares to its customers that are significantly below those of traditional carriers:

- Simple fleet – using a single aircraft type (Boeing 737 – most of which are also quite new) simplifies maintenance, training and crew scheduling.
- Secondary airports – using airports away from major cities keeps landing charges low, sometimes as little as £1 per passenger against £10 at a major airport.
- Fast turnrounds – staff typically turn an aircraft around between flights in 25 minutes, compared to

Thierry Tronnel/Corbis

an hour for older airlines. This enables aircraft to spend more time in the air, earning revenue (11 hours compared to 7 at British Airways).
- Simplified operations – not assigning seats at check-in simplifies ticketing and administrative processes, and also ensures that passengers arrive early to get their preferred seat. Flying directly between cities avoids the problems of transferring passengers and baggage between flights, which is where costly mistakes and delays frequently occur.
- Cabin staff collect rubbish before and after landing, saving the cost of expensive cleaning crews which the established carriers choose to use.

Source: *Economist*, 10 July 2004; O'Connell and Williams (2005); and other published information.

Case questions 1.1

- What functions is Ryanair performing?
- What did 'management' contribute to the growth of the airline?
- Give examples of three points at which managers changed what the organisation does and how it works.

1.1   Introduction

An **entrepreneur** is someone with a new venture, project or activity, and is usually associated with creative thinking, driving innovation and championing change.

The Ryanair case illustrates several aspects of management. A group of **entrepreneurs** created an organisation to offer a new service they believed customers would want to buy. The company does this by bringing resources together and transforming them into something with greater value – which they sell to the customers. They differ from their competitors in that they use a different set of resources (e.g. secondary airports) and have different ways of transforming these into outputs (e.g. short turnrounds). They have been innovative in the way they run the business, such as in identifying what some customers value in a flight – cost rather than luxury – and carried a record 40 million passengers in 2006.

Innovation is the process of taking a creative idea and turning it into a useful product, service or method of operation.

Entrepreneurs such as Michael O'Leary of Ryanair are always looking for ways to **innovate** and make the most of new opportunities. Other managers face a different challenge – more demand with less resources. James Morris, who in 2006 was head of the United Nations World Food Programme, was struggling to raise funds to alleviate the famine in southern Africa. Food aid from global donors has fallen while the number of hungry people has increased. In almost every public healthcare organisation managers face a growing demand for treatment but find it difficult to secure the resources to meet it.

Organisations of all kinds – from rapidly growing operations such as Ryanair to established businesses like Royal Dutch Shell or H&M (the Swedish fashion retailer) – depend on people at all levels who can run the current business efficiently, and also innovate. This book is about the knowledge and skills that enable people to meet these expectations, and so build a satisfying and rewarding management career.

Figure 1.1 illustrates the themes of this chapter. It represents the fact that people draw resources from the external environment and manage their transformation into outputs that they hope are of greater value. They pass these back to the environment and the value they obtain in return (money, reputation, goodwill, etc.) enables them to attract new resources to continue in business (shown by the feedback arrow from output to input). If the outputs fail to attract sufficient resources then the enterprise will fail.

The chapter begins by examining the significance of managed organisations in our world. It then outlines what management means and introduces theories about the nature of managerial work. Finally, it introduces ideas on studying management.

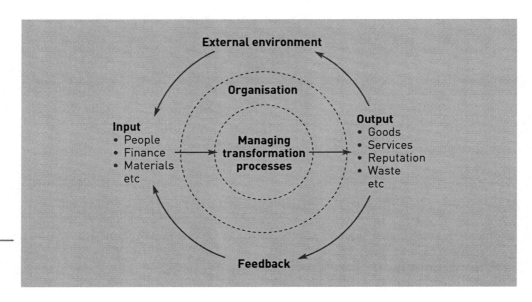

Figure 1.1

Managing organisation and environment

Activity 1.1   **What is management?**

Write a few notes summarising what you think 'management' means.

- You may find it helpful to think of instances in which you have encountered 'management' – such as when you have been managed in your school or university.
- Alternatively, reflect on an occasion when you have managed something, such as a study project. Keep the notes so you can refer to them.

1.2   Management and organisation

We live in a world of managed **organisations**. In a normal day we experience many of them – domestic arrangements of various kinds (family or flatmates), large public organisations (the postal service), small businesses (the newsagent), well-known private companies (which made our jar of coffee), or a voluntary group (the club where we attended a meeting). They have an effect on us and we make some judgement about the encounter. Did the transaction work smoothly or was it surrounded by chaos? Was the service good, reasonable or poor? Will you go there again?

> An **organisation** is a social arrangement for achieving controlled performance towards goals that create value.

Joan Magretta on the innovation of management   key ideas

What were the most important innovations of the past century? Antibiotics and vaccines that doubled, or even tripled, human lifespans? Automobiles and aeroplanes that redefined our idea of distance? New agents of communication, such as the telephone, or the chips, computers and networks that are propelling us into a new economy?

All of these innovations transformed our lives, yet none of them could have taken hold so rapidly or spread so widely without another. That innovation is the discipline of management, the accumulating body of thought and practice that makes organisations work. When we take stock of the productivity gains that drive our prosperity, technology gets all of the credit. In fact, management is doing a lot of the heavy lifting.

Source: Magretta (2002), p. 1.

While we conduct some human activities individually or in family and social groups, we depend on organisations to deliver most of what we use. As we become more specialised in our work we depend more on others, who are equally specialised, to meet our needs. That interdependence requires progressively more complex forms of organisation to make the work productive. Their form varies infinitely, and new types continually evolve – but without them little would get done. The work of management is to build organisations which work, in the sense that they use resources to create **value**: '[the genius of management] is turning complexity and specialization into performance' (Magretta, 2002, p. 2). Commercial organisations create material value, not-for-profit organisations create value through educating people, counselling the troubled or caring for the sick. Theatres, orchestras, museums and art galleries create value by offering inspiration, new perspectives or unexpected insights.

> **Value** is added to resources when they are transformed into goods or services that are worth more than their original cost plus the cost of transformation.

Well-managed organisations create value in many ways. If you buy a ticket from Ryanair you can easily measure the tangible value of a cheap flight. In other purchases the value is *in*tangible, as people judge a product by its appearance, what it feels or smells like, how trendy it is, or whether it fits the image they want to present to the world. Others value good service, or a clear set of instructions on how to assemble their purchase. Good managers understand what customers value, and build an organisation to deliver it – whether in commercial or non-profit enterprises.

management in practice   Creating value in a pub and brewery company

Ralph Findlay (a former geology student) has been Chief Executive of Wolverhampton and Dudley Breweries since 2001. In 2004 the company owned about 1600 pubs and brewed Banks's and Pedigree ales. Findlay knows that he works in an industry where success often comes down to paying attention to detail – such as a lick of paint or some flower-boxes. He says:

> We are in a business that is not actually that complicated. You can overcomplicate it ... A lot of the time it is about somebody in a place like this who has got a smile on his face and wants to welcome his customers. Provided he makes them feel good about coming in, they will keep coming back and that is what it is really about.

FT

Source: From an article by Adam Jones, *Financial Times*, 25 July 2003.

Although the purpose of managing is to add value and create wealth this does not always happen. People may produce goods and services inefficiently, using more resources than customers are willing to pay for. Their work may create pollution and waste, so destroying wealth: the growth of air travel increases carbon dioxide emissions and so contributes to climate change. Work can create value for some and destroy it for others. Motorway builders create value for road users, residents of by-passed villages, and their shareholders – but destroy value (from their opponents' perspective) if the route damages an ancient woodland rich in history and wildlife. From the latter perspective the company has used resources to destroy natural wealth and has reduced, not created, value. The idea of creating value is subjective and relative.

It is not only commercial organisations that create value by providing goods and services. To a degree that is not commonly recognised, voluntary and non-profit organisations (VNPOs) provide many services in health care, culture, environment, social services and education – Barnado's, The Salvation Army, Age Concern – and thousands more. Osborne (1996) points out that managing such organisations combines issues unique to the sector (maintaining good relationships with donors or funding bodies) with others which are common in commercial organisations (business planning, marketing or quality). Charities such as Oxfam or Greenpeace were created by a few like-minded individuals, and have become worldwide organisations with significant operations to raise funds and manage their activities. Donors and recipients expect them to manage resources well so that they add value (Lewis, 2001).

Other organisations add value by serving particular interests such as Unison, a trade union that represents workers in the UK public sector, or the Law Society, which defends the interests of lawyers. Firms in most industries create trade organisations to protect their interests by lobbying or public relations work. Organisations of all kinds can create value by providing psychological support for members and non-members. Corporate scandals at prominent companies such as Enron and Parmalat have indicated the greed and self-interest of some directors and senior managers, who saw them as vehicles for personal enrichment. Table 1.1 summarises these organisational functions.

Function	Description	Examples
Create value, wealth or human well-being	By providing goods and services that people value	Commercial, public sector, voluntary and non-profit, and non-governmental organisations (NGOs)
Articulate and implement ideals	Individuals with an interest in a topic, or a passion to change something, usually need the support of others	Charities, protest groups, political parties
Gain power to protect sectional interests	Large organisations have access to political and economic resources beyond those of individuals	Trade unions, professional associations, industry groups
Give people work, status and social contact	A source of jobs, training, careers, contact with others, a wider outlook, a source of structure in life	Any long-lasting and respected organisation
Enrich directors or senior managers	When those in charge work for personal gain by providing misleading information to shareholders or regulators	Scandals at Enron (US), Ahold (The Netherlands) or Parmalat (Italy)

Table 1.1

Some functions of organisations

Activity 1.2   Managing in a voluntary organisation

The Charities Commission (which regulates charities in England and Wales) estimates that the 190,000 charities in England and Wales have an annual income of £38 billion – equal to about 3.4 per cent of gross domestic product. Ninety per cent of this income is received by the 10,000 largest charities such as Age Concern and the Royal Society for the Protection of Birds (Charities Commission Annual Report for 2005–06, available at **www.charitycommission.gov.uk**). Running a large charity is at least as demanding a management job as running a commercial business.

- If you are connected with a charity or voluntary group, reflect on how it is managed.
- What management issues have you been aware of in that work?

Whatever its function, how well an organisation performs its value-creating role depends on those who work within it. Luck plays a part, but most of the time it is the quality of management that determines whether an organisation fails or succeeds.

1.3   Meanings of management

Management as a universal human activity

People called managers are not alone in requiring the skills of management. As individuals we run our lives and careers: in this respect we are managing. Family members manage children, elderly dependants and households. Management is both a **universal human activity** and a distinct occupation. In the first sense, people manage an infinite range of activities:

Management as a universal human activity occurs whenever people take responsibility for an activity and consciously try to shape its progress and outcome.

When human beings 'manage' their work, they take responsibility for its purpose, progress and outcome by exercising the quintessentially human capacity to stand back from experience and to regard it prospectively, in terms of what will happen; reflectively, in terms of what is happening; and retrospectively, in terms of what has happened. Thus management is an expression of human agency, the capacity actively to shape and direct the world, rather than simply react to it. (Hales, 2001, p. 2)

A manager is someone who gets things done with the aid of people and other resources.

Management is the activity of getting things done with the aid of people and other resources.

Rosemary Stewart (1967) expressed this idea when she described a **manager** as someone who gets things done with the aid of people and other resources, which leads to a definition of management as the activity of getting things done with the aid of people and other resources. So described, **management** is a feature of most human circumstances – domestic, social and political – as well as in formally established organisations.

In pre-industrial societies people typically work alone or in family units. They retain control of the time and other resources used in producing goods and services. They decide what to make, how to make it and where to sell it, combining work and management to create value. Self-employed craftworkers, professionals in small practices and those in a one-person business do this every day. We all do it in household tasks or voluntary activities in which we do the work (planting trees or selling tickets for a prize draw) and the management activities (planning the winter programme).

Activity 1.3   Think about the definition

Choose some domestic, community or business activity you have undertaken.

- What, specifically, did you do to 'get things done with the aid of people and other resources'?
- Decide if the definition accurately describes 'management'.
- If not, how would you change it?

Management as a distinct role

Management as a distinct role develops when activities previously embedded in the work itself become the responsibility not of the employee, but of owners or their agents.

Human action can also separate the 'management' element of a task from the 'work' element, thus creating 'managers' who are in some degree apart from those doing the work. **Management as a distinct role** emerges when external agents, such as a private owner of capital, or the state, gain some control of a work process that a person used to complete themselves. Such agents then have more say in decisions about what to make, how to make it and where to sell it. They take responsibility for some management tasks previously integrated with the work – even if their job titles do not include the term 'management'. Previously independent workers become employees, selling their labour rather than the results of their labour. During the process of industrialisation in western economies, factory owners took control of the physical and financial means of production. They also tried to take control of the time, behaviour and skills of those who were now employees rather than autonomous workers.

A role is the sum of the expectations that other people have of a person occupying a position.

The same evolution occurs when an individual starts an enterprise, initially combining the management and ownership functions. He or she performs all the management functions as well as the work itself. If the business grows and the owner engages employees, he or she will probably spend more of their time on management activities, while employees concentrate more on the work. This creates the distinct role of management – a **role** being the sum of the expectations that others have of a person occupying a position.

This separation of management and non-management work is not inevitable or permanent. People deliberately separate the roles, and can also bring them together. As Henri Fayol (1949) (a French writer, of whom you will read more in Chapter 2) observed:

Management ... is neither an exclusive privilege nor a particular responsibility of the head or senior members of a business; it is an activity spread, like all other activities, between head and members of the body corporate. (p. 6)

Tony Watson on separating roles   key ideas

All humans are managers in some way. But some of them also take on the formal occupational work of being managers. They take on a role of shaping ... work organisations. Managers' work involves a double ... task: managing others and managing themselves. But the very notion of 'managers' being separate people from the 'managed', at the heart of traditional management thinking, undermines a capacity to handle this. Managers are pressured to be technical experts, devising rational and emotionally neutral systems and corporate structures to 'solve problems', 'make decisions', 'run the business'. These 'scientific' and rational—analytic practices give reassurance but can leave managers so distanced from the 'managed' that their capacity to control events is undermined. This can mean that their own emotional and security needs are not handled, with the effect that they retreat into all kinds of defensive, backbiting and ritualistic behaviour which further undermines their effectiveness.

Source: Watson (1994), pp. 12–13.

Someone in charge of part of an organisation, say a production department, will usually be treated as a manager, and referred to as one. The people who operate the machines will be called something else. In a rapidly growing business such as Ryanair the boundary between 'managers' and 'non-managers' is likely to be very fluid, with all being ready to perform a range of tasks, irrespective of their title.

1.4   Specialisation between areas of management

As an organisation grows, senior managers create separate functions and a hierarchy, so that management itself becomes divided.

Functional specialisation

General managers typically head a complete unit of the organisation, such as a division or subsidiary, within which there will be several functions. The general manager is responsible for the unit's performance, and relies on the managers in charge of each function. A small organisation will have just one or two general managers, who will also manage the functions. At Shell UK the most senior general manager in 2007 was James Smith, the chairman.

Functional managers are responsible for an area of work – either as line managers or staff managers. **Line managers** are in charge of a function that creates value directly by supplying products or services to customers: they could be in charge of a retail store, a group of nurses, a social work department or a manufacturing area. Their performance significantly affects business performance and image, as they and their staff are in direct contact with customers or clients. At Shell, Andrew Kerr was (in 2007) the distribution manager responsible for the storage, scheduling and delivery of Shell's bulk fuel sales in the UK, while Ken Rivers was manager of the Stanlow Refinery.

General managers are responsible for the performance of a distinct unit of the organisation.

Functional managers are responsible for the performance of an area of technical or professional work.

Line managers are responsible for the performance of activities that directly meet customers' needs.

The store manager – fundamental to success

A manager with extensive experience of retailing commented:

The store manager's job is far more complex than it may at first appear. Staff management is an important element and financial skills are required to manage a budget and the costs involved in running a store. Managers must understand what is going on behind the scenes – in terms of logistics and the supply chain – as well as what is happening on the shop floor. They must also be good with customers and increasingly they need outward-looking skills as they are encouraged to take high-profile roles in the community.

Source: Private communication from the manager.

Staff managers are responsible for the performance of activities that support line managers.

Project managers are responsible for managing a project, usually intended to change some element of an organisation or its context.

Staff managers are in charge of activities such as finance, personnel, purchasing or legal affairs that support the line managers, who are their customers. Staff in support departments are not usually in direct contact with external customers, and so do not earn income directly for the organisation. Managers of staff departments operate as line managers within their unit. At Shell, Rachel Fox was Head of Legal, and Paul Milliken led the unit responsible for UK employment policies including remuneration and benefits.

Project managers are responsible for a temporary team created to plan and implement a change, such as a new product or system. Mike Buckingham, an engineer, managed a project to implement a new manufacturing system in a van plant. He still had line responsibilities for aspects of manufacturing, but worked for most of the time on the project, helped by a team of technical specialists. When the change was complete he returned to full-time work on his line job.

Management hierarchies

As organisations grow, senior managers usually create a hierarchy of positions. The amount of 'management' and 'non-management' work within these positions varies.

Performing direct operations

People who perform direct operations do the manual and mental work to make and deliver products or services. These range from low-paid cleaners or shop workers to highly paid pilots or lawyers. The activity is likely to contain some aspects of management work, though in lower-level jobs this will be limited. People running a small business combine management work with direct work to meet customer requirements.

Managing staff on direct operations

Sometimes called supervisors or first-line managers, they typically direct and control the daily work of a group or process, 'framed by the requirement to monitor, report and improve work performance' (Hales 2005, p. 484).

They allocate and coordinate tasks, monitor the pace of work and help to overcome difficulties. Sometimes they become involved with middle managers in making operational decisions on staffing levels or work methods. Examples would include the supervisor of a production team, the head chef in a hotel, a nurse in charge of a hospital ward or the manager of a bank branch. They may continue to perform some direct operations, but will spend less time on these than their subordinates.

Managing managers

Usually referred to as middle managers, they – such as an engineering manager at Ryanair – are expected to ensure that first-line managers work in line with company policies. They translate long-term strategies into short-term operational tasks, mediating between senior management vision and operational reality. They may help to develop strategy by presenting information about customer expectations or suggesting alternative strategies to senior managers (Floyd and Wooldridge, 2000; Currie and Proctor, 2005). They provide a communication link – telling first-line managers what they expect, and briefing senior managers about current issues. Some have close links with managers in other organisations (suppliers or customers) on whom they depend.

In voluntary organisations an important task is to manage relationships with the governing body (similar to the board of directors in a commercial business). Harris and Rochester (1996) describe this as 'one of the most difficult challenges of voluntary and non-profit ... management' (p. 30), since their existence depends on sufficient volunteers being willing to serve as governors, formulating policy and ensuring it raises the necessary resources.

Managing the business

Managing the business is the work of a small group, usually called the board of directors. They establish policy and have a particular responsibility for managing relations with people and institutions in the world outside, such as shareholders, media or elected representatives. They need to know broadly about internal matters, but spend most of their time looking to the future or dealing with external affairs. Depending on local company law, the board usually includes several non-executive directors – senior managers from other companies who are intended to bring a wider, independent view to discussions, supplementing the internal view of the executive directors. Such non-executive directors can enhance the effectiveness of the board, and give investors confidence that the board is acting in their interests. They can 'both support the executives in their leadership of the business and monitor and control executive conduct' (Roberts *et al.*, 2005, p. S6) by challenging, questioning, discussing and debating issues with the executive members. The board will not usually spend time on current operational issues.

The Board of Alliance Boots   www.allianceboots.co.uk   management in practice

The board of directors, which in 2007 consisted of six executive and seven non-executive directors, determines the strategic direction of the company, and meets regularly to review the operating and financial position of the group. The non-executive directors include Guy Dawson, an investment banker who chairs the Audit Committee; Tim Parker, chief executive of the Automobile Association; and Helene Ploix, chairman of a private investment company. The executive directors are led by Richard Baker, the chief executive, and are responsible respectively for Community Pharmacy, Finance, Health and Beauty Retail, and Wholesale and Commercial affairs.

Source: Company website.

1.5   Influencing through the process of managing

Stakeholders
are individuals, groups or organisations with an interest in, or who are affected by, what the organisation does.

Whatever their role, people add value to resources by influencing others, including internal and external **stakeholders** – those parties who affect, or who are affected by, an organisation's actions and policies. The challenge is that stakeholders will have different priorities, so managers need to influence them to act in ways they believe will add value.

They do this directly and indirectly. Direct methods are the interpersonal skills (see Chapter 14) that managers use – persuading a boss to support a proposal, a subordinate to do more work, or a customer to change a delivery date. Managers also influence others indirectly through:

- the process of managing (Rosemary Stewart, Henry Mintzberg and Fred Luthans);
- the tasks of managing (Section 1.6); and
- shaping the wider context (Section 1.7).

key ideas   Rosemary Stewart – how managers spend their time

What are managers' jobs like? Do they resemble an orderly, methodical process – or a constant rush from one problem to the next? One of the best-known studies was that conducted by Rosemary Stewart (1967), an academic at Oxford University, who persuaded 160 senior and middle managers to keep a diary for four weeks, which allowed the researchers to establish how the managers spent their time. This showed that managers typically worked in a fragmented, interrupted fashion. Over the four weeks, the managers had, on average, only nine periods of 30 minutes or more alone, with 12 brief contacts each day. They spent 36 per cent of their time on paperwork (writing, dictating, reading, calculating) and 43 per cent in informal discussion. They spent the remainder on formal meetings, telephoning and social activities.

The research team also found great variety between managers when they analysed the data to show different profiles of management work, based not on level or function but on how they spent their time. They identified five profiles:

1 **Emissaries** spent much of their time out of the organisation, meeting customers, suppliers or contractors.
2 **Writers** spent most of their time alone reading and writing, and had the fewest contacts with other managers.
3 **Discussers** spent most of their time with other people and with their colleagues.
4 **Troubleshooters** had the most fragmented work pattern of all, with many diary entries and many fleeting contacts, especially with their subordinates.
5 **Committee members** had a wide range of internal contacts, and spent much time in formal meetings.

They spent half their time in discussions with more than one other person.

Source: Stewart (1967).

Henry Mintzberg – ten management roles

Mintzberg (1973) used structured observations to gather data on how managers spent their time – though from only five chief executives. Despite this limitation others (e.g. Martinko and Gardner, 1990) have supported Mintzberg's main conclusion that managers' work was varied and fragmented (see also Key Ideas). He identified ten management roles in the three categories shown – informational, interpersonal and decisional – all of which are means of influencing other people. Table 1.2 lists these roles, with the right-hand column giving contemporary examples from an account by the manager of a project to distribute funds to schools to improve nutrition.

Table 1.2

Mintzberg's ten management roles

Category	Role	Activity	Examples from a school nutrition project
Informational	**Monitor**	Seek and receive information, scan reports, maintain interpersonal contacts	Collect and review funding applications; set up database to monitor application process
	Disseminator	Forward information to others, send memos, make phone calls	Share content of applications with team members by e-mail
	Spokesperson	Represent the unit to outsiders in speeches and reports	Present application process at internal and external events
Interpersonal	**Figurehead**	Perform ceremonial and symbolic duties, receive visitors	Sign letters of award to successful applicants
	Leader	Direct and motivate subordinates, train, advise and influence	Design and coordinate process with team and other managers
	Liaison	Maintain information links in and beyond the organisation	Become link person for government bodies to contact for progress reports
Decisional	**Entrepreneur**	Initiate new projects, spot opportunities, identify areas of business development	Use initiative to revise application process and to introduce electronic communication
	Disturbance handler	Take corrective action during crises, resolve conflicts amongst staff, adapt to changes	Holding face-to-face meetings with applicants when the outcome was negative; handling staff grievances
	Resource allocator	Decide who gets resources, schedule, budget, set priorities	Ensure fair distribution of grants nationally
	Negotiator	Represent unit during negotiations with unions, suppliers, and generally defend interests	Working with sponsors and government to ensure consensus during decision making

Source: Based on Mintzberg (1973), and private communication from the project manager.

Informational roles

Managing depends on obtaining information about external and internal events, and passing it to others. The *monitor role* involves seeking out, receiving and screening information to understand the organisation and its environment. It comes from papers and reports, and from chance conversations with customers or new contacts at conferences and exhibitions. Much of this information is oral (gossip as well as formal meetings), building on personal contacts. In the *disseminator role* the manager shares information by forwarding reports, passing on rumours or briefing staff. As a *spokesperson* the manager transmits information to people outside the organisation – speaking at a conference, briefing the media or giving the department's view at a company meeting. Michael O'Leary at Ryanair is renowned for flamboyant statements to the media about competitors or officials in the European Commission with whose policies he disagrees.

Interpersonal roles

Interpersonal roles arise directly from a manager's formal authority and status, and shape relationships with people within and beyond the organisation. In the *figurehead role* the manager is a symbol, representing the unit in legal and ceremonial duties such as greeting a visitor, signing legal documents, presenting retirement gifts or receiving a quality award. The *leader role* defines the manager's relationship with other people (not just subordinates), including motivating, communicating and developing their skills and confidence. As one manager commented:

> I am conscious that due to conflicting priorities I am unable to spend as much time interacting with staff members as I would like. I try to overcome this by leaving my door open whenever I am alone as an invitation to staff to come in and interrupt me, and to encourage the staff to come to me to discuss any problems that may arise.

The *liaison role* focuses on contacts with people outside the immediate unit. Managers maintain a network in which they trade information and favours for mutual benefit with clients, government officials, customers and suppliers. For some managers, particularly chief executives and sales managers, the liaison role takes a high proportion of their time and energy.

---

management in practice   **Strengthening interpersonal roles**

A company restructured its regional operations, closed a sales office in Bordeaux and transferred the work to Paris. The sales manager responsible for south-west France was now geographically distant from her immediate boss and the rest of the team. This caused severe problems of communication and loss of teamwork. She concluded that the interpersonal aspects of the role were vital as a basis for the informational and decisional roles. The decision to close the office had broken these links.
   She and her boss agreed to try the following solutions:

- a 'one-to-one' session of quality time to discuss key issues during monthly visits to head office;
- daily telephone contact to ensure speed of response and that respective communication needs were met;
- use of fax and e-mail at home to speed up communications.

These overcame the break in interpersonal roles caused by the location change.

Source: Private communication.

Decisional roles

Creativity is the ability to combine ideas in a unique way or to make unusual associations between ideas.

In the *entrepreneurial role* managers demonstrate creativity and initiate change. They see opportunities and create projects to deal with them. Managers play this role when they introduce a new product or create a major change programme – as when Lars Kolind became chief executive of Oticon (Chapter 10 case), determined to change an established and inflexible business, unsuited to deal with new competition. Managers play the *disturbance-handler role* when they deal with problems and changes that are unexpected.

management in practice

Two examples of handling disturbance

In early 2004 Doreen Tobin, chief financial officer of Vivendi Universal, the French media and communications group that has owned Universal Music Group since 2000, announced that it planned to cut €400 million from its cost base by 2005. The company had just reported a loss of €1.1 billion, which she blamed on the recent contraction in the music industry. The saving will come from cuts in back-office staff, lower royalties to artists, and a reduction in the number of artists whose work it promotes.

In the same year the chief executive of Lego, the Danish toy maker, unveiled a wide-ranging restructuring programme, under which it would cut jobs, reduce costs and sell non-core businesses. He said that it had recently misjudged part of the market and lost substantial sales, but that it now wanted to deal with its serious earnings crisis by improving its competitive edge and returning the focus to basic play materials.

Source: Various published information.

The *resource-allocator role* involves choosing amongst competing demands for money, equipment, personnel and other resources. How much of her budget should the housing manager quoted on p. 23 spend on different types of project? What proportion of the budget should a company spend on advertising or to improve a product? The manager of an ambulance service regularly decides between paying overtime to staff to replace an absent team member or letting service quality decline until a new shift starts. This is close to the *negotiator role*, in which managers seek agreement with other parties on whom they depend. When managers at Ryanair want to change the fees they pay to an airport they try to negotiate a new deal with the owners.

Activity 1.4   Gather evidence about Mintzberg's model

Recall a time when you have been responsible for managing an activity.

- Do the ten roles cover all of the roles you performed, or did you do things that are not included in his list? What were they?
- Give examples of what you did under (say) five of the roles.
- Were there any of these roles to which you should have given more time? Or less?
- If possible compare your results with other members of your course.
- Decide if the evidence you have collected supports or contradicts Mintzberg's theory.

Mintzberg proposed that every manager's job combines these roles, with their relative importance varying between the manager's level and their type of business. Managers usually recognise that they use many of the roles as they influence others to add value.

Managers often highlight two roles missing from Mintzberg's list – manager as subordinate and manager as worker. Most managers have subordinates but, except for those at the very top, they are subordinates themselves. Part of their role is to advise, assist and influence their boss – the role of 'managing up', to influence people over whom they have no formal authority. Managers often cannot wait for a decision to be resolved through formal channels, and need to persuade people higher up the organisation of a proposal's value or urgency. A project manager recalled:

Ryanair – the case continues   www.ryanair.com   C A S E   S T U D Y

The company has continued to grow rapidly, announcing in December 2006 that it had carried a record 40 million passengers that year. Passenger volumes rose by 20 per cent in the year to March 2007 to 42.5 million, following a 26 per cent rise the previous year. However it expected growth in the year to March 2008 to be only about 5 per cent. It was now one of the world's most profitable airlines, and continued to seek new bases from which to operate its growing European network. Despite the growing passenger numbers managers continued to seek ways to cut costs and raise revenues. They decided that their new aircraft would not have window blinds, headrests, seat-pockets or reclining seats: this would save money, and managers believed passengers would not miss these 'frills' as most journeys are less than an hour.

In 2005 the company earned £55 million from selling refreshments to passengers, and in 2006 began to charge customers for checking in their baggage. Each time a passenger rents a car or books a hotel room on the Ryanair website, it earns a commission. It now sells scratch cards on board, plans to offer in-flight gambling and online gaming over its website: the chief executive thinks that gambling could double Ryanair's profits over the next decade. A report by Paul Vallely for *The Independent* in late 2006 noted that:

Currently he's offering advertisers the opportunity to repaint the exteriors of Ryanair's planes. Effectively turning them into giant billboards: Hertz, Jaguar and Vodafone have purchased space on the fuselages of Ryanair's 737s.

Applicants for jobs as first officers are charged £50 to apply online, which is refunded if they are successful. They must also pay a non-refundable £200 for a simulator check. The company expects that in 2007 it will introduce a scheme enabling passengers to use in-flight mobile phones, and believes that revenue from such ancillary activities will continue to grow more rapidly than passenger revenue.

Sources: *Economist*, 10 July 2004; *Independent*, 7 October 2006; *Financial Times*, 7 June 2006; Kumar (2006); and company website.

Case questions 1.2

- Which of Mintzberg's management roles can you identify being exercised in the latest stage of the Ryanair case?
- Decide which two of these roles are likely to be most critical in the next stage of the company's development, and explain why.

This is the second time we have been back to the management team, to propose how we wish to move forward, and to try and get the resources that are required. It is worth taking the time up front to get all members fully supportive of what we are trying to do. Although it takes a bit longer we should, by pressure and by other individuals demonstrating the benefits of what we are proposing, eventually move the [top team] forward.

Many managers spend some time doing the work of the organisation. A director of a small property company helps with sales visits, or an engineering director helps with difficult technical problems. A lawyer running a small practice performs both professional and managerial roles.

Fred Luthans – managers as networkers and politicians

Does the focus of a manager's influencing activities affect performance? Mintzberg's study gave no evidence on this point, but work by Luthans (1988) showed that the relative amount of time spent on specific roles did affect outcomes. The team observed 292 managers in four organisations for two weeks, recording their behaviours in agreed categories.

Managerial work in small businesses

O'Gorman *et al.* (2005) studied the work of ten owner-managers of small growth-oriented businesses to establish empirically if the nature of their work differs from those in the large businesses studied by Mintzberg. They concluded that managerial work in these businesses is in some ways similar to that in large organisations, finding brevity, fragmentation and variety; mainly verbal communication; and an unrelenting pace.

Another observation was that managers moved frequently between roles, switching from, say, reviewing financial results to negotiating prices with a customer. They were constantly receiving, reviewing and giving information, usually by telephone or in unscheduled meetings. They reacted immediately to live information by redirecting their attention to the most pressing issues, so that their days were largely unplanned, with frequent interruptions. They spent only a quarter of their time in scheduled meetings compared to Mintzberg's finding that managers in large organisations spent almost 60 per cent of their time in this way. Finally, the owners of these small businesses spent 8 per cent of their time in non-managerial activities – twice that of those in Mintzberg's study.

The research shows that the nature of managerial work in small growth-oriented businesses is in some ways similar to, and in others different from, that in large organisations. There is the same brevity and fragmentation, but more informal communication.

Source: O'Gorman *et al.* (2005).

The research also distinguished between levels of 'success' (relatively rapid promotion) and 'effectiveness' (work-unit performance and subordinates' satisfaction). The behavioural categories were:

Communicating	Exchanging information and paperwork
Traditional management	Planning, decision making, controlling
Networking	Interacting with outsiders, socialising/politicking
Human resource management	Motivating, managing conflict, staffing, training

The conclusion was that *successful* managers spent considerably more time networking (socialising, politicking, interacting with outsiders) than the less successful managers. Human resource management took least time. In contrast, *effective* managers spent most time on communication and human resource management activities. They spent little time networking. These results implied that managers who want to rise to more senior positions should spend relatively large amounts of time and effort on networking and on the political skills of management – confirmed by Aslani and Luthans (2003). Noordegraaf and Stewart (2000) provide an extensive review of research into the managerial role, especially into differences and similarities between contexts, sectors and nations.

1.6   Influencing through the tasks of managing

A second way in which managers influence others is when they manage the transformation of resources into more valuable outputs. Building on Figure 1.1, this involves the **management tasks** of planning, organising, leading and controlling the use of resources to 'get things done'. The amount of each varies with the job and the person, and they do not perform them in sequence: they do them simultaneously, switching as the situation requires.

Management tasks are those of planning, organising, leading and controlling the use of resources to add value to them.

Figure 1.2 illustrates the elements of this definition. It expands the central 'transforming' circle of Figure 1.1 to show the tasks that together make up the transformation process. People draw inputs (resources) from the environment and transform them through the tasks of planning, organising, leading and controlling. This results in goods and services that they pass as output into the environment. The feedback loop indicates that this output is the source of future resources.

Environment

Organisations depend on the external environment for the resources to sustain them. These are most clearly those of finance, people, ideas, materials and information. They also include intangible resources such as goodwill, licences, permissions and authorisations to undertake certain activities. An organisation also depends on people in the external environment being willing to buy or recognise what it produces, and so provide the cash, recognition or reputational resources it needs to survive. Commercial firms sell goods and services and use the revenue to buy resources. Public organisations depend on the authorities being sufficiently satisfied with their performance to provide future budgets. Charities depend on convincing donors that they have used their contributions well. Part 2 of the book deals with the external environment.

Planning

Planning deals with the overall direction of the work to be done. It includes forecasting future trends, assessing resources and developing objectives for performance. It inevitably means making decisions about the areas of work in which to engage, and how to use resources. Managers therefore invest time and effort in developing a sense of direction for the organisation, or their part of it, and express this in a set of objectives. Part 3 of the book deals with planning.

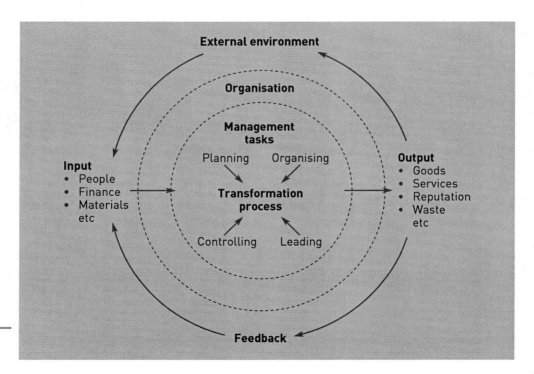

Figure 1.2

The tasks of
management

David Simon – planning targets at BP   www.bp.com

David Simon was chairman and chief executive of BP from 1992 to 1995. He believes that setting simple goals is an important part of developing a culture of continual performance improvement. He made it clear to BP employees that they should be cost and profit conscious. He has a golden rule for attaining goals: 'Targeting is fundamental to achieving. If you do not target, you do not measure and you do not achieve.' He believes that:

> Picking the right targets is a skill in itself. The difficulty of leadership is picking the targets and having a dialogue as you progress towards that goal so that, when it is achieved, it seems the easiest thing in the world. Then you can pick another target.

One top executive described Simon's accomplishment: 'What he has done so well is pull the company together in a very calming way, setting clear targets and telling people how they can achieve them.'

Source: See BP Case Study at the end of Part 2.

Organising

Organising is the activity of moving abstract plans closer to realisation, by deciding how to allocate time and effort. It includes creating a structure for the organisation, developing policies for HRM and deciding what equipment people need. Part 4 deals with organising.

Reorganising Diageo's distribution in the US   www.diageo.com

Diageo, based in the UK, is the world's leading premium drinks business, whose brands include Smirnoff, Guinness, J&B and Baileys. To make the most of its already strong position in the United States it announced in 2004 that it had completed a major reorganisation of its distribution in that country. It had reduced the number of distributors in each state, and in return required those remaining to do more – such as employ some staff who only sell Diageo brands. The benefits included better retail displays – a key influence on a customer's choice of drink. The company believed that this change in organisation had contributed to a 10 per cent growth in sales and a small increase in market share.

Source: Company announcement of half-yearly results, February 2004, available at www.diageo.com.

Leading

Leading is the activity of generating effort and commitment, including motivating individuals and teams. As organisations become more complex, so does the task of securing commitment and action. People exercise choice, and managers cannot assume that they will act as managers would like them to. For David Simon at BP, setting targets was itself a vital part of his leadership. Part 5 deals with this topic.

Controlling

Control is the task of monitoring progress, comparing it with plan, and taking corrective action. Managers set a budget for a housing department, an outpatients' clinic, or for business travel. They then ensure that there is a system to collect information regularly on expenditure or performance – to check they are keeping to budget. If not, they need to decide how to bring actual costs back into line with budgeted costs. Are the outcomes consistent with the objectives? If so, they can leave things alone. But if by Wednesday it is clear that staff will not meet the week's production target then managers need to act. They may deal with the deviation by a short-term response – such as authorising overtime. Other deviations are so severe that the board decides to leave a business altogether – the Prudential decided to sell Egg, their online bank, to Citibank in 2006, as it was losing so much money.

> **management in practice** The dangers of less control at Shell www.shell.com
>
> In early 2004 Shell received some damaging publicity when the (then) chairman admitted the company had overstated its oil reserves – a key part of an oil company's value. Many observers believed that the source of the trouble lay in the company's history – including the dismantling of well-established systems of internal controls during a period of growth in the 1990s. As senior managers encouraged growth and a more entrepreneurial spirit ('people were wearing T-shirts saying "grow at 15 per cent a year"') controls were gradually removed as a hindrance. Where previously systems were in place to track projects, it became almost impossible to find out how much money had been committed. Executive committees for main business units were given more responsibility, and were expected to make speedier decisions, with fewer restrictions and checks. This decreased internal control, and opened the way for top management to manipulate data – but it was not seen as dangerous at the time.
>
> Source: Based on an article by Ian Bickerton, *Financial Times*, 18 June 2004.

Control also provides an opportunity to learn from past events. The ability of managers to learn from their experience is crucial to their performance. This does not mean sending people on external courses, but creating and using opportunities to learn from what they are doing. The box gives an example of this; Part 6 deals with control.

> **management in practice** Encouraging learning
>
> The organisation is a national charity that runs residential homes for people with severe learning disabilities. It has a high reputation for the quality of the care it gives and for the way it treats the carers. Managers take whatever opportunities they can to help staff gain confidence in the difficult and often stressful work. An example:
>
> > Staff in one area described how their manager supported their studies by creating a file for them containing information on relevant policies and legislation. The same manager recognised that a night-shift worker doing a qualification was not getting the range of experience necessary to complete college assessments: 'So she took me to a review last week and also took me to a referral for a service user. I'd never seen that side before – but now I can relate to the stuff that will come up at college. It's about giving you the fuller picture, because sometimes the night shift can be quite isolating.'
>
> Source: Unpublished research.

The tasks in practice

Managers typically switch between tasks many times a day. They deal with them intermittently and in parallel, touching on many different parts of the job, as this manager in a housing association explains:

> My role involves each of these functions. Planning is an important element as I am part of a team with a budget of £8 million to spend on promoting particular forms of housing. So planning where we will spend the money is very important. Organising and leading are important too, as staff have to be clear on which projects to take forward, clear on objectives and deadlines. Controlling is also there – I have to compare the actual money spent with the planned budget and take corrective action as necessary.

And a manager in a legal firm:

> As a manager in a professional firm, each assignment involves all the elements to ensure we carry it out properly. For example, I have to set clear objectives for the assignment, organise the necessary staff and information to perform the work, supervise staff and counsel them if necessary, and evaluate the results. All the roles interrelate and there are no clear stages for each one.

Activity 1.5 Gather evidence about the tasks of managing

Recall your work on Activity 1.4.

- Do the four tasks of managing cover all of your work, or did you do things that are not included? What were they?
- Give an example of something you did in each of the tasks.
- Were there any of these to which you should have given more time? Or less?
- If possible compare your results with other members of your course.

1.7 Influencing through shaping the context

A third way in which managers influence others is through changing aspects of the context in which they work. Changing an office layout, a person's reporting relationships, or the rewards they obtain, alter their context and perhaps their actions. The context is both an influence on the manager and a tool with which to influence others (Johns, 2006):

> It is impossible to understand human intentions by ignoring the settings in which they make sense. Such settings may be institutions, sets of practices, or some other contexts created by humans – contexts which have a history, within which both particular deeds and whole histories of individual actors can and have to be situated in order to be intelligible. (Czarniawska, 2004, p.4)

Managers continually aim to create contexts that they hope will influence others to act in ways that meet their objectives.

Dimensions of context

Internal context

Figures 1.1 and 1.2 showed the links between managers, their organisation and the external environment. Figure 1.3 enlarges the 'organisation' circle to show more fully the elements that make up the internal environment within which managers work. Any organisation contains these elements – they represent the immediate context of the manager's work. For example, as Jorma Ollilia built Nokia into a major business, he and his team made many changes to technology, business processes – and indeed to all the elements shown in the figure (Steinbock, 2001), which later chapters examine:

- **objectives** (Chapters 6 and 8) – a desired future state of an organisation or unit;
- **culture** (Chapter 3) – norms, beliefs and underlying values that characterise the unit;
- **structure** (Chapter 10) – how tasks are divided and coordinated to meet objectives;
- **technology** (Chapter 12) – the facilities and equipment that people use to transform inputs into useful outputs;
- **power** (Chapter 14) – the amount and distribution of power with which to influence others;
- **people** (Chapter 15) – their knowledge, skills, attitudes and goals;
- **finance** (Chapter 19 – the financial resources available;
- **business processes** (Chapter 20) – activities that people and technologies perform on materials and information.

Models such as this show that managers work within constraints – they are to some degree helped or hindered by the elements in Figure 1.3. Effective managers do not accept their context passively – they initiate change to create the combination of elements to meet their objectives (Chapter 13).

Historical context

Managing takes place within the flow of history as what people do now reflects the influence of past events and future uncertainties. Managers typically focus on current issues, ensuring that things run properly, and that the organisation works. At the same time, history exerts an influence through the structure and culture. People remember successes and failures, which affects how they respond to current proposals.

However good the present situation, effective managers look to the future. They question present systems and seek improvements, observe changes in the environment and what they imply. Are resources being wasted, requiring some changes in method? What

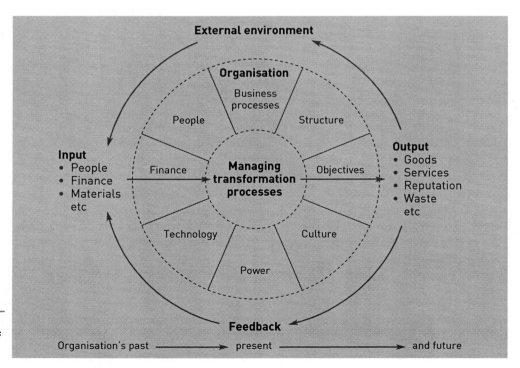

Figure 1.3

The internal and external context of management

are others doing? Questions such as these are resolved through the tasks and processes of management. The arrow at the foot of the figure represents the historical context.

External context

Finally there is the world outside. Chapter 3 shows that the external context includes an immediate competitive (micro) environment and a wider (or macro) environment. All of these affect performance, and part of the manager's work is to identify emerging changes and adapt the organisation. Managers at major food retailers have noted growing consumer interest in healthy food, and are working with suppliers to meet this.

Table 1.3 summarises the last two sections and illustrates how managers can influence others as they perform tasks affecting internal, micro and macro contexts.

	Internal (organisational)	Micro (competitive)	Macro (general)
Planning	Clarifying the objectives of a business unit, and communicating them clearly to all staff	Reducing prices in the hope of discouraging a potential competitor from entering the market	Lobbying for a change in a trade agreement to make it easier to enter an overseas market
Organising	Changing the role of a business unit	Reducing the number of suppliers in exchange for improved terms	Lobbying government to change planning laws to enable longer trading hours
Leading	Redesigning tasks and training staff to higher levels to improve motivation	Arranging for staff to visit customers so that they understand more fully what they need	Sending staff on overseas study tours to raise awareness of changes in the macro context
Controlling	Ensuring the information system keeps an accurate output record	Implementing an information system directly linked to customers and suppliers	Lobbying for tighter procedures to ensure all countries abide by trade agreements

Table 1.3

Examples of managing tasks in each context

Theories of managers and their context

Anyone managing a business uses a theory (even if subconsciously) of the link between context and action. This section sets out three alternative models – determinism, choice and interaction – which Chapter 13 develops more fully.

Determinism

The determinist view is that people have no influence on events, which are the result of forces beyond their control. Performance, on this view, depends on micro and macro factors such as the industry one is in or the rate of economic growth. Managers must adapt to external changes and have little influence over the direction of the business. People expect banks to have cash machines and to offer Internet banking, so banks have little choice but to use these technologies. On this view, the context is an independent variable: Figure 1.4(a) represents this.

Choice

An alternative view is that people have free will and can influence events. People in powerful positions shape their environment, have minds of their own and choose which businesses to enter or leave, and the countries in which they operate. Many observers believe that managers in major companies lobby to influence taxation, regulations and policy generally to serve their interests. On this view, the context is a dependent variable, reflecting human activities – Figure 1.4(b).

Interaction

The interaction approach expresses the idea that people are influenced by, and can themselves influence, the context. People interpret the existing context and act to change it to promote personal, local or organisational objectives. A manager may see a change in the company's external environment, and respond by advocating the purchase of a computer system (technology) or a change in reporting relationships (structure). Others interpret this proposal in the light of *their* perspective. All the players try to influence decisions in a way that suits their interests. The outcomes from these interactions affect the context – which now provides the historical background to future action. The essential idea is that the relationship between the manager and the context works both ways – Figure 1.4(c). People shape the context, and the context shapes people. Throughout the book there are examples of managers interacting with their context.

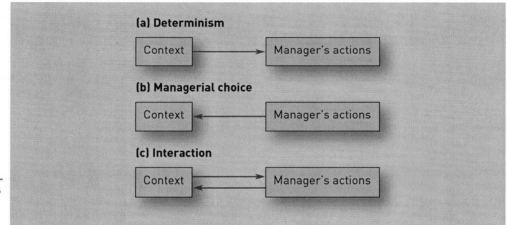

Figure 1.4

Alternative models of managers and their context

Ryanair – the case continues   www.ryanair.com   CASE STUDY

The company depends on securing agreements with airport operators, and also approvals from aviation authorities in the countries to which it flies. This often leads it into public disputes, such as one with the European Commission over subsidies. The regional government and the company operating Charleroi Airport in Belgium offered the company a subsidy to persuade it to fly there. The European Commission ruled that such subsidies were illegal, and the company feared that it would lose subsidies it receives at other airports: 'Bureaucrats in Brussels wish to prevent privately owned airlines from developing low-cost arrangements for the benefit of consumers', said Michael O'Leary, the chief executive. Ryanair's rivals lobbied in support of the Commission, urging them to stand firm against state aid.

In May 2006 Ryanair suspended planned flights between two Italian cities because the Italian National Civil Aviation Authority had refused to allow it to operate the route: the company claimed this was a deliberate attempt to protect the high-cost Italian national airline from competition.

Michael O'Leary takes a deliberately aggressive stance to these controversies, believing that 'as long as its not safety-related, there's no such thing as bad publicity'. He is dismissive of traditional high-cost airlines, the European Commission, airport operators, travel agents, and governments that try to protect established airlines from competition.

The rise in low-cost travel has affected where some people live and work. Some now choose to work in expensive cities such as London for perhaps four days a week, returning at weekends to their families in other countries. Entrepreneurs also offer new services. One Briton who bought a second home in Slovenia now helps local estate agents to sell properties to English-speaking buyers. Others arrange for Britons to have dental treatment in less expensive eastern European countries.

Source: *Economist*, 10 July 2004; *Business Week*, 8 May 2006; *Independent*, 7 October 2006; and other sources.

Case questions 1.3

- Which aspects of the external general environment have affected the company?
- How has the company affected these environments?

1.8 Critical thinking

As managers aim to add value to resources by influencing others, they continually receive data, information and knowledge about their business and its context – but cannot take what they receive at face value. They must test it by questioning the underlying assumptions, relating them to the context, considering alternatives available and recognising limitations. In doing so they develop the skills of critical thinking.

Critical thinking

Brookfield (1987) stresses the benefits of thinking critically, in that it

> involves our recognizing the assumptions underlying our beliefs and behaviors. It means we can give justifications for our ideas and actions. Most important, perhaps, it means we try to judge the rationality of these justifications ... by comparing them to a range of varying interpretations and perspectives. (p. 13)

Critical thinking is a productive and positive activity that enables people to see a future with many possibilities, rather than as a single, fixed path. Critical thinkers 'are self-confident about their potential for changing aspects of their worlds, both as individuals and through collective action' (Brookfield, 1987, p. 5). He offers four components of critical thinking.

Critical thinking identifies the assumptions behind ideas, relates them to their context, imagines alternatives and recognises limitations.

Identifying and challenging assumptions

Critical thinkers look for the assumptions that underlie taken-for-granted ideas, beliefs and values, and question their accuracy and validity. They are ready to discard those that no longer seem valid guides to action, in favour of more suitable ones. A manager who presents a well-supported challenge to a theory of marketing that seems unsuitable to their business, or who questions the need for a new business division, is engaging in this aspect of critical thinking.

Recognising the importance of context

Critical thinkers are aware that context influences thought and action. Thinking uncritically means assuming that ideas and methods which work in one context will work equally well in others. What we regard as an appropriate way to deal with staff reflects a specific culture: people in another culture – working in another place or at a different time – will have other expectations. Critical thinkers look for approaches suitable for the relevant context.

Imagining and exploring alternatives

Critical thinkers develop the skill of imagining and exploring alternative ways of managing. They ask how others have dealt with a situation, and seek evidence about the effectiveness of different approaches. This makes them aware of realistic alternatives, and so increases the range of ideas that they can adapt and use.

Seeing limitations

Critical thinking alerts people to the limitations of knowledge and proposals. They recognise that because a practice works well in one situation does not ensure it will work in another. They are sceptical about research whose claims seem over-sold, asking about the sample or the analysis. They are open to new ideas, but only when these are supported by convincing evidence and reasoning.

Thinking critically will deepen your understanding of management. It does not imply a 'do-nothing' cynicism, 'treating everything and everyone with suspicion and

---

key ideas   Techniques to help develop your ability to think critically

1 **Identifying and challenging assumptions**
   - Reflect on recent events that worked well or not so well; describing what happened and your reactions to it may help to identify assumptions that were confirmed or challenged by events.
   - Do the same for an achievement of which you are most proud.
   - Imagine that you have decided to leave your job, and are advising the committee who will appoint your replacement: list the qualities they should look for in that person. That may indicate the assumptions you hold about the nature of your job, and what it takes to do it well.

2 **Recognising the importance of context**
   - Select a practice that people in your organisation take for granted; ask people in other organisations how they deal with the matter, and see if the differences relate to context.
   - Repeat that with people who have worked in other countries.

3 **Imagining and exploring alternatives**
   - Brainstorming – trying to think of as many solutions to a problem as you can in a short period, by temporarily suspending habitual judgements.
   - Gather evidence about how other businesses deal with an aspect of management that interests you: the more alternatives you find, the easier it may become to think of alternatives that could work for you.

4 **Seeing limitations**
   - Acknowledging the limited evidence behind a theory or prescription.
   - Asking if it has been tested in different settings or circumstances.

Source: Based on Brookfield (1987) and Thomas (2003), p. 7.

doubt' (Thomas, 2003, p. 7). Critical thinking lays the foundation for a successful management career, as it helps to ensure that proposals are supported by convincing evidence and reasoning.

Managing your studies

Studying management is itself a task to be managed. Each chapter sets out some learning objectives – to which you can add. The text, including the activities and case questions, help you work towards these objectives, and you can check your progress by using the review questions at the end of each chapter. The questions reflect objectives of varying levels of difficulty (Anderson and Krathwohl, 2001), which Table 1.4 illustrates. Working on these will help develop your confidence to think critically in your studies and as a manager.

Studying is an opportunity to practise managing. You can plan what you want to achieve, organise the resources you need, generate personal commitment and check your progress. The book provides opportunities to improve your skills of literacy, reflection (analysing and evaluating evidence before acting), critical thinking, communicating, problem solving and teamwork.

The most accessible sources of ideas and theory are this book (including the 'further reading' and websites mentioned), your lectures and tutorials. Draw on the experience of friends and relatives to help with some of the activities and questions. These help you to gather information about current practices, which you can compare with members of your tutorial group and with the theories. As you go about your educational and social lives you are experiencing organisations, and in some cases helping to manage them. Actively reflecting on these experiences will support your study of management.

Table 1.4

Types of learning objective in the text

Type of objective	Typical words associated with each	Examples
Remember – retrieve relevant knowledge from memory	Recognise, recall	State or write the main elements and relationships in a theory
Understand – construct meaning from information	Interpret, give examples, summarise, compare, explain, contrast	Compare two theories of motivation; contrast two strategies, and explain which theory each reflects
Apply – use a procedure in a specified situation	Demonstrate, calculate, show, experiment, illustrate, modify	Use (named theory) to show the issues that managers in the case should consider
Analyse – break material into parts, showing relationship to each other and to wider purpose	Classify, separate, order, organise, differentiate, infer, connect, compare, divide	Collect evidence to support or contradict (named theory); which theory is reflected in (example of practice)?
Evaluate – make judgements based on criteria and standards	Decide, compare, check, judge	Decide if the evidence presented supports the conclusion; should the company do A or B?
Create – put parts together into a coherent whole; reorganise elements	Plan, make, present, generate, produce, design, compose	Present a marketing plan for the company; design a project proposal

Source: Adapted from Anderson and Krathwohl (2001), p. 31.

1.9   Current themes and issues

Each chapter of this book concludes with a section relating the topic to three related themes:

- the challenging performance expectations that many managers face;
- while also acting responsibly in general and over climate change in particular; and
- doing so in an increasingly international economy.

Performance

Many companies are in markets where customers are becoming more demanding, expecting more individual products or services, and who have more opportunities to take their custom elsewhere if they are not satisfied. Managers in the public sector face similar pressures, being expected to provide better services with the same or fewer resources. Taxpayers routinely demand better services but resist higher taxes, while employees may resist attempts to increase efficiency.

To meet these demands managers try to identify trends in the external context, and build an organisation that can meet them, by changing some or all of the elements in Figure 1.3. The next Management in Practice feature illustrates how one company is successfully meeting external demands by developing internal capabilities.

---

management in practice   Balancing external and internal at H&M   www.hm.com

H&M, the trading name of Swedish fashion retailer Hennes & Mauritz, is one of Europe's top performing companies. In 2005 sales rose by 14 per cent compared to 2004, and profit by 23 per cent. In 2007 it had over 1000 stores in 24 countries, selling fashionable clothes to young, style-conscious customers. The company's secret weapon is its quick turnround time: H&M's in-house design team of 95 designers can move a garment from the design board to shop floor in as little as three weeks. Quick reflexes enable H&M to stay on the cutting edge of trends and minimise the impact of fashion disasters. Costs are kept low by outsourcing manufacturing to a network of more than 900 apparel contractors in low-wage countries such as Bangladesh, China and Turkey.

Source: *Business Week*, 28 July 2003, 24 June 2004; company website.

The H&M story shows how rapidly improving information and transport systems have enabled them to draw supplies from low-wage countries, while internally they have created processes and structures that allow them to manage a very rapid design-to-delivery system.

Managers meet the challenge of rising performance expectations in conjunction with two other factors – responsibility and internationalisation.

Responsibility

The pressure on H&M managers (as in all commercial companies) originates primarily with those who own the business – the shareholders. They expect managers to focus on adding value to resources in a way that most benefits their (the shareholders') financial interests, and that can be a daunting challenge in itself. As Chapter 5 will show, many other interest groups now expect managers to act in a way that benefits their (the stakeholders') interests. Many now interpret responsible action as that which takes account of a wide range of stakeholders. These wider interest groups press a range of issues: better treatment of employees, dealing fairly with suppliers, selling healthy food, protecting the environment, limiting effects on climate change, or improving the conditions of workers in developing countries. These demands often conflict, in that meeting the performance expectations of one group of stakeholders may make it more difficult to meet the expectations of others.

Internationalisation

The international economy can both help and hinder managers as they balance multiple performance expectations. They can often meet the expectations of their customers and shareholders by moving activities to suppliers in developing countries who are able to supply goods and services much more cheaply than those in the developed world. H&M is typical of this, able to draw suppliers around the world to meet customer demands – which is also profitable for shareholders. However, is that meeting other expectations of responsible behaviour? Workers in the domestic economy have lost employment, the transport of products over vast distances contributes to climate change, and suppliers in developing countries typically work to lower environmental and labour standards than those in developed countries. Meeting social expectations in a European country may mean becoming uncompetitive with companies operating under different regulations. Yet moving production abroad leads trade unions to accuse managers of not acting responsibly towards employees in their home country.

Summary

1 **Summarise the functions of organisations and how management affects their performance**

   ● Organisations enable people to create value by transforming inputs into outputs of greater value – though the concept of creating value is subjective and open to different interpretations. Management is the process of building organisations in which inputs are transformed into more valuable outputs.

2 **Give examples to show how management is both a universal human activity and a distinct role**

   ● Management is an activity that everyone undertakes to some extent as they manage their daily lives. In another sense management is an activity within organisations, conducted in varying degrees by a wide variety of people. It is not exclusive to people called 'managers'. People create the distinct role when they separate the management of work from the work itself and allocate the tasks to different people. The distinction between management and non-management work is fluid and the result of human action.

3 **Compare the roles of general, functional, line, staff and project managers**

   ● General managers are responsible for a complete business or a unit within it. They depend on functional managers who can be either in charge of line departments meeting customer needs, such as manufacturing and sales, or in staff departments such as finance that provide advice or services to line managers. Project managers are in charge of temporary activities usually directed at implementing change.

4 **Explain how managers influence others to add value to resources**

- The processes of managerial work (Stewart, Mintzberg and Luthans). Rosemary Stewart drew attention to the fragmented and interrupted nature of management work, while Mintzberg identified ten management roles in three groups that he labelled informational, interpersonal and decisional. Luthans observed that successful managers were likely to be those who spent most time networking and politicking.

- Arranging the tasks (or content) of managerial work. Planning is the activity of developing the broad direction of an organisation's work, to meet customer expectations, taking into account internal capabilities. Organising is the activity of deciding how to deploy resources to meet plans, while leading seeks to ensure that people work with commitment to achieve plans. Control monitors activity against plans, so that people can adjust either if required.

- Shaping the contexts within which they and others work. The organisational context consists of eight elements that help or hinder the manager's work – objectives, technology, business processes, finance, structure, culture, power and people. The historical context also influences events, as does the external context made up of the competitive and general environments.

5 **Evaluate a manager's approach to the role by analysing how they influence others**

- You can achieve this objective by arranging with a manager to discus their role, and organise your questions or discussion around the theories of the processes, contents and contexts of managerial work outlined in the chapter. If possible compare your results with others on your course, and try to explain any differences you find.

6 **Explain the elements of critical thinking and use some techniques to develop this skill**

- Critical thinking is a positive approach to studying, as it encourages people to develop the skills of identifying and challenging assumptions; recognising the importance of context; imagining and exploring alternatives; and seeing the limitations of any idea or proposal.

7 **Current themes and issues**

Managers are expected to meet:

- challenging expectations of financial performance or service standards;

- while also acting responsibly in general and over climate change in particular; and

- to do so in an increasingly global economy, where competitors may work to less demanding expectations.

Review questions

1 Apart from delivering goods and services, what other functions do organisations perform?

2 What is the difference between management as a general human activity and management as a specialised occupation? How has this division happened, and what are some of its effects?

3 What examples are there in the chapter of this boundary being changed, and what were the effects?

4 Describe, with examples, the differences between general, functional, line, staff and project managers.

5 Give examples from your experience or observation of each of the four tasks of management.

6 How does Mintzberg's theory of management roles complement that which identifies the tasks of management?

7 What is the significance to someone starting a career in management of Luthans' theory about roles and performance?

8 How can thinking critically help managers do their job more effectively?

9 Review and revise the definition of management that you gave in Activity 1.1.

Concluding critical reflection

Think about the way managers in your company, or one with which you are familiar, go about their work. If you are a full-time student, draw on any jobs you have held or on the management of your studies at school or university. Review the material in the chapter, and make notes on these questions:

- Which of the issues discussed in this chapter are most relevant to the way you and your colleagues manage?

- What **assumptions** about the role of management appear to guide the way you, or others, manage? If these assumptions are supported by the evidence of recent events – have they worked, or not? Which aspects of the content and process of managing are you expected to focus on – or are you unsure? Does your observation support, or contradict, Luthans' theory?

- What aspects of the historical or current **context** of the company appear to influence how you, and others, interpret your management role? Do people have different interpretations?

- Can you compare and contrast your role with that of colleagues on your course? Does this suggest any plausible **alternative** ways of constructing your management role, in terms of where you devote your time and energy? How much scope do you have to change it?

- What **limitations** can you see in the theories and evidence presented in the chapter? For example, how valid might Mintzberg's theory (developed in large commercial firms) be for those managing in small business, or in the public sector? Can you think of ways of improving the model – e.g. by adding elements to it, or being more precise about the circumstance to which it applies?

Further reading

Magretta, J. (2002), *What Management Is (and why it is everyone's business)*, Profile Books, London.

This small book by a former editor at the *Harvard Business Review* offers a brief, readable and jargon-free account of the work of general management. Highly recommended.

Thompson, P. and McHugh, D. (2002), *Work Organisations: A critical introduction* (3rd edn) Palgrave, Basingstoke.

Alvesson, M. and Wilmott, H. (1996), *Making Sense of Management,* Sage, London.

Both provide very detailed discussion of management from a critical perspective, with numerous further references.

Handy, C. (1988), *Understanding Voluntary Organizations,* Penguin, Harmondsworth.

This chapter has stressed that management is not confined to commercial organisations, and Handy's book offers a valuable perspective for anyone wanting to consider management in the voluntary sector more fully.

Drucker, P. (1999b), *Management Challenges for the 21st Century,* Butterworth/Heinemann, London.

Worth reading as a collection of insightful observations from the enquiring mind of this great management theorist.

Finkelstein, S. (2003), *Why Smart Executives Fail: And what you can learn from their mistakes,* Penguin, New York.

A thoroughly researched and elegantly written analysis of the causes of failure – from which he draws many valuable insights into the complexities of managing.

Noordegraaf, M. and Stewart, R. (2000), 'Managerial behaviour research in private and public sectors: distinctiveness, disputes and directions', *Journal of Management Studies*, vol. 37, no. 3, pp. 427–444.

A scholarly review of research into the role of managers, which summarises and relates the main contributions, including those who have studied management in the public sector.

Mezias, J.M. and Starbuck, W.H. (2003), 'Studying the accuracy of managers' perceptions: a research odyssey', *British Journal of Management,* vol. 14, no. 1, pp. 3–17.

Since this chapter has stressed the significance of managers interpreting and interacting with their context, this paper is a timely reminder of how fallible those perceptions can be. The other articles in this symposium provide valuable insights into how managers see their world.

Currie, G. and Proctor, S.J. (2005), 'The antecedents of middle managers' strategic contribution: the case of a professional bureaucracy', *Journal of Management Studies*, vol. 42, no. 7, pp. 1325–1356.

An empirical study comparing how middle managers contributed to strategy in three hospitals, showing the ambiguities in their changing roles, and how contextual factors affected performance.

Hales, C. (2005), 'Rooted in supervision, branching into management: continuity and change in the role of first-line managers', *Journal of Management Studies*, vol. 42, no. 3, pp. 471–506.

Reviews the literature on supervisors and first-line managers, as an introduction to an empirical study (135 organisations) of their changing, and continuing, role.

Weblinks

These websites have appeared in the chapter:

www.ryanair.com

www.charitycommission.gov.uk

www.allianceboots.com

www.bp.com

www.shell.com

www.diageo.com

www.hm.com

Visit two of the business sites in the list, or those of other organisations in which you are interested, and navigate to the pages dealing with recent news, press or investor relations.

● What are the main issues which the organisation appears to be facing?

● Compare and contrast the issues you identify on the two sites.

● What challenges may they imply for those working in, and managing, these organisations?

Annotated weblinks, multiple choice questions and other useful resources can be found on www.pearsoned.co.uk/boddy

Chapter 2

Models of management

Aim

To present the main theoretical perspectives on management and to show how they relate to each other.

Objectives

By the end of your work on this chapter you should be able to outline the concepts below in your own terms and:

1 Explain the value of models of management, and compare unitary, pluralist and critical perspectives

2 State the structure of the competing values framework and evaluate its contribution to our understanding of management

3 Summarise the rational goal, internal process, human relations and open systems models and evaluate what each can contribute to a manager's understanding of their role

4 Use the model to classify the dominant form in two or more business units, and to gather evidence about the way this affects the roles of managing in those units

5 Explain the influence on management of uncertain conditions and the assumptions of non-linear models of management.

Key terms

This chapter introduces the following ideas:

model (or theory)	open system
metapho	system boundary
scientific management	feedback
operational research	subsystem
bureaucracy	sociotechnical system
administrative management	contingency approach
human relations approach	non-linear system
system	

Each is a term defined within the text, as well as in the Glossary at the end of the book.

Robert Owen – an early management innovator

www.newlanark.org.uk

Robert Owen (1771–1856) was a successful manufacturer of textiles, who ran mills in England and at New Lanark, about 24 miles from Glasgow, in Scotland. David Dale built the cotton-spinning mills at New Lanark in 1785 – which were then the largest in Scotland. Since they depended on water power Dale had built them below the Falls of Clyde – a well-known tourist attraction throughout the eighteenth century. Many people continued to visit both the Falls and New Lanark, which combined both manufacturing and social innovations.

Creating such a large industrial enterprise in the countryside meant that Dale (and Owen after him) had to attract and retain labour – which involved building not just the mill but also houses, shops, schools and churches for the workers. By 1793 the mill employed about 1200 people, of whom almost 800 were children, aged from 6 to 17: 200 were under 10 (McLaren, 1990). Dale provided the children with food, education and clothing in return for their working 12 hours each day: visitors were impressed by these facilities.

One visitor was Robert Owen, who shared Dale's views on the benefits to both labour and owner of good working conditions. By 1801 Dale wanted to sell New Lanark to someone who shared his principles and concluded that Owen (who had married Dale's daughter) was such a man. Owen had built a reputation for management skills while running mills in England, and did not approve of employing children in them.

Having bought the very large business of New Lanark, Owen quickly introduced new management and production control techniques. These included daily and weekly measurements of stock, output and productivity; a system of labour costing and measures of work in progress. He used a novel control technique: a small, four-sided piece of wood, with a different colour on each side, hung beside every worker. The colour set to the front indicated the previous day's standard of work – black indicating bad. Everyone could see this measure of the worker's performance, which overseers recorded to identify any trends in a person's work: 'Every process in the factory was closely watched, checked and recorded to increase labour productivity and to keep costs down' (Royle, 1998, p. 13).

Most adult employees, at this stage of the Industrial Revolution, had no experience of factory work, or of living in a large community such as New Lanark. Owen found that many 'were idle, intemperate, dishonest [and] devoid of truth' (quoted in Butt, 1971). Evening patrols were introduced to stop drunkenness, and there were rules about keeping the residential areas clean and free of rubbish. He also had 'to deal with slack managers who had tolerated widespread theft and embezzlement, immorality and drunkenness' (Butt, 1971).

During Owen's time at the mill it usually employed about 1500 people, and soon after taking over he stopped employing children under 10. He introduced other social innovations: a store at which employees could buy goods more cheaply than elsewhere (a model for the Co-operative Movement), and a school that looked after children from the age of 1 – enabling their mothers to work in the mills.

Sources: Butt (1971); McLaren (1990); Donachie (2000).

Case questions 2.1

● What management issues was Owen dealing with at New Lanark?

● What assumptions guided his management practices?

2.1 Introduction

The brief historical sketch of Robert Owen illustrates three themes that run through this book. First, he was active in devising management systems to improve mill performance, and paid particular attention to controlling the workforce to ensure productive activity. Second, Owen engaged with the wider social system: he criticised the effects of industrialisation on that social system and tried to influence local and national policy by advocating the end of child labour. (Providing nurseries for employees' children from the age of 1 would be rare even today.) Third, he was managing at a time of transition from an agricultural to an industrial economy, and many of the practices he invented were attempts to resolve the conflicts between these systems.

Indeed, Owen was an entrepreneur in many ways. His attempts to change worker behaviour was innovative, and he was equally creative in devising management systems and new ways of working. Managers today cope with similar issues. They need to recruit willing and capable staff, and ensure that their work creates value. Many share Owen's commitment to responsible business practice: they see that working conditions affect family circumstances – which in turn affect staff performance – and try to balance the two. Some subsidise child care and offer flexible hours to make it easier for people with family responsibilities to continue working. A new and widespread concern is that climate change will affect all businesses in ways that are not yet clear.

They also operate in a world experiencing changes equal to those facing Owen. In the newer industrial countries of eastern Europe and Asia the transition is again from agriculture to industry. Everywhere the Internet is enabling great changes in how people organise economic activity, equivalent to the Industrial Revolution of which Owen was part. All are coping with the transition to a world in which ever more business is done on a global scale.

In coping with such changes managers, like Owen before them, have searched for ways to manage their enterprises in a way that adds value. They all make assumptions about the best way to do things – and through trial and error develop management methods for their circumstances. Managers today can use their knowledge of these methods in deciding how to manage their business. No single approach will suit all conditions – managers need to draw critically and selectively on several perspectives.

The next section introduces the idea of management models, and how they can support a manager's work. Section 2.3 presents the competing values framework – a way of seeing the contrasts and complementarities between four theoretical perspectives – and the following sections outline the major ideas within each approach. The final section indicates some of the issues facing managers today – and new models that may represent these conditions.

2.2 Why study models of management?

A model (or theory) represents a complex phenomenon by identifying the major elements and relationships.

A **model (or theory)** represents a more complex reality. Focusing on the essential elements and their relationship helps to understand that complexity, and how change may affect it. Most management problems can be understood only by examining them from several perspectives, so no model offers a complete solution. Those managing a globally competitive business require flexibility, quality and low-cost production. Managers at Ford or DaimlerChrysler want models of the production process that help them to organise it efficiently from a technical perspective. They also want models of human behaviour which will help them to organise production in a way that encourages enthusiasm and commitment. The management task is to combine both approaches into an acceptable solution.

Managers act in accordance with their model (or theory) of the task. To understand management action we need to know the models available and how people use them, though Pfeffer and Sutton (2006) suggest why people frequently ignore such evidence: see Key Ideas.

Pfeffer and Sutton on why managers ignore evidence

key ideas

In making the case for evidence-based management, Pfeffer and Sutton (2006a) observe that experienced managers frequently ignore new evidence relevant to a decision because they:

- trust personal experience more than they trust research;
- prefer to use a method or solution that has worked before;
- are susceptible to consultants who vigorously promote their solutions;
- rely on dogma and myth – even when there is no evidence to support their value;
- uncritically imitate practices that appear to have worked well for famous companies.

Their paper outlines the benefits of basing practice on sound evidence – similar to the ideas of critical thinking presented in Chapter 1.

Source: Pfeffer and Sutton (2006a).

Models identify the variables

Models (theories) aim to identify the main variables in a situation, and the relationships between them: the more accurately they do so, the more useful they are. Since every situation is unique, many experienced managers doubt the value of theory. Joan Magretta's answer is that:

> without a theory of some sort it's hard to make sense of what's happening in the world around you. If you want to know whether you work for a well-managed organization – as opposed to whether you like your boss – you need a working theory of management. (Magretta, 2002, p. 10)

We all use theory, acting on (perhaps implicit) assumptions about the relationships between cause and effect. Good theories help this universal process by identifying variables and relationships. They provide a mental toolkit to deal consciously with a situation. The perspective we take reflects the assumptions we use to interpret, organise and makes sense of events – see Alan Fox in Key Ideas.

As managers seek to influence others to add value to resources, they use their mental model of the situation to decide where to focus effort. Figure 2.1 develops Figure 1.3 (the internal context within which managers work) to show some variables within each element: 'structure' could include more specific variables such as roles, teams or control systems. In 2006 Willie Walsh took over as chief executive of British Airways, and one of his objectives (set by his predecessor) was to raise operating profits to 10 per cent of sales. Figure 2.1 suggests ways of meeting this:

objectives – retaining a reputation for premium travel (a different market than Ryanair);

people – continuing the policy of reducing the number of employees;

technology – opening Terminal 5 at Heathrow;

business processes – new procedures for dealing with passengers and baggage.

key ideas   Alan Fox and a manager's frame of reference

Alan Fox (1974) distinguished between unitary, pluralist or radical perspectives on the relationship between managers and employees. Which assumption a person holds affects how they interpret the tasks of managing. Fox argued that those who take a:

● **unitary perspective** believe that organisations aim to develop rational ways of achieving common interests. Managerial work arises from a technical division of labour, and managers work to achieve objectives shared by all members.

● **pluralist perspective** believe that the complex division of labour in modern organisations creates groups with distinctive interests. Some conflict over ends and/or means is inevitable, and managerial work involves gaining sufficient consent to meet all interests in some mutually acceptable way.

● **radical perspective** challenge both unitary and pluralist models, arguing that they ignore the fact that the horizontal and vertical division of labour sustains unequal social relations within capitalist society. As long as these exist managers and employees will be in conflict.

Source: Alan Fox (1974).

In each area there are theories about the variables and their relationships – and about which changes will best add value. A change in one element may affect others – the aim of reducing staff will need to be handled sensitively to avoid hindering the aim of providing a premium service. Any change would depend on available *finance* – and on the chief executive's *power* to get things done. External events (Chapter 3) such as rising fuel prices or changes in general economic conditions shape all of these.

Managers need to influence people to achieve their value-adding objectives: people who are aware, thinking beings, with unique experiences, interests and objectives. This affects what information they attend to, the significance they attach to it and how they act. There is an example in Chapter 3 of a retail business in which senior managers, store

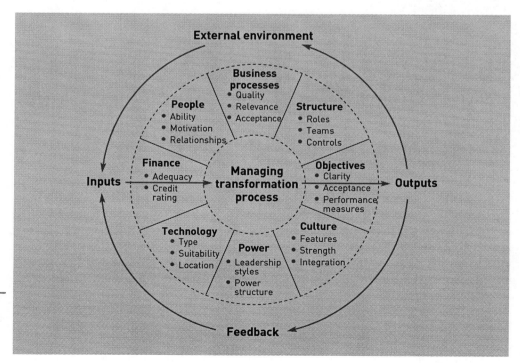

Figure 2.1

Some variables within the internal context of management

managers and shop-floor staff attached different meanings to the culture in which they worked. People interpret information subjectively, which makes it hard to predict how they will react: the Management in Practice feature illustrates two managers' contrasting assumptions about how to deal with subordinates.

Practice reflects managers' theories

These examples illustrate contrasting theories about motivation.

Motivating managers: Tim O'Toole, who became chief executive of London Underground in 2003, put in a new management structure, appointing a general manager for each line to improve accountability.

> Now there's a human being who is judged on how that line is performing and I want them to feel that kind of intense anxiety in the stomach that comes when there's a stalled train and they realise that it's their stalled train.

(From an article by Simon London, *Financial Times*, 20 February 2004)

Motivating staff to be innovative: Joe Roelandts is CEO of Xilinx (a company that makes advanced products in the electronics industry) and which (exceptionally) did not make staff redundant during a period of low industry demand.

> The decision to avoid lay-offs was a better business decision. It protected the minds of the people who work on the future; it keeps their minds free to continue to innovate. No one can innovate when they are worried about their jobs.

(From an article by Simon London, *Financial Times*, 22 January 2003)

Find out more at **www.xilinx.com**.

FT

Case questions 2.2

- Give examples of the variables in Figure 2.1 that Robert Owen was attempting to influence.
- Which of the variables were influencing the performance of his mill?
- Is there a conflict between the need to control workers and Owen's creative approach to management?

Models reflect their context

People develop models in response to circumstances: in this case this means the most pressing issues facing managers at the time. In the late nineteenth century skilled labour was scarce and unskilled labour plentiful: the most pressing problem for managers such as Robert Owen was to recruit and control workers. Entrepreneurs trying to meet growing demand wanted theories about making production more efficient. They looked for ways to simplify tasks so that they could use less skilled employees, and early management theories gave priority to these issues. People often refer to this focus on efficiency as a manufacturing mindset.

Peter Drucker (1954) observed that customers do not buy products, but the satisfaction of needs: what they value may be different from what producers think they are selling. Manufacturing efficiency is necessary, but not sufficient. Managers, Drucker argued, should develop a marketing mindset, focused on what customers want, and how

A **metaphor** is an image used to signify the essential characteristics of a phenomenon.

much they will pay. As managers try to meet changing customer needs quickly and cheaply they seek models of flexible working. As business becomes more global, they seek theories about managing across the world.

---

key ideas   Gareth Morgan's images of organisation

Since organisations are complex creations, no single theory can explain them adequately. We need to see them from several viewpoints, each of which will illuminate one aspect or feature – while also obscuring others. Gareth Morgan (1997) shows how alternative mental images and **metaphors** can represent organisations. Metaphors are a way of thinking about a phenomenon, attaching labels that vividly indicate the image being used. Images help understanding – but also obscure or distort understanding if we use the wrong one. Morgan explores eight ways of seeing organisations as:

- **machines** – mechanical thinking and the rise of the bureaucracies;
- **organisms** – recognising how the environment affects their health;
- **brains** – an information-processing, learning perspective;
- **cultures** – a focus on beliefs and values;
- **political systems** – a view on conflicts and power;
- **psychic prisons** – how people can become trapped by habitual ways of thinking;
- **flux and transformation** – a focus on change and renewal;
- **instruments of domination** – over members, nations and environments.

Critical thinking helps improve our mental models

The ideas on critical thinking in Chapter 1 help managers to improve the accuracy and usefulness of the theories they use to guide their action. Working effectively depends on being able and willing to test the validity of any theory, and to revise it in the light of experience by:

- identifying and challenging assumptions
- recognising the importance of context
- imagining and exploring alternatives
- seeing limitations.

As you work through this chapter, there will be opportunities to practise these components of critical thinking.

2.3   The competing values framework

People have developed a succession of models of management to understand and deal with current management issues. While academics or practitioners put forward new models, many managers continue to use earlier approaches – perhaps because they still suit their situation, or because they are familiar. Quinn *et al.* (2003) believe that successive models (which they term 'rational goal', 'internal process', 'human relations' and 'open systems') complement, rather than contradict, each other as they are all:

symptoms of a larger problem – the need to achieve organizational effectiveness in a highly dynamic environment. In such a complex and fast-changing world, simple solutions become suspect … Sometimes we needed stability, sometimes we needed change. Often we needed both at the same time. (p. 11)

While each model adds to our knowledge of management, none is sufficient in itself – the four are complementary elements in a larger whole. The 'competing values' framework integrates them by highlighting their underlying values – see Figure 2.2.

The vertical axis represents the tension between flexibility and control. Managers seek flexibility as they try to cope with rapid change. Others try to increase control – apparently the opposite of flexibility. The horizontal axis distinguishes an internal focus from an external one. Some managers focus on internal issues, while others focus on the world outside. Successive models of management relate to the four segments.

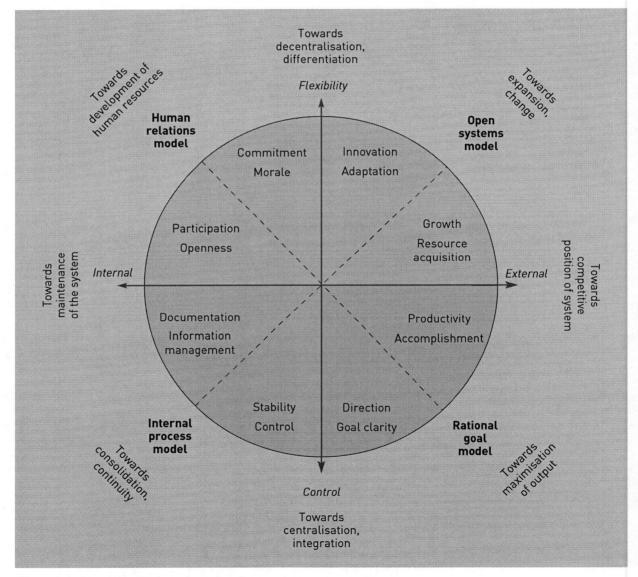

Figure 2.2 Competing values framework
Source: Quinn *et al.* (2003), p. 13.

The labels within the circle indicate the primary criteria of effectiveness that are the focus of models in that segment, shown around the outside. The human relations model, upper left in the figure, stresses the human criteria of commitment, participation and openness. The open systems model (upper right) stresses criteria of innovation, adaptation and growth. The rational goal model in the lower right focuses on productivity, direction and goal clarity. The internal process model stresses stability, documentation and control. Finally, the outer ring indicates the values associated with each model – the dominant value in the rational goal model is that of maximising output, while in human relations it is developing people. Successive sections of the chapter outline theories associated with each segment.

---

management in practice **Competing values at IMI?** www.imiplc.com

When Martin Lamb took control of IMI (the UK's seventh largest engineering group) in 2001 he introduced significant changes. He rebuilt the group, which had suffered a decline in business like many other engineering businesses, by switching more manufacturing to low-cost countries and began to change the culture to encourage close links with key customers and to boost innovation. He also concentrated the business on five sectors of engineering, each associated with high-value products and a strong chance of growth in the next few years. About 40 skilled engineers at 'vision centres' had to identify technologies from other industries that IMI could adapt to its own use. Mr Lamb said: 'This is a fundamental transition, aimed at moving IMI away from an old-established manufacturing enterprise to a company focused on product development and applications of knowledge.'

Someone who knew the company well commented: 'I always had the feeling ... that IMI was a bit introverted and anything that [makes] the company more aggressive on the sales side is to be applauded.'

FT

Source: Extracts from an article in *Financial Times*, 4 February 2004.

Activity 2.1   **Critical reflection on the model**

Using the model to reflect on IMI

- Which of the competing values were most dominant in 2000, and which were most dominant at the time of this report?
- What examples can you find in the case that correspond to the open systems model?

Using the model to reflect on your organisation

- Which of the competing values are most dominant in, say, three separate departments?
- What evidence can you find of how that affects the way people manage?
- Does your evidence support or contradict the model?

2.4   Rational goal models

A rarely quoted example of early entrepreneurs developing ways to manage large numbers of people is found in the slave plantations in the United States, where several 'modern management practices were to be found in the operation of the ante-bellum plantations' (Cooke, 2003). Cooke quotes a contemporary account of work on a cotton plantation that records how owners divided slaves into gangs according to their abilities, and then allocated predetermined tasks to each:

> 1st the best hands, embracing those of good judgement and quick motion. 2nd those of the weakest and most inefficient class. 3rd the second class of hoe hands. Thus classified, the first class run ahead and open a small hole about seven to ten inches apart, into which the second class drop from four to five cotton seed, and the third class follow and cover with a rake. (Fogel, 1989: quoted in Cooke, 2003, p. 1908)

More widely, the availability of powered machinery during the Industrial Revolution enabled the transformation of manufacturing and mining processes. These technological innovations encouraged, but were not the only reason for, the growth of the factory system. The earlier 'putting-out' system of manufacture, in which people worked at home on materials supplied and collected by entrepreneurs, allowed great freedom over hours, pace and methods of work. However, it was difficult to control the quantity and quality of output. Emerging capitalist entrepreneurs found that they could secure more control if they brought workers together in a factory. Having all workers on a single site meant that:

> coercive authority could be more easily applied, including systems of fines, supervision ... the paraphernalia of bells and clocks, and incentive payments. The employer could dictate the general conditions of work, time and space; including the division of labour, overall organisational layout and design, rules governing movement, shouting, singing and other forms of disobedience. (Thompson and McHugh 2002, p. 22)

This still left entrepreneurs across Europe and later the United States (and now China – see Management in Practice) with the problem of how to manage these new factories profitably. Although domestic and export demand for manufactured goods was high, so was the risk of business failure.

Incentives at TCL, China   www.tcl.com   **management in practice**

TCL Corporation is one of the top producers of electronics products in China, and management is proud of the long hours employees work. Signs posted next to production lines encourage workers to push themselves to do even more. 'If you don't diligently work today', one warns ominously, 'you'll diligently look for work tomorrow'. The company is growing rapidly and has won many awards for design and quality.

Source: Based on 'Bursting out of China', *Business Week*, 17 November 2003, pp. 24–25; company website.

key ideas   Adam Smith and Charles Babbage

Adam Smith, the Scottish economist, had written enthusiastically in 1776 of the way in which pin manufacturers in Glasgow had broken a job previously done by one man into several small steps. A single worker now performed each of these steps repetitively. This greatly reduced the discretion that workers had over their work but, because each was able to specialise, output increased dramatically. Smith believed that this was one of the key ways in which the new industrial system was increasing the wealth of the country.

Charles Babbage supported and developed Smith's observations. He was an English mathematician better known as the inventor of the first calculating engine. During his work on that project he visited many workshops and factories in England and on the Continent. He then published his reflections on 'the many curious processes and interesting facts' that had come to his attention (Babbage, 1835). He believed that 'perhaps the most important principle on which the economy of a manufacture depends is the division of labour amongst the persons who perform the work' (p. 169).

Babbage also observed that employers in the mining industry had applied the idea to what he called 'mental labour'. 'Great improvements have resulted ... from the judicious distribution of duties ... amongst those responsible for the whole system of the mine and its government' (p. 202). He also recommended that managers should know the precise expense of every stage in production. Factories should also be large enough to secure the economies made possible by the division of labour and the new machinery.

Source: Babbage (1835).

Frederick Taylor

Scientific management
The school of management called 'scientific' attempted to create a science of factory production.

The fullest answer to the problems of factory organisation came in the work of Frederick W. Taylor (1856–1915), always associated with the ideas of scientific management. An American mechanical engineer, Taylor focused on the relationship between the worker and the machine-based production systems that were in widespread use:

> the principal object of management should be to secure the maximum prosperity for the employer, coupled with the maximum prosperity for each employee. The words 'maximum prosperity' ... mean the development of every branch of the business to its highest state of excellence, so that the prosperity may be permanent'. (Taylor, 1917, p. 9)

He believed the way to achieve this was to ensure that each worker reached their state of maximum efficiency, so that each was doing 'the highest grade of work for which his natural abilities fit him' (p. 9). This would follow from detailed control of the process, which would become the managers' primary responsibility: they should concentrate on understanding the production systems, and use this to specify every aspect of the operation. In terms of Morgan's images, the appropriate image would be the machine. Taylor advocated five principles:

1 use scientific methods to determine the one best way of doing a task, rather than rely on the older 'rule of thumb' methods;
2 select the best person to do the job so defined, ensuring that their physical and mental qualities were appropriate for the task;
3 train, teach and develop the worker to follow the defined procedures precisely;
4 provide financial incentives to ensure people work to the prescribed method; and
5 move responsibility for planning and organising from the worker to the manager.

Taylor's underlying philosophy was that scientific analysis and fact, not guesswork, should inform management. Like Smith and Babbage before him, he believed that efficiency rose if tasks were routine and predictable. He advocated techniques such as time and motion studies, standardised tools and individual incentives. Breaking work into small, specific tasks would increase control. Specialist managerial staff would design these tasks and organise the workers:

> The work of every workman is fully planned out by the management at least one day in advance, and each man receives in most cases complete written instructions, describing in detail the task which he is to accomplish, as well as the means to be used in doing the work ... This task specifies not only what is to be done but how it is to be done and the exact time allowed for doing it. (Taylor, 1917, p. 39)

Taylor also influenced the development of administrative systems such as record keeping and stock control to support manufacturing.

Using work study in the 1990s

management in practice

Oswald Jones recalls his experience as a work study engineer in the 1990s, where he and his colleagues were deeply committed to the principles of scientific management:

> Jobs were designed to be done in a mechanical fashion by removing opportunities for worker discretion. This had dual benefits: very simple jobs could be measured accurately (so causing [fewer] disputes) and meant that operators were much more interchangeable which was an important feature in improving overall efficiency levels. (p. 647)

Source: Jones (2000).

Managers in industrialised economies adopted Taylor's ideas widely: Henry Ford was an enthusiastic advocate. When he introduced the assembly line in 1914 the time taken to assemble a car fell from over 700 hours to 93 minutes. Ford also developed systems of materials flow and plant layout, a significant contribution to scientific management (Williams *et al.*, 1992; Biggs, 1996).

Increased productivity often came at human cost (Thomson and McHugh, 2002). Trade unions believed Taylor's methods increased unemployment, and vigorously opposed them. Many people find work on an assembly line boring and alienating, devoid of much human meaning. In extreme cases the time taken to complete an operation is less than a minute, and uses few human abilities.

Ford's Highland Park plant

management in practice

Ford's plant at Highland Park, completed in 1914, introduced predictability and order

> that eliminates all questions of how work is to be done, who will do it, and when it will be done. The rational factory, then, is a factory that runs like a machine. (Biggs, 1996, p. 6)

Biggs provides abundant evidence of the effects of applying rational production methods:

> The advances made in Ford's New Shop allowed the engineers to control work better. The most obvious and startling change in the entire factory was, of course, the constant movement, and the speed of that movement, not only the speed of the assembly line, but the speed of every moving person or object in the plant. When workers moved from one place to another, they were instructed to move fast. Laborers who moved parts were ordered to go faster. And everyone on a moving line worked as fast as the line dictated. Not only were workers expected to produce at a certain rate in order to earn a day's wages but ▶

they also had no choice but to work at the pace dictated by the machine. By 1914 the company employed supervisors called pushers (not the materials handlers) to 'push' the men to work faster.

The 1914 jobs of most Ford workers bore little resemblance to what they had been just four years earlier, and few liked the transformation ... As early as 1912, job restructuring sought an 'exceptionally specialized division of labor [to bring] the human element into [the] condition of performing automatically with machine-like regularity and speed'. (Biggs, 1996, p. 132)

Frank and Lillian Gilbreth

Frank and Lillian Gilbreth (1868–1924 and 1878–1972) worked as a husband and wife team, and enthusiastically promoted the development of scientific management. Frank Gilbreth had been a bricklayer, observing practices that made the work slow and output unpredictable. He filmed men laying bricks and used this to set out the most economical movements for each task. He specified exactly what the employer should provide, such as trestles at the right height and materials at the right time. Supplies of mortar and bricks (arranged the right way up) should arrive at a time that did not interrupt work. An influential book (Gilbreth, 1911) gave precise guidance on how to reduce unnecessary actions (from 18 to 5) and hence fatigue, while laying bricks. The rules and charts would help apprentices:

> [They] will enable the apprentice to earn large wages immediately, because he has ... a series of instructions that show each and every motion in the proper sequence. They eliminate the 'wrong' way [and] all experimenting. (quoted in Spriegel and Myers, 1953, p. 57)

Lillian Gilbreth focused on the psychological aspects of management, and on the welfare of the individual worker. She also advocated the ideas of scientific management believing that, properly applied, they would enable individuals to reach their full potential. Through careful development of systems, careful selection, clearly planned training and proper equipment, workers would build their self-respect and pride. In *The Psychology of Management* (1914) she argued that if workers did something well, and that was made public, they would develop pride in their work and in themselves. She recognised that workers had enquiring minds, and that management should take time to explain the reasons for work processes:

> Unless the man knows why he is doing the thing, his judgment will never reinforce his work ... His work will not enlist his zeal unless he knows exactly why he is made to work in the particular manner prescribed. (quoted in Spriegel and Myers, 1953, p. 431)

Activity 2.2   What assumptions did they make?

What assumptions did Frederick Taylor and Lillian Gilbreth make about the interests and abilities of industrial workers?

Operational research

Operational research is a scientific method of providing (managers) with a quantitative basis for decisions regarding the operations under their control.

Another practice within the rational goal model is **operational research** (OR). This originated in the early 1940s, when the UK War Department faced severe management problems – such as the most effective distribution of radar-linked anti-aircraft gun emplacements, or the safest speed at which convoys of merchant ships should cross the Atlantic (see Kirby (2003) for a non-technical introduction to the topic). To solve these it formed operational research teams, which pooled the expertise of scientific disciplines such as mathematics and physics. These produced significant results: Kirby points out that while at the start of the London Blitz 20,000 rounds of ammunition were fired for each enemy aircraft destroyed: 'by the summer of 1941 the number had fallen ... to 4,000 as a result of the operational research [teams] improving the accuracy of radar-based gun-laying' (Kirby 2003, p. 94).

After the war, managers in industry and government saw that operational research techniques could also help to run complex civil organisations. The scale and complexity of business was increasing, and required new techniques to analyse the many interrelated variables. Mathematical models could help, and computing developments supported increasingly sophisticated models. In the 1950s the steel industry needed to cut the cost of transporting iron ore: staff used OR techniques to analyse the most efficient procedures for shipping, unloading and transferring it to steelworks.

The method is widely used in both business and public sectors, where it helps planning in areas as diverse as maintenance, cash flow, inventory and crew scheduling (e.g. Lezaun *et al.*, 2006). Willoughby and Zappe (2006) illustrate how a university has used the technique to help allocate students to seminar groups. One difficulty is that some managers find the mathematical basis forbidding. A second is that OR cannot take into account human and social uncertainties, and the assumptions built into the models may be invalid, especially if they involve political interests. The technique clearly contributes to the analysis of management problems, but is only one part of the solution.

Current status

Table 2.1 summarises principles common to rational goal models and their modern application.

Principles of the rational goal model	Current applications
Systematic work methods	Work study and process engineering departments develop precise specifications for processes
Detailed division of labour	Where staff focus on one type of work or customer in manufacturing or service operations
Centralised planning and control	Modern information systems increase the scope for central control of worldwide operations
Low-involvement employment relationship	Using temporary staff as required, rather than permanent employees

Table 2.1

Modern applications of the rational goal model

Examples of rational goal approaches are common in manufacturing and service organisations. Cooper and Taylor (2000) show how the work of accounting staff has been transformed by the steady application of scientific management techniques, while Aquiar (2001) presents a similar story from the building cleaning industry. You may have experienced the frustration of speaking to a customer service adviser on the telephone who is compelled to provide only a scripted response, without deviation, to try to make a further sale.

Case questions 2.3

- Which of the ideas in the rational goal model was Owen experimenting with at New Lanark?
- Would you describe Owen's approach to management as low involvement?
- What assumptions did he make about the motivation of workers?

The methods are widely used in the mass production industries of emergent economies such as China and Malaysia. Gamble *et al.* (2004) found that in such plants 'Work organization tended to be fragmented (on Taylorist lines) and routinized, with considerable surveillance and control over production volumes and quality' (p. 403).

Human resource management policies were consistent with this approach – the recruitment of operators in Chinese electronics plants was

> often of young workers, generally female and from rural areas. One firm said its operators had to be 'young farmers within cycling distance of the factory, with good eyesight. Education is not important'. (p. 404)

Activity 2.3   Finding current examples

Try to find an original example of work that has been designed on rational goal principles. There are examples in office and service areas as well as in factories. Compare your examples with those of colleagues.

2.5   Internal process models

Max Weber

Bureaucracy is a system in which people are expected to follow precisely defined rules and procedures rather than to use personal judgement.

A major contribution to the search for ways of managing organisations efficiently came from Max Weber (1978). Weber (1864–1920) was a German social historian who drew attention to the significance of large organisations. As societies became more complex, responsibility for core activities became concentrated in specialised units. They could only operate with systems that institutionalised the management process by creating rules and regulations, hierarchy, precise division of labour and detailed procedures. Weber was one of the first to observe that the process of **bureaucracy** was bringing routine to office operations just as machines had to production.

Bureaucratic management is usually associated with the characteristics in the next Key Ideas box.

key ideas   The characteristics of bureaucratic management

Rules and regulations The formal guidelines that define and control the behaviour of employees while they are working. Adherence to rules and regulations ensures uniform procedures and operations, regardless of an individual's wishes. Rules enable top management to coordinate middle managers and, through them, first-line managers and employees. Managers leave, so rules bring stability.

Impersonality Rules leads to impersonality, which protects employees from the whims of managers. Although the term has negative connotations, Weber believed it ensured fairness, by evaluating subordinates objectively on performance rather than subjectively on personal considerations. It limits favouritism.

Division of labour Managers and employees work on specialised tasks, with the benefits originally noted by Adam Smith – such as that jobs are relatively easy to learn and control.

Hierarchical structure Weber advocated a clear hierarchy in which jobs were ranked vertically by the amount of authority to make decisions. Each lower position is under the control of a higher position.

Authority structure A system of rules, impersonality, division of labour and hierarchy forms an authority structure – the right to make decisions of varying importance at different levels within the organisation.

Rationality This refers to using the most efficient means to achieve objectives. Managers should run their organisations logically and 'scientifically' so that all decisions help to achieve the objectives.

Activity 2.4   Bureaucratic management in education?

Reflect on your role as a student and how rules have affected the experience. Try to identify one example of your own to add to those below or that illustrates the point specifically within your institution:

- rules and regulations – the number of courses you need to pass for a degree;
- impersonality – admission criteria, emphasising previous exam performance, not friendship;
- division of labour – chemists not teaching management, and vice versa;
- hierarchical structure – to whom your lecturer reports, and to whom they report;
- authority structure – who decides whether to recruit an additional lecturer;
- rationality – appointing new staff to departments that have the highest ratio of students to staff.

Compare your examples with those of other students and consider the effects of these features of bureaucracy on the institution and its students.

Weber was aware that, as well as creating bureaucratic structures, managers were using scientific management techniques to control production and impose discipline on factory work. The two systems complemented each other. Formal structures of management centralise power, and hierarchical organisation aids functional specialisation. Fragmenting tasks, imposing close discipline on employees and minimising their discretion ensures controlled, predictable performance (Thompson and McHugh, 2002).

Weber stressed the importance of a career structure clearly linked to the position a person held. This would allow them to move up the hierarchy in a predictable, defined and open way, which would increase their commitment to the organisation. Rules about selection and promotion brought fairness to these at a time when nepotism and favouritism were common. He also believed that officials should work within a framework of rules. The right to give instructions was based on a person's position in the hierarchy, and a rational analysis of how staff should work. This worked well in large public and private organisations, such as government departments and banks.

While recognising the material benefits of modern methods, Weber also saw their costs:

> Bureaucratic rationalization instigates a system of control that traps the individual within an 'iron cage' of subjugation and constraint ... For Weber, it is instrumental rationality, accompanied by the rise of measurement and quantification, regulations and procedures, accounting, efficiency that entraps us all in a world of ever-increasing material standards, but vanishing magic, fantasy, meaning and emotion. (Gabriel, 2005, p. 11)

Activity 2.5   Gathering evidence on bureaucracy

Rules often receive bad publicity, and we are all sometimes frustrated by rules that seem obstructive. To evaluate bureaucracy, collect some evidence. Think of a job that you or a friend has held, or of the place in which you work.

- Do the supervisors appear to operate within a framework of rules, or do they do as they wish? What are the effects?
- Do clear rules guide selection and promotion procedures? What are the effects?
- As a customer of an organisation, how have rules and regulations affected your experience?
- Check what you have found, preferably combining it with that prepared by other people on your course. Does the evidence support the advantages, or the disadvantages, of bureaucracy?

Henri Fayol

Administrative management is the use of institutions and order rather than relying on personal qualities to get things done.

Managers were also able to draw on the ideas of **administrative management** developed by Henri Fayol (1841–1925), whose work echoes that of Taylor and Weber. While Taylor's scientific management focused on production systems, Fayol devised management principles that would apply to the whole organisation. Like Taylor, Fayol trained as an engineer, graduating at the age of 19 as the most distinguished student in his year. In 1860 he joined Commentry–Fourchambault–Decazeville, a coal mining and iron foundry company, rising rapidly through the company to become managing director in 1888 (Parker and Ritson, 2005). By the time he retired in 1918 it had become one of the success stories of French industry. Throughout his career he kept detailed diaries and notes about his management experiences, and his reflections on these formed the basis of his work after retirement, when he sought to stimulate debate and thinking about management in both private and public sectors. His book *Administration, industrielle et générale* only became widely available in English in 1949 (Fayol, 1949).

Fayol credited his success as a manager to the methods he used, not to his personal qualities. He believed that managers should use certain principles in performing their functions, and these are listed in the next Key Ideas box. The term 'principles' did not imply they were rigid or absolute:

> It is all a question of proportion ... allowance must be made for different changing circumstances ... the principles are flexible and capable of adaptation to every need; it is a matter of knowing how to make use of them, which is a difficult art requiring intelligence, experience, decision and proportion. (Fayol, 1949, p. 14)

In using terms such as 'changing circumstances' and 'adaptation to every need' in setting out the principles, Fayol anticipated the contingency theories that were developed in the 1960s (see Chapter 10). He was also an early advocate of management education: 'Elementary in the primary schools, somewhat wider in the post-primary schools, and quite advanced in higher education establishments' (p. 16).

Fayol's principles of management

key ideas

1 **Division of work** If people specialise, the more can they concentrate on the same matters and so acquire an ability and accuracy, which increases their output. However, 'it has its limits which experience teaches us may not be exceeded'.

2 **Authority and responsibility** The right to give orders and to exact obedience, derived from either a manager's official authority or his or her personal authority. 'Wherever authority is exercised, responsibility arises.'

3 **Discipline** 'Essential for the smooth running of business ... without discipline no enterprise could prosper.'

4 **Unity of command** 'For any action whatsoever, an employee should receive orders from one superior only' – to avoid conflicting instructions and resulting confusion.

5 **Unity of direction** 'One head and one plan for a group of activities having the same objective ... essential to unity of action, co-ordination of strength and focusing of effort.'

6 **Subordination of individual interest to general interest** 'The interests of one employee or group of employees should not prevail over that of the concern.'

7 **Remuneration of personnel** 'Should be fair and, as far as possible, afford satisfaction both to personnel and firm.'

8 **Centralisation** 'The question of centralisation or decentralisation is a simple question of proportion ... [the] share of initiative to be left to [subordinates] depends on the character of the manager, the reliability of the subordinates and the condition of the business. The degree of centralisation must vary according to different cases.'

9 **Scalar chain** 'The chain of superiors from the ultimate authority to the lowest ranks ... is at times disastrously lengthy in large concerns, especially governmental ones.' Fayol pointed out that if a speedy decision was needed it was appropriate for people at the same level of the chain to communicate directly, as long as their immediate superiors approved. 'It provides for the usual exercise of some measure of initiative at all levels of authority.'

10 **Order** Materials should be in the right place to avoid loss, and the posts essential for the smooth running of the business filled by capable people.

11 **Equity** Managers should be both friendly and fair to their subordinates – 'equity requires much good sense, experience and good nature'.

12 **Stability of tenure of personnel** A high employee turnover is not efficient – 'Instability of tenure is at one and the same time cause and effect of bad running.'

13 **Initiative** 'The initiative of all represents a great source of strength for businesses ... and ... it is essential to encourage and develop this capacity to the full. The manager must be able to sacrifice some personal vanity in order to grant this satisfaction to subordinates ... a manager able to do so is infinitely superior to one who cannot.'

14 **Esprit de corps** 'Harmony, union among the personnel of a concern is a great strength in that concern. Effort, then, should be made to establish it.' Fayol suggested doing so by avoiding sowing dissension amongst subordinates, and using verbal rather than written communication when appropriate.

Source: Fayol (1949).

Current status

Table 2.2 summarises some principles common to the internal process models of management and indicates their modern application.

Table 2.2

Modern applications of the internal process model

Some principles of the internal process model	Current applications
Rules and regulations	All organisations have these, covering areas such as expenditure, safety, recruitment and confidentiality
Impersonality	Appraisal processes based on objective criteria or team assessments, not personal preference
Division of labour	Setting narrow limits to employees' areas of responsibility – found in many organisations
Hierarchical structure	Most company organisation charts show managers in a hierarchy – with subordinates below them
Authority structure	Holders of a particular post in the hierarchy have authority over matters relating to that post, and not to matters which are the responsibility of others
Centralisation	Organisations balance central control of (say) finance or online services with local control of (say) pricing or recruitment
Initiative	Current practice in some firms is to increase the power and responsibility of operating staff
Rationality	Managers are expected to focus on achieving the organisation's objectives, and assess issues on the basis of evidence, not personal preference

Some organisations use these methods, especially in the public sector and in commercial businesses with geographically dispersed outlets – such as hotels, retailers and banks. Customers expect them to deliver a predictable service in each location, so they centralise design and development activities. Manuals set out how to deliver the service, and the procedures managers should follow – how to recruit and train staff, what the premises must look like and how to treat customers. Walton (2005) found that the model of bureaucratic control outlined by Weber is still widely used (see also Greenwood and Lawrence, 2005), in organisations where predictability and order are important. If managers work in situations that require change, innovation and willing commitment, they need other models.

2.6 Human relations models

In the early twentieth century writers such as Follett and Mayo recognised the limitations of the scientific management perspective.

Mary Parker Follett

Mary Parker Follett (1868–1933) graduated with distinction from Radcliffe College (now part of Harvard University) in 1898, having studied economics, law and philosophy. She took up social work and quickly acquired a reputation as an imaginative and effective professional. She realised the creativity of the group process, and the potential it offered for truly democratic government – which people themselves would have to create.

She advocated replacing bureaucratic institutions by networks in which people themselves analysed their problems and implemented their solutions. True democracy depended on tapping the potential of all members of society by enabling individuals to take part in groups organised to solve particular problems and accepting personal responsibility for the result. Such ideas are finding renewed relevance today in the work of institutions such as community action and tenants' groups.

Mary Parker Follett on groups

key ideas

Follett saw the group as an intermediate institution between the solitary individual and the abstract society, and argued that it was through the institution of the group that people organised cooperative action. In 1926 she wrote:

> Early psychology was based on the study of the individual; early sociology was based on the study of society. But there is no such thing as the 'individual', there is no such thing as 'society'; there is only the group and the group-unit – the social individual. Social psychology must begin with an intensive study of the group, of the selective processes which go on within it, the differentiated reactions, the likenesses and the unlikenesses, and the spiritual energy which unites them.

Source: Graham (1995), p. 230.

In the 1920s Follett became involved in the business world, when managers invited her to investigate business problems. She again advocated the application of the self-governing principle that would facilitate the growth of individuals and the groups to which they belonged. Conflict was inevitable if people brought valuable differences of view to a problem: the group must then resolve the conflict to create what she called an integrative unity amongst the members.

She acknowledged that organisations had to optimise production, but did not accept that the strict division of labour was the right way to achieve this (Follett, 1920), as it devalued human creativity. The human side should not be separated from the mechanical side, as the two are bound up together. She believed that people, whether managers or workers, behave as they do because of the reciprocal response that occurs in any relationship. If managers tell people to behave as if they are extensions of the assembly line they will do so. This implied that effective managers would not manipulate their subordinates, but train them in the use of responsible power: 'managers should give workers a chance to grow capacity or power for themselves'. Graham (1995) provides an excellent review of Follett's work.

Elton Mayo

Elton Mayo (1880–1949) was an Australian who, from 1911 to 1922 taught logic, psychology and ethics at the University of Queensland. In 1922 he moved to the United States, and in 1926 became Professor of Industrial Research at Harvard Business School, applying psychological methods to industrial conflict. He was an accomplished speaker, and his ideas aroused wide interest in the academic and business communities (Smith, 1998).

In 1924 managers of the Western Electric Company initiated a series of experiments at their Hawthorne plant in Chicago to discover the effect on output of changing defined factors in the physical environment. The first experiments studied the effect of lighting. The researchers established a control and an experimental group, varied the level of illumination and measured the output. As light rose, so did output. More surprisingly, as light fell output continued to rise. Even stranger was the fact that output in the control group also rose, even though there had been no change in their lighting. Clearly the physical conditions had only a small effect and the team set up a more comprehensive experiment to identify other factors.

They assembled a small group of workers in a separate room and altered variables in turn. These included the working hours, the length of breaks and the provision of refreshments. The experienced workers were assembling small components into telephone equipment. A supervisor was in charge and there was also an observer to record the experiments and how the workers reacted. Great care was taken to prevent external factors disrupting the effects of the variables under investigation. The researchers were careful to explain what was happening and to ensure that the workers understood what they were expected to do. They also listened to employees' views of working conditions.

The researchers varied conditions every two or three weeks, while the supervisor measured output regularly. This showed a gradual, if erratic, increase – even when the researchers returned conditions to those prevailing at an earlier stage, as Figure 2.3 shows.

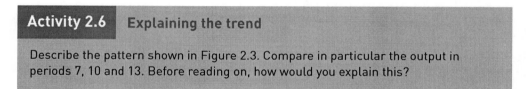

Activity 2.6   Explaining the trend

Describe the pattern shown in Figure 2.3. Compare in particular the output in periods 7, 10 and 13. Before reading on, how would you explain this?

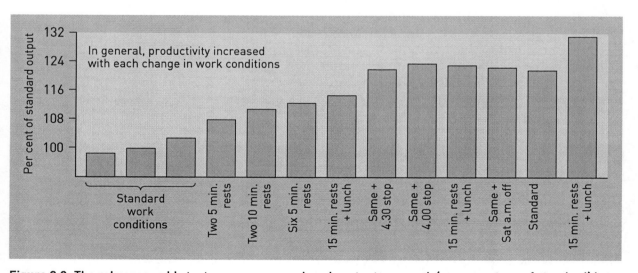

Figure 2.3 The relay assembly test room – average hourly output per week (as percentage of standard) in successive experimental periods

Source: Based on data from Roethlisberger and Dickson (1939). From *Behavior in Organizations*, 6th edition, Greenberg and Baron, © 1997. Reprinted by permission of Pearson Education, Inc. Upper Saddle River, NJ.

In 1928 senior managers invited Mayo to interpret the experiments and present his conclusions to a wider audience (Smith, 1998). Mayo undertook this work enthusiastically, reconciling the different interests in the research teams and bringing additional staff from Harvard into the team now conducting and publicising the research (Roethlisberger and Dickson, 1939; Mayo, 1949).

Their conclusions from the relay-assembly test room experiments were that the increase in productivity was not related to the physical changes, but to a change in the social situation in which the group was working:

> the major experimental change was introduced when those in charge sought to hold the situation humanly steady (in the interests of critical changes to be introduced) by getting the co-operation of the workers. What actually happened was that 6 individuals became a team and the team gave itself wholeheartedly and spontaneously to co-operation in the environment. (Mayo, 1949, p. 64)

The group felt special: managers asked for their views, were involved with them, paid attention to them and they had the chance to influence some aspects of the work.

The research team also observed another part of the factory, the bank wiring room, which revealed a different aspect of group working. Workers here were paid according to a piece-rate system, in which management pays workers a set amount for each item, or piece, that they produce. Such schemes reflect the assumption that financial incentives will encourage staff to work. The researchers observed that employees regularly produced less than they could have done. They had developed a sense of a normal rate of output, and ensured that all adhered to this rate, believing that if they produced, and earned, too much, management would reduce the piece-rate. Group members exercised informal sanctions against colleagues who worked too hard (or too slowly), until they came into line. Members who did too much were known as 'rate-busters' while those who did too little were 'chisellers'. Anyone who told the supervisor about this was a 'squealer'. Sanctions included being 'binged' – tapped on the shoulder to let them know that what they were doing was wrong. Managers had little or no control over these groups, who appointed their leader.

Finally, the research team conducted an extensive interview programme. They began by asking employees about the working environment and how they felt about their job, and then some questions about their life in general. The responses showed that there were often close links between work and domestic life. Work affected people's wider life much more than had been expected, and domestic circumstances affected their feelings about work. This implied that supervisors needed to think of a subordinate as a complete person, not just as a worker.

Activity 2.7   A comparison with Taylor

Compare this evidence with Frederick Taylor's belief that piece-rates would be an incentive to individuals to raise their performance. What may explain the difference?

Mayo's reflections on the Hawthorne studies drew attention to aspects of human behaviour that practitioners of scientific management had neglected. He introduced the idea of 'social man', in contrast to the 'economic man' who was at the centre of earlier theories. While financial rewards would influence the latter, group relationships and loyalties would influence the former, and may outweigh management pressure.

On financial incentives, Mayo wrote:

> Man's desire to be continuously associated in work with his fellows is a strong, if not the strongest, human characteristic. Any disregard of it by management or any ill-advised attempt to defeat this human impulse leads instantly to some form of defeat for management itself. In [a study] the efficiency experts had assumed the primacy of financial incentive; in this they were wrong; not until the conditions of working group formation were satisfied did the financial incentives come into operation. (Mayo, 1949, p. 99)

People had social needs that they sought to satisfy – and how they did so may support management interests or oppose them.

Later analysis of the experimental data by Greenwood *et al.* (1983) suggested that the team had underestimated the influence of financial incentives. Becoming a member of the experimental group in itself increased the worker's income. Despite the possibly inaccurate interpretation of the data, the findings stimulated interest in social factors in the workplace, adding another dimension to knowledge of management. Scientific management stressed the technical aspects of work. The Hawthorne studies implied that management should give at least as much attention to human factors, leading to the **human relations approach**. This advocates that employees will work more effectively if management shows some interest in their well-being, such as through humane supervisory practices.

The **human relations approach** is a school of management that emphasises the importance of social processes at work.

> ## Case questions 2.4
> - Which of the practices that Robert Owen used took account of workers' social needs?
> - Evaluate the extent to which he anticipated the conclusions of the Hawthorne experiments.

Current status

The Hawthorne studies have been controversial, and the interpretations questioned (Gillespie, 1991). Also, the idea of social man is itself now seen as an incomplete picture of people at work. Providing good supervision and decent working environments may increase satisfaction, but not necessarily productivity. The influences on performance are certainly more complex than Taylor assumed – but are also more complex than the additional factors Mayo identified in the Hawthorne studies.

Other writers have followed and developed Mayo's emphasis on human factors. McGregor (1960), Maslow (1970) and Alderfer (1972) have suggested ways of integrating human needs with those of the organisation as expressed by management. Some of this reflected a human relations concern for employees' well-being. A much stronger influence was the changing external environments of organisations, which have become less predictable since the time of Taylor and Mayo. These changes encouraged scholars to develop open systems models.

Ricardo Semler and Semco   www.semco.locaweb.com.br

Semco is a successful Brazilian company which in 2007 employed 2500 people in three countries. It was founded by Ricardo Semler's father in the early 1950s and is now a federation of about ten companies engaged in highly engineered, high-quality products that they offer in carefully chosen market niches. These include industrial machinery, cooling systems for commercial properties, managing buildings and properties, and environmental consulting.

The most distinctive feature of the company is the philosophy that underlies the way people work. Semler believes that: 'the repetition, boredom and aggravation that too many accept as an inherent part of working can be replaced with joy, inspiration and freedom' (p. x). Semler does not plan the future of the company: he believes that the employees shape it with their effort, interests and initiatives. See the Chapter 14 Case for more on Semco.

Source: Semler (2003).

2.7   Open systems models

The open systems approach builds on earlier work in general systems theory, and has been widely used to help understand management and organisational issues. The basic idea is to think of the organisation not as a **system**, but as an **open system**.

The open systems approach draws attention to the links between the internal parts of a system, and to the links between the whole system and the outside world. The system is separated from its environment by the **system boundary**. An open system imports resources such as energy and materials, which enter it from the environment across this boundary, undergo some transformation process within the system, and leave the system as goods and services. The central theme of the open systems view of management is that organisations depend on the wider environment for inputs if they are to survive and prosper. Figure 2.4 (based on Figure 1.1) is a simple model of the organisation as an open system.

A **system** is a set of interrelated parts designed to achieve a purpose.

An **open system** is one that interacts with its environment.

A **system boundary** separates the system from its environment.

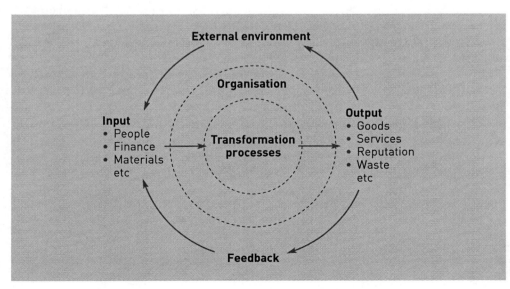

Figure 2.4

The systems model

The figure shows input and output processes, conversion processes and feedback loops. The organisation must satisfy those in the wider environment well enough to ensure that they continue to provide resources. The management task is to sustain those links if the organisation is to thrive. **Feedback** refers to information about the performance of the system. It may be deliberate, through customer surveys, or unplanned, such as the loss of business to a competitor. Feedback enables those managing the system to take remedial action.

Another idea is that of **subsystems**. A course is a subsystem within a department or faculty, the faculty is a subsystem of a university, the university is a subsystem of the higher education system. This in turn is part of the whole education system. A course itself will consist of several systems – one for quality assurance, one for enrolling students, one for teaching, another for assessment, and so on. In terms of Figure 2.1, each of the organisational elements is itself a subsystem – there is a technical subsystem, a people subsystem, a finance subsystem and so on, as Figure 2.5 shows.

These subsystems interact with each other, and how well people manage these links affects the functioning of the whole system: when a university significantly increases the number of students admitted to a popular course, this affects many parts of the system – such as accommodation (*technology*), teaching resources (*people*), and examinations (*business processes*).

A systems approach emphasises the links between systems, and reminds managers that a change in one will have consequences for others. What counts as the environment

Feedback (in systems theory) refers to the provision of information about the effects of an activity.

Subsystems are the separate but related parts that make up the total system.

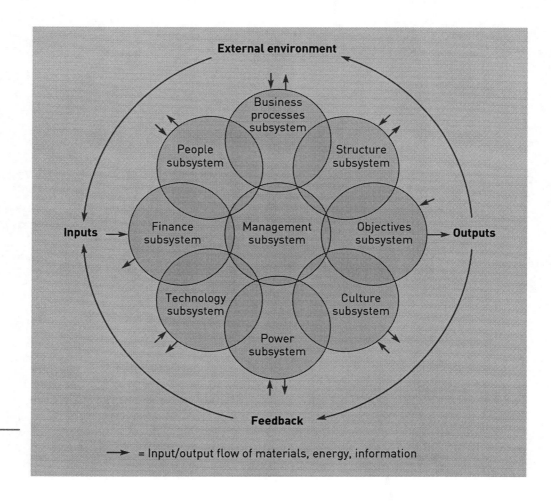

Figure 2.5

Interacting subsystems in organisations

depends on the level at which the analysis is being conducted. If a team at British Airways is discussing a new strategy to concentrate on business passengers, the relevant environmental factors will be mainly external – competing airlines, the expected level of demand, whether they can negotiate suitable facilities at airports. If the discussion is about reservations procedures, then the relevant environment will be mainly internal – such as their information systems, reservations staff and available capacity. In either case the principle is the same: take account of the systems that surround the immediate one. That implies being ready and able to scan those environments, to sense changes in them, and to act accordingly.

Robert Owen – the case continues
www.newlanark.org.uk

CASE STUDY

Owen actively managed the links between his business and the wider world. On buying the mills he quickly became part of the Glasgow business establishment, and was closely involved in the activities of the Chamber of Commerce. He took a prominent role in the social and political life of the city. He used these links in particular to argue the case for reforms in the educational and economic systems, and was critical of the effect that industrialisation was having upon working-class life.

Owen believed that education in useful skills would help to release working-class children from poverty. He provided a nursery for workers' children over 1 year old, allowing both parents to continue working, and promoted the case for wider educational provision. He also developed several experiments in cooperation and community building, believing that the basis of his successful capitalist enterprise at New Lanark (education, good working conditions and a harmonious community) could be applied to society as a whole.

These attempts to establish new communities (at New Harmony in the United States, and at Harmony in Hampshire, England) cost him a great deal of money,

but soon failed (Royle, 1998), because of difficulties over admission, finance and management processes.

More broadly, he sought new ways of organising the economy to raise wages and protect jobs, at a time of severe business fluctuations. In 1815 he persuaded allies in Parliament to propose a bill making it illegal for children under 10 to work in mills. It would also have limited their working hours to ten a day. The measure met strong opposition from mill owners and a much weaker measure became law in 1819.

Sources: Butt (1971), Royle (1998).

Case questions 2.5
- Draw a systems diagram detailing the main inputs, transformation and outputs of Robert Owen's mill.
- What assumptions did Owen make about the difference between running a business and running a community?

Sociotechnical systems

An important variant of systems theory is the idea of the **sociotechnical system**. The approach developed from the work of Eric Trist and Ken Bamforth (1951) at the Tavistock Institute in London. Their most prominent study was of an attempt in the coal industry to mechanise the mining system. Introducing what were in essence assembly line technologies and methods at the coalface had severe consequences for the social system that the older pattern of working had encouraged. The technological system destroyed the social system, and the solution lay in reconciling the needs of both.

A **sociotechnical system** is one in which outcomes depend on the interaction of both the technical and social subsystems.

This and similar studies showed the benefits of seeing a work system as a combination of a material technology (tools, machinery, techniques) and a social organisation (people, relationships, constitutional arrangements). Figure 2.6 shows that an organisation has technical and social systems: it is a socio-technical system. Each affects the other, so people need to manage both.

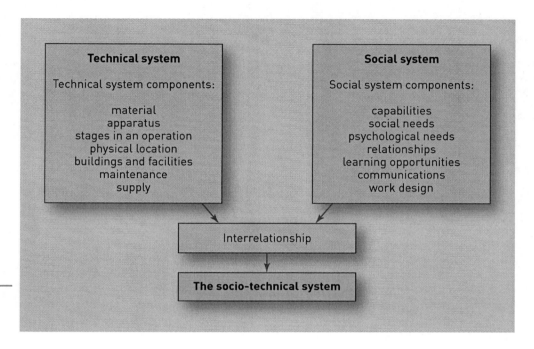

Figure 2.6
The organisation as a socio-technical system

A sociotechnical analysis aims to integrate the social and technical components: optimising one while ignoring the other is likely to be unproductive. Cherns (1987) developed a set of principles for redesigning organisations on socio-technical principles.

Contingency management

A further development of the open systems view is the contingency approach (Chapter 10). This arose from the work of Woodward (1958) and Burns and Stalker (1961) in the United Kingdom, and of Lawrence and Lorsch (1967) in the United States. The main theme is that to perform well managers must adapt the structure of the organisation to match external conditions: 'performance is determined not so much by the environment or the firm's actions, but by the congruence of the two' (Child *et al.*, 2003, p. 4).

The **contingency approach** looks for those aspects of the environment that managers should take into account in deciding how to shape the organisation – see the Management in Practice feature.

As the environment becomes more complex managers can use contingency perspectives to examine what structure best meets the needs of the business. Contingency theorists emphasise creating organisations that can cope with uncertainty and change, using the values of the open systems model: they also recognise that some functions need to work in a stable and predictable way, using the values of the internal process model.

Contingency approaches
to organisational structure are those based on the idea that the performance of an organisation depends on having a structure that is appropriate to its environment.

Successful Hong Kong firms adapt to the environment in China

Child *et al.* (2003) studied the experience of Hong Kong companies managing affiliated companies in China, predicting that successful firms would be those that adapted their management practices to suit those conditions. Because the business environment at the time was uncertain and difficult for foreign companies, they proposed that a key aspect of management practice in these circumstances would be the extent to which affiliated companies are controlled by, and integrated with, the parent company. Their results supported this – in the environment of this transitional economy, successful firms kept their mainland affiliates under close supervision, by maintaining frequent contact and allowing them to make few decisions.

Source: Child *et al.* (2003).

Current status

An open systems perspective emphasises that people need to adjust objectives and plans more rapidly to external change, and also find new ways of motivating people to act appropriately in these new conditions. Organisations in themselves achieve nothing: any change depends on the initiative and action of individuals. Open systems models draw attention to the wide range of issues that potentially affect an organisation. Yet these only affect internal affairs when a person notes an issue and in some way ensures that it is on the management agenda – that people begin to take notice of it. It is the goals, interests and power of individuals that determine whether an issue is noticed, interpreted, and acted upon. Factors such as these facilitate employee capability to act creatively and drive innovation.

2.8   Management theories for uncertain conditions

Although theories of management develop at particular times in response to current problems, this does not mean that newer is better. While new concerns bring out new theories, old concerns usually remain. Hence, while current theories are heavily weighted towards ways of encouraging flexibility and change, management still seeks control. Rather than thinking of theoretical development as a linear process, see it as a circular or iterative process in which certain themes recur as new concerns arise. The competing values approach captures the main theoretical developments in one framework and shows the relationships between them – as Table 2.3 shows.

The emerging management challenges come from many sources. One is the increasingly global nature of the economic system. Another is the deregulation of many areas of activity, allowing new competitors to enter previously protected markets (airlines, financial services). Still another is the closer integration between many previously separate areas of business (telecommunications, consumer electronics and entertainment). Consumer expectations are increasing and computer-based information systems are developing rapidly. Managers look for radical solutions – just as at the start of the Industrial Revolution.

Table 2.3

Summary of the models within the competing values framework

Features/model	Rational goal	Internal process	Human relations	Open systems
Main exponents	Taylor Gilbreths	Fayol Weber	Mayo Follett Barnard	Trist and Bamforth Woodward Burns and Stalker Lawrence and Lorsch Peters and Waterman
Criteria of effectiveness	Productivity, profit	Stability, continuity	Commitment, morale, cohesion	Adaptability, external support
Means/ends theory	Clear direction leads to productive outcomes	Routinisation leads to stability	Involvement leads to commitment	Continual innovation secures external support
Emphasis	Rational analysis, measurement	Defining responsibility, documentation	Participation, consensus building	Creative problem solving, innovation
Role of manager	Director and planner	Monitor and coordinator	Mentor and facilitator	Innovator and broker

Peters and Waterman – In Search of Excellence

In 1982 Peters and Waterman published their best-selling book *In Search of Excellence*. As management consultants with McKinsey & Co., they set out to discover the reasons for the success of what they regarded as 43 excellently managed US companies. One of their conclusions was that they had a distinctive set of philosophies about human nature and the way that people interact in organisations. They did not see people as rational beings, motivated by fear and willing to accept a low-involvement employment relationship. Instead, the excellent companies regarded people as emotional, intuitive and creative social beings who like to celebrate victories, however small, who value self-control, but who also need and want the security and meaning of achieving goals through organisations. From this, Peters and Waterman deduced some general rules for treating workers with dignity and respect. This was not out of a sense of philanthropy, but to ensure that people did quality work in an increasingly uncertain environment.

In Search of Excellence had a significant influence on management thinking and practice. It reflected a move away from rational goal approaches that emphasised complex and usually quantitative analytical techniques as the route to effective management. Peters and Waterman believed that management had relied too much on analytical techniques at the expense of the more intuitive and human aspects of business. In this they developed the ideas associated with the human relations school and introduced the idea of company culture – discussed in the next chapter.

Non-linear systems

Another new theme in management thinking in such volatile conditions is to consider the implications of feedback. People in organisations, both as individuals and as members of a web of working relationships, can choose how they react to an event or to an attempt to influence their behaviour. That reaction in turn leads to a further response – setting off a complex feedback process. Figure 2.7 illustrates this for three individuals, X, Y and Z.

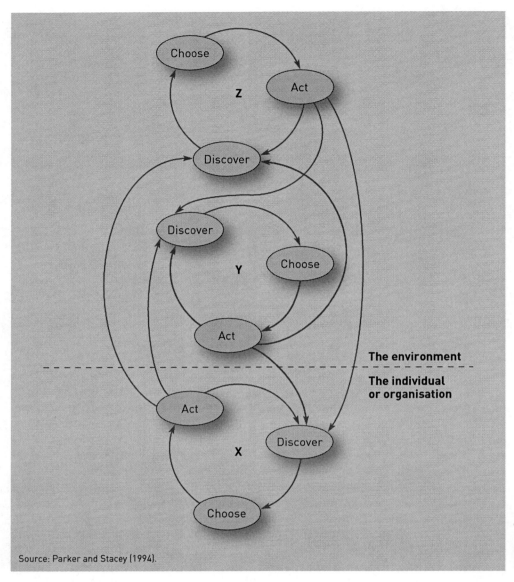

Source: Parker and Stacey (1994).

Figure 2.7
Feedback in
non-linear
systems

If we look at the situation in Figure 2.7 from the perspective of X, then X is in an environment made up of Y and Z. X discovers what Y and Z are doing, chooses how to respond and then acts. That action has consequences for Y and Z, which they discover. This leads them to choose a response, which has consequences that X then discovers, and acts on. This continues indefinitely. Every act X takes feeds back to have an impact on Y and Z's next action – and the same is true of Y and Z. Hence, as they interact, they make up a feedback system – and what is true of individuals as depicted in the diagram can also be used to indicate the interactions of three groups or three organisations. It can then extend to large numbers of organisations operating in their economic and social environment.

This way of thinking about organisations distinguishes between what are called 'linear' and 'non-linear' systems. 'Linear' describes a system in which an action leads to a predictable reaction. If you light a fire in a room, the thermostat will turn the central heating down. Non-linear systems are those in which outcomes are less predictable. If managers reduce prices they will be surprised if sales exactly match the forecast – they cannot predict the reactions of competitors, changes in taste, or new products.

Non-linear systems are those in which small changes are amplified through many interactions with other variables so that the eventual effect is unpredictable.

Table 2.4

Contrasting assumptions in linear and non-linear systems

Linear	Non-linear
The organisation is a closed system. Generally, what it decides to do will take place without too much disruption from outside events.	The organisation is a complex open system, constantly influenced by, and influencing, other systems. Intended actions will often be diverted by external events or by the internal political and cultural processes.
The environment is stable enough for management to understand it sufficiently well to develop a relevant detailed strategy. That strategy will still be relevant when implemented.	The environment is changing too rapidly for management to understand it and to develop a detailed strategy. By the time a strategy is implemented the environment will have changed.
There are defined levers within an organisation that cause a known response when applied (cut staff numbers, increase profits).	Actions lead to unexpected consequences, which can be either positive or negative.

Circumstances in the outside world change in ways that management cannot anticipate, so while short-term consequences of an act may be clear, long-run ones are not.

Glass (1996) argues that the modern business world corresponds much more closely to this non-linear world, and Table 2.4 contrasts the two models.

In linear systems, negative or damping feedback brings the system back to the original or preferred condition. People used to such systems think in terms of 'what actions can we take to return to the desired equilibrium?' (Glass, 1996, p. 102). Glass argues many of today's growth industries have come from aggressively exploited scientific breakthroughs. He goes on:

> A manager's way of thinking and acting are quite different if they see the world as being in something near stable equilibrium, than if they believe they are operating in chaos ... In stable equilibrium the manager is constantly trying to bring a situation back to a pre-planned state. In chaos, managers have goals but are also looking for the kind of positive amplification that can give extraordinary, rather than just ordinary, results. (p. 102)

Robert Owen – the case continues
www.newlanark.org.uk

CASE STUDY

The mills at New Lanark continued to operate after Owen's departure in 1825. Competition from new sources of supply meant that the mills eventually became unprofitable, and they closed in 1968, threatening the survival of the village community. There had been little new building since Owen left, so the site (with its high mills and rows of workers' cottages) represented a time capsule of industrial and social history. The New Lanark Conservation Trust was created to restore it as a living community, and as a lasting monument to Owen and his philosophies.

Visitors can see the mills and examples of the machinery they contained, visit many of the communal buildings Owen created (such as the store that was the inspiration for the worldwide Co-operative Movement), and some of the workers' housing. New Lanark is not just a tourist destination – it is a living community with most of the houses occupied by people who work elsewhere in the area.

Sources: Published sources and company website.

2.9   Current themes and issues

Performance

The theories outlined in this chapter have usually been developed as a means to improving performance. Many practitioners dismiss the value of theory and systematic evidence, preferring to follow what they call the lessons of experience.

Pfeffer and Sutton (2006a) present the case for basing management actions on substantiated theories and relevant evidence. They acknowledge the difficulties of putting that into practice, given that the demands for decisions are relentless and that information is incomplete. They also acknowledge that evidence-based management depends on being willing to put aside conventional wisdom. They identify practices that help managers to foster an evidence-based approach:

> If you ask for evidence of efficacy every time a change is proposed, people will sit up and take notice. If you take the time to parse the logic behind that evidence, people will become more disciplined in their own thinking. If you treat the organization like an unfinished prototype and encourage trial programs, pilot studies, and experimentation – and reward learning from these activities, even when something new fails – your organization will begin to develop its own evidence base. And if you keep learning while acting on the best knowledge you have and expect your people to do the same – if you have what has been called 'the attitude of wisdom' – then your company can profit from evidence-based management. (p. 70)

Pfeffer and Sutton's advice to demand evidence, examine logic, be willing to experiment and to embrace the attitude of wisdom can guide your approach to using the theories in this chapter. They are all potentially useful as part of an evidence-based approach, but only if you treat them critically, by asking about their underlying assumptions, how well they relate to the context you are considering, examining what alternatives may be available, and recognising the limitations of any theory. Used in that way, they can help you develop the skills of thinking critically about management theory, and using that to enhance performance.

Responsibility

Chapter 5 shows that many observers now believe that performance should be judged against the interests of a wide range of stakeholders, not just those with a financial stake in the enterprise. Although developed long before current concerns over the environment and climate change, the competing values model makes it possible to relate these theories to that topic. Those who believe that managers should act responsibly towards a wider range of stakeholders are taking an open systems view, in that they recognise the wide and interconnected nature of organisational and environmental factors.

There is still considerable scope for understanding the forces that shape managers' responses to these issues – in other words whether they act solely out of philanthropic motives or because they see responsible behaviour and image as helpful to their wider strategy. Applying the techniques of evidence-based management and critical thinking to the topics in Chapter 5 will help clarify how managers can act responsibly while still meeting performance expectations.

Internationalisation

The theories outlined here were developed when most business was conducted within national boundaries, although of course with substantial foreign trade in certain products and services. They take little direct account of the explosion in global trade, and the way in which many organisations are reorganising themselves as international or global businesses. However, the competing values framework provides a useful starting point, by highlighting the importance of underlying assumptions behind a theory, and how this relates to particular contexts. The fact that a theory based on, say, open systems values works well in some economies does not necessarily mean that it will be suitable in others. As Chapters 3 and 4 point out, cultural factors affect performance, yet it is still unclear how multiple national cultures interact with the corporate culture of an international business.

There is no shortage of prescriptions on offer to managers operating in global businesses, offering advice on all aspects of the process, from creating strategies to redesigning the organisation and implementing global changes. Many popular books are based on the practices of successful companies, without explaining the circumstances that enabled them to use the practices advocated. Learning to distinguish good theory and bad is the first step towards a style of management that balances proper regard for theory with respect for the lessons of practice.

Summary

1 **Explain the value of models of management, and compare unitary, pluralist and critical perspectives**
   ● Models represent more complex realities, help to understand complexity and offer a range of perspectives on the topic. Their predictive effect is limited by the fact that people interpret information subjectively in deciding how to act.

   ● A unitary perspective emphasises the common purpose of organisational members, while the pluralist draws attention to competing interest groups. Those who take a critical perspective believe that organisations reflect deep divisions in society, and that attempts to integrate different interests through negotiation ignore persistent differences in the distribution of power.

2 **State the structure of the competing values framework and evaluate its contribution to our understanding of management**
   ● A way of integrating the otherwise confusing range of theories of management. Organisations experience tensions between control and flexibility and between an external and an internal focus. Placing these on two axes allows theories to be allocated to one of four types – rational goal, internal process, human relations and open systems.

3 **Summarise the rational goal, internal process, human relations and open systems models and evaluate what each can contribute to a manager's understanding of their role**
   ● Rational goal (Taylor, the Gilbreths and operational research):
     – clear direction leads to productive outcomes, with an emphasis on rational analysis and measurement.

- Internal process (Weber, Fayol):
  - routinisation leads to stability, so an emphasis on defining responsibility and on comprehensive documentation and administrative processes.

- Human relations (Follett, Mayo):
  - people are motivated by social needs, and managers who recognise these will secure commitment. Practices include considerate supervision, participation and seeking consensus.

- Open systems (socio-technical, contingency and chaos):
  - Continual innovation secures external support, achieved by creative problem solving.

These theories have contributed to the management agendas in these ways:

- Rational goal – through techniques such as time and motion study, work measurement and a variety of techniques for planning operations; also the narrow specification of duties, and the separation of management and non-management work.

- Internal process – clear targets and measurement systems, and the creation of clear management and reporting structures. Making decisions objectively on the basis of rules and procedures, rather than on favouritism or family connections.

- Human relations – considerate supervision, consultation and participation in decisions affecting people.

- Open systems – understanding external factors and being willing and able to respond to them through individual and organisational flexibility.

4 **Use the model to classify the dominant form in two or more business units, and to gather evidence about the way this affects the roles of managing in those units**

- You can achieve this objective by asking people (perhaps others on your course) to identify which of the four cultural types in the competing values framework most closely correspond to the unit in which they work. Ask them to note ways in which that cultural type affects their way of working. Compare the answers in some systematic way, and review the results.

5 **Explain the influence of uncertain conditions on management and the assumptions of non-linear models of management**

- Uncertain conditions mean that it is hard to predict the outcome of an action. Complex feedback loops between the many elements in a situation mean that outcomes are affected by small differences in conditions. The eventual effect is out of all proportion to the initial action or event.

- Linear – closed system, relatively stable environment in which planning is feasible, and identifiable actions with predictable effects are available.

- Non-linear – open system, influenced by other systems; rapidly changing environment, and actions lead to unexpected consequences.

Review questions

1 Name three ways in which theoretical models help the study of management.

2 What are the different assumptions of the unitary, pluralist and critical perspectives on organisations?

3 Name at least four of Morgan's organisational images and give an original example of each.

4 Draw the two axes of the competing values framework, and then place the theories outlined in this chapter in the most appropriate sector.

5 List Taylor's five principles of scientific management and evaluate their use in examples of your choice.

6 What was the particular contribution that Lillian Gilbreth made concerning how workers' mental capacities should be treated?

7 What did Follett consider to be the value of groups in a community as well as business?

8 Compare Taylor's assumptions about people with those of Mayo. Evaluate the accuracy of these views by reference to an organisation of your choice.

9 Compare the conclusions reached by the Hawthorne experimenters in the relay assembly test room with those in the bank wiring room.

10 Is an open system harder to manage than a closed system, and if so, why?

11 How does uncertainty affect organisations and how do non-linear perspectives help to understand this?

Concluding critical reflection

Think about the way your company, or one with which you are familiar, approaches the task of management, and the theories that seem to lie behind the way people manage themselves and others. Review the material in the chapter, and perhaps visit some of the websites identified. Then make notes on these questions:

● What examples of the issues discussed in this chapter are currently relevant to your company?

● In responding to these issues, what **assumptions** about the nature of management appear to guide what people do? Do they reflect rational goal, internal process, human relations or open systems perspectives? Or a combination of several? Do these assumptions reflect a unitary or pluralist perspective, and if so, why?

● What factors such as the history or current **context** of the company appear to have influenced the prevailing view? Does the approach appear to be right for the company, its employees, and other stakeholders? Do people question those assumptions, in the way that Semler does within Semco?

● Have people put forward **alternative** ways of managing the business, or even a small part of it, based on evidence about other companies? Does the competing values model suggest other approaches to managing, in addition to the current pattern? How might others react to such alternatives?

● What **limitations** can you see in the theories and evidence presented in the chapter? For example, how valid might the human relations models be in a manufacturing firm in a country with abundant supplies of cheap labour, competing to attract overseas investment? Will open systems models be useful to those managing a public bureaucracy?

Further reading

Drucker, P. (1954), *The Practice of Management*, Harper, New York.

Still the classic introduction to general management.

Taylor, F.W. (1917), *The Principles of Scientific Management*, Harper, New York.

Fayol, H. (1949), *General and Industrial Management*, Pitman, London.

The original works of these writers are short and lucid. Taylor (1917) contains illuminating detail that brings the ideas to life, and Fayol's (1949) surviving ideas came from only two short chapters, which again are worth reading in the original.

Biggs, L. (1996), *The Rational Factory*, The Johns Hopkins University Press, Baltimore, MD.

A short and clear overview of the development of production systems from the eighteenth to the early twentieth centuries in a range of industries, including much detail on Ford's Highland Park plant.

Graham, P. (1995), *Mary Parker Follett: Prophet of management*, Harvard Business School Press, Boston, MA.

The contribution of Mary Parker Follett has been rather ignored, perhaps overshadowed by Mayo's Hawthorne studies – or perhaps it was because she was a woman. This book gives a full appreciation of her work.

Gillespie, R. (1991), *Manufacturing Knowledge: A history of the Hawthorne experiments*, Cambridge University Press, Cambridge.

Alvesson, M. and **Wilmott, H.** (1996), *Making Sense of Management*, Sage, London.

Thompson, P. and **McHugh, D.** (2002), *Work Organisations: A critical introduction*, Palgrave, Basingstoke.

Morgan, G. (1997), *Images of Organisation*, Sage, London.

These last four books discuss the ideas in this chapter from a critical perspective.

Semler, R. (2003), *The Seven Day Weekend: Finding the work/life balance*, Century, London.

Worth reading for an absorbing insight into a radically different approach to managing.

Gamble, J., Morris, J. and Wilkinson, B. (2004), 'Mass production is alive and well: the future of work and organisation in east Asia', *International Journal of Human Resource Management*, vol. 15, no. 2, pp. 397–409.

Smith, J.H. (1998), 'The enduring legacy of Elton Mayo', *Human Relations*, vol. 51, no. 3, pp. 221–249.

Walton, E.J. (2005), 'The persistence of bureaucracy: a meta-analysis of Weber's model of bureaucratic control', *Organisation Studies*, vol. 26, no. 4, pp. 569–600.

Three papers that show the continued application in successful business of early theories of management.

Mumford, E. (2006), 'The story of socio-technical design: reflections on its successes, failures and potential', *Information Systems Journal*, vol. 16, no. 4, pp. 317–342.

A review of socio-technical design from one of its leading practitioners.

Weblinks

These websites have appeared in the chapter:

www.newlanark.org.uk
www.xilinx.com
www.imiplc.com
www.tcl.com
www.semco.locaweb.com.br

Visit two of the business sites in the list, or those of other organisations in which you are interested, and navigate to the pages dealing with recent news, press or investor relations.

● What are the main issues the organisations appear to be facing?

● Compare and contrast the issues you identify on the two sites.

● What challenges may they imply for those working in, and managing, these organisations?

Annotated weblinks, multiple choice questions and other useful resources can be found on www.pearsoned.co.uk/boddy

Chapter 6
Planning

Aim

To describe the purposes of planning in organisations, and illustrate the iterative tasks in the planning cycle.

Objectives

By the end of your work on this chapter you should be able to outline the concepts below in your own terms and:

1 Explain the purposes of planning and the content of different types of plan
2 Compare alternative planning processes, and evaluate when each may be most suitable
3 Outline the seven iterative steps in planning, and describe techniques used in each
4 Use theory to evaluate the motivational effect of the goals stated in a plan
5 Use a framework to evaluate whether a plan is sufficiently comprehensive
6 Evaluate the context that will affect the ability of managers to implement a plan.

Key terms

This chapter introduces the following ideas:

planning
goal (or objective)
business plan
strategic plan
strategic business unit
operational plans
corporate strategy
planning system
SWOT analysis
critical success factors
sensitivity analysis
scenario planning
mission statement
stated goal
real goal

Each is a term defined within the text, as well as in the Glossary at the end of the book.

CASE STUDY

© DSM

In 1902 the Dutch government created Dutch State Mines (DSM) as a state-owned coal mining company. Although it stopped mining coal years ago, its headquarters are at Heerlen in the south of The Netherlands, close to the original mines. It has been through many changes since then, and is now a speciality chemicals business. The Dutch government sold the firm in 1989 and it now operates entirely in the private sector.

By 2007 the company had almost 22,000 employees working in over 200 offices and production sites in 40 countries. It has a decentralised structure, with 13 business groups that are empowered to perform all business functions. They form four strategic clusters – Nutrition, Pharma, Performance Materials and Industrial Chemicals. Each of the 13 companies is headed by a business group director, who reports directly to the managing board of directors. This has five members, responsible for strategy, the portfolio (the range of businesses in the company) and resource allocation.

Until the mid-1990s the company operated a traditional strategic planning process, with a corporate planning department setting out three- to five-year plans, supplemented by an annual budget cycle. Senior managers became dissatisfied with this as it was 'owned' by the corporate planning department, and had become a routine 'numbers' exercise.

The company therefore introduced a new arrangement. There is a Corporate Strategic Dialogue (CSD)

every three years, in which about 50 executives take part. It develops a long-term strategy for the business, deciding on the portfolio, investment priorities and geographical spread. The result of the last such exercise – 'Vision 2010: Building on Strengths' – is now being implemented through the business groups.

This strategic plan will build on Vision 2005, through which the company's portfolio shifted towards speciality products in the areas of life sciences and performance materials, in the search for higher and more stable earnings. The plan is to accelerate growth in the most profitable and innovative areas, by investing heavily in research and development and in new production facilities and staff.

Source: Based on Bloemhof *et al.* (2004). Copyright 2004 INSEAD, Fontainebleau, France; *DSM Annual Report, 2005* (on website).

Case questions 6.1

Visit the DSM website.

- What are the main elements of 'Vision 2010: Building on Strengths'?
- What effects may the plan have on what managers in the business do?
- What kind of environment do you think the company is operating in (Chapter 3, Section 3.4)?

6.1 Introduction

The DSM story outlines how managers in that company developed an approach to planning that seeks to balance the need for overall strategic direction with a high degree of autonomy for the main business units. DSM operates around the world in several technologically advanced businesses – like many other prominent companies. They too face the issue of how to identify external trends and plan changes accordingly.

Changes in external forces create uncertainty, and planning offers a systematic way to cope with that, and to adapt to new conditions. It enables people to set objectives, to specify and coordinate actions to achieve them, and to monitor progress. It is concerned with both ends (what to do) and means (how to do it).

Some plans are informal – not written down, nor widely or consistently shared. This can work perfectly well in managing domestic and social life, or in small businesses where the owner-manager and a few staff can see what everyone is doing and adapt to changing circumstances. Some larger organisations also manage with little formal planning – though they run the risk of duplication or of ignoring important information.

The focus here is on more formal plans, which express the goals of a business or unit for some future period, and the actions to achieve them, in written form. Warburton's, a family-owned Lancashire-based bread company, has a goal of reaching every UK household, challenging the two dominant firms. To achieve this it had to plan and build new capacity – it opened a bakery in North London in 2003, and is now searching for a site to the south of London. When two entrepreneurs decided to create the City Inn hotel chain they planned in detail the kind of hotels they would be – contemporary, city centre, newly built, 'active and open' atmosphere, and a consistent room design across the group. Plans like this can then be communicated to relevant players, to ensure they act consistently.

Figure 6.1 provides an overview of the themes. At the centre are seven generic tasks in planning – but people vary the order, and how much attention they give to each. How they manage these issues will affect whether planning helps or hinders performance.

The chapter outlines the benefits of planning and distinguishes the content of plans. Later sections examine the process of planning, and its seven generic steps – stressing throughout that these take place iteratively, and that their form depends on circumstances.

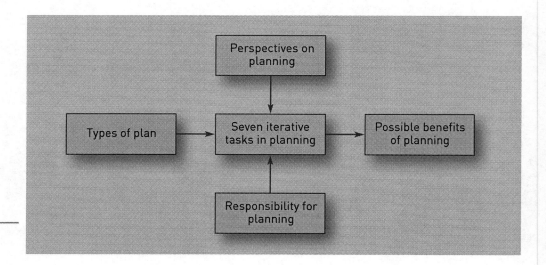

Figure 6.1

An overview of the chapter

6.2   Purposes of planning

While people use different terms, the activity of **planning** essentially involves establishing the **goals** (or **objectives**) for the task being planned, specifying how to achieve them, implementing the plan and evaluating the results. Goals represent the desired future state of an activity or organisational unit, and planning to meet them typically includes allocating the resources and specifying what people need to do.

Planning is the task of setting objectives, specifying how to achieve them, implementing the plan and evaluating the results.

Planning, if done well, brings four main benefits in that it:

- it clarifies direction;
- motivates people;
- helps to use resources efficiently; and
- provides a way to measure progress.

A goal (or objective) is a desired future state for an activity or organisational unit.

The act of planning may in itself add value, by ensuring that people base decisions on a wider range of evidence than if there was no planning system (Sinha, 1990). If done badly, planning has the opposite effect, leading to confusion, frustration and waste.

Good plans give direction to the people whose work contributes to their achievement. If everyone knows the purpose of a larger activity and how their task contributes, they can work more effectively. They can adjust their work to the plan (or vice versa), and cooperate and coordinate with others. It also helps them cope with the unexpected, since if they understand the end result they can respond to unexpected changes – without having to ask or waiting to be told. People like to know how their task fits into the larger whole, as it adds interest and enables them to take more responsibility.

---

management in practice

More planning at SABMiller   www.sabmiller.com

South African Brewers (SAB) purchased the US brewer Miller in 2002, to form SABMiller. The chief executive of SAB, Graham Mackay, was reported to be very critical of the company he had bought, saying that it was not a finely tuned, focused, effective organisation. In recent years it had lost market share to Anheuser-Busch and Coors. He would be exporting the South African company's direct management style to Miller's Milwaukee home, bringing a tighter focus on planning, objective setting and appraisal of Miller staff. The typical middle manager at Miller will be working to clearer objectives as well as having their pay more closely linked to performance: 'There will be a very much stronger management of consequences than there has been in the past. People will be held accountable for performance.'

Source: *Financial Times*, 22 November 2002.

FT

Planning reduces overlapping activities, and at the same time ensures that someone is responsible for each activity. A plan helps people coordinate their separate tasks, so saving time and resources; without a plan they may work at cross purposes. If people are clear on the end result they can spot inefficiencies or unnecessary delays in the activity, and correct or eliminate them.

Finally, planning establishes goals and standards that help people to monitor progress towards them. Setting final and interim goals lets people know how well they are progressing, and when they have finished. Comparing actual progress against the intended goals enables people to adjust the goal or change the way they are using resources.

key ideas   Does planning help new ventures?

Delmar and Shane (2003) studied whether planning helps new ventures, gathering data from over 200 new firms in Sweden. They hypothesised that planning would support new ventures by:

- enabling quicker decisions;
- providing a tool for managing resources to minimise bottlenecks;
- identifying actions to achieve broader goals in a timely manner.

They gathered extensive data from the firms at their start-up in 1998, and then at regular intervals for three years. The results supported each of their hypotheses, leading them to conclude that planning did indeed support the creation of successful new ventures.

Source: Delmar and Shane (2003).

The content of a plan is the subject matter – *what* aspect of the business it deals with: the next section distinguishes strategic, business unit, operational and special purpose plans. The one after that focuses on the process of planning.

Activity 6.1   Critical reflection on the purpose of plans

Gather examples of the plans that people prepare in an organisation – try to get one example of each of the types listed here.

- For one of the plans, ask someone who is familiar with it what the purpose of the plan is, and whether it achieves that purpose.
- Ask whether the plan is too detailed, or not detailed enough.
- What do they regard as the strengths and weaknesses of the planning process?

6.3   The content of plans

A **business plan** is a document that sets out the markets the business intends to serve, how it will do so and what finance they require.

People starting a new business or expanding an existing one prepare a **business plan** – a document that sets out the markets the business intends to serve, how it will do so and what finance they require (Blackwell, 2004). They do so to convince potential investors to lend money. Managers in divisions of a business (such as DSM) seeking capital investment or other corporate resources need to convince senior managers to allocate a share of the capital budget to them – which they do by presenting a convincing divisional plan. People in the public sector do the same – a director of roads (for example) needs to present a plan to convince the chief executive or elected members that planned expenditure on roads is a better use of resources than competing proposals from (say) the director of social work or cultural services. Service managers inevitably compete with each other for limited resources, and develop plans to support their case.

A **strategic plan** sets out the overall direction for the business, is broad in scope and covers all the major activities.

Plans vary in the level and breadth of the business they cover and in how far ahead they look. **Strategic plans** apply to the whole organisation or business unit. They set out the overall direction and cover major activities – markets and revenues, together with plans for marketing, human resources and production. Chandler (1962, p. 13) defined strategic plans as determining 'the basic long-term goals and objectives of an enterprise and the adoption of courses of action and the allocation of resources necessary for carrying out these goals'. Strategy is concerned with deciding what business an organisation should be in, where it wants to be and how it is going to get there. These decisions involve major resource commitments and usually require a series of consequential operational decisions. The benefits of central planning, especially at the strategic level, have long been advocated (Ansoff 1965, 1991; Armstrong, 1982) to coordinate actions and to spur adaptive strategic thinking. Glaister and Falshaw (1999) found that most senior managers regularly engage in strategic planning.

DSM – the case continues   www.dsm.com   CASE STUDY

In October 2005 DSM presented its new five year strategy – 'Vision 2010' – which was the outcome of the regular corporate strategic dialogue (CSD). This focuses on accelerating the profitable and innovative growth of its specialties portfolio, with the overall objective of strong value creation. This will be accomplished in three ways:

1 **Market-driven growth and innovation** Based on existing product leadership, DSM plans to grow sales in four *emerging business areas* – personalised nutrition, speciality packaging, biomedical materials and industrial biotechnology. This growth will be accelerated by innovation in the target markets. The company plans that by 2010 60 per cent of sales will come from speciality products, compared with 40 per cent in 2005. To boost innovation, 250 people will be recruited to work in business-driven innovation teams. About 15 per cent of capital expenditure will be dedicated to this effort.

2 **Increased presence in emerging economies** DSM plans to continue the trend of improving its globally balanced presence by accelerating the internationalisation of its asset base and workforce. Identified growth in demand in selected emerging economies has led the company to significantly increase its growth efforts in these regions. When evaluating investment proposals DSM will take this aim into account.

3 **Operational excellence** The company plans to continue building on its strong operational skills to enhance the cost competitiveness of the business. Over the previous five years it had implemented several operational excellence programmes, standardising business processes in manufacturing, order fulfilment, finance, and information technology. These will be extended to purchasing, pricing and productivity.

Source: DSM *Annual Report 2005* (on website).

Case questions 6.2

- How are the strategic plans being supported by operational plans?
- Visit the company website and look for information about recent developments in the business that may affect these plans.

In a large business there will be divisional plans for each major unit. If subsidiaries operate as autonomous **strategic business units** (SBUs) they develop their plans with limited inputs from the rest of the company, as it manages distinct products or markets.

Strategic plans are usually long term in form, looking up to three years ahead – though in businesses with long lead times (energy production or aircraft manufacture) they look much further ahead. Ryanair plans to grow capacity rapidly to meet demand, and makes a plan showing the financial and other implications of enlarging the fleet, recruiting staff and opening new routes.

A **strategic business unit** consists of a number of closely related products for which it is meaningful to formulate a separate strategy.

management in practice

Fiat's restructuring plan www.fiat.co.uk

In 2003 Fiat Group, owner of the Italian car maker, decided to retain the struggling Fiat Auto, and to invest in returning the company to profit. The plan included:

- cutting manufacturing costs by £700 million
- increasing research and development expenditure by £750 million
- reducing European capacity to 1.6 million vehicles a year
- boosting sales in Europe by 9 per cent with the launch of new models
- investing £100 million a year for three years to expand the dealer network.

Within that broad plan, the sports car division that makes the Alfa-Romeo was making its own plans to restore excitement to the range before re-entering the US market in 2007.

Source: *Business Week*, 21 April 2003.

Operational plans detail how the overall objectives are to be achieved, by specifying what senior management expects from specific departments or functions.

Corporate strategy 'is concerned with the firm's choice of business, markets and activities' (Kay, 1996), and thus it defines the overall scope and direction of the business.

Operational plans detail how the overall objectives are to be achieved. They are narrower in scope, indicating what senior management expects individual departments or functions to do, so that they support the overall plan. So there may be a family of related plans forming a hierarchy – a strategic plan for the organisation and main divisions, and several operational plans for departments or teams. Each will contain linked objectives and plans that become more specific as they move down the organisation, but aiming to be consistent with the overall **corporate strategy**. Table 6.1 shows this hierarchical arrangement, and how the character of plans changes at each level.

Most organisations also prepare annual plans that deal mainly with the financial aspects of the business and set out budgets for the coming year, but necessarily include sales, marketing, production or technology plans as well. These short-term plans are expected to be consistent with the longer-term strategy, but take account of immediate developments and changes since the strategic plan was prepared.

Activity plans are short-term plans that deal with immediate production or service delivery – a sheet scheduling which orders are to be dealt with next week, or planning who is on duty when. Some use a method called enterprise resource planning to integrate the day-to-day work of complex production systems – Chapter 12 describes this technique in section 12.6.

Table 6.1

A planning hierarchy

Type of plan	Strategic	Operational	Activity
Level	Organisation or business unit	Division, department, function or market	Work unit or team
Focus	Direction and strategy for whole organisation	Functional changes or market activities to support strategic plans	Actions needed to deliver current products or services
Nature	Broad, general direction	Detail on required changes	Specific detail on immediate goals and tasks
Timescale	Long term (2–3 years?)	Medium (up to 18 months?)	Very short term (hours to weeks?)

Figure 6.2 contrasts specific and directional plans. Specific plans have unambiguous, mainly quantified objectives and leave little room for discretion in how to achieve them. A manager who seeks to increase his or her unit's work output by 8 per cent over the next 12 months could establish clear procedures, budgets and schedules of activities to reach that goal.

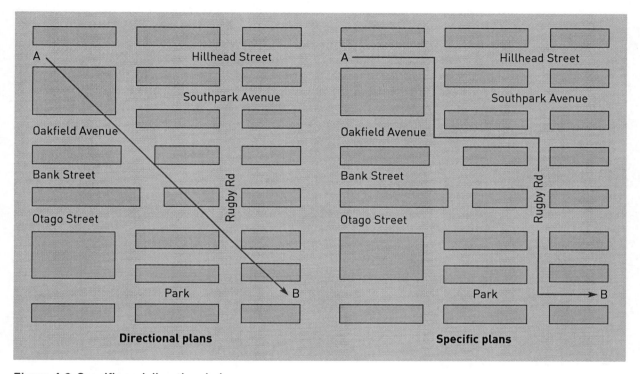

Figure 6.2 Specific and directional plans

In uncertain conditions management will need to respond to unexpected changes, and then directional plans are preferable. They give a looser guidance – providing focus but not directing managers to specific actions. The Chapter 7 case (Wipro) describes how in the early days of the company the founder, Azim Premji, held weekly telephone conversations with his regional managers, in which he set their targets for the following week – but they were free to decide how to meet them. He held them accountable for meeting the target, but not for how they did so (provided they met his high ethical standards).

Managers also prepare special-purpose plans for projects or aspects of the business. They may have plans for disaster recovery (after, say, a major computer failure or terrorist action), and develop project plans to organise and implement specific changes, such as introducing a new computer system or launching a new product. When The Royal Bank of Scotland took over NatWest Bank managers quickly developed a collection of over 160 interlocking plans to incorporate NatWest operations into those of RBS to secure the cost savings they had promised investors (Kennedy *et al.*, 2006). On a smaller scale, a manager who needs to recruit a new member of staff will make a simple plan to organise the task. Standing plans specify how to deal with routine, regularly recurring issues such as recruitment or dealing with customer complaints. People plan throughout an organisation, at all levels and in all degrees of formality.

6.4 The process of planning

The process of planning refers to the way plans are produced – are they developed from the top of the organisation, or from the bottom up? How frequently are they revised? Who takes part in creating them? The organisation's planning system organises and coordinates the activities of those involved in the planning process. The content of a plan, and how well it serves the organisation, is shaped by the process that produces it. Designing and maintaining a suitable planning system is part of the planning task.

Participation is one issue – who is involved in making the plan? One approach is to appoint a group of staff specialists to be responsible for producing plans, with or without consultation with the line managers or staff concerned. Others believe the quality of the plan, and especially the ease of implementing it, will be increased if staff familiar with local conditions help to create the plan.

A planning system refers to the processes by which the members of an organisation produce plans, including their frequency and who takes part in the process.

management in practice A new planning process at Merck www.merck.com

In the early 1990s Merck was the world's leading pharmaceutical company, but by 2006 it was ranked only eighth. Dick Clark, the new chief executive, was charged with reviving the company: one of his first actions was to make radical changes in its planning process. Teams of employees were asked to present the business cases to senior managers to test possible directions for the company – such as whether to build a generic drugs business. This process was vital, said Mr Clark, as it showed the 200 senior executives that Merck would now operate in an atmosphere where assumptions would be openly questioned by anyone. He has also changed the way the company sets its earnings projections. Formerly set by top managers, projections are now set by lower-level teams. 'It wasn't like Dick Clark said "We're going to have double-digit growth, go out and find it!" We tested it and tweaked it ... but it was legitimate and we believe in it, so let's go public with it. And that's the first time we'd done that as a company.'

Source: From an article by Christopher Bowe, *Financial Times*, 27 March 2006, p. 10.

FT

key ideas The benefits of participation and communication

Ketokivi and Castañer (2004) studied the strategic planning process in 164 manufacturing plants in five countries and three industries (automotive supplies, machinery and electronics). It has long been recognised that organisational members tend to focus on the goals of their unit or function, rather than on those of the enterprise – known as 'position bias'. The study sought to establish empirically whether position bias existed, and, more importantly, whether strategic planning reduced this. The evidence confirmed the tendency to position bias. It also showed that having employees participate in strategic planning, and communicating the outcome to them, significantly diminishes it. If top management wants to reduce position bias, they should incorporate participation and communication into the strategic planning process.

Source: Ketokivi and Castañer (2004).

A related debate (developed more fully in Chapter 8, Section 8.6) is between those who advocate a rational approach to planning and those who favour what are variously called learning or emergent approaches (also called logical incrementalism (Quinn, 1980)). They argue that when a company is in dynamic context plans must be essentially temporary and provisional, so that managers can adapt them to suit changing circumstances, drawing on new information from the frequent interaction of a wide range of participants (Fletcher and Harris, 2002; Papke-Shields *et al.*, 2006).

Jennings (2000) shows how companies change their approach to planning as conditions change. A study of the UK electricity generating company PowerGen (now owned by the German company E.on) that was privatised in 1991 traced the evolution since then of the company's corporate planning process. It had retained a formal process with a five-year planning horizon, but it was more devolved. A small central team focuses on overall strategy while business units develop strategy for their particular situations. Business unit plans have become shorter and are no longer required to follow a prescribed format. The overall planning cycle is completed in a shorter period of time. All of these developments have created a more adaptive style of planning that is consistent with the increased uncertainty of the company's business environment.

Figure 6.3 shows the seven generic tasks that people can perform when they make a plan. They use them iteratively, often going back to an earlier stage when they find new information which implies, say, that they need to reshape the original goals. And of course they may miss a stage, or spend too little or too much time on each: the figure only indicates a way of analysing the stages of planning.

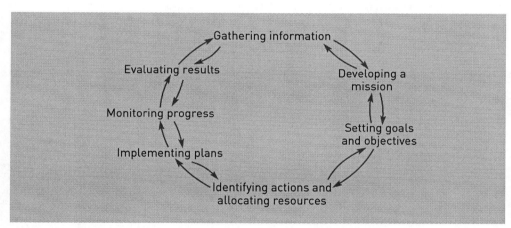

Figure 6.3

Seven iterative tasks in making a plan

6.5   Gathering information

Any plan depends on information that people can use to guide their choices in building the plan. This includes both informal, soft information gained from casual encounters with colleagues, competitors and customers, and from formal analyses of economic and market trends. This will reflect the form of plan, but an indication of the range available can begin with the strategic level – people use a simpler version for plans that are more limited in level or scope.

Chapter 3 outlined the competitive and general environments, and those involved in planning will usually begin by drawing on information about these, collecting, analysing and interpreting information from internal and external sources. Computer-based information systems usually hold a great deal of valuable information about a company's customers. The main benefit of loyalty cards for retailers is that they can track each customer's purchasing patterns and map them against the personal information in the database, obtained when they applied for the card. Tesco has been particularly skilled at analysing customer data, enabling planners to predict likely demand, especially for new products.

management
in practice **Electrolux asks its customers**   www.electrolux.com

When Hans Straberg became chief executive of Electrolux, the world's second largest maker of domestic appliances, he faced major problems with both costs and product design. He tackled the former by closing many western European and US manufacturing plants and transferring the work to countries with lower costs. To ensure the company designed products that customers wanted, the company conducted in-depth interviews with 160,000 customers from around the globe. To analyse the data 53 employees, including designers, engineers and marketers gathered in Stockholm in November 2005 for a week-long brainstorming session to search for insights to stimulate the next generation of new products. This open, cross-functional approach to dealing with information was a radical departure from traditional ways of planning at the company.

Source: *Business Week*, 27 February 2006, pp. 42–43.

External sources include government economic and demographic statistics, industry surveys and general business intelligence services. Managers also commission market research on, for example, individual shopping patterns, attitudes towards particular firms or brand names, and satisfaction with existing products or services. Many firms use focus groups to test consumer reaction to new products (for more on this see Chapter 9).

DSM – the case continues   www.dsm.com   CASE STUDY

The new strategy presented in October 2005 was the outcome of the corporate strategy dialogue. This 12-month process thoroughly analysed global economic and social trends and conditions, technological developments, and price scenarios for energy and raw materials. It also studied likely differences in growth in the various geographical regions and end markets, fac- tors that might affect the company's portfolio, and likely developments within each of DSM's business areas. This led to a clear set of conclusions about the future of each business area, and specifically to the need to focus more on those speciality innovative products in which it had a leading position in the industry.

Source: DSM *Annual Report 2005* (on website).

SWOT analysis

A **SWOT analysis** is a way of summarising the organisation's strengths and weaknesses relative to external opportunities and threats.

At a strategic level, planning will usually combine an analysis of external environmental factors with an internal analysis of the organisation's strengths and weaknesses. A **SWOT analysis** does this, bringing together the internal strengths and weaknesses and the external opportunities and threats. Internally, managers would analyse the strengths and weaknesses of the resources within, or available to, the organisation (Grant, 1991) – such as a firm's distinctive research capability, or its skill in integrating acquired companies. The external analysis would probably be based on PESTEL and Porter's (1980a) five forces model (see Chapter 3). These tools help to identify the main opportunities and threats that people believe could affect the business.

A SWOT analysis at Cable & Wireless   www.cw.com

Cable & Wireless is a global telecommunications business. One of its most successful areas has been its Caribbean operation, but in 2002 it experienced growing competition from new rivals, especially a company called Digicel. C&W took the threat sufficiently seriously to commission a report that compared the company with Digicel, using the SWOT technique. This provides a useful public example of the technique.

Strengths
- Established customer base
- Diversified revenue structure that can absorb losses
- Strong knowledge of local culture
- Strong technical support

Weaknesses
- C&W network not as good as Digicel's
- Capital spending restrictions
- Poor image across the Caribbean
- Low motivation of sales team

Opportunities
- Take advantage of regionalisation and economies of scale
- Offer more coverage before Digicel arrives
- Market growth potential
- Ability to remain the market leader

Threats
- Global entrants to market
- Loss of key staff to competitors
- Rapid technological innovation
- Poor market image

Source: Based on *Financial Times*, 10 December 2002.

While the method appears to be a rational way of gathering information, its usefulness depends on recognising that it is a human interpretation of internal and external factors. It is only a representation of reality – and participants are likely to differ about the significance of a factor, or even if it should be included at all. Debate about the factors is itself a potentially valuable part of the planning process.

Activity 6.2   Conducting a SWOT analysis

Choose one of the companies featured in the text (or any that interests you).

- Gather information from the company's website and other published data to prepare a SWOT analysis.
- Compare your analysis with that of a colleague on your course.
- Identify any differences between you in terms of the factors identified, and the significance given to them. What do those differences tell you about the value of the SWOT method?

Given the diversity and complexity of organisational environments it is easy to have too much information. Managers need to focus on the few trends and events that are likely to be of greatest significance. De Wit and Meyer (2004) report that planners at Royal Dutch/Shell focus on critical factors such as oil demand (economic), refining capacity (political and economic), the likelihood of government intervention (political) and alternative sources of fuel (technological).

Critical success factors analysis

Critical success factors are those aspects of a strategy that *must* be achieved to secure competitive advantage.

In considering whether to enter a new market, a widely used planning technique is to assess the **critical success factors** (Hardaker and Ward, 1987) in that market. These are the things which customers in that particular market most value about a product or service – and they therefore play a key role as people plan whether to move into a line of business. Some value price, others quality, others some curious aspect of the product's features – but in all cases they are things that a company must be able to do well to succeed in that market.

Forecasting

Forecasts or predictions of the future are often based on an analysis of past trends in factors such as input prices (wages, components, etc.), sales patterns or demographic characteristics. All forecasts are based on assumptions. In relatively simple environments people can reasonably assume that past trends will continue, but in uncertain conditions they need alternative assumptions. A new market might support rapid sales growth, whereas in a saturated market (e.g. basic foods, paid-for newspapers) it might be more realistic to assume a lower or nil growth rate.

Forecasting is big business, with several organisations selling analyses to business and government, using techniques such as time-series analysis, econometric modelling and simulation. However, because forecasts rely heavily on extrapolating past trends, users learn to question the assumptions inherent in them.

Sensitivity analysis

A **sensitivity analysis** tests the effect on a plan of several alternative values of the key variables.

One way of testing the assumptions is by including a **sensitivity analysis** of key variables in a plan to increase confidence in the choice made. A plan may assume that the company will attain a 10 per cent share of a market within a year: what will be the effect on the calculations if they secure 5 per cent, or 15 per cent? What if interest rates rise, increasing the cost of financing the projects? This enables those making the decision to compare the robustness of the options they are examining and so be better able to assess the relative risks. It gives people greater confidence in the decision, or alternatively may show that it is too risky to be worthwhile. Johnson *et al.* (2006) give a worked example that illustrates the method (pp. 372–373).

Scenario planning

Scenario planning is an attempt to create coherent and credible alternative stories about the future.

Forecasting is still relevant in dynamic and complex situations but cannot be relied on as uncertainty increases and where the rate of environmental change shows signs of discontinuity (marked and often rapid changes from trend). In these situations some companies build scenarios of what the future may look like. Cornelius *et al.* (2005) note that: '**scenarios** are not projections, predictions or preferences; rather they are coherent and credible stories about the future.'

Scenarios typically begin by considering how some major forces in the external environment such as the Internet, an ageing population, global terrorism or climate change might affect a company's business over the next five to ten years. Doing so can bring new ideas about their environment into the heads of managers, thus enabling them to recognise new and previously unthinkable possibilities. No one can predict the future, but advocates (Van der Heijden, 1996; Schwartz, 2005) claim two main benefits of scenario planning. The first is that it discourages reliance on what is sometimes referred to as 'single-point forecasting' – a single view of the future; second it encourages managers to develop contingency plans to cope with outcomes that depart from the most likely scenario. However, few companies use the technique as it is time consuming and costly. Moreover, while systematic thinking about possible futures may yield new information, that only becomes useful if senior managers make noticeable adjustments to strategy as a result.

Scenario planning at Shell www.shell.com

management in practice

In today's global and fast-changing environment, extrapolating from historical performance using medium- and long-term forecasting techniques has not proved very reliable, and managers in some companies use scenarios to test their plans. Royal Dutch/Shell was one of the earliest to adopt this approach. Traditionally, Shell planners would forecast refining plant requirements for several years ahead by extrapolating from current demand. However, the volatility in the oil market makes accurate prediction difficult. Shell underestimated oil demand in the 1950s and 1960s and overestimated it in the 1970s.

Rather than rely on one projection, Shell develops a range of possible scenarios for, say, future crude oil supply. One scenario could be that it continues as now, another that many new fields become available and a third that Saudi Arabia experiences major political turmoil and ceases to export oil. Major capital investment projects are evaluated against each scenario, with the aim of ensuring that they have a positive return under each. Scenario planning helps generate projects that are more robust under a variety of alternative futures. It also encourages people to ask deeper questions – for example about whether the oil companies, or the political leaders in the oil-rich countries where the wells are drilled, would be deciding the supply of oil.

Scenario thinking now underpins the established way of thinking at Shell. It has become a part of the culture, such that people throughout the company, dealing with significant decisions, normally will think in terms of multiple, but equally plausible, futures to provide a context for decision making. (Van der Heijden, 1996, p. 21)

Source: Van der Heijden (1996).

A combination of PESTEL and five forces analysis should ensure that managers recognise all the major influences in the external environment. Forecasting and scenario planning then enable them to consider the possible implications for the business at the start of the planning process.

DSM – the case continues www.dsm.com

CASE STUDY

The planning process introduced at DSM requires that each business group conducts a business strategy dialogue (BSD) about every three years. The purpose of a BSD is to provide a consistent method and terminology to structure the development process and improve its quality. Usually the whole management team of the business group conducts the dialogue, supported by specialists from within the organisation. The reviews have five phases:

1 **Characterising the business situation** Collecting information on questions such as what business are you in, who are the competitors, how attractive is the industry in terms of growth and profitability, how do you compare with competitors, what are the main trends?

2 **Analysing the business system (macro)** Analysing the industry in which the business unit competes, using Porter's five forces model. It also analyses the strategies that competitors are using, to identify the ▶

different ways in which a business could compete in an industry.

3 Analysing the business system (micro) This looks at the internal processes of the business, including its internal value chain, benchmarking of functions, and the strengths and weaknesses of the unit.

4 Options and strategic choice This phase compares the results of earlier phases – the competitive environment and the key success factors required, and its internal capabilities. This allows the unit to choose which strategic option it should pursue and what is required for successful implementation.

5 Action planning and performance measurement The chosen strategy is then turned into an action plan and linked to performance measurement. The team sets performance indicators such as market share, new product development, customer satisfaction and cost per unit of output. These enable managers to monitor the implementation of the strategy.

Each unit reviews progress on the implementation of its BSD quarterly in its management reporting, and annually in the annual strategic review (ASR). With these building blocks from the businesses, the ASR monitors progress on DSM's overall execution of its strategic plan.

Source: Based on Bloemhof *et al.* (2004). Copyright 2004 INSEAD, Fontainebleau, France.

Case questions 6.3

- Comment on the main features of the content and process of planning at DSM.
- What are their main methods of gathering information?
- The process must be very costly to the company. What features of their business explain why they are willing to incur these costs?
- How does it compare with the planning process at your organisation?

6.6 Developing a mission and goals

Mission statements

A clear plan depends on being clear about the ultimate purpose of a task – whether this concerns the whole organisation or a single unit. This seems obvious, but studies of managerial work (Stewart, 1967) show that managers are drawn towards action rather than planning – especially the ambiguities of agreeing on purposes. Yet until a team has spent time thinking, debating and clarifying the wider purpose, they will find it difficult to agree on details.

A fashionable medium for expressing purpose at the level of the whole organisation is the **mission statement** – a way of expressing a vision of what the future could be if the plan were to succeed. The same idea can be expressed at departmental or business unit level – setting out what participants see as distinctive about their activities.

A **mission statement** is a broad definition of an organisation's operations and scope, aiming to distinguish it from similar organisations.

Goals

Goals turn the generalities of mission statements into specific commitments – what is to be done by when. They provide the focus or reference point for other decisions and the criteria against which to measure performance. Most plans include quantified objectives in the areas of financial objectives – such as earnings per share, return on shareholders' funds and cash flow. They are also likely to quantify sales targets, cost reductions, and R&D expenditure. Table 6.2 lists some stated goals of high-profile projects.

Company	Published goals
Merck Pharmaceuticals – Recovery plan to 2010	Annual earnings growth of at least 10% Focus drug research on 9 disease areas, rather than 32 Restructure manufacturing operations
British Airways – Future shape and size (2001–2005)	Deliver operating margins of at least 10% Reduce capacity and destinations served Reduce aircraft fleet by 10%
Volkswagen – Recovery plan to 2008	Pre-tax profit target of €5.1 billion (up from €1.1 billion in 2004) Reduce jobs by at least 30,000 A restructuring 'more drastic than people can imagine' (company executives)
Nestlé – long-term growth target	In 2003 set new targets of 5–6% organic growth over three to five years, to focus managers' efforts on profit margins rather than sales

Source: Company announcements.

Table 6.2

Examples of published goals

Activity 6.3 Developing a mission and goals

- Go to the websites of some companies that interest you and collect examples of mission statements.
- Does the organisation you work for have a mission statement? If so, how was it developed?
- Gather examples of goals at either organisational, operational or activity levels. If you can, ask those affected by them about the process by which they were set. Also ask if this has affected their attitudes towards them.

A hierarchy of goals

A way of relating goals to each other is to build them into a hierarchy, in which the overall goals are transformed into more specific goals for different parts of the organisation – such as marketing, finance, operations and human resources. Managers in those areas develop plans setting out the actions they must undertake to meet the overall goal. Figure 6.4 illustrates this by using IKEA's plan to expand in Japan. To meet its planned sales growth managers intend to open many stores across Asia, of which the first group will be in Japan. That has evolved into a plan for their probable location, and then into a precise plan for two near Tokyo, for which land has been bought. That in turn is leading managers to develop progressively more detailed plans for the thousands of details that will need to be in good order if the venture is to succeed.

Plans of this sort need to be flexible, as there is no knowing what may change between design and completion. Managers often stress their firm commitment to the highest-level goals – but leave staff with much more discretion over the lower-level plans through which they achieve them.

However convincingly set out, statements of goals only have value if they guide action. Effective goal setting involves balancing multiple goals, considering whether they meet the SMART criteria (see below), and evaluating their likely motivational effects.

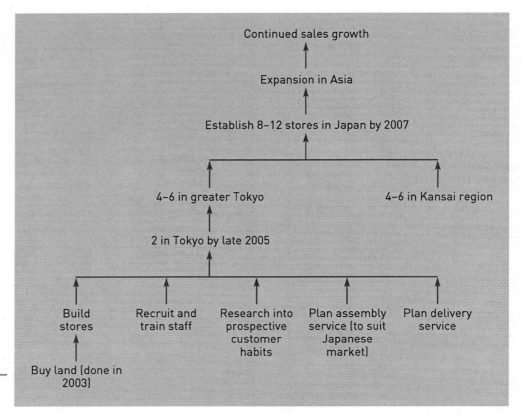

Figure 6.4

Developing a plan for IKEA (Japan)

Single or multiple goals?

Company statements of goals – whether long term or short – are usually expressed in the plural, since a single measure cannot indicate success or failure. Emphasis on one goal, such as growth, ignores others such as dividends for shareholders. Growth takes time and investment – which takes away from profits available for distribution to shareholders now. Managers have to balance multiple, possibly conflicting objectives, of even one group of stakeholders. As Gerry Murphy, who became chief executive of Kingfisher (a UK DIY retailer) in 2004, recalled:

> Alan Sheppard, my boss at Grand Metropolitan and one of my mentors, used to say that senior management shouldn't have the luxury of single point objectives. Delivering growth without returns or returns without growth is not something I find attractive or acceptable. Over time we are going to do both. (*Financial Times*, 28 April 2004, p. 23)

As senior managers try to take account of stakeholders other than those with shares in the company, they anticipate their various expectations. This means balancing profits (or growth) to satisfy shareholders, quality to satisfy customer interests, and sustainability to satisfy environmental interests. All are legitimate, but mean that managers are juggling conflicting goals. This can lead to conflict between stated goals, as reflected in public announcements, and real goals, which are those to which people work. **Stated goals** are those that appear and are given prominence in company publications and websites. Establishing the **real goals** – those to which people give most attention – depends on observing what they do. Actions reflect the priorities that senior managers express through what they say and do within the company, and how they reward and discipline managers.

Stated goals are those that are prominent in company publications and websites.

Real goals are those to which people give most attention.

Criteria for assessing goals

The SMART acronym summarises some criteria for assessing a set of goals. What form of each is effective depends on circumstances (specific goals are not necessarily better than directional ones). The list simply offers some measures against which to evaluate a statement of goals.

- **Specific** Does the goal set specific targets? People who are planning a meeting can set specific goals for what they hope to achieve, such as:

  By the end of the meeting we will have convinced them to withdraw their current proposal, and to have set a date (within the next two weeks) at which we will start to develop an alternative plan.

  Having a clear statement of what the meeting (or any other activity in a plan) is intended to achieve helps people to focus effort.
- **Measurable** Some goals may be quantified ('increase sales of product X by 5 per cent a year over the next three years') but others, equally important, are more qualitative ('to offer a congenial working environment'). Quantitative goals are not more useful than qualitative ones – what can be measured is not necessarily important. The important point is that goals be defined precisely enough to measure progress towards them.
- **Attainable** Goals should be challenging, but not unreasonably difficult. If people perceive a goal as unrealistic, they will not be committed. Equally goals should not be too easy, as that too undermines motivation. Goal-setting theory (see Key Ideas) predicts the motivational consequences of goal setting.
- **Rewarded** People need to see that attaining a goal will bring a reward – this gives meaning and helps ensure commitment.
- **Timed** Does the goal specify the time over which it will be achieved, and is that also a reasonable and acceptable standard?

Practical uses of goal-setting theory   key ideas

Goal-setting theory offers some practical implications for those making plans:

- **Goal difficulty**: set goals for work performance at levels that will stretch employees but are just within their ability.
- **Goal specificity**: express goals in clear, precise and if possible quantifiable terms, and avoid setting ambiguous or confusing goals.
- **Participation**: where practicable, encourage staff to take part in setting goals to increase their commitment to achieving them.
- **Feedback**: provide information on the results of performance to allow people to adjust their behaviour and perhaps improve their achievement of future plans.

Source: Locke and Latham (2002).

Activity 6.4   Critical reflection on goals

Choose a significant plan that someone in your organisation has produced within the last year. Assess the goals that it expresses – are they mutually consistent? Do they meet the criteria of being motivational? Are they SMART? Then try to set out how you would amend the goals to meet these criteria more fully. Alternatively, comment on how the criteria set out in the text could be modified, in the light of your experience with these goals.

6.7   Identifying actions and communicating the plan

This part of the planning process involves deciding what needs to be done, who will do it, and communicating that. In a small activity such as planning a project in a club this would just mean listing the tasks and dividing them clearly amongst a few able and willing members. At the other extreme, Ford's plan to build a new car plant in China probably runs to several volumes.

Identifying what needs to be done and by whom

Figure 1.3 (reproduced as Figure 6.5) provides a model to help envisage the implications of a goal, by enabling managers to ask what, if any, changes need to be made to each element.

If the goal is to launch a new product, the plan could identify which parts of the organisation will be affected (structure), what investment is needed (finance), how production will fit with existing lines (business processes) and so on. New technology

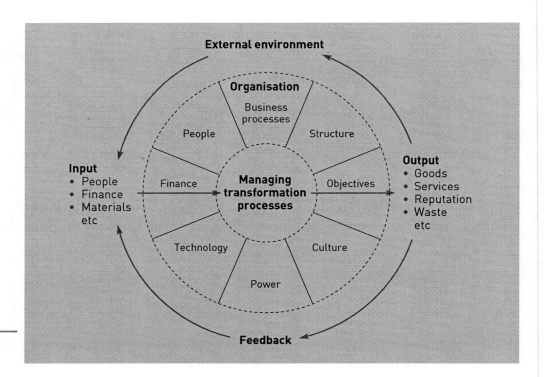

Figure 6.5

Possible action areas in a plan

projects often fail because those planning them pay too much attention to the technological aspects, and too little to the human aspects of structure, culture and people (Boddy *et al.*, 2005). Each main heading will require further actions that people can identify and assign.

Lynch (2003) points out that managers handle this aspect of planning comprehensively, incrementally or selectively.

- **Comprehensive (specific) plan** This happens if managers decide to make a clear-cut change in direction, in response to a reassessment of the market, a financial crisis or a technological development. They assume that success depends on driving the changes rapidly and in a coordinated way across the organisation – which implies a comprehensive plan.
- **Incremental (directional) plan** People use this approach in uncertain conditions – such as volatile markets or when direction depends on the outcome of research and development. Tasks, times and even the objective are likely to change as the outcomes of current and planned activities become known – 'Important strategic areas may be left deliberately unclear until the outcomes of current events have been established' (Lynch, 2003, p. 633).
- **Selective plan** This approach may work when neither of the other methods is the best way forward – such as when managers wish to make a comprehensive change, but are unable to do so because of deep opposition in some area affected by the plan. They may then try to implement the major change in only some areas of the business which, while not their preferred choice, may enable them to make some progress towards the objectives.

Communicating the plan

In a small organisation or where the plan deals with only one area, communication in any formal way is probably unnecessary. Equally, those who have been involved in developing the objectives and plans will be well aware of it. However, in larger enterprises managers will probably invest time and effort in communicating both the objectives and the actions required throughout the areas affected. They do this to:

- ensure that everyone understands the plan;
- allow them to resolve any confusion and ambiguity;
- communicate the judgements and assumptions that underlie the plan;
- ensure that activities around the organisation are coordinated in practice as well as on paper.

6.8   Implementing plans and monitoring results

However good the plan, nothing worthwhile happens until people implement it, acting to make visible, physical changes to the organisation and the way people work within it. Many managers find this the most challenging part of the process – when plans, however well developed, are brought into contact with the processes people expect them to change. Those implementing the plan then come up against a variety of organisational and environmental obstacles – and possibly find that some of the assumptions in the plan are incorrect. When a new chief executive took over at Woolworths he commented that he had joined the group because of the great opportunities it offered to recover after a difficult trading period:

but I did not know how much of the work to be done was executional and how much about strategic positioning. Now I know that it is 80 per cent executional.

Organisations are slower to change than plans are to prepare – so events may overtake the plan. Miller *et al.* (2004) tracked the long-term outcomes of 150 strategic plans to establish how managers put them into action and how that affected performance. They defined implementation as

> all the processes and outcomes which accrue to a strategic decision once authorisation has been given to ... put the decision into practice (p. 203)

Their intention was to identify the conditions in which implementation occurs, the managerial activities involved in putting plans into practice, and the extent to which they achieved the objectives. They concluded that success was heavily influenced by:

- managers' experience of the issue; and
- the readiness of the organisation for the change.

> Having relevant experience of what has to be done ... enables managers to assess the objectives [and to] specify the tasks and resource implications appropriately, leading [those affected to accept the process]. (p. 206)

Readiness means a receptive organisational climate that enables managers to implement the change within a positive environment.

The statistical results were illustrated by cases that showed, for example, how managers in a successful company were able to implement a plan to upgrade their computer systems because they had *experience* of many similar changes. They were 'able to set targets, detail what needed doing and allocate the resources ... That is, they could plan and control the implementation effectively'. In another illustration, a regional brewer extending into the London area had no directly relevant experience, and so was not able to set a specific plan. But people in the organisation were very *receptive* to new challenges, and could implement the move with little formal planning.

The authors concluded that the activities of planning do not in themselves lead to success, but are a means for gaining acceptance of what has to be done when it is implemented. Planning helps by inducing confidence in the process, leading to high levels of acceptability. 'Planning is a necessary part of this approach to success, but it is not sufficient in itself' (Miller *et al.* (2004) p. 210).

The final stage in planning is to set up a system that allows people to monitor progress towards the goals. This happens at all levels of planning – from a project manager monitoring and controlling the progress of a discrete project to a board committee monitoring the progress of a broad strategic change that affects many parts of the business – such as integrating an acquisition, or entering a new line of business. This is sometimes called a programme, and monitoring then focuses on the interdependencies between many smaller specific projects.

Project plans define and display every task and activity, but someone managing a programme of linked projects would soon become swamped with such detail. The programme manager needs to maintain a quick-to-understand snapshot of the programme. This should show progress to date, the main events being planned, interdependencies, issues, and expected completion dates. This also helps the programme manager to communicate with senior executives and project managers. One way to do this is to create a single chart with a simplified view of each project on an indicative timeline. Figure 6.6 illustrates this. Details vary but the main features are usually:

- an indicative timeline, along which the individual projects are plotted;
- a simplified representation of the major milestones in each project or change;
- descriptions of progress made against that expected for each project;
- indications of interdependencies between projects.

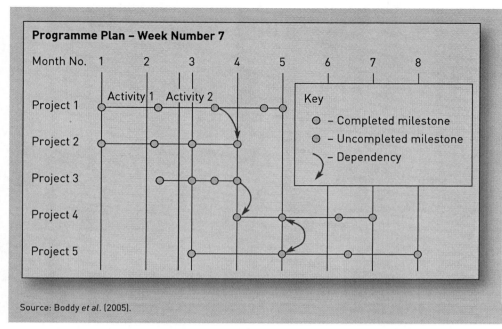

Figure 6.6
A programme
overview chart

Source: Boddy *et al.* (2005).

6.9   Current themes and issues

Performance

Section 6.3 introduced the continuing controversy over whether planning affects performance, especially in conditions which are so uncertain that they are likely to change
before a plan lasting longer than a year has been implemented. While most managers
regularly engage in some form of strategic planning (Glaister and Falshaw, 1999), an
influential group of writers (notably Mintzberg, 1994a) question the role of centralised
planning, instead focusing on the autonomous actions of managers throughout the
organisation. They argue that action by those familiar with local circumstances are the
sources of significant strategic change, which planning tends to inhibit.

Andersen (2000) sought to reconcile these views by studying the use of strategic planning and autonomous action in three industries with different external conditions. He
concluded that strategic planning was associated with superior organisational performance in all industrial settings. Whether industries were complex and dynamic or stable
and simple, companies that planned performed better than those that did not. In addition, he found that in complex dynamic industries a formal planning process was
accompanied by autonomous actions by managers, which further enhanced performance.

Responsibility

Many companies are now responding to the challenges posed by climate change, and are
developing policies to reduce carbon emissions and other environmentally damaging
practices. Such policy statements will depend on the quality of the plans managers
develop – unless they make detailed plans they will be no more than good intentions.
Some idea of the planning required to make a difference can be gained from Marks &
Spencer's 'Plan A', announced in 2007 (see Chapter 8 case), illustrated in the
Management in Practice feature.

management in practice   The M&S 'Plan A'   www.marksandspencer.com

Plan A is a business-wide 'eco-plan' that will affect every part of the business over the next five years. The 100-point plan means that by 2012 the company will:

- become carbon neutral
- send no waste to landfill
- extend sustainable sourcing
- set new standards in ethical trading
- help customers and employees live a healthier lifestyle.

The plan sets targets in each area, and specifies about 20 more specific plans in each. For example, the item on reducing waste includes plans to:

- stop sending waste to landfill
- reduce packaging by 25 per cent
- use food waste to generate green energy
- use packaging from sustainable or recycled sources.

Source: Company press release, 15 January 2007 (on website).

In each of these areas more detailed plans will be required to bring the plan into reality – including ensuring that suppliers also plan changes in the way they operate.

Internationalisation

A theme in all international businesses is the extent to which they should plan the business on a global scale, or leave local managers with autonomy to adapt to local conditions. As Chapter 4 pointed out, the globalisation of markets was observed, and advocated, by Theodore Levitt, who noted the trend in the early 1980s for global brands to displace local products, with identical goods being sold across the globe without modification. This enabled consumer companies such as Coca-Cola and McDonald's to develop as identical global brands, with standard practices and a centralised management structure: it also implied a high degree of centralised planning, with major decisions being made at the centre and local companies implementing them.

This approach began to lose favour as local companies fought back, with customers often finding that new local brands offered better value. Global brands, offering standard products regardless of local tastes, lost market share. So rather than 'going global' they began to 'go local' – adapting products to suit local tastes.

The dilemma this raises is how far to plan globally, and how much to leave to local managers. Managers typically identify some features that are important to the overall health of the brand – such as ingredients or design, advertising or promotional style, and to the health of the business – such as financial performance. They are likely to plan these issues at the global level. They leave other matters, such as choice of suppliers or methods of distribution, to local planners. Establishing that balance in planning is likely to affect the value they add to resources.

Summary

1 **Explain the purposes of planning and the content of different types of plan**

- Effective plans can clarify direction, motivate people, use resources efficiently and allow people to measure progress towards objectives.

- Plans can be at strategic, tactical and operational levels, and in new businesses people prepare business plans to secure capital. Strategic business units also prepare plans relatively independently of the parent. There are also special-purpose or project plans, and standing plans. All can be either specific or directional in nature.

2 **Compare alternative planning processes, and evaluate when each may be most suitable**

- Plans can be formal/rational/top down in nature, or they can be adaptable and flexible (logical incrementalism); accumulating evidence that a combination of approaches is most likely to suit firms in volatile conditions.

3 **Outline the seven iterative steps in planning and describe techniques used in each**

- Recycling through the tasks of gathering information, developing a mission, setting goals, identifying actions and allocating resources, implementing plans, monitoring progress and evaluating results.

- Planners draw information from the general and competitive environments using tools such as Porter's five forces analysis. They can do this within the framework of a SWOT analysis, and also use forecasting, sensitivity analysis, critical success factors and scenario planning techniques.

4 **Use theory to evaluate the motivational effect of the goals stated in a plan**

- Goal-setting theory predicts that goals can be motivational if people perceive the targets to be difficult but achievable.

- Goals can also be evaluated in terms of whether they are specific, measurable, attainable, rewarded and timed.

5 **Use a framework to evaluate whether a plan is sufficiently comprehensive**

- The 'wheel' provides a model for recalling the likely areas in an organisation that a plan should cover, indicating the likely ripple effects of change in one area on others.

6 **Evaluate the context that will affect the ability of managers to implement a plan**

- The value of a plan depends on people implementing it, but Miller's research shows that that depends on the experience of those implementing it, and the receptivity of the organisation to change.

Review questions

1 What types of planning do you do in your personal life? Describe them in terms of whether they are (a) strategic or operational, (b) short or long term, (c) specific or directional.

2 What are four benefits that people in organisations may gain from planning?

3 What are the main sources of information that managers can use in planning? What models can they use to structure this information?

▶

4 In what ways can a goal be motivational? What practical things can people do in forming plans that take account of goal-setting theory?

5 What is meant by the term 'hierarchy of objectives', and how can that idea help people to build a consistent plan? What else would managers need to do once they have agreed a hierarchy of objectives?

6 Explain the term 'organisational receptivity', and how people can use the idea in developing a plan that is more likely to work.

7 What are the main ways of monitoring progress on a plan, and why is this so vital a task in planning?

8 As environments become more uncertain, will planning become more or less useful? How can managers plan effectively in a rapidly changing environment?

Concluding critical reflection

Think about the way your company, or one with which you are familiar, makes plans. Review the material in the chapter, and perhaps visit some of the websites identified. Then make notes on these questions:

- What examples of the themes discussed in this chapter are currently relevant to your company? What types of plans are you most closely involved with? Which of the techniques suggested do you and your colleagues typically use, and why? What techniques do you use that are not mentioned here?

- In responding to these issues, what **assumptions** about the nature of planning in business appear to guide your approach? Are the prevailing assumptions closer to the planning or emergent perspectives, and why do you think that is?

- What factors in the **context** of the company appear to shape your approach to planning – what kind of environment are you working in, for example? To what extent does your planning process involve people from other organisations – and why is that?

- Have you compared your planning processes with those in other companies to check if they use **alternative** methods to yours? How do they plan?

- Have you considered the **limitations** of your approach – such as whether you plan too much, or too little? What limitations can you see in some of the ideas presented here – for example the usefulness of scenario planning or SWOT analyses?

Further reading

Johnson, G., Scholes, K. and Whittington, R. (2006), *Exploring Corporate Strategy* (7th edn.), Financial Times/Prentice Hall, Harlow.

> The best-selling European text on corporate strategy. Although more detailed than required at introductory level, a number of sections usefully build on this chapter.

Dobson, P., Starkey, K. and Richards, J. (2004), *Strategic Management: Issues and cases*, Blackwell, Oxford.

Smith, R.J. (1994), *Strategic Management and Planning in the Public Sector*, Longman/Civil Service College, Harlow.

> Both cover the main elements in the strategic planning process and explain, with the use of examples, some planning tools in addition to those covered in this chapter. Smith's book also contains useful chapters on definitions and terminology and options analysis.

Weblinks

These websites have appeared in the chapter:

www.dsm.com
www.sabmiller.com
www.fiat.co.uk
www.merck.com
www.electrolux.com
www.cw.com
www.shell.com
www.powergen.co.uk
www.marksandspencer.com
www.cocacola.com

Visit two of the sites in the list, and navigate to the pages dealing with corporate news, or investor relations.

- What planning issues can you identify that managers in the company are likely to be dealing with?
- What kind of environment are they likely to be working in, and how will that affect their planning methods and processes?

Annotated weblinks, multiple choice questions and other useful resources can be found on www.pearsoned.co.uk/boddy

Chapter 7

Decision making

Aim

To identify major aspects of decision making in organisations and to outline alternative ways of making decisions.

Objectives

By the end of your work on this chapter you should be able to outline the concepts below in your own terms and:

1 Explain the tasks in making a decision and how decision processes affect the outcome
2 Explain, and give examples of, programmed and non-programmed decisions
3 Distinguish between certainty, risk, uncertainty and ambiguity
4 Contrast rational, administrative, political and garbage can decision models
5 Give examples of common sources of bias in decisions
6 Explain the contribution of Vroom and Yetton, and of Irving Janis, to our understanding of decision making in groups.

Key terms

This chapter introduces the following ideas:

decision
decision making
problem
opportunity
decision criteria
decision tree
programmed decision
procedure
rule
policy
non-programmed decision
certainty
risk
uncertainty

ambiguity
rational model of decision making
administrative model of decision making
bounded rationality
satisficing
incremental model
heuristics
prior hypothesis bias
representativeness bias
illusion of control
escalating commitment
groupthink

Each is a term defined within the text, as well as in the Glossary at the end of the book.

Wipro www.wipro.com

Wipro provides a growing range of IT services to companies around the world. In the year to March 2006 it reported that sales had reached $US 2.4 billion – 33 per cent above the previous year. It employed over 50,000 staff (23,000 in 2004). Azim Premji is chairman of the company and follows an exhausting work routine even though he is India's richest person:

[His day begins at 7 with] meetings with visiting customers or government officials. That's followed by meetings where he focuses on the minutiae of business. Before the sun is overhead Premji has already worked seven hours, with another seven to go. Frequently he ends his day on a commercial flight – there is no corporate jet – to Bombay, San Francisco or London – anywhere his sales team needs a boost.

The company has grown from being a small producer of cooking oil (Western India Vegetable Products) founded by his father. He took charge in 1966 when he was 21 and immediately began to professionalise the company. He held staff meetings by telephone every Monday morning at which regional managers reported on their performance and were set new goals for the following week.

He empowered his managers. They were free to set prices in their regions as they saw fit. But they were also held accountable for their performance. These were innovations for India, which (had a tradition of bureaucracy and government control). (Hamm, 2007, p. 34)

Sales grew, but Premji wanted to broaden the business. He had no long-term plan, but saw opportunities in new areas – diversifying into toilet soaps and beauty products, and into manufacturing construction equipment. His next diversification laid the foundations for the modern company.

In 1977 the Indian government passed new rules that required foreign companies to operate through local, Indian-owned partners. IBM, then the world's dominant computer company, left the country, creating an opportunity for Indian companies to enter the market for computer hardware. Premji recalls: 'When IBM left, it created a vacuum. So we decided to zero in on info tech.'

By 1981 the company was selling the computers it had designed, which were India's top-selling machines for several years. In 1984 it moved into software with a spreadsheet and word-processing package.

Wipro

In the early 1990s the rules changed again, with serious consequences. The Indian government liberalised its business regulations, which enabled the world's top computer companies to move into the country again. Their R&D resources and sales volumes would soon allow them to overcome Wipro. The head of the IT unit, Sridhar Mitta, had the idea of selling the company's expertise to the world's top tech companies:

We saw that while the door was open for others to come in, it was also open for us to go out. So we decided to become a global company.

As a relatively unknown company growth was slow, but a large contract from a major US company, General Electric in 1990 helped Wipro's credibility. Initially the work was in low-value software coding and maintenance, but has extended into more advanced areas of designing software and complete IT systems. Premji has also expanded his reach into the Middle East where US companies are unwelcome.

Recent decisions have involved moving the technology division's HQ to California to be closer to the customers, and acquiring smaller companies that will add to the range of expertise and services it can offer.

Sources: Based on *The Economist*, 6 February 2003; Hamm (2007); Wipro *Annual Report 2005-06* from the company website.

Case questions 7.1

- Make a note of the decisions that Mr Premji has made in the story so far.
- How have they affected the development of the business?
- Visit Wipro's website, and note examples of recent decisions that have shaped the company.

7.1   Introduction

The case recounts the recent history of one of India's biggest and most successful companies, which is now a global player in the market for IT services. To develop the business from a local cooking oil firm to its present position senior managers at Wipro needed to decide where to allocate time, effort and other resources. Over the years their decisions paid off and they now face new issues, such as how to attract customers and well-qualified staff against competition from established global companies. Wipro also faces political reactions from foreign governments about the loss of local jobs when work is outsourced. How managers decide to deal with matters such as these will shape Wipro's future.

The performance of every organisation reflects (as well as luck and good fortune) the decisions that people make, and there are many studies of the activity – Buchanan and O'Connell (2006) provide a historical review. People continually make choices (including that of ignoring an issue and avoiding a decision), as they see problems that may need attention, and ideas or proposals they may be able to use. Resources are limited, there are many demands on them, and people have different goals. Their choices relate to all aspects of the management task – decisions about inputs (how to raise capital, who to employ), outputs (what products to make, how to distribute them) and transformations (how to organise the delivery of a new service, how to manage the finances). Decisions affect how well the organisation uses resources, and whether it transforms them in a way that creates sufficient value (as seen by customers) to ensure it survives: 'Like management itself, decision-making is a generic process that is applicable to all forms of organised activity' (Harrison, 1999, p. 8). Choice is a source of tension as it makes us worry about 'what if' we had selected the other option (Schwartz, 2005).

J.K. Rowling (estimated, in 2007, to be the wealthiest person in the media business) offered the manuscript of the original Harry Potter story to several leading publishers, whose editors decided to reject it: an editor at Bloomsbury decided to accept it. The managers of the European Airbus 380 project decided in July 2004 to increase production from 20 to 30 a year. By 2007 technical difficulties were delaying deliveries by two years – so airlines that had ordered the aircraft needed to decide whether to cancel their order or accept the delay and seek compensation.

Figure 7.1 illustrates the themes of the chapter, showing that decision making involves:

- identifying the type of decision
- identifying the conditions surrounding the decision
- using one or more models to guide the approach
- selecting a decision-making style
- working through the process and implementing the decision.

The chapter begins with the tasks through which people make decisions and identifies types of decision. It compares four models of the decision-making process, and finally examines a method for deciding how much to involve others in making decisions.

7.2   Tasks in making decisions

A **decision** is a specific commitment to action (usually a commitment of resources).

A **decision** is a specific commitment to action (usually a commitment of resources). People make such choices at several levels – individual, group, organisational and societal (Harrison, 1999) – and will be influenced to some extent by decisions made at the other levels.

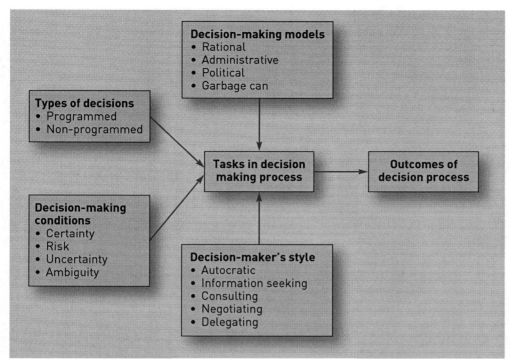

Figure 7.1

An overview of decision making in organisations

- **Individual** People make individual choices about all aspects of their lives, and in relation to organisations they make choices about careers, whether to change job or not, how hard to work, whether to apply for promotion or make a complaint.
- **Group** Members of a group continually make decisions about how to work together, accomplish a task or choose a new member. They are still individuals, but their decisions reflect relationships and mutual expectations.
- **Organisational** These decisions are made by people in their organisational roles. They are still individuals and will often be part of a team resolving a problem – but will be aware of what others expect, and of organisational policies and practices.
- **Societal** People outside the organisation make decisions that affect those within it – either directly (awarding a contract) or indirectly (changing a tax). People within organisations also seek to influence, and be part of, these external processes.

Managers at Nokia, seeking to maintain the company's dominant position in the mobile phone market, constantly have to choose between several possible models to launch. In 2003 they made some wrong decisions, favouring models that customers did not like, and lost sales. Later choices must have been better, since by 2007 sales were rising again and the company had recovered its position. Such decisions are part of a wider process of **decision making** – which includes identifying problems, opportunities and possible solutions. It involves effort before and after the actual choice. In deciding whether to select Jean, Bob or Rasul for a job the manager would probably, amongst other things, have to:

Decision making is the process of identifying problems and opportunities and then resolving them.

- identify the need for a new member of staff
- perhaps persuade his or her boss to authorise the budget
- decide where to advertise the post
- interview candidates
- select the preferred candidate
- decide whether or not to agree to their request for a better deal, and
- arrange their induction into the job so that they work effectively.

At each of these stages the manager may have to go back in the process to reconsider what to do, or to deal with another set of decisions – such as the sensitive area of who to include on the selection committee. In Nokia's case the choice of model would have been preceded by choices about the basic design concept and which groups of customers to target – and would be followed by choices about production volumes, features and price.

The effect on performance depends on the actions that follow the decision – when someone implements it. The visible, public actions that tell us about a decision will have been preceded by many invisible choices. A manager is making small but potentially significant decisions all the time – which of several urgent jobs to deal with next, whose advice to seek about them, which report to read, which customer to call. These shape the way people use their time, and the issues they decide are sufficiently important to earn a place on the agenda.

As we make decisions we attend to the tasks shown in Figure 7.2 – the arrows showing the iterative nature of the process, as we move back and forwards between the tasks. As we move through an activity we find new information, reconsider what we are doing, go back a stage or two and perhaps decide on a different route. People may also miss a step, or pay too much attention to some and too little to others. Putting enough time into each step is a decision-making skill.

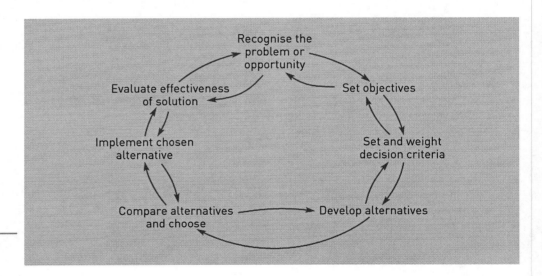

Figure 7.2
Tasks in making decisions

Paul Nutt on why decisions fail

Paul Nutt studied over 400 decisions involving major commitments of resources. He distinguished between a 'discovery process' that usually led to success, and an 'idea imposition process' which usually led to failure. Decision makers select tactics that push their process towards one or other of these types, and Nutt argues that by being aware of these managers have a better chance of success than failure.

Those following a discovery process spend time at the start looking beyond the initial claim that 'a problem has arisen that requires a decision': they spend time *understanding the claims* – by talking to stakeholders to judge the strength of their concerns and their views. This leads to a better-informed expression of the 'arena of action' on which to take a decision. They also identify at the outset the forces that may block them from *implementing the preferred idea*, as this helps to understand the interests of stakeholders whose support may be required.

These early actions enable decision makers *to set a direction* – an agreed outcome of the decision. Dealing thoroughly with these three stages makes the remaining stages – *uncovering and evaluating ideas* – comparatively easy, as they help build agreement on what the decision is expected to achieve. Those following an idea imposition process

skip some stages ... jump to conclusions and then try to implement the solution they have stumbled upon. This bias for action causes them to limit their search, consider very few ideas, and pay too little attention to people who are affected, despite the fact that decisions fail for just these reasons. (Nutt, 2002, p. 49)

Source: Nutt (2002).

Recognising a problem and setting objectives

People make decisions that commit time and other resources towards meeting an objective. They do so when they become aware of a **problem** – a gap between an existing and a desired state of affairs, or an **opportunity** – the chance to do something not previously expected. An example to illustrate the steps would be a manager who needs to decide whether to buy new laptops for members of their sales team. The team have been complaining that their present machines are too slow and do not have enough capacity for the volume of work. The sales manager now has a problem, but in real life few problems are that obvious. Is a 5 per cent drop in sales a problem? Identifying a problem as significant is a subjective, possibly contentious matter. Before a problem (or opportunity) gets on to the agenda, enough people have to be aware of it and feel sufficient pressure to act. Managers at Microsoft were slow to realise that Linux software was a serious threat to their growth, and this delay lost valuable time.

A **problem** is a gap between an existing and a desired state of affairs.

An **opportunity** is the chance to do something not previously expected.

Denial at P&G www.pg.com

management in practice

Procter & Gamble (P&G), the world's largest consumer products company (brands include Tide, Pampers and Crest), is undergoing radical change to increase profitability. This drive is being led by A.G. Laffley, a long-term manager at the company, who became CEO in 2000.

For most of its history P&G was one of the United States' leading companies, with brands that have become household names in many parts of the world. Many of its management techniques have also been widely adopted – such as the idea of having competing brands within the same company, to encourage performance. But by the 1990s P&G was in danger of becoming another Eastman Kodak or Xerox, a once-great company that had lost its way. Sales of most of its top 18 brands were slowing; the company was losing ground to more focused rivals such as Kimberly-Clark and Colgate-Palmolive. At the same time, the dynamics of the industry were changing as power shifted from manufacturers to massive retailers.

Through all of this, much of senior management was in denial. Laffley says: 'Nobody wanted to talk about it. Without a doubt [I and a few others] were in the camp of "We need a much bigger change".'

Source: *Business Week*, 7 July 2003.

Managers become aware of a problem as they compare existing conditions with the state they desire. If things are not as they should be – the sales reps are complaining that their slow laptops prevent them doing their jobs properly – then there is a problem.

People are only likely to act if they feel pressure to do so – such as a rep threatening to leave or a customer complaining about the time it takes to download the latest prices. Pressure comes from many sources – and people differ in whether they pay attention to the signals: some will react quickly, others will ignore uncomfortable information and postpone a difficult (to them) decision.

Setting and weighting the decision criteria

Decision criteria define the factors that are relevant in making a decision.

To decide between two or more options people need some **decision criteria** – the factors that are relevant to the decision. Until people set these, they cannot choose between options: in the laptop case criteria could include usefulness of features, price, delivery, warranty, compatibility with other systems, ease of use and many more. Some criteria are more important than others and the decision process needs to represent this in some way – perhaps by assigning 100 points between the factors depending on their relative importance. We can measure some of these criteria (price or delivery) quite objectively, while others (features, ease of use) are subjective.

Like problem recognition, setting criteria is subjective: people vary in the factors they wish to include, and the weights they assign to them. They may also have private and unexpressed criteria – such as 'will cause least trouble', 'will do what the boss expects', 'will help my career'. Changing the criteria or their relative weights will change the decision – so the manager in the laptop case also has to decide whether to set and weight the criteria herself, or to invite the views of the reps.

Developing alternatives

Another task is to identify several alternative solutions to the problem. In the laptop case this is a matter of identifying currently available brands and is not difficult. In more complex problems the alternatives themselves may need to be developed. A practical issue is how many alternatives to develop – and how much time and effort to put into the process. Developing too few limits choice, but developing too many will be costly and may overwhelm decision makers. Barry Schwartz (2005) found this in his study of individual decision making – giving people more choices beyond a certain point can be counter-productive. More choice means more stress, frustration and anxiety that they may make the wrong decision – see Key Ideas.

key ideas   Too many jams to choose

Iyengar and Lepper (2000) demonstrated that consumers protect themselves from the stress of too much choice by refusing to purchase. In an experiment conducted in a food store, they set up a tasting booth offering different types of jam. When 24 types were on display, about 60 per cent of passers-by stopped at the booth, compared with just 40 per cent when only 6 jams were shown. But when it came to choosing a pot of jam to buy, the proportions changed. Just 3 per cent of the visits to the 24 jam booth resulted in a purchase, while 30 per cent of those who visited the smaller display made a purchase. The limited selection was the most effective in converting interest into sales.

Source: Iyengar and Lepper (2000).

Comparing alternatives and making a choice

As in daily life, management decisions depend on a system for comparing alternatives and making a choice. Which bar, where to holiday, whether to bid for a house – people compare alternatives and decide between them. In a simple case, the chosen criteria may quickly show the best choice. Since criteria and their weights are subjective, a choice that is made by several people can end in argument and disagreement – those who do not like the choice may reopen the debate by proposing different criteria.

Figure 7.3 illustrates the tasks in making a decision through a simple personal example. Although superficially simple, people find these choices difficult – mainly in the area of setting criteria. Some are easy to state and compare (price, warranty) but others are inherently subjective (in fashion?) and so are open to wide differences of interpretation. The more people involved, the more difficult it may be to resolve these issues.

Another way to structure a situation in which there are several alternative actions is to draw a **decision tree**. This helps to assess the relative suitability of the options by assessing them against identified criteria – successively eliminating the options as each relevant factor is introduced. Figure 7.8 is an example of a decision tree – it shows how a manager can decide the most suitable method of solving a problem by asking a succession of questions about the situation, leading to the most likely solution for those circumstances. The main challenge in using the technique is to identify the logical sequence of intermediate decisions and how they relate to each other.

A **decision tree** helps someone to make a choice by progressively eliminating options as additional criteria or events are added to the tree.

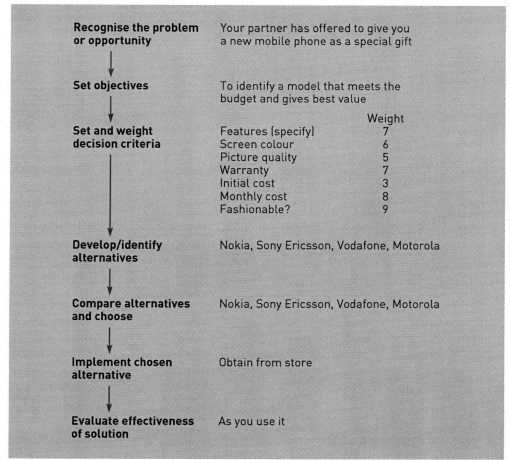

| Recognise the problem or opportunity | Your partner has offered to give you a new mobile phone as a special gift |
| Set objectives | To identify a model that meets the budget and gives best value |

Set and weight decision criteria		Weight
	Features (specify)	7
	Screen colour	6
	Picture quality	5
	Warranty	7
	Initial cost	3
	Monthly cost	8
	Fashionable?	9

Develop/identify alternatives	Nokia, Sony Ericsson, Vodafone, Motorola
Compare alternatives and choose	Nokia, Sony Ericsson, Vodafone, Motorola
Implement chosen alternative	Obtain from store
Evaluate effectiveness of solution	As you use it

Figure 7.3

Illustrating the decision-making tasks – a new mobile phone

Activity 7.1   Critical reflection on making a decision

Work through the steps in Figure 7.3 for a decision you currently face – such as where to go on holiday, which courses to choose next year, or which job to apply for. Then do the same for a decision that involves several other people, such as which assignment to do in your study group or where to go for a night out together.

If you work in an organisation, select two business decisions as the focus of your work.

- How did working through the steps affect the way you reached a decision?
- Did it help you think more widely about the alternatives?
- How did the second decision, involving more people, affect the usefulness of the method?
- Then reflect on the technique itself – did it give insight into the decision process? What other tasks should it include?

 **key ideas**   Mintzberg's study of major decisions

Henry Mintzberg and his colleagues studied 25 major, unstructured decisions in 25 organisations, finding that rational techniques could not cope with the complexity of strategic decisions. They concluded that:

- Whether people recognised the need for a decision depended on the strength of the stimuli, the reputation of the source and the availability of a potential solution.
- Most decisions depended on designing a custom-made solution (a new organisation structure, a new product or a new technology).
- The choice phase (see Figure 7.2), was less significant than the design phase: it was essentially ratifying a solution that was determined implicitly during design.

Source: Mintzberg *et al.* (1976).

Implementing the chosen alternative

In the laptop case this is a simple matter – provided the manager has conducted the process satisfactorily. In bigger decisions this will be a much more problematic stage as it is here that the decision is translated, or not, into visible action. Even then it depends on what is meant by 'implementation'. If the decision concerns a new computer system then one measure of implementation could be that the equipment is bought and installed. Another (and more useful) view would be that implementation refers to the wide acceptance and use of the system so that people are using it effectively to improve the service they offer.

This will be a much more protracted process, and will depend on people making many other decisions elsewhere in the organisation. This is also where the way in which a person conducts the decision-making process will become evident. If implementation depends on the cooperation of other people (for example, a major change in the way they work) then their willingness to cooperate will be affected by the extent to which they were involved in the decision process.

Wipro – the case continues   www.wipro.com

Decide quickly, and don't be afraid to switch

A company facing rapidly changing technical and business conditions needs to be able to make decisions quickly. Wipro has evolved a management rhythm that is organised around the type of decisions managers have to make. There are:

- weekly meetings in each business unit about spotting and fixing problems, or exploiting opportunities (continuing the meetings with regional managers in the cooking oil business);
- monthly IT management meetings to introduce and adjust tactics;
- quarterly strategy council meetings to decide longer-term issues.

In each of these meetings, the spirit of experimentation is pervasive. Managers are inclined to try things and get them going fast – essentially pilot projects. They track the projects closely, so if something doesn't work, they spot it quickly and make adjustments, or even pull the plug. (Hamm, 2006, p. 286)

Source: Hamm (2007).

> **Case questions 7.2**
>
> - Compare this account with Nutt's analysis (p. 210) of why decisions fail, and try to identify how closely Wipro's approach matches Nutt's recommendations.
> - What are the advantages and disadvantages of quick decision making?

Evaluating the decision

The final stage is evaluation – looking back to see if the decision has resolved the problem, and what can be learned. It is a form of control, which people are often reluctant to do formally, preferring to turn their attention to future tasks rather than reflect on the past. That choice inhibits their ability to learn from experience.

Having given this simplified overview of the process, the following sections outline different types of decisions, and some models that seek to explain how people make them.

7.3   Types of decisions

Strategic and operational decisions

Strategic decisions have greater implications for the organisation than operational ones. As Chapter 8 shows, strategy is the business of developing the future direction of the organisation, by committing major resources to one area rather than another. Strategic decisions relate to the world outside the organisation – to develop a new product, acquire a competitor, enter an overseas market or increase a price. Strategic decisions affect the future of large parts of the organisation – such as when managers at Philips decided to change from being a traditional electronic manufacturer to a healthcare and technology group. This in turn led to the disposal of its interests in semiconductor manufacturing and the purchase of medical equipment companies.

management in practice **McDonald's decides on a new menu** www.mcdonalds.com

In 2004 McDonald's, the world's largest fast food chain and a popular target for those concerned about obesity, announced that it would introduce a new range of salads in its European restaurants. Dennis Hennequin, executive vice-president for Europe, promised that space for the new products would be created by eliminating two traditional burgers from the menu. The company has also stopped selling several super-size portions of fries and drinks. Mr Hennequin had taken on his present job earlier in the year, in recognition of his success in turning France into McDonald's fastest-growing European market. His decisions there to upgrade restaurants and modernise menus will be the template for what will be done elsewhere in Europe. The menu will include many new ingredients and reflect Hennequin's belief that the company must start catering to a new customer awareness of the need for a well-balanced diet.

Source: Based on *Financial Times*, 9 March 2004.

Operational (or activity-related) decisions are shorter term, often on day-to-day matters, and within established policy: whether to recruit staff, to replace a machine or to offer a discount to a customer.

Programmed and non-programmed decisions

A **programmed decision** is a repetitive decision that can be handled by a routine approach.

A **procedure** is a series of related steps to deal with a structured problem.

A **rule** sets out what someone can or cannot do in a given situation.

A **policy** is a guideline that establishes some general principles for making a decision.

Programmed decisions (Simon, 1960) deal with problems that are familiar, and where the information required is easy to define and obtain – the situation is well structured. If a store manager notices that a product is selling more than expected there will be a simple, routine procedure for deciding how much extra to order from the supplier. Decisions are structured to the extent that they arise frequently and can be dealt with routinely by following an established **procedure** – a series of related steps, often set out in a manual, to deal with a structured problem. They may also reach a decision by using an established **rule**, which sets out what someone can or cannot do in a given situation. They may also refer to a **policy** – a guideline that establishes some general principles for making a decision.

People make programmed decisions to resolve recurring problems – to reorder supplies when stocks drop below a defined level, to set the qualifications required for a job, to decide whether to lend money to a bank customer. Once managers formulate procedures, rules or policies others can usually make the decisions. Computers handle many decisions of this type – the checkout systems in supermarkets calculate the items sold and order new stock.

Simon (1960) also observed that people make **non-programmed decisions** to deal with situations that are unstructured, and so require a unique solution. The issue has not arisen in quite that form, and the information required is unclear, vague or open to many interpretations. Major management decisions are of this type – such as the choice that managers at Virgin faced over whether to delay their order for Airbus 380 planes for 18 months until the weight of the new airliner was reduced to that originally promised. Several solutions were being tested, but it was not clear when they would be ready, nor how passengers would react to them. Most issues of strategy are of this type, because they involve great uncertainty and many interests.

A **non-programmed decision** is a unique decision that requires a custom-made solution when information is lacking or unclear.

People need to deal with programmed and non-programmed decisions in different ways. The former are amenable to procedures, routines, rules and quantitative analytical techniques such as those associated with operational research. They are also suitable for resolution by modern information systems. Non-programmed decisions depend on judgement and intuition.

Figure 7.4 relates the type of decision to the levels of the organisation. Those lower in the organisation typically deal with routine, structured problems that they can resolve by applying procedures. As people move up the hierarchy they face correspondingly more unstructured decisions. It is easy to see why this happens – lower-level staff hand decisions that do not fit the rules to someone above them to deal with; those higher up pass routine matters to subordinates.

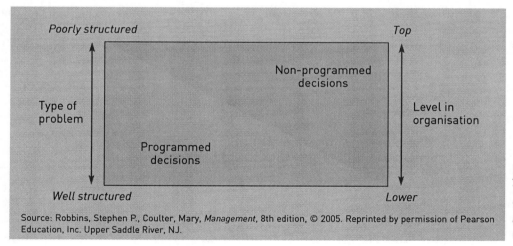

Source: Robbins, Stephen P., Coulter, Mary, *Management*, 8th edition, © 2005. Reprinted by permission of Pearson Education, Inc. Upper Saddle River, NJ.

Figure 7.4

Types of decision, types of problem and level in the organisation

Many decisions have elements of each type – non-programmed decisions probably contain elements that can be handled in a programmed way.

Non-programmed decisions – growth goals and the Wipro way

In 1999 Premji hired Vivek Paul (from GE Medical Systems) as head of Wipro Technologies, with the goal of accelerating growth. Paul had seen the capabilities of Wipro staff, and was eager for the chance to run the global technology business. However, other tech businesses were also growing rapidly, and he feared this would make it difficult to retain and excite staff. He decided that Wipro was not thinking big enough. He and his aides came up with a challenging growth goal – to be a $4 billion company by the end of 2004 (the 4 × 4 plan): 'We decided to dream big, and people had the confidence we could actually achieve it.'

Paul left in 2005, and the company faced challenges from other Indian companies such as Tata and Infosys, and from overseas competitors. To attack these issues, Premji took personal charge of the technology business, deciding that Wipro needed to be more aggressive about growing revenues, both organically and through acquisition. He sought more innovative solutions, and continued the practice of frequent reorganisations.

He and his executive team also decided to formalise the company's core philosophy – the Wipro Way. This gives all managers and employees a clear target at which to aim. It identifies Wipro's four pillars of strength – customer centred, process excellence, people management and career development. Then it sets a high bar for each of them – such as to have the best customer satisfaction ratings of any company in the industry.

Source: Hamm (2007).

Activity 7.3   Programmed and non-programmed decisions

Identify examples of the types of decision set out above. Try to identify one example of your own to add to those below or that illustrates the point specifically within your institution:

- **programmed decision** – whether to reorder stock
- **non-programmed decision** – whether to launch a new service in a new market.

Compare your examples with those of other students and consider how those responsible made each decision. What examples of programmed and non-programmed decisions can you see in the Wipro case? How easy is it to divide decisions between these two categories – how useful are they as distinguishing characteristics?

Dependent or independent

Another way to categorise decisions is in terms of their links to other decisions. People make decisions in a historical and social context and so are influenced by past and possible future decisions and the influence of other parts of the organisation.

Many decisions are influenced by previous decisions – that constrain, or enable, what can be done now. When Hutcheson began to offer third-generation (3G) mobile services in 2004 it was able to offer more competitive prices than established companies. The latter were concerned that if they cut charges on their third-generation services this would affect revenues from existing customers. Hutcheson, as the new entrant, did not depend on revenues from earlier decisions. Legacy computer systems (the result of earlier decisions) frequently constrain how quickly a company can adopt new systems.

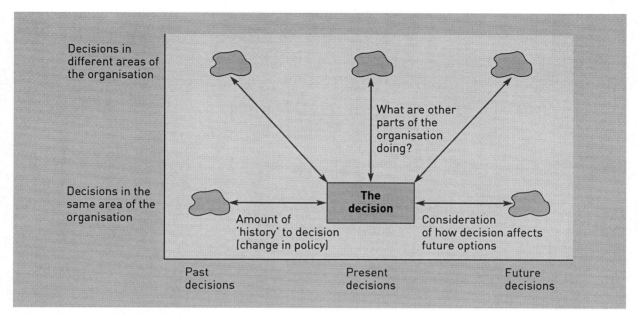

Figure 7.5 Possible relationships between decisions
Source: Cooke and Slack (1991), p. 24.

Some decisions have few implications beyond their immediate area, but others have significant ripples around the organisation. Changes in technology, for example, usually require consistent, supportive changes in structures and processes if they are to be effective – but decisions on these areas are harder to make than those affecting the technology. More generally, local units may be limited in their decisions by wider company policies. Figure 7.5 illustrates this.

7.4   Decision-making conditions

Decisions arise within a wider context, and the conditions in this context, as measured by the degree of **certainty, risk, uncertainty** and **ambiguity**, materially affect the decision process.

A major factor distinguishing structured from unstructured decisions is the degree of certainty managers deal with in making the decision. Some aspects of a decision are unknowable – what Nokia's competitors will be charging next year, whether GSK's pharmaceutical research programme will deliver the new drugs the company needs to keep revenue growing. Decisions based on assumptions about these future conditions may not turn out as people hope. Managers try to obtain information about the options facing them to reduce this uncertainty.

Figure 7.6 relates the nature of the problem to the type of decision. People can deal with conditions of certainty by making programmed decisions, but many situations are both uncertain and ambiguous. Here people need to be able to use a non-programmed approach.

Certainty describes the situation when all the information the decision maker needs is available.

Risk refers to situations in which the decision maker is able to estimate the likelihood of the alternative outcomes.

Uncertainty is when people are clear about their goals but have little information about which course of action is most likely to succeed.

Ambiguity is when people are uncertain about their goals and how best to achieve them.

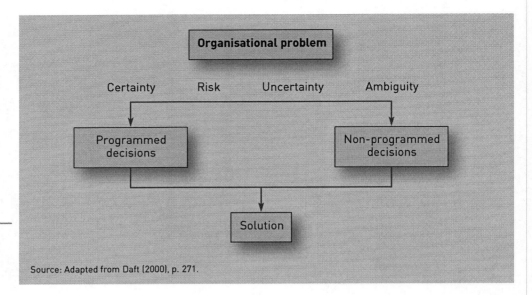

Figure 7.6

Degree of uncertainty and decision-making type

Source: Adapted from Daft (2000), p. 271.

Certainty

Certainty is when the decision maker has all the information they need – are fully informed about the costs and benefits of each alternative. A company treasurer wanting to place reserve funds can readily compare rates of interest from several banks, and calculate exactly the return from each. Few decisions are that certain, and most contain risk and/or uncertainty.

Risk

Risk refers to situations in which the decision maker can estimate the likelihood of the alternative outcomes, possibly using statistical methods. Banks have developed tools to assess credit risk, and so reduce the risk of a borrower not repaying a loan. The questions on an application form for a loan (home ownership, time at this address, employer's name, etc.) enable the bank to assess the risk of lending money to that person.

Uncertainty

Uncertainty means that people know what they wish to achieve but do not have enough information about alternatives and future events to estimate the risk confidently. Factors that may affect the outcomes of deciding to launch a new product (future growth in the market, changes in customer interests, competitors' actions) are difficult to predict.

Managers at GSK, the pharmaceutical group, experienced great uncertainty in a decision to allocate research funds. Scientists who wished to develop a new range of vaccines had to persuade the board to divert resources to their project. Uncertainties included the fact that the science was evolving rapidly, discoveries could be made elsewhere, and it would be many years before the research produced commercial results. The board approved the investment, and the line of work is now a major product within GSK Biologicals.

Ambiguity

Ambiguity describes a situation in which the intended goals are unclear, and so the alternative ways of reaching them are equally fluid. Ambiguity is by far the most difficult decision situation. Students would experience ambiguity if their teacher created student groups, told each group to complete a project, but gave them no topic, direction or guidelines. Ambiguous problems are those where people have difficulty in coming to grips with the issues, and they are often associated with conflicts over ends and means, rapidly changing circumstances and unclear links between decision elements – see Management in Practice.

Ambiguity at EADS defers a decision www.eads.com   **management in practice**

EADS is the parent company of Airbus, and has experienced long-running conflicts between French and German shareholders. In 2007 the board was under pressure to approve a cost-cutting plan proposed by the chief executive of Airbus, necessary because of the delays to the A380, which has increased losses at the company. It is also trying to launch a project to build a new fleet of aircraft to compete with Boeing's Dreamliner, but has been unable to agree how to divide the work between operations in France, Germany, Spain and the United Kingdom. National political conflicts at the highest level over this long-term issue were preventing the board from deciding the short-term restructuring issue.

Source: *Financial Times*, 20 February 2007.

Case questions 7.3

- Reflect on the decisions at Wipro that you identified earlier. What risks, uncertainties or ambiguities were probably associated with them?
- When the company moved its technology division to California, what dependencies would that have involved (use Figure 7.5 to structure your answer)?
- If the company expands its business in the Middle East, what dependencies might that raise?

7.5   Decision-making models

James Thompson (1967) distinguished decisions on two dimensions – agreement or disagreement over goals, and the beliefs that decision makers hold about the relationship between cause and effect. A decision can be mapped on these two dimensions – whether or not there is agreement on goals, and how certain people are about the consequences of their decisions. Figure 7.7 shows these, and an approach to making decisions that seems best suited to each cell.

Computational strategy – rational model

The **rational model of decision making** is based on economic assumptions. Traditional economic models suggested that the role of a manager was to maximise the economic return to the firm, and that they did this by making decisions on economically rational criteria. The assumptions underlying this model are that the decision maker:

The **rational model of decision making** assumes that people make consistent choices to maximise economic value within specified constraints.

- aims for goals that are known and agreed, and that the problem is structured;
- strives for conditions of certainty, gathering complete information and calculating the likely results of each alternative;
- selects the alternative that will maximise economic returns;
- is rational and logical in assigning values, setting preferences and evaluating alternatives.

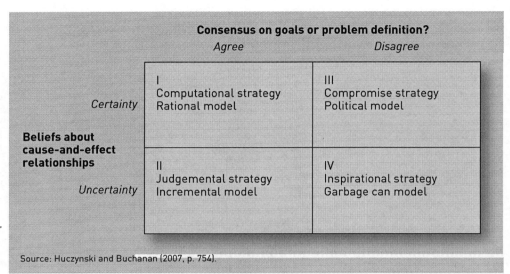

Figure 7.7

Conditions favouring different decision processes

Source: Huczynski and Buchanan (2007, p. 754).

The rational model is normative, in that it defines how a decision maker should act – it does not describe how managers actually make decisions. It aims to help decision makers act more rationally, rather than rely solely on intuition and personal preferences, and is most valuable for programmed decisions where there is little conflict. Where the information required is available and people can agree the criteria for choice, the approach can work well.

key ideas   Evidence-based management?

Pfeffer and Sutton (2006a) note that managers frequently make decisions without considering the evidence about what works, and what does not. They often base decisions on:

experience (which may or may not fit current circumstances);
solutions with which they are familiar;
accepting commercially motivated claims about a technique;
dogmas or beliefs for which there is no reliable evidence.

After enumerating the possible reasons for this, they advocate that evidence-based management could change the way every manager thinks and acts:

We believe that facing the hard facts and truth about what works and what doesn't, understanding the dangerous half-truths that constitute so much conventional wisdom about management, and rejecting the total nonsense that too often passes for sound advice will help organizations perform better. (p. 74)

Source: Pfeffer and Sutton (2006a).

Developments in technology have encouraged some observers to anticipate that computers would be able to take over certain types of decisions from managers and professionals. While many early attempts to apply artificial intelligence or decision support systems failed, Davenport and Harris (2005) report new applications in many organisational settings. They are well suited where decisions depend on the rapid analysis of large quantities of data, with complex relationships – such as in power supply, transport management and banking. Automated decision systems: 'sense online data or conditions, apply codified knowledge or logic and make decisions – all with minimal amounts of human intervention' (Davenport and Harris, 2005, p. 84). Table 7.1 gives examples.

Type of decision	Example of automated decision application
Solution configuration	Mobile phone operators who offer a range of features and service options: an automated programme can weigh all the options, including information about the customer, and present the most suitable option to the customer.
Yield optimisation	Widely used in the airline industry to allow companies to vary prices frequently depending on available capacity and present time relative to departure. Spreading to companies in transport generally, retailing and entertainment to increase revenue.
Fraud detection	Credit card companies and tax authorities use some automated screening techniques to help detect and deter possible fraud.
Operational control	Power companies use automated systems to sense changes in the physical environment (power supply, temperature or rainfall), and respond rapidly to changes in demand, by redirecting supplies across the network.

Source: Based on Davenport and Harris (2005).

Table 7.1

Examples of the application of automated decision systems

Such applications will continue to spread, supporting companies where many decisions can be handled by using rational, quantitative methods. When decisions are more complex and controversial, the rational approach itself will not be able to resolve a decision – it can play a part, but only as one input to a wider set of methods.

A behavioural theory of decision making   key ideas

Richard Cyert, James March and Herbert Simon (Simon, 1960; Cyert and March, 1963; March, 1988) developed an influential model of decision making. It is sometimes referred to as the behavioural theory of decision making since it treats decision making as an aspect of human behaviour. Also referred to as the administrative model, it recognises that in the real world people are restricted in their decision processes, and therefore have to accept what is probably a less than perfect solution. It introduced the concepts of bounded rationality and satisficing to the study of decision making.

Judgemental strategies – administrative, incremental and intuitional

Administrative models

Simon's (1960) **administrative model of decision making** aims to describe how managers make decisions in situations that are uncertain and ambiguous. Many management problems are unstructured and not suitable for the precise quantitative

The **administrative model of decision making** describes how people make decisions in uncertain, ambiguous situations.

analysis implied by the rational model. People rely heavily on their judgement to resolve such issues.

Simon based the model on two central concepts – bounded rationality and satisficing. **Bounded rationality** expresses the fact that people have mental limits, or boundaries, on how rational they can be. While organisations and their environments are complex and uncertain, people can process only a limited amount of information. This constrains our ability to operate in the way envisaged by the rational model, which we deal with by **satisficing** – we choose the first solution that is 'good enough'. While continuing to search for other options may eventually produce a better return, identifying and evaluating them costs more than the benefits. Suppose we are in a strange city and need coffee before a meeting. We will look for the first acceptable coffee shop that appears to provide what we need. We have neither the time nor the knowledge to explore several alternatives for variety and price – we satisfice by choosing one that looks good enough for the immediate problem. In a similar fashion, managers generate alternatives for complex problems only until they find one they believe will work.

The administrative model focuses on the human and organisational factors that influence decisions. It is more realistic than the rational model for non-programmed, ambiguous decisions. According to the administrative model, managers:

- have goals that are typically vague and conflicting, and are unable to reach a consensus on what to do – as indicated by the EADS example on p. 221;
- have different levels of interest in the problems or opportunities facing the business, and interpret information subjectively;
- rarely use rational procedures, or use them in a way that does not reflect the full complexity of the issue;
- limit their search for alternatives;
- usually settle for a satisficing rather than a maximising solution – having both limited information and only vague criteria of what would be 'maximising'.

The administrative model is descriptive, aiming to show how managers make decisions in complex situations rather than stating how they should make them.

Bounded rationality is behaviour that is rational within a decision process which is limited (bounded) by an individual's ability to process information.

Satisficing is the acceptance by decision makers of the first solution that is 'good enough'.

---

management in practice — Satisficing in an IT project

Symon and Clegg (1991) studied a project to introduce a computer-aided design and computer-aided manufacturing (CAD-CAM) system into a manufacturing plant. The system itself was technically complex, but to secure the fullest benefits managers would also need to make significant changes throughout the organisation. The processes for managing orders would need to change, as would the work of staff and the responsibilities of managers. After several years of operation the system was producing some modest benefits, but nothing like the benefits that investment could have produced. The research team concluded that managers had unconsciously decided to satisfice – it was working, and producing some benefits that they could demonstrate: to secure the full potential would require more effort than they were willing to give.

Source: Symon and Clegg (1991).

Incremental models

Charles Lindblom (1959) developed what he termed an **incremental model**, which he observed people used when they were uncertain about the consequences of their choice. In the rational model these are known, but people face many decisions in which they cannot know what the effects will be. Lindblom built on Simon's idea of bounded rationality to show that if people made only a limited search for options their chosen solution would differ only slightly from what already existed. Current choices would be heavily influenced by past choices – and would not move far from them.

> People use an **incremental model** of decision making when they are uncertain about the consequences. They search for a limited range of options, and policy unfolds from a series of cumulative small decisions.

On this view, policy unfolds not from a single event but from many cumulative small decisions. Small decisions help people to minimise the risk of mistakes, and to reverse the decision if necessary. Lindblom called this incrementalism, or the 'science of muddling through'. Instead of looking rationally at the whole problem and a range of possible ways forward, the decision maker simplifies the problem by contemplating only marginal changes. The incremental model (like the administrative one) recognises human limitations.

Intuitional models

George Klein (1997) studied how effective decision makers work, including those working under extreme time pressure such as surgeons, fire fighters and nurses. He found they rarely used classical decision theory to weigh the options: instead they used pattern recognition to relate the situation to their experience. They acted on their intuition – a subconscious process of making decisions on the basis of experience and accumulated judgement – sometimes called 'tacit knowledge'. Klein concluded that effective decision makers use their intuition as much as formal processes – perhaps using both formal analysis and intuition as the situation demands. Experienced managers can act quickly on what seems like very little information. Rather than do a formal analysis, they draw quickly on experience and judgement to decide what to do. It may be that intuition is better described as 'recognition'.

When people build a depth of experience and knowledge in an area the right decision often comes quickly and effortlessly, as the subconscious mind recognises information that the conscious mind has forgotten. Jurgen Schrempp, CEO of DaimlerChrysler, is said to be such a person – a risk-taker who always trusts his instincts, and to whom the need for bold moves is so evident that he becomes annoyed when investors question his strategy. In similar vein Sadler-Smith and Shefy (2004) argue that both rationality and intuition have a part to play in making decisions.

Compromise strategy – political model

The political model examines how people make decisions when managers disagree over goals and how to pursue them (Pfeffer, 1992; Buchanan and Badham, 1999). It recognises that an organisation is not only a working system, but also a political system, which establishes the relative power of people and functions. A significant decision will enhance the power of some people or units and limit that of others. People will pursue goals relating to personal and sub-unit interests, as well as those of the organisation as a whole. They will evaluate a decision in terms of its likely effects on those possibly conflicting objectives. Chapter 13 contains an example in Section 13.4 – the Management in Practice feature on 'Pensco'.

They will often try to support their position by building a coalition with those who share their interest. This gives others the opportunity to contribute their ideas and enhances their commitment if the decision is adopted.

The political model assumes that:

● Organisations contain groups with diverse interests, goals and values. Managers disagree about problem priorities and may not understand or share the goals and interests of other managers.
● Information is ambiguous and incomplete. Rationality is limited by the complexity of many problems as well as personal interests.
● Managers engage in the push and pull of debate to decide goals and discuss alternatives – decisions arise from bargaining and discussion.

Inspirational strategy – garbage can model

This approach is likely when those concerned are not only unclear about cause-and-effect relationships, but are also uncertain about the outcome they seek. James March (1988) observed that in this situation the processes of reaching a decision become separated from the decisions reached. In the other models there is an assumption that the processes that the decision makers pass through lead to a decision. In this situation of extreme uncertainty the elements that constitute the decision problem are independent of each other, coming together in random ways.

March argued that decisions arise when four independent streams of activities meet – and when this happens will depend largely on accident or chance. The four streams are:

1	Choice opportunities	Organisations have occasions at which there is an expectation that a decision will be made – budgets must be set, there are regular management meetings, etc.
2	Participants	A stream of people who have the opportunity to shape decisions.
3	Problems	A stream of problems that represent matters of concern to people – a lost sale, a new opportunity, a vacancy.
4	Solutions	A stream of potential solutions seeking problems – ideas, proposals, information – that people continually generate.

In this view, the choice opportunities (scheduled or unscheduled meetings) act as the container (garbage can) for the mixture of participants, problems and solutions. One combination of the three may be such that enough participants are interested in a solution, which they can match to a problem – and take a decision accordingly. Another group of participants may not have made those connections, or made them in a different way, so creating a different outcome.

This may at first sight seem an unlikely way to run a business, yet in highly uncertain, volatile environments this approach may work. Creative businesses depend on a rapid interchange of ideas, not only about specified problems but on information about new discoveries, research at other companies, what someone heard at a conference. They depend on people bringing these solutions and problems together – and deliberately foster structures that maximise opportunities for face-to-face contact and rapid decisions. The practical implication is that encouraging frequent informal contact between creative people will improve decisions, and performance.

Oticon builds a better garbage can   www.oticon.com

Oticon, a leading maker of sophisticated hearing aids, underwent a massive transformation in the early 1990s, in which the chief executive, Lars Kolind, broke down all barriers to communication. He realised that the key to success in the face of severe competition was to ensure that the talents of staff in the company were applied to any problems that arose. In March's terms, problems were expressed as a project, for which a member of staff (a participant) took responsibility, depending on other staff to suggest or help develop a solution.

> Any and all measures were taken to encourage contact and informal communication between employees. Elevators were made inoperable so that employees would meet each other on the stairs, where they were more likely to engage in conversation. Bars were installed on all three floors where coffee was served and meetings could be organised – standing up. Rooms with circular sofas were provided, complete with small coffee tables, to encourage discussion. (Rivard *et al.*, 2004, p. 170)

These discussions centred on reaching fast and creative decisions about problems and new product ideas – and the arrangement is credited with helping the continuing success of the company.

Source: Rivard *et al.* (2004); see also Chapter 10 Case.

Table 7.2 summarises these four models.

Table 7.2 Four models of decision making

Rational	Administrative/incremental	Political	Garbage can
Clear problem and goals	Vague problems and goals	Conflict over goals	Goals and solutions independent
Condition of certainty	Condition of uncertainty	Uncertainty/conflict	Ambiguity
Full information about costs and benefits of alternatives	Little information about costs and benefits of alternatives	Inconsistent views about costs and benefits of alternatives	Costs and benefits unconnected
Rational choice to maximise benefit	Satisficing choice – good enough	Choice by bargaining amongst players	Choice by accidental merging of streams

7.6   Biases in making decisions

Since people are subject to bounded rationality (limited capacity to process information) they tend to use heuristics – simple rules, or short cuts, that help us to overcome our limited capacity to deal with information and complexity (Khaneman and Tversky, 1974). While these short cuts help us to make decisions, they expose us to the danger of biases – four of which are prior hypothesis, representativeness, illusion of control and escalating commitment (Schwenk, 1984).

Heuristics Simple rules or mental short cuts that simplify making decisions.

Prior hypothesis bias

People who have strong prior beliefs about the relationship between two variables tend to make decisions based on those beliefs, even when presented with evidence that shows the beliefs are wrong. In doing so they fall victim to the **prior hypothesis bias**: their bias

Prior hypothesis bias results from a tendency to base decisions on strong prior beliefs, even if the evidence shows that they are wrong.

is strengthened by a tendency to use information consistent with their beliefs, and ignore or discredit that which is inconsistent. People recall vivid events more readily that ones that stir no particular emotions or did not have a memorable outcome. The ones they recall will bias decisions about the likelihood of an event occurring, even if circumstances have changed.

Representativeness bias

Representativeness bias results from a tendency to generalise inappropriately from a small sample or a single vivid event.

A common source of bias is to generalise from a small sample or a single episode. It uses the similarity of one object to another to infer that the first object acts like the second, and this can lead people to ignore other relevant information. Examples include:

- believing that expensive-looking packaging means a high-quality product;
- predicting the success of a new product on the basis of an earlier success;
- appointing someone with a certain type of experience because a previous successful appointment had a similar background.

Illusion of control

The **illusion of control** is a source of bias resulting from the tendency to overestimate one's ability to control activities and events.

Other errors in making decisions result from the **illusion of control**, which is the human tendency to overestimate our ability to control activities and events. Those in senior positions, especially if they have a record of successes, seem particularly prone to this. Having worked their way to the top, they tend to have an exaggerated sense of their ability to shape destiny. This bias causes them to overestimate the odds of a favourable outcome, and so end up making poor decisions – such as the ability to grow a company successfully by acquisition.

Escalating commitment

Escalating commitment is a bias that leads to increased commitment to a previous decision despite evidence that it may have been wrong.

Having already made decisions that have committed significant resources to a project, some managers continue to commit more resources even though there is abundant evidence that the project is failing. Feelings of personal responsibility for a project, and the resources already consumed bias their analysis and lead to an escalating commitment – see Management in Practice. They may also be influenced by the phenomenon known as the **escalation of commitment**, which is an increased commitment to a previous decision despite evidence that it may have been wrong (Drummond, 1996). People are reluctant to admit mistakes, and may persist in committing further resources to a project despite its evident failure. Rather than search for a new solution, they increase their commitment to the original decision.

management in practice   A study of escalation – Taurus at the Stock Exchange

Helga Drummond studied the attempt by management at the London Stock Exchange to implement a computerised system to deal with the settlement of shares traded on the Exchange. The project was announced in May 1986 and was due to be completed by 1989 at a cost of £6 million. After many crises and difficulties, the Stock Exchange finally abandoned the project in March 1993. By that time the Exchange had spent £80 million on developing a non-existent system. Drummond interviewed many key participants to explore the reasons for this disaster – which occurred despite the commitment of the system designers.

She concluded that the project suffered from fundamental structural problems, in that it challenged several powerful vested interests in the financial community, each of whom had their own idea about what should be done. Each new demand, reflecting this continuing power struggle, made the system more complicated. However, while many interests needed to work together, structural barriers throughout the organisation prevented this. There was little upward communication, so that senior managers were largely unaware of staff concerns about the timetable commitments being made.

Senior managers continued to claim the project was on track until a few days before it was finally, and very publicly, terminated. The lack of proper mechanisms to identify pressing issues lulled those making decisions into a false sense of security about the state of the project.

Source: Drummond (1996).

7.7   Group decision making

Many organisational decisions are made by groups, rather than by individuals acting alone, as groups have several potential advantages over individuals. When managers work as a team they are less likely to experience the biases which the previous section identified: other members are more likely to challenge them. They are also able to draw on a wide range of experience and perspectives, and so more likely to deal fully with dimensions of a decision that an individual may overlook. There is also evidence that if the group includes those who will be responsible for implementing the decision, the chances of acceptance are greater.

However, groups can take longer than individuals to reach decisions, and not all decisions are suitable for a participative approach. In addition, groups too can be liable to bias, which reflects the phenomenon of groupthink.

Vroom and Yetton's decision model

The idea behind Vroom and Yetton's (1973) contingency model of decision making is to influence the quality and acceptability of decisions. This depends on the manager choosing how best to involve subordinates in making a decision – and being willing to change their style to match the situation. The model defines five leadership styles and seven characteristics of problems. Managers can use these characteristics to diagnose the situation. They can find the recommended way of reaching a decision on that problem by using the decision tree shown in Figure 7.8. The five leadership styles defined are:

1 *AI (Autocratic)* You solve the problem or make the decision yourself using information available to you at that time.
2 *AII (Information seeking)* You obtain the necessary information from your subordinate(s), then decide on the solution to the problem yourself. You may or may not tell your subordinates what the problem is in getting the information from them. The role played by your subordinates in making the decision is clearly one of providing the necessary information to you rather than generating or evaluating alternative solutions.
3 *CI (Consulting)* You share the problem with relevant subordinates individually, getting their ideas and suggestions without bringing them together as a group. Then *you* make the decision that may or may not reflect your subordinates' influence.
4 *CII (Negotiating)* You share the problem with your subordinates as a group, obtaining their collective ideas and suggestions. Then you make the decision that may or may not reflect your subordinates' influence.

5 *G (Group)* You share the problem with your subordinates as a group. Together you generate and evaluate alternatives and attempt to reach agreement (consensus) on a solution. Your role is much like that of a chairperson. You do not try to influence the group to adopt 'your' solution, and you are willing to accept and implement any solution that has the support of the entire group.

The idea behind the model is that no style is in itself better than another. Some believe that consultative or delegating styles are inherently preferable to autocratic approaches, as being more in keeping with democratic principles. Vroom and Yetton argue otherwise. In some situations (such as when time is short or the manager has all the information needed for a minor decision) going through the process of consultation

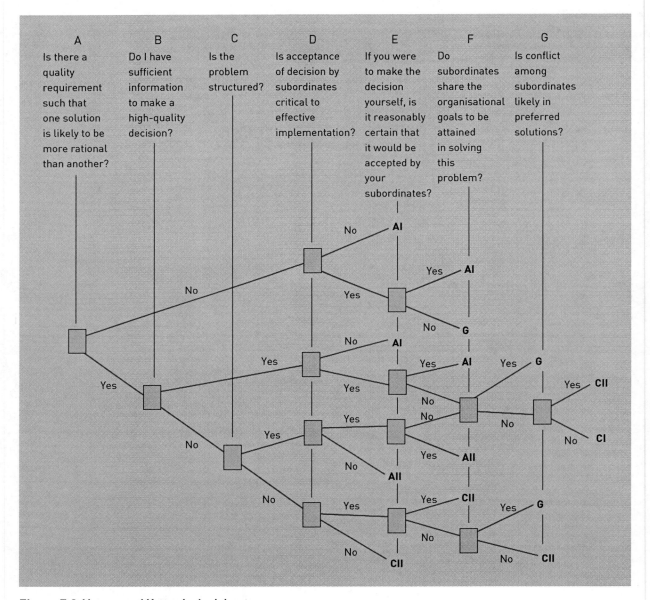

Figure 7.8 Vroom and Yetton's decision tree

Source: Reprinted from Vroom and Yetton (1973), p. 188 by permission of the University of Pittsburgh Press, copyright © 1973 by University of Pittsburgh Press..

will waste time and add little value. In other situations, such as where the subordinates have the relevant information, it is essential to consult them. The point of the model is to make managers more aware of the range of factors to take into account in using a particular decision-making style.

The problem criteria are expressed in seven diagnostic questions:

1 Is one solution likely to be better than another?
2 Does the manager have enough information to make a high-quality decision?
3 Is the problem structured?
4 Is acceptance of the decision by subordinates critical to effective implementation?
5 If the manager makes the decision alone, is it likely to be accepted by subordinates?
6 Do subordinates share organisational goals?
7 Is conflict likely amongst subordinates over preferred solutions?

The Vroom–Yetton decision model implies that managers need to be flexible in the style they adopt. The style should be appropriate to the situation rather than consistent amongst all situations. The problem with this is that managers may find it difficult to switch between styles, perhaps several times a day. Although the approach appears objective, it still depends on the manager answering the questions. Requiring a simple yes or no answer to complex questions is too simple, and managers often want to say 'it all depends' – on other historical or contextual factors.

Decision-making style at Rexam   www.rexam.com

management in practice

Rexam is a UK-based packaging business (and the world's leading beverage can maker), run by Chief Executive Swede Rolf Borjesson from 1996 until 2004 (when he became chairman). His management style is described by colleagues as collegial, combined with ruthlessness in delivering results. When it comes to key decisions about the business he says:

> I want to test where the organisation is, or where my closest colleagues are, when it comes to important decisions, and then I have to make up my mind what to do. It is very, very critical to the success of the company that the team is very much involved. If you try to run it yourself and you take all the decisions, you turn around to look back and there is no one behind you.

Source: *Financial Times*, 18 November 2002.

Nevertheless the model is used in management training to alert managers to the style they prefer to use and to the range of options available. It also prompts managers to consider systematically whether that preferred style is always appropriate. They may then handle situations more deliberately than if they relied only on their preferred style or intuition.

Delegation

The model also relates to the issue of *delegation* that managers frequently face – whether or not to delegate more of their tasks to others, including how far to enable them to participate in decisions. As managers cope with increasingly demanding and uncertain conditions and as staff become more educated and confident, it will often make sense to widen the range of people taking part in decisions. This enables a wider range of experience and perspectives to be brought into consideration, as well as the motivational and development benefits.

However, the model indicates that this may not always be the best approach – such as if time is too short for wide consultation, or if conflicting views would delay, but not necessarily affect, the implementation of a decision. Equally if the decision is in effect already made for reasons beyond the manager's control, staff would see a show of participation as an empty gesture. The model brings in the notion of management style being contingent on the specific situation, a topic to which later parts of the book will return.

Irving Janis and groupthink

Groupthink is 'a mode of thinking that people engage in when they are deeply involved in a cohesive in-group, when the members' striving for unanimity overrides their motivation to realistically appraise alternative courses of action' (Janis, 1972).

Groupthink is a pattern of biased decision making that occurs in groups which become too cohesive – members strive for agreement amongst themselves at the expense of accurately and dispassionately assessing relevant, and especially disturbing, information. An influential analysis of how it occurs was put forward by the social psychologist Irving Janis. His research (Janis, 1972) began by studying major and highly publicised failures of decision making, looking for some common theme that might explain why apparently able and intelligent people were able to make such bad decisions – such as President Kennedy's decision to have US forces invade Cuba in 1961. One common thread he observed was the inability of the groups involved to consider a range of alternatives rationally, or to see the likely consequences of the choice they made. Members were also keen to be seen as team players, and not to say things that might end their membership of the group. Janis termed this phenomenon 'groupthink', and defined it as:

> a mode of thinking that people engage in when they are deeply involved in a cohesive in-group, when the members' striving for unanimity overrides their motivation to realistically appraise alternative courses of action. (Janis, 1972, p. 9)

He identified eight symptoms of groupthink, shown in Key Ideas.

---

key ideas   Irving Janis on the symptoms of groupthink

Janis (1977) identified eight symptoms that give early warning of groupthink developing – and the more of them that are present the more likely it is that the 'disease' will strike. The symptoms are:

1 **Illusion of invulnerability** The belief that any decision they make will be successful.
2 **Belief in the inherent morality of the group** Justifying a decision by reference to some higher value.
3 **Rationalisation** Playing down the negative consequences or risks of a decision.
4 **Stereotyping out-groups** Characterising opponents or doubters in unfavourable terms, making it easier to dismiss even valid criticism from that source.
5 **Self-censorship** Suppressing legitimate doubts in the interest of group loyalty.
6 **Direct pressure** Strong expressions from other members (or the leader) that dissent to their favoured approach will be unwelcome.
7 **Mindguards** Keeping uncomfortable facts or opinions out of the discussion.
8 **Illusion of unanimity** Playing down any remaining doubts or questions, even if they become stronger or more persistent.

Source: Based on Janis (1977).

management
in practice

Groupthink in medicine

An experienced nurse observed three of the symptoms of groupthink in the work of senior doctors:

- **Illusion of invulnerability** A feeling of power and authority leads a group to see themselves as invulnerable. Traditionally the medical profession has been very powerful and this makes it very difficult for non-clinicians to question their actions or plans.
- **Belief in the inherent morality of the group** This happens when clinical staff use the term 'individual clinical judgement' as a justification for their actions. An example is when a business manager is trying to reduce drug costs and one consultant's practice is very different from those of his colleagues. Consultants often reply that they are entitled to use their clinical judgement. This is never challenged by their colleagues, and it is often impossible to achieve change.
- **Self-censorship** Being a doctor is similar to being in a very exclusive club, and none of the members want to be excluded. Therefore doctors will usually support each other, particularly against management. They are also extremely unlikely to report each other for mistakes or poor performance. A government scheme to encourage 'whistle blowing' was met with much derision in the ranks.

Source: Private communication.

When groupthink occurs, pressures for agreement and harmony within the group have the unintended effects of discouraging individuals from raising issues that run counter to the majority opinion. An often-quoted example is the Challenger disaster in 1986, when the space shuttle exploded shortly after take-off. Investigations showed that NASA and the main contractors, Morton Thiokol, were so anxious to keep the Shuttle programme on schedule that they ignored or discounted evidence that would slow the programme down. When two Thiokol engineers warned that a component was likely to fail in cold weather, endangering safety, they were overruled by the team, which authorised the launch in cold weather. Turner and Pratkanis (1998) review research on groupthink, including studies that have taken a critical view of the phenomenon.

7.8 Current themes and issues

Performance

As performance standards become more demanding and circumstances more volatile, the task of making decisions becomes correspondingly more challenging. Nutt's analysis (Nutt, 2002) identifies the causes of failure in decision making and points towards practices that he claims increase the chances of a successful outcome. His suggestions include:

- Avoid making premature commitments – the hazard of grabbing hold of the first idea that comes up.
- Maintain an exploratory mindset – keep an open mind towards other possibilities.
- Let go of the quick fix – defer choice until understanding has been gained.
- Pause to reflect – even if this means resisting demands for a quick fix.
- Use resources to evaluate options, not just the preferred solution (or current quick fix).
- Pay attention to both the rational and the political aspects of a decision process.

Adopting such practices would undoubtedly add to the quality of anyone's approach to decision making: the challenge is whether they will be able to resist the pressures from others to deal with issues quickly, to deal with rapid external change. Wipro has developed the approach of making decisions quickly – and being willing to change quickly if the decision turns out to be wrong. Defending a wrong decision in the face of evidence is a sure way to destroy value.

Responsibility

Decisions often raise ethical issues – which can arise at any point in the process. A problem that may appear ethically neutral to those promoting a project – to alter recruitment policies, to build a manufacturing or distribution facility or to launch a new consumer product – may not seem like that to others. Ethical issues often arise when there is a mismatch between those who benefit from a decision and those who lose. Failure to take account of ethical concerns in the decision-making process can lead to delay, protest and a diversion of management time.

One way of addressing this is to attend to the structure of the decision-making process, to ensure that those whose interests will be affected are included from the outset. Including relevant stakeholders in the decision-making process may seem like a costly investment, but it could pay off if it brings better and more acceptable decisions. Some companies ensure that ethical issues have a higher place on the management agenda by appointing a director with an explicit remit in the area of ethics or corporate responsibility.

Internationalisation

The structure of decision-making processes also arises as companies become international. Decisions will cross the boundaries between managers at global headquarters, those in local business units and perhaps a regional grouping in between. Neither of the extreme possibilities is likely to work. If decision making tilts too far in favour of global managers at the centre, local preferences are likely to be overlooked, and local managers are likely to lack commitment to decisions in which they have had no say. Leaving too many decisions to local managers can waste opportunities for economies of scale or opportunities to serve global clients consistently.

A solution may be to identify the major ways in which the company adds value to resources, and align the decision-making processes to make the most of them. For example, it may be that procurement can best be done on a global scale, with contracts being negotiated at the centre to supply the whole of the company's needs. Once supply contracts are agreed, however, responsibility for operating them could pass back to the local level. Conversely, they might leave decisions on pricing or advertising expenditure to local managers. The central issue is to spend time on the difficult choices about the location of each set of decisions, to achieve an acceptable balance between global and local expectations.

Summary

1 Explain the tasks in making a decision and how decision processes affect the outcome

- Decisions are choices about how to act in relation to organisational inputs, outputs and transformation processes. The chapter identifies seven *iterative* steps in the process:

  1 Recognise the problem – which depends on seeing and attending to ambiguous signals.

  2 Set and weight criteria – the features of the result most likely to meet problem requirements, and that can guide the choice between alternatives.

  3 Develop alternatives – identify existing or develop custom-built ways of dealing with the problem.

  4 Compare and choose – using the criteria to select the preferred alternative.

  5 Implement – the task that turns a decision into an action.

  6 Evaluate – check whether the decision resolved the problem.

  7 Most decisions affect other interests, whose response will be affected by how the decision process is conducted, in matters such as participation and communication.

2 Explain, and give examples of, programmed and non-programmed decisions

- Programmed decisions deal with familiar issues within existing policy – recruitment, minor capital expenditure, small price changes.

- Non-programmed decisions move the business in a new direction – new markets, mergers, a major investment decision.

3 Distinguish between certainty, risk, uncertainty and ambiguity

- Certainty – decision makers have all the information they need, especially the costs and benefits of each alternative action.

- Risk – where the decision maker can estimate the likelihood of the alternative outcomes. These are still subject to chance, but decision makers have enough information to estimate probabilities.

- Uncertainty – when people know what they wish to achieve, but information about alternatives and future events is incomplete. They cannot be clear about alternatives or estimate their risk.

- Ambiguity – when people are unsure about their objectives and about the relationship between cause and effect.

4 Contrast rational, administrative, political and garbage can decision models

- Rational models are based on economic assumptions which suggest that the role of a manager is to maximise the economic return to the firm, and that they do this by making decisions on economically rational criteria.

- The administrative model aims to describe how managers actually make decisions in situations of uncertainty and ambiguity. Many management problems are unstructured and not suitable for the precise quantitative analysis implied by the rational model.

- The political model examines how people make decisions when conditions are uncertain, information is limited, and there is disagreement amongst managers over goals and how to pursue them. It recognises that an organisation is not only a working system, but also a political system, which establishes the relative power of people and functions.

- The garbage can model identifies four independent streams of activities that enable a decision when they meet. When participants, problems and solutions come together in a relevant forum (a 'garbage can'), then a decision will be made.

5 Give examples of common sources of bias in decisions

- Sources of bias stem from the use of heuristics – mental short cuts that allow us to cope with excessive information. Four biases are:

    1 representativeness bias – basing decisions on unrepresentative samples or single incidents;

    2 prior hypothesis bias – basing decisions on prior beliefs, despite evidence they are wrong;

    3 illusion of control – excessive belief in one's ability to control people and events;

    4 escalating commitment – committing more resources to a project despite evidence of failure.

6 Explain the contribution of Vroom and Yetton, and of Irving Janis, to our understanding of decision making in groups

- Vroom and Yetton introduced the idea that decision-making styles in groups should reflect the situation – which of the five ways to use of involving subordinates in a decision (Autocratic, Information seeking, Consulting, Negotiating and Delegating) depended on identifiable circumstances – such as whether the manager has the information required.

- Irving Janis observed the phenomenon of groupthink, and set out the symptoms which indicate that it is affecting a group's decision-making processes.

Review questions

1 Why does the quality of decisions that people make in an organisation affect its performance?

2 Explain the difference between risk and ambiguity. How may people make decisions in different ways for each situation?

3 List three decisions you have recently observed or taken part in. Which were programmed, and which unprogrammed?

4 The Vroom–Yetton model describes five styles. How should the manager decide which style to use?

5 What are the major differences between the rational and administrative models of decision making?

6 What is meant by satisficing in decision making? Can you illustrate the concept with an example from your experience? Why did those involved not try to achieve an economically superior decision?

7 What did Henry Mintzberg's research on decision making contribute to our understanding of the process?

Concluding critical reflection

Think about the ways in which your company, or one with which you are familiar, makes decisions. Review the material in the chapter, and perhaps visit some of the websites identified. Then make notes on these questions:

- What examples of the issues discussed in this chapter struck you as being relevant to practice in your company?

- Are people you work with typically dealing mainly with programmed or non-programmed decisions? What **assumptions** about the nature of decision making appear to guide their approach – rational, administrative, political or garbage can? On balance, do their assumptions accurately reflect the reality you see?

- What factors such as the history or current **context** of the company appear to influence the way people are expected to reach decisions? Does the current approach appear to be right for the company in its context – or would a different view of the context lead to a different approach? (Perhaps refer to some of the Management in Practice features for how different contexts encourage different approaches.)

- Have people put forward **alternative** approaches to decision making, based on evidence about other companies? If you could find such evidence, how may it affect company practice?

- Can you identify **limitations** in the ideas and theories presented here – for example are you convinced of the 'garbage can' model of decision making? Can you find evidence that supports or challenges that view?

Further reading

Bazerman, M.H. (2005), *Judgment in Managerial Decision Making* (6th edn), Wiley, New York.

Comprehensive and interactive account, aimed at developing the skill of judgement amongst students, thus enabling them to improve how they make decisions.

Harrison, E.F. (1999), *The Managerial Decision-Making Process* (5th edn), Houghton Mifflin, Boston, MA.

Comprehensive interdisciplinary approach to the generic process of decision making, with a focus on the strategic level. The author draws on a wide range of scholarly perspectives and presents them in a lucid and well-organised way.

Schwartz, B. (2005), *The Paradox of Choice*, Ecco, New York.

An excellent study of decision making at the individual level. It shows how people in modern society face an ever-widening and increasingly bewildering range of choices, which is a source of increasing tension and stress. Many of the issues the author raises apply equally well to decision making in organisations.

Buchanan, L. and O'Connell, A. (2006), 'A brief history of decision making', *Harvard Business Review*, vol. 84, no. 1, pp. 32–41.

Informative overview, placing many of the ideas mentioned in the chapter within a historical context. Part of a special issue of the *Harvard Business Review* devoted to decision making.

Weblinks

These websites have appeared in the chapter:

www.wipro.com
www.pg.com
www.mcdonalds.com
www.eads.com
www.oticon.com
www.rexam.com

Visit two of the business sites in the list, or any other company that interests you, and navigate to the pages dealing with recent news or investor relations.

- What examples of decisions that the company has recently had to take can you find?
- How would you classify those decisions in terms of the models in this chapter?
- Gather information from the media websites (such as **www.ft.com**) that relate to the companies you have chosen. What stories can you find that indicate something about the decisions the companies have faced, and what the outcomes have been?

Annotated weblinks, multiple choice questions and other useful resources can be found on www.pearsoned.co.uk/boddy

Corporations and Corporate Governance

Capitalism is an economic system of business based on private enterprise. Individuals and businesses own land, farms, factories, and equipment, and they use those assets in an attempt to earn profits. Capitalism provides rewards for those who work hard and who are inventive and creative enough to figure out new or improved products and services. One potential reward for creating value in an economy is the accumulation of personal wealth. The wealth incentive provides the fuel to generate new ideas and to foster economic value that provides jobs and raises our standard of living.

The main goal of a company is to create an environment conducive to earning long-term profits, which stem from two main sources. First, a large portion of a firm's value derives from the current and future profits of the products and/or services it provides to its customer base. Finding ways to increase profits from these core operations can increase economic value. Second, increased profits can come from growth in the sales of an existing product or from introducing new products. The ability to access capital and to control risk is important in the success or failure of a firm. Expansion usually requires additional money, or capital, that must be raised by the company. Business activities also entail risk as there is no guarantee that new products will be successful or that existing products will continue to be successful. As these are important attributes for companies, capital requirements and risk sharing affect the manner in which a company or firm is organized. A small part-time business may operate as a sole proprietorship (i.e., one owner), while a major international business is more likely to be a publicly traded corporation.

In this chapter, we first describe different forms of business, with emphasis on the publicly traded corporation. We then describe the structure of publicly traded corporations, including the separation of owners and managers that is required to effectively run such a company. As this separation means that the owners of the company do not control day-to-day operations, there is a potential for managers to take actions other than those that the owners would prefer.

An integrated system of checks and balances known as corporate governance has evolved to address this potential conflict. Throughout this chapter, we outline the parties who have some impact on the governance of corporations. Then, in the following chapters, each of the parties involved in corporate governance is analyzed individually.

FORMS OF BUSINESS OWNERSHIP

In general, a business can be a sole proprietorship, a partnership, or a corporation. Other forms exist,[1] but we will focus on these three as this is the most general distinction. Each organizational form involves different advantages and disadvantages. A **sole proprietorship** is a business owned by a single person. These businesses are relatively easy to start up and business tax is computed at the personal level. Due to its simplicity, sole proprietorships are ubiquitous, representing more than 70 percent of all U.S. businesses.[2] However, there are several significant drawbacks. Such firms often have a limited lifespan (they die with the owner's death or retirement), they have a limited ability to obtain capital, and the owner bears unlimited personal liability for the firm.

A **partnership** is similar to a sole proprietorship but there is more than one owner. As such, a partnership shares the advantages and disadvantages of the sole proprietorship. While one obvious advantage of a partnership is the ability to pool capital, this advantage may not be as important as combining service-oriented expertise and skill, especially for larger partnerships. Examples of such partnerships include accounting firms, law firms, some investment banks, and advertising firms. The biggest disadvantage to partnerships is that each partner bears unlimited personal liability for the activities of the partnership.

This book focuses on the third business form, the **corporation**. Fewer than 20 percent of all U.S. businesses are corporations but they generate approximately 90 percent of the country's business revenue.[3] The corporation is its own legal entity, as if it were a person. This means the corporation can sue and be sued in court, and that the corporation is a taxpayer that must pay taxes regardless of the fact that its owners already pay taxes.[4] Even though it exists as a legal person that has unlimited life, real individuals are required to act on behalf of the corporation. This is the role of the corporate officers who act as agents for the corporation.

A corporation is formed by filing a document with the state government that sets forth how many shares of stock are authorized for issuance to shareholders. Once the corporation is formed, shareholders contribute capital in exchange for shares of stock. The shareholders then elect a board of directors to run the corporation and the board appoints officers to handle the day-to-day operations. While these corporate officers (also known as "executives" or "management") control the activities of the corporation, the board of directors and the shareholders each retain some power to govern the corporation.

One of the primary reasons for choosing the corporate form of organization is to limit the liability of the owners of the company. Shareholders' investment in a corporation is limited to the amounts they paid for their shares. If the company fails and owes large amounts to creditors, the creditors can only collect from the corporate assets. The shareholders, as owners of the corporation, are not required to put any additional funds into the company to cover the losses of the creditors.[5]

The other important reasons for choosing to operate as a corporation are the ability to raise capital and to share risk. Issuing shares of stock in a corporation is an efficient method for raising capital. As new shares of stock can be created by fiat by the corporation, there is no limit to the amount of shares that can be issued. These new shares also have the effect of an increased sharing of risk because the new shareholders have effectively taken over some of the risk of the corporation's failure.

Examples of the benefits of a corporation can be seen in the history of large companies such as Apple and Google. Each was started by two individuals and operated initially as a partnership. Apple was started in a garage by Steven Jobs and Steve Wozniak; Google was started at Stanford University by Larry Page and Sergey Brin. As the potential for success of these companies readily became apparent, there was a need for capital to expand. Each did this expansion in the same way—they found a large investor to bankroll their startup and converted the business to a corporation. Soon after, both companies became public corporations and sold shares of stock to the general public. In this way, the growing companies took advantage of the corporation's ability to raise capital as Apple sold $65 million in stock in 1980 and Google sold $1.6 billion worth in 2004. The risk of expanding their businesses into wide distribution was also spread across a large number of shareholders.

The advantages of the corporate business form are appealing, but there are also major disadvantages. Corporate profits are subject to business taxes before any income goes to shareholders in the form of dividends.[6] Subsequently, shareholders must also pay personal taxes on dividend income. Therefore, shareholders are exposed to double taxation. In addition, running a public corporation can be expensive. For example, the costs of hiring accountants and legal experts, the costs of communicating with all shareholders, the costs of complying with regulations, and so forth, can cost millions of dollars per year. Finally, and perhaps the most important disadvantage, large corporations suffer from potentially serious governance problems. The separation of ownership from management results in a situation where many investors own only a small stake of a large public corporation, so they consequently do not have much of an incentive to get involved in monitoring the activities of mangers of the firms in which they own stock. Management may also not be as careful in spending money when managers are not major shareholders because they are effectively spending someone else's money.

SEPARATION OF OWNERSHIP AND CONTROL

In 1932, Adolf Berle and Gardiner Means wrote what was to become a famous book about the corporate form of business.[7] They pointed out that corporations were becoming so large that the ownership and control was separated. The stockholders own the firm and managers (technically, officers or executives) control the firm. This situation comes about because the thousands, or even hundreds of thousands, of investors who own public firms cannot collectively make the daily decisions needed to operate a business. Hence the need for specialized management.

Most shareholders do not wish to take part in a firm's business activities. These shareholders act like passive investors, not active owners. The difference is subtle but important. An active owner is like a sole proprietor who is focused on the business performance of the firm. In contrast, a passive investor is an investor who does not have the time or desire to get involved in running the company and instead focuses on the risk and return of the investment. While diversifying reduces risk for the investor, ownership of many companies also makes participation and influence in those companies less likely. Therefore, investors tend to be inactive shareholders of many firms.

Hence, there is a problem with this separation of ownership and control. Why would the managers care about the owners? Berle and Means pointed out that with managers being freed from vigilant owners, managers would only pursue enough profit to keep stockholders satisfied while managers sought self-serving gratification in the form of perks, power, and/or fame. In academic terms, this situation is known as the principal-agent problem or the agency problem. The owners are the principal and the manager is the agent who is supposed to work for the owner. If shareholders cannot effectively monitor the managers' behavior, then managers may be tempted to use the firm's assets for their own ends, all at the expense of shareholders. This should not be hard to imagine. Secretaries may take home office supplies. When traveling, mid-level managers may order as much food as allowed for on their expense accounts. Executives might prefer fancy oak furniture for their offices and the use of corporate jets when traveling. All of these actions are at the expense of shareholders. If people feel they can get away with these minor offenses, what else might they try?

Among all employees, the agency problem is the greatest with the executives of a corporation because they have the most power and control in the corporation. Mid-level managers have bosses who look at expense reports. But who watches the executives? The primary monitor of the executives is the board of directors of the corporation who are appointed by the shareholders to run the corporation on behalf of the shareholders. It is the board that appoints the executives and removes them if they take actions that harm the corporation. However, if the shareholders are passive investors without an incentive to monitor closely, will the shareholders make sure the board does its job? If not, then what is to stop the executives from including the directors in the activities that personally benefit them at the expense of the shareholders?

Solutions to this problem tend to come in two categories: incentives and monitoring. The incentive solution attempts to tie the wealth of the executive to the wealth of the shareholders, so that executives and shareholders want the same thing. This is called aligning executive incentives with shareholder desires. Managers would then act and behave in a way that is also best for the other shareholders. How can this be done? For most U.S. companies, executives are given stock, restricted stock, stock options, or combinations of these as a significant component of their compensation. A similar approach is frequently considered with directors as well. If all directors own stock or have options on stock, then directors will personally benefit if the firm does well. The advantages and disadvantages of this incentive solution for executives are explored in Chapter 2. The incentive problem with the board of directors is covered in Chapter 4. Suffice it to say, there are troubles with incentives as a solution to the agency problem.

The second solution is to address the weaknesses in the monitoring by the board and to set up additional monitoring mechanisms for monitoring the behavior of managers. Several monitoring mechanisms are discussed shortly in this chapter, and they are importantly discussed throughout this book.

CAN SHAREHOLDERS INFLUENCE MANAGERS?

Theoretically, managers (executives) work for owners (shareholders). In reality, because shareholders are usually inactive and the board does as management asks, the firm actually seems to belong to management. Some active shareholders have tried to influence management and/or change the directors on the board, but they are often met with defeat. Recent evidence of unsuccessful outcomes of shareholder proposals is quite telling. Shareholders of public corporations have the power to make proposals that can be voted on at the annual shareholders meeting. There are generally two types of proposals, those related to governance (e.g., suggesting changes in board structure) and those oriented to social reform (e.g., proposing to stop selling chemicals to rogue countries). About half of all shareholder-initiated proposals progress far enough in the process to reach the voting stage. When there is a vote, such proposals usually are defeated.[8]

A huge factor in whether a proposal is successful depends on management's opinion. Without management approval, proposals have little chance of succeeding. The reason for this is that management is permitted to ask shareholders who will not be able to attend a meeting to return proxy statements voting as management suggests. Traditionally, shareholders have trusted management to know what is best for the firm, so most passive shareholders will go along with whatever management wants. The result is that management effectively controls a large block of votes due to the proxies of uninvolved shareholders and it is unlikely that activist shareholders will prevail. The same issue arises in shareholder voting to replace directors. It is difficult for outside shareholders to mount a serious challenge to the directors nominated by the company.

Monitors

There are a variety of potential monitors of the actions of corporate executives that jointly make up the current system of corporate governance.

EXAMPLE 1.1   Carly Fiorina's Takeover of Compaq

For an illustration of management control and influence, consider the 2002 merger between Hewlett-Packard (HP) and Compaq.[9] Carly Fiorina, the CEO of Hewlett-Packard, announced on September 4, 2001, that HP would acquire Compaq for $25.5 billion. The stock markets, industry experts, and the business media reacted negatively to the news. Hewlett-Packard stock was down 18 percent following the announcement, and even Compaq's stock declined by 10 percent, which is rare for a target firm. Of particular note, David W. Packard and Walter Hewlett, both significant shareholders (when including the Packard Foundation, the pair owned 18 percent of HP stock) and sons of HP's founders, were also strongly opposed to the acquisition. In fact, they took out newspaper ads asking other HP shareholders to vote against the merger.

However, Fiorina went ahead with her plan, despite attacks from both Packard and Hewlett, and on March 19, 2002, the plan was approved by the shareholders. Despite the controversy and the drop in stock prices, most shareholders voted with management's wishes and approved the acquisition. This example reinforces the idea that even though some investors may want to influence business strategy and direction, management controls the firm.

Figure 1.1 illustrates the separation of ownership and control between stockholders and managers. In addition, the figure shows that monitors exist inside the corporate structure, outside the structure, and in government.

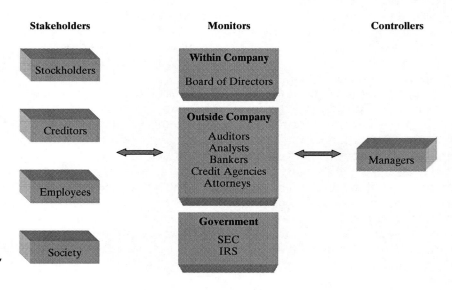

FIGURE 1.1 Separation of Ownership, Monitoring, and Control

The monitoring role inside a public corporation falls on the board of directors who oversee management and are supposed to represent shareholders' interests. The shareholders elect directors at the annual meeting each year. These directors have a legal obligation to represent the shareholders' interests in running the corporation. One of the most important roles the board carries out is to appoint the executives who will actually run the day-to-day operations of the company. The board hires the executives and can replace them if the board is unhappy with management for any reason. The board can also design compensation contracts to tie management's salaries to the firm's performance.

You may remember that Apple Computer was cofounded by Steve Jobs. When the firm became a public corporation, Jobs was the largest shareholder, and he also became CEO, which is the highest executive at a corporation. However, the Apple board of directors felt that Jobs was not experienced enough to steer the firm through its rapid expansion. Therefore, they hired John Sculley as CEO in 1983. In 1985, a power struggle ensued for control of the firm, and the board backed Sculley. Jobs was forced out of Apple and no longer had a say in business operations even though he was the largest shareholder. (Interestingly, when Apple Computer experienced difficulties in the late 1990s, the board hired Jobs back as CEO!)

As shown in the figure, outsiders—including auditors, analysts, investment banks, credit rating agencies, and outside legal counsel—all interact with executives and the board and monitor manager activities (as well as the actions of the board). Auditors examine the firm's accounting systems and comment on whether financial statements fairly represent the financial position of the firm. Investors and other stakeholders use these public financial statements to make decisions about the firm's financial health, prospects, performance, and value. Even though investors may not have the ability or opportunity to validate the firm's activities, accountants and auditors can attest to the firm's financial health and verify its activities.

Investment analysts who follow a firm conduct their own, independent evaluations of the company's business activities and report their findings to the investment community. Analysts are supposed to give unbiased and expert assessments. Investment banks also interact with management by helping firms access the capital markets. When obtaining more capital from public investors, firms must register documents with regulators that show potential investors the condition of the firm. Investment banks help firms with this process and advise managers on how to interact with the capital markets.

The U.S. government also monitors business activities through federal laws covering securities, taxes, antitrust, foreign trade, and other aspects that affect large corporations. Federal laws have created the Securities and Exchange Commission (SEC), the Internal Revenue Service (IRS), and other federal agencies with jurisdiction over publicly traded companies. The SEC regulates public firms for the protection of public investors, and it makes policy and prosecutes violators. The IRS enforces the tax rules to ensure corporations comply with the tax code in paying its taxes. Violations of federal law by executives can lead to large fines and even jail time.

In response to corporate and investment community scandals, the U.S. government enacted the Sarbanes-Oxley Act of 2002. Overall, the act created a new oversight body to regulate auditors, created laws pertaining to corporate responsibility, and increased punishments for corporate white-collar crime. Similarly, the two largest stock exchanges, the NYSE and NASDAQ, both developed and adopted their own governance-focused listing standards to address the problems.

More recently, the government has impacted corporate governance in the firms asking for financial help during the 2008 and 2009 economic recession. In formulating a bailout package for the big three American auto companies, Congress first demanded the three CEOs accept compensation of only $1. Later, as the government helped GM navigate through the bankruptcy court process quickly, it demanded CEO Rick Wagoner's resignation. Also, U.S. Treasury is providing capital to financial firms from the Troubled Asset Relief Program (TARP) in exchange for debt and equity stakes in the firms. This makes the government an investor stakeholder in these firms. It is unclear how this new relationship will impact the corporate governance of the firms and what incentives might have been created. However, we have already seen Congress interfere with compensation bonus payments at American International Group, Inc., (AIG).

Another monitor of management is market forces. If a manager is not doing a good job, either because he is bad at managing or because he is abusing his managerial discretion, then his firm might get taken over and he is subsequently fired. On the contrary, an executive who avoids agency problems and is successful in increasing the value of shareholders' investments at one firm will be in demand in the marketplace by other firms who are looking for an effective leader. In this sense, the fear of a potential takeover and the reward of a CEO position at a more prestigious company each might represent powerful disciplinary mechanisms to make sure that managers perform to the best of their abilities and to make sure that managerial discretion is controlled.

Other potential monitors include: stockholders, such as large institutional investors like pension funds, who are active monitors; creditors and credit rating agencies who analyze whether the firm can handle its current debt level; employees, such as internal auditors, who monitor the firm to make sure it is healthy; and others in the corporation's community who can instill a sense of corporate citizenship to the firm so that firm executives feel a sense of responsibility toward their community.

As a group, this is a pretty impressive set of monitors. Unfortunately, all of these mechanisms can fail at one time or another. An important purpose of this book is to describe each of these corporate monitors and the problems that may exist with each of them.

AN INTEGRATED SYSTEM OF GOVERNANCE

The corporate governance system is integrated and complicated. The potential incentives for executives, auditors, boards, banks, and so on, to misbehave are intertwined. By focusing on one part of the system, readers

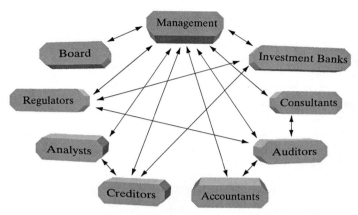

FIGURE 1.2   Interlinking Relationships among Business Participants

might not fully understand how the governance system can break down. Consider the diagram of corporate participants in Figure 1.2. The arrows show the relationships between the groups. Note that these relationships are interconnected.

For example, analysts talk to management to gauge the prospects of the firm. Managers want to paint a rosy picture so that analysts will recommend a "buy" rating and the stock price will rise. However, this situation may also cause analysts to predict a high profit forecast for the company, and the managers may struggle to meet the high profit forecast. If the business activities of the firm do not merit the high profit forecast, managers might then pressure their accounting department to help. In some cases, consultants are hired who recommend aggressive accounting techniques to help show increased profits.

The public auditors for the firm may have had a long and fruitful relationship with the company, auditing the books for many years. The auditors are proud to have a prestigious corporation as a client and do not want to end this relationship; consequently they may not press too hard on limiting aggressive accounting methods. Why are managers so obsessed with pushing hard for smooth and increasing profits? Why are they obsessed with gaining analyst favor? It is because a board (which is largely picked by the managers) awards them stock options and stock incentives. If managers can increase the price of the stock, then they can cash in their options and stock and earn far more than their base compensation level.

Government regulators also monitor managers' behavior. However, regulators often have experience as partners in the consulting firms, auditing firms, or law firms that are an integral part of the system. By participating in the corporate system, regulators know how it works. Unfortunately, they might also have their own conflicts of interest.

This book describes the following monitors or monitoring mechanisms:

- incentive contracts that supposedly align executive incentives with shareholder interests;
- accountants and auditors who check the firm's financial statements;
- boards of directors who represent shareholders;
- investment banks and analysts who bring securities to the public for sale and evaluate them;
- creditors and credit rating agencies who monitor the firm's ability to handle debt;
- shareholders themselves;
- the corporate takeover market where supposedly good firms take over bad firms;
- the Securities and Exchange Commission who are the official regulators of the securities industry;
- government and the governance of international firms;
- the government's role in the survival of firms; and
- corporate citizenship that should instill a sense of corporate responsibility to the executives.

INTERNATIONAL MONITORING

Other capitalist countries use the types of monitoring and incentives used in the United States to align the interests of executives and shareholders. However, important differences do occur. Some countries use different compensation contracts and have different accounting standards. Many countries do not have the same institutional investing environment as the United States. Some countries are bank oriented rather than capital markets oriented. A country's legal environment can explain some of the differences. However, corporate scandals can occur in every country. In this book, every chapter contains an international perspective on that chapter's topic.

Summary

The corporate form of business allows firms that need capital to obtain it and expand, thereby helping the economy. This form also allows people with money to provide those funds and profit from having ownership in business. The disadvantage of public corporations lies in the relation between ownership and control. Managers who control the firm can take advantage of the investors who own the firm. To inhibit poor managerial behavior, boards of directors try to align the executives' interests with shareholders' interests through incentive programs involving stock and stock options. In addition, the corporate system has several different groups of people that monitor managers. Unfortunately, both alignment incentives and monitoring groups bring to the table their own set of problems. The corporate system has interrelated incentives that combine to create an environment where people might act unethically. The following chapters discuss each aspect of the incentive and monitor system of corporate governance.

Review Questions

1. What are the three basic forms of business owner-ship? What are the advantages and disadvantages of each?
2. How can executive compensation align managers interests with shareholders interests?
3. Name and describe the different groups that moni-tor a firm.
4. Describe the separation of ownership and control. Explain how that separation comes about and why it leads to problems.

Discussion Questions

1. Figure 1.1 shows monitors and stakeholders. In your opinion, which group is in the best position to monitor the firm? Explain why. Which group has the potential to be the weakest monitor? Explain why.
2. Figure 1.2 shows how business participants are in-terlinked. In your opinion, which links potentially create the greatest problems for stockholders? Explain why.
3. In your opinion, how do you think U.S. corpora-tions became as important and as large as they are today?

4. In general, and in your personal experience, which has been the most effective way to get people to do what you want:
   (i) provide incentives for good behavior;
   (ii) closely monitor them; or
   (iii) give punishments for bad behavior?

From what you have seen, read, and heard from the mass media, journalists, politicians, and so on, what do these people think is the best way to get executives to behave ethically? If your answers to these two ques-tions are different, then try to reconcile the differences.

Exercises

1. This chapter described how Carly Fiorina exerted control over Hewlett-Packard despite objections from large shareholders. Find another example of how management went against shareholders' wishes and describe what happened.
2. Do some research and explain how U.S. corpora-tions became as important and as large as they are

today. Some academics have discussed the "theory of the firm" or the "nature of the firm." To what extent, and how, do these theories explain U.S. corporations today? How do agency problems play a role in these theories?

Exercises for Non-U.S. Students

1. Figure 1.2 shows how business participants are interlinked in the United States. Create a figure showing the interlinkages among business partici-pants in your country. Explain the interlinkages.
2. How severe is the agency problem in your coun-try? Explain. Also, provide real examples.
3. In your country, which ideology seems to be used in resolving agency conflicts:

   (i) providing incentives to executives for good behavior;
   (ii) closely monitoring the executives; or
   (iii) giving punishments to executives for bad behavior?

Do you think it is working? Explain why or why not.

Endnotes

1. There are other common forms of business organizations, such as the Limited Liability Company (LLC) and limited partnership (LP). These are "hybrids" that combine the limited liability of corporations with the tax benefits of partnerships. Depending on the size and structure of LLCs and LPs, they could be managed similar to large corporations or to sole proprietorships.

2. William J. Megginson, *Corporate Finance Theory* (Reading, MA: Addison-Wesley, 1997), p. 40.

3. Ibid.

4. In contrast, the sole proprietor and partnership are not taxpayers. Income from the companies are charged directly to the owners on their tax returns.

5. In contrast, the owner of the sole proprietorship or a partner in a partnership would be legally liable for paying off the creditor in full. Note, also, that the limitation of liability is not absolute in corporations, as there are rare cases where a court "pierces the corporate veil" and assigns personal liability to shareholders in cases where the court finds the corporate form was abused for personal gain.

6. Corporations with small numbers of shareholders can elect to become "S" corporations where the only tax is at the shareholder level. Public corporations, however, are required to be "C" corporations with double taxation.

7. Adolf Berle and Gardiner Means, *The Modern Corporation and Private Property* (New York, MacMillan, 1932).

8. See, for example, Stuart Gillan and Laura Starks, "A Survey of Shareholder Activism: Motivation and Empirical Evidence," *Contemporary Finance Digest* 2, no. 3 (1998):10–34; Cynthia Campbell, Stuart Gillan, and Cathy Niden, "Current Perspectives on Shareholder Proposals: Lessons from the 1997 Proxy Season," Financial Management 28, no. 1 (1999):89–98; and Gordon and Pound, "Information, Ownership Structure, and Shareholder Voting: Evidence from Shareholder-Sponsored Corporate Governance Proposals," *Journal of Finance* 47, no. 2 (1993):697–718.

9. Larry Magid, "Many Would Lose in Hewlett-Packard, Compaq Merger," *Los Angeles Times*, *www.larrysworld.com/articles/synd.hpmerger. htm;* Mike Elgan and Susan B. Shor, "Gloves Are Off in Merger Fight," *HP World* 5, no. 2, *www. interex. org/hpworldnews/hpw202/01news.html.*

Chapter 8

Strategic management

Aim

To describe and illustrate the main elements of strategy and to show the flexible nature of the process.

Objectives

By the end of your work on this chapter you should be able to outline the concepts below in your own terms and:

1 Explain the significance of strategic management to all organisations
2 Describe the main steps in the strategic management process
3 Use the product/market matrix to compare corporate level strategies
4 Use the concept of generic strategies to compare business level strategies
5 Give examples of alternative methods of delivering a strategy
6 Compare planning, learning and political perspectives on strategy.

Key terms

This chapter introduces the following ideas:

strategic management
strategy
competitive strategy
value for money
institutional advantage
mission statement
strategic capability
tangible resource
intangible resource
unique resources
competences
core competences
value chain
cost leadership strategy
differentiation strategy
focus strategy
emergent strategy

Each is a term defined within the text, as well as in the Glossary at the end of the book.

Marks & Spencer   www.marksandspencer.com

Originating in 1884 as a market stall, Marks & Spencer (M&S) is today one of the UK's leading retailers of clothes, food, home products and financial services, with a turnover of £7.8 billion in the year to April 2006. There are 455 UK stores, employing 65,000 people. Each week, 15 million people shop at M&S and three-quarters of UK adults have shopped there in the last 12 months. There are 198 M&S-branded franchised stores in Europe, the Middle East, Asia and the Far East. Until April 2006 the company owned the US supermarket group Kings Super Markets. Following an unprecedented programme of expansion at home and abroad in the late 1990s, profits started to slide.

Clothing accounts for 45 per cent of M&S's UK retail sales. There is a wide range of clothing for all ages and, although sales fell in 2003, the company still held an 11 per cent share of the UK market. Food sales account for 50 per cent of UK turnover and grew by 5 per cent in 2003. New 'metro' store concepts were being tested in city centre and high street stores.

At the 2004 AGM the new CEO, Stuart Rose, conceded that the brand was in decline and that customer relationships were weakening due to confusion and disappointment. Although it still had a high share of the market, there was intense rivalry with competitors who can establish strong brands in well-defined segments. Some thought that M&S was targeting too many segments and losing understanding of customer needs.

The traditional bases for competition (quality, trust) for which customers paid a premium appeared to be changing: differentiating competitors (Next, Gap) offered more attractive ranges at similar prices; cost competitors (Matalan, TK Maxx, Tesco) offered basic clothing at lower prices.

The new management team were debating whether to change the traditional strategy and if so, how. Another possibility was that the traditional strategy was still valid, but had been poorly implemented in recent years. By the end of 2006 the new strategy appeared to be paying off, with the company reporting a strong growth in sales and profits, and M&S was about to begin

© Marks and Spencer PLC.

a large investment programme to make the stores more attractive.

Source: M&S *Annual Reports* 2003–2006; company website; *Financial Times* (various, 2006–2007).

Case questions 8.1

Visit an M&S store, and also visit their website – especially the section on 'the company'.

- Note the sales and profit performance in the most recent period compared to an earlier one.
- What do the chairman and chief executive write about the company's current strategy?
- What challenges do they say the company is facing?

8.1 Introduction

Strategic management is the set of decisions and actions intended to improve the long-run performance of an organisation.

Marks & Spencer illustrates the value of **strategic management**. For many years it occupied a leading position in the UK retailing industry, but in the late 1990s its performance declined. Some reasons were external – new competitors and changing customer tastes – while others were internal – little investment in modern stores and poor clothing design. New senior managers were appointed in 2003, and began to adjust the company's strategy – investing to improve the stores, making the all-important women's clothing line more fashionable and developing a new line of 'Just Food' stores. By 2007 the company was doing well again, as the new strategies began to show through in rising sales and profits. It still faces strong challenges from new brands that focus on a cheaper range or a narrower group of customers. Managers also know that entrepreneurs such as Phillip Green could use any sign of trading weakness as an opportunity to try to take the company over (as he attempted to do in 2005).

All organisations (not just those in trouble) face issues of strategic management. Established businesses such as BT are in a growing and diversifying telecommunications market – but face new competition that threatens their core business. Should the company try to compete in all areas, or concentrate on one sector, as Vodafone has done? Should Virgin continue to extend the brand into ever more diverse areas of activity, or would it gain more by building profits in the existing areas, and achieving more synergies across the group? Some charities face declining income – should their managers continue as they are now, or will they serve their cause better by initiating a radical review of their strategy? Strategic management enables companies to be clear about how they will add value to resources, even though much is changing in their world. Table 8.1 gives examples of the strategic issues managers face, and how they have responded: you can easily collect current examples. Comparing the performance of companies serving similar markets shows the importance of strategy: while all work in the same business and competitive environment, some perform better than others – probably because they adopted a more suitable strategy.

Table 8.1

Examples of organisations making strategic changes

Organisation and strategic issue	Strategic decisions or moves
BAE Systems (UK military equipment) – how to increase sales in the US www.baesystems.com	Acquired United Defense, US armoured vehicles maker in 2005, becoming sixth biggest contractor to Pentagon.
Procter & Gamble (world's largest supplier of consumer goods e.g. soap and toothpaste) – how to ensure long term-growth **www.pg.com**	Changed from focus on people in rich economies to those in poor countries – affects R&D, market research and manufacturing to identify and make suitable products.
Nestlé (global food and beverage company) – how to stimulate sales and profits in a mature business www.nestle.com	Increased emphasis on healthy foods, by adapting current products and taking over companies with established reputations for healthy products.

Strategy links the organisation to the outside world, and Chapter 3 showed how this influences management practice. Porter's model (1985) identifies the forces specific to an industry's competitive environment while the PESTEL framework summarises factors common to all organisations. Changes in these represent opportunities and threats: understanding strategic management enables you to observe more analytically the moves that companies make, and to think about possible alternatives.

Linn Products, suppliers of hi-fi equipment   www.linn.co.uk

Linn Products was founded in 1972 with a clear purpose: 'to reproduce, through superior sound, the thrills and emotion of a live performance'. The commitment is to quality and accurate performance. Linn is an independent precision-engineering company specialising in top-performance sound reproduction. It makes a portfolio of products, including CD players, tuners, amplifiers and speakers, which it exports to more than 50 countries. Linn entertainment systems can be found throughout the world in royal residences, luxury homes, performance motorcars and yachts.

A market leader in specialised sound systems, Linn exhibits a clear, consistent philosophy, being true to the music and being directly coupled to its sources. As the sound technology leader, Linn has earned a unique reputation in the world of specialist hi-fi and multi-channel sound recording and reproduction, providing pitch-accurate sound reproduction. Linn has its own record label with a list of 275 jazz, classical and Celtic titles: artists include Claire Martin, Barb Jungr and Carole Kidd. This helps Linn to control, monitor and compare every stage in the sound reproduction process, from performance to listener.

Market channels are strictly controlled: agents and distributors are intensively trained in the Linn philosophy. The jeans-clad, single-minded founder and CEO, Ivor Tiefenbrun:

> the traditional [dealer] approach is inadequate to sustain growth in our industry. And retailers who want to build a business, or who want to grow with their customers, have to meet their changing requirements.

Today, the Linn mission is 'To thrill customers who want the most out of life from music, information and entertainment systems that benefit from quality sound'. Reflecting changes in technology, it now offers digital downloads of all its music titles, allowing customers to receive high-quality music more quickly than through traditional channels, and making the titles more widely available around the world.

Competition is growing more active. Tiefenbrun says:

> I don't think there's much wrong with the way hi-fi's sold now in the sense that the people who sell it and the people who buy it are quite happy with that programme. But hi-fi is falling down people's lists of priorities. Our customers are changing, and we recognise that the world has changed from the time of the classic enthusiast like myself 20 years ago. There are more products and more issues competing for those individuals' attention.

Source: Interviews with managers, published information and company website.

Activity 8.1   Comparing practice with the model

- What features of Linn's business could be a source of challenge in formulating strategy?
- What are the bases of competition in this market?

The chapter begins by outlining the strategic management process, and then examines each step – mission, external and internal analyses, formulating, implementing and review. It compares structured, emergent and political theories of the strategy process and concludes with a commentary on three current themes.

8.2   Purposes of strategy – and how they vary with context

Benefits of setting strategy

A structured approach to strategy can benefit all organisations, though its nature varies with circumstances. Common benefits are that it:

- **Reduces uncertainty** It obliges managers to look ahead, anticipate change and develop appropriate responses; it also encourages them to consider the risks of each option.
- **Links long term and short term** It helps people to relate current operational activities and decisions to the longer-term strategic objectives they are intended to support.
- **Clarifies and unifies purpose** By setting the overall strategic objectives and what these imply for those at operational level it helps departments to work towards common goals.
- **Enables control** By setting clear objectives, it provides standards against which to measure performance.

> **Strategy** is concerned with deciding what business an organisation should be in, where it wants to be, and how it is going to get there.

While people use different terms, the activity of **strategy** essentially involves dealing with what is to be achieved, for whom and how. In traditional strategic planning, people establish a vision and/or mission, set some more tangible goals, and then design the strategy – how to achieve the goals. As you will see, strategic planning is rarely as neat as this – strategies can emerge, alter and disappear, sometimes very quickly.

For most organisations the purpose of developing strategy is to perform well against competitors over the long term. It helps to identify the factors that give it a sustained advantage, the basis for higher levels of profitability or other measures of performance. Identifying sustainable sources of competitive advantage clarifies the organisation's **competitive strategy**. This sets the direction and scope of the organisation, by establishing how it will use resources to meet the expectations of stakeholders.

> **Competitive strategy** is concerned with the basis on which an organisation (or unit within it) might achieve competitive advantage in its market.

Strategy and type of business

While the common benefits of developing a strategy are clear, the process varies with the type of organisation. One difference is that the concept of competitive advantage does not apply directly to not-for-profit (NFP) organisations (Goold, 1997). While NFPs have some similar characteristics to the profit-seeking firm, there are fundamental differences in (a) their goals, (b) their funding and external influence, and (c) their internal power relationships (Bowman and Asch, 1996). Some NFPs have direct competitors: Oxfam competes for donations and for customers through shop and mail order networks. Others compete for resources, media attention and volunteers.

> **A value for money** service is one that is provided economically, efficiently and effectively.
>
> **Institutional advantage** 'is when a not-for-profit body performs its tasks more effectively than comparable organisations' (Goold, 1997).

The analogue to profit in the public and NFP sector (Smith, 1995) is frequently **value for money**, that is, providing a project or service as economically, efficiently and effectively as possible. Goold (1997) suggests that in these sectors a better term is **institutional advantage**, which 'is held when a not-for-profit body performs its tasks more effectively than ... comparable organisations'.

Porter (1990) has also written about competition between nations. Nation states (and cities within them) compete with each other to secure investment by multinational companies, the right to host events such as the Olympic Games, or to hold titles such as 'European City of Culture'. Such events can bring valuable income and to gain this countries and cities identify sources of their competitive advantage, such as an educated workforce or an attractive physical environment. Table 8.2 summarises the strategic issues that arise in different settings.

Table 8.2

Strategic issues in
different settings

Type of organisation	Distinctive strategic issues	Examples in this text
Large multinational corporations (MNCs)	Structure and control of global activities Allocating resources between units	Procter & Gamble (this chapter); BP (Part 2 case)
Small and medium enterprises (SMEs)	Strongly influenced by founders or owners; lack of capital limits choices	Linn Products (this chapter)
Manufacturing	Relative contribution to competitive advantage of the manufacturing (physical product) or service aspect (delivery, customer support) of the offer.	Wipro (Chapter 7 case); BMW (Chapter 11)
Firms in innovative sectors	Competitive advantage depends on ability to change the rules of the game, and so on creating a culture of questioning and challenge	Nokia (Chapter 3); Oticon (Chapter 10)
Public sector	Competition centres on fight for resources, and so on ability to demonstrate best value in outputs; problems increasingly require cooperation between agencies, complicating strategy.	HM Revenue and Customs (Chapter 11)
Voluntary and NFP sector	Balancing the influence of ideology and values with interests of funding sources; balancing central control (consistency) with local commitment (volunteers and local staff).	Charity with residential homes (Chapter 1); Housing Association (Chapter 10); The Big Issue (Chapter 9)
Professional service organisations	Strategy process influenced by partnership nature of their structure, requiring time to reach consensus.	

8.3   Steps in the strategic management process

Figure 8.1 illustrates the six steps in the strategic management process – which will be carried out iteratively and, in many circumstances, continually.

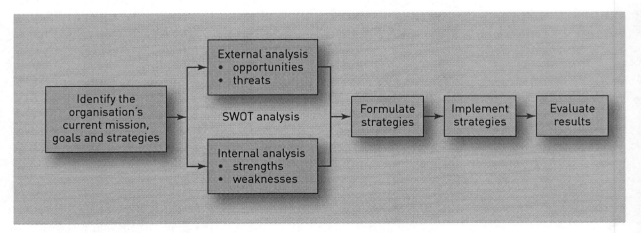

Figure 8.1 The strategic management process

Identifying current mission, goals and strategies

A mission statement is a broad statement of an organisation's scope and purpose, aiming to distinguish it from similar organisations.

Defining an organisation's mission is intended to identify the scope of its customers, products or services: it provides a focus for work. A broad statement of mission (or purpose) can guide those setting more specific goals and the strategies to achieve them. A useful **mission statement** also expresses the underlying beliefs and values held within the organisation – the emphasis given to matters such as innovation, customer care or climate change. Dobson *et al.* (2004) suggest that a mission statement should clarify:

- principal business or activities
- key aims or objectives
- key beliefs and values – what it represents
- main stakeholders.

Missions should be short and easy to understand: the Management in Practice feature gives examples.

---

management in practice **Examples of mission and vision statements**

IKEA (www.ikea.com)
A better everyday life. The IKEA business idea is to offer a wide range of home furnishings with good design and function at prices so low that as many people as possible will be able to afford them. And still have money left!

Unilever (www.unilever.com)
Unilever's mission is to add vitality to life. It meets the everyday needs for nutrition, hygiene and personal care with brands that help people feel good, look good and get more out of life.

Royal Society for the Protection of Birds (www.rspb.org.uk)
The RSPB is the UK charity working to secure a healthy environment for birds and wildlife, helping to create a better world for us all.

Higher Education Funding Council for England (www.hefce.ac.uk)
Working in partnership, HEFCE promotes and funds high-quality, cost-effective teaching and research, meeting the diverse needs of students, the economy and society.

Nokia (www.nokia.com)
By connecting people, Nokia helps fulfil a fundamental human need for social connections and contact. Nokia builds bridges between people – both when they are far apart and face to face – and also bridges the gap between people and the information they need.

Activity 8.2 **Critical reflection on mission statements**

- Decide whether the examples above satisfy the requirements of a good mission statement (as defined by Dobson *et al.*, 2004).
- Does the M&S statement of vision, mission and values meet those requirements?
- Give examples of the ways in which the company's values are reflected in its business activities.
- Does your organisation have a mission statement, and does it meet the criteria of Dobson *et al.* (2004)? If not, edit it so that it would fit, or suggest why it is better as it is.

The dangers of mission statements

Some question the value of mission statements, especially if they are an idealistic aspiration rather than a realistic guide to action. A study of local government in Britain (Leach, 1996) found that while in some authorities mission statements had clarified the dominant values and culture, in others staff saw them only as symbolic public relations documents. Another danger is that management fails to develop a belief in the mission throughout the organisation. People only come to believe in, and act upon, the mission statement if they see others doing the same – especially senior managers. The mission needs to be cascaded through the structure to ensure it guides day-to-day actions.

Marks & Spencer – the case continues
www.marksandspencer.com

CASE STUDY

The M&S brand is strongly associated with the company's values of quality, value, service and trust. These were severely tested during the difficulties between 2001 and 2004, but the new management team built their recovery plan on the company's 'unique fundamental strengths'. One of these is that it works to high ethical trading standards and a strong sense of environmental and social responsibility. In January 2007 it announced 'Plan A', a five-year plan to tackle some of the biggest challenges facing the business and the world. It covered:

climate change – aiming to become carbon neutral by minimising energy use and using renewable energy sources where possible;

waste – aiming to stop sending waste to landfill and reducing the amount of packaging on products;

raw materials – ensuring that raw materials come from the most sustainable resources possible;

fair partner – trading fairly to improve the lives of hundreds of thousands of people in its supply chain and in its local communities;

healthy eating – continuing to set good food standards, helping customers and employees to live a healthier lifestyle.

Sources: M&S *Annual Reports* 2003–2006; company website, *Financial Times* (various, 2006–2007).

Case questions 8.2

● What encouraged the company to extend its ethical policies by launching Plan A (see the website)?

● Do you think these commitments will give M&S a competitive advantage? How?

External analysis

Chapter 3 established that the external environment is made up of competitive and general environments. At the micro-level, Porter's five forces analysis helps management to assess the state of competition within the industry. At the macro-level, the PESTEL framework helps to identify the major drivers of change. Lei and Slocum (2005) distinguish industries in terms of the stage of their life cycle, and their rate of technological development. In the early stages of an industry's growth there are few barriers to entry, so many firms enter the market and seek different ways of attracting consumers. These will change as the industry matures, growth slows, and customers become familiar with the product. Their second point is that industries vary in their rate of technological change. At one extreme, firms experience a slow accumulation of minor changes, while at the other they face a constant stream of radical new technologies that change the basis of competition. The chapter also showed that external stakeholders, such as government and pressure groups, also influence organisations.

Case questions 8.3
Referring to the analytical frameworks in Chapter 3:

● What are the main external factors affecting M&S at present?
● How do these differ between the food and clothing businesses?

Kay (1996) defined strategy as the match between the organisation's external relationships and its internal capabilities, describing 'how it responds to its suppliers, its customers, its competitors, and the social and economic environment within which it operates'. Before establishing a direction, managers need an internal analysis to show how well they can cope with external changes.

Internal analysis: resources and capabilities

Managers analyse the internal environment to identify the organisation's strengths and weaknesses. This means identifying what the organisation does well, where it might do better and whether it has the resources and competences to deliver a preferred strategy. Those that are considered essential to outperforming the competition constitute critical success factors.

Johnson *et al.* (2006) define **strategic capability** as the ability to perform at the level required to survive and prosper. That depends on the resources available to the organisation, and its competence in using them. **Tangible resources** are the physical assets such as buildings, equipment, people or finance, while **intangible resources** include reputation, knowledge or information. **Unique resources** are those which others cannot obtain – such as a powerful brand or access to a unique source of raw material.

While the amount and quality of these resources matter, how people use them has a more sustained effect on performance. If a manager encourages staff to develop higher skills, cooperate with each other, be innovative and creative, the company is likely to perform better than one where staff are unable to use their talents. The first company gains because it has developed **competences** – activities and processes that enable it to deploy resources effectively.

Understanding competitive advantage requires a further distinction between those capabilities (resources and competences) that are at the threshold level and those that give competitive advantage. Threshold capabilities are those an organisation must have to compete in a market – adequate IT systems, for example. **Core competences** are the activities and processes which people use to deploy resources in ways that gain them a competitive advantage, because others cannot imitate them. Ryanair has prospered not just because it has a fleet of modern, standard aircraft – other airlines could have a similar resource, but be unprofitable. The difference is that Ryanair has developed core competences that enable it to use its aircraft more efficiently than competitors.

Management's task in internal analysis is to identify those strengths (capabilities) that distinguish the organisation in the minds of the customer and thereby support its competitive advantage. One of these strengths is the overall balance of activities that the organisation as a whole undertakes – the product or service portfolio. Does it have sufficient interests in growing rather than declining markets? Does it have too many new products (which tend to be a drain on resources) relative to established ones?

At the divisional or strategic business unit level, the ability to compete effectively depends on:

Strategic capability is the ability to perform at the level required to survive and prosper, and includes resources and competences.

Tangible resources are physical assets such as buildings, equipment, people or finance.

Intangible resources are non-physical assets such as reputation, knowledge or information.

Unique resources are resources that are vital to competitive advantage and which others cannot obtain.

Competences are the activities and processes through which an organisation deploys resources effectively.

Core competences are the activities and processes through which resources are deployed to achieve competitive advantage in ways that others cannot imitate or obtain.

- **The resource base:** includes physical resources (buildings and production facilities), human resources (employees' skills, knowledge, attitudes, etc.), financial resources (growth prospects, debt–equity mix, liquidity position, financial control systems, etc.) and intangibles (such as 'goodwill', or good relationships with suppliers). Each can be assessed for their adequacy in supporting a strategy.
- **The competence base:** how the organisation performs the activities of designing, producing, marketing, delivering and supporting its products or services – and manages the linkages between them. These are critical since the key to performance lies in the competences that add extra value to the resources available to the organisation.

Value chain analysis

The concept of the **value chain**, introduced by Porter (1985), is derived from an accounting practice that calculates the value added at each stage of a manufacturing or service process. Porter applied this idea to the activities of the whole organisation, as an analysis of each activity could identify sources of competitive advantage.

Figure 8.2 shows primary and support activities. *Primary* activities transform inputs into outputs and deliver them to the customer:

A **value chain** 'divides a firm into the discrete activities it performs in designing, producing, marketing and distributing its product. It is the basic tool for diagnosing competitive advantage and finding ways to enhance it' (Porter, 1985).

- **Inbound logistics:** activities such as receiving, storing and distributing the inputs to the product or service. They include material handling, stock control, etc.
- **Operations:** transforming these into the final product or service, such as machining or packing.
- **Outbound logistics:** moving the product to the buyer – collecting, storing and distributing; in some services (a sports event) these activities will include bringing the customers to the venue.
- **Marketing and sales:** activities to make consumers aware of the product.
- **Service:** enhancing or maintaining the product – installation, training, repairs.

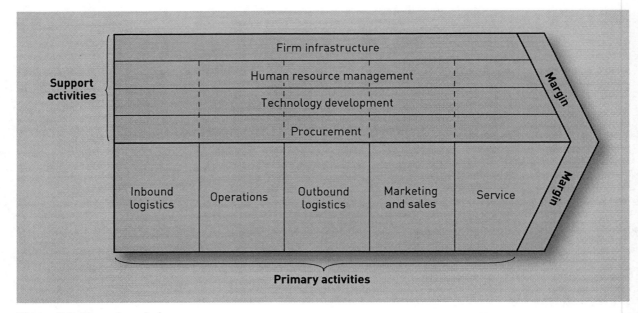

Figure 8.2 The value chain

Source: Porter (1985), copyright © 1985 Michael E. Porter, reprinted with permission of The Free Press, a division of Simon & Schuster.

These depend on four *support* activities:

1 **firm infrastructure**: organisational structure, together with planning, financial and quality systems;
2 **human resource management**: recruitment, training, rewards, etc.;
3 **technology development**: relate to inputs, operational processes or outputs;
4 **procurement**: acquiring materials and other resources.

Case questions 8.4

As part of the recovery plan, M&S improved the design of its products, outsourced the supply of many to cheaper suppliers overseas, improved store design, spent heavily on training, and introduced an online service.

- How do these changes fit into the value chain?
- What new challenges may they have raised for the linkages between stages in the chain?

Value chain analysis enables managers to consider which activities are of particular benefit to customers, and which are more troublesome – perhaps destroying value rather than creating it. It might, say, be good at marketing, outbound logistics and technology development – but poor at operations and human resource management. That awareness may lead managers to consider which activities in the value chain it should concentrate on – perhaps outsourcing the others to specialist firms. Even if they decide to outsource, say, after-sales service they must still ensure that those who deliver that service on its behalf do so in a way that contributes to overall quality.

Each activity in the chain 'can contribute to a firm's relative cost position and create a basis for differentiation' (Porter, 1985) – the two main sources of competitive advantage. While a threshold level of competence is necessary in all value chain activities, management needs to identify the core competences that the organisation has (or needs) to compete effectively. Analysing the separate activities in the value chain helps management to consider:

- Which activities have most effect on reducing cost or adding value? If customers value quality more than costs, then that implies a focus on ensuring quality of suppliers.
- What linkages do most to reduce cost, enhance value or discourage imitation?
- How do these linkages relate to the cost and value drivers?

SWOT analysis

Strategy follows from finding a 'fit' between external environment and internal capabilities. Management therefore needs to identify the key issues from each analysis and draw out the strategic implications. A SWOT analysis (strengths, weaknesses, opportunities and threats – discussed) in Chapter 6 is a convenient way to summarise the internal and external issues, and to identify the developments most likely to be profitable – shown schematically in Figure 8.3.

The value chain and comparative analysis usually identify internal strengths and weaknesses (compared with the competition). The PESTEL and five forces analyses usually identify the opportunities and threats in the external environment. A potential customer locating a plant near a firm might constitute an opportunity, but competition from cheaper imports could pose a threat.

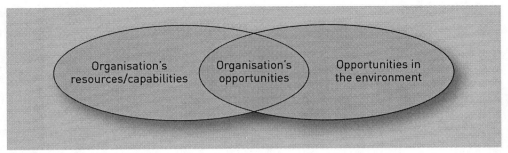

Figure 8.3
Identifying the organisation's opportunities

Formulate strategy

Once the SWOT analysis is complete, managers can develop and evaluate strategic alternatives, aiming to select those that make the most of internal strengths and external opportunities. These may need to be developed for corporate, business and functional levels.

Managers are usually advised to focus on identifying strengths that give the company an edge over its competitors and constitute its core competences, which can be sustained in the long term. If there is a threat from an external factor that could erode them, can they be enhanced (e.g. through technology or training) or protected from imitation (e.g. patenting of innovation)? If erosion is inevitable then a new strategy is required. Management also needs to assess the critical success factors to ensure they have the resources and competences needed to achieve the strategy.

Case questions 8.5

Drawing on your answers to previous questions:

- Make a summary SWOT analysis for Marks & Spencer's clothing business.
- Consult the website to read recent statements from the CEO and other information.

Examples of objectives

management in practice

The Kingfisher Group's mission is to be the world's best international home improvement retailer. It has three core objectives for its home improvement division: (1) major growth at B&Q, Costorama, Brico and Screwfix; (2) driving best practice and scale benefits throughout the sector; and (3) building an international store network beyond the United Kingdom and France.

With a more specific set of objectives to hand, managers can then plan how to achieve them. Given its stated mission to be the best in the world, Kingfisher, for example, could expand internationally by building new stores, by buying overseas companies, or both.

Implement strategy

Implementation turns strategy into action, moving from corporate to operational levels. Many strategies fail to be implemented, or fail to achieve as much as management expected. A common mistake is to assume that formulating a strategy will lead to pain-less implementation. Sometimes there is an 'implementation deficit', when strategies are not implemented at all, or are only partially successful. A common reason for this is that while formulating strategy may appear to be a rational process, it is often a political one. Those who were content with the earlier strategy may oppose the new one if it affects their status, power or career prospects. Chapter 13 shows how implementing major change is a complex, often conflicting process.

Evaluate results

Managers, shareholders (current and potential) and financial analysts routinely compare a company's performance with its published plans. Only by tracking results can these and other interested parties decide if performance is in line with expectations or if the company needs to take some corrective action. Many targets focus on financial and other quantitative aspects of performance, such as sales, operating costs and profit. Table 8.3 shows the high-lights of the Marks & Spencer results for the half-year to 30 September 2006.

Table 8.3

Summary of Marks & Spencer results for 26 weeks to end September 2006

Indicator	2006 (£m)	2005 (£m)	Growth (%)
Total revenue	3,929	3,542	11
Profit before tax	407	306	33
Earnings per share	16.6p	12.7p	31
Interim dividend per share	6.3p	4.8p	31

Source: M&S *Interim Report to Shareholders* on company website.

Given the wide-ranging interests of stakeholders, companies do not restrict their reporting to this type of information. In the public services, measures of quality and fairness of service outcomes may be more important to consumers and service users, but financial performance may be of greater interest to government and other funders.

Although monitoring is shown as the last stage in the strategy model, it is not the end of the process. This is continuous as organisations adjust to changes in their business environment. Regular monitoring alerts management to the possibility that targets might not be achieved and that operational adjustments are needed. Equally, and in conjunction with continuous scanning of the external environment, performance monitoring can prompt wider changes to the organisation's corporate and competitive strategies.

Case questions 8.6

Review Marks & Spencer's most recent annual reports (on the website), including the summary financial statements (not the detailed version).

- What measures does the company use to assess performance?
- What measures does it use (or is it planning) in respect of its commitment to society?
- Is the emphasis on hard (quantitative) or soft (qualitative) measures?

8.4   Levels of strategy

Managers in large enterprises will typically develop strategies at corporate, business and functional levels, though in smaller organisations there will be less complexity. Figure 8.4 shows this.

Corporate level strategy

At corporate level the strategy reflects the overall direction of the organisation, and the part which the respective business units will play in that. Should it remain focused on a small range of activities or diversify? Should it remain a local or national business, or seek to operate internationally? These decisions establish the direction of the organisation.

Strategies can aim for growth, stability or renewal. A growth strategy seeks to increase the organisation's business by expanding the number of products offered or markets served. A stability strategy is one in which the organisation plans to continue offering the same products and services to much the same group of customers. A commercial business may do this after a period of rapid growth (perhaps through acquisition), and it wishes to conserve managerial resources to manage the current business, rather than seek further growth in the short term. Many public sector organisations operate a stability strategy: since resources are limited, they will usually have little opportunity to engage in growth. Many owners of small businesses wish to retain their business at its present size so that they are able to remain in sole control.

A renewal strategy often follows a period of trouble within a business: if performance has been poor management will be required to make major changes to the strategy to return profits to an acceptable level – perhaps involving significant changes to the business to secure the required turnround.

Managers can decide how to achieve their chosen option by using the product/market matrix, shown in Figure 8.5. They can achieve growth by focusing on one or more of the quadrants; stability by remaining with existing products and services; and renewal by combining withdrawal from some existing products and markets, followed (perhaps) by entry into some new products or markets.

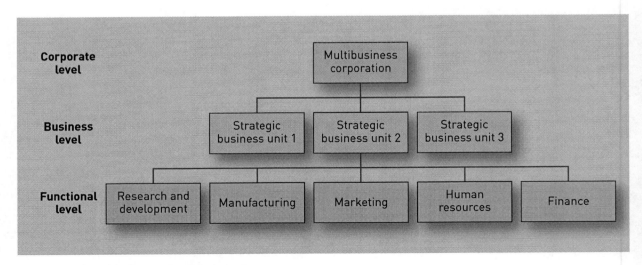

Figure 8.4 Levels of organisational strategy

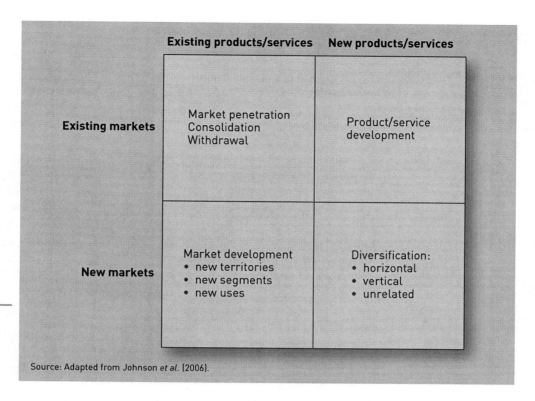

Figure 8.5

Strategy development directions – the product/market matrix

Source: Adapted from Johnson *et al.* (2006).

Existing markets, existing product/service

Choice within this segment depends on whether the market is growing, mature, or in decline. The box shows several possibilities:

- A market penetration strategy aims to increase market share, which will be easier in a growing than in a mature market. It could be achieved by reducing price, increasing advertising or improving distribution.
- Consolidation aims to protect the company's share in existing markets. In growing or mature markets this could mean improving efficiency and/or service to retain custom. In declining markets management might consolidate by acquiring other companies.
- Withdrawal is a wise option when, for instance, competition is intense and the organisation is unable to match its rivals: staying in that line of business would destroy value, not create it. In the public sector, changing priorities lead to the redeployment of resources. Health boards have withdrawn accident and emergency services from some hospitals to make better use of limited resources.

Existing markets, new products/services

A strategy of product or service development allows a company to retain the relative security of its present markets while altering products or developing new ones. In retail sectors such as fashion, consumer electronics and financial services, companies continually change products to meet perceived changes in consumer preferences. Car manufacturers compete by adding features and extending their model range. Some new products, such as 'stakeholder pensions' in the United Kingdom, arise out of changes in government policy. Many new ideas fail commercially, so that product development is risky and costly.

New markets, existing products/services

Market development aims to find new outlets by:

- extending geographically (from local to national or international);
- targeting new market segments (groups of customers, by age, income or lifestyle); or
- finding new uses for a product (a lightweight material developed for use in spacecraft is also used in the manufacture of golf clubs).

P&G targets poorer customers   www.pg.com

Procter & Gamble, the world's largest consumer goods company, built its success on selling detergent, toothpaste and beauty products to the world's wealthiest 1 billion consumers. When Chief Executive AG Lafley arrived in 2002 and said, 'We're going to serve the world's consumers' he surprised the company's staff. One recalled:

> We realised that we didn't have the product strategy or the cost structure to be effective in serving lower-income consumers. What's happened in the last five years has been one of the most dramatic transformations I've seen in my career. We now have all of our functions focused on meeting the needs of poorer consumers.

By 2005 it was devoting 30 per cent of the annual research and development budget to low-income markets, a 50 per cent increase on five years earlier. Developing markets are expected to grow twice as fast as developed markets over the next five years. The transformation has been evident in three areas:

1 how the company finds out what customers want;
2 how this affects R&D; and
3 manufacturing facilities.

Source: Published sources and company website.

New markets, new products/services

Often described as diversification, this can take three forms:

1 **Horizontal integration** Developing related or complementary activities, such as when mortgage lenders extend into the insurance business, using their knowledge of, and contact with, existing customers to offer them an additional service. The advantages include the ability to expand by using existing resources and skills – such as Kwik-Fit's use of its database of depot customers to create a motor insurance business.
2 **Vertical integration** Moving either backwards or forwards into activities related to the organisation's products and services. A manufacturer might decide to make its own components rather than buy them from elsewhere. Equally, it could develop forward, for instance into distribution.
3 **Unrelated diversification** Developing into new markets outside the present industry. Virgin has used its strong brand to create complementary activities in sectors as diverse as airlines, trains, insurance and soft drinks. The extension by some retailers into financial services is another example. It is a way to spread risk where demand patterns fluctuate at different stages of the economic cycle, and to maintain growth when existing markets become saturated.

Alternative development directions are not mutually exclusive: companies can follow several at the same time. Nevertheless, managers need to decide where to focus their effort, as some directions will bring higher sales than others. Terri Dial was appointed as head of retail banking at Lloyds TSB in 2005, charged with introducing a three-year turnround programme. Commenting on her job she said: 'I am a big believer that what you aspire to be is a diversified retail financial services firm ... Diversification is important as the only way to meet customers' needs.'

Sales through branches were declining in the third quarter of last year, but by the first quarter of 2006 she had reversed the trend and sales were increasing. Ms Dial believes Lloyds has concentrated too much on cross-selling more products to existing customers, and not enough on innovation and attracting new customers. (*Financial Times*, 16 August 2006, p. 17)

Marks & Spencer – the case continues
www.marksandspencer.com

CASE STUDY

Appointed as chief executive in 2003, Stuart Rose and his new management team built their three-year recovery plan on the company's strengths, while also looking for new opportunities. The company's scale facilitates innovation and also gives it buying power, although the close supplier relationships for which M&S is renowned were damaged by its decision to increase overseas sourcing in search of cost advantage.

It has a good record of product development. In food it has a leading share in fast-growing markets, such as ready meals; it has strong food development capabilities, changing a quarter of its food range every year, and has introduced bakeries, butcher's shops and hot food counters. Of the company's lines, 40 per cent are suitable for vegetarians and it was the first retailer in the world to respond to customers' health and nutrition concerns by appointing food technologists and animal welfare specialists.

In clothing, product ranges are constantly upgraded and the company is proud of its innovative 'magic fabrics' such as non-iron cotton, machine-washable wool and non-polish shoes. In 2006 the number of people visiting the stores had risen to the levels last achieved in 2002, as the company improved its core women's wear range with up-to-date fashion at Limited Collection and a buoyant Per Una:

'We had been making tractors for people who wanted wheelbarrows,' joked Mr Rose, saying he was pleased with the current designs. He also said he was thinking about broadening the range by experimenting with branded electrical products.

In April 2006 M&S completed the sale of the Kings Super Markets in the United States, the last part of the programme to refocus the group.

By 2006 financial analysts were becoming enthusiastic about the business again, as it appeared that the plan was six months ahead of target. Results for the year to April 2006 showed that group sales were higher than the previous year, while pre-tax profits had risen from £556 million to £751 million. Observers noted that the new team had increased both total sales and the profit margin on those sales – a significant milestone on the road to recovery. It was growing market share in all clothing categories, including the vital women's wear collection.

The recovery plan centred on reviving the existing business of selling high-quality clothing, food and household items through large, well-designed stores. In 2007 the company was continuing to develop its 'Simply Food' concept – a range of smaller stores aimed at those who wanted easy access to that part of the company's product range. It was also planning an e-commerce initiative in conjunction with Amazon.com.

Sources: M&S *Annual Reports* 2003–2006; company website; *Financial Times* (various, 2006–2007).

Case questions 8.7

- Use the product/market matrix to classify the elements of Marks & Spencer's current strategy.
- How has the company chosen to deliver changes in strategic direction?
- In the light of your reading and answers to previous questions, what kind of competitive strategy do you think M&S is following in respect of clothing and foods? Provide examples to support your answer.

Business level strategy

At the business unit level, firms face a choice about how to compete. Porter (1980b, 1985) identified two basic types of competitive advantage: low cost or differentiation. From this he developed the idea that there are three generic strategies that a firm can use to develop and maintain competitive advantage: cost leadership, differentiation and focus. Figure 8.6 shows these strategies. The horizontal axis shows the two bases of competitive advantage. Competitive scope, on the vertical axis, shows whether company's target market is broad or narrow in scope.

Cost leadership

Cost leadership is a strategy whereby a firm aims to compete on price rather than on, say, advanced features or high levels of customer service. Firms following this strategy typically sell a standard no-frills product and place a lot of emphasis on minimising direct input and overhead costs. This requires economies of scale in production and close attention to efficiency and operating costs, although other sources of cost advantage, such as preferential access to raw materials, also help. However, a low cost base will not in itself bring competitive advantage – consumers must see that the product represents value for money. Retailers that have used this strategy include Wal-Mart (Asda in the United Kingdom), Argos and Superdrug; Dell Computers is another example, as is Ryanair (Chapter 1 case).

A cost leadership strategy is one in which a firm uses low price as the main competitive weapon.

Differentiation

A differentiation strategy is seen when a company offers a service that is distinct from its competitors, and which customers value. It is 'something unique beyond simply offering a low price' (Porter, 1985) that allows firms to charge a high price or retain customer loyalty. Chatterjee (2005) shows the strategic benefits of identifying very clearly

Differentiation strategy consists of offering a product or service that is perceived as unique or distinctive on a basis other than price.

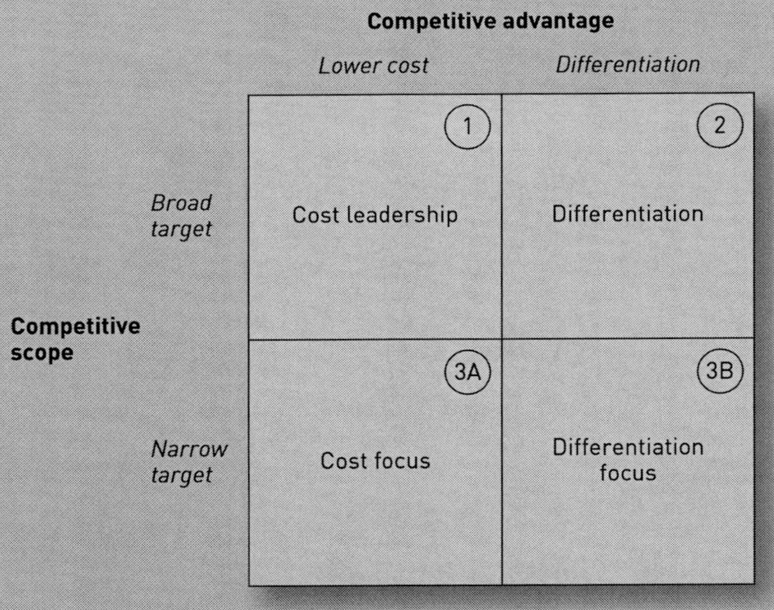

Competitive advantage

	Lower cost	*Differentiation*
Broad target	① Cost leadership	② Differentiation
Narrow target	③A Cost focus	③B Differentiation focus

Competitive scope

Source: Porter (1985), copyright © 1985 Michael E Porter, reprinted with permission of The Free Press, a division of Simon & Schuster.

Figure 8.6

Generic competitive strategies

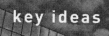

key ideas The experience curve

An important feature of cost leadership is the effect of the experience curve, in which the unit cost of manufacturing a product or delivering a service falls as experience increases. In the same way that a person learning to knit or play the piano improves with practice, so 'the unit cost of value added to a standard product declines by a constant percentage (typically 20–30 per cent) each time cumulative output doubles' (Grant, 2002). This allows firms to set initial low selling prices in the knowledge that margins will increase as output grows and costs fall. The rate of travel down the cost experience curve is a crucial aspect of staying ahead of the competition in an undifferentiated market and underlines the importance of market share – if high volumes are not sold, the cost advantage is lost. Examples of products where costs have fallen as volumes have risen are semiconductors, watches, cars and online reservations.

the outcomes that customers value, and Sharp and Dawes (2001) contrast companies' methods of differentiation:

- Nokia achieves differentiation through the individual design of its product.
- Sony achieves it by offering superior reliability, service and technology.
- BMW differentiates by stressing a distinctive product/service image.
- Coca-Cola differentiates by building a widely recognised brand.

The form of differentiation varies. In construction equipment durability, spare parts availability and service will feature in a differentiation strategy, while in cosmetics differentiation is based on images of sophistication, exclusivity and eternal youth. Cities compete by stressing differentiation in areas such as cultural facilities, available land or good transport links.

Focus

A focus strategy
is when a company
competes by targeting
very specific segments of
the market.

A focus strategy involves targeting a narrow market segment, either by consumer group (teenagers, over-60s, doctors) or geography. The two variants – cost focus and differentiation focus – are simply narrow applications of the broad strategies. Examples include:

- Saga offers travel and insurance for those over 50.
- Rolls-Royce offers luxury transport to the wealthy.
- NFU Mutual offers insurance for farmers, Female Direct offers motor insurance for women.
- Co-operative Financial Services appeals to consumers with social concerns.

management in practice British Airways' differentiation strategy www.ba.com

After several years of poor performance British Airways has been renewing its strategy. It is seeking to differentiate itself from other airlines by focusing on business travellers rather than those travelling in economy class. Business passengers pay the full fare for their ticket, and expect a high-quality service. BA gradually reduced the number of seats available in economy class, and took fewer low-cost passengers travelling on connecting flights with other airlines. It sold GO (its low-cost airline) in early 2001, as this was not consistent with the new strategy. Through this clear differentiated strategy, BA has lost passenger volume to the low-cost airlines but sustains the higher-paying business passenger, who needs flexibility.

At the same time, BA has cut many fares on its website, even though they still provide some frills. In its desire to satisfy multiple segments, the company is essentially hyper-differentiating, a situation in which competitive companies must respond more rapidly to customers' changing demands.

Activity 8.3   Critical reflection on strategy

- Select two companies you are familiar with, and in each case gather evidence to help you decide which generic strategy they are following.
- Then consider what features you would expect to see if the company decided to follow the opposite strategy.

Porter initially suggested that firms had to choose between cost leadership and differentiation. Many disagreed, observing how companies often appeared to follow both strategies simultaneously. By controlling costs better than competitors, companies can reinvest the savings in features that differentiate them. Porter (1994) later clarified his view:

> Every strategy must consider both relative cost and relative differentiation ... a company cannot completely ignore quality and differentiation in the pursuit of cost advantage, and vice versa ... Progress can be made against both types of advantage simultaneously. (p. 271)

However, he notes that there are trade-offs between the two and that companies should 'maintain a clear commitment to superiority in one of them'.

Is the Porter model valid in the Internet age?

key ideas

Kim *et al.* (2004) asked whether strategy perspectives developed when the competitive landscape contained only offline firms are still relevant in the Internet age. The Internet allows firms to overcome barriers of time and distance, to serve large audiences more efficiently while also targeting groups with specific needs, and to reduce many operating costs. However Kim *et al.* also noted that some things stay the same – especially the need to invest in a clear and viable strategy. Their analysis led them to propose that the generic strategies of differentiation and cost leadership still apply to online businesses. However the strategy of focus will not be as viable as it has been for offline firms: since the Internet enables companies to reach both large and tightly defined audiences very cheaply, focus will be a competitive imperative rather than an option.

They also proposed a third approach – an 'integrated strategy' – that combines features of cost leadership and differentiation, and which will be superior to both. They suggested that online strategies could form a continuum, as shown in Figure 8.7.

Source: Kim *et al.* (2004).

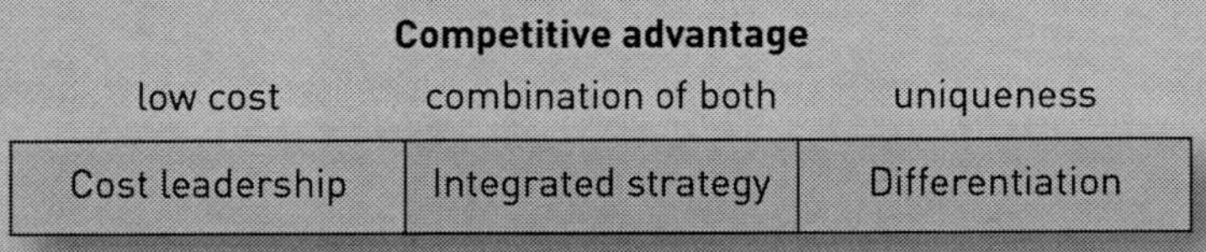

	Competitive advantage	
low cost	combination of both	uniqueness
Cost leadership	Integrated strategy	Differentiation

Figure 8.7 E-business competitive strategy as a continuum
Source: Kim *et al.* (2004).

Functional level strategy

Business level strategies need the support of suitable functional level strategies – Chapters 9 (Marketing) and 11 (Human Resources) give examples.

8.5   Alternative ways to deliver strategy

Corporate and business strategies can be delivered by internal development, acquisition or alliance – or a combination.

Internal development

The organisation delivers the strategy by expanding or redeploying relevant resources that it has or can employ. This enables managers to retain control of all aspects of the development of new products or services – especially where (such as at Linn Products) the product has technologically advanced features. Microsoft develops its Windows operating system in-house.

Public sector organisations typically favour internal development, traditionally providing services through staff whom they employ directly. Changes in the wider political agenda have meant that these are often required to compete with external providers, while some – such as France Telecom, Deutsche Post or the UK Stationery Office – have been partially or wholly sold to private investors.

Merger and acquisition

One firm merging with, or acquiring, another allows rapid entry into new product or market areas and is a quick way to build market share. It is also used where the acquiring company can use the other company's products to offer new services or enter new markets. Companies such as Microsoft and Cisco Systems frequently buy small, entrepreneurial companies and incorporate their products within the acquiring company's range. A company might be taken over for its expertise in research or its knowledge of a local market. Financial motives are often strong, particularly where the merger leads to cost-cutting. When The Royal Bank of Scotland acquired NatWest it achieved major economies by merging the two companies' computer systems. Other mergers extend the range of activities. Vodafone made several large acquisitions in its quest to become the world's largest mobile phone company.

Mergers and acquisitions frequently fail, destroying rather than adding value. When Sir Roy Gardner took over as chairman of Compass (a UK catering company) at which profits and the share price had fallen rapidly, he was critical of the previous management:

> [They] concentrated far too much on growing the business through acquisition. They should have stopped and made sure [that] what they had acquired delivered the expected results. Compass was being run by its divisional managers, which resulted in a total lack of consistency. (*Financial Times*, 19 January 2007, p. 19)

Joint developments and alliances

Organisations sometimes turn to partners to cooperate in developing products or services. Arrangements vary from highly formal contractual relationships to looser forms of cooperation but there are usually advantages to be gained by both parties. One attraction of this method is that it limits risk. For example, the large UK constructor John Laing announced an infrastructure joint venture in July 2004 with the Commonwealth Bank of Australia. It is a 50:50 joint venture with the bank to invest in UK hospital and European road projects, which allows both parties to limit the risk and to operate in areas in which they are strong. Rather than simply borrow from the bank, Laing shares the risk (and the reward) with the bank.

GSK's drug development strategy   www.gsk.com

management in practice

Half of the new drug discovery projects at GlaxoSmithKline may be undertaken by external partners by the turn of the decade as part of a radical overhaul designed to improve the pipeline of new drugs at the group. The research and development will be coordinated by GSK's Centre of Excellence for External Drug Discovery (CEEDD) which the company created in 2005 to boost innovation. The company's research director estimated that between one-quarter to one-third of GSK's existing research pipeline of new drugs already involved work conducted with external partners and a growing role would be played by the CEEDD, managing a 'virtual' portfolio of research run by such companies: 'In the future we are going to have many more external projects.'

Source: *Financial Times*, 31 May 2006, p. 22.

A second reason for joint ventures (JVs) is to learn about new technologies or markets. Alliances also arise where governments want to keep sensitive sectors, such as aerospace, defence and aviation, under national control. Airbus, which competes with Boeing in aircraft manufacture, was originally a JV between French, German, British and Spanish manufacturers. Alliances – such as the Star Alliance led by United Airlines of the United States and Lufthansa of Germany – are also common in the airline industry, where companies share revenues and costs over certain routes. As governments often prevent foreign ownership, such alliances avoid that barrier.

Other forms of joint development include franchising (common in many retailing activities – M&S has 198 franchised stores overseas), licensing and long-term collaboration between manufacturers and their suppliers.

Alliances and partnership working have also become commonplace in the public sector. In many cities alliances or partnerships have been created between major public bodies, business and community interests. Their main purpose is to foster a coherent approach to planning and delivering services. Public bodies often act as service commissioners rather than as direct providers, developing partnerships with organisations to deliver services on their behalf.

8.6   Perspectives on the strategy process

While most managers recognise the steps outlined earlier as the basic content of strategic planning there are differing views on how the *process* actually works in practice. Some views are *prescriptive* in that they seek to explain how management *should* make strategy, while others are *descriptive* in that they try to set out how management *does* make strategy. Table 8.4 shows three perspectives.

Table 8.4 Alternative perspectives on the strategy process

	Planning	Learning	Political
Approach	Prescriptive; assumes pure rationality	Descriptive; based on bounded rationality	Descriptive; based on bounded rationality
Content	Extensive use of analytical tools and techniques; emphasis on forecasting; extensive search for alternative options, each evaluated in detail	More limited use of tools and techniques and more limited search for options: time and resources don't permit	As learning view, but also some objectives and options disregarded as politically unacceptable
Nature of process	Formalised, systematic, analytical; top down – centralised planning teams	Adaptive, learning by doing; bottom up and top down	Characterised by bargaining and negotiation; use of power to impose objectives and strategies; top down and bottom up
Outcomes	Everything planned in advance; plans assumed to be achieved as set out	Plans are made but not all are 'realised'; some strategies are not planned but emerge in course of 'doing'	Plans are made but often couched in ambiguous terms to secure agreement; need interpretation in course of implementation; outcomes reflect compromises
Context/ environment	Stable environment; assumption that future can be predicted; if complex, use of more sophisticated tools	Complex, dynamic, future unpredictable	Stable or dynamic, but complex; stakeholders have diverging values, objectives and solutions

Planning view

The 'planning view' is prescriptive and based on a belief that the complexity of strategic decisions requires an explicit and formalised approach to guide management through the process. In the 1960s and 1970s a wide literature, most notably the work of Ansoff (1965), espoused this structured approach. At this time, strategy was seen as a systematic process, following a prescribed sequence of steps and making extensive use of analytical tools and techniques. This was the 'one best way' to develop strategy that, if followed, was believed almost to guarantee corporate success. Implicit in this view are assumptions that people behave rationally and that events and facts can be expressed or observed objectively. Those who challenge assumptions of rationality and objectivity advocate two possible alternative views – the learning and the political (Brews and Hunt, 1999).

Learning view

The learning view sees strategy as an *emergent* or adaptive process. Mintzberg (1994a, b) regards formal strategic planning as a system developed during a period of stability, and designed mainly for centralised bureaucracies typical of manufacturing industry. This style of planning may be appropriate for them, but not for businesses in more rapidly changing sectors: they require a more flexible approach.

Emergent strategies are those that result from actions taken one by one which converge in time in some sort of consistency or pattern.

Mintzberg (1994a) distinguished between intended and **emergent strategy** (see Figure 8.8). He acknowledges the validity of strategy as a plan, setting out intended courses of action, and recognises that some deliberate intentions may be realised. But he challenges managers to review how closely their realised strategies fit the original intention. As well as realising some intended strategies, it is also likely that some plans were not implemented (unrealised strategies) and that others which he describes as 'emergent strategies' were not expressly intended. They resulted from 'actions taken one by one, which converged in time in some sort of consistency or pattern' (p. 25).

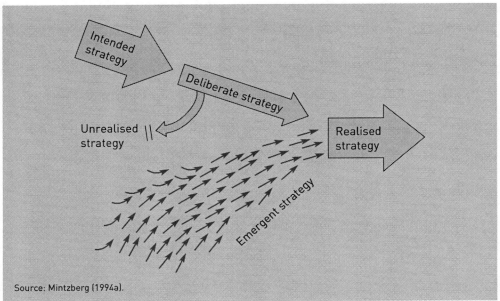

Source: Mintzberg (1994a).

Figure 8.8

Forms of strategy

A flexible approach to strategy is one which recognises that 'the real world inevitably involves some thinking ahead of time as well as some adaptation en route' (Mintzberg, 1994a, p. 26). The essence of the learning view is this process of adaptation, the ability to react to unexpected events, to exploit or experiment with new ideas 'on the ground'. Mintzberg gives the example of a salesperson coming up with the idea of selling an existing product to some new customers. Soon all the other salespeople begin to do the same, and 'one day, months later, management discovers that the company has entered a new market' (p. 26). This was not planned but learned, collectively, during implementation.

management in practice — Emergent strategy at IKEA

Barthélemy (2006) offers an insight into the strategy process at IKEA (Chapter 15 case). Their strategy has clearly been highly successful, but how did it come about? A close examination of the company's history shows that many of the specifics of the strategy were not brought about through a process of deliberate formulation followed by implementation:

> Instead, the founder, Ingvar Kamprad started with a very general vision. IKEA's specific strategy then emerged as he both proactively developed a viable course of action and reacted to unfolding circumstances. (p. 81)

Examples include:

- The decision to sell furniture was an adaptation to the market, not a deliberate strategy – furniture was initially a small part of the retail business, but was so successful that he soon dropped all other products.
- The flat-pack method which symbolises the group was introduced to reduce insurance claims on the mail order business – its true potential only became clear when the company started opening stores, and realised that customers valued this type of product.
- The company only began to design its own furniture because other retailers put pressure on established furniture companies not to sell to IKEA.

Source: Barthélemy (2006).

Political view

Strategy as an emergent process has much in common with political perspectives, since both draw on the concepts of bounded rationality and satisficing behaviour (Chapter 7). While the learning view reflects the logic that 'prior thought can never specify all subsequent action' (Majone and Wildavsky in Mintzberg, 1994a, p. 289), the political view adds dimensions of power, conflict and ambiguity.

Drawing on his experiences in the public policy sphere, Lindblom (1959) was an early proponent of the political view (see also Chapter 7). He drew attention to the way value judgements influence policy and to the conflicting interests of stakeholders that frustrate attempts to agree objectives or strategies to achieve them. He concluded that strategic management is not a scientific, comprehensive or rational process, but an iterative, incremental process, characterised by restricted analysis and bargaining between the players or stakeholders involved. Lindblom labelled this the method of 'successive limited comparisons' whereby 'new' strategy is made by marginal adjustments to existing strategy: 'Policy is not made once and for all; it is made and remade endlessly ... [through] ... a process of successive approximation to some desired objectives.' It is not a comprehensive, objective process but a limited comparison of options, restricted to those that are politically acceptable and possible to implement.

Activity 8.4 Reviewing mission statements

Refer back to the examples of mission statements earlier in the chapter. Do you consider any of these stated intentions to be unclear or vague? If so, consider why they might have been expressed in this way.

Both the learning and the political views of strategy oppose the rigid planning view of strategy, but ultimately accept that a structured approach to strategy has its place: 'Too much planning may lead us to chaos, but so too would too little, and more directly' (Mintzberg, 1994a, p. 416). The planning style of the 1960s seemed to suit the relative stability that characterised the period. The highly competitive, increasingly global and fast-moving markets that characterise the present time may be better matched by a learning, adaptive or even 'real-time strategy' (Taylor, 1997).

8.7 Current themes and issues

Performance

Several studies have claimed to show that strategic planning improves company performance, though a review of research by Greenley (1986) was more sceptical, concluding that the evidence of a link between planning and performance was at best inconclusive. Pfeffer and Sutton (2006b) suggest that strategic planning can be valuable in providing a focus for a business and its staff, helping them to set priorities and allocate resources – provided it is done intelligently. Strategy is typically seen as an activity of senior managers and their advisers, with details of implementation left to those lower in the hierarchy:

the view that strategy setting is top management's central activity remains dominant. Because of the obvious importance of focus and the need to optimize the allocation of scarce resources, it became almost axiomatic that strategy was the most important single cause of a firm's success. (Pfeffer and Sutton, 2006b, p. 138)

In view of the inconclusive evidence, they advocate supplementing top down approaches with more flexible, responsive methods. While some top down planning is valuable, there are other ways of ensuring that effort is focused and scarce resources are allocated productively. These include:

- ensuring that managers listen to customers and employees, and act on what they say;
- not confusing implementation problems with the need to change strategy;
- expressing strategies in simple, actionable terms;
- balancing attention to strategy with attention to the details of implementation:

    too many companies overemphasize strategy which detracts time, resources and focus from the less glamorous and gritty details of implementation and undermines adaptation to shifting conditions. (2006, p. 156)

Responsibility

Issues of corporate responsibility arise in many aspects of management, and managers debate how these relate to strategy. Chapter 5 contrasted the 'Friedmanite' and 'stakeholder' perspectives – the former arguing that the business leaders should focus on the financial interests of shareholders, while the latter believe that managers have responsibilities to a wider constituency. Claims for and against the idea that corporations should act responsibly often reflect deeply held moral and ethical principles, and this makes it a challenge to relate them to a company's strategic decisions. A perspective that can help to clarify the issue was suggested by Vogel (2005), who concludes that while advocates of corporate responsibility are genuinely motivated by a commitment to social goals, CR is only sustainable if 'virtue pays off'. Responsible action is both made possible and constrained by market forces.

Virtuous behaviour can make business sense for some firms in some areas in some circumstances, but does not in itself ensure commercial success. Companies that base their strategy on acting responsibly may be commercially successful, but equally they may fail – responsible behaviour carries the same risks as any other kind of business behaviour. While some consumers or investors will give their business to companies that appear to be acting responsibly, others will not. Some customers place a higher priority on price, appearance or any other feature than they do on whether goods are produced and delivered in a sustainable way. As Vogel (2005) observes: 'There *is* a place in the market economy for responsible firms. But there is also a large place for their less responsible competitors' (p. 3).

While some companies can benefit from a strategy based on acting responsibly, market forces alone cannot prevent others from having a less responsible strategy, and profiting from doing so.

Internationalisation

As the business world becomes ever more international, companies inevitably face difficult strategic choices about the extent to which they develop an international presence, and the way in which they develop their international strategy. The nature of the challenge is shown by the fact that while many companies have done very well from international expansions, many overseas ventures fail, destroying value rather than creating it.

Chapter 4 outlined the nature of the challenges faced as companies respond to what they perceive to be international opportunities. They need, for example, to deal with complex structural and logistical issues when products are made and sold in several countries, ensure that there are adequate links between research, marketing and production to speed the introduction of new products, and facilitate the rapid transfer of knowledge and ideas between the national components of the business. These are complex enough issues in themselves, but the extra dimension is that solutions which work in one national context may not work as well in another. Differences in national culture mean that people will respond in perhaps an unexpected way to strategies and plans, especially if these are perceived in some way to be inconsistent with the local culture (as the examples cited in Chapter 4 of Coca-Cola in India or Egg in France testify).

The content of an international strategy will be shaped by the process of its production – and the extent to which different players in the global enterprise take part in it.

Summary

1 **Explain the significance of strategic management to all organisations**
   - Strategy is about the survival of the enterprise; the strategy process sets an overall direction with information about the external environment and internal capabilities. Defining the purposes of the organisation helps to guide the choice and implementation of strategy.

2 **Describe the main steps in the strategic management process**
   - Figure 8.1 identified the steps of identifying mission and goals, external and internal analysis, formulating, implementing and evaluating strategy.

3 **Use the product/market matrix to compare corporate level strategies**
   - Strategy can focus on existing or new products, and existing or new markets. This gives four broad directions, with options in each – such as market penetration, product development, market development or diversification.

4 **Use the concept of generic strategies to compare business level strategies**
   - Key strategic choices are those of cost leader, differentiation or a focus on a narrow segment of the market.

5 **Give examples of alternative methods of delivering a strategy**
   - Strategy can be delivered by internal (sometimes called organic) development by rearranging the way resources are deployed. Alternatives include acquiring or merging with another company, or by forming alliances and joint ventures.

6 **Compare planning, learning and political perspectives on strategy**
   - The planning approach is appropriate in stable and predictable environments; while the emergent approach more accurately describes the process in volatile environments, since strategy rarely unfolds as intended in complex, changing and ambiguous situations. A political perspective may be a more accurate way of representing the process when it involves the interests of powerful stakeholders. It is rarely an objectively rational activity, implying that strategy models are not prescriptive but rather frameworks to guide managers.

Review questions

1 Distinguish between a corporate and an operating strategy.

2 In what ways does the concept of competitive advantage apply to for-profit organisations, non-profits, cities and countries?

3 Describe the main elements in the strategy process in your own terms.

4 Discuss with a manager from an organisation how his or her organisation developed its present strategy. Compare this practice with that set out in the model. What conclusions do you draw from that comparison?

5 Compare the strategies of Marks & Spencer and The Body Shop, and list any similarities and differences.

6 What are the main steps to take in analysing the organisation's environment? Why is it necessary to do this?

7 Can you describe clearly each of the stages in value chain analysis and illustrate them with an example? Why is the model useful to management?

8 The chapter described three generic strategies that organisations can follow. Give examples of three companies each following one of these strategies.

9 Give examples of company strategies corresponding to each box in the product/market matrix.

Concluding critical reflection

Think about the way your company, or one with which you are familiar, approaches issues of strategy. Review the material in the chapter, and perhaps visit some of the websites identified. Then make notes on these questions:

● What examples of the issues discussed in this chapter are currently relevant to your company – such as whether to follow a differentiation or focus strategy, or the balance between planning and learning?

● In responding to these issues, what **assumptions** about the strategy process appear to have guided what people have done? To what extent do these seem to fit the environmental forces as you see them? Do they appear to stress the planning or the learning perspectives on strategy?

● What factors such as the history or current **context** of the company appear to have influenced the prevailing view? Is the history of the company constraining attempts to move in new directions? How well are stakeholders served by the present strategy – how would they benefit from a significantly different one?

● Have people put forward **alternative** strategies, or alternative ways of developing strategy, based on evidence about other companies? If you could find such evidence, how may it affect company practice?

● What limitations can you see in any of the ideas presented here? For example, does Porter's value chain adequately capture the variable most relevant in your business, or are there other features you would include? What limitations are there in the way strategy is formed in an organisation with which you are familiar?

Further reading

Johnson, G., Scholes, K. and Whittington, R. (2006), *Exploring Corporate Strategy* (7th edn.), Financial Times/Prentice Hall, Harlow.

> The best-selling European text on corporate strategy. Although more detailed than required at introductory level, a number of sections usefully build on this chapter.

Smith, R.J. (1995), *Strategic Management and Planning in the Public Sector* (2nd edn), Longman/Civil Service College, Harlow.

> Covers the main elements in the strategic planning process and explains, with the use of examples, some tools of strategic analysis in addition to those covered in this chapter. It also contains useful chapters on definitions and terminology, and on options analysis.

Kay, J. (1996), *The Business of Economics*, Oxford University Press, Oxford.

> Presents a readable account of competitive strategy written from an economic perspective, illustrated by a wide range of European and other international examples.

Mintzberg, H., Ahlstrand, B. and Lampel J. (1998), *Strategy Safari*, Prentice Hall Europe, Hemel Hempstead.

> Excellent discussion of the process of strategy-making from various academic and practical perspectives.

Moore, J.I. (2001), *Writers on Strategy and Strategic Management* (2nd edn), Penguin, London.

> Summarises the work of the major contributors to the fields of strategy and strategic management – Part One contains a useful overview of the work of the 'movers and shakers', including Ansoff, Porter and Mintzberg.

Greenley, G.E. (1986), 'Does strategic planning improve company performance?', *Long Range Planning*, vol. 19, no. 2, pp. 101–109.

> Valuable study that shows the benefits of a sceptical view towards claims about the planning–performance link, and also a good example of a systematic literature analysis.

Cummings, S. and Angwin, D. (2004), 'The future shape of strategy: lemmings or chimera?', *Academy of Management Executive*, vol. 18, no. 2, pp. 21–36.

> Based on research amongst executives in Europe and Australasia, this article develops an approach to strategy formulation that takes account of the current need to manage multiple customer groups in complex environments.

Weblinks

These websites have appeared in the chapter:

www.marksandspencer.com
www.baesystems.com
www.pg.com
www.nestle.com
www.linn.co.uk
www.ikea.com
www.unilever.com
www.rspb.org.uk
www.hefce.ac.uk
www.nokia.com
www.ba.com
www.gsk.com

Visit two of the business sites in the list, or any other company that interests you, and navigate to the pages dealing with news or investor relations.

● What are the main strategic issues the companies seem to be facing?
● What information can you find about their policies?

Annotated weblinks, multiple choice questions and other useful resources can be found on www.pearsoned.co.uk/boddy

Shareholders and Shareholder Activism

If a company is poorly governed, the effect is felt by shareholders through a loss in value of the shares they own. What can shareholders do to improve corporate governance or change the actions of managers? Unfortunately, in terms of direct action, not much. However, shareholders are not entirely powerless. There are a number of indirect actions that can affect corporate governance. At the company's annual meeting, shareholders can vote to replace ineffective directors and shareholders can make proposals to change the way the firm is governed. And, of course, shareholders also have legal rights they can pursue if management or the board is looting the company for personal advantage. Shareholders can bring a lawsuit against directors and/or officers to recover damages or force them to comply with the law.

When shareholders try to change the way the corporation is run, the actions are referred to as "shareholder activism." While the list of corporate governance control actions by shareholders seems impressive at first, in practice, shareholders rarely have much success influencing corporate governance. One reason is that it is costly to be a monitor. If you own a small amount of stock in a company, the benefit to your personal wealth from improving this stock's performance is much smaller than the cost of forcing a change. Hence, only large shareholders typically find it worthwhile to be a shareholder activist. The other reason shareholder activism is not successful is that the rules allowing such activism are stacked in favor of management and the board. As we will discuss in the following text, winning a proxy fight to change directors or getting a shareholder proposal passed at the annual meeting are both low probability events. Nonetheless, there are always poorly performing or incompetent managers, which means there are always disgruntled shareholders who decide to become activists. And if enough shareholders try to change corporate governance, some will have an effect. Hence, shareholder activism remains an important part of corporate governance.

A high profile example of shareholder activism is found in the recent fallout after Microsoft failed in its bid to acquire Yahoo! After spurning a merger proposed by Microsoft at a price of $31 per share in February 2008, Yahoo!'s stock price slid throughout the year until it dropped below $10 at one point. This extreme decrease in price was a serious loss in value for Yahoo! shareholders who would have been much wealthier if the Yahoo! board accepted Microsoft's offer. The actions of disgruntled shareholders included all the responses discussed in the preceding text: one large shareholder, Carl Icahn, nominated replacement directors for the entire Yahoo! board and started a campaign to build support among shareholders; another shareholder proposed at the shareholder meeting that management bonuses be more tightly tied to performance to give management an incentive to pull Yahoo! out of its slump; and numerous lawsuits were filed by other shareholders against officers and directors seeking to punish those whose decisions destroyed shareholder value.

In the following text, we discuss the incentives of small and large shareholders to become activists, and the types of activism: shareholder proposals, director election contests, and lawsuits. The details of the Microsoft-Yahoo! failed merger are presented throughout to show a high-profile example of shareholder activism in action.

WHAT IS SHAREHOLDER ACTIVISM?

There is no formal definition of shareholder activism. Loosely speaking, any time shareholders express their opinions to try to affect or to influence a firm they are being activist shareholders. Shareholders who submit proposals to be voted on at annual shareholder meetings could certainly be considered an activist. Even writing a letter to management regarding some aspect of the firm's operations or social policies could be considered investor activism. We discuss the activism by three kinds of shareholders: individual shareholders, large shareholders (defined as the owner of a large portion of a firm's shares), and institutional shareholders. Note that these shareholder types are not mutually exclusive. Either an individual or institutional investor can be a large shareholder.

Activism by Individual Shareholders

An individual investor with only a modest number of shares is able to attend shareholder meetings, submit proposals to be voted by at those meetings and vote at those meetings. Lewis Gilbert is generally credited with being the first individual shareholder activist.[1] In 1932, as the owner of 10 shares of New York's Consolidated Gas Company, he attended its annual meeting. While at the meeting, he was surprised and appalled that he was not given a chance to ask questions. After all, he was a part-owner (albeit a small one) of the firm. Subsequently,

Gilbert and his brother pushed for reform and, in 1942, the SEC created a rule to allow shareholders to submit proposals that could be put to a vote.

Lee Greenwood is an activist shareholder well-known to General Mills management. Greenwood once simply suggested that Wheaties® should appear on airlines and in hotels.[2] Among individual shareholder activists, Evelyn Y. Davis is perhaps the most well-known and has been featured in *People* magazine.[3] As the modest shareholder of about 120 firms, Davis attends about 40 shareholder meetings each year. What does she do at these meetings? As everyone from journalists to executives seems to put it, she "raises hell." Davis has berated executives for everything from questionable merger decisions to the enormous size of their pay. Most individual shareholder activists use less dramatic methods. However, enough people like Evelyn Y. Davis vigorously and frequently make themselves heard to have been deemed "corporate gadflies."

EXAMPLE 7.1 **Individual Investors in Action**

During 2000, the stock price of Computer Associates (CA) had dropped from a $70 high in January to about $30 in September. In the following year, Sam Wyly sponsored a proposal to unseat four CA board members.[4] After a highly publicized and expensive campaign, Wyly's proposal was defeated, primarily because it also sought to unseat the firm's cofounder and board chairman, Charles Wang. This example does not mean, however, that proposals, and even defeats, are fruitless or that shareholders should give up. Robert A. G. Monks spent $250,000 to run for a board seat at Sears in 1991. His effort resulted in defeat but the publicity eventually caused Sears to make massive changes on its own.[5]

Proposals do sometimes gain majority support. John Chevedden sponsored a proposal in 2001 to change the way board members are elected at Airborne Freight and he gained the support of 71 percent of the voting shareholders.[6] During that same year, Guy Adams beat tremendous odds with his bid for a board seat. As the owner of 1,100 shares of Lone Star restaurant stock, or 0.005 percent of the company, he was disgruntled because his stock had plummeted in value while the CEO's income rose. Consequently Adams ran for a board seat, one held by the restaurant CEO Jamie B. Coulter. Despite the fact that Adams had never before served on a corporate board and had no restaurant experience, Adams actually won. What does he plan to do with his newfound authority and power? He says he will be a watchdog for other Lone Star investors.[7]

Monitoring by Large Shareholders

Is it good for firms to have a large shareholder? Anecdotally, the answer seems to be "yes" for shareholders but "maybe not" for managers. For example, for many years Kirk Kerkorian was the largest shareholder of Chrysler and because of his large vested interest in that company he battled with former Chrysler chairman Robert Eaton for years over how the firm should be run.[8] Eaton probably felt he had to listen to Kerkorian as Kerkorian could have probably influenced Eaton's salary and even job security. For example, in 1996, Kerkorian was able to force Chrysler to disburse much of its cash holdings to shareholders in the form of stock repurchases or dividends. Chrysler's minority shareholders benefited from having a fellow shareholder who was active and influential. However, Kerkorian was both active and influential probably because he was a large shareholder.

Some managers of firms can also be one of its large shareholders. For example, Bill Gates owns over 8 percent of Microsoft Corporation, which probably explains why he seems to have such a strong vested interest in Microsoft's growth and financial success. Microsoft's minority shareholders directly benefit from Gates's shared interest to enhance the value of Microsoft shares. Note that a key difference between Gates being a large owner and Kerkorian being a large owner is that Gates is actually both a manager and an owner of Microsoft, while Kerkorian is simply an owner. So in the case of Microsoft, a person whose wealth is significantly tied to a firm is also directly responsible for running the firm. This duality minimizes conflict of interest problems between owners and managers (note also that as a top manager, Gates can also monitor his fellow managers). In the case of Chrysler and Kerkorian, the existence of a large outside shareholder seemed to exacerbate the conflicts between management and owners. However, in both cases, minority shareholders seem to come out as clear beneficiaries.

In the academic literature, large shareholders (both manager-owners and just plain owners) are in fact found to be active monitors of the firm.[9] This should not be surprising as they have the incentive *and* the power to be effective monitors. Think of it this way: if two firms are identical in every way but one firm has one or two large shareholders who own 10 percent of the firm each, while the other firm has dispersed shareholders where no single shareholder owns more than 0.1 percent of the firm, then which firm might be better monitored by its shareholders? Probably the firm with the large shareholders. It is also worth pointing out that the latter hypothetical firm probably resembles many real public firms for at least two reasons. Some public firms can be so large that it would take a lot of wealth to own a significant fraction of it. Further, most investors may not wish to forgo the benefits of portfolio diversification by investing so heavily in any one particular firm. So, while large shareholders are useful monitors, there may not be a lot of investors who have the capital or the desire to be a large shareholder.

Institutional Shareholders: An Overview

Institutional shareholders have the potential to exert effective influence. One academic study finds that proposals sponsored by institutional shareholders have a much greater chance of success than ones sponsored by individuals.[10] Fortunately, institutional shareholders, especially public pension funds, have become more active in their oversight of companies. One reason for their increased activity is their increasing ownership stakes. That is, institutional investors are large shareholders. The pie charts in Figures 7.1 and 7.2 show the percentage of U.S. equities held by different shareholder types for the years 1970 and 2002. [11]

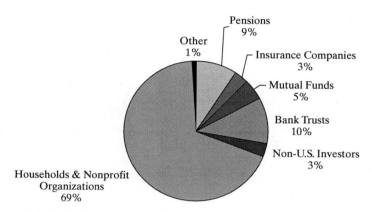

FIGURE 7.1   Shareholders of Stocks by Investor Type in 1970

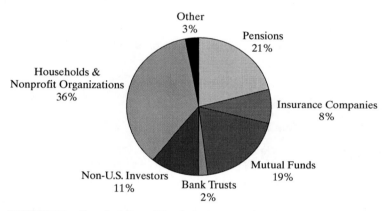

FIGURE 7.2   Shareholders of Stocks by Investor Type in 2002

From these charts, it can be seen that institutions now own a larger per-centage of shares than they did in 1970. The most dramatic increases are with pension funds and mutual funds. In fact, according to anecdotal evidence, we might expect fewer than 100 funds to hold about half of the U.S. stock market in any given year during the 2000s.[12] As such, these funds do have the eco-nomic incentive to be more active, and some actually have been.

Further, note that both pension funds and mutual funds actually man-age money on behalf of many smaller investors. In fact, under the Employee Retirement Income Security Act (ERISA), pension funds have a fiduciary re-sponsibility to their plan participants and beneficiaries. Hence, pension funds in particular are in a position to be active shareholders. They also have fewer restrictions compared to mutual funds on how much of a firm they can own. Pensions can take on a relatively large ownership stake and subsequently en-gage in a long-term active ownership role in the firm. In contrast, mutual funds have to diversify their holdings into at least 20 separate companies or the mutual fund may face additional taxation.[13] Therefore, not surprisingly, public pension funds often lead the way with regard to institutional shareholder activism.

Since the early 1990s, a few public pension funds have taken on a relational investor role with a long-run mindset. These funds have tried to influence the firms they own, mainly through direct communication with management and other shareholders, by identifying poor corporate performers and through pushing for reforms.[14] For example, the public pension fund CalPERS, which has $190 billion in assets and serves 1.4 million members, has targeted Sears and Westinghouse in the past and has pushed for them to divest laggard divisions. Also, during July 2002, the chairmen of 1,754 major U.S. firms all received a letter from the TIAA-CREF, the country's largest pension fund, asking them to account for stock options as an expense.[15] Activism by TIAA-CREF is quite common; they constantly monitor firms and make numerous recommendations for reform.

To help increase their influence, many pension funds belong to a coalition called the Council of Institutional Investors (CII), whose primary objective is to help members take an active role in protecting their assets. Given that pension funds control more than $3 trillion worth of assets, they certainly do have an incentive to come together and exert influence.

TYPES OF SHAREHOLDER ACTIVISM

Shareholder Proposals

The first type of shareholder activism is shareholder proposals. SEC rules permit anyone owning more than $2,000 or 1 percent of a firm's stock on a continuous basis for at least one year to submit a proposal to be considered and voted on at a meeting of the shareholders. With Rule 14a-8, the SEC gives shareholders a method to suggest changes in corporate governance. The shareholder proposal rules require all publicly traded companies to solicit proposals prior to their shareholder meetings. If these proposals meet the requirements of the company's bylaws and are sufficiently related to the company's business, then the company is required to include a summary of the proposal in the proxy statement issued to all shareholders at the annual meeting.[16] At the annual meeting, the shareholder proposal will then be voted on by all shareholders. If it passes, the proposal can be either binding or advisory on management, depending on the nature of the proposal and the rules for each type of proposal.

One prohibition in shareholder proposals is that nominations for the election of directors are not allowed. Instead, directors are nominated under the company's internal bylaws or through an independent campaign seeking the votes of shareholders called a contested election of directors or **proxy fight**. This form of activism is covered in the next section.

More than a thousand shareholder proposals are submitted each year. Many shareholder proposals are governance-oriented, primarily attempting to forge an alignment between shareholder views and managerial actions. For example, proposals may address issues related to antitakeover amendments, shareholder voting rules, or board composition.[17] For example, following the failed Microsoft-Yahoo! merger in 2008, many shareholders of Yahoo! were not happy about how poorly management had run the company. One shareholder, the United Brotherhood of Carpenters Pension Fund, offered a shareholder proposal at the annual meeting that proposed that executives be paid bonuses only for superior performance and not for average performance or simply for serving as executives long enough.[18] If this proposal passed, it would have the effect of tying the incentive of management more closely to successful results for Yahoo!. At the 2008 annual meeting, the proposal, identified as Proposal No. 3, was rejected by voters by a 2-1 margin. Why didn't more shareholders vote for something that would apparently be helpful to the company? As will be discussed in more detail in the following text, management usually resists shareholder amendments quite strongly and the mechanics of collecting votes are stacked against shareholder activists.

EXAMPLE 7.2   Fictitious Excerpt of Notice of Pretend Company Shareholder Meeting

Item No. 4

Ms. Gwen Smith, 1234 Main St., South Park, MI 48199, owner of approximately 101 shares of common stock, has given notice that she intends to present for action at the annual meeting the following resolution:

> To be resolved: "That the Board of Directors no longer issue executive stock options, nor allow any current stock options to be repriced or renewed.
>
> REASON: 'The firm appears to be issuing too many stock options. Instead, executives should be compensated with actual stock instead of options. Actual stock may better align management and shareholders. If you AGREE please mark your proxy FOR this resolution.'"

The Board of Directors recommends a vote AGAINST the adoption of this proposal for the following reasons:

Pretend Company has granted stock options for many years and believes it to be a useful incentive compensation tool.

Management endorses the granting of stock options as an incentive to generate long-term stock price appreciation. Eliminating executive options may impair the firm's ability to retain high quality executives and to achieve sustained future growth.

The Board of Directors recommends a vote AGAINST this stockholder proposal, Item No. 4. Proxies solicited by the Board of Directors will be so voted unless stockholders specify a different choice.

Other shareholder proposals are related to social goals such as not dealing with countries that abuse human rights. While it may appear that these proposals are not business related, there is a link in the sense that boycotts are a reality of the business world and there is potentially a large loss in sales if a powerful political group is offended by a company's action. Accordingly, there are frequently shareholder proposals to limit a company's involvement with countries or businesses with offensive policies. Continuing with the Yahoo! example, at the 2008 annual meeting, there were two proposals related to Yahoo!'s involvement with the issue of human rights: Proposal No. 4 requested a corporate policy against cooperating with other countries" requests to censor the Internet; and Proposal No. 5 establishing a Board Committee on Human Rights.[19]

Although shareholder proposals appear to be a useful way to change corporate governance, in practice, most shareholder proposals do not pass, especially those that go against management desires. Typically, management and the board resist shareholder proposals forcefully and the proposals cannot muster enough votes. In the case of Yahoo!'s 2008 shareholder meeting, the Board of Yahoo! recommended voting against all three proposals. Proposal No. 3 earned only 33 percent of votes cast, which was far more than Proposals No. 4 and 5, which earned 5.8 percent and 3.1 percent, respectively.[20] These results are typical of the votes on shareholder proposals, as shareholder activists are usually unsuccessful.

One reason shareholder proposals fail is that it is difficult and expensive for one shareholder to communicate with all other shareholders. This creates an uneven playing field because expense is not a concern for management and the board who can freely spend the company's money in lobbying against shareholder proposals. As an individual shareholder, how much of your own money are you willing to spend in an uphill battle to change governance? Most spend little and hope that the description in the company's proxy statement is enough to convince shareholders to vote in favor of the proposal. Another reason it is hard to win approval of a shareholder proposal is that management collects proxy cards before the meeting that show how shareholders want to vote. These proxy cards give management the authority to act on behalf of the shareholder in voting. If no vote is registered for a proposal, then management can choose how to vote those shares on that proposal. In other words, management controls the votes of the uncommitted shareholders who return their voting proxy but do not take a position on the shareholder proposals.

For both reasons, it is difficult to change governance through submission of shareholder proposals. To successfully win a vote on a proposal, you have to overcome the board's money advantage in lobbying against proposals and you have to collect enough votes to counter management's control of the proxy votes of disinterested shareholders. Nonetheless, proposals are one of the only ways small shareholders can express concern with management actions. So they remain a common feature of a company's annual meeting. Further, if a large shareholder supports a shareholder amendment, it is more likely that money will be spent on lobbying other shareholders and the prospects of passing improve. Later in this chapter, we consider how large shareholders such as institutional investors may be more active monitors of management using shareholder proposals and other techniques.

Contested Election of Directors (Proxy Fights)

Another action shareholder activists can take is to try to replace directors serving on the board. After all, the directors are the shareholders' representatives at the firm, so the directors should be accountable to shareholders and subject to replacement if the company is performing poorly. While it seems like it would be easy for shareholders to replace an ineffective board, the rules of the game are structured to make it quite difficult. As an example, consider again the Microsoft-Yahoo! failed merger. One of the first things disgruntled Yahoo! shareholders tried to do in April 2008 was to replace the board that had rejected the Microsoft offer. One large shareholder, Carl Icahn, took the lead in nominating nine new directors to entirely replace the existing directors. However, after a contentious fight for the votes of shareholders, Icahn gave up the battle and agreed to a compromise solution. The deal added Icahn and two of his nominated directors to an expanded Yahoo! board, while leaving in place eight of the nine directors who rejected Microsoft.[21] In other words, only one director lost his position following a high-profile proxy fight.

The Yahoo! case shocked many because, if ever there was a situation where directors would be replaced, this seemed to be it. Icahn was willing to spend significant resources to campaign for his slate of directors, neutralizing the company's financial advantage. And there were many disgruntled shareholders who wanted a change. However, these forces still had to counter the advantages held by Yahoo! management and the board under the rules for nominating directors.

The first difficulty shareholders have in replacing board members is that the nomination of board members is typically handled by a committee of the current board. This means the current board has the power to pick the candidates who will be voted on by shareholders. If shareholders believe the current board is incompetent, shareholders will probably not like the new director nominees chosen by a committee made up of incompetent board members. Further limiting shareholder choice, there is usually only one nominee for each seat, so the only power an unsatisfied shareholder has is to vote "no" for a director nominee and hope the board picks a better candidate next time.

To counter the board's control of director nominees, two avenues are available to shareholders. First, shareholders can make suggestions to the board as to who to nominate. The rules for making these suggestions differ depending on company bylaws. But there is no guarantee that the nominating committee will agree with the suggestions and the board will probably propose its own directors anyway. The second approach is to go around the board's nominating process and present your choice for director directly to the shareholders. This is called a proxy solicitation, which is governed by a complicated set of SEC rules under Rule 14A.[22] If you start a proxy solicitation, this creates a contested election of directors or, more commonly, a proxy fight. The proxy fight is fairly uncommon action by shareholder activists because of the expense required. The SEC requires a shareholder contesting a director election to make numerous mailings to all shareholders, to file many detailed documents with the SEC and to potentially make payments to the Company for their costs in providing shareholder information and conducing mailings.

In addition to cost, the proxy fight also has an uncertain outcome because management and the board have several advantages. As mentioned in the preceding text in discussing shareholder proposals, the voting rules favor management. Many shareholders return proxies to management that do not check a box for votes or that vote as management requests. This allows management to control the votes of disinterested shareholders who do not invest any time in determining who to vote for. Another issue that benefits management is that institutional investors like pension fund managers will often stick with management because they do not want to gain a reputation of opposing corporate management. In other words, to the extent pension funds primary business is administering the retirement plan of large companies, the pension funds might be afraid that corporate activism would cause managers to choose other pension funds for their employees. This issue is discussed further in the following section on the effectiveness of institutional activism.

In the Yahoo! proxy fight, it appeared several large institutional shareholders were going to side with management. This institutional support, combined with management and board ownership of 10 percent and management's control of the proxy votes from disinterested shareholders, may have been enough to win the fight.[23] Presumably, this is why Icahn agreed to settle for only 3 seats on an 11-seat board, instead of pushing for 9 seats on a 9-seat board. Overall, it was a disappointment to many Yahoo! shareholders that this was the best they could do to unseat a poorly performing board.

Given the difficulty and expense of replacing directors in a proxy fight, the SEC has proposed a rule that may help shareholders increase control. The proposed rule allows large shareholders to use the shareholder proposal rules to change the way directors are nominated in the company by laws.[24] For example, this would allow for shareholders to propose for vote a bylaw provision that required the board to nominate several candidates for each board seat and let shareholders have a real choice. In this way, shareholders could gain more control over the choice of directors without requiring an expensive proxy fight. While this proposed rule would probably help with corporate governance, its status is uncertain because, as of this writing, the rule has not been adopted as a final rule by the SEC more than a year after the required comment period ended. Also, the proposed rule limits the shareholders who can make a proposal to change the bylaws to large shareholders with more than 5 percent of the outstanding shares. So, small shareholders could not benefit directly under this rule. Only after a large shareholder opened up the nominating process would small shareholders potentially increase their control over nominations to the board.

Shareholders Lawsuits

Shareholders who are unhappy with the action of managers or the board can also turn to the legal system seeking relief. Because officers and directors have a fiduciary duty to act in the best interest of the shareholders, misconduct by officers and directors gives shareholders legal grounds to bring a lawsuit. The goal of the lawsuit could be to force the executives to follow company bylaws in the actions they take, or the goal could be to force the offending party to pay the shareholders for the lost value of their stock. The difference between these goals is that one has a direct impact on corporate governance and the other an indirect impact. If you sue only seeking a money judgment, this will not directly affect the governance of the company. Nonetheless, there is some corporate governance effect because it is a real wakeup call for an executive or director when a court orders you to pay shareholders because your misconduct has lowered the value of the stock.

There are two types of lawsuits that shareholders bring. The first is known as a derivative lawsuit, which is a special lawsuit brought in the company's name against the executives and/or directors. The idea behind the derivative lawsuit is that, even though the board is appointed as the agents of shareholders, the shareholders retain the right to step in and enforce the rules of the company if the directors are ignoring them.[25] In other words, if the board is ignoring its responsibility to monitor and punish executives who are involved in misconduct, the shareholders can bring an action on behalf of the company to force the directors and officers to comply with the rules. The shareholders can also force the directors and officers to repay money to the corporation. This lawsuit is called a "derivative" lawsuit because the shareholders are not actually the parties suing. The effect of this distinction is that, any money paid in a settlement of a derivative lawsuit goes to the company only and not to shareholders.

The other type of lawsuit is a direct suit where shareholders themselves file a lawsuit against officers and directors of a company. In a direct suit, the legal argument is that the officers and directors are agents of the shareholders who owe a duty to the shareholders to act in the shareholders best interest. A direct lawsuit typically alleges the officers or directors intentionally took actions that harmed the shareholders. If any amounts are paid under a direct suit, they go into the shareholders' pockets, not the company coffers.

Recent Research

How do derivative lawsuits improve corporate governance? Other than forcing a company to follow its own internal rules, are there any other effects on corporate governance? Recent research has shown that derivative lawsuits can be an effective corporate governance mechanism because they lead to changes in the composition of the board. Professors Ferris, Jandik, Lawless, and Makhija identified 215 derivative lawsuits filed against 174 companies over the period 1982–1999. For each company, they compared the following key variables related to corporate governance at the time the lawsuit was filed and three years after the lawsuit date: board size, percentage of inside directors, percentage of outside directors, chair of board/CEO same person, and board departure rate. To control for changes in the overall economy during the same period, the authors constructed a control sample with one comparable non-sued company chosen for each company that was sued.

The strongest result of the study was a statistically significant decrease in the percentage of inside directors on the board of sued companies three years after the lawsuit (and a corresponding increase in outside directors). As discussed in the board chapter, it typically improves corporate governance to have outsider directors more involved. Hence, the derivative lawsuits appear to improve corporate governance. Another interesting result was that there was

Continued

a statistically significant decrease in the percentage of CEOs who were also board chair. Again, this is typically seen as an improvement in corporate governance because someone other than the CEO controls the board meetings. Overall, these results demonstrate that there were real effects on corporate governance in the firms that were sued three years after the derivative lawsuits were filed.

A different question is why an individual shareholder would pay the costs of bringing a shareholder lawsuit. If you had $10,000 invested in Yahoo! in early 2008, the decrease in value from the Yahoo! board turning down the Microsoft deal was about 20 percent depending on the date used for the calculation. This translates into a loss of $2,000 on your investment, which is not enough to support the high cost of bringing either a derivative or direct lawsuit. Nonetheless, there were at least 10 lawsuits brought against the Yahoo! board and some of its officers. Why would so many shareholders sue? One reason is that they are large shareholders who have a lot of money at stake. If your investment in Yahoo! was $100 million, then the potential to recover $20 million may be enough to support a lawsuit. A more important reason for a direct lawsuit is that there is a provision in federal law that allows for a **class action lawsuit,** which is a type of lawsuit where all shareholders join together in a single lawsuit. Most direct securities lawsuits are of the class action type and even if they are not initially class action, as in the Yahoo! case, a court will frequently combine them into a class action to save on court time of litigating the same suit over and over. At the time of this writing, the Yahoo! lawsuits have been consolidated into a class action (which also allows others to easily join). The effect of the class action lawsuit is that shareholders share the cost of prosecuting the lawsuit.

For both types of lawsuits, however, the biggest reason why shareholders might be willing to bring a costly suit is that, if the shareholders win the lawsuit, the company is required to pay the legal fees of the shareholders. The prospect of recovering attorneys'

fees has led to a situation where there are large law offices that actively look for opportunities to file class action lawsuits or derivative lawsuits. In many cases, the attorneys pay for the case and the shareholders reimburse them only if the case wins. In other words, the shareholders do not pay for the costs of the suit if it loses. This system where attorneys profit from successful shareholder lawsuits has led to changes in securities laws. The Private Securities Litigation Reform Act of 1995 was passed to reduce the number of frivolous lawsuits.[26] But according to the Securities Class Action Clearinghouse at Stanford Law School, there have been a steady stream of class action lawsuits since the new law in 1995.[27] As demonstrated by the examples of poor corporate governance throughout this book, there are apparently always some executives taking actions against shareholder interests—which means that there will always be nonfrivolous issues to sue over.

While it is still open for debate how many lawsuits filed by shareholders are merely attempts by attorneys to earn big fees, there is no question that lawsuits also play a role in corporate governance. If officers and directors are potentially liable to pay shareholders for their losses, this is a real disincentive to take actions that harm shareholders. Hence, there is a role for shareholder lawsuits in deterring opportunistic behavior by managers. One limitation on this power of deterrence should be noted, however. Directors and officers are typically covered by Directors and Officers (D&O) insurance policies and the company also agrees to indemnify officers and directors for payments made to settle lawsuits. This means that most shareholders actually collect from insurance company money and not from the pockets of the offending parties.[28]

Stephen P. Ferris, Tomas Jandik, Robert M. Lawless, and Anil Makhija, "Derivative Lawsuits as a Corporate Governance Mechanism: Empirical Evidence on Board Changes Surrounding Filings," *Journal of Financial and Quantitative Analysis*, 42 (2007): 143–166.

If you are a disgruntled shareholder, how do you decide which type of lawsuit to bring? It depends on whether you are more concerned with fixing the situation at the company or with getting back the lost value of the stock you own. The derivative lawsuit does not benefit shareholders directly, but can be useful to force compliance with company policies. On the other hand, the direct lawsuit is all about collecting money damages to cover the loss in stock value caused by the actions of officers and directors.

DOES INSTITUTIONAL SHAREHOLDER ACTIVISM WORK?

All of the types of shareholder activism described earlier were more likely to be undertaken by large shareholders because they have a greater incentive to take action. This raises the question of whether large shareholders like institutions regularly take advantage of the available actions. Determining whether activism bears positive results is difficult because, more often than not, good subsequent firm performance cannot be directly linked to increased activism. According to one study commissioned by CalPERS, Steven Nesbitt of Wilshire Associates conducted a before and after analysis of 42 firms targeted for reform by CalPERS. After being targeted, the aggregate stock returns of these 42 firms over a five-year period were 52.5 percent higher than the returns of the S&P (Standard & Poor's) 500 Index. Prior to being targeted, these same firms had under-performed the S&P 500 by 66 percent over a five-year period.[29] Michael P. Smith of the Economic Analysis Corporation conducted an independent study of CalPERS' activism and found that the combined gain to CalPERS for their activities related to 34 targeted firms was $19 million during the 1987–1993 period, while the total cost to their monitoring was only $3.5 million.[30] His evidence also suggests that CalPERS' activism works.

However, counter evidence also exists. In one academic study, the authors found that shareholder proposal submission did not lead to any obvious improvements in firm performance, even for those firms where the proposals passed.[31] In a study that examined the effects of targeting by CII, the authors found no subsequent improvement for the targeted firms and little evidence of the efficacy of shareholder activism.[32] Due to the inconsistent evidence, whether activism really changes firms for the better is unknown. Perhaps one of the main problems is that activism has its own set of shortcomings, which we discuss next.

POTENTIAL ROADBLOCKS TO EFFECTIVE SHAREHOLDER ACTIVISM

Mutual funds and pension funds try to earn a high return on their portfolios. However, many active investors have a speculative or short-run view of the stock markets and they make trading and investment decisions based on short-term trends. The short-term view of these investors limits their desire to be activists.

Institutional investors might be interested in good performance for the short term and then subsequently sell the stock to move on to something else. John Bogle makes the same contention; he has been calling on mutual fund managers to engage in more activism but instead he witnesses mutual funds engaging in speculative investing. According to anecdotal evidence, it is not uncommon for equity funds to turn their portfolio over at an annual rate of more than 100 percent.[33] If the equity funds do not like the future prospects of a firm, they simply sell the stock instead of working to change the firm.

Other than the activism of public pension funds, what about private (or corporate) pension funds? Are these groups active? Private pension funds are extremely quiet on the activism front. Jamie Heard, CEO of Institutional Shareholder Services, is not aware of a single corporate pension fund that has become a governance activist.[34] In total, private pension funds own almost 50 percent more assets than public pension funds. As a group they could be a strong monitoring force and exert influence to protect shareholders. However, private fund advisors face a huge conflict of interest problem: Corporate executives hire them to manage pension assets. If these advisors take an aggressive approach with the firm's management, then they will not be retained to manage the assets for very long. Executives probably do not want to see activism by shareholders because it interferes with their activities. Therefore, they would not hire pension fund advisors who are activists. This being the case, private funds usually just go along with the firm's management, even though their fiduciary duty is supposed to be with their beneficiaries, the employees, and retirees. A recent study confirms this. The authors find that mutual funds that manage a firm's 401(k) plans often voted with management.[35] In other words, mutual funds will not bite the hand that feeds them.

The regulatory and political environment may also hinder large institutional shareholders from engaging in activism. Under the Investment Company Act, mutual funds that own more than 10 percent of any one company must face additional regulatory and tax burdens. Half of the mutual fund assets must be vested in at least 20 firms (that is, a firm cannot constitute more than 5 percent of half the fund's portfolio). These ownership restrictions apply to pension funds as well. Specifically, ERISA imposes a rather strict diversification standard. As stated by Bernard S. Black, a Columbia law professor and well-known advocate of shareholder activism, "pension funds are encouraged by law to take diversification to ridiculous extremes."[36]

Why do these restrictions exist? Bernard S. Black and another law professor, Mark J. Roe, have adamantly argued that legal restrictions stand in the way of large investors engaging in the beneficial oversight of corporations.[37] The pair contends that the legal and regulatory environment prohibits or discourages institutional investors from becoming too large, from acting together, and from becoming significant owners. At the same time these investors face tremendous SEC paperwork if they do wish to accumulate a significant stake in a firm, while also facing unfavorable tax ramifications in the process. Meanwhile, only a few laws actually encourage or make it easier for institutions to be effective owners.

To see what shareholder activism by institutions could look like if there were no legal restrictions, consider the case of hedge funds, which are large investment funds that operate outside of most regulations. In a recent study, hedge fund activism over the period 2001–2006 was examined and the authors found that the hedge funds had success or partial success two-thirds of the time when they proposed strategic, operational, and financial remedies for companies in which they were large shareholders.[38]

INTERNATIONAL PERSPECTIVE

The public firms in the United States and in the United Kingdom have the most dispersed ownership structures in the world. This should not be surprising. For an individual investor, it costs a lot of money to own even 1 percent of these large, publicly traded firms. Institutional investors might have enough capital to be significant owners but they have regulatory restrictions preventing them from owning a significant fraction of any one firm.

In many other countries, however, there is greater ownership concentration where large shareholders are more prevalent. The two most common types of large shareholders are family-owners and state-owners. These large shareholders, especially family-owners, actively participate in management. For example, the Li Ka-Shing family owns and controls some of the largest firms in Hong Kong. The Wallenberg family owns and controls some of the largest firms in Sweden (such as ABB).

To own and to control the firm might seem like an optimal governance arrangement, as owner-controllers are unlikely to behave suboptimally and consequently minority (i.e., small) shareholders reap the benefits as well. However, because these owners have to be active in management and give up having diversified portfolios, there is a cost of this ownership structure to the large owners. Further, there is a chance that these family-owners may enjoy some private benefits of control (e.g., perks, large salaries, etc.) at the expense of their other smaller shareholders. That is, someone might have to monitor the family-owners.

In recent years, shareholder activist groups have begun to pop up in countries where family-ownership is prevalent. For example, the specific focus of the People's Solidarity of Participatory Democracy (PSPD), a leading shareholder activist organization that began its activism activities in the late 1990s in Korea, is to target family-owned firms (known as *chaebols*) for reform. Whether or not these shareholder activist groups will be successful remains to be seen.

Finally, it should be mentioned that a poor corporate governance infrastructure might have led to the prevalence of family-ownership and control to begin with. Some countries might not offer shareholders strong shareholder rights. With a poor governance environment, investors may have felt that they had to look out for themselves so they concentrated their wealth and maintained control. Therefore, significant governance reforms, ones that would protect minority shareholder rights, may probably have to be put in place before family-owners are willing to delegate control and diversify their wealth.

Summary

Shareholders have several actions they can take when managers are opportunistic and destroy shareholder value. One option, of course, is to sell their shares and walk away. But if the shareholders want to remain as shareholders and improve the corporate governance of their company their choices are shareholder proposals, proxy fights, and lawsuits. While each of these choices can be useful, they often have low probabilities of success and, even if they are successful, most small investors will not receive enough of a benefit to justify the cost of activism. Institutional investors, on the other hand, are large shareholders, so they may be able to monitor effectively through shareholder activism. In fact, institutional investors, such as pension funds, actually invest on behalf of their plan participants. Therefore, it could be argued that these investors should be activist shareholders.

There are some institutional investors that do earnestly try to engage in shareholder activism.

However, for the most part, most institutions are not active shareholders. This situation may exist because institutional investors face incentive problems, conflict of interest dilemmas, and regulatory constraints. Should we give institutional shareholders more power? Or is there a downside to them having too much ownership and power over U.S. public firms?

Web Info about Shareholder Activism

CalPERS Shareholder Forum
www.calpers-governance.org/forumhome.asp

Council of Institutional Investors (CII)
www.cii.org

Teachers Insurance and Annuity Association College Retirement Equities Fund (TIAA-CREF)
http://www.tiaa-cref.org/about/governance/index.html

Review Questions

1. Compare and contrast the ability of different types of investors to engage in shareholder activism.
2. What can investors do to monitor and influence a company?

3. How successful is investor activism?
4. Describe the roadblocks to effective shareholder activism.

Discussion Questions

1. The text states that perhaps there are some firms that require large shareholders and some that do not. What kinds of firms might belong in each category? Might this contention apply to other monitors? How?
2. Do you think institutional shareholders should be allowed to be larger shareholders of individual firms? Why or why not?
3. Which approach to shareholder activism (shareholder proposals, proxy fights, lawsuits) do you

think is more effective in monitoring managers and improving corporate governance? Can you think of any changes you would make to any of these forms of corporate activism that would make them more effective?
4. In your opinion, do you think shareholder activism works? Why or why not?

Exercises

1. Do some research and describe what is involved in submitting a shareholder proposal.
2. Describe the corporate governance objectives of institutional investor activist CalPERS (or TIAA-CREF).

3. Go to the Council of Institutional Investors Web page (*www.cii.org*). What shareholder initiatives are they following?

4. Pick two firms in the same industry and identify their largest shareholders. If their ownership structure is similar or different, try to identify why this might be. Pick two firms in different industries and identify their largest shareholders. If their ownership structure is similar or different, try to identify why this might be.

5. Do some research and find both types of shareholder lawsuits. Who is suing in each type of lawsuit? What are the allegations against officers and directors and what are the shareholders seeking?

6. Do some research and identify and describe the current regulations that mutual funds and pension funds must adhere to. In particular, discuss regulations that might hinder their ability to be more active shareholders.

Exercises for Non-U.S. Students

1. Who are the largest shareholders in your country? How do they control the firms that they own? Do you think having these large shareholder types (e.g., the family or state) is good or bad for minority shareholders? Explain.

2. Do small individual investors have any significant power in your country? Why or why not? If not, then do you foresee improvements in this regard in the near future? Why or why not?

3. Are pension funds and mutual funds significant shareholders in your country? Why or why not?

4. Is it easy for shareholders to change the directors of companies in your country? Can individual shareholders nominate director candidates to be voted on by all shareholders?

Endnotes

1. See, for example, "Ending the Wall Street Walk," a commentary on the Corporate Governance Web site *www.corpgov.net*.
2. Lee Clifford, "Bring Me the Head of Your Board Chairman!" *Fortune*, October 2, 2000, 252.
3. Richard Jerome, "Evelyn Y. Davis for America's Most Dreaded Corporate Gadfly," *People*, May 20, 1996, 69.
4. David Shook, "Rebel Stockholders are on the Move," *BusinessWeek*, September 6, 2001, *www.businessweek.com/investor/content/sep2001/pi2001096_073.htm*.
5. Robert A.G. Monks and Nell Minow, "Sears Case Study," *www.thecorporatelibrary.com*.
6. David Shook, "Rebel Stockholders are on the Move," *BusinessWeek*, September 6, 2001, *www.businessweek.com/investor/content/sep2001/pi2001096_073.htm*.
7. David Grainger, "Driving a Stake into Lone Star" *Fortune*, August 13, 2001, 32–34.
8. Daneil Mcginn, "Don't Cry for Krik," *NewsWeek*, Feburary 19, 1996, *www.newsweek.com/id/101518/output/print*.
9. Perhaps the most well-known academic studies that discuss the benefits of having large shareholders include Harold Demsetz and Kenneth Lehn, "The Structure of Corporate Ownership: Causes and Consequences," *Journal of Political Economy* 93 (1985): 1155–1177; Andrei Shleifer and Robert Vishny, "Large Shareholders and Corporate Control," *Journal of Political Economy* 94 (1986): 461–488; and Randall Morck, Andrei Shleifer, and Robert Vishny, "Management Ownership and Market Valuation: An Empirical Analysis," *Journal of Financial Economics* 20 (1988): 293–315.
10. Stu Gillan and Laura Starks, "Corporate Governance Proposals and Shareholder Activism: The Role of Institutional Investors," *Journal of Financial Economics* 57 (2000): 275–305.
11. Source: NYSE Fact Book Online, */www.nyxdata.com/factbook*.
12. Marc Gunther, "Investors of the World, Unite!" *Fortune*, June 24, 2002, 78–86.
13. See Internal Revenue Code Section 851(b)(3).
14. "Ending the Wall Street Walk," Corporate Governance Web site, *www.corpgov.net*: Stu Gillan

and Laura Starks, "A Survey of Shareholder Activism," *Contemporary Finance Digest* 2 (1998): 10–34.

15. The letter is available for viewing on the TIAA-CREF Web site, *www.tiaa-cref.org.*

16. The rules for shareholder proposals are found at 17 C.F.R. 240.14a-8.

17. Stu Gillan and Laura Starks, "Corporate Governance Proposals and Shareholder Activism: The Role of Institutional Investors," *Journal of Financial Economics* 57 (2000): 275–305.

18. See Proposal No. 3, Yahoo! Notice of Annual Meeting of Stockholders, Proxy Statement, June 9, 2008.

19. Yahoo! Notice of Annual Meeting of Stockholders, Proxy Statement, June 9, 2008.

20. Yahoo! Announces Results of 2008 Annual Stockholder Meeting, press release, August 1, 2008.

21. Yahoo! Revised Definitive Proxy Statement, July 28, 2008.

22. The rules for proxy solicitation are found at 17 C.F.R. 240.14a.

23. Market Watch, Yahoo Proxy May Come Down to Battle of Big Funds, July 18, 2008.

24. Securities and Exchange Commission, Shareholder Proposals, Proposed Rule, Release No. 34-56160, July 27, 2007.

25. Depending on the applicable state corporation law, there is usually a requirement of showing that the board has failed to act before a derivative lawsuit can be brought. For more information on the details of derivative lawsuits, see *http://en.wikipedia.org/wiki/Derivative_suit.*

26. *http://en.wikipedia.org/wiki/Private_Securities_Litigation_Reform_Act*

27. *http://securities.stanford.edu/index.html*

28. Intentional fraud is typically not covered by either insurance or indemnification by the company, so executives in cases like Enron were required to pay their own funds to shareholders in settlement of lawsuits.

29. Source: "Ending the Wall Street Walk," Corporate Governance Web site, *www.corpgov.net.*

30. Michael P. Smith, "Shareholder Activism by Institutional Investors: Evidence from CalPERS," *Journal of Finance* 51 (1996): 227–252.

31. Jonathan M. Karpoff, Paul H. Malatesta, and Ralph A. Walkling, "Corporate Governance and Shareholder Initiatives: Empirical Evidence," *Journal of Financial Economics* 42 (1996): 365–395.

32. Wei-Ling Song, Samuel H. Szewczyk, and Assem Safieddine, "Does Coordinated Institutional Investor Activism Reverse the Fortunes of Underperforming Firms?" *Journal of Financial and Quantitative Analysis* 38 (2003): 317–336.

33. Remarks by John C. Bogle before the New York Society of Security Analysts on February 14, 2002. For the text of the speech, go to *www.vanguard.com.*

34. "Ending the Wall Street Walk," Corporate Governance Web site, *www.corpgov.net,* Stu Gillan and Laura Starks, "A Survey of Shareholder Activism," *Contemporary Finance Digest* 2 (1998): 10–34.

35. Gerald Davis and E. Han Kim, "Business Ties and Proxy Voting by Mutual Funds," *Journal of Financial Economics* 85 (2007): 552–570.

36. Bernard S. Black, "Institutional Investors and Corporate Governance: The Case for Institutional Voice," in *The Revolution in Corporate Finance*, 3rd Edition (Oxford: Blackwell Publishers, 1998).

37. Mark J. Roe, "Political and Legal Restraints on Ownership and Control of Public Companies," *Journal of Financial Economics* 27 (1990): 7–41.

38. Alon Brav, Wei Jang, Frank Partnoy, and Randall Thomas, "Hedge Fund Activism, Corporate Governance, and Firm Performance," *Journal of Finance,* 63 (2008): 1729–1775.

Corporate Takeovers:
A Governance Mechanism?

Mergers and acquisitions (M&A) are significant and dramatic events. Yet they are relatively commonplace in corporate America when compared to the rest of the world. In recent years, the United States has experienced some of the largest M&A ever. For example, Pfizer agreed to acquire Wyeth in 2009, America Online (AOL) acquired Time Warner in 2001, Exxon and Mobil merged in 1999, and SBC Communications merged with Ameritech, also in 1999. These mergers, among others, created some of the largest firms within their industries. During the 1990s and 2000s, the United Kingdom seemed to ride its own merger wave. Some of these recent large mergers have been cross-border mergers, such as Vodafone's (United Kingdom) acquisition of AirTouch (United States). Less than one year later, Vodafone Air Touch acquired Mannesmann (Germany). Other European firms such as Netherland's InBev are frequent acquirers of other firms. In a high-profile transaction in 2008, InBev acquired Anheuser-Busch, the largest brewer in the United States, creating the world's largest beer company.

The number and value of U.S. M&A transactions, for each year from 1980 to 2008, is presented in Figure 8.1. The number of acquisitions spiked in the mid-1980s; the wide availability of junk debt to finance corporate acquisitions is a common explanation for the spike. The figure also highlights the dramatic rise in M&A activity that took place during the 1990s, with a decrease in activity around the recessionary early-2000s. Since then, M&A activity has increased to the highest levels on the chart in terms of number of deals and dollar value.

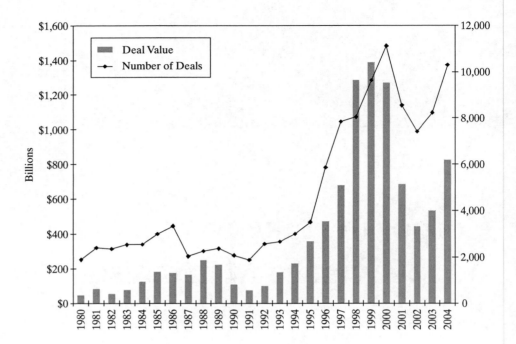

FIGURE 8.1 United States and U.S. Cross-Border M&A Transactions

Data Source: Mergerstat

There are many characteristics associated with M&A. Mergers can be characterized by:

- the type;
- the valuation of the firms involved;
- the payment;
- the new corporate structure; and
- the legal issues.

The legal effect of a merger is that two firms combine their operations into a single firm. The merger type could be between firms in the same industry or different industries, or they could even be vertical mergers where a firm might acquire one of its suppliers. The firm that is buying is called the **acquirer** and the firm that is being sold is called the **target**. Mergers where both the acquirer and the target firm's management and board agree to the deal are known as **friendly** mergers. If the target firm management and board does not want to be acquired, the attempt to take over control of the target is called a **hostile takeover.**

In friendly mergers, management and the boards of both firms negotiate over what is a "fair" price and the deal is not finalized until shareholders of both firms approve the deal. In a hostile takeover, the acquirer attempts to buy all the stock of the firm by making a temptingly high offer to the shareholders to buy their stock. Once a controlling block of stock is acquired, the acquiring firm then uses the voting power of this stock to approve a merger. Many takeovers start hostile and end friendly. If the target company resists negotiation, the acquirer may make an offer to shareholders as a way of putting pressure on target management to approve the deal. In either type of acquisition, payment can be made with a combination of cash, borrowed money (often known as leveraged buyouts [LBOs]), and newly issued stock of the acquiring firm.

What will the new corporate structure look like? Who will be in charge and, which managers or business lines will be retained? Government agencies try to determine if a merger significantly reduces competition, in which case it may be deemed illegal, and therefore challenged, by the federal government. There is also the general issue of costs and benefits of conducting M&A, to both the firms and to society. Many business schools have separate courses that treat M&A as a stand-alone topic.

At this point a question that business students might ask is, "Why is a book on corporate governance discussing M&A?" During the 1980s, there were occasions where "bad" firms were acquired by other corporations and even (famously) by individual investors, who then subsequently imposed dramatic changes (such as firing the target firm's top managers) to improve the acquired firm's profitability. These kinds of corporate acquisitions were often resisted by the target firm's management because they were afraid of losing their jobs after their firms were acquired. These kinds of hostile takeovers are sometimes known as "disciplinary takeovers" because they represent one process in which "bad" managers and/or "bad" operating procedures can be eliminated once their firms are taken over. In other words, if a firm is poorly managed, one way to force management and the board to make changes is to buy all of the shares of stock in the company and then use the voting power of this stock to replace the board and management.

We first provide a brief overview of M&A. However, this chapter is not about M&A *per se*; students are highly encouraged to read other corporate finance books if they wish to learn more about this exciting topic. After the brief introduction, we then discuss hostile takeovers in more detail and also characterize the nature of the disciplinary takeover. Perhaps most importantly, we then discuss how firms and their managers are able to defend against unwanted takeovers. We believe that these takeover defenses (both at the firm-level and at the U.S. state-level) may have severely hindered the disciplinary takeover market during the last two decades. We then offer some international perspective on takeovers.

BRIEF OVERVIEW OF MERGERS AND ACQUISITIONS

Mergers and acquisitions can occur for a variety of reasons. Firms can merge for strategic reasons to improve operational or financial synergies. In 1999, the merger between Exxon and Mobil led to reduced oil exploration costs. Firms can merge to diversify by expanding into new businesses. The AOL and Time Warner merger brought together new and old media (i.e., AOL's Internet service and Time Warner's cable [CNN, HBO] and print media [*Time, People, Sports Illustrated*]).

Mergers can be both synergistic and diversifying. The Morgan Stanley and Dean Witter merger brought together an investment bank that underwrote securities and a retail brokerage firm that sold securities. A diversifying merger can also be extreme in the sense that two very different businesses are joined together. General Electric's acquisition of the television company, NBC, during the 1980s, is a classic example of an extreme diversifying merger. Corporate diversification can make the combined firm's profits more stable but there is some debate about whether or not diversifying mergers are good for shareholders.[1]

Most of the recent mergers have occurred for growth and for increased market power. Mergers between Oracle and PeopleSoft, between Hewlett-Packard (HP) and Compaq, and between NationsBank and BankAmerica, can be viewed as market-power enhancing mergers. In recent years, these kinds of mergers seem to be popular with banks, pharmaceuticals, oil companies, and telecommunication firms. In a broad sense, we could classify all of these merger types into one category: they are *synergistic* in nature through the cutting of costs and risks and through economies of scale.

While we generally view mergers and acquisitions as being somewhat different (a merger is often viewed as a combination of two firms, whereas an acquisition is viewed as one firm buying another), almost all mergers are essentially acquisitions, as there is often an explicit buyer and seller when two firms are joined together. ExxonMobil is often thought of as a merger between equals but in reality Exxon acquired Mobil. Or put another way, Exxon "took over" Mobil. AOL purchased Time Warner. Daimler purchased Chrysler.[2]

Are corporate takeovers good for shareholders? In the first chapter, we mentioned that Hewlett-Packard's takeover of Compaq was not viewed positively by some HP shareholders nor was it viewed positively by the stock market. When HP announced its plans to acquire Compaq, HP share price immediately declined. There is a popular view that smaller firms are more nimble and more *focused* than larger firms in their ability to generate profits. In addition, some believe that managers want to take over companies simply to increase their "empire." This kind of acquisition is often referred to as "empire building." If both of these beliefs are true (and they are both widely popular beliefs), then takeovers may not be good for the acquiring firms' shareholders. Today there are people who believe that the HP-Compaq merger was bad for both of these reasons—which may be why CEO Carly Fiorina lost her job.

THE TARGET FIRM

Most of the time the target firm (i.e., the firm being acquired or taken over) will enjoy a share price *increase* when its acquisition is announced to the public. Why might this be? A firm, or even an individual investor, may be interested in taking over a target firm because they believe that that firm is not performing up to its full potential or that it could become an even better performer under someone else's control. The acquirer's goal under these circumstances would be to take over the firm and then to turn it around (i.e., to make it profitable) by cutting its fixed or variable costs (either by getting rid of unnecessary expenses or through financial synergy with the acquiring firm), improving its operational efficiency, or by getting rid of its "bad" managers.

Sometimes students new to finance might think it is odd that a successful firm would want to acquire an unsuccessful firm but the rationale is pretty simple. If a firm or an individual were to acquire a successful firm then they would have to pay a large sum for it and the subsequent net gains after the takeover may be limited. However, if a firm or an individual were to acquire an unsuccessful firm then they would only have to pay a relatively small sum for it. The subsequent net gains may be significant if they are able to convert the unsuccessful firm into a successful one. Unfortunately for the acquirer, because the stock market anticipates these subsequent improvements in target firms once they are taken over, the target firms' share price will *immediately* increase when its acquisition is announced. Acquirers almost always end up paying a significant premium for target firms. As the gains go to the target shareholders in most acquisitions, firms making offers typically offer a premium when making a bid for the target shares. An extreme example of this is the $60 per share bid News Corporation (News Corp.) offered in May 2007 to acquire Dow Jones, whose stock was trading at $37.12 per share.[3] An interesting debate among academics and among financial experts in general is whether or not the premium paid for target firms is ever fully recovered. That is, does the acquisition end up being a positive NPV (net present value) project for the acquirer?

Because the acquirer often pays a premium for the target firm, the target firms' shareholders might like it when their firms are taken over. However, the target firms' management team and board of directors may oppose being acquired. Once firms are acquired, many of the target firms' managers are then subsequently fired so that the acquirer can install their own management team into the newly acquired firm. Board members are also frequently replaced. As you can easily imagine, corporate CEOs and presidents generally do not like being fired. When management and the board balks at a takeover bid from an interested acquirer, the acquirer may then try to take their takeover bid directly to the target firm's shareholders in a hostile takeover. However, it can be argued that whether or not a takeover is "hostile" is in the eye of the beholder. Many initial hostile acquisitions are eventually approved by the target firm. Also some firms, fearing a hostile takeover, may try to work out a "friendly" deal with a potential acquirer. In both of these cases, the firms involved may publicly state that their merger was a friendly one.

EXAMPLE 8.1	**Microsoft Fails in Hostile Takeover Attempt of Yahoo!, But Who Is the Real Loser?**

Throughout 2007, Yahoo! was losing ground to Google in their competition for Internet search advertising. To try and revive a stagnant stock price, Yahoo! replaced its CEO in June 2007 with company founder Jerry Yang. However, changes in strategy under the new CEO did not improve Yahoo!'s success and Microsoft initiated discussions of a proposed acquisition of Yahoo!. The benefits of this acquisition would be access to Microsoft's ample resources, as well as a restructuring of Yahoo!'s operations to make Yahoo! more profitable. In other words, this merger would be part strategic and part disciplinary takeover. The Yahoo! board, led by Jerry Yang, rejected Microsoft's proposal. In January 2008, Yahoo!'s performance had fallen even further and the company was forced to lay off 1,000 employees. Its stock price fell below $20 per share, which was the lowest price in years.[4]

In February 2008, Microsoft decided to again try to takeover Yahoo!, but this time it went around the board and offered $31 per share directly to the shareholders. This represented a 62 percent premium above the previous day closing price of $19.18 per share.[5] With this offer, Microsoft was trying to create pressure on the board and management of Yahoo! to negotiate a deal. The Yahoo! board, however, rejected the Microsoft offer, claiming it substantially undervalued Yahoo!.[6] In follow-up negotiations, Microsoft raised its offer to $33, but the Yahoo! board's minimum price was $37. Further complicating the deal, Yahoo! enacted a "poison pill" severance plan that would require more than a billion dollars be paid to employees who lost their jobs or were adversely affected by a takeover. This effectively raised the cost of a takeover beyond the price per share offered.

The combination of the board resisting the proposed takeover and the poison pill caused Microsoft to walk away from the deal. While the Yahoo! board claimed they were driving a better bargain on behalf of shareholders and were protecting employees who would be hurt by the takeover, the numerous lawsuits filed claim the board and management were protecting their own jobs at the expense of the shareholders. In fact, the aftermath of the failed Microsoft-Yahoo! takeover suggests the shareholders of Yahoo! were the big losers. On the day Microsoft announced it was walking away, the stock price fell to $23 and then in the next few months fell below $20. Compared to a price over $30 per share in a takeover, Yahoo! shareholders lost at least a third of the value of their investment. Following a high-profile proxy fight led by Carl Icahn to oust all the directors on the board because they rejected the Microsoft bid, Yahoo! was forced to make changes. The company added additional outside board members and eventually replaced its CEO in January 2009.[7] However, as of March of 2009, the value of Yahoo! stock remained below $15 per share, less than half of Microsoft's offer.

The Notion of the Disciplinary Takeover

Most of the time, when a firm takes over another firm, we generally do not think of it as a "disciplinary takeover." Profitable firms can also be taken over. Time Warner was making about $27 billion in revenue when it was taken over by AOL, which was making less than $5 billion in revenue (though the merged firm has struggled since the 2001 merger, suffering a $99 billion write-off of the value of AOL in 2002[8]). Even hostile takeovers are not always viewed as disciplinary takeovers. PeopleSoft was a profitable firm in the process of trying to take over J. D. Edwards (combined, they were expected to make about $3 billion in annual revenue) when Oracle made a hostile takeover bid for PeopleSoft during the summer of 2003.[9]

However, because some (if not most) firms that get taken over are poorly performing firms, there are many people (such as academics) who view takeovers as an important governance mechanism. If a manager is not doing a good job, either because he is bad at managing or because he is abusing his managerial discretion (i.e., he is using his power for self-serving ends), then his firm might get taken over and he will subsequently be fired. In this sense, the fear of a potential takeover might represent a powerful disciplinary mechanism to make sure that managers perform to the best of their abilities and to make sure that managerial discretion is controlled.[10] In a study of over 250 takeovers during 1958–1984, the study's authors found that over half of the target firm's top manager (usually the CEO but sometimes the president) was fired within two years of the takeover. These statistics are probably representative of today's takeover landscape. Even though Oracle's takeover of PeopleSoft might not have started off as a disciplinary takeover, many of PeopleSoft's top management team eventually got fired after Oracle's takeover. PeopleSoft's CEO, Craig Conway, was even fired just before the takeover was consummated because PeopleSoft's board felt that Conway was responsible for losing $2 billion in shareholder value.[11] While Conway's ability as a CEO can be debated, a takeover (or the fear of a takeover) represents a potentially powerful way to dismiss managers (or to motivate managers) that might not be looking out for their shareholders' best interest otherwise.

Therefore, in addition to the synergy motive for mergers mentioned previously, we could classify a second broad merger category as the disciplinary takeover. It is important to note that mergers can be for both reasons. It could easily be argued that Daimler's acquisition of Chrysler was both a synergistic merger (the two automakers produce different types of cars and primarily serve different geographic markets) and a disciplinary takeover (Chrysler was struggling to maintain sales growth and Daimler felt that Chrysler could make a turnaround if it had Daimler-style management). Similarly, the takeover of Dow Jones by News Corp. was both a synergistic merger because it added to one of the world's largest media empires, as well as a disciplinary takeover because one goal was making changes in a company with lackluster performance.

However, while takeovers may be viewed as a governance mechanism, it is not clear that they are an *effective* one. That is, we might *not* be able to rely on them as being an efficient contributor to the corporate governance system. First, as mentioned above, an acquirer may have to pay too much for a target. Second, takeovers could occur for the wrong reasons (e.g., empire building, corporate diversification). Third, even if the acquirer is able to pay a "fair" price for a target, the amount usually is still significant.

While the idea of disciplinary takeovers as a governance device might be new to some, it may be a more familiar idea to those of us who remember the "corporate raiders" of the 1980s. Corporate raiders, such as Carl

Icahn and T. Boone Pickens were well known to identify firms that could not control their spending. For example, Carl Icahn took over TWA (Trans World Airlines) in 1985 and then dramatically cut TWA's costs. Corporate raiders are obviously *not* seeking a synergistic-type takeover; their takeovers are clearly of the disciplinary type. These disciplinary takeovers benefited target firms' shareholders. They got rid of "bad" managers and in the process they themselves also enjoyed a profit. *However*, we would be remiss if we did not mention an alternative viewpoint. These corporate raiders were also seen as villains. Because raiders often cut jobs to control costs, many people viewed raiders as heartless cost-cutters who only cared about making profits.

Once raiders obtain enough shares of a firm, they can force management to make changes. Kirk Kerkorian, a large shareholder of Chrysler for many years has always been an activist shareholder. For example, in 1996, he forced Chrysler to disburse their large cash holdings to repurchase stock. Kerkorian's large purchase of General Motors (GM) stock, in the spring of 2005, had many analysts predicting future improvements at GM. By the end of 2006, however, Kerkorian had sold all of his GM stock and GM shareholders lost a potentially important monitor of management and shareholder activist. GM shares have fallen steadily since from about $30 per share to worthless in GM's 2009 bankruptcy. Another example of a corporate raider forcing change was discussed in Chapter 7 where Carl Icahn bought a large block of shares in Yahoo! and forced his way on the board through a proxy fight.

If a disciplinary takeover is profitable, in and of itself (even in the absence of a synergy motive) and if it is an effective governance mechanism, then the question that begs asking is why did we not see more of them during the 1990s and 2000s, as we did in the 1980s? Even when bad firms were taken over in recent years, a synergy-oriented reason rather than a pure investment-oriented reason was usually cited. There are several possible reasons. First, management opportunism and questionable actions such as "cooking the books" can lead to a temporary, but artificially, high stock price. No one would want to pay an artificially high price to take over a firm and fix things so that the true lower price was revealed. Second and mentioned previously, it costs a lot of money to buy a firm. In the 1980s, junk debt was a popular financing vehicle for takeovers but this form of capital is no longer widely available. A third reason, and perhaps the most important, is that today there are too many defenses against takeovers. That is, firms can install takeover defenses, which may have effectively disabled this governance device from playing an active role in our corporate governance system. These takeover defenses are discussed next.

TAKEOVER DEFENSES

For the United States, we can place takeover defenses into two categories: those at the firm-level and those at the U.S. state-level. Firm-level defenses can be broken down further into pre-emptive defenses that try to prevent takeovers and reactionary defenses that are enacted after a takeover attempt has begun. State-level defenses are state laws that regulate and limit takeovers. Firms lobby the state to enact such laws. We discuss firm-level takeover defenses first.

Firm-Level Pre-Emptive Takeover Defenses

The term **poison pill** represents any strategy that makes a target firm less attractive immediately after it is taken over. Most poison pills are simply favorable rights given to its shareholders. One popularly used poison pill gives target firm shareholders the right to buy the acquirer's stock for a deep discount if its firm is acquired. For example, in November 2004, News Corp. adopted a plan that, in the event a shareholder obtained a 15 percent stake in the company, offered all the other shareholders the chance to buy one share of News Corp. at half price.[12] The effect of this policy was to dilute the owner-ship percentage of a potential acquirer, making acquisition more difficult. Of course this makes the firm much less attractive to takeover from the acquirer's standpoint.

A related poison pill is to create **blank-check preferred** which means the company gives the board the right to issue preferred stock at any time with any voting rights the board determines. This allows the board to resist a takeover because they can put super-voting preferred stock in friendly hands. Other types of poison pills involve a firm's debt becoming immedi-ately due once it is taken over or an immediate deep-discount selling of fixed assets once it is taken over. Well over half of the S&P 500 firms have a poison pill.[13]

A **golden parachute** is an automatic payment made to managers if their firm gets taken over. Because the acquirer ultimately bears the costs of these parachutes, their existence make those firms less attractive to take over. An example of a golden parachute was adopted by Yahoo! in February 2008 after Microsoft made an offer to buy the shares from Yahoo! shareholders. Yahoo!'s golden parachute plan is triggered by a takeover attempt and allows any employee who resigns after an "adverse change" in his or her duties to receive immediate vesting of options and a severance payment of 18–24 months' salary.[14] According to Carl Icahn, the cost of this plan was about $2.4 billion, which was a real disincentive to a firm such as Microsoft considering a takeover of Yahoo!

Other takeover defenses are **supermajority rules** where two-thirds, or even 90 percent, of the shareholders have to approve a hand-over in control. Firms can also have **staggered boards**, where only a fraction of the board can get elected each year to multiple-year terms, thereby making it difficult to gain control of the board in any one particular year.

Firm-Level Reactionary Takeover Defenses

Greenmail is like a bribe that prevents someone from pursuing a takeover. For example, David Murdoch owned 5 percent of Occidental Petroleum in 1984 and because Occidental's management feared a hostile takeover bid by Murdoch, they bought his shares at a significant premium.[15]

Other reactionary defenses to unwanted takeover bids include the firm's management trying to convince its shareholders that the offer price is too low (from Example 8.1, note that Polaroid management did this in their defense against Shamrock's hostile takeover), raising antitrust issues, finding another acquirer (also known as a *white knight*) who might not fire management after the takeover, or finding an investor to buy enough shares (also known as a *white squire*) so that he can have sufficient power to block the acquisition.

State-Level Antitakeover Laws

In general there are five common state-level antitakeover laws. **Freeze-out** laws stipulate a length of time (usually about three years) that a bidder that gains control has to wait to merge the target with its own assets. **Fair price** laws make sure that shareholders who sell their shares during a later stage of an acquisition get the same price as any other shareholder who sold their shares to the acquirer earlier. Individual firms can also adopt this type of provision. **Poison pill endorsement laws** protect the firm's rights to adopt poison pills. A **control share acquisition** law requires shareholder approval before a bidder can vote his shares. A **constituency** statute allows managers to include non-shareholders' (such as employees or creditors) interests in defending against takeovers.

Three states have rather extreme antitakeover statutes. Pennsylvania and Ohio allow target firms to claim the short-term profits made by acquirers and Massachusetts mandates staggered boards.

There are also federal acts (e.g., Sherman Act, Clayton Act) that prevent mergers that would significantly reduce competition but these acts are designed to ensure a competitive environment rather than to protect firms from unwanted takeovers. This task falls to the Bureau of Competition of the Federal Trade Commission (FTC) and the Antitrust Division of the Department of Justice (DOJ). These two government agencies uphold antitrust policy. Their main focus is on anti-competitive business practices and on ensuring a competitive industry environment in the face of mergers between companies.

EXAMPLE 8.2	States that have at Least Four of the Mentioned Antitakeover Laws[16]:		
Arizona	Florida	Georgia	Idaho
Illinois	Indiana	Kentucky	Massachusetts
Maryland	Minnesota	Missouri	New Jersey
Nevada	New York	Ohio	Oregon
Pennsylvania	Rhode Island	South Dakota	Tennessee
Virginia	Wisconsin		

EXAMPLE 8.3   **Oracle's Hostile Takeover of PeopleSoft**

On June 2, 2003, PeopleSoft announced that it would be acquiring rival J. D. Edwards, which would make the combined firm the second largest enterprise application software vendor behind SAP.[17] Four days later, Oracle, also an enterprise application software vendor, made an unsolicited offer to acquire PeopleSoft for $16 per share. PeopleSoft management issued a negative response to the bid. Twelve days later, Oracle upped the bid to $19.50 per share. Over the course of the next year and a half, numerous dramatic events played out. For one, DOJ filed a lawsuit against Oracle citing antitrust issues, as the merger would dramatically reduce competition in the industry. In addition to challenging the DOJ suit, Oracle was lobbying its own battles against PeopleSoft. In particular it tried to put its own slate of nominated candidates up for election to PeopleSoft's board and they challenged PeopleSoft's poison pills, one of which would have flooded the market with millions of PeopleSoft shares if it were acquired and another that would have automatically refunded PeopleSoft's customers two to five times their license fees if the firm were acquired. It was also speculated that a white knight, possibly IBM, would come to PeopleSoft's rescue. Meanwhile PeopleSoft's stock price was crumbling, prompting its board to fire its CEO, Craig Conway. At the end of 2004, PeopleSoft's board approved a takeover deal with Oracle for $26.50 per share.

ASSESSMENTS OF TAKEOVER DEFENSES

Are Takeover Defenses Bad for the Governance System?

It is hard to say whether or not these takeover defenses are the only cause of the demise of the disciplinary takeover. Most of these takeover devices (both firm-level defenses and state-level antitakeover laws) were invented and implemented during the mid-to-late 1980s, in direct response to the high level of hostile takeovers that were taking place at the time. We may surmise, therefore, that takeover defenses at least contributed to the end of disciplinary takeovers.

If takeover defenses prevent disciplinary takeovers then their existence causes us to be left with one less governance mechanism. In this sense, takeover defenses are bad for the governance system. Studies have shown that when a firm adopts an antitakeover mechanism, their firm's stock price declines on the news.[18] However, this is not to say that we staunchly advocate eliminating antitakeover mechanisms. The matter is simply not clear-cut. Corporate raiders are often looking for quick profits. We generally encourage managers and investors to have a long-run focus. Further, we can certainly sympathize with those who viewed the corporate raiders of the 1980s as heartless villains.

In the least, however, we should continue to evaluate the pros and cons of antitakeover defenses in light of the reevaluation of corporate governance that is taking place today. Perhaps there is a middle ground that can be achieved. Some antitakeover devices appear only to benefit managers. For example, golden parachutes directly benefit outgoing managers, but who else? Also there is a lot of evidence that the extreme antitakeover laws in Pennsylvania, Ohio, and Massachusetts have harmed firm value and thus shareholders.[19]

On the other hand, many firms with takeover defenses do eventually agree to be acquired. When they do the acquisition price tends to be much higher than the original offer. Therefore fighting against the merger for a while may cause the bid price to increase, thereby increasing wealth to the target firm's shareholders. For example, in the failed Microsoft-Yahoo! takeover, Microsoft raised its offer from $31 per share to $33 per share, but was still rejected by management and the board of Yahoo![20] In their defense to the various lawsuits filed by shareholders, management and the board of Yahoo! argue they were acting in shareholders' best interest in rejecting the offers because they were driving a harder bargain.

INTERNATIONAL PERSPECTIVE

The United Kingdom seems to be experiencing its own merger wave since the early 1990s. In fact, Vodafone's (United Kingdom) recent takeover of Mannesmann (Germany) is the largest ever hostile takeover. The United States and the United Kingdom probably have the most antitakeover laws, yet they also have the most M&A activity in the world. Figure 8.2 shows the fraction of

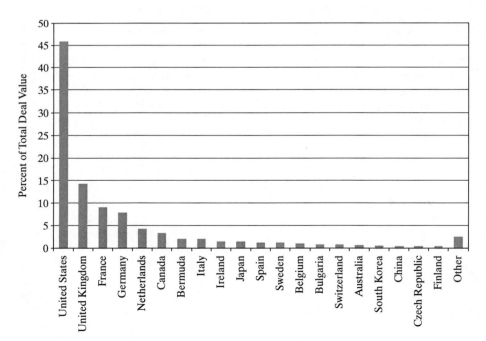

FIGURE 8.2 Percentage of Acquisition Deal Value by Country (Identified by Location of Target Firm), 2004

Data Source: ZEPHYR: published by Bureau van Dijk Electronic Publishing

M&A activity (out of all M&A activity worldwide) that was conducted in each country in 2004. The United States and the United Kingdom comprise 60 percent of all the M&A that took place.

In bank-centered financial systems, unlike the U.S. capital markets system, banks seem to play a significant role in determining which firms merge. For example, a study finds that banks are influential in German mergers.[21] Japan is also a bank-based system and, in general, it is a country that has believed in protecting its firms from hostile takeovers, especially from foreigners.[22] However, Japan has been suffering a protracted bear market since its market crash in 1990, so it is hard to argue that its opposition to hostile takeovers has been good for shareholders (but, of course, this is not to say that M&A are the cure for Japan's economy either).

After the Asian financial crisis of 1997–1998, many Asian governments relaxed the foreign ownership restrictions of their firms. This action will attract foreign capital and at the same time a larger presence of outside investors may lead to an improvement in firm-level governance. However, whether or not the presence of outside investors (or an acquirer of an entire firm) will lead to better governance remains to be seen.

Within Asian countries and in many other countries around the world, they also have their own unique set of circumstances that make M&A difficult. For example, in Japan multiple corporations cross-own one another and in Korea, families are powerful controlling shareholders of many firms. Both of these arrangements make it difficult for an acquirer from outside these tight networks to take over a firm. The strength of Japan's cross-ownership has been weakening in recent years. And there is a lot of pressure on family-run businesses in Korea, from both within and outside that country, to break up their multiple business conglomerates. In the future, we may see more hostile takeovers in other parts of the world, but whether or not they will be viewed as an important corporate governance mechanism also remains to be seen.

EXAMPLE 8.4   **The Largest Hostile Takeover Did Not Occur in the United States**

In late October 1999, German telecommunication and engineering giant, Mannesmann, made a bid for Orange, a telecommunication firm in the United Kingdom.[23] Vodafone, the largest telecommunication firm in Britain, perhaps fearing a new competitor in its own backyard, responded with its own takeover bid of Mannesmann. Vodafone's Chris Gent sought out Mannesmann's Klaus Esser to make a friendly merger offer but Esser refused it. Gent then made his offer directly to Mannesmann shareholders. In the following months, a very public battle took place, where each firm took out full-page ads with each side trying to convince Mannesmann shareholders that they were in the right. In February 2000, the two firms finally agreed to merger terms and consummated the largest hostile takeover in the world valued at $173 billion.

Summary

In the United States, mergers and acquisitions have been on the rise since the 1980s. In the beginning many of these acquisitions could have been characterized as hostile takeovers, as acquiring firms were looking to take over target firms whose management and boards did not want their firm to be bought. Many of these acquirers believed they could take over a poorly performing firm and then convert them into profitable firms. In this way M&A can be viewed as a corporate governance device, and thus these hostile takeovers were viewed as "disciplinary takeovers." However, the recent mergers we have seen seem to be more focused on simply increasing market power. What happened to the disciplinary takeover? In response to the hostile takeover activity of the 1980s, many firms and states adopted antitakeover devices, thereby weakening a potentially powerful corporate governance device. Besides the United States, takeover activity is only common in the United Kingdom. However, given collapses in corporate governance around the world, there is a good chance that we may see a new increased worldwide M&A activity in the near future.

WEB Info about Mergers and Acquisitions

Mergerstat
www.mergerstat.com

Zephyr
www.bvdep.com/ZEPHYR.html

Bureau of Competition, Federal Trade Commission
www.ftc.gov/bc/index.shtml

Antitrust Division, Department of Justice
www.usdoj.gov/atr/

Review Questions

1. What are the two broad rationales for takeovers? What are some of the specific rationales?
2. Discuss how takeovers can be viewed as a governance mechanism.
3. List and describe various takeover defenses.
4. Discuss why takeover defenses might be bad for shareholders.

Discussion Questions

1. In your opinion, who benefits when firms have takeover defenses? Who is hurt when firms have takeover defenses? In sum, which is greater the benefits or the costs?
2. Do you believe that takeovers can effectively contribute to the corporate governance system? Why or why not?

Exercises

1. Daimler Benz was adamant that its takeover of Chrysler was really a "merger between equals." From Daimler's viewpoint, why was it important that Chrysler shareholders believed this? Do some background research.
2. Find a recent hostile takeover attempt not mentioned in this chapter. Was it successful? How did it eventually get resolved? Regardless of the outcome, do you think the target firm is now better off? Explain your answer.

3. Conduct some research and discuss the costs and benefits of state antitakeover laws. In particular, what benefit is it to the states to have these laws?

4. Find a firm with a poison pill and describe it. Find another firm from the same industry that does not have a poison pill and identify why one firm has a poison pill and the other does not.

5. This chapter suggests that hostile takeovers might be good for corporate America. Do some research and argue that hostile takeovers are bad for corporate America.

Exercises for Non-U.S. Students

1. Compare and contrast the M&A market in your country to the United States. Also, do some research to work out what led to the differences between the two countries (e.g., if you find that M&A activity is low in your country, then what might be the cause; is it historical, economic, social, political, ownership related, etc.?).

2. This chapter did not discuss foreign acquisitions in detail. Does your country have foreign ownership restrictions? Do you think having a more active international acquisition market can improve the corporate governance environment in your country and worldwide?

3. Do you think hostile acquisitions are going to occur more often in your country? Do you think there should be more hostile acquisitions? Support your contentions.

Endnotes

1. A firm operating in multiple and diversified businesses are known as conglomerates. A good academic article about the economic costs of diversified firms is Phil Berger and Eli Ofek, "Diversification's Effect on Firm Value," *Journal of Financial Economics* 37 (1995):39–65. A good general article about the costs and benefits of diversified firms is Amar Bhide, "Reversing Corporate Diversification," in Donald H. Chew (ed.), *The New Corporate Finance*, 2nd edition (Irwin McGraw Hill, 1999, New York, New York).

2. When two large firms join together, it is often hailed as a "merger between equals." The Daimler-Chrysler merger is an interesting case. It had been highly publicized as a merger between equals, but in fact Daimler bought Chrysler. After the merger, Daimler CEO Juergen Schrempp even stated that he too viewed the merger as a takeover. Kirk Kerkorian, the largest shareholder of Chrysler before the merger, tried to sue Daimler-Chrysler arguing that he had been misled into thinking that it was a "merger between equals" but he lost his lawsuit in 2005. More background details of the story can be found at *http://www.nytimes.com/2006/09/27/automobiles/27daimler.html?_r=1&dlbk*.

3. *http://money.cnn.com/2007/05/01/news/companies/newspapers/index.htm*.

4. *http://en.wikipedia.org/wiki/Yahoo!*

5. *www.microsoft.com/presspass/press/2008/feb08/02-01CorpNewsPR.mspx*.

6. *http://yhoo.client.shareholder.com/press/ releasedetail.cfm?ReleaseID=293129*.

7. *http://yhoo.client.shareholder.com/press/ releasedetail.cfm?ReleaseID=359016*.

8. Information on the aftermath of the merger is summarized at *http://en.wikipedia.org/wiki/Time-Warner*.

9. Information on the legal fight between the three firms is summarized at *www.internetnews.com/bus-news/article.php/2220981*.

10. A good overview of disciplinary takeovers of the 1980s is Michael Jensen, "The Modern Industrial Revolution, Exit, and the Failure of Internal Control Systems," *Journal of Finance* 48 (1993): 831–880.

11. *www.eweek.com/article2/0,1895,1665096,00.asp*.

12. This information comes from *http://www.forbes.com/2005/10/13/newscorp-liberty-malone-murdoch-cx_sc_1013intrepid.html*. Interestingly, News Corp. removed its poison pill and staggered board of directors in 2008.

13. *http://207.36.165.114/Toronto/bizjak.pdf.*

14. Yahoo! Inc. Change in Control Employee Severance Plan, filed with the SEC 2/27/2008 as attachment 10.18 to the 10-K (Annual Report).

15. A good description of this incident is on page 727 in Mark Grinblatt and Sheridan Titman, *Financial Markets and Corporate Strategy*, 2nd edition (Irwin McGraw Hill Publishers, 2001, New York, New York).

16. Grant Gartman, *State Antitakeover Laws* (Washington, DC : Investor Responsibility Research Center, 2000).

17. This information comes from various news clips from *http://news.cnet.com/2030-1012-1018823.html.*

18. A good example of such a study is Gregg Jarrell and Annette Poulsen, "Shark Repellents and Stock Prices: The Effects of Antitakeover Amendments since 1980, *Journal of Financial Economics* 19 (1987):127–168.

19. Sam Szewczyk and George Tsetsekos, "State Intervention in the Market for Corporate Control: The Case of Pennsylvania Senate Bill 1310," *Journal of Financial Economics* 31 (1992):3–23; Michael Ryngaert and Jeff Netter, "Shareholder Wealth Effects of the 1986 Ohio Antitakeover Law Revisited, Its Real Effects, *Journal of Law, Economics and Organization* 6 (1990):253–262; and Robert Daines, "Do Staggered Boards Affect Firm Value? Massachusetts and the Market for Corporate Control," New York Law School working paper (2001).

20. *http://money.cnn.com/2008/05/03/technology/ microsoft_yahoo/?postversion=2008050412.*

21. Julian Franks and Colin Mayer, "Bank Control, Takeovers, and Corporate Governance in Germany, *Journal of Banking and Finance* 22 (1998): 1385–1403.

22. A good illustration of Japanese firms' resistance to foreign hostile takeovers is Koito Manufacturing preventing T. Boone Pickens from getting on its board. The account can be found in Kenichi Miyashita and David Russell, *Keiretsu: Inside the Hidden Japanese Conglomerates* (McGraw-Hill, 1994, New York).

23. *www.businessweek.com/1999/99_48/b3657017.htm.*

Corporate Citizenship

The previous chapters discuss corporate governance from the perspective of agency theory. As described in the first chapter, agency theory focuses on the separation of ownership and control. Shareholders (owners) are the central point of concern. From this perspective, corporate governance is mainly about the incentive systems and monitors designed to protect shareholder interests. The primary goal of the firm is to create wealth for these shareholders.

However, this is not the only perspective from which to consider corporate governance. Many believe that companies should have a greater responsibility to society. Proponents argue that companies have unique opportunities to improve society. This *stakeholder* view of the firm describes the firm as having many different groups with legitimate interests in the firm's activities. Corporate governance is then defined as the mechanisms that ensure corporations take responsibility for directing their activities in a manner fair to all stakeholders. Strategic management concepts argue that this is based on creating positive relationships with stakeholders. Through creating these positive relationships, firms can create sustainable economic wealth.

In particular, agency theory has been an important perspective for formulating governance rules, laws, and policy in the United States. However, many other countries have operated under the idea that large corporations have a greater responsibility in society than just maximizing shareholder wealth. Their governance rules tend to be influenced to a greater extent by this duty to an expanded set of stakeholders.

If U.S. firms believed they had a social obligation to be good citizens, then this sense of responsibility for the greater good could serve as yet another governance device. However, do firms have a sense of social responsibility? Some might say that they do not, but others may argue that they should. We discuss the stakeholder view of the firm and we also describe problems with the view, which make it difficult to use this view to ensure good governance.

STAKEHOLDER VIEW OF THE FIRM

A company must maintain relationships with several groups that affect or are affected by its decisions.[1] Stakeholders are identified as people or groups with legitimate interests in various aspects of the company's activities. Note that stakeholders are defined by their interest in the corporation, not whether the corporation has any interest in them. Companies have varying responsibilities to each of their stakeholders. While some relationships may be more valuable (or important) than others, no one group should be able to dominate all of the others. These relationships between managers and stakeholders are based on a moral or ethical foundation.

Clearly groups, such as stockholders, employees, and creditors have a strong interest in the firm. But what other groups might be considered stakeholders? Figure 11.1 shows the different types of groups that might be considered stakeholders of the firm. The primary stakeholders (sometimes called contractual stakeholders) have direct, contractually determined relationships. While the stockholder is considered a very important stakeholder, other groups are also important. Company employees have short-term interests in the firm in the form of pay and working conditions and long-term interests

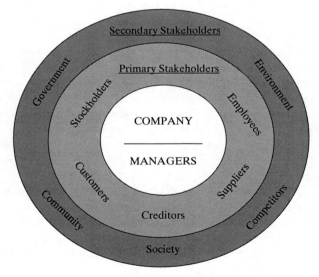

FIGURE 11.1 Company Stakeholders

in the form of pension and health care. Employees often have labor unions to manage their relationship with the firm. Creditors, customers, and suppliers also have legitimate interests in the organization. The secondary (or diffuse) stakeholders are impacted by the firm's actions but have limited contractual connection to it. Examples of secondary stakeholders may be its competitors and environmental activists. Certainly, local communities, governments, and all of society may be affected by the company's decisions.

The figure shows just one way to categorize the different stakeholders of a firm. Other distinctions could be made. For example, groupings can be based on the various activities of the firm and those that they impact. It can be based on a resource view, or industry structure, or by social and political affiliations. Or these stakeholders can be grouped by institutional, economic, and ethical interests. There is no consensus on how these stakeholders should be categorized. However, all the stakeholder views illustrate a much different perspective than agency theory—companies have responsibilities to groups other than to stockholders.

A stakeholder view of the firm places its executives at the center of managing relations with each stakeholder group. The managerial objective in this view is to maximize sustainable organizational wealth (all stakeholders' utilities) by optimizing these relationships. Many companies now have an organizational unit tasked with communicating with stakeholders. These units may have camouflaged names like "corporate communication department" or "public affairs department." Others use more direct names like "sustainability group" or "corporate social responsibility committee."

EXAMPLE 11.1 **Wal-Mart's Battle with Stakeholders**

Wal-Mart operates over 4,100 discount stores in the United States (Wal-Mart, Super Centers, and Sam's Clubs). The firm generates over $13 billion in profits per year. The company is the largest corporate employer in the United States, with 1.4 million employees and plans to open about 200 new stores every year.

But Wal-Mart seems to be coming under increasing pressure from different social groups for its business practices. Coalitions of community groups have worked to keep Wal-Mart from coming to their towns. Hundreds of communities have been successful. A recent class-action lawsuit was filed against Wal-Mart on behalf of female employees, arguing that they were being paid less than their male counterparts. Many politicians have noticed that a large percentage of Wal-Mart's employees end up on public health care assistance. The firm has endured allegations of child labor law violations, the hiring of illegal immigrants, and violations of worker rights.

Wal-Mart's view is much different. It claims that its low prices help everyone in the community. Also by giving $296 million to charity last year, it is the largest corporate cash contributor in the United States. Wal-Mart targets 90 percent of its charitable contributions at the local level where Wal-Mart customers and associates live and work.

Whether Wal-Mart has been a good corporate citizen or not is being actively debated. However, one thing seems obvious—Wal-Mart has done a poor job of actively engaging many of its stakeholders to optimize their mutual interests. Having adversarial relationships with employees, potential customers, politicians, and civil rights activists do not seem like wise business choices.

Legal Foundations

The legal underpinnings of the stakeholder view of the firm stems from property rights. This may seem ironic because it is the stockholders who own the firm. If stockholders are the owners, do not they have the property rights? Not necessarily. The definition of property can be expressed as a "bundle" of rights, which may be limited.[2] Owners of property have the right to engage in a limited set of activities.

Consider a landowner. Building a home requires a building permit. The government agency that grants the permit must first approve the building plans. The building must meet adequate safety and appearance criteria. Land is also zoned for specific uses. These laws and procedures protect citizens who may go on the property (safety) and the landowners in the area (appearance and use). Although they are not owners of the land, these citizens and nearby property owners are stakeholders of this land. They also have rights.

The U.S. government, various state governments, and courts have formalized the rights of stakeholders in corporations. Many states have adopted statutes that extend the concern of corporate boards beyond that of the shareholders to other stakeholders, such as employees, creditors, suppliers, customers, and communities. The determination of which rights are held by the corporation (and its owners) and which rights belong to various stakeholders continues to evolve.

Corporate Social Responsibility

The modern evolution of the stakeholder view of the firm advocates that management develop specific relationships with stakeholder groups. Proponents of this view argue that companies have a social obligation to operate in ethically, socially, and environmentally responsible ways. This active approach is referred to as corporate social responsibility[3] (CSR) or corporate citizenship.

What is a company's responsibility to society? Archie Carroll has offered a four-part taxonomy of CSR that lends itself to corporate citizenship from a managerial perspective. A firm should conduct its business in a manner that meets its economic, legal, ethical, and philanthropy expectations:[4]

Level I: Economic—the first and foremost social responsibility of a firm is economic. The firm must survive by producing goods and services at a profit.

Level II: Legal—society expects firms to operate their business within the legal framework.

Level III: Ethical—these responsibilities are those over and above the ones codified in laws and are in line with societal norms and customs. They are expected, though not required, by society even though they may be ill-defined. This could include things such as environmental ethics.

Level IV: Philanthropy—corporate giving is discretionary, although increasingly desired by stakeholder communities.

The economic responsibilities (Level I) have the highest priority. A firm must be efficient and survive over the long term, in order to be useful to society. However, it must execute its business activities in a legal (Level II) and ethical (Level III) way. Philanthropy (Level IV) is the least important priority. Reconsider the Wal-Mart example through this model of CSR. Corporate social responsibility proponents might argue that any failure of Wal-Mart in higher-priority responsibilities, such as legal and ethical considerations, cannot be to offset through greater participation in lower-priority responsibilities, such as corporate giving.

While corporate citizenship might include charity or philanthropy (Level IV), the concept focuses more on engagement with stakeholders to achieve mutual goals (Levels II and III). Proponents of CSR argue that the main drivers of the citizenship trend include the following:

- globalization, the worldwide expansion of business and market economies;
- greater power of global firms should fill the activities formerly left to governments;
- pressure from assertive social activists;
- an increasingly popular environmental movement; and
- a rising desire in the capital markets to punish firms not meeting ethical standards.

Some corporations have responded to this trend by including CSR-oriented statements in their corporate values and goals. These statements recognize that CSR has value in a code of conduct or ethics, a commitment to local communities, an interest in employee health and education, an environmental consciousness, and recognition of social issues (e.g., diversity, social fairness, etc.).

By embracing citizenship goals, advocates claim corporations will insulate themselves from many activist actions, establish stakeholder confidence in management, enhance the firm's reputation, and demonstrate an emphasis on prevention rather than corrective actions.[5] As a result of these perceptions, firms may find that their goodwill opens doors to new communities and additional sales.

However, social responsibility is a dynamic process. It stems from the making of decisions balancing the interests of all stakeholders. But these decisions can only be made from an ongoing conversation among affected parties. For this to occur over time, social awareness must become an integral part of the corporate culture. Ethical considerations become central to this process.

When Enron executives were falsifying revenue and taking excessive risks, they not only hurt their shareholders but other stakeholders as well. Enron hurt their customers who now have to find other vendors, suppliers who depended on Enron's orders, employees who could have worked elsewhere, and the future local economy as current and future jobs have now been taken away. In addition, because the government spent millions investigating and prosecuting Enron executives, society as a whole is harmed as well, as that money could have been spent elsewhere for a greater good. For these Enron executives, where was their sense of corporate citizenship? Can citizenship, or a sense of corporate responsibility to society, be considered a type of monitor?

EXAMPLE 11.2 **Corporate Citizenship at American Express**

American Express is the world's largest travel agency and a large issuer of credit cards. It has a presence in 160 countries and more than 40 percent of its 84,000 employees work outside the United States. The firm has had "company values" long before the term became vogue. American Express values:[6]

- developing relationships that make a positive difference in their customers' lives;
- providing outstanding products and unsurpassed service;
- upholding the highest standards of integrity in all actions;
- working together across boundaries, to meet the needs of their customers and to help the company win;
- valuing employees, encouraging their development, and rewarding their performance;
- being citizens in the communities in which employees live and work;
- exhibiting a strong will to win in the marketplace and in every aspect of the business;
- being personally accountable for delivering on commitments.

Note that only three of the eight values can be clearly identified as relating to the business bottom line of the firm. Many of these values are clearly grounded in moral and social objectives.

These values are far more than just statements for the company coffee mug. American Express ensures that these values become an integral part of mainstream operations by surveying each employee on how the company has performed with respect to these values. The results of this survey are then used as one of several measurements used to determine compensation issues of managers. Social goals can really only be effective in the long run when objectives can be measured and when progress success or failure is tied to managerial compensation.[7]

GOVERNANCE AND STAKEHOLDER THEORY

Can stakeholder theory play a role in corporate governance? In the agency theory view of the firm, governance is about aligning managerial incentives and providing monitoring of management behavior. In the stakeholder view of the firm, how can management be forced to internalize the welfare of stakeholders?

Managerial incentives can be provided by rewarding management on the basis of some measure of the welfare of the stakeholders.[8] This process requires clear objectives and performance measurements. Defining acceptable, multiple missions suitable to all stakeholder groups can be tricky. Another key problem to be overcome is whether a measure of stakeholder welfare is available. It is harder to measure the firm's performance to its employees, customers, and so on than to its stockholders. There is no *accounting* measure (like earnings) or *market* value measure (like stock price) of the impact of past and current managerial decisions on stakeholder welfare. The result is that aligning managerial incentives with multiple stakeholder groups and measuring overall performance can become a noisy and chaotic process.

To date, there is no consensus on how to measure and report on changes in stakeholder welfare. Ideas that have supporters are the balanced scorecard[9] approach and the "triple bottom line."[10] The balanced scorecard measures performance in four perspectives: customer, internal processes, employee learning and growth, and financial success. Triple bottom line accounting expands the traditional company-reporting framework to take into account financial, environmental, and social outcomes. While both systems are used by some companies, neither has been generally adopted.

Regardless of the overall measurement of outcomes, organizational theory states that the firm will only value CSR goals if the company executive exhibits strong leadership in instilling corporate responsibility within the company's culture. The values of the culture influence the processes by which the company will try to solve a problem.[11] Executives signal which values are important through both employee incentives and through organizational structure.[12] The primary means is that of setting the criteria for recruitment and promotion. CSR goals are best executed when individual employees have promotion criteria incentives tied to those goals. A secondary means are the design of organizational structure and procedures that are aligned with the values. Mission statements, which reflect CSR goals and organizational units tasked with interacting with stakeholders, are examples of structural means of promoting culture values. The values set at the top of the company filter down throughout the organization. Therefore, leadership in corporate responsibility is critical to its adoption by a firm.

CRITICISMS

The authors, researchers, and practitioners of the stakeholder view of the firm use the concepts in different ways and often use contradictory evidence and arguments to support the theory. For example, some characterize stakeholder theory as a **descriptive theory**. It is used to describe what firms are doing and how they are doing it. Others use stakeholder theory from an **instrumental perspective**. This approach provides principles and practices that should be implemented to achieve (or avoid) certain results. They portent that if corporate performance results A, B, and C are desired, then the firm should implement standards and practices X, Y, and Z. Lastly, the stakeholder view is used to advocate how firms should behave based on ethical and philosophical principles. Advocates of CSR or corporate citizenship use this **normative approach**.

Is the stakeholder view correct? Should we view firms from a stakeholder perspective? If so, then how can we operationalize it? Because the stakeholder view is not a well-defined theory, it is difficult to assess. As an example, consider one of the primary stakeholders—employees. Providing employees with high-quality health care seems consistent with the tenets of the stakeholder view of the firm. The descriptive approach might ask how many companies are providing quality health care. The instrumental approach would be interested in how the providing of quality health care impacts the firm's stock returns and operating performance. The normative approach advocates that firms should provide quality health care because it is the moral thing to do. However, none of these provide the chance to accept or reject the validity of the stakeholder view.

Since the stakeholder view of the firm is difficult to empirically validate or reject, can it be philosophically criticized? Even critics of corporate citizenship agree that companies should act responsibly and should be seen doing so. After all, this is often good for business. However, that is different than aggressively pursuing the CSR doctrine advocated today. Indeed, critics argue that deviating too far from the profit-maximizing role of companies would be harmful to society.

The critics' argument stems from the experience that economic progress comes from profit-related activities. The primary role of business in society is to act as a vehicle for economic development. In a market-oriented economic system, economic progress results from entrepreneurial opportunities and competitive pressures. Successfully introduced new or improved products enhance profits while increasing the quality of life in society. Competition forces business to continually work to provide goods and services more effectively and more efficiently.

When managers have to take into account a wider range of goals and involve themselves in stakeholder engagement activities, higher costs and impaired business performance are likely to follow. When trying to serve "many masters," managers often become ineffective in achieving any of the goals.[13] Indeed, more exacting environmental and social standards will bring more regulation. Overregulation exacts an enormous cost on society in the form of limiting competition, narrowing opportunities, and worsening economic performance. History shows that when the economy is intentionally focused on social goals, such as employment, production, and so on, society becomes worse off. The poor economic performance of the former Soviet Union, Cuba, and China (before its more recent move toward a market-based economy) shows this.

EXAMPLE 11.3   Dow Jones STOXX Sustainability Index

One way to measure the success of firms engaged in corporate citizenship activities is to form a stock index of such firms. The SAM (sustainable asset management) Group measures a company's "corporate sustainability" and forms an index of the best companies (in cooperation with Dow Jones Indexes and STOXX Limited).

The SAM Group purports that "corporate sustainability is a business approach that creates long-term shareholder value by embracing opportunities and managing risks deriving from economic, environmental, and social developments." Specifically, the SAM Group quantifies the quality of a company's strategy and management in dealing with economic, environmental, and social opportunities. Competence is measured in areas such as strategy, financial performance, customer relationships, stakeholder engagement, governance standards, and employee satisfaction.

The Dow Jones STOXX 600 Index is designed to provide a broad representation of the European market, by including 600 firms from Austria, Belgium, Denmark, Finland, France, Germany, Greece, Ireland, Italy, Luxembourg, the Netherlands, Norway, Portugal, Spain, Sweden, Switzerland, and the United Kingdom. The narrower Dow Jones STOXX Sustainability Index (DJSI) tracks the performance of the top 20 percent (in terms of sustainability) of the companies in the Dow Jones STOXX 600 Index. This index started at the beginning of 1999. As of March 27, 2009, the DJSI STOXX included 161 companies.

Figure 11.2 shows both the DJ STOXX Index and the DJSI[14] since the creation of the DJSI. The DJ STOXX Index was scaled to 100 on January 1, 1999

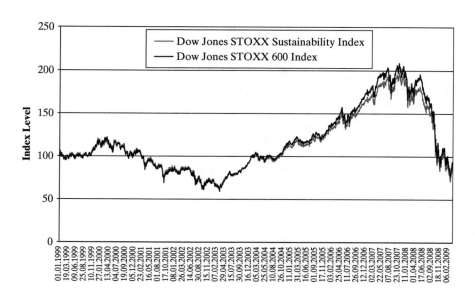

FIGURE 11.2 DJ STOXX 600 Index and DJSI, Since January 1, 1999

to equal the DJSI. Notice that performance of both indexes is nearly identical. In late 2001 and 2002, the sustainability index seems to be higher than the broader index. However, this reverses in 2004 as the sustainability index lags behind by a small amount for the next few years. This evidence does not seem to support the argument of corporate citizenship critics that companies serving multiple masters often become ineffective at achieving any of the goals. Neither does the evidence support proponents' argument that corporate citizenship maximizes company wealth. The sustainability index performs no better than the broader index.

INTERNATIONAL PERSPECTIVE

Corporate citizenship has different historical roots in different regions of the world and therefore is viewed with different perspectives. For example, CSR in the United States derived from the conflict between stockholder-focused managers and social activists. This unenthusiastic relationship between companies and some activist groups created a negative attitude toward stakeholder theory in the business community. Over the past few decades, many U.S. business groups have slowly began to embrace CSR ideas. In the United Kingdom and Europe, corporate citizenship has been viewed less negatively and is currently a more holistic concept. In India, the lack of government efficacy in the provision of social welfare has caused corporations to step into the role of helping society. Stakeholder concern is integrated within the firm and is based on family values.

A stakeholder view of the firm is also reflected in many laws internationally. In the United Kingdom, company directors are mandated to include the interests of employees in decision-making (the United Kingdom's Companies Act of 2006). In Germany, employee representation is required on one of the two-tier boards (codetermination laws). The European Union (EU) permits corporations to take into account the interests of employees, creditors, customers, and potential investors (harmonization laws). In Japan, after World War II, corporations were tasked with the responsibility for rebuilding the Japanese economy. The same was true for Korea after the Korean War in the 1950s. Korean companies that focused on exporting were even given tax breaks to help them bring capital into Korea.

How actively are managers engaging stakeholders? This is a difficult question to assess. The Conference Board surveyed over 700 companies on the issues of corporate citizenship between 2000 and 2001.[15] The firms tended to be very large (over 95 percent of the firms surveyed recorded over $1 billion in sales annually). The companies that respond to such surveys are those that have a positive attitude toward corporate citizenship. Instead of declaring a negative attitude, managers that do not value CSR simply do not complete the survey. Therefore we should consider the survey responses as a survey of firms actively engaged in CSR.

In the surveys, CEOs were asked what their firm's role would play in creating good business and good society. They were given the choices of

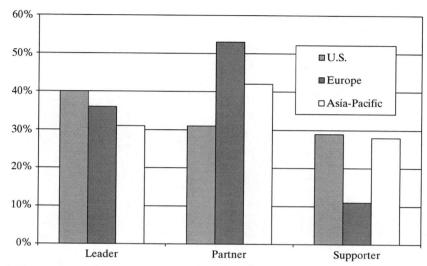

FIGURE 11.3 What Role Will Your Company Play in Increasing Good Business and Good Society?

Data Source: *Corporate Citizenship in the New Century: Accountability, Transparency, and Global Stakeholder Engagement*, The Conference Board. Research Report # R-1314-02-RR, July 2002.

being a leader, a partner, or a supporter. Results are shown in Figure 11.3 by geographical region for the companies completing the survey. Note that the most frequent answer from U.S. managers was to be a leader. European managers and those in the Asia-Pacific region most often chose to be partners. In general, managers from Europe and Asia-Pacific generally believed that the government should assume the leadership role in designing social good standards and activities.

The surveys also asked managers about how effective they were in implementing standards, codes, and programs that will result in achieving their corporate citizenship goals. Figure 11.4 shows that these companies believe they still have much room for improvement. Keep in mind, however, that it is more difficult to achieve higher-standard goals than lower goals. Nevertheless, there appears to be a large difference between U.S. and European firms and those in the Asia-Pacific. Over 50 percent of the firms from the United States and Europe responded as being either extremely effective or somewhat effective in their efforts. Only 20 percent of the Asia-Pacific firms believed they were so effective. Any lack of effectiveness may arise from not having a structured program to engage stakeholders on a regular basis. Only 60 percent of the responding firms have a structured program. Nevertheless, many companies are learning how to deal with this new area of corporate accountability.

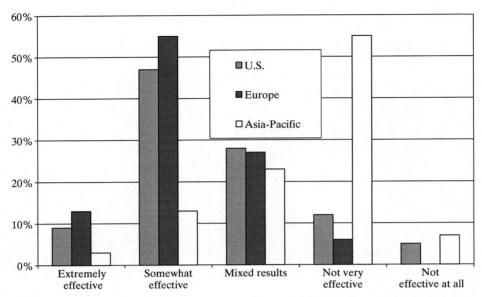

FIGURE 11.4 How Effective Are Your Efforts Today to Address the Citizenship Factors That Will Assure Your Success Tomorrow?

Data Source: Corporate Citizenship in the New Century: Accountability, Transparency, and Global Stakeholder Engagement, The Conference Board. Research Report # R-1314-02-RR, July 2002.

Summary

The stakeholder view of the firm does not focus on the maximization of shareholder wealth but rather on the optimization of the sustainable economic wealth of all stakeholders. Stockholders, employees, customers, communities, and the environment are just some examples of stakeholders. Their legitimate interest in the firm arises from the perspective that these stakeholders have property rights in the firm. Corporate stakeholder relationships have different historical roots in different regions of the world and therefore are viewed with different perspectives.

The modern evolution of the stakeholder view of the firm, called CSR or corporate citizenship, advocates that companies have a social obligation to operate in ethically, socially, and environmentally responsible ways. By embracing citizenship goals, corporations may insulate themselves from activist actions, enhance the firm's reputation, and find that their goodwill opens doors to new communities and additional sales. Therefore, a sense of corporate citizenship potentially represents another way to affect business people's behaviors and actions. In this sense, it can be considered a monitor. But is the CSR concept good for society? It is difficult to do well while doing good. A company can fail in its social goals and still succeed as a business, but it cannot fail as a business and still succeed in its social goals. In addition, how do we create a governance system based on this sense of citizenship?

WEB Info about Corporate Citizenship

The Conference Board
www.conference-board.org

CSR Europe
www.csreurope.org

The Corporate Citizenship Company
www.corporate-citizenship.co.uk

Review Questions

1. Name and describe as many stakeholders of the corporation as you can.
2. Describe the differences between agency theory and stakeholder theory.
3. Name and describe the four levels of CSR.
4. What are the criticisms of a profit-maximization focus?
5. What are the criticisms of the stakeholder view of the firm?

Discussion Questions

1. Do you think corporations should have a responsibility to society in general? Explain.
2. Let's say companies should be good citizens. How can this be measured? How can it be enforced?
3. How should we solve a stakeholder crisis? Who would be the monitors? Who should be the monitors? What regulations can be imposed?

Exercises

1. Report on the latest developments of CSR as described by The Conference Board (*www.conference-board.org*).
2. Go to *www.wakeupwalmart.com*. Describe the current stakeholder problems with Wal-Mart. Also go to *www.walmart.com* and determine what Wal-Mart is doing to engage the stakeholders.
3. How might corporations engage environmental activists in a productive and legal way?
4. Investigate and report on the standards of corporate social responsibility issued by the Social Venture Network (*www.svn.org*).

Exercises for Non-U.S. Students

1. Does your country subscribe to an agency view or the stakeholder view of the firm? Explain.
2. In what ways are firms in your country viewed differently from U.S. firms? Are they seen as contributors to the national economy? Are corporate executives looked upon as greedy or as important social leaders?
3. What is your overall opinion of the role of your country's firms in your country? Is it good for the long run? What criteria (profits, environment, etc.) should be applied?

Endnotes

1. An early organization of the stakeholder theory concepts is provided in E. R. Freeman, *Strategic Management: A Stakeholder Approach*, (Boston, MA: Pitman, 1984).

2. Thomas Donaldson and Lee E. Preston, "The Stakeholder Theory of the Corporation: Concepts, Evidence, and Implications," *Academy of Management Review* 20, no. 1 (1995):65–91.

3. Andrew Carnegie is generally credited with creating the term *corporate social responsibility* in his 1889 essay entitled "The Gospel of Wealth."

4. See Archie B. Carroll, "A Three-Dimensional Conceptual Model of Corporate Performance," *Academy of Management Review* 4 (1979):497–505 and Archie B. Carroll, "Corporate Social Responsibility: Evolution of a Definitional Construct," *Business & Society* 38, no. 3 (1999):268–295.

5. Paine, Lynn S., *Value Shift: Why Companies Must Merge Social and Financial Imperatives to Achieve Superior Performance* (New York: McGraw-Hill, 2003).

6. See *www.americanexpress.com*.

7. For an example of American Express's commitment to corporate responsibility, see "Recognizing Responsibility: American Express Company 2007/2008 Corporate Citizenship Report" at *http://home3.americanexpress.com/corp/gb/cresp/pdf/cresp.pdf*.

8. See Jean Tirole, "Corporate Governance," *Econometrica* 69, no. 1 (2001):1–35.

9. Robert Kaplan and David Norton, *The Balanced Scorecard: Translating Strategy into Action* (Harvard Business School Press, 1996).

10. John Elkington, *Cannibals With Forks: The Triple Bottom Line of 21st Century Business* (New Society Publishers, Stony Creek Creek, Connecticut, 1998).

11. Diane Swanson, "Toward an Integrative Theory of Business and Society: A Research Strategy for Corporate Social Performance," *Academy of Management Review,* 24 (1999):506–521.

12. Edgar Schein, *Organizational culture and leadership*, 2nd ed. (San Francisco, CA: Jossey-Bass, 1992).

13. Michael Jensen, "Value Maximization, Stakeholder Theory, and the Corporate Objective Function," *Journal of Applied Corporate Finance* 14, no. 3 (2001): 8–21.

14. Data is from *www.sustainability-indexes.com*.

15. Sophia A. Muirhead, Charles J. Bennett, Ronald E. Berenbeim, Amy Kao, and David J. Vidal, *Corporate Citizenship in the New Century: Accountability, Transparency, and Global Stakeholder Engagement* The Conference Board, Research Report # R-1314–02-RR, July 2002.

CHAPTER 14

Leadership

LEARNING OUTCOMES

After studying this chapter, you should be able to:

1 suggest reasons why leadership at work in the twenty-first century might be more challenging than ever before;

2 identify various criteria of leader effectiveness;

3 specify some common personality characteristics of leaders;

4 define the terms consideration and structure as they are used in leadership research;

5 define the key concepts and propositions of Fiedler's contingency and cognitive resource theories of leadership;

6 define five leader decision-making styles (with varying degrees of participation, and several features of the problem situation) identified by Vroom and Jago;

7 name and define four aspects of transformational leadership and two aspects of transactional leadership and examine the nature of charismatic leadership;

8 discuss the extent to which transformational and charismatic leadership influence performance at work and discuss some drawbacks of charisma and transformational leadership;

9 examine the circumstances in which leadership might be seen as relatively unimportant;

10 describe how concepts of leadership held by subordinates and in society generally give an alternative perspective on leadership;

11 explain why and in what ways effective leader behaviour may differ between countries and cultures;

12 list the cultural groupings within Europe, and describe their distinctive views of leadership.

Opening Case Study   ## Corporate leaders on a quest for meaning

Chief executives are reluctant to talk publicly about the difficulties of the job. In private, however, they admit to a fear of failure, qualms about their leadership style and worries about winning employees' commitment. Anonymous interviews with 30 European chief executives over the past three months reveal consistent concerns despite wide variations in culture and management style.

'The things keeping them awake at night would be to do with their own personal performance as a leader, not their business performance,' says Mike Walsh, chairman of Ogilvy Europe, Africa and Middle East, part of Ogilvy & Mather, the advertising company, which carried out the research. Strikingly, only two of the 30 had been groomed for the job, highlighting the rapid rate of CEO turnover and the difficulties, or even absence, of succession planning. While they were worried about handling external economic pressure, they felt the absence of 'textbook' solutions most acutely in relation to their personal style and effectiveness.

'Coming fresh to this role, many were tempted or persuaded to do things in which they did not believe,' says the report, *Today's CEO*.

> They learned that this did not work, primarily because the people who were expected to follow and implement such decisions could detect their lack of sincerity. The greatest mistake was to try to be something one was not: to claim to know more, do more, be more than one actually was.

The interviewees said they wanted to build relaxed, non-hierarchical working cultures, but in many cases they were part of a much larger organisation for which that was too big a step. Many needed to understand better how their employees think and feel, especially as they tried to squeeze more productivity out of them. Increasingly, they realised this need. 'There is a degree of introspection today that wasn't there three years ago, inspired by a fear of failure and loss of office', the report says.

Senior executives are increasingly searching for meaning in their lives, says Mark Watson, a coach, and director or Purple Works, a UK learning and communications group. Top jobs confer less influence and power than most people think but entail huge responsibility, and life can be a grind. 'In big organisations you're hemmed in by board committees, corporate governance protocol and expectations to perform. Many of these people also find themselves detached from the real operations.'

Source: Financial Times, *21 September 2001.*

Introduction

If the article above is to be believed, corporate leaders are not happy people. They think a lot about how they should go about being a leader. The styles they adopt are influenced by their own past experience and by the opportunities and constraints of the context. At times they feel they are expected to pay attention to the needs of others while their own needs are overlooked. They need to increase the productivity of their workgroups and organisations and they wonder how to achieve that without inducing burnout and alienation.

Many argue that demands on leaders are changing in their nature and also increasing (Dess and Picken, 2000). Work organisations are increasingly reliant upon rapid and skilful innovation and use of information at all levels. Leadership based upon monitoring and control of subordinates is often no longer appropriate or even possible. Subordinates and leaders sometimes work in different locations, which makes close supervision very difficult (*see* Chapter 10). The task of leaders, even at quite low levels in an organisation, is said to be managing continuous change and delegating responsibility while maintaining an overall sense of direction. Yet this may not come naturally to either leaders or followers. To quote an analysis of leadership from South African and American perspectives:

> What is killing us is the illusion of control: that things can be predictable, consistent and forever under control. What is also killing us is that followers require their leaders to be in control, on top of things, and to take the blame when things go wrong. Nearly all the new management programmes on TQM, re-engineering, right-sizing, just-in-time, this or that, are really old wine in new bottles – more efforts to design control systems that ask the workers to try harder; do better and be even more productive.
>
> *(April et al., 2000, p. 1)*

Key Learning Point

Leadership is especially challenging nowadays because of the pace of change, the illusion of control and the high expectations of followers.

In this chapter we examine some of the many academic approaches to leadership. There is quite a long history of research in this area, and it would be impossible to cover all of it. Particularly influential work will receive most attention, along with applicability in twenty-first century workplaces. In many of the early sections of this chapter you will see that we identify issues that will be discussed later in this chapter: this is because many early theories of leadership fail to account for important aspects of leadership behaviour. We also consider whether contemporary theories of leadership are successful in addressing these deficiencies. In accordance with the increasing internationalisation of the organisational realm, we will also examine the extent to which national cultures affect perceptions and impact of leaders.

Some important questions about leadership

Leadership can be considered to be the personal qualities, behaviours, styles and decisions adopted by the leader. One attempt at defining leadership in a cross-culturally valid way comes from the Global Leadership and Organisational Behavior Effectiveness (GLOBE) Project, to which we will return later. After ample discussion, scholars representing 56 countries defined leadership as 'the ability of an individual to influence, motivate, and enable others to contribute towards the effectiveness and success of the organisation of which they are members' (House *et al.*, 2004).

A leader can be defined as the 'person who is appointed, elected, or informally chosen to direct and co-ordinate the work of others in a group' (Fiedler, 1995, p. 7). This definition acknowledges that the formally appointed leader is not always the real leader, but it confines the notion of leader to a group context. If we take the word 'group' literally, this definition *excludes* leaders of larger collectives such as nations, large corporations and so on (except in so far as they lead a small group of senior colleagues, such as a cabinet of government ministers, or other members of a board of company directors). You will probably notice that this goes against how we often view leaders: we also tend to see those who are indirect supervisors at much higher levels in organisations as leaders.

When most followers do not have direct contact with the leader, the dynamics of leadership may differ from those when they do. This is an important point because many leadership theories were developed for the situation of *close supervision* rather than more distant leadership. Waldman and Yammarino (1999) have argued that similar concepts can be used to describe leadership styles in these two situations, but the ways in which followers form impressions of the leader differ. For those close to the leader, impressions are derived from day-to-day interaction. For those distant from the leader impressions depend more on leaders' stories, vision and symbolic behaviours and on how well their organisations perform.

Key Learning Point

The real leader of a group may not be the person who was formally appointed to the role.

Over the years several distinct but related questions have been asked about leaders and leadership, including:

■ Who becomes a leader and how do leaders differ from other people? Can we predict the *emergence* of leadership?

■ How can we describe their leadership?

It is difficult to consider these questions without bringing in the notion of effectiveness. So we can also ask questions like:

■ What determines the *effectiveness* of leaders? What are effective leaders like (e.g. what characteristics do they possess, what do they do, what do they say?) and how do effective leaders differ from ineffective ones?

■ What characteristics of the various situations that leaders find themselves in help or hinder a leader's effectiveness?

How can we tell whether or not leaders are effective? One method might be to assess the performance of their groups relative to other similar groups with different leaders. This assumes both that such comparison groups are available and that performance is easy to measure. However, some teams perform unique, new and knowledge-intensive tasks: this makes their performance harder to 'see'. Also, in many jobs, performance is difficult to define objectively and measure accurately in all aspects, especially in the long-term. Then there is also the problem that performance is often determined by many things other than leadership. The current state of the employment market is an obvious example of such a factor affecting performance while not being directly under the leader's control. Employees may be aware that they can get better pay for doing a similar job elsewhere, and hence underperform despite good leadership. They might also leave when there are plenty of jobs available, rendering voluntary turnover as an inaccurate measure of good leadership. Sometimes group members' satisfaction with the leader is used as a measure of leader effectiveness, but who is to say that high levels of satisfaction with the leader are always good? At times good leaders probably need to ruffle a few feathers. Although too much tends to be harmful to the organisation, some turnover might be healthy. In short, there is no perfect measure of leader effectiveness. Group performance is used most often, probably correctly, but we must remember not to expect an especially strong association with leadership: too many other factors come into play.

Key Learning Point

There is no one perfect indicator of leadership effectiveness, but the work performance of the leader's workgroup or organisation is probably the best (although the influence of other factors on workgroup performance also needs to be taken into account).

The early leader-focused approaches to leadership

You will have noticed that for many of the chapters in this book we examine the simple ideas before moving to the complex theory and research. This is the approach we will take with leadership. Most theory and practice up to the 1960s (and some since) had two key features:

1   Description of the leader in terms of their characteristics and/or behaviours rather than the dynamics of the leader's relationship with subordinates.

2   Attempts to identify the characteristics/behaviour of 'good leaders' *regardless* of the context in which they lead.

Leader characteristics

One of the questions early leadership research tried to answer was: which characteristics differentiate leaders from non-leaders, or effective leaders from ineffective ones? Some early work (reviewed by Stogdill, 1974; House and Baetz, 1979) found that leaders tended to be higher than non-leaders on:

■ intelligence;

■ dominance/need for power;

■ self-confidence;

■ energy/persistence;

■ knowledge of the task.

Many other personality traits (for example good adjustment, emotional balance and high integrity) were found in some early studies to be more common among leaders than non-leaders (e.g. Bass, 1990). Although this early search for what makes a leader did yield some interesting results, researchers did not find a definitive, consistent profile of characteristics among effective leaders. Also, this research was of variable quality which made it difficult to identify reliable findings.

More recently, meta-analysis has allowed researchers to isolate the common, reliable findings from the vast amount of previous research. Judge *et al.* (2004a) reviewed a large number of studies of leadership and discovered a modest but significant overall positive correlation ($r = 0.27$) between intelligence and leadership. Meta-analysis has also helped us to better understand the relationship between personality and leadership. Judge *et al.* (2002) found that, overall, the Big Five model of personality (*see* Chapter 3) had a multiple correlation of 0.48 with leadership. This indicates that when traits are organised according to the five-factor model and they are all included, there is a moderate relationship between them and leadership. Looking at each of the Big Five in turn, this study showed that those who are more likely to emerge as leaders, and be more effective, tend also to be:

- high in extroversion, openness to experience and conscientiousness (with there being relatively small positive correlations between these and the emergence of leadership and leadership performance).

- low in neuroticism (with there being a small, negative correlation between this and leadership emergence and performance).

This comprehensive analysis of personality and intelligence concluded that no one trait stood out as the single most important determinant of effective leadership. One possible explanation that Judge *et al.* suggest for this is that traits may interact with each other to determine the quality of leadership. For example, high levels of intelligence may only lead to effective leadership if the individual also possesses the *other traits* that are also necessary to show effective leadership in any given context (Judge *et al.*, 2004b):

> It is possible that leaders must possess the intelligence to make effective decisions, the dominance to convince others, the achievement motivation to persist, and multiple other traits if they are to emerge as a leader or be seen as an effective leader. If this is the case, then the relationship of any one trait with leadership is likely to be low.
>
> (Judge et al., 2004b, pp. 549–50).

Key Learning Point

Although no single characteristic or trait fully explains leadership, personal characteristics such as intelligence and personality appear to be important for the emergence of leaders and the effectiveness of leaders.

Therefore, there is enough reliable research evidence that intelligence and sociability play a role in determining which people emerge as leaders (although as we will see later they are only part of the story). However, these same characteristics that help leaders to reach the top may also subsequently prove their undoing. For example, a high level of dominance and need for personal power may help people reach leadership positions, but once there such traits may prevent a leader maintaining good relationships with their team or superiors, and this may precipitate their removal (Conger, 1990).

In addition, the characteristics of people who attain leadership positions have been found to depend partly on their motives for being leaders, and the acceptability of those motives to those who appoint them. Research in the Netherlands compared Chief Executive Officers (CEOs) in the 'not-for-profit' sector (e.g. organisations campaigning for children's rights or environmental protection) with CEOs in the commercial sector. Those in the commercial sector scored *lower on the power motive and higher on the social responsibility motive* (De Hoogh *et al.,* 2005; De Hoogh and Den Hartog, 2008). These pieces of research also showed CEOs in the voluntary sector were also generally seen as exhibiting more power-sharing leader behaviour and less despotic leader behaviour than those in commercial organisations. These findings fit with the idea that leaders are likely to be attracted to organisations that fit their personality and values (e.g. Schneider, 1987). People with a high concern for responsibility may be more attracted to jobs in not-for-profit organisations, as they feel these organisations have a social and morally responsible orientation. Therefore, when leaders use their power for purely personal goals in such organisations, they may be perceived to be acting against the organisation's altruistic values.

A more democratic ideology, or leader motive, emphasising the decentralisation of power, fits the context of the 'not for profit' organisation. In commercial organisations top leadership positions are often where legitimate power is concentrated. In these organisations authority is generally directed downward through a hierarchy which provides a more conducive context for leaders who are motivated by, and show, dominance and personal power (De Hoogh and Den Hartog, 2008). Thus, the acceptability of leaders' motives is likely to vary in different contexts or for different 'audiences' and organisational contexts. We will return to this issue when we examine leadership in different cultures. However, it should also be noted that there are some findings that are applicable in many different organisational settings. House and Baetz (1979) have argued that the very nature of the leadership role must mean that sociability, need for power and need for achievement are at least somewhat relevant, across different organisations and organisational cultures. Two of their insights are generally accepted by many studying leadership:

1   A leader's personal characteristics must be expressed in their observable behaviour if those characteristics are to have an impact on others and their performance.

2   Different types of tasks may require somewhat different leader characteristics and behaviours.

Key Learning Point

The leadership characteristics that are desired and acceptable may vary across different organisational contexts.

Of course, one of the most evident and difficult to change personal characteristics is one's gender. It can be argued that most leadership roles are typically described in stereotypically masculine terms, which might mean that women have more difficulty in (i) being selected for leadership roles, and (ii) being seen as good leaders even when they are selected. On the other hand, one might expect women to do better precisely because only the most able ones make it to leadership roles. In a meta-analysis, Eagly *et al.* (1995) found no overall difference in leadership performance between men and women. However, men had an advantage in military and outdoor pursuits (i.e. stereotypically masculine settings), while there was no difference or a slight advantage for women in business, education and government settings. Research by Lewis (2000) suggested a rather subtle disadvantage for women leaders relative to men. Lewis asked students to view videotapes showing a male or female company chief executive displaying anger, sadness or emotional neutrality in response to a company's poor performance. The student's ratings of the leaders' effectiveness tended to be *lower* if leaders expressed emotion than if they were neutral. However, displays of anger damaged the ratings of female leaders more than they damaged those of male leaders. Lewis suggested that this result showed the importance of followers' perceptions of leaders' behaviour. In this study it was suggested that whereas a man's anger might be perceived as assertiveness, a woman's anger may be perceived as aggression or instability. Later in this chapter we will examine how leaders might be able to influence their followers' interpretation of a leader's behaviour.

Key Learning Point

Personality characteristics in themselves do not make leaders inherently effective. What matters is how those characteristics are expressed in leaders' behaviour, and how that behaviour is understood by others.

Task orientation and person orientation

In the 1950s, one research team at Ohio State University and another at Michigan University launched independent projects on leader behaviour. Rather than focusing on the *characteristics* of leaders, they focused instead on how leaders *behaved*. They did this simply by asking primarily subordinates to describe the leader's behaviour. This produced a very long initial list of leaders' behaviours, within which there seemed to be two separate groups of behaviour (i.e. two general underlying dimensions). One focused on how leaders facilitate group maintenance and the other on what leaders do to ensure task accomplishment. These were described as follows (Fleishman, 1969):

1 *Consideration*: the extent to which a leader demonstrates that they trust their subordinates, respect their ideas and show consideration of their feelings.

2 *Initiating structure*: the extent to which a leader defines and structures their own role and the roles of subordinates toward goal attainment. The leader actively directs group activities through planning, communicating information, scheduling, criticising and trying out new ideas.

The Michigan team started by classifying leaders into two groups (as effective or ineffective) and then looked for behaviours that distinguished these two groups. Behaviours associated with relationships (consideration) and task orientation (initiating structure) differentiated the effective and ineffective managers: effective managers seemed concerned about both the task and their subordinates. Based on this, Blake and Mouton's (1964) Managerial Grid (still used in some management training courses) encourages leaders to examine their own style on these two dimensions: the suggestion is that it is usually best to be high on both consideration and initiating structure.

However, when trying to achieve different outcomes, might one style be more effective than another? Meta-analysis (Judge *et al.*, 2004a) of leadership research has revealed that both consideration (correlation, $r = 0.48$) and initiating structure ($r = 0.29$) have moderately strong relationships with different leadership outcomes. Although both dimensions were related to all studied outcomes, consideration was more strongly related to follower satisfaction (both with the leader and the job), motivation and leader effectiveness. Initiating structure was slightly more strongly related to leaders' job performance and group/organisation performance. This suggests that followers may prefer considerate leaders, but seem to perform at least as well for structuring leaders (Judge *et al.*, 2004a).

This research was very useful in demonstrating what impact these leadership styles might have on followers. However, it did not show exactly *how* these styles impact on followers. It seems likely that mediating mechanisms play a role: for example, leaders' behaviour may provoke an emotional reaction among followers, or it may have some impact on followers' working conditions (Nielsen *et al.*, 2008a). Also, so far, much of the research we have discussed has assumed that there was a linear relationship between exposure to these styles of leadership and outcomes have been assumed (i.e. the more the better). However, Fleishman (1995), for example, argued for curvilinear relationships, i.e. that there are diminishing returns to the increased use of consideration and structure on the part of the leader.

In any case, structuring and consideration refer to quite specific styles of day-to-day behaviour. They give little indication of how *well* the leader structures tasks or expresses consideration. They also give no indication of how well the leader is thinking strategically about what the workgroup is trying to achieve, and by what routes. The extent to which leaders working at the highest levels of large organisations use structure and consideration with immediate subordinates may have little or no impact on the wider organisation. Later, we will return to the more strategic angle when we discuss providing an overarching vision as an important element of leadership.

Key Learning Point

Consideration and initiating structure are useful concepts that have stood the test of time in analysing leadership. However, they focus on the leader's day-to-day behaviour rather than their overall strategy.

Participation and democracy

Another behavioural style that received much attention is participation. This concerns the extent to which the leader is democratic or autocratic (i.e. has a participatory leadership style). It is clearly related to the dimensions already discussed, but not identical. For example, the definition of structure given earlier does not necessarily exclude subordinates from influencing the direction given by the leader. In discussing the nature of the democratic leadership, Gastil (1994) emphasises that it is not just a case of letting the subordinates get on with their work, rather, the three key elements of democratic leadership are:

1   *Distributing responsibility*: ensuring maximum involvement and participation of every group member in group activities and setting of objectives.

2   *Empowerment*: giving responsibility to group members, setting high but realistic goals, offering instruction but avoiding playing the role of the 'great man'. Keller and Dansereau (1995) found that use of empowerment by leaders can both help them get the performance they want from subordinates and increase subordinates' satisfaction with their leadership.

3   *Aiding deliberation*: by playing an active part in the definition and solution of group problems, without dictating solutions.

In the aftermath of the Second World War it was hoped and believed that democratic or participative leadership was superior to autocratic leadership. In fact, the evidence is that on the whole participation has only a small positive effect on performance and satisfaction of group members (Wagner, 1994). As Filley *et al.* (1976) observed, where the job to be done is clearly understood by subordinates, and within their competence, participation is not going to make much difference because there is little need for it. On the other hand, in many less straightforward situations, participation does aid group performance. This is another theme that we will return to later in this chapter when we discuss more contemporary theories of leadership.

Key Learning Point

A democratic leader is active in group affairs: they do not just sit back and let the rest of the group sort everything out.

STOP TO CONSIDER

As you will have gathered, theories that focus on leader characteristics do not provide a complete explanation of leaders' success. However, we have also seen that they do provide some useful information. At this point, if you were going to develop a selection process that would be used to identify people with strong leadership potential, what would you try to measure?

Contingency theories of leadership

The above approaches to leader behaviour contribute to our understanding of what leaders do and the effects of their behaviour. In their original forms these approaches have an important feature in common. They all describe leader behaviour without paying much attention to the situation or context in which the leader acts.

To oversimplify a little, they are stating that in order to be effective, leaders need to perform certain behaviours regardless of the context or the particular demands of the situation.

However, consideration, initiating structure and participation can all be used more flexibly. The key idea behind contingency theories is that some situations demand one kind of behaviour from leaders, while other situations may require others. Do we really need a leader high on consideration and low on structure in an emergency such as a bomb scare? Probably not – we need someone who will quickly tell us what to do. We can do without a leader who asks us, at that specific moment, how we feel about the bomb scare. On the other hand, if a leader is responsible for allocating already well-defined tasks to a group of junior managers, we might hope for some sensitive consideration of the managers' skills, preferences, career development plans, etc. You might also want to think about which types of leadership behaviour might suit different types of organisational change (*see* Chapter 16).

Contingency theories assume that optimal leader behaviour is contingent upon (i.e. depends upon) the situation. As a result, contingency theories are fairly complex. They specify not only which leader behaviours are crucial, but also which aspects of the situation matter most, and how leader behaviour and the demands of different situations interact with each other. Of course, this leaves plenty of room for disagreement between different contingency theorists. Without being exhaustive, we will examine some of the most influential and controversial contingency theories.

Key Learning Point

Contingency theories of leadership propose that different situations demand different leader behaviours.

Fiedler's contingency theory of leadership

Fred Fiedler put forward his contingency theory of leadership in the 1960s (Fiedler, 1967). Fiedler argued that leaders have fairly stable personal characteristics, leading to a characteristic behavioural style. In his view, the key personal characteristic concerns how positively leaders view their least preferred co-worker (or LPC). His questionnaire had leaders describe their least preferred co-worker on 16 dimensions, such as pleasant–unpleasant, boring–interesting and insincere–sincere. A high LPC score signifies a positive view (and a low score a negative view) of the least preferred co-worker.

Exactly what an LPC score means remains unclear. It could be quite similar to consideration (high LPC) and structuring (low LPC), though this assumes that consideration and structuring are opposite ends of the same continuum rather than independent constructs. Indeed, high LPC leaders are often referred to as person-oriented – after all, they must be if they can be positive even about people they do not like! Low LPC leaders are often thought of as task-oriented. No doubt these approaches overlap. Yet Fiedler and others have argued that LPC also reflects the leader's deeper pattern of motivation. Some suggest that LPC is strongly linked to cognitive complexity. High LPC leaders may score higher on cognitive complexity than low LPC leaders because they can differentiate between a person's inherent worth and their work performance or likeability (i.e. they have a more complex and multifaceted way of evaluating their followers).

Key Learning Point

In his original contingency theory Fiedler assumed that a leader's perception of their least preferred co-worker indicates how person-oriented the leader is.

Fiedler argued that in some situations having a high LPC leader at the helm is best, while others call for a low LPC leader. He proposed three aspects of the situation which together define its favourableness to the leader, namely:

1 Leader–member relations: whether or not subordinates trust and like their leader.

2 Task structure: are the group's tasks, goals and performance are clearly defined?

3 Position power: does the leader control rewards and punishments for subordinates?

Fiedler's research found that in highly favourable and in very unfavourable situations, group performance was better for low LPC leaders (i.e. task-oriented). In situations of moderate to quite low favourability, high LPC leaders were best (i.e. person-oriented). It is not clear why this should be. One common-sense explanation is that where the situation is good, the leader does not need to spend time on interpersonal relationships. They are already sufficient for smooth functioning. Similarly, where the situation is very bad, things are so difficult that it is not worth spending time on interpersonal relationships. Improvement would take too long even if it was possible at all. Forging ahead with the task is best. Where the situation falls between the extremes, keeping group members happy becomes more important. A leader needs high LPC to hold the group together, so that tasks can be tackled. Fiedler's theory asserts that leaders have a fairly stable LPC score, so training them to do things differently is not very useful. Instead, he argued for matching the leader to the situation and viewed placement as more useful than training (Fiedler and Chemers, 1984).

Key Learning Point

Fiedler proposed in this original contingency theory that task-oriented leaders are best in very favourable and unfavourable situations, and that people-oriented leaders are best in moderately favourable or moderately unfavourable situations.

Many problems with Fiedler's theory have been identified. Apart from the unclear nature of LPC (i.e. what factors drive a leader's LPC rating), there is doubt about whether the LPC score is indeed stable. Perhaps it depends too much on just how undesirable the leader's least preferred co-worker really is – that is, the LPC

Table 14.1   Predictions of Fiedler's contingency theory of leadership

	Situation highly favourable I	II	III	IV	V	VI	VII	Situation highly unfavourable VIII
Leader–member relations	Good	Good	Good	Good	Poor	Poor	Poor	Poor
Task structure	Structured	Structured	Un-structured	Un-structured	Structured	Structured	Un-structured	Un-structured
Leader position power	Strong	Weak	Strong	Weak	Strong	Weak	Strong	Weak
Desirable leader LPC score	Low	Low	Low	High	High	High	High	Low

score may say more about the co-worker than the leader. Another issue concerns Fiedler's concept of the situation. For example, in the medium and long-term, leader–member relations (which Fiedler defined as a dimension of the favourableness of the situation) are most likely a result of the leader and subordinates' behaviours. Is it therefore valid to treat leader–member relations as part of the situation, rather than a product of the actions of leaders and followers?

Despite these doubts, Peters *et al.* (1985) reported partial support for the theory in an extensive meta-analysis. Schriesheim *et al.* (1994) also found general support by reviewing studies comparing leader performance in different situations. As predicted by Fiedler's theory, low LPC leaders did better in the two most favourable situations and the least favourable one (Table 14.1). High LPC leaders did better in moderately favourable and moderately unfavourable situations. The researchers point out that if we assume that most leadership situations are moderate, we can simply say that high LPC leaders are better, rather than going to the trouble of engineering situations to fit leader styles.

Cognitive resource theory

Fiedler built on his earlier work in his cognitive resource theory (CRT). CRT builds upon LPC theory by examining how the cognitive resources of leaders and subordinates affect group performance (e.g. Fiedler and Garcia, 1987). As Fiedler (1995, p. 7) puts it: 'the relationship between cognitive resources and leadership performance is strongly dependent on such factors as the leader's situational control over the group's processes and outcomes, and the stressfulness of the leadership situation'. Referring to situational control demonstrates the links with Fiedler's earlier theory (since situational control relates to leader–member relations, position power and task structure). The stressfulness of the situation is also linked with this because

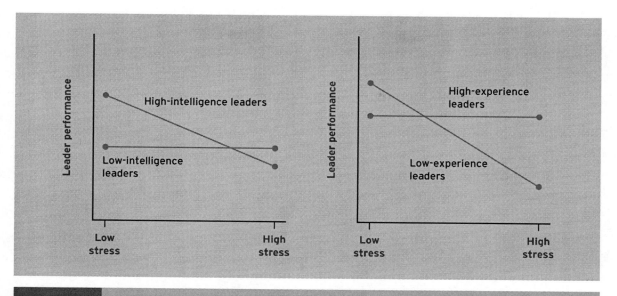

Figure 14.1   **Predictions of leader performance in Fiedler's cognitive resource therapy**

less favourable situations tend to be more stressful. Fiedler (1995) also sees stress as coming from the leader's own boss being unsupportive, hostile or over-demanding. Some of the key predictions of CRT are shown in Figure 14.1.

Fiedler argues that cognitive performance is inhibited in high-stress situations. That is, when leaders feel anxious or overloaded, they are unable to think clearly. In difficult situations they are likely to fall back on well-learned patterns of behaviour that result from their experience (Fiedler, 1996). Hence, in high-stress situations experience plays a more important role than intelligence in determining a leaders' performance.

Sternberg (1995) argues that experience is a disguised measure of so-called crystallised intelligence; that is, our store of know-how and knowledge about the world. This is essentially what Fiedler refers to when he uses the word intelligence. When a lot of our cognitive resources are being used in coping with a difficult situation, we use 'automatic' behaviour, which we can deploy without having to think too much about it. CRT theory proposes that leaders' automatic behaviour in such situations is more likely to be appropriate and effective if it is based on long experience.

Key Learning Point

Fiedler's cognitive resource theory introduces new factors about the leader and the situation. It proposes that, in difficult situations, leaders need to rely on their experience rather than their fluid intelligence.[1]

---

[1] Fluid intelligence is relatively context-free and drives logic and problem-solving. More detailed information on the distinction between crystallised and fluid intelligence can be found in Chapter 3.

Not all psychologists are convinced by CRT. Vecchio (1990, 1992) argued that there is not much empirical support for it, but Fiedler *et al.* (1992) claimed that it was simply not yet tested properly. Fiedler (1995) reports a number of studies showing results that are consistent with CRT. A recent meta-analysis examining intelligence and leadership provides support for the two moderators suggested by CRT: fluid intelligence and leadership were more strongly related when leader stress was low and when leaders exhibited directive behaviours (Judge *et al.*, 2004a).

Thus, Fiedler suggests both experience and fluid intelligence as key criteria in selecting leaders. His recent work suggests that the concept of matching leader to situation must be based on the leader's intelligence and experience as well as LPC and situational characteristics. Stress-reduction programmes are now thought to help leaders utilise their cognitive resources, and thus avoid the problems that might occur when leaders are placed in a situation where they might over-rely on 'automatic' responses.

Exercise 14.1   Using Fiedler's theories of leadership

For the last year, Debbie Walsh has been head of the ten staff of the market analysis department of a garden furniture company. The company sells its products through selected garden centres and do-it-yourself shops. The department's tasks are well established. For example, it monitors sales of each product at each outlet. It evaluates the viability of potential alternative outlets. It checks the products and prices of competitors. Debbie is a high-flyer academically, having obtained a first-class honours degree and an MBA with Distinction. The managing director has great faith in her, and has given her complete discretion over awarding salary increases to her staff and most other aspects of people management in the marketing department. This is Debbie's first marketing job: most of her previous four years' work experience were spent in general management at a knitwear company. Other staff do not resent Debbie. They feel her appointment demonstrates the truth of the company's pledge to put ability ahead of experience in promotion decisions. They may in future benefit from that policy themselves, since most of them are young and well qualified.

Debbie takes a no-nonsense approach to her work and colleagues. She responds well to business-like people who come straight to the point. She has little patience with those who are slower to get to the heart of a problem, or who do not share her objectives. Most of her present staff have a similar approach to hers. However, in one of Debbie's previous jobs her hostility toward several slow and awkward colleagues was a major factor in her decision to leave.

Suggested exercises

1   In Fiedler's terms, how favourable is Debbie Walsh's leadership situation?

2   Using Fiedler's contingency and cognitive resources theories, decide whether Debbie is well suited to her situation.

Vroom and Jago's theory of leader decision-making

Vroom and Yetton (1973) proposed a contingency theory of leader decision-making (extended by Vroom and Jago, 1988). They took a different approach from Fiedler by focusing exclusively on specific decisions, big and small, that leaders have to make.

They suggested that leaders are able to adapt their behaviour from situation to situation (remember that Fiedler's approach suggested that different leaders might be needed for different situations).

Certainly, most leaders say they do adapt their behaviour. The theory identifies five styles of leader decision-making that leaders might choose to use. The options on this 'menu' range from autocratic styles to democratic styles (*see also* the section Participation and democracy, above):

- AI: the leader decides what do to, using information already available.

- AII: the leader obtains required information from subordinates, then makes the decision about what to do. The leader may or may not tell subordinates what the problem is.

- CI: the leader shares the problem with each subordinate individually, and obtains their ideas. The leader then makes the decision.

- CII: the leader shares the problem with subordinates as a group, and obtains their ideas. The leader then makes the decision.

- GII: the leader shares the problem with subordinates as a group. They discuss options together and try to reach collective agreement. The leader accepts the decision most supported by the group as a whole.

Vroom and Jago (1988) identified some key features of situation to consider that together indicate the style a leader should adopt in that particular situation. The situational features are shown in Figure 14.2.

Also, Vroom and Jago argued that two further factors are relevant if the situational factors shown in Figure 14.2 allow for more than one recommended style to be used. These factors are (i) the importance to the leader of minimising decision time and (ii) the importance to the leader of maximising opportunities for subordinate development. Computer software has been developed that allows a leader to input answers to the questions listed in Figure 14.2. It then calculates an overall 'suitability score' for each possible style. The specific formulae are beyond our scope here, but general rules of thumb include:

- where subordinates' commitment is important, more participative styles are better;

- where the leader needs more information, AI should be avoided;

- where subordinates do not share organisational goals, GII should be avoided;

- where both problem structure and leader information are low, CII and GII tend to be best.

Key Learning Point

Vroom and Jago assume that leaders are able to alter their decision-making style to fit the situation they are in. Many factors in the situation can help determine appropriate styles, including time pressure, clarity of the decision parameters and attitudes of subordinates.

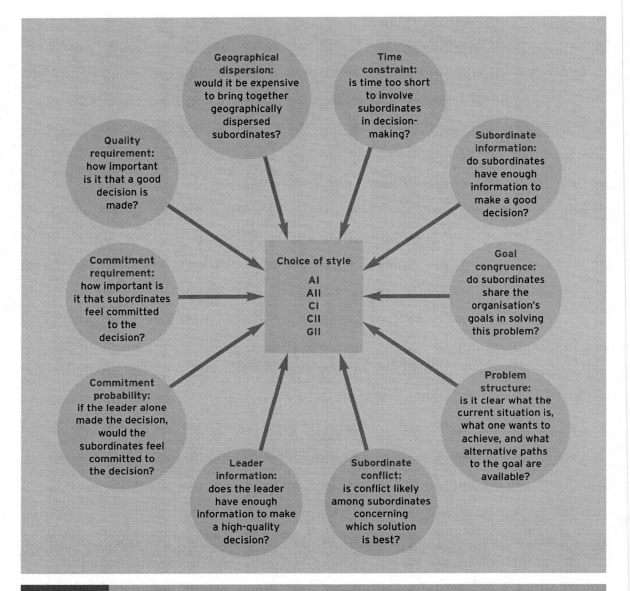

Figure 14.2   **Vroom and Jago's features of leadership situations**

The model has not been examined much in the published research literature. There is some evidence that the skill with which leaders put their selected style into action is at least as important as choosing an appropriate style in the first place (Tjosvold *et al.*, 1986). This suggests that it's not only what the leader does, but the way that they do it. In practice, the model's complexity makes it difficult for leaders to use quickly and easily in their everyday decision-making. Due to their subjectivity, a leader's answers to the questions posed by the model (e.g. whether subordinates share organisational values) may say as much about the leader's personality and values (i.e. how they perceive the situation) as about the reality of the situation itself. Vroom and Jago nevertheless suggest that knowledge of the general principles such as those presented here will often be useful, and sometimes even sufficient, for managers.

Other contingency approaches: is a leader really necessary?

In their situational leadership theory (SLT), Hersey and Blanchard (1982) proposed that leader effectiveness depends on the interplay between leader style (i.e. relationship or task orientation) and the maturity of the follower. Follower maturity refers to the subordinates' understanding of the job and their commitment to it, but length of time in the job is often used as a proxy to measure it in research. The idea of the theory is that during the early stages of an employee's tenure, leadership is more about orienting employees to the task. Therefore, a low level of relationship orientation coupled with high task orientation is ideal. As employees gain maturity and start to cope with the task, the need for supervisory social-emotional support increases, while the need for structuring decreases. At the highest levels of employee maturity, supervisory behaviours (both task-related and social emotional ones) become superfluous to effective employee performance. In other words, this approach suggests that once employees master with both task and social relationships, they are perhaps best left to get on with it. Vecchio (1987) found that among 303 teachers in America, the theory's predictions were fairly accurate for subordinates with low maturity and reasonably accurate for those with moderate maturity. However, the theory was not at all accurate for those with high maturity.

Perhaps the crucial message of Vecchio's results is that even when subordinates are mature, it is not a good idea for leaders to neglect both task and relationships. This echoes studies showing that a laissez-faire (or non-active) leader style is unlikely to be effective (e.g. Bass, 1990) and seems to argue against an extension of SLT principles proposed by Kerr and Jermier (1978). They proposed that in some circumstances leaders are unnecessary. This approach is labelled *substitutes for leadership*. It suggests that some factors can neutralise the impact of leadership. Examples of proposed substitutes for leadership are: intrinsically interesting tasks for employees (*see* Chapter 8); the ability, experience, training and knowledge of subordinates; and availability of senior staff other than the leader. Research suggests that the presence of substitutes for leadership does not fully eliminate effects of leadership style on satisfaction and performance. This may be partly because measures of the substitutes for leadership are not very good (Williams *et al.*, 1988). However, it also seems likely that in most situations leadership does matter. The apparent lack of efficacy of substitutes for leadership suggests either (i) that leadership tasks cannot easily be distributed around a group or (ii) that we have a psychological need for a leader: this issue we return to discuss later in this chapter.

Key Learning Point

Several contingency theories analyse leader style in terms of consideration and structuring, even if the words used are different.

Transformational leadership and charisma

The theories already discussed in this chapter show that both task- and relationship-oriented behaviours are important for effective group leadership. However, as we have highlighted, these theories did not explain the effectiveness of leaders in all situations. An important leadership function was rarely considered: leaders often provide a uniting vision, or overarching goal, for followers to strive for. In essence, much of the early research on leadership viewed the leader as a *tactician*, not as an *inspirational figure* with a strategic role. If we consider successful leaders in business and politics they are frequently portrayed as heroes and heroines who unite, inspire and motivate their followers by offering attractive strategic visions of a better tomorrow. Thus, in the 1990s, many scholars turned their attention to qualities such as vision, charisma and other related concepts. These added an important new element to the study of leadership.

What is meant by a leader's vision? Leaders often present a vision that describes a better future in ideological terms. Effective leaders tend to present a vision that is congruent with the dearly held values of followers, and this vision helps leaders to integrate and align followers' efforts. Through formulating a vision a leader interprets reality for listeners and gives meaning to events. The leader communicates this vision through words as well as deeds, modelling desired behaviour. Visionary leaders instil pride, gain respect and trust and increase a sense of optimism and hope in followers. An attractive vision of the future helps give followers a sense of vision and inspires acts as a powerful motivating force for those who share the vision (Bass, 1985; Conger, 1990; Shamir *et al.*, 1993). Earlier in this chapter we highlighted how early theories of leadership largely ignored the issue of how leaders' behaviour is perceived by followers. In contrast, the way leaders influence followers' perceptions of their behaviour is central to the theories of transformational leadership.

Theorists in this area make a clear distinction between transactional and transformational leadership (Burns, 1978; Bass, 1985, 1997). Transactional leaders try to motivate subordinates by observing their performance, identifying the rewards they desire and distributing rewards for desired behaviour. The underlying idea is that transactional leadership is based on exchanges, or transactions, with subordinates. Leaders define work goals and the behaviour deemed appropriate for reaching them. They offer clarity and the desired rewards, and in return subordinates contribute effort and skill.

Table 14.2	Components of transformational, transactional and laissez-faire leadership

The four components of transformational leadership

1 *Individualised consideration*: the leader treats each follower on their own merits, and seeks to develop followers through delegation of projects and coaching/mentoring

2 *Intellectual stimulation*: the leader encourages free thinking, and emphasises reasoning before any action is taken

3 *Inspirational motivation*: the leader creates an optimistic, clear and attainable vision of the future, thus encouraging others to raise their expectations

4 *Idealised influence*, or *charisma*: the leader makes personal sacrifices, takes responsibility for their actions, shares any glory and shows great determination

The two components of transactional leadership

1 *Contingent reward*: the leader provides rewards if, and only if, subordinates perform adequately and/or try hard enough

2 *Management by exception*: the leader does not seek to change the existing working methods of subordinates so long as performance goals are met. They intervene only if something is wrong. This can be *active* where the leader monitors the situation to anticipate problems, or *passive* where the leader does nothing until a problem or mistake has actually occurred

Laissez-faire leadership
The leader avoids decision-making and supervisory responsibility, and is inactive. This may reflect a lack of skills and/or motivation, or a deliberate choice by the leader.

Transformational leaders, on the other hand, go beyond this skilled use of inducements by developing, inspiring and challenging the intellects of followers so that they become willing to go beyond their self-interest in the service of a higher collective purpose, mission or vision. To be effective, this vision needs to be ambitious but realistic, and articulated clearly and in inspirational ways. Transformational leaders encourage followers by setting a personal example and followers become motivated and emotionally attached to the leader (Bass, 1985, 1997). Bass (1985) developed a questionnaire called the Multifactor Leadership Questionnaire (MLQ) to assess the extent to which subordinates perceive their leader to exhibit different components of transformational and transactional leadership (as well as a laissez-faire approach to leadership). The measured components are described in Table 14.2.

Key Learning Point

Transformational leadership is about inspiring and challenging subordinates, providing an overarching goal and setting a personal example.

Although the components described in Table 14.2 can be theoretically distinguished, in research in practice this is harder. Leaders' MLQ scores on the four components of transformational leadership often covary. In other words, when leaders are seen to exhibit one of these, they also tend to be rated high on the others. For example, Den Hartog *et al.* (1997) found high correlations (of 0.61 to 0.75) between the different components of transformational leadership in ratings of their leaders of about 700 people in eight Dutch organisations. Geyer and Steyrer (1998) also report similar findings in their sample of over 1400 employees of Austrian banks, as did Tracey and Hinkin (1998) in their sample of hotel employees in the United States. This shows that the components of transformational leadership tend to 'hang together' in followers' perceptions of leader behaviour.

Furthermore, contingent reward, a component of transactional leadership, also tends to go hand in hand with transformational leadership. In other words, transformational leaders also tend to administer contingent rewards. Such rewards can be tangible (e.g. money) but also intangible in nature (e.g. praise or symbolic appreciation). In some studies it seems that transformational leaders tend to also engage in active management by exception. This may be a matter of context: in a high-risk context 'good' leaders might need to or be expected to engage in monitoring.

It has often been argued over the years that transactional and transformational leadership are not mutually exclusive (e.g. Bryman, 1992), and that leaders can demonstrate one or the other, both or neither. Both and neither seem to be more common than one or the other. Therefore although they examine qualitatively different behaviours, measures of transformational and transactional behaviour are often highly correlated (e.g. Nielsen *et al.*, 2008b). Transformational leaders also tend to be perceived as executing the transactional elements of their job effectively.

Not surprisingly, the extent to which a leader is transformational seems to depend partly on his or her personality. For example, Judge and Bono (2000) found that transformational leaders tended to score higher than others on the personality traits extroversion, agreeableness and openness to experience (*see* Chapter 3). This might seem to suggest that we have come full circle back to the old trait-based approaches to leadership. However, they concluded that the connections between personality and leadership style were not strong enough to consider transformational leadership a personality-based theory: transformational leadership also appears to be about learned behaviour.

Key Learning Point

In the behaviour of real leaders, the four components of transformational leadership tend to go together with (i) each other and (ii) elements of transactional leadership.

Other work has taken a closer look at one particular element of transformational leadership: *charismatic leadership* (Conger and Kanungo, 1998). Charisma, as you might imagine, has been a difficult construct for researchers to define. It tends to be viewed by researchers as a *perception of a leader held by followers* as well as a *characteristic of the leader*. Intuitively we might think that charisma is something a leader is (or is not) born with. However, Frese and Beimel (2003) report a study which suggests that leaders can be trained to perform some of the behaviours associated with charisma. Also, as Gardner and Avolio (1998) put it, perceptions of charisma are in the eye of the beholder and thus do not always stem directly or only from the leader's behaviour. Most researchers agree that a leader is not charismatic unless described as such by their followers. Success plays a role in this: more successful leaders are often seen as more charismatic regardless of whether they had full control over getting there. For example, House *et al.* (1991) found that the perceived success of past US presidents was associated with how charismatic they were thought to be.

In order to isolate a definition of charismatic leadership, Conger *et al.* (2000) collected data from about 250 managers on five aspects of charismatic leadership in a business context. They found that there were five key elements to charismatic leadership:

1   The leader formulates a strategic vision, and articulates that vision.

2   The leader takes personal risks in pursuit of the vision.

3   The leader is sensitive to the opportunities and limitations provided by the environment (e.g. in terms of technology, money, people).

4   The leader is sensitive to others' needs.

5   The leader sometimes does unusual or unexpected things.

Although this is labelled charisma, it clearly has a wider meaning than the more specific charisma component of transformational leadership in Table 14.2. Sensitivity to others' needs resembles individualised consideration, and articulating strategic visions resembles inspirational motivation. So this model of charismatic leadership forms an alternative way of viewing transformational leadership. Rowold and Heinitz (2007) find a strong overlap between transformational leadership measured with the MLQ and charismatic leadership as measured with Conger *et al.*'s measure.

Key Learning Point

The components of charisma as defined by Conger and Kanungo go beyond the narrower charisma dimension of the Bass model. Combined, these components are similar to transformational leadership as a whole as defined by Bass.

Of course, there is great interest in whether transformational and/or charismatic leadership measurably helps improve the work performance, satisfaction, attitudes and well-being of individuals, groups and organisations, and if so how. In other words, does transformational leadership 'work'? The simple answer seems to be yes. The extent to which leaders are perceived to use elements of transformational leadership is positively correlated with subordinates' perceptions of their effectiveness, satisfaction and effort and with performance measures such as percentage of group targets reached, and supervisory evaluations of workgroup performance (e.g. Hater and Bass, 1988; Bass and Avolio, 1994). Several MLQ meta-analyses summarise the relationships of transformational, transactional and laissez-faire leadership with outcomes. Transformational leadership shows highest correlations with outcomes such as follower and leader satisfaction and effectiveness, follower motivation, leader job performance and group performance. Perhaps not surprisingly, contingent reward is positively related to a range of outcomes. Recent work also shows that inactive leaders are not, generally, effective: laissez-faire leadership was generally associated with negative outcomes. Management by exception is inconsistently related to performance criteria (e.g. Judge and Piccolo, 2004).

Geyer and Steyrer (1998) carried out a particularly well-designed study of the impact of transformational leadership. They took a careful look at the nature and measurement of transformational leadership and obtained objective measures of the performance of bank branches in Austria such as volumes of savings, loans and insurance products. They also took into account local market conditions for each branch (for example, the average income in the area). Staff then rated branch managers on the MLQ. Core transformational leadership (intellectual stimulation, inspirational motivation and charisma) was a significant predictor of branch performance. So was contingent reward, though to lesser extent. Rowold and Heinitz (2007) also found that transformational leadership shows a stronger relationship to profit than transactional leadership shows to profit.

In addition, Geyer and Steyrer found that core transformational leadership, individualised consideration and contingent reward were strongly associated with the effort that branch staff said they exerted. Passive management by exception was associated with less effort and lower branch performance. The correlations between ratings of leadership and branch performance were not especially high (around 0.25) but with a large number of branches and high volume of business, this small effect of transformational leadership could mean a big impact on profitability company-wide. The impact of transformational leadership does not appear to be limited to financial outcomes. In a longitudinal study Nielsen *et al.* (2008a) found that transformational leadership has a positive impact on employee well-being, partly due to the influence that transformational leadership behaviour has on shaping the nature of the work carried out by employees. Research by Conger *et al.* (2000) found that when followers perceive their leader as charismatic, they form more of a sense of group identity, empowerment and reverence (i.e. awe or extreme admiration) for the leader. Using a range of different measures of transformational leadership, studies find that charismatic leadership is related to top team effectiveness (De Hoogh *et al.*, 2004), followers' positive emotions (Bono and Ilies, 2006) and organisational citizenship behaviours (e.g. Den Hartog *et al.*, 2007). In the US, Waldman *et al.* (2001) and in the Netherlands, De Hoogh *et al.* (2004) found positive relationships between charismatic leadership of CEOs and financial outcomes, but only in dynamic and challenging market contexts.

Key Learning Point

Transformational and charismatic leadership tend to be associated with good performance of workgroups and organisations.

Exercise 14.2　Transactional and transformational leadership

Marc LeBlanc is manager of the claims department of a medical insurance company. He is rather unlike many of his colleagues, in that he dresses unconventionally and has long hair, which he ties into a pony tail. The department's job is to process claims by clients who have spent time in hospital. Marc considers himself scrupulously fair with his staff of 17 administrators and clerks. He thinks that if something (such as a training course) is good for one of them, then it is good for all. He has successfully resisted senior management's wish for performance-related pay, arguing that group solidarity will ensure that everyone pulls their weight. ▶

Marc thinks of his job as making sure that the members of the department know where it is going and why. In contrast to his predecessor, he never tires of telling his staff that their job is to 'play a proper part in the client's return to good health' rather than to contest every doubt, however tiny, about a client's claim. He has been known to invite claimants to the office when he thinks they are being treated badly by the company, and to force his bosses to see them. Marc has a noticeboard for displaying complimentary letters from clients grateful for prompt and trouble-free processing of their claims. He frequently emphasises the need to look at things from the client's point of view. He tells his staff to focus on certain key aspects of the long and complicated claim form, and only briefly inspect most of the rest of it. Marc checks whether they are doing this, but only when a complaint is received from a client or the company's own internal claims auditors. In such cases he defends his staff, provided they have conformed to the department's way of doing things. He is less sympathetic if they have taken decisions about claims on other criteria, even if those claims have some unusual features.

Suggested exercises

1   Marc LeBlanc scores high on just one aspect of transformational leadership. Which one and why?

2   He scores high on one aspect of transactional leadership. Which one and why?

3   In what respects, if any, might Marc's leadership be described as charismatic?

4   The performance of the claims department could be measured with more than one criterion. Think of one respect in which Marc's style enhances the department's performance, and one respect in which his style hinders performance.

Critiquing transformational leadership

The concepts of transformational and charismatic leadership clearly represent an important advance in our understanding of how leadership can be described and of how to be an effective leader. In the complex twenty-first century world many feel we need a leader we can believe in. However, even with all this evidence to support it, this approach too has several limitations. We highlight four of these.

First, researchers have speculated, but so far scarcely investigated, whether the type of situation in which leaders and followers find themselves affects the suitability of transformational leadership. A few exceptions are starting to show that contingency models are needed for this form of leadership too. More challenging, uncertain contexts seem to offer more room for transformational leadership to have effects (e.g. Shamir and Howell, 1999). For example, several studies on charisma indicated that its effect on performance, effectiveness and organisational citizenship is context-dependent. More research on this is needed however before firm conclusions can be drawn.

Second, until recently, there seems to have been an implicit assumption that the leader is the source of most of what happens. The reality may be that followers have as much impact on the leader as the leader does on the follower. Barker (1997) noted that too much (transformational) leadership research ignores the fact that any workplace has conflict and competition. Leaders and followers do not necessarily have the same goals. Barker argues that the 'ship' in leadership has too often led to leadership being seen as a set of skills (as in craftsman*ship*) rather than a political phenomenon (as in relation*ship*).

Third, writers such as Tourish and Pinnington (2002) argue that the notion of transformational leadership moves too close to cult leaders who are revered by their followers as people who can do no wrong. Over a period of time, this may encourage authoritarianism, which is not helpful for democracy, nor for the development of employees as mature and responsible adults. For example, Kark *et al.* (2003) show how transformational leadership relates both to followers' empowerment and their dependence on the leader. Thus, although such leaders may intellectually stimulate followers and help them take responsibility they may also increase their need for leadership.

Fourth, transformational leadership glosses over the issue of whether the leader is forming and articulating an appropriate vision of the future. History tells us that some transformational leaders fail, or even cause terrible harm. In any case, followers may reject the leader's vision as being inappropriate. These concerns coupled with recent ethical scandals and sustainable management issues fuelled research on different forms of authentic and ethical leader behaviour (e.g. Avolio *et al.*, 2004; Brown and Treviño, 2006). Different theories that pay much more attention to the moral aspects of leadership emerged. Recently, researchers have begun to consider ethical leadership as a behavioural style in itself rather than focusing only on ethical aspects of other leadership styles (Brown *et al.*, 2005; De Hoogh and Den Hartog, 2008).

Brown *et al.* (2005) take a social learning approach to ethical leadership and focus on the exemplary behaviour of the leader. They define ethical leadership as 'the demonstration of normatively appropriate conduct through personal actions and interpersonal relationships, and the promotion of such conduct to followers through two-way communication, reinforcement, and decision-making' (p. 120). They find a correlation between ethical and transformational leadership, but show the two do not overlap completely (i.e. they appear to be different concepts). Others have defined ethical leadership as something more than the perceived normative appropriateness of leadership behaviour. Factors such as the leader's social influence, the purpose of the behaviour of the leader and the consequences of that behaviour for the leader and others are also important in determining ethical leadership (e.g. De Hoogh and Den Hartog, 2008; Turner *et al.*, 2002). For example, Kanungo (2001) states that the leader, in order to be ethical, must engage in virtuous acts or behaviours that benefit others, and must refrain from evil acts or behaviours that harm others.

Key Learning Point

Transformational leadership has construed the leader as a 'great person', although increasingly research is starting to pay some attention to how followers behave, ethical leadership and the impact of the situation on leader effectiveness.

Perceiving leadership

As we have seen, many leadership theories have focused on what leaders do, rather then how those actions are perceived. In recent years, increasing attention has been paid to how and when we perceive leadership to be important. A related issue is how we identify someone as a leader. Some authors have focused on these questions, using ideas from the social psychology of person perception. Other analyses recognise that leadership is partly in the eye of the beholders, something that may be particularly important for charismatic leadership. However, Meindl and colleagues go further and argue that perceptions of leadership are entirely constructed by followers and observers and have little to do with the behaviour of leaders. In an article entitled 'The romance of leadership', Meindl *et al.* (1985, p. 79) argued that:

> we may have developed highly romanticised, heroic views of leadership – what leaders do, what they are able to accomplish, and the general effects they have on our lives. One of the principal elements in this romanticised conception is the view that leadership is . . . the premier force in the scheme of organisational processes and activities.

Meindl *et al.* (1985) further argued that our conception of leadership as important and influential should lead us to consider leadership a key factor where performance is either very good or very bad. When things go really well, we attribute it to the leader's skill. When things go really badly, we blame the leader's ineptitude. But when things go averagely well, we are less likely to say it was primarily due to average leadership. This is because we have a shared understanding of leadership as a big concept which has big effects, not moderate ones. Meindl *et al.* support this claim in several ways. For example, they searched the *Wall Street Journal* (WSJ) between 1972 and 1982 for articles about 34 firms representing a range of American industries. They then related the proportion of WSJ articles about each company mentioning the leadership of top management to company performance. A higher proportion of 'leadership' articles appeared when firms were doing especially well or especially badly – particularly the former. They also conducted experiments presenting case studies of corporate success and failure, and asking participants to rate the importance of various possible causes of that success or failure, including leadership. Again, leadership was seen as a more important cause of extreme (especially good) performance than of medium performance. Pillai and Meindl (1991) expanded this and found that the charisma of the CEO in a hypothetical case study of a fast-food company was rated as very high if the case described a crisis followed by success for the company (and very low if the crisis was followed by decline).

Findings such have these have provoked some to question whether leadership can be defined objectively. Gemmill and Oakley (1992) have argued that leadership is a *culturally defined concept*. They argue that we use it to protect ourselves from anxiety brought about by uncertainty concerning what we should do ('no need to worry, the leader will decide'), and from various uncomfortable emotions and wishes that arise when people try to work together. They also argue that the cost of using the concept of leadership to organise our social world is *alienation* – that is, feeling distant from our true self and devoid of authentic relationships with others. This could be because we give too much responsibility to people we label leaders, and therefore it can feel difficult to lead purposeful lives, or to view ourselves as purposeful, *self-managing individuals*. This is a rather radical view that draws partly on psychoanalytic theory and challenges both common-sense and academic leadership theories that are well-supported by well-designed research. Most people working in organisations would probably find it difficult to agree that leadership is illusory as they take on leadership roles, or report to people in leadership positions and functions. The point that Gemmill and Oakley make is that as employees we may try to transfer responsibilities or tasks to leaders that it would be better to take on ourselves. This brings us back to a point made earlier in relation to democratic leadership: democratic leaders may have to insist that their subordinates take a share of the responsibility (Gastil, 1994).

All of this seems like good evidence for a romanticised view of leadership, where we tend to grossly overestimate its importance, but this is not necessarily true. Meindl *et al.* (1985) did not demonstrate that we are wrong to make these attributions about leadership, only that we make them. Others, such as Yukl (1998), and the numerous sources of evidence cited in this chapter, argue that the quality of leadership really does make a difference to outcomes that matter in the real world.

> **Key Learning Point**
>
> Leadership is partly in the eye of the beholder. We may be inclined to overestimate the impact of leaders, particularly when performance is very good or very bad. However, this does not mean that leadership is an illusory concept or unimportant.

Global leadership

The globalisation of markets brought about by communications technology and the mobility of production resources mean that more and more people work in countries and cultures that are novel to them. For many managers, this means leading people of different backgrounds and outlooks from their own. There has been much recent interest in identifying the cultural dimensions along which countries can differ: this has a number of implications for leadership that we will examine in this section. The work which started it all was carried out by Hofstede (1980, 2001), who collected data from employees of IBM across many countries. He identified four cultural dimensions:

1 *Power distance*: the extent to which members of a society accept that there should be an unequal distribution of power between its members.

2 *Uncertainty avoidance*: the extent to which members of a society wish to have a predictable environment, and have set up institutions and systems designed to achieve this.

3 *Masculinity* vs. *femininity*: a masculine society values assertion, success and achievement, while a feminine one is oriented more towards nurturing and caring.

4 *Individualism* vs. *collectivism*: the former reflects a belief that individuals should be self-sufficient while the latter emphasises people's belongingness to groups in which there is mutual support.

It would be strange if there were not differences between countries with respect to the preferred, most used and most effective leadership styles. Using Hofstede's cultural dimensions we might expect autocratic styles to be more effective in high power distance cultures than in low ones. Leaders whose style is high on structure will probably be most appreciated in high uncertainty-avoidance cultures. Dickson *et al.* (2003) provide a very informative review of research on cross-cultural leadership.

They discuss in detail some of the reasons why the dimensions of culture identified by Hofstede and others might affect which styles of leadership are expected and effective. They argue that the search for leadership styles that work across the whole world is (or should be) accompanied by more research into indigenous models (i.e. models of how leadership works in specific culture, rather then across cultures) as well as exactly how culture and leadership affect each other.

GLOBE is a long-term study concerning how societal and organisational cultures affect leadership (House *et al.*, 1999). Over 60 countries from all major regions of the world are represented, making it the most extensive investigation of cross-cultural aspects of leadership to date. The core quantitative study looks at what the images of outstanding leadership are in different cultures, and includes over 17,000 middle managers from some 800 organisations in the financial, food and/or telecommunications industries in over 60 countries. These managers were asked to describe leader *attributes* and *behaviours* that they perceived to enhance or impede outstanding leadership in their respective organisations.

What were the findings? Attributes reflecting integrity (i.e. *trustworthy, just* and *honest*) contributed to outstanding leadership in all cultures. Also, an outstanding leader in all studied cultures shows many attributes reflecting transformational leadership: these include the leader being described as *encouraging, positive, motivational, a confidence builder, dynamic* and *having foresight*. Team-oriented leadership is also universally seen as important (i.e. such a leader is effective in team-building, communicating and coordinating). Other universally endorsed attributes included *excellence-oriented, decisive, intelligent,* and a *'win–win' problem solver.* The GLOBE study also shows that several attributes are universally viewed as ineffective including: *being a loner, being non-cooperative, ruthless, non-explicit, irritable* and *dictatorial.* Interestingly, many different leadership attributes were found to be culturally contingent. In other words, a high positive rating was obtained in some and a low or even negative rating in other cultures. Examples include being *unique* (i.e. different from the 'norm'), *indirect, status-conscious, intuitive* and *habitual*. These are examples of attributes that are considered desirable for outstanding leadership in some cultures but impediments in others (Den Hartog *et al.*, 1999).

The attributes seem to reflect underlying culture differences. For instance, country means for the attribute '*Subdued*' range from 1.32 to 6.18 on a 7-point scale and for '*Enthusiastic*' from 3.72 to 6.44. Thus, in some countries acting in a subdued manner is highly relevant to being an outstanding leader and in others such an approach is described as highly inefficient. Similarly, showing enthusiasm is relevant for outstanding leadership in some, but not in other cultures. This seems to reflect cultural rules regarding the expression of emotion. In some cultures, displaying emotion is interpreted as a lack of self-control and thus perceived a sign of weakness: not showing one's emotions is the norm. In other cultures, it is hard to be an effective communicator and leader without showing emotions.

Other culture dimensions are also reflected. For instance, several of the differences in attributes seem to reflect different levels of uncertainty avoidance. People in uncertainty-avoidance cultures want things to be unambiguous, predictable and easy to interpret and in such cultures technologies, rules and rituals are used to ensure this. This is reflected in several of the cross-culturally varying attributes. For instance, the attributes *risk-taking, habitual, procedural, able to anticipate, formal, cautious* and *orderly* are seen to impede outstanding leadership in some countries and enhance it in others.

Similarly, several attributes reflect high power distance versus egalitarianism in society. For example, *status and class-conscious, elitist, domineering* and *ruler* are attributes that fit a high power distance society, but are seen in a negative light in egalitarian societies. Also, several of the attributes reflect the culture dimension of individualism, for instance, *autonomous, unique* and *independent* are more important for outstanding leaders in individualistic than in collectivist societies.

GLOBE research offers further insights into leadership perceptions across Europe. Brodbeck *et al.* (2000) have reported perceptions of what makes a good leader in 22 European and ex-Soviet countries. They asked managers to indicate the extent to which 112 words (such as *foresight, honest, logical, dynamic, bossy*) were characteristic of outstanding leaders. The 112 words were grouped into 21 scales, which were given names such as Visionary, Diplomatic, Administrative and Conflict-inducer. The researchers then searched their data for consistent patterns *both within and between* countries. There were some substantial similarities across all European countries regarding perceptions of good leadership. For example *Integrity* and *Inspirational* were seen as highly desirable leader characteristics, and *Face-saver* and *Self-centred* as highly undesirable. But there were also some differences. To a large extent these replicated other work (Ronen and Shenkar, 1985) suggesting the European cultural groupings and characteristics shown in Table 14.3. France did not fit clearly into any of the groupings.

Table 14.3	Cultural groupings in Europe	
Grouping	Countries	Five most valued leadership attributes (most important first)
1. Anglo	UK, Ireland	Performance, Inspirational, Visionary, Team integrator, Integrity
2. Nordic	Sweden, Netherlands, Finland, Denmark	Integrity, Inspirational, Visionary, Team integrator, Performance
3. Germanic	Switzerland, Germany, Austria	Integrity, Inspirational, Performance, Non-autocratic, Visionary
4. Latin	Italy, Spain, Portugal, Hungary	Team integrator, Performance, Inspirational, Integrity, Visonary
5. Central	Poland, Slovenia	Team integrator, Visionary, Administratively competent, Diplomatic, Decisive
6. Near east	Turkey, Greece	Team integrator, Decisive, Visionary, Integrity, Inspirational

Source: Adapted from Brodbeck *et al.* (2000). With permission from Professor Dr. Felix Brodbeck.

It is clear that some of the differences between clusters are quite small. Nevertheless, it is notable that, for example, the Anglo cluster is the only one to have *Performance* at the top of the list, whereas *Performance* is not even in the top 5 for the central and near east clusters. Integrator is more important in south and east Europe (i.e. clusters 4, 5 and 6) than in north and west Europe. Although not shown in Table 14.3, it is also the case that *Status consciousness* was seen as slightly unhelpful to good leadership in north and west Europe but slightly helpful in the south and east.

There is also a question of whether actual leader behaviour is interpreted differently in different cultures and countries. Some research (Smith *et al.*, 1989; Peterson *et al.*, 1993) sought to discover whether similar leader styles are described using the same dimensions across different cultures. Using data from electronics firms in the United Kingdom, the United States, Japan and Hong Kong, Smith *et al.* (1989) concluded that what they call maintenance and performance leadership styles (similar to the consideration and structuring dimensions described earlier in this chapter) do indeed exist in different cultures. However, they also stated that 'the specific behaviours associated with those styles differ markedly, in ways which are comprehensible within the cultural norms of each setting' (p. 97). For example, one of the questions asked by Smith *et al.* was: 'When your superior learns that a member is experiencing personal difficulties, does your superior discuss the matter in the person's absence with other members?' In Hong Kong and Japan, this behaviour is seen as highly characteristic of maintenance (consideration). In the United Kingdom and the United States it is not: probably most Western subordinates would regard this as 'talking about me behind my back'. Not that all other British and American perceptions were identical: as Smith *et al.* (1989) noted, in the United Kingdom, consideration can be expressed by talking about the task, but this is not so in the United States. This also holds for other behaviours and attributes. For example, Bernard Bass describes that 'Indonesian inspirational leaders need to persuade their followers about the leaders' own competence, a behaviour that would appear unseemly in Japan' (Bass, 1997, p. 132). He goes on to say that, not withstanding the fact that it can be expressed in different ways, the concept of inspiration appears 'to be as universal as the concept of leadership itself'.

Political changes in some countries, for example in Eastern Europe, also have implications for the way managers are expected to lead in different contexts. Maczynski (1997) has shown that Polish leaders' preferred problem-solving styles shifted towards more participation between 1988 and 1994: this was the time during which time communism was toppled. Smith *et al.* (1997) found some differences even between neighbouring Eastern European countries. Managers in the Czech Republic and Hungary tended to report that they made great use of their own experiences and those of others around them. This is an individualistic style consistent with those countries' long-standing links with Western Europe: it can easily be contrasted with Romanian and Bulgarian managers' self-reported reliance on widespread beliefs held in their country to guide their behaviour.

These insights are very important as work organisations become increasingly international, with employees working across national and cultural boundaries. Assuming that leaders can identify which style they wish to adopt, they need to make sure they behave in ways which are interpreted as consistent with that style. Those behaviours differ somewhat between countries and cultures. The very fact that people are willing to try to describe leaders in terms of personal characteristics supports the attributional view that we carry around in our heads conceptions of what leaders are like. It also suggests that we believe we know what a good leader is like, regardless of the situation. Nevertheless, historically the situations faced by countries may well have influenced cultural norms about what constitutes good leadership.

Key Learning Point

Both long-standing cultural differences and major social and political change can influence actual leader behaviour and the behaviour desired by subordinates.

STOP TO CONSIDER

In this chapter we have looked at a number of different approaches to leadership. From what you have read, which is the most convincing? Do the various approaches offer competing explanations of leadership (i.e. if one is valid then the other cannot be)? Or might there be elements from some approaches that overlap with others? If you were to extract the most important and most valid elements from each approach to form a 'super theory' of leadership, which elements would you select – and what would this 'super theory' look like?

Summary

This chapter has explored many approaches to leadership. Consideration, initiating structure, charisma, cognitive complexity/intelligence and participation have been identified as some key leader characteristics and behaviours. Other less discussed notions such as the extent of the leader's knowledge of the industry and organisation must not be overlooked. There is considerable overlap between the various leadership concepts, and some tidying up and increased precision is needed. The same is true of the various situational variables proposed by contingency theorists. It is therefore not surprising that several of these theories are equally (and moderately) good at explaining leadership phenomena. Several approaches contain useful practical guidance about how to go about being an effective leader. Transformational and charismatic leadership models presented a significant step forwards, but more detailed knowledge is needed. Future theory and practice in leadership need to combine concepts from the better theories in a systematic way. There is also increasing recognition that leadership is not only about leaders. It also concerns followers and their preferences, characteristics and behaviours and cultural and individual perceptions of what leaders should be as well as about the relationships between leaders and followers. Greater attention to the question of whether and how leaders can be trained or selected not only to do the desirable things, but to do them well and in an ethical and sustainable manner, is also needed.

Exercise 14.3   Leadership and policy implementation

It was a turbulent time in the health and safety department of Super Chem's Hamburg plant. The multinational chemical company had recently adopted a policy of developing managers by giving them international experience. A consequence of this policy had been that a 32-year-old Spaniard, José Alonso, had been put in charge of the department. José's German was more than adequate for the task, but this was his first assignment outside Spain, a country seen by many in the company as peripheral to its operations. He had much to learn when he first arrived, especially about German health and safety legislation. He was, however, an experienced health and safety manager, having been head of health and safety at two plants in Spain for two years each.

Almost as soon as he arrived, José was pitched into an interesting situation. Two major accidents at other plants had caused a high-level health and safety policy review. The resulting report had come out in favour of more stringent inspection and a tougher approach from company health and safety departments. The recommendations were clear and specific, and had quickly become company policy.

José knew that his presence was resented by his six staff, who had worked together for some time and tended to think alike. They felt they had more specialist knowledge than he did. Most were older than him, and they could not understand why the deputy head, Gunter Koenig, had not been promoted. Koenig himself was understandably especially bitter. José felt that he could not follow his staff around as they inspected the plant: it would look too much like snooping. On the other hand, he needed to tap into his staff's knowledge of the plant and of how things had always been done there. Existing documents were too incomplete or too out of date to be of much help.

José had reason to believe that his staff typically adopted a collaborative approach with the plant managers whose areas they inspected. They preferred to use friendly persuasion and gentle hints rather than the precise written reports and threats for non-compliance required by the new policy. It had always worked at that plant, they said, and it would continue to do so. Yet José knew that exactly the same had been said at the plants where major accidents occurred. What was worse for José was that it was fairly clear that the plant manager privately agreed with José's staff. José's position was all the more difficult because he was known to be on a two-year secondment, after which the previous head (who had herself been seconded elsewhere) was expected to return in his place. Therefore he was not in a position to exert a long-term influence on the careers of his staff. His inclination would have been to intervene in his subordinates' work only when something was clearly wrong, but the new policy did not permit that approach. José himself was answerable not only to the plant manager but also to the company health and safety chief, who was the chief proponent of the new policy.

José knew that he was not a particularly creative or imaginative individual. He enjoyed the precision and rules and regulations of health and safety work. He preferred to focus on implementing the detail of policies rather than the big picture. He was usually inclined to draw up detailed plans of work for himself and others, and to keep a careful check on implementation of those plans. He liked to formulate work plans in a collaborative manner, encouraging his subordinates to think for themselves about what was required and how best to go about it. He felt he could understand how his staff felt about his appointment as their head without their consent: he had been landed with an unwelcome boss himself a few years earlier. He did not blame them for their attitude, and, characteristically, he was always keen to emphasise what he genuinely saw as the many strengths of his subordinates. He took time to discuss their work with each of them individually and tried to assign them work that would broaden their skills.

Despite the complicated situation, José felt that his task was clear enough. A decision had to be made concerning exactly how the department's practices would need to change in order to implement the new health and safety policy. Also, it had to be made in time for a visit by the health and safety chief six weeks later.

Suggested exercises

1   Analyse this case study using Fiedler's theories. What kind of situation is it? How well suited to it is José Alonso? What should he do next? What important features of this case study, if any, are neglected by Fiedler's ideas?

2   Analyse this case study using the Vroom and Jago theory. What kind of situation is it? What should José Alonso do next? What important features of this case study, if any, are neglected by Vroom and Jago?

3   In what respects, if any, can José's leadership style be described as (i) transformational and (ii) transactional? What scope is there for him to change, and would it make any difference if he did?

4   In what respects are national and cultural differences in perceptions of leadership relevant to this case study?

Closing Case Study   ## Lion King and the politics of pain

Junichiro Koizumi is the most popular prime minister in Japan's history and he is turning the country's staid political world on its head. For most of the past half-century, the country's politics have been predictable and dull, with barely a change of government, let alone the earth-shaking of the past few months. Until Koizumi took power in April 2001, the possibility of the country producing an iconic statesman capable of inspiring both hope and fear was unimaginable.

When Koizumi appears in parliamentary debates, millions tune in to watch live broadcasts. When he handed out a trophy at a recent sumo tournament, he stole the show, and the following day's headlines, from the sumo champion. The prime minister is a fashion leader, too. His Armani suits and permed 'Lion King' hairstyle are the talk of afternoon TV gossip shows. Fans are so desperate for a piece of 'Jun'chan', as he is nicknamed, that schoolgirls are queuing up at his party headquarters to buy mobile phone straps decorated with little Koizumi dolls. Off-duty salarymen wear T-shirts printed with their hero's chiselled profile drawn in the style of the famous Che Guevara ▶

poster, with the message: 'It's not just my challenge, it's our challenge.' Housewives subscribe to his personal webzine, Lionheart, where he shares insights into his family life. Depicted as a cartoon cuddly, big-hearted lion, Koizumi confides that high office feels 'like being trapped in a cage'. Among Tokyo's Asian neighbours, however, his unapologetic nationalism and mass appeal ignite fears that he may become a Japanese Hitler, a dictator who will lead the country back down the path of militarism.

Last month, Koizumi's approval ratings hit a staggering 90 per cent. Almost entirely as a result of his personal popularity, the ruling Liberal Democratic Party, which looked dead and buried at the start of the year, won a convincing victory in the upper house election. And his means of achieving such pre-eminence defy conventional political logic: Koizumi has wooed his party and the public with the bleakest of messages. Ask any Japanese citizen what words they most associate with the prime minister, and the answer will almost certainly be 'pain, pain and more pain'. Koizumi says he is willing to accept two years of recession, unemployment and bankruptcy as the price for restructuring an economy that has been described by former prime minister Yasuhiro Nakasone as 'the sick man of Asia'.

It all looked very different in 1989, when Tokyo was the envy of the world. From the ruins of the Second World War, the 'Japanese miracle' had transformed this nation of 126 million, small geographically, into the richest country on the planet. People worked hard, but in return they had the smallest gap between rich and poor in the world, the safest streets and the longest average lifespan.

Since 1989, shares on the Tokyo stock exchange have lost three-quarters of their value and land prices have more than halved. Economic growth – the *raison d'être* of postwar Japan – has virtually ground to a halt. Two years of falling prices have left the country on the edge of a deflationary spiral not seen in an industrialised nation since the great depression of the 1930s. The government has already pushed most of the emergency levers, to little effect. Even a 'money-for-nothing' policy of zero interest rates put in place by the Bank of Japan has failed to find takers.

All this would be a nightmare in any country, but it hurts more in Japan because the entire social system is built on the assumption of growth and the principle of deferred reward: men put up with low pay, long hours and short holidays; in return, they are guaranteed a job for life, steady promotion and a generous allowance when they retire. Women carry the burden in the home in return for a share of the security provided for their husbands. With a prolonged economic contraction, this unwritten contract has been broken. Faced by the trauma of restructuring, so many middle-aged salarymen are committing suicide that the average male lifespan has actually gone down.

The prime minister's family background and political record raise many questions about his claim to be a daring reformer who will shake up the country's semi-feudal political system. Like almost a third of Japanese MPs, Koizumi is a political aristocrat who inherited his father's constituency, support group and factional allegiances. He won the family seat in 1972 and has been re-elected 10 times, pushing him higher and higher up the LDP hierarchy. He has been consistently ambitious – running twice for the party leadership before this year's victory.

'He is a very unusual Japanese leader because he has a broad vision of society and culture, rather than a deep understanding of particular issues of industries', observed the governor of Okinawa, Kenichi Inamine. 'He's a weirdo', said LDP law-maker Tanaka, before she became foreign minister and declared herself Koizumi's 'political wife'. In office, Koizumi has already shaken the old hierarchy with the for-mation of a cabinet that, for once, does not merely reflect the old Confucian bias to-wards geriatric male timeservers. In terms of sex, age and background, Koizumi has picked the most diverse administration in the country's history. Many in the cabinet stress their loyalty to the premier ahead of the party. 'I'm not doing this for LDP, I'm doing it for Koizumi', says Tanaka. For the public, this is thrilling stuff. For the first time, politics is being played out in the open rather than in smoke-filled rooms. There is a clear diversity of opinion in the cabinet and public debate about key issues. It is chaotic, exciting and not a little frightening.

It is more for his promise of economic reform than for his nationalism that the pub-lic love Koizumi. But, at times, they are disturbingly protective of their would-be sav-iour. Opposition politicians who dare criticise the prime minister are bombarded with hate mail. The two parties that launched the most vociferous opposition to the gov-ernment's policies were almost wiped out in the last election. 'It frightens me that parties who criticise Koizumi or Tanaka during parliamentary debates receive death threats', says Kyosen Ohashi, an opposition lawmaker. 'LDP candidates think they can get elected just by posing for a campaign poster with Mr Koizumi. It is so far away from democracy that it worries me.'

Source: The Guardian, *August 2001.*

Suggested exercises

1   **To what extent and in what ways can Koizumi be considered a successful leader?**

2   **Which leadership characteristics are most evident in this article?**

3   **What aspects of the situation and the followers (i.e. the Japanese population) might have contributed to perceptions of Koizumi's leadership?**

Test your learning

Short-answer questions

1 Describe the strengths and weaknesses of alternative measures of leader effectiveness.

2 What are major pressures facing corporate leaders in the early twenty-first century?

3 Briefly, what factors other than the leader's personality traits influence their effectiveness?

4 Define consideration and structure.

5 Describe the key features of democratic leadership.

6 Outline the main features of Fiedler's contingency theory. Suggest two strengths and two weaknesses of the theory.

7 Outline the main features of Fiedler's cognitive resource theory.

8 List the leadership styles and problem-situation features identified in Vroom and Jago's theory of leadership.

9 Name and define four aspects of transformational leadership and two aspects of transactional leadership.

10 Describe some possible outcomes of transformational and charismatic leadership.

11 Briefly describe three or more possible weaknesses or limitations of the notion of transformational leadership.

12 Provide some examples of universally appreciated leadership characteristics and of cross-culturally contingent ones.

13 List the main cultural groupings of European countries in terms of perceptions of leadership.

Suggested assignments

1 Discuss the proposition that all of the aspects of leadership style identified in research essentially amount to person-orientation and task-orientation.

2 Examine the extent to which different contingency theories of leadership share the same key ideas.

3 Examine the implications for leadership of research which views leadership as a socially constructed phenomenon.

4 Discuss how and why leaders need to adjust their behaviour to different cultures.

5 Do theories of leadership concentrate too much on the leader as an individual?

6 Discuss the proposition that theories of leadership pay too much attention to specific aspects of the leader's behaviour, and not enough to their overall strategy.

Relevant websites

In the UK, the Council for Excellence in Management and Leadership has been working since 2000 to promote good practice – as indicated by its strap-line of 'Managers and Leaders: Raising our Game'. Its web address is http://www.managementandleadershipcouncil.org/. You can find quite a lot of useful information there, including reports prepared for the Council.

An example of how some consultancy companies promote leadership training can be found at http://www.ldl.co.uk/inspirational-leadership-management-training-course.htm. This shows the close connections between leadership and motivation, as well as the current concern with leaders who are inspirational.

One of the most influential and long-standing organisations promoting leadership research and practice is the Center for Creative Leadership, which is based in the USA but also has substantial operations in Europe (Brussels) and Asia (Singapore). Its home page is http://www.ccl.org/leadership/. There is a lot there to illustrate how ideas from theory and research are applied in management development.

 For further self-test material and relevant, annotated weblinks please visit the website at **www.pearsoned.co.uk/workpsych**

Suggested further reading

Full details for all references are given in the list at the end of this book.

1   *The Nature of Leadership* edited by Antonakis, Cianciolo and Sternberg, published in 2004, is a readable overview of leadership theory which expands on many of the themes of this chapter.

2   Keith Grint's edited book published in 1997 entitled *Leadership: Classical, contemporary and critical approaches* provides a scholarly analysis of a variety of leadership theories.

3   Gary Yukl has produced a thorough text on many areas of the field called *Leadership in Organizations*. The sixth edition was published in 2006.

4   The academic journal *The Leadership Quarterly* published by Elsevier is an important source for the latest research and theorising.

HUMAN RESOURCE MANAGEMENT

The efficiency and performance of staff, and their commitment to the objectives of the organisation, are fostered by good human relationships at work. This demands that proper attention be given to human resource management and harmonious employee relations. The manager needs to understand the importance of good managerial practices and how to make the best use of the people resource. The promotion of good human relations is an integral part of the process of management and improved organisational performance.

Learning outcomes

After completing this chapter you should be able to:

- explain the nature and responsibilities of human resource management (HRM);
- analyse HRM policies, activities and functions;
- outline a strategic approach to HRM and the organisation of the HRM function;
- examine the importance and benefits of training and talent management;
- explore the system and main features of performance management;
- explain the nature of employee relations and the employment contract;
- review the importance of the HRM function for individual and organisational performance.

Critical reflection

'The human resource department has no executive authority, it is non-productive and provides only a support and administrative function to other departments and managers. The title of "human resource manager" is arguably a complete misnomer.'

Do you agree? What alternative title would you suggest?

THE NATURE OF HUMAN RESOURCE MANAGEMENT

However the activities of management are identified, and whatever the nature of organisational processes, an essential part of the process of management is that proper attention be given to the efficient use of resources, in particular human resources. The human element plays a major part in the overall success of the organisation. There must be effective management of human resources.

The significance of human resources and people as the most important asset of any organisation is emphasised by *Gratton*. As the basis of her 'Living Strategy', Gratton puts forward four basic propositions:

1 there are fundamental differences between people as an asset and the traditional assets of finance or technology;
2 an understanding of these fundamental differences creates a whole new way of thinking and working in organisations, a shift in mindset;
3 business strategies can only be realised through people;
4 creating a strategic approach to people necessitates a strong dialogue across the organisation.[1]

The personnel management/HRM debate

You will be aware that in recent years there has been a noticeable popularity in the use of the term 'human resource management' to replace the term 'personnel management'. The personnel management/HRM debate is now a well-trodden path and much has been written about the subject. Discussion generally centres on the extent to which HRM is a new and distinctive philosophy with a paradigm shift towards a more strategic approach to people management, or simply 'new wine in old bottles' and in reality no more than a different term for what good personnel managers have always been doing.

There seems little to be gained in proliferating this debate except perhaps in summary to suggest that it is difficult to escape the thought that the increasing use of the term HRM has been associated with those engaged in personnel work seeking to enhance their status and influence. Not, however, that there is anything **necessarily** to criticise about this. The essential point is that it does not follow that HRM however it is described will, *per se*, result in a higher level of motivation and job satisfaction or organisational performance than would be achieved with a traditional personnel management approach. It is, however, recognised that developments in information and communications technology (ICT), new forms of work organisation and structure, and increasing attention to empowerment, flexible working arrangements and new psychological contracts (discussed in Chapter 1) certainly provide a challenge to traditional personnel management (or HRM) theories and practices.

Definitions of HRM

HRM is often defined in very general and broad terms. For example, according to *Fisher et al.*: '**Human resource management (HRM)** involves all management decisions and practices that directly affect or influence the people, or **human resources**, who work for the organisation.'[2]

The Chartered Institute of Personnel and Development is a professional body for all those concerned with the management and development of people. The Institute provides the following definition: 'The design, implementation and maintenance of strategies to manage people for optimum business performance including the development of policies and processes to support these strategies and the evaluation of the contribution of people to the business.'[3]

Interestingly, apart from a change in title from personnel management to human resource management, a more detailed definition given by *Torrington and Chapman* in 1979[4] remains largely unchanged today.

Human resource management is a series of activities which: first enables working people and the organisation which uses their skills to agree about the objectives and nature of their working relationship, and secondly, ensures that the agreement is fulfilled.[5]

A strategic approach

It seems reasonable to conclude that there is no clear distinction between personnel management and human resource management. However, the increasing emphasis on effective employee relations and the importance of securing the involvement and commitment of staff to the aims of the organisation may, at least in part, be argued as justification for the change in title. *Crainer* refers to the change from personnel management to human resource management.

With hierarchies decreasing and the growing emphasis on becoming leaner and fitter, the onus is increasingly on corporations extracting the best possible performance from all employees. In (best) practice this means recruiting well-qualified and highly skilled people and developing the skills of everyone in the organisation. With increased acceptance of its importance, personnel management has become human resource management. The emerging role of human resource management is radically different from that of the past when it dealt with the bureaucracy of employing people and little else. From being a caring role, human resources is being realigned as a strategic role, focused on the business needs and strategic plans of the corporation.[6]

Competencies-based human resource management

Effective HRM is critical to organisational performance and success. In most organisations, people are the largest asset. Without taking a strategic approach to the management of that asset, its skills and ability, knowledge development and deployment, even the best business strategy may not succeed. Success is also not guaranteed by having an HR strategy that simply stems from the business strategy. Only by having a truly strategic approach where HR influences all discussions regarding activities, priorities and goals, and thereby designs individual policies with these wider organisational goals and with each other, is the organisation more likely to succeed in achieving these goals.

The viewpoint of HR being realigned as a strategic role is consistent with a survey that was carried out by the CIPD in 2007[7] which reported that 53 per cent of organisations had restructured their HR function in the preceding five years, in most cases to enable the HR function to become a more strategic contributor. Alongside this, HR in many organisations has devolved certain operational personnel tasks, such as recruitment and selection and absence management, from the central specialists to the line manager.

HUMAN CAPITAL MANAGEMENT

Attention to a strategic approach to HRM has given rise to the idea of **human capital management**. However, according to a DTI report, although the expression 'human capital management' is now widely used, there is no generally agreed definition. In the report the term is used to denote a strategic approach to people management that focuses on the issues that are critical to an organisation's success. The report maintains that greater transparency on how value is created through effective people policies and practices will benefit organisations and their stakeholders.

The Accounting for People Task Force believes that the way organisations manage their people affects their performance. Human Capital Management (HCM) – an approach to people management that treats it as a high level strategic issue and seeks systematically to analyse, measure and evaluate how people policies and practices create value – is winning recognition as a way of creating long-term sustainable performance in an increasingly competitive world.[8]

Gratton refers to three elements of human capital – intellectual capital, emotional capital and social capital – which have implications for both individuals and organisations:

- **Intellectual capital** is at the heart of individual development and the creation of knowledge and personal value. This enables the exercise of choice.
- **Emotional capital** enables the continual growth and fulfilment of ambition. It is maintained through self-awareness and insight.
- **Social capital** arises from the forging of relationships. Traditional hierarchical roles and responsibilities are now being replaced by integrated structures and relationships of trust and reciprocity.

Gratton suggests that the three elements, or personal assets, are highly interrelated. It is through their combination, the feedback-loops and connectivity, that they bring advantage to the organisation and to the individual. Taken together the three elements form the basis for strong and supportive relationships and for developing the courage and grit necessary for entrepreneurship and taking action.[9]

The CIPD has more recently provided a slightly different focus to that of Gratton, seeking human capital as part of intellectual capital. The CIPD suggest that intellectual capital is made up of three elements:

- Human capital – defined by knowledge, skills, abilities and capacity to develop and innovate, as possessed by people in an organisation;
- Social capital – defined as 'the structures, networks and procedures that enable those people to acquire and develop intellectual capital represented by stocks and flows of knowledge derived from relationships within and outside the organisation';
- Organisational capital – defined as the 'institutionalised knowledge possessed by an organisation which is stored in databases, manuals etc.' The CIPD notes that this includes HR policies and processes.[10]

The CIPD also notes, like Gratton, that there are clear interrelations between different forms of capital.

People, strategy and performance

According to *Coppin*, 'human capital' is simply the knowledge, skills and competencies of people, which generates wealth for organisations. However, despite increasing evidence to show that HCM can and does improve business performance, UK companies appear to be slow in putting it into practice. There is a need for: (i) further training and development of board members in HR management with the aim of seeing people as balance sheet assets rather than costs, and (ii) devising relevant measures as human capital is somewhat intangible and more difficult to measure than financial key performance indicators.

Coppin suggests that HR professionals within an organisation should be more than staffing, training and remuneration helpers, and need to contribute on matters that show real bottom-line impact. 'Of course, human capital measurement is not enough in itself. If it and HR management that underpins it are to be key to competitive advantages they need to be embedded in the holistic management of a business, linking people, strategy and performance.'[11]

A similar point is made by *Reeves*, who suggests that although organisations have bought the notion that people are a vital asset, the trouble is they have precious little idea how to invest in them. Organisations, and the HR profession in particular, still need a clearer idea on what they should actually be doing. To stand any chance of being seen as a strategic business partner, HR professionals need to be more thoughtful about the interaction between people and other investments, and more consistent in the application of existing policies.[12]

The CIPD also note that the difficulty of measuring human capital to enable the organisation can demonstrate impact on the bottom line. They note the difficulty, due to many internal and external factors, of measuring impact on

- customer satisfaction,
- innovation, and
- service delivery.[13]

The management of people

Whatever the debate on comparative meanings, terms such as 'human resource management' or 'human capital', despite their (present) popularity, have overtones of a cold, impersonal approach. Referring to people as resources, assets or capital is an instrumental approach implying a means to an end. Human resources are clearly the most important asset of any organisation and a resource that needs to be managed, but it is important to remind ourselves that, unlike physical resources, people are not owned by the organisation. People are individuals who bring their own perceptions, feelings and attitudes towards the organisation, systems and styles of management, their duties and responsibilities, and the conditions under which they are working. It is people who make the organisation. Without its members, an organisation is nothing. It is pleasing, therefore, to see what appears to be the increasing use of the terminology 'people management' or the 'management of people'.

> *The best HR people are a form of hybrid: one part pastor, who hears all sins and complaints without recrimination, and part parent who loves and nurtures, but gives it to you fast and straight when you're off track . . . They see the hidden hierarchies in people's minds – the invisible org chart of political connections that exists in every company.*
>
> Jack Welch, Former Chairman and Chief Executive of General Electric[14]

HRM POLICIES, ACTIVITIES AND FUNCTIONS

Recognition of the needs and wants of staff and of the nature of their grievances is a positive step in motivating them to perform well. The efficiency of staff, their commitment to the aims of the organisation, and the skills and attitudes they bring to bear on the quality of service offered are fostered by good human relationships and effective HRM policy and practice. The effective management of people is influenced by the philosophy of top management and the attitudes they bring to bear on relationships with staff, and the problems which affect them. HRM policies therefore should emanate from the top of the organisation. They should be subject to consultation with employee and union representatives, defined clearly and communicated through managers and supervisors to staff at all levels. An example is the need for a clearly stated policy on the use of ICT resources (including email and the internet) that is clear about prohibited activities and consequences of failure to adhere to the policy such as disciplinary action and potential sanctions.

Underlying philosophies

The formulation of HRM policies, and the implementation of practices and procedures, should be based on underlying philosophies of managerial behaviour and employee relationships. Such philosophies should embrace:

- the recognition of people's needs and expectations at work;
- respect for the individual;
- justice in treatment and equitable reward systems;
- stability of employment;
- good working environment and conditions of service;
- opportunities for personal development and career progression;
- democratic functioning of the organisation; and
- full observance of all laws and codes of conduct relating to employment.

In overall terms, HRM policies can be seen to embrace:

- designing an effective organisation structure;
- staffing the structure with suitable people;
- defining work roles and relationships; and
- securing optimum working arrangements.

The objective is to develop and maintain a level of morale and human relationships that evoke willing and full co-operation of all people in the organisation in order to attain optimum operational performance. This is the total concept of the HRM function. It is important to remember, however, that no matter how genuine and well intended are HRM policies, they must also be practically and effectively implemented, and integrated vertically and horizontally throughout the organisation. In a truly strategic vision of HR, these policies are designed to promote the organisation's vision and achievement of goals whilst at the same time influencing the direction of that vision and the setting of the organisation's goals.

Ethical dimensions of HRM

Winstanley and Woodall also draw attention to the ethical dimension of HRM. They suggest that ethical frameworks and principles can be applied through action on three levels:

- **academic debate** – including incorporation of ethical aspects into HRM and organisational behaviour curricula at both undergraduate and postgraduate level;
- **academic research** – including evidence-based research to identify the full range of ethical concerns and practices, and to explore relationships between humanism and employee performance; and
- **professional HR practice** – including a role for the CIPD in promoting ethical debate, and for HR professionals to become a champion, architect and steward of ethical management of people.[15]

ORGANISATION OF THE HRM FUNCTION

The organisation of the HRM function is primarily determined by the nature of the requirement that the business places upon it. Is it a strategic partner or operational task master? Are line management to be responsible for functional tasks or is there a centralised specialised function? The size of the enterprise concerned also has a significant impact.

Line management role or need for a specialist function

Smaller organisations may not justify a specialist human resource manager or a separate department. But **it is still necessary to have an effective HRM function**, whether it is the responsibility of the owner or of a manager or an administrative assistant. Even in the smallest organisations, or in organisations where a specialist department has not been established, there will be a need to recruit staff, to train them, to motivate and reward them, and to comply with the law relating to employment. HR work must still be carried out even if an organisation is too small to justify a separate department or chooses not to establish one.

In the larger concerns, where more time is taken up with problems of organisation and the management of people, there is greater need for a specialist member of staff to whom are delegated full-time responsibilities for advising top management on human resource matters and for the development and implementation of clearly defined policies which permit consistent HRM practices. For example, high staffing costs together with increasing employment legislation and the changing nature of the work organisation (discussed in previous chapters) combine to suggest that personnel activities and employee relations are areas of increasing specialisation. There continues to be much debate about the value of the HR function to the bottom line. This has inevitably contributed to the changing nature of the personnel function and increasing specialisation of the role.[16]

The human resource manager

Even where personnel work is established as a separate, specialist function, it is not easy to define closely the activities of the HRM department. The range of responsibilities varies from one organisation to another, as do the title and status of the head of the department and position in the management structure. In the larger organisations activities might be divided between two or more specialists, so that it would be possible to have, for example, a human resource manager, training officer and employee relations adviser. Whatever the range of responsibilities, the manager operates by consent, by delegated authority. How much consent is dependent upon the attitudes of top management, the role they see the personnel specialist(s) performing and formal organisational relationships with 'line' managers.

Line managers are departmental or unit managers with responsibility for the 'production' process – for the operational functions directly related to the purpose and aims of the organisation. They form a hierarchical level in the chain of command throughout the organisation structure and are responsible for the management of their own staff. However, although line managers are specialists in their own area of work, they are not necessarily specialists in human resource management. Just as line managers turn to specialists on legal and accounting matters and the use of technology, so they will need help, guidance and specialist advice on HRM activities.

WORKING IN PARTNERSHIP WITH LINE MANAGERS

The HRM function is part of the generality of management and the responsibility of all managers and supervisors. The HR manager, as a separate entity, operates in terms of a 'functional' relationship: that is, as a specialist adviser on matters of policy and their implementation through all departments of the organisation. It is the job of the HR manager to provide specialist knowledge and services for line managers, and to support them in the performance of their jobs. In all other respects the HR manager's relationship with other managers, supervisors and staff is indirect: it is an advisory relationship. It is the line managers who have authority and control over staff in their departments and who have the immediate responsibility for personnel activities, although there will be times when they need specialist help and advice. **If the HRM function is to be effective there has to be good teamwork, and co-operation and consultation between line managers and the HR manager.**

This is made easier when top management take an active part in fostering goodwill and harmonious working relationships among departments. It is important to have clear role relationships and to attempt to avoid difficulties with role incongruence or role conflict (discussed in Chapter 8). Top management should agree clear terms of reference for the HR manager within a framework of sound personnel policies. The effective management of people involves a partnership between managers and HR specialists. Within this framework the HRM function can be seen as operating at two levels: the organisational level and the departmental level (*see* Figure 13.1).

The organisational level

At the organisational level the detailed involvement of the work activities of several departments, available time and the need for specialisation suggest that the HR manager has a prominent role to play and is the main executor of policies but acting in consultation with, and taking advice from, line managers. On this basis the HR manager would be concerned mainly with broader aspects of procedures that affect the organisation as a whole or staff generally. This could include such activities as human resource planning, procedures for recruitment and selection, induction and training, consultations with trade unions or staff representatives, employee development, compliance with the law relating to employment, maintaining records and statistics, and liaison with outside bodies such as ACAS, employers' organisations, government agencies, the Criminal Records Bureau, training organisations and professional associations.

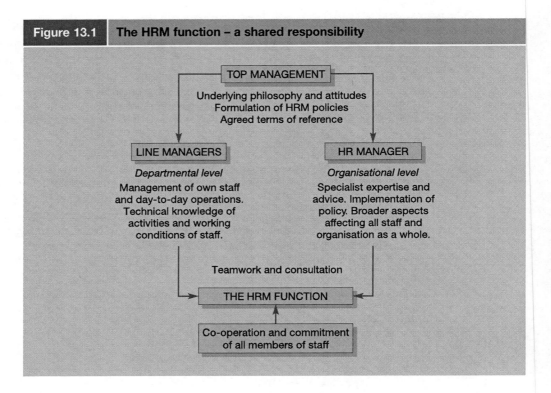

Figure 13.1 The HRM function – a shared responsibility

The departmental level

At the departmental or unit level line managers might assume a prominent role for day-to-day personnel matters, with the HR manager as adviser and if necessary as arbitrator. Line managers would be more concerned, at least in the first instance, with the operational aspects of HR activities within their own departments, for example the organisation of work and allocation of duties, minor disciplinary matters, standards of work performance, safety, on-the-job training, communication of information, and grievances from staff. In this respect it could be said that **all line managers are their own human resource managers**. Line managers are on hand to observe directly the performance of their staff. They will actually see, and be directly affected by, for example, lateness of staff, unsatisfactory work, insufficient training, low morale, staff unrest, or poor planning of work duties and responsibilities.

Whatever the respective roles of the HR manager and line managers, the HRM function can be effective only if it is based and implemented on sound policies and procedures. It also requires the co-operation and commitment of all members of staff, whatever their duties or positions within the organisation. The HRM function cannot be housed within one discrete department or as the sole responsibility of selected members of staff. It permeates all levels of the organisation and all phases of its operations.

Critical reflection

'HRM is an integral part of any managerial activity. Line managers have the right and the duty to be concerned with the effective operation of their own department, including the well-being of their staff. Having a separate HR department only leads to line managers abdicating responsibility for their people.'

What are your views? Do you think line managers should act as their own human resource manager?

Decision by top management

The extent to which authority and responsibility for the HR function is devolved to line managers is a decision for top management and is likely to be influenced by the nature, culture, structure and characteristic features of the particular industry or organisation. For example, in the hospitality industry, *Rocco Forte* has emphasised the importance of a caring and efficient personnel function to assist line managers in what is one of their primary responsibilities. The nature of the hospitality business, with many separate units of differing size, location and mix of skills, means of necessity the personnel function is decentralised and prime responsibility has to be with line management.

> *However, even if we have had a choice, I believe we would elect to put the prime responsibility for personnel on line management rather than on specialists. The nature of our work calls for active participation by management in day-to-day operations and they need to know that line management has the authority and responsibility for taking actions which vitally affect them in their work and in their working environment. The link therefore must be a direct one.*[17]

This philosophy is still very much part of the structure of many hospitality organisations.

The concern of all managers

It is clear, then, that the human resource management function is a shared responsibility among top management, line managers and supervisors, and the HR manager. *Johnson et al.* also maintain that people-related issues are a central concern and responsibility of most managers in organisations and not confined to a specialist human resource function.

> *Indeed, although formal HR systems and structures may be vitally important in supporting successful strategies, it is quite possible that they may hinder strategy if they are not tailored to the types of strategies being pursued. Also the relationship between people and successful strategies goes beyond the traditional agenda of the HR function and is concerned with behaviours as much as competencies. The ability to change behaviours may be the key ingredient for success. Creating a climate where people strive to achieve success and the motivation of individuals are crucial roles of any manager and are a central part of their involvement in their organisation's strategy.*[18]

A STRATEGIC BUSINESS PARTNERING APPROACH

We have already noted the strategic approach to HR becoming more prominent with the change from personnel management to HRM. *Ulrich* contributed further to this debate with the introduction of the concept of the strategic business partner role. Ulrich refers to serious and widespread doubts about HR's contribution to organisational performance but suggests that it has never been more necessary. The question for senior managers is not 'should we do away with HR?', but 'what should we do with HR?'. Companies today face five critical business challenges: globalisation, profitability through growth, technology, intellectual capital, and change, change and more change. These challenges provide HR with an opportunity to play a leadership role in the development of new capabilities to meet the challenges. However, Ulrich maintains that HR cannot transform itself alone and the primary responsibility belongs to the CEO and every line manager who must achieve business goals.

The five challenges present a new mandate for human resource management in order to help deliver organisational excellence in the following four ways. It should become:

- a partner with senior and line managers in strategy execution;
- an expert in the way work is organised and executed to ensure costs are reduced and quality maintained;
- a champion for employees, vigorously representing their concerns to senior management and working to increase employee contribution and commitment; and
- an agent of continuous transformation, shaping processes and a culture to improve an organisation's capacity for change.[19]

Ulrich's model, often referred to as the 'three-legged stool' model, has been embraced by many large organisations in the reorganisation of the HR function. Many HR functions now contain:

- shared service centres – typically in recruitment and selection, and payroll/HR administration, providing low-cost and effective administration;
- centres of excellence – teams of expert practitioners offering specialist knowledge in areas such as reward, learning and development and employee relations;
- strategic business partners – senior HR professionals working closely with business leaders, constantly influencing and steering strategy and supporting strategy implementation.[20]

Effectively these partners shape what HR does by implementing and understanding the business strategy and supporting this by commissioning the necessary services to implement these strategies, from the shared service centres and centres of excellence. In the public sector in particular, business partners are likely to have a significant role in the service level agreement approach, detailing the requirements of the client department or organisation to the HR service, and working with HR to develop a specification and defined cost for the services that meet these requirements.

THE IMPORTANCE OF HRM

Whatever the choice of terminology or decisions on organisation, effective HRM and the successful implementation of personnel activities are essential ingredients for improved organisational performance. *Lynch* refers to the importance of people as a vital resource for sustainable competitive advantage. 'For most organisations, people are a vital resource. There are some industries where people are not just important but are the *key factor* for successful performance.'[21]

According to *Delany*, organisations that get the people things right are the organisations likely to be around in the future.

> *Some organisations regard human resources as a purely transactional item: recruitment, salaries, laying off. Others try to go beyond that and try to develop a meaningful people strategy but fail. But the successful organisations keep the people issues at the forefront of their thinking and at the core of their decision making and planning . . . The human resource element has to be a vital part of the planning process – just as vital as the financial forecasts. Companies need a people vision which will support the vision for a business.*[22]

Strategic HR, according to the CIPD, has become a 'commercial necessity'. It notes that organisations need 'HR functions that can deliver skilled, creative, motivated, flexible and committed employees'.[23]

It is not the purpose of this chapter to provide detailed coverage of HRM – this is covered well in specialist books on the subject area.[24] It is important, however, to recognise the broader context in which the process of management takes place and to provide an insight into particular areas of interest for the study of organisational behaviour, including training and development, talent management, performance management and employee relations.

TRAINING AND DEVELOPMENT

One major area of the HRM function of particular relevance to the effective management and use of people is training and development. Recent years have seen training teams renamed as training and development or learning and development. There are some fundamental differences between each of these terms:

- training is a content-based activity, normally away from the workplace with an instructor leading and aiming to change individual behaviour or attitudes;

- learning is a self-managed process of acquiring new knowledge and skills with the aim of increasing performance;
- development is wider than both training and learning and is a longer-term, structured learning process involving a number of activities, including training.

The nature of learning, and coaching and mentoring, are discussed in Chapter 5. Management development is discussed in more detail in Chapter 20. This section focuses purely on training as an area of the HRM function.

Few would argue against the importance of training as a major influence on the success of an organisation. Staff are a crucial, but expensive, resource. In order to sustain economic and effective performance it is important to optimise the contribution of employees to the aims and goals of the organisation.

> *Skills shortages are often the result of short-termism and little or no analysis of present or future training needs . . . Keeping skilled workers is one of the first business goals.*
>
> Sir Brian Wolfson, Chairman of Investors in People UK[25]

The importance of training as a central role of management has long been recognised by leading writers. According to *Drucker* (writing in 1977), the one contribution a manager is uniquely expected to make is to give others vision and ability to perform. A basic operation in the work of the manager is to develop people and to direct, encourage and train subordinates.[26] The general movement towards flexible structures of organisation and the nature of management moving towards the devolution of power to the workforce give increasing emphasis to an environment of coaching and support. Training is necessary to ensure an adequate supply of staff who are technically and socially competent, and capable of career advancement into specialist departments or management positions. There is, therefore, a continual need for the process of staff development, and training fulfils an important part of this process.

> *It is morally wrong to give a person a leadership role without some form of training – wrong for them and those who work with them.*[27]

The benefits of training

The purpose of training is to improve knowledge and skills and to change attitudes. It is one of the most important potential motivators. This can lead to many possible benefits for both individuals and the organisation. Training can:

- increase the confidence, motivation and commitment of staff;
- provide recognition, enhanced responsibility and the possibility of increased pay and promotion;
- give a feeling of personal satisfaction and achievement and broaden opportunities for career progression; and
- help to improve the availability, quality and skills of staff.

Training is therefore a key element of improved organisational performance. Training increases the level of individual and organisational competence. It helps to reconcile the gap between what should happen and what is happening – between desired targets or standards and actual levels of work performance. Although many employers continue to have reservations about the cost and the extent of tangible business returns from training, the development of vocational skills has been identified as a key factor in sharpening competitiveness and delivering hard, bottom-line improvement in profits.[28]

Investment in people is fundamental to employee well-being.

This means actively facilitating the learning, growth and development of individuals. An extensive capability and commitment to training must be an integral part of the organisation's business strategy. Essential components of the training policy will be:

- *the view that continuous training is the norm;*
- *the assumption that training will be a life-long process;*
- *recognition of the need to update existing skills, replace redundant skills and train for new skills;*
- *the need for multi-skilling to cope with change.*[29]

However, although the potential benefits of training may appear obvious, it does not necessarily follow that training, *per se*, will lead to improved performance. There has to be an appropriate training culture. Training has to be relevant to the needs and requirements of the organisation and there is increasing emphasis placed on the value of vocational education. *Tate* acknowledges that training is an important lever to bring about improvement and change but questions whether individual competence would lead automatically to corporate competence, and emphasises the importance of a sound business agenda and the distinction between training and education.

Training can easily become an agenda for conformity and the status quo – good at instilling uniformity and compliance with someone else's model of current best practice. Genuine education – with which training is so clumsily lumped much of the time – is its polar opposite. Education is liberating and challenging; it offers us choice, because it opens our eyes and our minds. Training works outside-in; education works inside-out . . . Training will only help if organisations learn to be wise in how they use an individual's capability, marrying talent with healthy cultures, systems and processes, serving well conceived business goals.[30]

THE MANAGEMENT OF TRAINING

Training should be viewed as an investment in people. This is important at any time, but particularly so with the increasing pace of technological, structural and social change. But training for its own sake achieves little. It must be real, operational and rewarding. As a function, it may sit within the strategic responsibility of the HR function, or it may sit as a discrete department and function of its own. Either way, training requires the co-operation of line managers, adequate finance and resources, time, skilled staff and a supporting appraisal system. There has to be a genuine commitment – from top management and throughout all levels of the organisation.

Stern argues that 'staff training and development have become matters of vital strategic importance'. It is, however, necessary to take an individual approach based on competencies and development needs.

In selecting training and development programmes, one size will not fit all. Nor can one course or degree be expected to do the whole development job. It is the menu of options that is offered, a complementary range of learning opportunities that will make sure new skills and learning are properly embedded, helping managers to raise their game and fulfil their potential. Practical, interpersonal or presentational skills training may fill the gaps left by more formal or more academic work.[31]

Stern's view is reflective of the wider strategic approach to learning and development, taken in recent years. A strategic learning and development approach, when effectively managed, offers a commitment to a range of individualised development opportunities. These include training, but also include coaching, mentoring, shadowing and other planned activities, all aimed at improving knowledge, developing skills and changing attitudes.

A planned and systematic approach

In order to secure the full benefits of successful training there must, therefore, be a planned and systematic approach to the effective **management of training**.

- There must be a **clear commitment to training throughout all levels of the organisation**. This should include seeking the co-operation of line managers and, where appropriate, trade unions or staff representatives. Top management should set the scene by giving active support and encouragement to the training process, and through the provision of adequate finance, resources, time and skilled staff.

- There should be effective **training needs analysis** at organisational, departmental and individual levels. The training needs analysis must examine current skills and attitudes and the future needs based on the strategic vision of the organisation, the external environmental influences and likely future staffing requirements. Through this process, gaps in knowledge, skills and attitudes required for the organisation, department and individual to reach their potential, will become evident.

- It is important that **staff themselves should also feel a sense of involvement** and know how they can play their part in achieving the goals and objectives of the organisation. They should be given 'ownership and partnership' in the training process.

- There should be **a clear set of objectives and a defined policy for training**. This will enable the design of a carefully planned programme of training. The programme should address such questions as: Who is to be trained and why? What should they be taught? How and where should the training be undertaken, and by whom? How will the training be assessed and evaluated? The expected results of training should be understood clearly and realistically and be seen as reasonably attainable. Wherever possible, desired objectives should be stated in behavioural terms such as: Exactly what, after training, should the trainee now be able to do?

- People cannot absorb a large amount of information at any one time. **The training programme should therefore be planned carefully**, reflect the priority areas within the training needs analysis, and avoid overload by being staggered over a reasonable period of time.

- Consideration must be given **to the choice of the most appropriate methods of training**. These can include internal courses, external courses and distance learning. The particular needs of the organisation reflect the nature of the knowledge, skills or attitudes, subject to the training and reflect where possible, employees preferred learning styles. Guidance should be given on how to prepare for training and how to deal with the various material or situations presented.

- Consideration should also be given to **external courses and training opportunities linked to the educational system**. These include programmes designed to provide improved employment opportunities and centred on standards of occupational competence; those that are essentially vocational in nature; and relevant professional, diploma and degree courses.

- Full regard should be given to the **training needs of minority groups** within the workforce. Special consideration should be given to barriers to accessing training and the most appropriate methods of training for ethnic minority groups, disabled workers, gender groups, flexible workers and also younger and older groups of staff.

- There should be **an effective system of review and evaluation** including the ongoing monitoring of progress, a supporting performance management system and the maintenance of suitable training records. Evaluation should involve assessment by the trainers, line managers and supervisors, and the trainees. The review process should include identification of those areas to which greater attention should be given in future training programmes.

- Wherever possible **evaluation should be related to objective, measurable factors**, for example: increased output or sales; reduced scrap or wastage; fewer accidents at work; fewer errors or customer complaints. Other measurable factors may include reduced staff turnover, absenteeism or sickness. However, such measures are difficult to isolate in terms of a single cause and effect. The ultimate evaluation of training is, of course, the extent to which it contributes to improved organisational performance and effectiveness; and to the quality, job satisfaction and prospects of employees. As an example, Hampshire

County Council ask for three learning outcomes and then 6–8 weeks after the training course individuals discuss with their managers reinforcement of the learning and how their working practices have changed as a result of their training.

Training in people skills

With the rapidly changing nature of the business world and the need to maintain competitive advantage, organisations need to ensure that staff are fully trained not only in knowledge of their products and/or services and technical skills, but also in their human relations skills. *Douglas* draws attention to the need for companies in all industrial and commercial sectors to be more serious about helping their technical people to master the so-called 'soft skills' and for training in their people skills and how to work with maximum effectiveness as part of a team.

> *Indeed, it is an accepted truism that some people who are truly gifted from a scientific and technical point of view find their career progress checked by their fundamental difficulties with managing people. They cannot be blamed for their lack of facility in this area: their entire training has been based around acquiring the rigorous knowledge they need to succeed at a technical level in their profession or industry. Expecting them automatically to excel at managing people is at best naïve, and at worst quite unreasonable.*[32]

This is equally true of line managers, particularly as the HR departments have been devolving much of the traditional personnel function to line managers to enable the HR function to have a greater focus on the strategic HRM approach. Chapter 20 discusses the development of managers in more detail.

E-LEARNING

Learning via technology – **e-learning** – is now a global phenomenon and is central to many organisations. It is not difficult to see why on-line learning is growing in popularity. It offers the opportunity to provide a standard message to a large number of widely geographically dispersed people with the minimum disruption to their working and private lives. And, where large numbers of learners are involved, learning materials delivered online can bring the cost per learner to negligible proportions. Thus, learning becomes more accessible than ever before.

While e-learning is making progress as far as learners are concerned, the other key group that needs to be convinced of its efficacy is the trainers and lecturers. These people can fear for their jobs on the introduction of e-learning. Traditionally, trainers gave knowledge to a group of people. The challenge involved in on-line learning is not simply teaching in a different way. Rather, it means rethinking the whole nature of the learning/teaching process. E-learning is also discussed in Chapter 5.

Forms of e-learning

E-learning arises in a number of forms. These include:

■ web-based training which provides information-based content without support or interaction with a trainer
■ supported learning which provides content-based learning which is supported by trainers or lecturers through additional dialogue with students and interaction between students at residential or other events.

Another example which could tenuously be linked to e-learning is that of social networking. There are numerous chatrooms and message boards available which enable individuals with particular questions or queries to ask peers within the same profession or to collaborate with those peers more substantially.

Benefits and limitations

According to *Sweeten*, however, the success rate for implementations of technology-based training over the past 20 years has not been high and large numbers of companies have spent countless millions on failed initiatives of what is now called e-learning. In order to make investment in technology work, those responsible for training need to be clear on the difference between learning and reference, the difference between training and education, and understanding what e-learning is good at and not so good at. Sweeten suggests that there are skills that you cannot impart through an e-learning course, for example to e-learn how to ride a bicycle.

> *However, you can deliver knowledge and understanding more effectively by computer than by any other way, and all the skills are underpinned and enhanced by knowledge and understanding. Achieving this through e-learning frees you to put more life into your live training with practical exercises, role-playing, etc.*[33]

It is clear that e-learning is more appropriate for the acquisition of knowledge and there are doubts about its application to training in social skills. Despite all of these reservations, as communications technology develops and as people want to learn exactly what they need to know, with the minimum disruption to their lives, e-learning will become an increasingly significant part of training, either pre-course preparation or post-course evaluation and refreshment of knowledge. *Burns* suggests that e-learning can be a powerful addition to conventional training, review and project support, saving both time and money, and has particular relevance for quality training. 'E-learning can be applied to three major aspects of quality: training, reviewing already learned material or communicating with employees to help them learn about quality, and supporting improvement teams.'[34]

The CIPD suggest that there are a number of benefits associated with e-learning including:

- immediate availability
- ease and flexibility of access
- consistency and simultaneous message
- cost reductions (reduced trainer cost and reduction in trainee time)
- ease of tracking course completion.

The CIPD also note that there are issues around technological infrastructure, IT skills, line management support, employee reluctance and quality of content, which can all restrict the ability to deliver the benefits outlined above.[35]

> ### Critical reflection
>
> 'The concept of e-learning may have popular appeal, especially as it is associated with modern technology, but it arguably has only limited potential and is no more than flavour of the month. In reality effective training can be achieved only through individual or small-group, face-to-face interactions and personal feedback.'
>
> *To what extent do you agree with this point of view?*

INVESTORS IN PEOPLE

The **Investors in People** Standard is a business improvement tool designed to advance an organisation's performance through the training and development of its people. It is a flexible framework that organisations of any size or sector can work with.

The Investors in People framework is outcome-focused, outlining what organisations need to achieve, but never prescribing how. This flexible approach allows thousands of different employers of every sector and size to use the same framework. Investors in People's flexibility is enhanced by focusing all their advice and assessment around meeting organisations' needs. This means the process starts with Investors in People finding out what organisations' performance targets or key priorities are. These targets and priorities then become central to all their work with the organisation, so they support the business plan and maximise the value customers can gain from working with Investors in People.

The Investors in People framework has three core principles:

- **Plan:** Develop strategies to improve performance.
- **Do:** Take action to improve performance.
- **Review:** Evaluate and improve performance.

The three principles break down into ten indicators, as you can see in the wheel diagram, Figure 13.2. 'Plan' has four strategies, starting with Business strategy. There are then four action-focused indicators to help organisations 'Do' what is in their plan. And finally 'Review' encourages organisations to evaluate results and feed them into continuous improvement for the future.

Figure 13.2	Investors in People Indicators

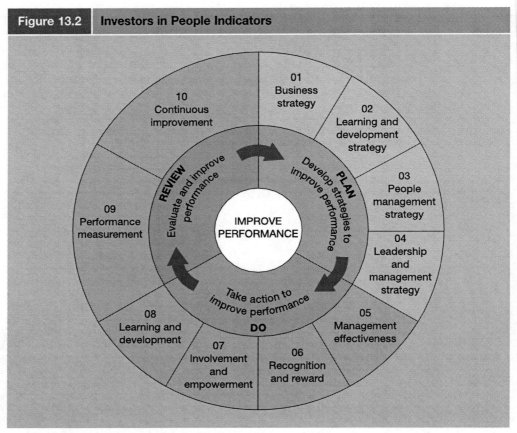

Source: Investors in People, Copyright © Investors in People 2009.

Much of Investors in People's success is down to the versatility of these three core principles. Essentially you can take any business issue and apply their 'plan, do, review' approach to it. Investors in People now have additional recognition for organisations that would like an extra stretch. The Standard is now complemented by Bronze, Silver and Gold recognition, which are designed to celebrate success as well as signpost areas for further improvement.

TALENT MANAGEMENT

Recent years have seen the emergence of the concept of **talent management** as a strategic approach to gaining competitive advantage. It encompasses many areas that fall within the responsibility of HRM practitioners including recruitment and selection, performance management, training and development, succession planning, and employee engagement. The CIPD defines talent management as 'the systematic attraction, identification, development, engagement/retention and deployment of those individuals with high potential who are of particular value to an organisation'.[36]

As this indicates, talent management is about more than simply attracting high potential to the organisation. It is inextricably linked with the human capital management approach with these particularly valuable individuals being seen as assets who should be invested into via development, appropriate planned deployment, and engagement and retention initiatives. The competitive advantage secured is normally measured through indicators such as improved retention and succession planning of high performers, an increased reputation as an employer of choice, making the organisation more attractive to work in for external talent and other factors such as increased diversity of the workforce and ultimately the success of the organisation.

Talent management needs to be aligned to the direction of the organisation and it needs senior management endorsement if it is to succeed. Line managers need to understand the concept and be encouraged to view talent in their own teams as a corporate resource rather than be concerned about their local deployment and workload issues.

The importance of maximising talent

An in-depth study by the Chartered Management Institute and Ashridge Consulting draws attention to maximising talent as a key requirement for every organisation to perform effectively.

> There is a strategic imperative for organisations to manage talent. Changing demographic patterns mean that more people are approaching retirement than entering the workforce. Younger generations have different needs and are renegotiating their psychological contracts with their employer. They are quick to move if their organisation is not meeting their expectations. Retaining and developing key people in the organisation will be a critical success factor in the next five years. Senior managers report talent management as a strategic priority, yet over half of line managers are resistant to talent management processes.

The study points out that most talent processes and systems fall within the domain of HRM and line management. Although it is critical that the management systems should be integrated with the business strategy, in practice they often develop in isolation.[37]

'High potential' people

Blass refers to the difficulty in finding a clear definition of talent management as the process may differ between organisations. There is, however, a need for some common understanding, and Blass proposes the following definition:

> Talent Management is the additional management, processes and opportunities that are made available to people in the organisation who are considered to be 'high potential' or 'talent'.

Blass suggests that the talent management system represents the additional elements that are offered to high potentials/high performers. The definition of 'high potential' or 'talent' will differ for every organisation as well as for every strategic perspective and may also differ with the economic times.[38]

Talent management at Lloyds TSB

At Lloyds TSB talent is defined as 'Those individuals assessed as having the aspiration and capability to deliver a greater contribution in their current roles and the potential to develop into roles of greater depth and/or breadth over time'. Thus talent is defined as a factor of (current) performance, (future) potential and (cultural fit) behaviour.

Current performance is assessed through the individual balanced scorecard which is linked directly to the organisation's scorecard via team and business unit scorecards. Future potential is assessed through Group Leadership Capabilities and increasingly through a number of role or function specific profiles. These factors are jointly assessed by line managers and their individual reports through the annual career paths process.

Talent pools are notional or specific groupings of individuals assessed as having the potential to progress, either in key specialist areas or general management/leadership roles, whose development is managed and progress monitored to meet succession needs and to build core/critical business capability requirements. The way that these various pools are managed varies greatly across the group, across divisions and indeed within divisions. This is because pools are created for very specific purposes at specific times.

Managing talent

- Create a climate and a context in which learning potential is maximised.
- Have a strong commitment to personal and career development.
- Have a TM system for spotting and pushing high flyers.
- Recognise potential in all staff.
- Know your staff well in order to understand and meet their developmental needs for achieving and giving of their best.
- Demonstrate and encourage a willingness to experiment – and to make mistakes without fear of blame.
- Identify the real motivators to get staff to commit.
- Manage flexibly, treating and valuing people as unique individuals, and reward them on an individual basis.
- Support staff with feedback and guidance.

Source: Sue Mann, 'War Goes On for the Talent Pool', *Professional Manager*, vol. 17, no. 1, January 2008, p. 25. Reproduced with permission.

PERFORMANCE MANAGEMENT (PM)

The process of management involves making a continuous judgement on the skills, behaviours, activities and contributions of staff. It is important that members of the organisation know exactly what is expected of them and how their performance will be measured. **Performance management** is a process which brings together many aspects of people management. It is about performance improvement at individual, team, department and organisational levels. It is also about staff development as a means to both improve and enhance performance and as a means of managing behaviour and attitudes. It logically follows that if there are good working relationships, individuals and teams are more likely to perform well together than if poor relationships exist.

The CIPD suggest that:

Performance management is about establishing a culture in which individuals and groups take responsibility for the continuous improvement of business processes and their own skills, behaviours and contributions. It is about sharing expectations. Managers can clarify what they expect individuals and teams to do; likewise individuals and teams can communicate their expectations of how they should be managed and what they need to do their jobs. It follows that performance management is about inter-relationships and about improving the quality of relationships between managers and teams, between members of teams and so on, and is therefore a joint process.[39]

The appraisal as a tool of PM

One of the tools of PM is the performance appraisal or personal development review. This is the formalised regular review of the individual's performance where potential is highlighted and training and development needs identified. This meeting should review performance against agreed criteria and measures based on expectations and objectives which ultimately derive from the organisation's business plan. The annual review should not be a top-down process which is done to the employee but an opportunity for two-way dialogues about performance in the past year, expectations and objectives for the coming year and any learning and development needs that may arise as a result. In many organisations, the annual review forms the basis of review of financial rewards and planned career progression. With the introduction of the concept of talent management and organisations fighting a 'war for talent', performance and development reviews offer the opportunity to highlight potential that the organisation is keen to retain and to offer opportunities to nurture and develop this talent including lateral moves and horizontal progression.

Performance management and career plans

Performance management is therefore a crucial activity of the management of human resources. A comprehensive system can provide the basis for key managerial decisions such as those relating to allocation of duties and responsibilities, pay, empowerment and levels of supervision, promotions, training and development needs, and career progression. According to ACAS, the identification of individual training needs will best be supported by a performance review system that focuses on future development needs. The system should be used by managers and workers to:

■ create career plans which encompass not only training proposals but also areas of work experience, job goals and personal development;
■ consider career tracks which may be as much about lateral moves designed to expand learning and competence as upward promotion.

This policy will, in particular, highlight the need for greater use within organisations of open learning facilities and formalised human resource development programmes. With the support of the organisation, emphasis should be placed on individuals taking responsibility for their own personal development. The manager's role in this process is predominantly that of counsellor.[40]

Key elements of a performance review system

A performance review system requires specific attention to be focused on a number of basic questions including who should feed back to the individual on their performance, the frequency of reviews, whether there should be an open system, how it is integrated with other people management practices, and how performance is going to be measured. The traditional practice is for reviews to be carried out by the immediate manager or supervisor – as the person who allocates work and has the closest knowledge of the individual's duties and performance. There is, however, an argument in favour of review at a higher level. This would extend the lines of communication and feedback. This may also help to demonstrate 'fair play' and to overcome problems of individual managers or supervisors applying different standards. A third approach is for the immediate manager/supervisor to conduct the review and write the report. Senior management are then asked to comment, to monitor the system, to review the consistency of reporting and to countersign as confirmation of approval. The review can also be undertaken by a member of the HR department. The removal of middle levels of management, flatter structures and greater empowerment of self-managed teams also have possible implications for who should undertake the PM process.

Frequency

With the majority of schemes, staff receive an annual review, sometimes with interim reviews half way through the year, and for many organisations this may be sufficient. However, the frequency of reviews should be related to the nature of the organisation, the purpose and objectives of the scheme, and the characteristics of the staff employed. For some organisations, for example those operating in a dynamic, changing environment, more frequent reviews may be called for. More frequent reviews may also be appropriate for new members of staff, those recently promoted or appointed to a new position, or those whose past performance has not been up to the required standard.

Openness

The performance review should ideally be a two-way conversation. PM should be about providing information about performance and progress against targets. It should allow for open dialogue, and discussion would ideally come to some agreement about the nature of the individual's performance and any measures being put in place to address any concerns. There is an argument that suggests that open reporting restricts managers from giving a completely honest and frank review. However, the more staff see of their report – that is, the more 'open' the system – the more they are likely to accept the process of performance management. Staff are better able to check the consistency of the report with verbal feedback from the manager. With an open system of reporting, staff should be given the opportunity to sign the completed form and to add any comments on their perception of the accuracy of the review. When decisions such as salary are based on the report there is greater demand for a transparent system so that individuals understand clearly the basis for decisions.

Appeals procedure

In order to maintain the credibility of the system and to maintain goodwill, it will be necessary to establish a formal appeals procedure which is clearly understood by all members of staff. Appeals should be made to a manager in a more senior position than the reviewer or sometimes, where appropriate, to the HR department or a representative committee. The appeals procedure should include provision for staff to be assisted, if requested, by a union or staff representative.

Integrating the system

In order to ensure the establishment of a successful performance review system, the system should not be viewed in isolation but in relation to the corporate objectives of the organisation, and designed to suit its culture and particular requirements. The purpose and nature of the system should be made clear and continually reinforced. Top management should be seen to own the system and be fully committed to the concept of performance management. They should ensure full consultation with trade unions, staff representatives, and all managers and members of staff. The system should not be perceived as something that is the prerogative of the HR department or introduced for its benefit but as an element of the organisation's integrated people management processes. An effective administration system should aim to keep form-filling and paperwork to a minimum.

Regular reviews of performance reviews system

The system needs to be monitored regularly to ensure that reviews are carried out properly and to obtain feedback from managers and staff. The system should be kept under continual review and, where necessary, modified to meet changing environmental influences or the needs of the organisation. It is important to ensure that operation of the system and the criteria used for assessment satisfy equal opportunities, diversity and all other legal requirements. The system must be supported by appropriate follow-up action, for example seeing that work plans or changes in duties and responsibilities actually take place and that suitable arrangements are made to meet identified training or development needs. One of the particular concerns of a performance review system is the paperwork it generates. Systems should be continually reviewed with the aim of keeping form-filling and paperwork to a minimum.

> ### *Critical reflection*
>
> 'Formal annual performance reviews are a complete waste of time. If you learn anything new this only suggests that the continual monitoring of performance as part of the line manager's day-to-day role has not been undertaken properly.'
>
> *What do you think? What has been your experience of formal performance reviews?*

METHODS OF MEASUREMENT AND REVIEW

To be effective in reviewing and improving performance it is necessary to measure current performance. Measurement may be a combination of:

- 'quantitative' measures using some form of rating scale, such as, for example, (1) excellent, (2) exceeds expectations or requirements of the job, (3) meets the expectations or requirements, (4) some weaknesses in meeting expectations or requirements, (5) unsatisfactory performance, and
- 'qualitative' measures involving an unstructured, narrative report on specific factors and/or overall level of behaviour and work performance.

Behaviourally anchored rating scales (BARS)

The use of behaviourally anchored rating scales (BARS) is an attempt to overcome difficulties with conventional rating scales and provide measurement scales that are directly related to the job being reviewed. A sample group of managers/supervisors is asked to identify, independently, several key behavioural aspects of the job in question. The responses are then collated and returned to the same or a different group to agree examples of good, average or poor performance and to allocate a scale point for each example. Those examples which are consistently rated at the same point on the scale can then act as 'anchors' and provide behavioural examples for each point on the scale.[41] Reviewers can then use the BARS as guidance against which to assess the expected behaviour of each person being rated. The disadvantages with BARS are that they can be time-consuming and costly to construct, and require careful and detailed training in their correct use. They are also more likely to be appropriate only in larger organisations.

Achieving objectives

With this system, the manager agrees with members of staff set objectives at the beginning of the review period. The 'SMART' approach to setting objectives is based on Specific, Measurable, Achievable, Realistic and Timebound examples. The review is then based on the extent to which these stated objectives have been achieved. This method provides for participation by staff and also allows for at least some degree of self-appraisal. This method can be related therefore to a system of management by objectives (discussed in Chapter 12). A major consideration with this method is the extent to which circumstances beyond the control of the individual, such as changes in environmental influences, make the achievement of objectives unrealistic. Objectives need to be continually reviewed and revised in accordance with changing circumstances. Comparison with achieving objectives may not, by itself, provide a detailed assessment of performance. Therefore, some schemes combine this method with the use of rating scales.

Performance 'agreement' or 'contract'

A variant of the 'meeting objectives' method is proposed by *Stein*. A good review system could be the key by which companies get the most out of all their staff without making them feel exploited.[42] Stein puts forward an approach based on the use of a performance 'agreement' or 'contract'. Members of staff create a succinct document, agreed with their superior, which sets out the individual's proposed contribution to the business plan of the organisation. This document provides an agenda that can be referred to during the review period and modified as necessary. This agenda serves as the basis of the appraisal judgement. Instead of rating performance in terms of a traditional five-box scale, as A, B, C, D or E, the question is simply: 'Has the plan been met?' This approach turns the appraisal system into a dialogue. The extent to which staff meet their contract also gives an indication of whether the business plan is realistic.

Levels of competency

Competences and competencies can be used as a tool to measure performance. Competences are what people need to be able to perform a job and competencies are aspects of behaviour that influence a person's competent performance. For example, a legal professional requires competences in technical knowledge of the law, but also requires the ability to present a strong case at court, thus needing strong interpersonal skills to present this knowledge to the court. There are many methods for measuring competence and for providing development opportunities for improving competence.

360° FEEDBACK AND UPWARD FEEDBACK

The concept of performance management has progressed into systems of '**360° feedback**' and 'upward feedback'. The idea of 360° feedback normally involves feedback from different groups within the work situation – peers and subordinates as well as bosses, and possibly internal and external customers. In most cases, the individual completes a questionnaire themselves assessing their own performance and behaviour. The idea is to provide a broader review covering good working relationship, teamwork, leadership, decision-making and quality of service provided.

An **upward feedback** review system involves subordinates' appraisal of managers. This can help to judge, among other things, managers' ability to accept constructive criticism. This initially can be a daunting experience for managers and also for individuals asked for feedback as they may fear antagonising their manager. To be effective, upward feedback requires an appropriate organisation culture and open management style. It is also necessary to involve an independent third person who can supply confidential feedback and comment.

Crainer refers to the need for the appraisal process to embrace the goals of the organisation and those of the individual in the short and long term. The process must also be managed effectively. A vast number of companies have abandoned the traditional approach in favour of a new model that tends to be flexible, is continuous, revolves around feedback, involves many more people than one manager and a boss, and seeks to minimise bureaucracy.

> *As methods of appraisal go, 360-degree feedback is undoubtedly robust and rigorous . . . The attraction of 360-degree feedback is that it gives a more complete picture of an individual's performance. Different groups see an individual in a variety of circumstances and situations and can, as a result, give a broader perspective than that of a single boss. This, of course, relies on a high degree of openness and trust.*[43]

Potential drawbacks

Despite the apparent support for 360° feedback, *Pfau et al.* claim that this is a perfect example of how too many organisations base their human resources investment decisions on tradition, fads or competitors' practices, instead of on sound financial measures. Although it has been adopted by a growing number of organisations, Pfau *et al.* report on research studies which show that 360° feedback may hurt more than it helps and that companies using 360° feedback have on average a 10.6 per cent decrease in shareholder value; while the concept delivers valuable feedback there are serious problems relating to privacy, validity and effectiveness. However, despite the drawbacks, Pfau *et al.* suggest that this does not mean 360° feedback programmes should be abandoned but that they should be implemented for the right reasons. Companies should ask themselves what they want to gain from the reviews. HR managers should revisit their programmes and take the necessary steps to implement the concept in order to transform 360° feedback into a value creator, not destroyer.[44]

Butcher also reports that 360° feedback is increasingly common in appraisals and makes sense. However, making peers review one another's strengths and weaknesses often leads to political tensions, particularly if bonuses or promotions are at stake. 'People can also feel a conflict between their role as a supportive colleague and their responsibility as a hard-nosed judge. What's more, close-knit teams may see the process as too focused on individual achievements – basically a popularity contest in disguise.'[45]

An example of a 360° feedback is provided by Gary Kusin, CEO of Kinko, who received a low score in the area of rewards and recognition.

> *We adopted 360-degree feedback about a year after I came to Kinko's (this was before Kinko's partnered with FedEx). It was my first experience with having my performance reviewed by people who reported to me . . . I know that as a CEO, I'm not getting honest feedback a lot of the time, but I took these results as dead-on honest feedback. Also, I've got an ego, and that low score was a good motivator to change. If I were going to be an effective manager, a response was required . . . Every organisation at some point in its life will hit a rough patch. When this happens, whether it's belt-tightening or a reverse of direction, you'd like to have that foundation of trust to fall back on. Recognition is one of the things that builds trust over time. And I'd be way behind in this area had I not been slapped by that 360.*[46]

BENEFITS OF PERFORMANCE MANAGEMENT

The underlying objective of a performance review (PR) system is to improve the performance of individuals in order to lead to improvement in the performance of the organisation as a whole. Performance review systems in themselves are not performance management. Performance management is how the various people management policies are integrated to support organisational performance. Performance review is one aspect of this and an effective scheme, therefore, offers a number of potential benefits to both the individual and the organisation:

- It can identify an individual's strengths and areas of development and indicate how such strengths may best be utilised and weaknesses overcome.
- It can help to reveal problems that may be restricting progress and causing inefficient work practices.
- It can develop a greater degree of consistency through regular feedback on performance and discussion about potential. This encourages better performance from staff.
- It can provide information for human resource planning, to assist succession planning and talent management, and to determine suitability for promotion and for particular types of employment and training.
- It can improve communications by giving staff the opportunity to talk about their ideas and expectations, and how well they are progressing.

Potential problem areas

Despite the benefits of a PR system, the effectiveness of any such system relies heavily on the quality and reliability of assessment. Variations in the consistency of reporting standards can quickly lead to a feeling of dissatisfaction and injustice. There are many potential sources of rating errors including, for example, perceptual distortions such as stereotyping and the halo effect, discussed in Chapter 6. Where a senior manager has the opportunity to confirm the ratings and countersign the report, this may help to identify inconsistencies and those appraisers who appear to be too generous or too critical in their assessments.

However well-designed the PM system, it is not possible to apply a completely objective approach to every unique situation. The system should therefore always allow for at least a degree of discretion and personal judgement. The reporting system should give the reviewer an opportunity to record formally any necessary qualifications to the given ratings.

The elimination of bias

Tackey refers to the importance of eliminating bias in performance reviews. 'The evaluation of the performance of individuals in the workplace is fraught with difficulties even at the best of times. The difficulties are compounded when there are allegations of bias in such evaluation; and magnified out of recognition when the alleged bias has racial undertones.' Many problems with performance review systems arise from the application of the systems rather than inherent deficiencies in the systems themselves. For example it is important to understand whether certain behavioural descriptions are used more frequently to describe different groups. Questions also arise about issues of assessing actual, as opposed to perceived, performance and whether there are differences in perceptions of organisational and managerial support, career progression, etc. that may help explain 'poor' performance of minority ethnic employees. Success in general career development programmes for different organisational groups is more likely only when there is immense commitment in the top echelons of the organisation to equality of opportunity.[47]

Regular review of performance

It is particularly important that a formal PR system does not result in managers failing in their responsibilities for reviewing performance on a day-to-day basis. Reviews should not be limited to a formal event occurring once or twice a year but should be a continuous process of monitoring, feedback and review. There should be regular communications and contacts between managers and staff, and discussions of problem areas and plans for the future.

According to *Kermally*, many organisations still do not fully understand the importance of measuring employee performance effectively. 'Managers need to value and measure the contribution of those that work for them in order to understand how people contribute to organisational success. For this reason, it is also imperative that performance reviews and measurement are undertaken continuously' (*see* Figure 13.3).[48]

Butcher also refers to the importance of a continuous feedback. 'This is another point about appraisals that often gets lost in all the form-filling: they're pointless if they're not part of a culture of constant feedback, a formalising of conversations that happen on a day-to-day basis in corridors or taxis or over lunch.'[49]

Emphasis on form-filling

According to a report by *Law*, referring to a research study by Mabey, an emphasis on form-filling and bureaucratic systems is seriously undermining the effectiveness of staff appraisals in many organisations.

A lot of organisations almost have the worst of both worlds – they are using an appraisal system which feels mechanistic and takes up a lot of time without seeming to produce benefits . . . Where good appraisal systems are combined with discussion of development needs, career planning, fast-tracking

Figure 13.3	Continuous measurement diagram

**Make decisions/
Take actions**

**Set objectives/
Involve employees**

Continuous measurement

Many organisations set aside specific periods to
review employee performance – normally once or twice
a year. These are the formal review periods.
In some organisations these review periods are dreaded because
employees believe they are designed to identify mistakes and then the
information is used against them when it suits their bosses or
their organisations.
The philosophy behind employee performance reviews is to minimise or
eliminate employee weakness and capitalise on their strengths. Apart from being
a measurement tool it is a development tool, allowing skills gaps to be identified
and employees to be given the opportunity to gain new skills for the benefit of
the organisation.
Employees should look forward to review periods so that they can highlight their
achievements and capabilities. Potentially, there could be benefits all round if
they are arranged more frequently on an informal basis.
The concept of continuous improvement is regarded as a powerful tool for
building 'best practice' organisations. It provides a bridge between formal
reviews and should take place in the form of mentoring and coaching.
Because employee performance is so crucial to organisational
performance, it may well be too late for the business if feedback on
under-performance is only reported in the middle or at the end
of the year.
In my experience not many organisations are adequately
geared to measuring employee performance on
a continuous review basis.

**Provide
feedback**

**Monitor,
coach,
counsel**

Evaluate/Analyse

Review/Appraise

Source: From Kermally, S. 'Appraising Employee Performance', *Professional Manager*, July 2002, p. 31. Reproduced with permission from Chartered Management Institute.

schemes for high-flyers and a systematic evaluation of management development, there is a direct impact on business performance. This is manifested in improved quality of products or services, and ability to recruit and retain good staff . . . However in many organisations in the UK staff appraisals are tick-boxing exercises with little or no follow-up action. This causes cynicism and fails to capitalise on the potential benefits of linking staff development to organisational performance.[50]

A similar point is made by *Shellabear* who says that, used effectively, performance management enables an organisation to forward plan and develop staff but used ineffectively it is often reduced to a hurried appraisal system by overworked managers rushing to complete a series of forms once a year. 'At best, a performance management system has the potential to develop your people and significantly increase business results. At worst it can be perceived as a form of employee control or a tick box process that managers and staff feel obliged to implement.'[51]

A concept map on understanding the appraisal system is set out in Figure 13.4.

Figure 13.4   Concept map of understanding the appraisal system

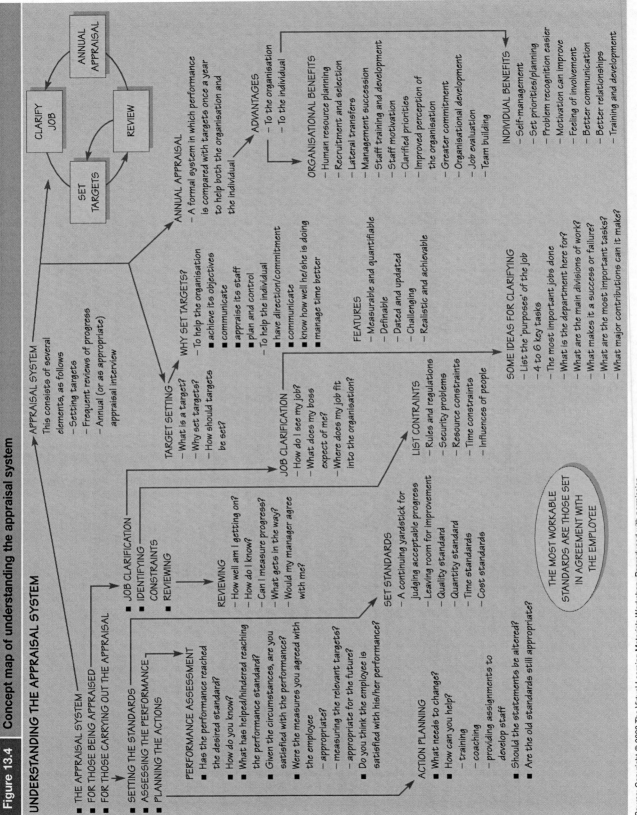

Source: Copyright © 2008 The Virtual Learning Materials Workshop. Reproduced with permission.

EMPLOYEE RELATIONS

Sound HRM policies help to foster good employee (or employment) relations. Broadly defined, **employee relations** is concerned with the relationships between the policies and practices of the organisation and its staff, and the behaviour of work groups. ACAS suggests that the employment relationship has many dimensions and wide-ranging implications, including legal, economic, social, psychological and political. It is not surprising that the employee relationship is one of the most difficult of relationships to manage.

> *A growing body of evidence suggests that it is the way the employment relationship is managed that makes the difference to the quality of working life and organisational performance. Skill levels and technology are important but not the complete answer. Effective employment relations is about the work organisation and whether it delivers maximum performance in terms of customer and employee satisfaction.*
>
> ACAS 'Employment Relations Matters'[52]

Employee relations policy

The nature and content of an employee relations policy will be influenced by such factors as:

- the type, nature and size of organisation;
- its structure and methods of operation;
- the nature of staff employed;
- arrangements for collective bargaining;
- the structure and strength of trade unions;
- preference of the parties for freedom of action from outside influences; and
- the philosophy of top management and their attitudes toward the management of employee relations.

To understand any employee relations situation it is necessary to take account of the institutions and parties involved, and their ideologies and motives. It is necessary to consider not only the legal dimensions but also the behavioural dimensions (discussed later in this chapter).

New kind of employee relations

The CIPD highlights the decline of the strength of trade unions, particularly in the private sector, and the growth of employee engagement as a new kind of employee relations. As unions have declined, organisations have sought to introduce opportunities for two-way communication and information sharing with employees, offering an opportunity for management seeking to improve efficiencies and for employee representatives to discuss workplace rights. The CIPD suggest that employee engagement 'offers managers a framework for monitoring of a range of indicators, including employee attitudes and behaviours, of the state of the employment relationship'.[53]

Whether undertaken through traditional routes of union/management conversations or via the concept of employee engagement, there is much more focus within employee relations generally, despite high-profile threatened and actual disputes, on working in partnership to improve productivity, than on conflict between management and employee representatives. This is supported by a growing belief among a number of employers that trade unions are much more sensitive to the business needs of enterprises than they ever were in the past and are more willing to co-operate with management in developing and helping to enforce workplace reform.

In any analysis of the transformation of Britain's employee relations we cannot neglect the changing nature of work. The influence of technological innovation, work restructuring and job redesign are all helping to reshape shopfloor attitudes among managers, unions and workers. The underlying shifts in labour markets with the modest but important relative growth in the number of those employed in part-time, temporary and contract work are also helping to determine the evolution of our employee relations in new ways.[54]

UNITARY AND PLURALISTIC PERSPECTIVES

In the search for effective employee relations and a common commitment to the goals of the organisation, consideration should be given to contrasting approaches which present two major ways of perceiving work organisations: the unitary perspective and the pluralistic perspective (referred to in Chapter 3 as contrasting views of conflict). While neither of the approaches can be seen as 'right' or 'wrong', these contrasting views will influence the nature of employee relations and the management of human resources.

The unitary perspective

With the **unitary perspective** the organisation is viewed as an integrated and harmonious whole with managers and other staff sharing common interests and objectives. There is an image of the organisation as a team with a common source of loyalty, one focus of effort and one accepted leader. Conflict is perceived as disruptive and unnatural and can be explained by, for example, poor communications, personality clashes or the work of agitators. Trade unions are seen as an unnecessary evil and restrictive practices as outmoded or caused by trouble-makers.

HR policies and managerial development can be seen as reflecting a unitary ideology. *Horwitz* suggests that the unitary perspective views company and trade union loyalty as mutually exclusive. He raises the question of human resource management as a reformation of a unitarist managerial ideology. Developments in HRM, in seeking to optimise co-operation and organisational loyalty, can be seen as imposing new forms of control. A managerial approach to facilitating organisational goals and the direct involvement of employees furthers a unitary perspective and can mask an underlying distaste for unionism.[55]

The pluralistic perspective

An alternative view suggested by *Fox* is the **pluralistic perspective** which views the organisation as made up of powerful and competing sub-groups with their own legitimate loyalties, objectives and leaders.[56] These competing sub-groups are almost certain to come into conflict. From the pluralist perspective, conflict in organisations is seen as inevitable and induced, in part, by the very structure of the organisation. Conflict is not necessarily a bad thing but can be an agent for evolution, and internal and external change.

Restrictive practices may be seen as a rational response from a group that regards itself as being threatened. The role of the manager would be less commanding and enforcing, and more persuading and co-ordinating. Fox suggests that the pluralistic perspective is a more realistic frame of reference. He argues the importance of viewing work situations through the different groups involved rather than attempting a wished-for unitary approach. According to *Horn*, 'these views were widely acceptable, particularly to trade unions, who saw this as legitimising their intervention into an increasing range of managerial prerogative areas'.[57] There are, however, relative shades of unitary and pluralistic perspectives, and the two can co-exist within the same organisation.

REGULATING THE EMPLOYMENT CONTRACT

A central feature of effective employee relationships is managing through people and regulating the employment relationship.[58] Whether as individuals or members of a group, the

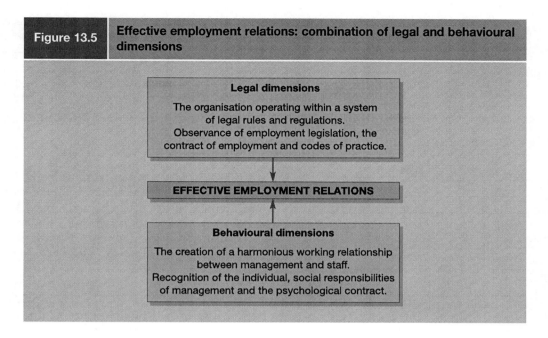

| Figure 13.5 | Effective employment relations: combination of legal and behavioural dimensions |

Legal dimensions

The organisation operating within a system of legal rules and regulations. Observance of employment legislation, the contract of employment and codes of practice.

↓

EFFECTIVE EMPLOYMENT RELATIONS

↑

Behavioural dimensions

The creation of a harmonious working relationship between management and staff. Recognition of the individual, social responsibilities of management and the psychological contract.

actions and decisions of people are governed by a set of underlying rules. In the work organisation these rules are implemented within a structured hierarchy of authority and responsibility. But regulating behaviour between people at work is a complex process. Effective employment relations are founded on a combination of legal and behavioural dimensions. The legal dimension embodies observance of employment legislation, the formal contract of employment and codes of practice. The behavioural dimension embodies recognition of the individual, the social responsibilities of management (discussed in Chapter 18) and the psychological contract (discussed in Chapter 1) (*see* Figure 13.5). Social responsibilities extend beyond terms and conditions of the formal contract of employment, and give recognition to the social and human needs of people at work, including greater emphasis on creating and integrating a work/life balance. The recognition of social responsibilities should form an integral part of corporate strategy and regulating the employment relationship.

Legal dimensions

The work organisation has to operate within a system of legal rules and regulations. Legal dimensions regulate the relationship between employers and employees, provide individual rights for employees and strengthen the position of trade unions. Legislation and codes of practice lay down rules that govern patterns of behaviour to ensure that 'managers act reasonably in the circumstances'. Some managers view these rules with trepidation and avoid taking necessary action to discipline employees. Others are unaware of the rules or choose to disregard them, terminating contracts without due cause. Either strategy is likely to result in behavioural problems among employees who will perceive avoidance or over-reaction as dysfunctional. A proper knowledge, understanding and respect of the law, coupled with appropriate managerial action, can turn a potentially difficult situation into an opportunity to motivate staff and improve organisational effectiveness.

Although it is not the purpose of this book to consider detailed aspects of employment law, it is important to recognise the existence of the legal framework within which organisations function and which affects employee relations. Traditionally, employee relations in Britain have been characterised by the concept of free collective bargaining between employees and employers. However, in recent years this philosophy has been underpinned by increasing amounts of employment law. The substance of British laws is also increasingly being influenced by the impact of EU legislation. Until the 1960s the law governing terms and conditions was based almost entirely on the concept of the contract of employment and attracted little statutory intervention. However, this area of law has been significantly extended, introducing new statutory rights for both those in employment and those seeking employment. Employees can seek redress through a tribunal system, and have rights concerning a range of issues from relatively minor matters such as time off for public duties, to the more important employment protection rights such as the right not to be unfairly dismissed.

Behavioural dimensions

While the observance of legal rules and regulations is clearly a necessary part of effective employment relations, this does not, by itself, make for a harmonious environment at work. Legal dimensions help to regulate the working relationships of people within the organisation. But rules and regulations do not by themselves ensure that disputes will be settled amicably. Human behaviour cannot be made to conform to prescribed rules and regulations just because such rules and regulations exist.

Harmonious employee relations can be effective only if sustained within a generally good relationship between management and staff, with a willing commitment from both sides.[59] Effective managers need to take note of both legal and behavioural perspectives, and to adopt a balanced view when making decisions that affect the employment relationship. Notwithstanding any legal obligations, the employer–employee relationship demands that attention be given to those factors that influence the behaviour of people at work, the psychological contract and the style of managerial behaviour. For example, there is a general duty placed on an employer to disclose, on request, to authorised representatives of independent trade unions information for the purposes of collective bargaining and which it would be good employee relations practice to disclose. However, many organisations now consider the broader behavioural considerations and choose as a matter of policy to report fully, and in non-technical terms, wider details of their financial results and performance direct to all employees.

Critical reflection

'The biggest problem with employee relations is that too much emphasis is placed on attempting to regulate the nature of jobs and work through increased legal requirements. Greater attention should be given to concern for the people–organisation relationship, understanding human behaviour and the effective management of people.'

To what extent do you support this point of view?

Responsibility for employee relations

It is sometimes suggested that in many organisations the responsibility for employee relations still lies with the line managers, who are often sceptical or even hostile towards HR ideas and techniques and who frequently reject the concept of an employee relations policy because it hampers their work and limits their flexibility. As with other aspects of the HRM function it is important that line managers are involved, at least to some extent, with employee relationships. But there must be good communications and close consultation with the HR department. There must be teamwork and a concerted organisational approach to the management of employee relations. This is made easier when top management take an active part in fostering goodwill and co-operation between departments and with official union representatives. Top management should agree clear terms of reference for both the HR manager and line managers within the framework of sound HRM policies.[60]

INTERNATIONAL DIMENSIONS OF HRM

The field of international human resource management comprises two distinct areas: (i) the management of employees in global businesses operating across national boundaries, and (ii) the comparison of human resource management activities and policies in different societies. *Budhwar* identifies four approaches to international staffing which may help to explain how businesses operating across national borders choose to co-ordinate their human resource management policies:[61]

1 **Ethnocentric approach.** Here managerial positions are normally filled by staff from the 'parent' country. It is likely that within this approach the home country's approach will be dominant with subsidiaries operating standardised HRM practices.
2 **Polycentric approach.** Under this heading local managers from the host country are more usually appointed. The approach may be useful when a global strategy is to be implemented on a regional basis. It can also be seen when a subsidiary develops local HRM practices.
3 **Geocentric approach.** In this approach managers are recruited from within the company or from outside with no importance attached to their nationality. It could be argued that such managers may possess greater cultural flexibility.
4 **Regiocentric approach.** Recruitment of managers is undertaken on a regional basis. This is more likely when subsidiaries operate as part of a regional strategy and HRM practices are, in turn, formulated regionally.

Increasingly, global corporations are both willing and able to adopt a flexible approach to staffing. For example, there are increasing examples of the shift of call centre operations from the UK and USA to new locations, in particular the Indian subcontinent, and press reports suggest that the transfer of jobs may prove to be a worldwide trend on a scale greater than previously envisaged.

Comparison of HRM in different societies

Human resource management practices, it is suggested, are influenced by the culture of the society in which they take place, being affected by both specific culturally derived attitudes and institutional factors. To take the example of recruitment and selection, *Koen* proposes that 'The methodology of recruitment and selection has never been uniform across the world. Moreover, whether a specific personnel selection practice should be adopted universally remains an unresolved issue. However, given the crucial role played by this personnel function, especially in managing a multinational workforce, understanding the similarities and dissimilarities of existing practices in different nations ought to be the first step taken by human resource managers and researchers.'[62]

In examining recruitment and selection methods in the USA, *Francesco and Gold* note that 'when making a hiring decision, people in an achievement-oriented country consider skills, knowledge and talent'.[63] This individual orientation will influence the selection methods typically chosen in such a society. Recruitment and selection in the United States has also been significantly affected by the relatively extensive laws prohibiting discrimination in employment, which can, in turn, be seen as an expression of a culture which places particular value on individual characteristics. It is also possible to view the largely American-derived battery of psychometric measures within this overall cultural framework.

It may also be that culturally based perceptions take effect in recruitment and selection in individual cultures. An executive from the Swedish company IKEA, cited by *Schneider and Barsoux*, provides one example of a culturally specific preference in this regard in the following quote. 'The most important quality for an Ikean is *odmjukhet* – a Swedish word that implies humility, modesty and respect for one's fellow man. It may be hard to translate, but we know it when we see it.'[64]

Grahl and Teague attempt to explain differences in the area of human resource management between countries in Europe with reference to a model contrasting competitive and constructive flexibility along a continuum.[65]

- **Competitive flexibility** as a concept states that national competitiveness may best be achieved by minimising restrictions on managerial prerogative – that is, implying a minimal level of legislation and the removal of barriers to workforce flexibility. This approach may be compared to some of the features of HRM as it evolved in the United States. In Europe, Grahl and Teague suggest that the UK is the country that is located furthest at the competitive end of their model.
- **Constructive flexibility** in contrast, while acknowledging the need for greater flexibility in all its dimensions – numerical, temporal and functional – aims to move towards this desired aim without exacerbating divisions within society. Here work employees may enjoy extensive legal rights and protection, and social costs to employers may be greater than in countries more closely associated with competitive flexibility. Constructive flexibility also presumes a social partnership model of co-operation within the enterprise whereby managers are required to consult with employee representatives before making decisions or conceivably to act jointly in conjunction with these representatives. Grahl and Teague find Germany and Sweden to be the two European countries most closely corresponding to constructive flexibility.

Industrial democracy in European countries

One example of how different cultural values and institutional arrangements combine to form distinctive philosophies and practices in the field of human resource management is evident in the concept of statutory industrial democracy prevalent in many European countries. This relates to the degree of consultation – or even joint decision-making – prescribed by national or pan-European law within individual workplaces. One illustration of how the concept can affect the management of people in practice is provided by the system operating in Germany.[66]

The German system

The German system of industrial democracy is the most comprehensive and has tended to be used by commentators as a model of its kind. The system comprises both the works council (*Betriebsrat*) and representation on boards of directors, the supervisory board (*Aufsichtsrat*) and the executive board (*Vorstand*).[67]

The works council

Works councils exist in organisations covering all sectors of the economy including both the private and public sector. Works council representatives are elected by fellow workers. They do not, however, stand on behalf of trade unions, and in elections stress their individual qualities and experiences. The works council has three rights: the right of information; the right of consultation; and the right of co-determination.

Representation on boards of directors

The supervisory board may include employee representatives. The composition of the executive board is most interesting in German organisations since it includes a labour director (*Arbeitsdirektor*). The labour director can be appointed only by a two-thirds majority of the worker representatives on the supervisory board. *French* shows how this director may be a worker representative, but equally may be a career personnel manager.[68] *Lawrence* suggests that increasingly personnel managers are labour directors and are thus represented on both boards of directors.[69]

Negotiation and discussion

It can be seen that in Germany, personnel managers are constrained by law from acting unilaterally, and are required to work jointly with the workforce representatives. Lawrence concludes that the personnel function in Germany is marked by a high degree of both legalism and formalism with laws, documents and written agreements being more salient than in Britain. The same author gives us a sense of the flavour of personnel management in that country as follows:

> *The works council is an important reference point for the German personnel manager and much of his time is spent in negotiation or discussion with the council.*[70]

EFFECTIVENESS OF THE HRM FUNCTION

The ultimate measure of the effectiveness of the HRM function is the contribution it makes to meeting the objectives of the business and to improved organisational performance. But achievement in the area of HRM is difficult to measure and it is not easy to establish satisfactory methods of assessment. There is also the more general problem of assessing managerial work where the end-product results from the efforts of other people. Cost is obviously a consideration but should not be viewed in isolation. Not every activity in the organisation can be identified clearly as making a direct contribution to profitability. A balance should be maintained between the more easily identified financial costs of the HRM function and the less readily apparent but very important long-term benefits which also make a positive contribution to the effectiveness of the organisation.

The contributions from an effective HRM function are not always readily apparent nor are they necessarily easy to identify. Account should be taken of intangible benefits such as the morale and job satisfaction of staff as well as their attitudes, behaviour and performance. Over a period of time, however, some quantified measures may serve to provide management with an indication of effectiveness. Possible examples include staffing costs, turnover and stability indexes; internal promotions and staff development; errors in work; levels of absenteeism and sickness; timekeeping; accidents at work; the number of discipline or grievance hearings, dismissals, labour disputes, employment tribunal cases; complaints from suppliers or customers.

Good HR policies and employment relations

According to *Slater*, 'Recognition that employees form the lifeblood of a company has highlighted the strategic role that the human resources department should now play.' For the first time HR professionals have the opportunity to add value to a business. There is a shift in emphasis in business and the bottom line is no longer all-important. Greater attention is placed on issues such as how well a company executes its business plan, employee well-being, corporate culture and organisational structure. Although the customer is still king, companies realise that it is their employees who deliver the performance of value to the customer.

> *Nowhere has this change impacted more greatly than in human resources. The need to focus more on internal 'customers' has put pressure on companies to release HR staff from a largely administrative role to a more strategic one that addresses increased productivity, employee commitment and career advancement. Only by addressing these issues will a company truly be able to leverage employee power . . . Freed from many routine tasks, the HR department will be able to devote more time to adding value to the business.*[71]

However the HRM function is organised or evaluated, proper attention to the establishment of good HR policies and employment relations will help to improve the efficiency of the workforce and standards of service to customers. Full use should be made of specialist HR staff, the involvement of line managers and modern methods and processes.

Browning lists ten ways to make HR effective:

1 *Be the catalyst for making things happen.*
2 *Avoid being the corporate soft touch.*
3 *Understand the whole business.*
4 *Keep people-management systems simple.*
5 *Remember line managers manage people, not HR.*
6 *Work with, not above, line managers.*
7 *Be super-efficient in the transactional stuff.*
8 *Be leaders in the transformational stuff.*
9 *Help the business to manage change.*
10 *Accept that good 'people ideas' exist outside HR.*[72]

HR and the future world of work

HR services provider Ceridian draws attention to dramatic changes in the workforce and workplace. People are living longer and face new caring responsibilities; the war for talent continues; generations X and Y present their own concerns; there is a struggle to raise productivity and for smarter not harder ways; there is the challenge of the management of outsourcing; and there is the dream of better technological solutions for improved efficiency and productivity.

> *This cocktail of changes presents HR professionals with a particular difficulty: can they make this new deal with their work people? Can we embrace change and make it work for us? Can we carry our staff with us on this arduous journey in to the future world of work? And do HR professionals have the skills required to engage with these strategic questions and provide the leadership their businesses and organ-isations need?*[73]

What is the real value of HR?

In a provocative feature in the *Financial Times*, *Johnson* suggests that HR, together with other divisions such as IT, legal and marketing, is probably the very definition of a necessary evil for the 21st-century business. HR is like many parts of modern business: a simple expense, and a burden on the backs of the productive workers. They don't sell or produce; they con-sume. They are the amorphous support services.[74]

Stern also questions the real value of HR professionals and suggests they are really only there for the nasty things in life, like sacking people – legally.

> *It may sound harsh, but the unfortunate truth is that of all the functional departments, HR vies only with IT for the amount of opprobrium it traditionally attracts from everyone else, and the sourness of the gibes made at its expense.*

Stern maintains that when in hard times harried line managers do contact colleagues in HR, too often they are met with an excessive level of bureaucracy, and it is no wonder no one takes them seriously. According to the Corporate Research Forum, HR profes-sionals will need to change if they are to succeed. HR professionals need to be seen to be contributing valuable insights and interventions. 'They need to be real business people, with a grasp of profit-and-loss realities . . . HR's efforts should be directed towards creating a high-performance work environment . . . HR needs . . . to be the guide and guardian of high-quality management . . . [and] think in terms of internal customer satisfaction and added value.'[75]

> ## Critical reflection
>
> 'Until HR professionals can produce hard and clear measures of their value to improved performance, it is perhaps no surprise that they are perceived as making only a marginal contribution to organisational effectiveness.'
>
> *Do you think HR professionals lack credibility among line managers? How would you attempt to measure the contribution of the HR department?*

SYNOPSIS

■ An essential part of the process of management is that proper attention be given to the efficient use of resources, in particular human resources. In recent years there has been increasing attention to a strategic approach to 'human resource management' (HRM) and also to the idea of 'human capital'. However, it is important to remember that it is people who are the most important asset of any organisation. Effective HRM requires strategic integration of people management policies and successful implementation if it is to impact on organisational performance.

■ Success in the field of human relationships stems from good HRM policies and practices which should be based on underlying philosophies of managerial behaviour and employee relations. The range and scope of HRM activities are wide, and a shared responsibility among top management, line managers and supervisors, and the HR manager. As an element function, HRM is part of the generality of management and part of the responsibility of all managers and supervisors. HRM has to operate at a strategic level and in partnership with line managers.

■ One major area of HRM work of particular relevance to the effective management and use of people is training and development. Training is a key element of improved performance and offers a number of potential benefits for both the individual and the organisation. In order to secure the full benefits of training there must be a planned and systematic approach and a continuous commitment to training standards. Learning via technology, e-learning, is growing in popularity and importance. Investors in People provides a national framework for training and development of people to achieve business goals. Another relatively new area of HRM of particular importance is talent management, which offers a strategic approach to gaining a competitive advantage through the people resource.

■ One way to review the performance and potential of staff is through a formal performance review system. An effective system offers a number of potential benefits to both individuals and the organisation but there are a number of important questions to be addressed. Consideration must be given to the design and implementation of the system, methods of appraisal, and potential problem areas. It is particularly important that a formal system does not detract from the manager's responsibility for reviewing performance on a day-to-day basis and that it should be seen as part of the PM strategy.

■ Sound HRM policies help to foster good employment relations. It is necessary to take account of the institutions and parties involved, and their ideologies and motives. There are two major and contrasting perspectives of work organisations, and the explanation and outcomes of conflict – the unitary and the pluralistic perspectives. These contrasting views influence the nature of employee relationships and the management of human resources. Good managerial strategies are important for effective employment relations that are founded on a combination of legal and behavioural dimensions.

■ It is important that line managers are involved, at least to some extent, with the responsibility for employment relations. HRM practices are influenced by the culture of the society in which they take place. Increasingly the European Union is seeking to harmonise employment practices among member states. The ultimate measure of effectiveness of the HRM function is the contribution to good human relationship at work and improved organisational performance, but this is not always readily apparent or easy to identify.

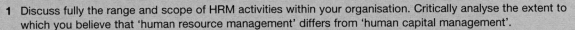

REVIEW AND DISCUSSION QUESTIONS

1   Discuss fully the range and scope of HRM activities within your organisation. Critically analyse the extent to which you believe that 'human resource management' differs from 'human capital management'.

2   'Every director an HR director, every line manager a HR manager.' In the light of this statement, discuss what you see as the role and functions of the human resource department in a large business organisation.

3   Explain fully what you understand by a strategic approach to HRM.

4   How would you justify to a group of sceptical line managers a high level of financial provision for training? Explain the steps you would take in order to ensure the effective management of training.

5   What are the potential benefits for both the individual and the organisation from a formal system of performance review?

6   Explain those factors that are likely to influence the nature and contents of an employment relations policy, and give specific examples from your own organisation. What is meant by the legal and behavioural perspectives of employee relations?

7   Discuss critically the extent to which line managers should be involved with the responsibility for employee relations. What arrangements exist in your organisation?

8   Comment critically on the accountability and measurement of the functioning of the HR department.

MANAGEMENT IN THE NEWS

The carrot and stick approach

FT

Alicia Clegg

Is the size of an employee's waistline any business of the employer? The notion of companies concerning themselves with their employees' lifestyles once seemed strange. But in the light of broader societal concerns about health, the role of employers in the provision of health care is more relevant than ever. The economist Julian Le Grand has even proposed that large employers should be legally required to 'automatically enrol their employees in a weekly exercise hour, unless the employee chose to opt out'.

Two years ago, Unilever invited its UK staff to undergo confidential health screening to assess their fitness. Now the company has launched 'Fit Business', a year-long pilot programme to encourage its people – more than half of whom were revealed to be overweight – to eat healthily, become physically active and monitor their blood pressure, body fat and cholesterol levels.

In the US, some businesses require workers to lose weight, exercise or stop smoking as a condition of employment or to qualify for benefits. In the UK, participation in health programmes is voluntary and pressure on people to adopt healthy habits is less intense. One potential problem with workplace programmes is that some people worry about

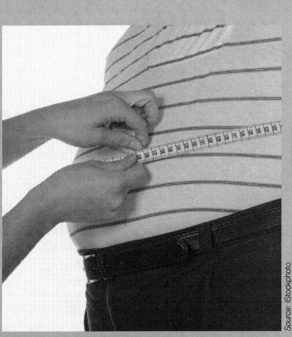
Source: iStockphoto

Organisations are increasingly rewarding employees for adopting 'healthy' lifestyles but should they be concerning themselves with the personal lives of their employees?

embarrassing themselves in front of fitter colleagues. Suggesting alternatives to formal exercise, such as taking the stairs and including walks as part of the daily commute, could be the solution, says Brent Pawlecki, corporate medical director at Pitney Bowes, the US-based postage services company.

As part of Unilever's health initiative, it offers weight loss programmes. Participants receive a set of scales and a Bluetooth-enabled wrist monitor, which records how physically active the individual has been and links to an on-line coaching programme that generates follow-up advice. The company stresses that participation is voluntary and only the employee concerned sees any personal data. But should organisations reward employees for adopting healthy lifestyles? Sarah Brown, an employee benefits principal at the Mercer consultancy, says giving cash or goods to employees for completing on-line health assessments has been shown to improve participation rates. But, she says, not everyone is happy with a practice that imposes extra costs on the employer. 'We get clients who ask: "Should we really be paying people to do something that's beneficial to their health?"'

In terms of improving eating habits, removing pies and puddings from canteen menus is guaranteed to put people's backs up. Pitney Bowes tries to nudge its employees towards health. It recently replaced potato crisps with carrots and celery as the default accompaniment to sandwiches, displays fruit instead of sweets by the check-out, and uses price subsidies to steer people's choices. 'The grilled chicken sandwich is a lot less expensive than the hamburger and fries,' says Dr Pawlecki. That said, even he recognises there is a limit to the nannying employees will tolerate. 'The cookies aren't easily reachable,' he says. 'But there isn't a hand that comes out and slaps you for grabbing them.'

Source: Clegg, A. 'The Carrot and Stick Approach', *Financial Times*, 28 May 2009. Copyright © 2009 The Financial Times Limited, reproduced with permission.

Discussion questions

1 Should employers require their workers to take exercise and eat healthily as a condition of employment? What are the arguments for such a policy, and how do you think you would respond as an employee?

2 What role could be played by a human resource or personnel manager in support of a 'healthy employee' policy, and how could it be linked to other employment policies such as recruitment, pay, training etc.?

ASSIGNMENT

Over fifty years ago, Peter Drucker first raised the question: 'Is personnel management bankrupt?' And he answered: 'No, it is not bankrupt. Its liabilities do not exceed its assets. But it is certainly insolvent, certainly unable to honour, with the ready cash of performance, the promises of managing worker and work it so liberally makes.'[76]

In view of the work of more recent writers, the changing nature of work organisations and developments in human resource management, how would *you* attempt to answer this question today? Set your response out as fully as possible and give supporting reasons.

PERSONAL AWARENESS AND SKILLS EXERCISE

Objectives

Completing this exercise should help you to enhance the following skills:

- Review options in dealing with difficult work situations.
- Play the role of manager, employee or observer.
- Appreciate sensitivities when dealing with issues related to poor performance.

Exercise

Working in a team of three people, you are required to participate in the following role-play exercise.

Personal awareness and skills exercise – continued

Role play A: Manager/Kirsty

You are a line manager and Steve is an administrator who reports to you. The other members of the team, while liking him personally, complain about his disorganisation and the image he gives the department.

His last performance review was six months ago and he was rated as just meeting his performance objectives. Since then Steve's performance has slipped steadily.

- 80 per cent of work has to be returned for correction, indicating that it has not been proofread or spell-checked.
- Computer files and cupboards are a mess. Other administrators fear standing in for him because of his poor organisation.
- He does not prioritise workload or respond well to urgent requests.
- He has left a confidential document on his desk overnight twice in the last month.
- His work area is untidy, with papers and half-empty coffee beakers all over the desk.

You have done your research and have determined that his performance is entirely unsatisfactory. You have asked to see Steve formally in your office so that you can make it clear to him that if his performance does not improve in all areas, his continued employment with the organisation is in jeopardy.

Decide how you will approach this difficult situation.

Role play B: Employee/Steve

You are an administrator with eight years' experience. Your manager has asked to see you and you are pretty sure that it's about your performance. She had a chat with you a while ago and said your work was not up to scratch. You know this is true but you are a friendly person and most people get on well with you. You usually manage to come up with the goods in the end. If only some of the people you work for would plan ahead a bit, then you wouldn't have to rush things so much and therefore would make fewer mistakes. Your manager has complained about the way you file things, but you usually find things when they are needed. You enjoy your work and certainly need the money. You are pretty confident you will be able to get out of any kind of scrape with your manager, as you can be quite persuasive when you choose to be.

Role play C: Observer

The outcome here needs to be that Steve is absolutely clear that if his performance doesn't improve dramatically then the usual, formal disciplinary procedure will be instigated.

Watch out for the following from the manager:

- clear, assertive but unemotional communication to Steve throughout the meeting;
- keeping clear of attacking Steve as a person;
- not allowing Steve to take over and blame others;
- checking that Steve is clear on the implications of not improving;
- pointing out clearly where Steve is going wrong and what improvements are expected;
- giving Steve a deadline and review date.

Discussion

- What have you learned from this exercise about the nature and management of performance review?
- What do you think is the best way to manage poor performance? What options are available?
- What other conclusions do you draw from this exercise?

The changing role of HRM

The Human Resource Management (personnel) profession has evolved to encompass a wide range of activities that surround the management of people in organisations. Its relationship with the subject of organisational behaviour is similar to that between engineering and mathematics; the one is a necessary foundation for the practical activities which form the other. Most managers have to manage staff-related issues (along with budgets, operations etc.) and the HR function should be there in some form to provide the necessary professional expertise to do so effectively and ensure the organisation doesn't find itself on the wrong end of an employment tribunal case. HRM is thus an important support activity, and as organisations grow so, in most cases, does the HR department.

Going outside
Four trends, perhaps, have contributed to the growing interest in the possibility of outsourcing the organisation's HRM function. Firstly, many organisations have gained first-hand experience of outsourcing a range of business processes to achieve efficiency gains and cost savings. The skills of contract management and the transactional nature of client–provider relationships are now well embedded in organisational life. Secondly, information technology has developed to an extent where instantaneous communication is not merely possible but routine; and internet-based software makes access to complex information simple. Well-designed web-based material allows detailed information to be searched and accessed without the need to trawl through lengthy manuals. Thirdly, the extent and complexity of much employment legislation, including that emanating from the European Union, requires a level of expertise in the development and management of HR policies which very few organisations can afford to hold in-house. For internationally operating organisations the variety and complexity is even greater. Finally, the HR profession (particularly in the UK) is seeking to position itself as a 'business partner' in organisational terms, not simply an administrative function. Outsourcing can be seen as an attractive way of offloading the more traditional elements of the job, thus freeing up HR managers to take a more strategic role.[77] The CIPD[78] recently summarised the top reasons given for outsourcing HR functions as including:

- cost cutting;
- making HR more strategic;

Are call centres the future for Human Resource Management professionals? There is a growing trend for HR to go online, but does this make it more effective.

Source: © Larry Lilac/Alamy

- service improvement;
- responding to changes in business;
- speeding up global transformation and streamlining the HR function;
- bringing in new technology and improving HR information.

Yet many administrative activities remain, and line managers rarely run the payroll or update employment contracts. And they still need advice about what they can and can't do about persistent absentees, how to handle maternity leave or how to deal with issues raised by trade union representatives. This is where the opportunities for a new type of HRM have opened up, by providing either single types of activity such as training courses, or complete 'bundles' of HRM services through a single contract.

The idea of outsourcing aspects of HRM is not new. External agencies commonly provide training and development activities and both the number and type of training consultants has increased rapidly in recent years. Payroll management is also a significant area of HR outsourcing, since it has a strong IT base and has often been part of the externalisation of wider IT support systems. Recruitment agencies have operated in different areas of the labour market for decades. The new departure, though, is a small but significant trend for organisations to engage in long-term contracts through which a provider offers a complete HRM service. In many cases a large company, often from the information technology or business consulting arena, has developed an HRM package as the core of a new consulting venture. ExcellerateHRO, for instance, began as a joint venture between EDS (Electronic Data Systems) and Towers Perrin, although the latter's share was bought out by Hewlett-Packard in 2009; and Convergys originated with Cincinnati Bell, in partnership with AT&T Solutions Customer Care in the late 1990s.

BT and Accenture

Accenture is the consulting company which split from accounting firm Arthur Andersen in 2000. In the late 1990s it noticed the business opportunity for the delivery of HR services to large, geographically spread organisations from central points of expertise using innovative technological applications. Its initial projects in this field were developed in 2000, and it created Accenture HR Services amongst whose first customers were to be BT and Accenture itself. At Accenture, the consolidation of the HR service, combined with a major redesign of its processes, permitted both individual staff and managers to have access to HR-related information from any internet-connected computer. Individuals were able to update important personal information and to access and edit their details and benefits data for themselves. The service covered 29 of Accenture's global locations, and was delivered from six 'hubs' and eight cities. The company found that its consolidated HR service not only improved the speed and quality of delivery but saved the business money, an estimated $3.3 million in 2003.[79] Convinced of the potential of its HR service, Accenture became an early player in this new market. It refined and developed its service, and the model now comprises four main elements:

- Business Partners; these are HRM generalists whose job involves researching organisational HR needs and offering advice which will help clients' HR policies and practices to align with their business needs.
- Centres of Expertise; these design HR programmes and each centre corresponds with a specific functional area, such as recruitment, compensation and learning/training.
- HR Shared Service Centres; these are the call centres which deal with individual problems and cases, and are staffed by HR administrators. They are, as the name suggests, shared by Accenture HR Services' client organisations.
- Self-service tools; these are the internet-based resources which enable employees to have personal access to specified data, and can provide tailored information packages for managers as the basis for initial enquiries about managing HR activities. If the on-line information is insufficient, then individual queries and cases are handled by one of the other three elements as appropriate.

By 2009 Accenture was employing more than 3,500 HR professionals in two hundred sites worldwide, and serving over fifty clients including Caja Madrid, Levi Strauss and Co., and the Victoria State Government of Australia.[80]

HR on call

As already noted, an early customer was BT, which went into partnership with Accenture in 2000; and the development of the service for BT helped shape Accenture HR Services' business model. By the late 1990s BT was a large and widespread organisation, operating from more than a hundred locations in the UK. It ran over forty individual HR systems and had personnel professionals located in over sixty areas, as well as an entirely separate training unit. In 1998 the pressure to deliver improved financial results from efficiency gains and costs savings post privatisation led BT to undertake a major rethink of its HR system. The development with Accenture resulted in the latter taking over the provision of what are described as 'end-to-end' HR services to 87,000 BT employees and 180,000 BT pensioners in the UK, using the four components of the Accenture business model described above. It was not all plain sailing, and initial difficulties and higher than anticipated costs seemed to threaten the new service (initially called e-peopleserve), and in 2002 BT paid £80m for the service against a projected cost of £75m.[81] One example of how this was happening included evidence that managers at BT didn't realise that the function was now run as a commercial contract, and did not appreciate that cancelling events such as training programmes would result in penalty charges to BT. Other cost and performance problems had to be resolved by a renegotiation of the contract through which BT sold its 50 per cent share in the business (which had started as a joint venture) and the clear separation of client from provider. By the end of the first period of the contract, costs savings for BT were estimated to have been approximately 20 per cent. In 2005 the two companies signed a new 10-year contract which extended the service to a further 10,000 BT employees. John Hindle of Accenture claims that

> The benefits of outsourcing have been more far-reaching than just direct cost savings. BT has rationalized its training catalog by 50 percent, reduced training waiting lists by 26 percent and saved $2.2 million in time and money lost because of sickness.[82]

Other benefits include a single HR telephone number for BT staff, a single and fully integrated HR reporting system which enables employees to self-service and a company-wide learning management system. Recruitment has speeded up considerably and jobs can be offered within 24 hours.

Organisational impact

The trend towards total outsourcing remains limited, but a number of large organisations have signed such deals with either individual or multiple external providers. Whirlpool for instance embarked on a major 'end-to-end' contract with Convergys in 2005;[83] whereas Essex County Council uses a range of suppliers to provide the majority of their HR service.[84] Yet others have found a compromise, and created similar centralised functions in-house. Standard Chartered Bank considered outsourcing, but decided to create its own global HR service centre based in Chennai, southern India.[85]

But apart from contractual and operational difficulties, there may be some unforeseen consequences of such a move. BAE outsourced the majority of its HR consultancy company Xchanging in 2000, and found that one unexpected result was the increasing influence of trade unions which stemmed from distancing HR from the workforce;

We had pulled out all the HR infrastructure and the relationship between the men and trade unions got stronger and stronger. And in the past 14 months we have put people back in the shipyards, and now have an Xchanging hub there.[86]

Perhaps direct human contact is important for the successful management of people after all.

Your tasks

1 Critically evaluate the extent to which an outsourced HR service might either support or undermine managers in carrying out the 'people' side of their work.

2 Review the position of an organisation like BT in relation to the model of HRM as a shared responsibility (Figure 13.1). To what extent does outsourcing disrupt this shared responsibility, and how?

3 The CIPD considers that HR professionals should become 'strategic business partners' rather than personnel administrators, and that outsourcing HR administration might be one route to achieving this aim. How do you think the trend towards creating centralised IT-based HR service centres might affect the nature of the HRM profession?

Notes and references

1 Gratton, L. *Living Strategy: Putting People at the Heart of Corporate Purpose*, Financial Times Prentice Hall (2000), p. xiii.

2 Fisher, C. D., Schoenfeldt, L. F. and Shaw, J. B. *Human Resource Management*, fifth edition, Houghton Mifflin (2003), p. 7.

3 Library and Information Services, CIPD, May 2009.

4 Torrington, D. and Chapman, J. *Personnel Management*, Prentice Hall (1979).

5 Torrington, D. Hall, L. and Taylor, S. *Human Resource Management*, seventh edition, Financial Times Prentice Hall (2008), p. 25.

6 Crainer, S. *Key Management Ideas: Thinkers That Changed the Management World*, third edition, Financial Times Prentice Hall (1998), p. 115.

7 'The Changing HR Function', Survey Report, CIPD (2007).

8 'Accounting for People', Report of the Task Force on Human Capital Management, DTI, October 2003, p. 3.

9 Gratton, L. *The Democratic Enterprise*, Financial Times Prentice Hall (2004).

10 'Human Capital: Factsheet', CIPD, November 2008.

11 Coppin, A. 'Getting the Measure of Your People Assets', *Professional Manager*, vol. 14, no. 5, September 2005, p. 37.

12 Reeves, R. 'People in the Equation', *Management Today*, November 2004, p. 31.

13 'Human Capital: Factsheet', CIPD, November 2008.

14 Welch, J. *Winning*, HarperCollins (2005), p. 102.

15 Winstanley, D. and Woodall, J. 'The Ethical Dimension of Human Resource Management', *Human Resource Management Journal*, vol. 10, no. 2, 2000, pp. 5–20.

16 See, for example, Purcell, J., Kinnie, N., Hutchinson, S. and Rayton, B. 'Inside the Box', *People Management*, 26 October 2000, pp. 30–8; and Cooper, C. 'Win by a Canvass', *People Management*, 25 January 2001, pp. 42–4.

17 Forte, R. 'How I See the Personnel Function', *Personnel Management*, vol. 14, no. 8, August 1982, p. 32.

18 Johnson, G., Scholes, K. and Whittington, R. *Exploring Corporate Strategy*, seventh edition, Financial Times Prentice Hall (2005), pp. 447–8.

19 Ulrich, D. 'A New Mandate for Human Resources', *Harvard Business Review*, vol. 76, no. 1, January–February 1998, pp. 124–34.

20 Arkin, A. 'Q&A with David Ulrich', *People Management*, 28 June 2007, p. 28; 'Business Partnering: Factsheet', CIPD, October 2008.

21 Lynch, R. *Corporate Strategy*, fourth edition, Financial Times Prentice Hall (2006), Chapter 7.

22 Delany, K. 'Futurising Human Resources: How to Achieve Sustainability', IBIS Best Practice Business Improvements, *Supplement, Management Today*, December 2001, pp. 8–9.

23 'Business Partnering: Factsheet', CIPD, October 2008.

24 See, for example, Torrington, D., Hall, L. and Taylor, S. *Human Resource Management*, seventh edition, Financial Times Prentice Hall (2008).

25 Wolfson, (Sir) B. 'Train, Retain and Motivate Staff', *Management Today*, March 1998, p. 5.

26 Drucker, P. F. *People and Performance*, Heinemann (1977).

27 Adair, J. 'Developing Tomorrow's Leaders', in CBI, *The Path to Leadership: Developing a Sustainable Model within Organisations*, Caspian Publishing (2005), p. 35.

28 'Training for Advantage', *Management Today*, May 1997, p. 89.

29 ACAS *Effective Organisations: The People Factor*, advisory booklet, ACAS (November 2001), p. 20.

30 Tate, W. 'Training – The Stuff of Legends', *Manager, The British Journal of Administrative Management*, September/October 1996, pp. 22–3.

31 Stern, S. 'Firm Choice', *Management Today*, October 2002, p. 6.

32 Douglas, M. 'Why Soft Skills Are an Essential Part of the Hard World of Business', *Manager, The British Journal of Administrative Management*, issue 34, New Year 2003, p. 34.

33 Sweeten, G. 'E-learning: How to Move Forward', *Manager, The British Journal of Administrative Management*, issue 36, Summer 2003, p. 25.

34 Burns, T. 'E-learning: The Future of Quality Training', *Quality Progress*, vol. 38, no. 2, February 2005, pp. 50–6.

35 'E-learning, Progress and Prospects: Factsheet', CIPD, April 2008.

36 'Talent Management, an Overview: Factsheet', CIPD, July 2008.

37 Blass, E. 'Talent Management: Maximising Talent for Business Performance', Chartered Management Institute, November 2007.

38 Blass, E. 'Talent for the Downturn', *Professional Manager*, vol. 18, no. 2, March 2009, pp. 26–8.

39 'Performance Management: An Overview: Factsheet', CIPD, February 2008.

40 ACAS *Effective Organisations: The People Factor*, advisory booklet, ACAS (November 2001), p. 21.

41 See, for example, *Employee Appraisal*, advisory booklet, ACAS (February 2003).

42 Stein, N. 'Remember, the Staff Is the Bread of Life', *Management Today*, July 1991, pp. 58–60.

43 Crainer, S. *Key Management Ideas: Thinkers That Changed the Management World*, third edition, Financial Times Prentice Hall (1998), pp. 134–7.

44 Pfau, B., Kay, I., Nowack, K. M. and Ghorpade, J. 'Does 360-degree Feedback Negatively Affect Company Performance?', *HR Magazine*, vol. 47, no. 6, June 2002, pp. 54–9.

45 Butcher, D. 'It Takes Two to Review', *Management Today*, November 2002, p. 57.

46 Kusin, G. 'A 360-Degree Spin', *Hemisphere Magazine*, United Airlines, October 2005, pp. 74–7.

47 Tackey, D. 'Eliminating Bias in Performance Management', *Manager, The British Journal of Administrative Management*, September/October 2001, pp. 12–13.

48 Kermally, S. 'Appraising Employee Performance', *Professional Manager*, July 2002, p. 19.

49 Butcher, D. 'It Takes Two to Review', *Management Today*, November 2002, p. 55.

50 Law, S. 'Appraisals Fail to Measure Up', *Professional Manager*, vol. 13, no. 3, May 2004, pp. 24–6.

51 Shellabear, S. 'Performance Management: An Art and a Science?', *Training Journal*, January 2005, pp. 48–51.

52 ACAS, 'Employment Relations Matters', Issue 1, Autumn 2004, p. 2.

53 'Employee Relations, an Overview: Factsheet', CIPD, July 2008.

54 Taylor, R. 'The Future of Employment Relations', Economic and Social Research Council (September 2001), pp. 7–8.

55 Horwitz, F. M. 'HRM: An Ideological Perspective', *International Journal of Manpower*, vol. 12, no. 6, 1991, pp. 4–9.

56 Fox, A. *Industrial Society and Industrial Relations*, HMSO (1966).

57 Horn, C. A. 'Management Style', *Administrator*, vol. 6, no. 4, April 1986, p. 14.

58 Mullins, L. J. and Peacock, A. 'Managing Through People: Regulating the Employment Relationship', *Administrator*, December 1991, pp. 32–3.

59 Mullins, L. J. and Peacock, A. 'Effective Employee Relations: Behavioural Dimensions', *Administrator*, April 1992, pp. 12–13.

60 For a fuller discussion on the part played by line managers and personnel specialists in the management of human resources, see, for example, Storey, J. *Developments in the Management of Human Resources*, Blackwell (1992).

61 Budhwar, P. S. 'International Human Resource Management', in Tayeb, M. (ed.) *International Management Theories and Practices*, Financial Times Prentice Hall (2003), Chapter 11.

62 Koen, K. *Comparative International Management*, McGraw-Hill (2005), p. 217.

63 Francesco, A. M. and Gold, B. A. *International Organizational Behavior: Text, Readings, Cases and Skills*, second edition, Prentice Hall (2005), p. 149.

64 Schneider, S. C. and Barsoux, J. *Managing Across Cultures*, second edition, Financial Times Prentice Hall (2003), pp. 151–3.

65 Grahl, J. and Teague, P. 'Industrial Relations Trajectories and European Human Resource Management', in Brewster, C. and Tyson, S. (eds) *International Comparisons in Human Resource Management*, Pitman Publishing (1991), pp. 67–91.

66 French, R. 'Employee Relations in the New Europe', *Administrator*, November 1992, pp. 25–6.

67 French, R. 'Employee Relations: The German Experience', *Administrator*, January 1993, pp. 29–30.

68 French, R. 'The Development and Structuring of Personnel Departments in Britain and West Germany', unpublished PhD thesis, Nottingham Polytechnic, 1985.

69 Lawrence, P. 'The Personnel Function: An Anglo-German Comparison', in Brewster, C. and Tyson, S. (eds) *International Comparisons in Human Resource Management*, Pitman (1991), pp. 131–44.

70 Ibid., p. 134.

71 Slater, L. 'Realising Your Assets', *Digital Britain: Management Strategies for the 21st Century*, Issue 6, p. 13, Supplement to *Management Today*, June 2001.

72 Browning, G. 'Ten Ways to Measure HR', *Management Today*, July 2002, p. 18.

73 'Surviving and Thriving in the Future World of Work', Ceridian (2005).

74 Johnson, L. 'The Truth about the HR Department', *Financial Times*, 29 January 2008.

75 Stern, S. 'What Is HR Really For?', *Management Today*, May 2009, pp. 52–6.

76 Drucker, P. F. *The Practice of Management*, Heinemann Professional (1955), pp. 267–82.

77 Clake, R. and Robinson, V. 'Stay Tuned', *People Management*, vol. 11, no. 10, May 2005, pp. 30–4.

78 CIPD 'The Guide to HR Outsourcing', *People Management*, February 2006.

79 Accenture website: http://www.accenture.com/Global/Services/Client_Successes/By_Subject/Talent_and_Organization/Human_Resources_Mgmt/TheResult.htm (accessed 1 August 2009).

80 Full details of Accenture's operation can be found at www.accenture.com.

81 Pollit, D. 'Outsourcing Connects BT with Better and Cheaper HRM', *HRM International Digest*, vol. 16, no. 1, 2008, pp. 10–12, http://www.emeraldinsight.com/10.1108/09670730810848261 (accessed 30 July 2009).

82 Ibid.

83 CIPD 'The Guide to HR Outsourcing', *People Management*, February 2006.

84 Clake, R. and Robinson, V. 'Stay Tuned', *People Management*, vol. 11, no. 10, May 2005, pp. 30–4.

85 CIPD 'Outsourcing Human Resources: A Framework for Decisions', CIPD, 2005, or in pdf format from www.cipd.co.uk.

86 Sallis, D., quoted in Pickard, J. 'Bridge the Divide', 'The Guide to HR outsourcing', CIPD, 2006.

ACADEMIC VIEWPOINT

Below you will find the title and abstract of a recent article in an academic journal which explores a topic relevant to the chapters in Part 4.

Wright, C. 'Reinventing Human Resource Management: Business Partners, Internal Consultants and the Limits to Professionalization', *Human Relations*, vol. 61, no. 8, 2008, pp. 1063–1086.

Abstract

The status of human resource management (HRM) and its standing as a managerial profession has been a recurring concern for practitioners over time. In recent years, a normative discourse has developed which asserts that the path to improved status for HR 'professionals' involves reinvention of their role as 'business partners' and 'internal consultants' promoting enterprise competitiveness. This article examines how HR managers interpret this new role and whether the internalization of this model results in an increase in professional identity. The findings suggest that while many gain greater self-esteem and organizational status from the identity and role of business partner/internal consultant, this does not equate to a broader identity as a member of an HR 'profession'. Two developments are central here. First, the focus on the business partner/internal consultancy role has served to undermine any pretence to a unitary and cohesive occupational identity, as the bifurcation between routine transactional and strategic transformational activities encourages competition within the HR profession between different sub-groupings. Second, this strategy of redefinition has reduced the entry barriers demarcating HR activities and facilitated the entry of new occupational groups and rival managerial specialisms.

Commentary

The article describes the struggles experienced by the HRM profession to gain credibility in business circles, and the way it has used the ideas of 'business partnership' or 'internal consultancy' to achieve higher status. Historically, personnel managers have been seen as having less to offer in terms of expertise that can solve crucial business problems than other managerial professions such as accountancy. In response, some have argued that a stronger identification with business objectives is the key to power: the business partner approach. Others consider that becoming a business partner results in the exact opposite: HR loses its professional independence and becomes a simple agent of capital.

The research described in the article attempts to demonstrate the extent to which being a business partner is more significant for the status of real practitioners than belonging to a professional HR association. The conclusions of the study suggest that HR may be polarising into two groups: high-status business partners who have limited regard for professional HR associations, and members of HR professional associations who remain focused on developing operational expertise and therefore relatively low in status.

The article might prompt you to consider the following questions.

- To what extent do you think that HRM is truly able to become a separate and independent profession? Whose interests *should* it represent, and how?

- How far do you think that it is true that all managers are, to some extent, HR managers? Does the attempt by HR associations to achieve professional closure result in more harm than good for HR specialists?

PART 4 CASE STUDY

Jamie Oliver: The Naked Manager?

It would seem that the British are media food junkies. The last decade has seen an apparently unstoppable growth in the number and type of television shows (generally with accompanying recipe books) by and about celebrity chefs. Scarcely any weekend newspaper is complete without its food and cookery section, and almost every possible type of cuisine and food-related angle is covered from domestic goddess to obsessive restaurateur, from food technologist to wilderness survivalist. Websites abound, and there are heated discussions about the quality and ethical provenance of our food. And yet, despite this obsession with reading about it, the British generally don't seem to like cooking and show very limited concern about the quality of what they, and perhaps more importantly their children, actually eat.[1] The catering industry remains one dominated by low pay, stressful working conditions and very limited prestige. Jamie Oliver (christened the 'Naked Chef' in an early series) is a British celebrity chef, and one who has spent his whole career in kitchens, albeit occasionally kitchens full of camera crew. In 2005 he became a campaigner for the provision of better-quality food in British schools after a startling series on Channel 4, *Jamie's School Dinners*.[2] This was followed in 2008 by a further attempt to get the British public weaned off ready meals and fast food through his 'Ministry of Food' initiative. But his approach to the recruitment, training and motivation of the first group of 15 young people to work in his new London restaurant gives a lively example of effective, if sometimes unconventional, managerial behaviour.

Jamie's kitchen: the project

Jamie himself went into the catering business at 16 after leaving school with no qualifications. His 2002 attempt to inspire some similarly unqualified young people to launch themselves into a career as chefs was followed by a Channel 4 documentary team.[3] The scheme itself was ambitious and required Jamie to fulfil several roles, first being the entrepreneur, as he was investing a substantial amount of his own money in the creation of a new restaurant (to be named 'Fifteen' for the 15 trainees who would work there). Secondly, he was the professional chef at the heart of the enterprise and his name, reputation and style of cooking would provide the basis of the business. And finally, he became a very public manager of people. The series shows his involvement in the recruitment and selection

In the heat of the kitchen, managerial skills are seen in the raw. Jamie Oliver shows how good management can encourage personal achievement as well as business success.

of the trainees, and his contributions to the design of the overall training programme which was in part sponsored by the UK government under the New Deal initiative, but also heavily reliant on Jamie's contacts in the industry to obtain access to work experience placements in some of London's top restaurants. It also shows him monitoring the trainees' development and follows his attempts to inspire and motivate them to achieve standards of performance which would match his own professional reputation and make the business successful. In other words, the series records a microcosm of management in a highly competitive and pressured business context.

Jamie's management style

The Oliver image is that of a tousled, cheeky but hugely enthusiastic cockney lad-made-good; and at a boyish 28 when the series was shot, not perhaps the stereotypical manager. The events of the series, however, show him very clearly in a managerial role, and some of the incidents illustrate significant managerial skill. Some of his trainees are what would generally be classed as 'difficult' staff; they are unskilled, at times some of them are seriously de-motivated and disruptive, and none of them has had successful experience of holding down a permanent job. What are the key components of Oliver's managerial approach to the trainees?

Vision

There is no doubt that Oliver has a very clear vision of what the business itself should be. His particular style of cooking is based around fresh ingredients, and he has an almost evangelical enthusiasm for the authenticity of produce and its 'traceability' (he emphasises the importance of knowing exactly where things come from, and building long-term relationships with growers and suppliers who share his values). He takes the trainees, many of whom have never really thought about the source of raw ingredients, on field visits to suppliers, farms and markets in order to communicate this vision. He has an equally clear goal, and one which is much harder to reach, of helping unemployed and unskilled people to launch themselves into a career as chefs. This is the people side of the vision:

It's about training unemployed people to a really professional level. I want them to be employable.[4]

The early episodes of the series show the recruitment of the initial fifteen potential trainees. A high profile, media-friendly project such as this attracted large numbers of applicants; but the selection process could not be based on more usual criteria such as knowledge, skills or experience since the whole purpose of the project was to offer opportunities for training to young people without these things. Instead, the selectors had to gauge potential and trainability, so a series of tests were constructed as a form of assessment centre, each stage taking place within a few days. At an open day, all applicants were asked to talk about food on camera; the purpose was to identify what Jamie considered an essential quality, enthusiasm or passion about food. The initial shortlist was largely based on these recordings. The next stage was an elimination day when the 60 chosen candidates were put through a 'taste test'. Jamie and three fellow chefs prepared two items for the candidates to taste: a butternut squash ravioli, and a tempura fried oyster. He deliberately chose items which he believed the candidates would not have tasted before, then challenged them to describe what they were eating in terms of textures and flavours. This was designed to find out how well candidates could use important sensory information. Very few were able to go beyond 'like' or 'don't like' and do what he asked, even when prompted. Students were then discussed and the four selectors finally agreed on 30 who would be put forward for a second test. This was a more detailed attempt to assess their ability to observe the method of preparing a simple dish of fried salmon and mixed vegetables, and then reproduce it in the kitchen. Having demonstrated and explained all the elements of the process, Jamie and the assessors were concerned to see how observant the candidates were, and also to watch the degree to which they took control of the process and reacted to the way the food was cooking. As they worked, the observers questioned them about what they were doing, often prompting them to remember the details of the process. The final selection was made on the basis of their approach to the work as much as on the quality of the finished dish.

Having recruited the trainees, Jamie participated in the training process. The trainees received instruction in basic skills at college, but as they progressed he began the attempt to shape them to the needs of his particular style and the standards which would be necessary in the restaurant. This involved classes and demonstrations followed by practical activity (for instance, in bread making) which additionally gave him the opportunity to pay detailed attention to each individual's ability to do the job. As the trainees began to realise the amount of work and mental effort which is involved in being a chef, some of them became de-motivated and failed to attend college. His approach to the weaker students was personal and supportive; he talked to them individually, paid for travel expenses to ensure they could attend college on time, and even visited some of them at home to discuss their problems. But he expected them to respond and so he also gave them some tough assignments to check their commitment. At one stage he sent them to work the night shift in a bakery for a week, a shift which he shared with them and used as a way to observe their growing skill and determination. Additionally, he was concerned to create a strong team spirit because of the importance of co-operation in a commercial kitchen environment. He took the group to spend a week camping (and of course catering for themselves as a group) on a Cumbrian farm, where they got to know about the business of livestock farming and observe first hand how to evaluate the quality of meat. This too would be important in the restaurant; chefs are responsible for ordering, and checking and assessing the quality of the goods being delivered. They also learned how to make sausages, including a chance to experiment and design their own.

Technical knowledge and understanding

As a chef, Oliver is both trained and experienced. His technical knowledge and ability is very important to the whole enterprise, as it provides him with part of his credibility amongst the young trainees as well as forming the basis for much of their training. The series shows him demonstrating basic techniques such as cutting and food preparation, as well as devising menus and improvising his way around the occasional disaster experienced by the trainees. The second half of Episode 5 shows Oliver putting the trainees together in a kitchen for the first time, with the task of cooking a set menu for 50 guests. He watches them carefully during prep (the hours prior to service), coaching individuals in the application of simple techniques they are learning at college, but which they forget under pressure: which knife to use for vegetables, how to shave parmesan, not to waste egg whites, even how to boil water efficiently to cook pasta to time. He then supervises with growing horror as service continues and many of the trainees fail to cope, but at the same time observing and praising those who are doing well, or who ask for the help they need to get things right. The orders pile up, some of the trainees become confused and prepare partial orders rather than complete ones, others forget key components so that dishes have to be sent back and re-done; and the time they take to prepare the main course runs to over 45 minutes. One or two become increasingly bad-tempered which causes them to make further mistakes; they argue with Jamie and waste more time. As the whole project descends into chaos, Oliver calls a halt; it was in fact only a simulation and there are no guests in the restaurant. However, the point of this training exercise was to create a real sense of urgency and not only to give the trainees a chance to practice their recently acquired technical skills, but also to give them a sense of the importance of teamwork. It underlined the need to stay calm under pressure, to concentrate on what they are doing and achieve the standards required and, most importantly for their future careers, to show respect for the chef. It is an important lesson for them to learn because the working culture of a restaurant kitchen is one of absolute respect and obedience; perhaps because the work is fast, dangerous in itself and potentially harmful to customers in a way which can cause a business to fold overnight.

Delegation and standards

Whilst he is very 'hands-on' in the management of the kitchen side of the enterprise, the series also shows that Jamie knows he can't do it all. The business side of the project involves accountants, project managers and builders, and the frustrations and problems involved in the actual creation of the premises clearly give Oliver serious headaches. We see the building project going over budget, and experience technical delays and setbacks; and at times it looks as if it will fail to hit schedule or even open at all. Oliver's personality often appears to be the only thing which keeps the project running, and he is not afraid to make unusual demands on his team to achieve the objective (he takes a similarly demanding approach with some of the school dinner ladies in the *Jamie's School Dinners* series). This is, in part, a reflection of the standards which he sets both by example and in his interactions with other professional members of the team and, indeed, with the trainees. However, he also knows he is a hard taskmaster, and when he gets that extra effort or sees a positive response, he acknowledges and praises the students. This 'hands-on' style shows the value of knowing what is going on as the result of personal observation and attention to detail. In Episode 6, he debriefs the students after they have delivered a successful charity dinner, a challenge which involved them having to cook in a tent in a field outside a stately

home, in the rain. He thanks them for their effort, encouraging them to feel proud of what they have achieved as a group. He also evaluates each of them individually, singling out both strengths and weaknesses in their technique and attitude.

Trust, respect and discipline

His technical knowledge aside, another important aspect of Oliver's credibility with this difficult group derives from his own experience as a young unqualified person and his natural empathy with some of the trainees' problems and circumstances. However, he does not let this empathy blind him to their faults and failings, or prevent him from dealing quickly and firmly with poor standards or breaches of discipline. He makes it clear that trust and respect have to run both ways: he bestows considerable trust upon the employees; in return he asks that they trust his judgement and do what he wants. Similarly he respects them as individuals and encourages them to respect each other – for instance by making sure that they all greet each other at the start of service and say goodbye at the end of the day.

If their behaviour is unacceptable then he does not hesitate to tell them so; nevertheless his emphasis is always on their behaviour, and what they need to do differently in the future in order to meet the required standards. One of the technically better students is eventually suspended from the course after aggressive and violent behaviour at college; this cannot be accepted in an already potentially dangerous working environment. In Episode 6 Oliver carries out a disciplinary interview which is in effect a final warning for another two of the trainees who have been absenting themselves without reason from both college and the kitchens where they have been doing their practical experience placement. His language is colourful but in essence he spells out the problem, explains how it affects all concerned and makes very clear what they need to do next. He explains that their absence not only causes him to waste time on unnecessary phone calls, but, and using the sort of language they will understand, that:

> If you treat them (the chefs hosting the trainees in their kitchens) like shit and you're unprofessional, one, they think I'm a wanker, two, they think the charity is a load of bollocks and three, they ain't going to take on another student. So you're not only disrespecting yourselves, you're disrespecting me and you're disrespecting the students who are going to come on this course for evermore. So this is what is going to happen; three strikes and you're out . . . You've got to behave like an adult, and in return I'll give you my time and I'll give you the connections . . . If you're not going to do that, then go away.

His approach to discipline is quick and consistent; when someone makes a mistake he points out what they have done, explains why it caused a problem, and tells them what to do to remedy the situation; after that it is over and forgotten – at least as far as he is concerned.

Success or failure?

Not all of the original 15 students completed the course successfully; however, some were able to retake exams and continue in the profession, and the scheme resulted in some real success stories for those who did achieve qualifications and subsequently pursued new careers as chefs. One of the successful students, Elisa Roche, has written about kitchen culture and the difficulty, particularly for women, of adapting to an aggressive, macho world.[5] On the other hand, the restaurant itself was a success, and established itself on the London food scene very quickly. The whole idea behind the restaurant and the training project attracted a certain amount of criticism in the press; it was accused of being a publicity stunt and essentially self-promotion by Oliver. The creation of a permanent foundation (originally called Cheeky Chops) to recruit

disadvantaged young people into the industry clearly shows this was more than a one-off stunt for the cameras. In 2004 Cheeky Chops was relaunched as The Fifteen Foundation[6] when Oliver and Liam Black, an experienced social entrepreneur, went into partnership to extend the programme. The majority of the money to run the Foundation came initially from fundraising events featuring Oliver, but by 2005 the profits from the original restaurant in London made a significant contribution to the Foundation.[7] Franchised versions of the restaurant, together with the associated training programme, form the nodes of the Foundation's activity, and the franchises are expected to make increasing contributions to its revenues in the future. The first franchise opened in Amsterdam in December 2004, the second in Cornwall in May 2006; and an Australian branch in Melbourne was recruiting in September of that year.[8] A further venture in the UK is an on-line shop (Fifteenshop.net), the profits from sales going to the Foundation. Far from being a one-off, Fifteen is becoming a serious global brand of social entrepreneurship.

Your tasks

- Using Mintzberg's classification, analyse the roles played by Jamie Oliver as a manager in the 'Fifteen' enterprise.

- Critically evaluate the idea that managers can be regarded as Theory X, Theory Y or Theory Z. Which is Jamie? Find evidence from the case to support your view.

- Carry out an analysis of the manager in this case using the framework provided in Figure 12.4.

- Assess Jamie Oliver's approach to human resource management activities such as recruitment and selection, training and appraisal, and disciplinary measures.

- Using evidence from the case, explain whether you consider his approach to the management of human resources as 'unitary' or 'pluralistic'?

Notes and references

1 Blythman, J. *Bad Food Britain*, Fourth Estate (2006).
2 See www.feedmebetter.com.
3 *Jamie's Kitchen*, Channel 4. Available on DVD.
4 *Jamie's Kitchen*, Episode 3.
5 Roche, E. 'If You Can't Stand the Heat . . . Get Some Balls', *The Guardian*, 28 January 2004.
6 The Fifteen Foundation website is at www.fifteen.net (accessed 5 August 2009).
7 Benjamin, A. 'Recipe for Success', *The Guardian*, 10 May 2006.
8 See www.fifteen.net (accessed 5 August 2009).

CHAPTER 8

Approaches to work motivation and job design

LEARNING OUTCOMES

After studying this chapter, you should be able to:

1 define the meanings and components of motivation;

2 describe three common-sense approaches to motivation;

3 describe Maslow's hierarchy of needs;

4 specify the strengths and weaknesses of need theories;

5 define the need for achievement and explain why it could affect productivity at work;

6 define valence, instrumentality and expectancy;

7 define and describe three forms of organisational justice;

8 outline the features of goals that usually enhance motivation;

9 draw a diagram describing the main features of goal-setting theory;

10 suggest how material rewards can affect motivation;

11 describe the typology of individual differences in motivation proposed by Leonard *et al.*;

12 list four techniques of job redesign;

13 draw a diagram to show the job characteristics model (JCM);

14 suggest four ways in which theory and research about the motivational features of jobs has moved beyond the JCM;

15 explain two features of Clegg and Spencer's model of work redesign that are different from other models.

Shop-floor reorganisation at Land Rover

Marin Burela, the new head of manufacturing at Land Rover, bounces gently up and down beside the refurbished assembly line at the carmaker's plant in Solihull, England. Looking at the floor, Mr Burela points out the springy 'anti-fatigue matting' as one sign of the transformation of once dingy and cramped working conditions. 'We have made a hell of a difference here. They don't call this the Bat Cave any more,' he says.

Mr Burela is one of a corps of Ford executives dispatched to Land Rover following its €2.9bn takeover this year. He is charged with turning round the loss-making brand, abandoned by Germany's BMW after the break-up of Rover Group. 'We have got to unlock the value in our assets and get the creative juices flowing,' he says. 'It's about instilling a sense of passion in Land Rover people.'

Ford executives privately admit they were shocked by some of what they found at Solihull. The production methods on the Defender line were antiquated. Other areas were poorly lit and untidy. Given the employees' dismay after BMW's sudden withdrawal this year, part of the task before Ford has been to hide its concerns and persuade the employees that they can make better cars. The trick for Land Rover's owners has been to win employees' backing for a restructuring that begins and ends with them. Ford is trying to persuade the workforce that it believes they are a top-quality asset that was either under-used or neglected by the former owner.

To preach its message, senior managers have held a series of US-style 'town hall meetings' with 200–500 workers at a time. Workers have been urged to match the best standards of Ford's premier automotive group, which includes Jaguar, Volvo, Lincoln and Aston Martin. Executives, rarely seen on the shop floor in the past, have been instructed to walk the line. They take cars at random from the assembly line for testing; they hold impromptu meetings with groups of workers. Everyone is encouraged to be on first-name terms. 'We're looking for visual management,' says Bob Dover, the new chief executive installed at Land Rover by Ford. 'You cannot expect high standards and a sense of passion if the management is invisible or if the roof leaks and the place is a mess.'

Mr Dover, formerly chief executive of Aston Martin, wants to start by removing unused temporary buildings: 'We probably have the biggest collection of Portakabins in the Midlands,' he says. 'We could start a Portakabin museum.' That effort and the investment in facilities will be coupled to what Mr Dover calls a 'culture of openness'. 'It sounds soft and stupid but we have to start by concentrating on people.' That means changing the outlook and profile of Land Rover's staff. Mr Dover points out that Land Rover sells cars to 140 countries. 'We have to include people from different backgrounds and more women.' Part of that overhaul mirrors the transformation of Jaguar, another neglected British brand acquired by Ford.

As Jaguar, Land Rover's people are invited to sign up to a system whereby they can suggest changes in production. If a junior employee feels quality is suffering, they can stop the entire line. In future, such employees are likely to have spent time on Volvo assembly lines in Gothenburg or Jaguar factories near Coventry. 'Nothing like this has happened in Land Rover's history,' says Mr Burela. 'There is tremendous enthusiasm . . . It's changing the way we do business.'

Source: Financial Times, *27 October 2000.*

Introduction

The Ford executives in charge of the Solihull Land Rover plant back in 2000 clearly had some ideas about what would motivate employees there. We suggest you take a few minutes now to identify what they are. The senior managers were looking for 'passion' from the staff, and thought they knew how to get it, but perhaps they were less clear about what behaviour would signify passion. Also it might be asked whether a person has to exhibit passion in order to be motivated at work.

In this chapter we therefore examine the concept of motivation and explore some of its implications. We look at some conflicting so-called 'common-sense' ideas about motivation. The chapter then turns to a description and evaluation of some of the old but enduring approaches to motivation, including need theories, the motivation to manage, expectancy theory, justice theories and goal-setting. The roles of the self and personality are also considered. Both theoretical and practical issues are covered. Textbook discussions of motivation theories are sometimes described as 'a walk through the graveyard of psychology', in the sense that many of the theories are both old and lacking life. However, there have been recent attempts to integrate the most valuable parts of the various theories, and these are discussed in this chapter. The idea that jobs can be designed to be motivating is also examined: this suggests that motivation is as much a feature of the job as of the person. The topic of motivation has received huge attention from work psychologists over very many years, so it is not possible to cover every relevant theory. The earlier ones were often designed to be big theories of human nature, whereas later ones have tended to confine themselves to specific aspects of motivated behaviour. In fact, some recent approaches scarcely have the label 'motivation' at all. So although motivation continues to be a very significant concept in work psychology, its boundaries are not easy to define.

Overview of motivation

As with many important concepts in psychology, there is no single universally accepted definition of motivation. Nevertheless, the word itself gives us some clues. To use a mechanical analogy, the motive force gets a machine started and keeps it going. In legal terms, a motive is a person's reason for doing something. As Locke and Latham (2004, p. 388) put it: 'motivation refers to internal factors that impel action and to external factors that can act as inducements to action'. Clearly, then, motivation concerns the factors that push us or pull us to behave in certain ways. Specifically, it is made up of three components:

1 *Direction*: what a person is trying to do. This is also sometimes called *choice*.

2 *Effort*: how hard a person is trying. This is also sometimes called *intensity*.

3 *Persistence*: how long a person continues trying. This is also sometimes called *duration*.

In a study of bank tellers (cashiers) Gary Blau (1993) assessed *effort* by filming each teller for a day and calculating the proportion of the time they were engaged in work behaviours. He assessed *direction* using a questionnaire that asked tellers to indicate how often they engaged in each of 20 different behaviours. Blau found that both the overall effort and the type of behaviours tellers engaged in (i.e. direction) predicted the quality of their work performance. This suggests that effort and direction are indeed separable, and that both are important. Some key points should be remembered:

- People are usually motivated to do *something*. A person may try hard and long to avoid work – that is motivated behaviour! Hence we should always remember the 'direction' component.

- It is easy to make the mistake of thinking that motivation is the only important determinant of work performance. Other factors, such as ability, quality of equipment and coordination of team members' efforts also affect performance.

- Like most concepts in work psychology, motivation is abstract. It cannot be observed directly. Quite often a person's work performance is used as a measure of their motivation, but as we have just seen, many factors other than motivation influence performance. Individuals' reports of how hard they are trying (i.e. effort) are sometimes used as an indicator of motivation, but direction and persistence rarely feature (Ambrose and Kulik, 1999). This needs to change. Many people have jobs that offer choices in what to do and pay attention to (i.e. direction), and in many jobs it is necessary to keep trying over a long period in order to succeed.

One often-made distinction is between *content* theories and *process* theories of motivation. The former focus on *what* motivates human behaviour at work. The latter concentrate on *how* the content of motivation influences behaviour. In fact, most theories have something to say about both content and process, but they do vary considerably in their relative emphasis.

Key Learning Point

Motivation concerns what drives a person's choice of what to do, how hard they try and how long they keep trying. It is not the only factor that influences work performance.

Common-sense approaches to motivation

McGregor (1960), Argyris (1964), Schein (1988) and others have collectively identified three broad common-sense approaches to motivation which are endorsed by different individuals or even by the same individual at different times. McGregor (1960) termed two of the three *theory X* and *theory Y*, though the reader should be clear that in neither case is the word 'theory' used in its formal academic sense. Schein (1988) added what can be called the *social* approach. In all three cases, we are essentially uncovering a general perspective on human nature. Briefly, they are as follows:

■ *Theory X*: people cannot be trusted. They are irrational, unreliable and inherently lazy. They therefore need to be controlled and motivated using financial incentives and threats of punishment. In the absence of such controls, people will pursue their own goals, which are invariably in conflict with those of their work organisation.

■ *Theory Y*: people seek independence, self-development and creativity in their work. They can see further than immediate circumstances and are able to adapt to new ones. They are fundamentally moral and responsible beings who, if treated as such, will strive for the good of their work organisation.

■ *Social*: a person's behaviour is influenced most fundamentally by social interactions, which can determine their sense of identity and belonging at work. People seek meaningful social relationships at work. They are responsive to the expectations of people around them, often more so than to financial incentives.

As you can probably see, theory X and theory Y are in most respects opposites, with the social approach different from both. Which of these common-sense approaches do you find most convincing? The authors' experience with business/ management undergraduates is that, if forced to choose one, about half go for the social approach, about 40 per cent for theory Y and about 10 per cent for theory X. Amongst practising managers, the overall distribution in our experience is about the same, but tends to differ between industries. The more physical the industry, the higher the proportion of theory X adherents. Which of the three approaches do you think is most evident in the opening case study of this chapter?

Key Learning Point

Common-sense views of motivation contradict each other but all have some truth.

None of these three 'common-sense' accounts is universally correct. However, as Schein (1988) pointed out, over time people may be socialised into their organisation's way of thinking about motivation. Ultimately, managers can influence their staff to see motivation their way. Of course they may also attract and select staff who are already inclined to see things their way. Nevertheless, none of the approaches can be forced on all of the people all of the time. Indiscriminate use of any could have disastrous results. Hence, although each of these approaches finds some expression in theories of motivation, the match between theory and common sense is not particularly close.

So what are the theories? Let us now examine some of the most widely known and extensively researched. Bear in mind that several of the theories are old, and nowadays rarely feature in research regarded as leading edge. That does *not* mean they are useless. They contain ideas that have found expression in subsequent work, and some practising managers say they are still useful in managing their staff.

Need theories

What are they?

Need theories are based on the idea that there are psychological needs, probably of biological origin, that lie behind human behaviour. When our needs are unmet, we experience tension or disequilibrium which we try to put right. In other words, we behave in ways that satisfy our needs. Clearly the notion of need reflects the *content* of motivation as opposed to process, but most need theories also make some propositions about how and when particular needs become salient – i.e. process. The notion of need has a long history in general psychology. It has, for example, formed the basis of at least one major analysis of personality (Murray, 1938). Two major traditions have been evident in the work setting. First, there are models based on the notion of psychological growth. Second, there are various approaches which focus on certain quite specific needs.

Need theories based on psychological growth

Easily the best known of these theories is that of Abraham Maslow (1943, 1954). Maslow was a humanistically oriented psychologist who offered a general theory of human functioning. His ideas were applied by others to the work setting.

Maslow proposed five classes of human need. Briefly, these are:

1 *Physiological*: need for food, drink, sex, etc., i.e. the most primitive and fundamental biological needs.

2 *Safety*: need for physical and psychological safety, i.e. a predictable and non-threatening environment.

3 *Belongingness*: need to feel a sense of attachment to another person or group of persons.

4 *Esteem*: need to feel valued and respected, by self and significant other people.

5 *Self-actualisation*: need to fulfil one's potential – to develop one's capacities and express them.

Maslow proposed that we strive to progress up the hierarchy shown in Figure 8.1. When one need is satisfied to some (unspecified) adequate extent, the next one up the hierarchy becomes the most important in driving our behaviour.

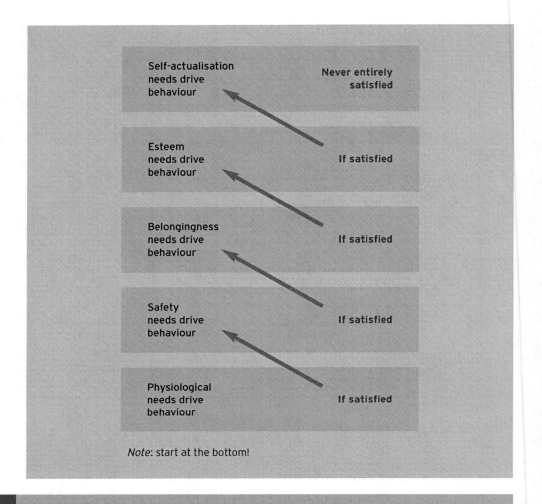

Figure 8.1   Maslow's hierarchy of needs

Other psychologists produced rather similar analyses. For example, Alderfer (1972) proposed three classes of need: existence, relatedness and growth. Existence equated to Maslow's physiological and safety needs. Relatedness can be matched to belongingness and the esteem of others. Growth is equivalent to self-esteem and self-actualisation. Both Maslow and Alderfer made propositions about how particular needs become more or less important to the person (i.e. process), but need theories are often thought of as examples of content theories because of their emphasis on describing needs.

For some years, need theories (especially Maslow's) dominated work motivation. Unfortunately, evaluations of them (e.g. Wahba and Bridwell, 1976; Salancik and Pfeffer, 1977; Rauschenberger *et al.*, 1980) revealed a number of significant flaws, such as:

- needs did not group together in the ways predicted;

- the theories were unable to predict when particular needs would become important;

■ there was no clear relationship between needs and behaviour, so that (for example) the same behaviour could reflect different needs, and different behaviours the same need;

■ needs were generally described with insufficient precision;

■ the whole notion of need as a biological phenomenon is problematic. It ignores the capacity of people and those around them to construct their own perceptions of needs and how they can be met. Some (e.g. Cooke *et al.*, 2005) have argued that Maslow's whole theory is a product of the context of the Cold War, with its tensions between religion and secularism, and between individualism and conformity.

Key Learning Point

Need theories have intuitive appeal and provide possible explanations for some human behaviour, but research suggests that they are difficult to apply successfully to the work context.

Hence these accounts of motivation based on needs have only limited value in understanding and managing work behaviour. They offer interesting and intuitively compelling ways of thinking about human functioning, but their theoretical foundation is doubtful and they have offered no clear guidance to managers about how to motivate individuals. However, that is not to say that needs are unimportant or non-existent. In their synthesis of different approaches to motivation (about which there will be more later in this chapter), Locke and Latham (2004) assume that needs are the starting point for motivation, even if not necessarily the most useful focal point for research and practice. Baumeister and Leary (1995) have reviewed a wide range of literature and concluded that the need to belong is powerful and pervasive. People seem strongly driven to form social bonds and are reluctant to break them. Deprivation of frequent interactions of a positive or at least non-conflictual nature has consequences for mental and physical health. Our interpersonal relationships affect the way we think, and how we interpret the situations we encounter. Laas (2006) has argued that the leaders and goals of some (desirable) social movements reflect self-actualisation quite well, whilst others are much more about imposing one view of the world at the expense of others.

Moreover, Maslow's work has provided a clear picture of the self-actualising person. Maslow regarded self-actualisation as the pinnacle of human growth and adjustment, but argued that few of us operate at that level. The truth of this assertion is difficult to evaluate because the exact nature of self-actualisation is both disputed and ambiguous. Leclerc *et al.* (1998) tried to resolve this by developing a long list of possible descriptions of a self-actualising person and asking 30 experts on the subject to indicate whether they agree that each description is accurate. They also invited the experts to add their own descriptions if they wished. Eventually there was consensus about 36 descriptions. Some of them are shown in Table 8.1. Leclerc *et al.* emphasised that this view of self-actualisation suggests that it is not some kind of special state of being, nor is it necessarily the highest stage of being. Instead, it portrays the characteristics of people who function well in the sense that they are open to all aspects of reality, are able to understand and communicate with others, and act accordingly. These observations led Leclerc and colleagues to suggest that self-actualisation can

Table 8.1	Fifteen characteristics of self-actualising people (based on Leclerc *et al.*, 1998)

1. Have a positive self-esteem
2. Consider themselves responsible for their own life
3. Give a meaning to life
4. Are capable of establishing meaningful relationships
5. Take responsibility for their actions
6. Are aware of their feelings
7. Are capable of intimate contact
8. Have a realistic perception of themselves
9. Are capable of commitment
10. Act according to their own convictions and values
11. Are able to resist undue social pressure
12. Are capable of insight
13. Feel free to express their emotions
14. Are able to accept contradictory feelings
15. Are aware of their strengths and weaknesses

be defined as 'a process through which one's potential is developed in congruence with one's self-perception and one's experience' (pp. 78–9).

STOP TO CONSIDER

Examine Table 8.1 to see whether you think you could be described as a self-actualising person. In the opening case study to this chapter, what evidence (if any) is there that Land Rover senior managers wanted a self-actualising workforce?

Maslow's ideas still enjoy some support, and some research claims to support some of his predictions, though often the connections between what is measured in the research and Maslow's original concepts looks rather weak (e.g. Reiss and Havercamp, 2005). In our experience students can often relate to his theory. Even some of those who want to amend his theory believe that it says something profound about human nature. For example, Rowan (1998, p. 81) said 'I am merely trying to tidy up the Maslow theory, which seems to me extraordinarily useful in general.' He proposes three amendments to the need hierarchy theory:

1. There are two types of esteem needs, and they need to be separated. One is the need for the esteem and respect of other people. This is really about self-image rather than the true self, and in some ways reflects needs for relatedness. The other type of esteem is that which we give ourselves. It comes from inside the self, not from other people.

2   The need for competence should be added to the hierarchy, probably between safety and belongingness. This need reflects our desire to master certain skills and do something well for the pleasure in being able to do it. It is evident from very early in life.

3   There may be two kinds of self-actualisation. The first is where a person is able to express their real self. The second is something more mystical – a sense of closeness with God or humanity as a whole which goes beyond (transcends) the self. This distinction was evident in some of Maslow's later work, which drew open ideas from Asian psychology and religion including Taoism and Zen Buddhism (Cleary and Shapiro, 1996).

Key Learning Point

There are at least two types of esteem, and also of self-actualisation. The need for competence is an important omission from some need theories.

Achievement, power and motivation to manage

Considerable success has been enjoyed by need-based approaches to motivation which concentrate on a small number of more specific needs. Need for achievement was one of the 20 needs underlying behaviour proposed by Murray (1938). It concerns the desire 'to overcome obstacles, to exercise power, to strive to do something difficult as well and as quickly as possible' (Murray, 1938, pp. 80–81, quoted by Landy, 1989, p. 73). Typically, people with high need for achievement seek tasks that are fairly difficult, but not impossible. They like to take sole responsibility for them, and want frequent feedback on how well they are doing. Need for achievement formed the basis of McClelland's (1961) theory of work motivation. McClelland argued that a nation's economic prosperity depends partly on the level of need for achievement in its population. He based this argument on a statistical relationship between the economic performance of countries and the prominence of themes of achievement in popular children's stories in each country. He also believed that people could be trained to have high need for achievement. As for personal success, Parker and Chusmir (1991) found that people with high need for achievement tend to feel more successful regarding status/wealth, professional fulfilment and contribution to society than those with lower need for achievement.

Need for achievement has attracted considerable attention in both theoretical and applied contexts (e.g. *see* Beck, 1983). It is not a simple construct, however, and several attempts have been made to identify its components (e.g. Cassidy and Lynn, 1989). Sagie *et al.* (1996) argued that it is important to restrict analysis to the level of tasks, as opposed to wider considerations of status and power. They proposed six task preferences that signal high need for achievement:

1   Tasks involving uncertainty rather than sure outcomes.

2   Difficult tasks rather than easy ones.

3   Tasks involving personal responsibility, not shared responsibility.

4   Tasks involving a calculated risk, rather than no risk or excessive risk.

5   Tasks requiring problem-solving or inventiveness, rather than following instructions.

6   Tasks that gratify the need to succeed, rather than ensuring the avoidance of failure.

Sagie *et al.* (1996) reported a five-country study of levels of achievement motivation. People from the United States generally scored highest on most components, followed by people from the Netherlands and Israel, with those from Hungary lower and those from Japan lower again, except on the first component, where Japanese people scored close to Americans. However, it is important to remember that need for achievement is not the only route to successful work performance. Also, need for achievement may be a very Western and individualistic concept, of little relevance to some other cultures. In fact, the link that McClelland claimed between achievement themes in children's stories and national prosperity has often been questioned. For example, an analysis of economic growth over up to 50 years by Beugelsdijk and Smeets (2008) found no relationship between growth and a country's need for achievement score based on McClelland's data from the mid-twentieth century. Of course, this may be because the need for achievement data were out of date, or indeed were inaccurate from the start.

A person's need for achievement is often assessed using *projective* tests, which involve the person interpreting ambiguous stimuli. For example, a person may be asked to make up a story about what is happening in a short series of pictures. It is assumed that people *project* their personality onto the stimuli through their interpretations. This general technique is derived from psychoanalytic theory (*see* Chapter 1). Need for achievement can also be assessed in a more straightforward manner using questions about the person's behaviour, thoughts and feelings as in a personality questionnaire. Spangler (1992) reviewed the relevant literature and found that scores on most assessments of need for achievement are indeed correlated with outcomes such as career success. Also, despite the generally poor record of projective tests in psychology, projective measures of need for achievement correlated more highly with outcomes than did questionnaire measures.

Key Learning Point

Need for achievement is a sufficiently specific and valid construct to explain some aspects of work behaviour, including managerial behaviour, at least in Western contexts.

One criticism of McClelland's work is that it was always unclear exactly how need for achievement translated into economic success. McClelland himself thought that it was partly through entrepreneurial activity. There is mixed evidence on this. For example, Hansemark (2003) did not find that people with a high need for achievement were more likely than others to start up their own business. However, Rauch and Frese (2007) did find that high need for achievement was modestly associated with success amongst people who were already entrepreneurs. Another line of thinking is that need for achievement makes people more inclined to be managers. John Miner (1964) developed the concept of *motivation to manage,* and a measure of it called the Miner Sentence Completion Scale (MSCS). The seven components of motivation to manage are shown in Table 8.2. The need for power and self-control,

Table 8.2	Components of the motivation to manage
Component	**Meaning**
Authority figures	A desire to meet managerial role requirements in terms of positive relationships with superiors
Competitive games	A desire to engage in competition with peers involving games or sports
Competitive situations	A desire to engage in competition with peers involving occupational or work-related activities
Assertive role	A desire to behave in an active and assertive manner involving activities that are often viewed as predominantly masculine
Imposing wishes	A desire to tell others what to do and to utilise sanctions in influencing others
Standing out from the group	A desire to assume a distinctive position of a unique and highly visible nature
Routine administrative functions	A desire to meet managerial role requirements of a day-to-day administrative nature

Source: Miner and Smith (1982, p. 298). Copyright © 1982 by the American Psychological Association. Adapted with permission.

and low need for affiliation probably underlie motivation to manage. So do some of the components of need for achievement.

STOP TO CONSIDER

Look again at the components of motivation to manage shown in Table 8.2. To what extent do you think they reflect what would be expected of managers across all organisational and national cultures?

Interesting studies by Miner *et al.* (1991) and Chen *et al.* (1997) investigated motivation to manage in China. They suggested that although China is a more collectivist society than Western ones, it is nevertheless sympathetic to competition and hierarchy, and that this would be one reason why the motivation to manage would be applicable there. Consistent with their arguments, they found that people in higher-level jobs scored higher on the MSCS than people in lower-level jobs. They also found that women scored no lower than men, and suggested that this might be a consequence of the assertive roles women were encouraged to take in China's cultural revolution of the late 1960s and 1970s, together with the Chinese government policy of no more than one child per family. Ebrahimi *et al.* (2001) also found no gender difference, but they did find that motivation to manage scores were generally higher in Hong Kong than in the People's Republic of China. This may have been due to the greater exposure of Hong Kong to Western influences at the time. Perhaps it would be different even a decade or so later.

Exercise 8.1   The motivation to manage

Marie Herzog is an administrative assistant at a large packaging factory in Lyons. She had previously been promoted from the factory floor and is keen to go higher. Her boss, Simone Trouchot, is not so sure - how keen is Marie? Simone made the following observations. Marie seemed rarely to impose her will on her clerical subordinates, even when they were obviously in the wrong. She got on well with the higher managers at the factory, and seemed willing to work closely to the remit they gave her. On the other hand, Marie rarely volunteered her department for trying out experimental new ideas. She seemed uncomfortable when the spotlight was turned on her and her department, even if the attention was congratulatory. Marie seemed happiest dealing with the routine administrative tasks she knew well. She was an accomplished athlete, and had recently been Lyons 400 metres champion two years in succession. Marie was extremely keen to get her department working better than other similar ones, and to ensure that she dealt with problems faster and better than others in similar jobs at the factory.

Suggested exercise

Consult Table 8.2 to judge the extent and nature of Marie Herzog's motivation to manage. Are there particular kinds of managerial roles in which she would feel particularly motivated?

Exercise 8.2   Need theory in the car factory

Look back at the opening case study of this chapter. Which of the needs described in this section do you think the Ford managers believed govern the motivation of the shop-floor workers? If possible, compare your answers with somebody else's, and discuss whether needs offer a useful guide to managers in improving motivation.

Expectancy theory: what's in it for me?

Whereas need theories place heavy emphasis on the content of motivation, expectancy theory concentrates on the process. Originally proposed by Vroom (1964), expectancy theory (also sometimes called VIE – valence, instrumentality, expectancy – theory or instrumentality theory) aimed to explain how people choose which of several possible courses of action they will pursue. This choice process was seen as a cognitive, calculating appraisal of the following three factors for each of the actions being considered:

1   *Expectancy*: if I tried, would I be able to perform the action I am considering?

2   *Instrumentality*: would performing the action lead to identifiable outcomes?

3   *Valence*: how much do I value those outcomes?

Vroom (1964) proposed that expectancy and instrumentality can be expressed as probabilities, and valence as a subjective value. He also suggested that force to act is a function of the product of expectancy, instrumentality and valence: in other words, V, I and E are multiplied together to determine motivation. This would mean that if any one of the components was zero, overall motivation to pursue that course of action would also be zero. This can be seen in Figure 8.2, where, for example, the instrumentality question is not even worth asking if a person believes they are incapable of writing a good essay on motivation.

Notice how little attention VIE theory pays to explaining *why* an individual values or does not value particular outcomes. No concepts of need are invoked to address this question. VIE theory proposes that we should ask someone how much they value something, but not bother about *why* they value it. This is an illustration of VIE theory's concentration on process, not content.

If correct, VIE theory would have important implications for managers wishing to ensure that employees were motivated to perform their work duties. They would need to ensure that all three of the following conditions were satisfied:

1   Employees perceived that they possessed the necessary skills to do their jobs at least adequately (expectancy).

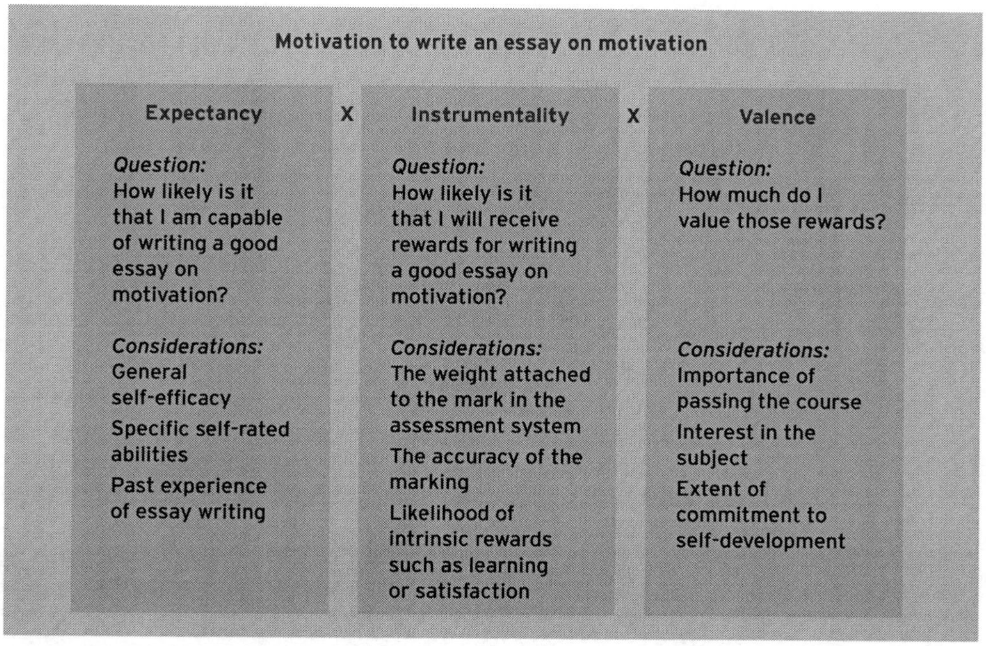

Motivation to write an essay on motivation		
Expectancy	X **Instrumentality**	X **Valence**
Question: How likely is it that I am capable of writing a good essay on motivation?	*Question:* How likely is it that I will receive rewards for writing a good essay on motivation?	*Question:* How much do I value those rewards?
Considerations: General self-efficacy	*Considerations:* The weight attached to the mark in the assessment system	*Considerations:* Importance of passing the course
Specific self-rated abilities	The accuracy of the marking	Interest in the subject
Past experience of essay writing	Likelihood of intrinsic rewards such as learning or satisfaction	Extent of commitment to self-development

Figure 8.2   An example of VIE theory in action

2   Employees perceived that if they performed their jobs well, or at least adequately, they would be rewarded (instrumentality).

3   Employees perceived the rewards offered for successful job performance to be attractive (valence).

Referring again to the Land Rover case study at the start of this chapter, to what extent do you think each of these three components of motivation was likely to have been a problem?

Key Learning Point

Expectancy theory proposes that people's choice of course of action depends upon their beliefs about (i) their own capabilities; (ii) whether the course of action will lead to rewards; and (iii) how valuable the rewards are.

Although it looks attractive, VIE theory has not done especially well when evaluated in research. Like need theories, it has rather gone out of fashion. Van Eerde and Thierry (1996) found 74 published research studies on VIE theory prior to 1990 but only 10 subsequently. Van Eerde and Thierry (1996), and also Schwab *et al.* (1979), summarised the available research and drew the following conclusions. The first four reflect badly on VIE theory as a whole. The other two are more to do with limitations of research design rather than the theory itself.

- Research studies that have not measured expectancy, or have combined it with instrumentality, have accounted for effort and/or performance better than studies that assessed expectancy and instrumentality separately.

- Behaviour is at least as well predicted by adding the three components V, I and E as it is by multiplying them.

- The theory does not work where any of the outcomes have negative valence (i.e. are viewed as undesirable) (Leon, 1981).

- The theory works better when the outcome measure is an attitude (for example intention or preference) than when it is a behaviour (performance, effort or choice).

- Self-report measures of V, I and E have often been poorly constructed.

- Most research has compared different people with each other (i.e. between-participants research design), rather than comparing different outcomes for the same person (i.e. within-participants design). The latter enables a better test of VIE theory because the theory was designed to predict whether an individual will prefer one course of action over another, rather than whether one person will favour a course of action more than another person does. Where within-participant designs are used, results tend to be more supportive of the theory.

Key Learning Point

Expectancy theory may over-complicate the cognitive processes involved in motivation, but is a helpful logical analysis of key factors in the choices made by individuals.

Expectancy theory is not quite dead and buried. It is still occasionally used in research. For example, Chiang and Jang (2008) found that expectancy, instrumentality and valence all made separate contributions to the motivation of hotel employees. However, they did not test whether multiplying the three terms together further improved prediction of motivation. Vansteenkiste *et al.* (2005) assessed the impact on people's reactions to being unemployed (e.g. general mental health) of (i) the value they placed on employment (valence) and (ii) their belief that they could get a job if they wanted to (expectancy). They found that both valence and expectancy mattered (especially valence), but multiplying them together did not improve prediction of reactions to unemployment.

Justice and citizenship theories: am I being fairly treated?

Justice theories are like expectancy theory, in that they focus on the cognitive processes that govern a person's decision whether or not to expend effort, but unlike expectancy theory they suggest that people want fairness above all. Some students and managers find it hard to believe that people might not always seek to maximise their gains, but let us suspend disbelief for the moment and consider the propositions of the original justice theory: equity theory.

Equity theory was derived from work by Adams (1965), originally in the context of interpersonal relationships. Huseman *et al.* (1987, p. 222) described the propositions of equity theory like this:

■ Individuals evaluate their relationships with others by assessing the ratio of their outcomes from and inputs to the relationship against the outcome:input ratio of a comparison other.

■ If the outcome:input ratios of the individual and comparison other are perceived to be unequal, then inequity exists.

■ The greater the inequity the individual perceives (in the form of either over-reward or under-reward), the more distress the individual feels.

■ The greater the distress an individual feels, the harder they will work to restore equity. Equity restoration techniques include altering or cognitively distorting inputs or outcomes, increasing or decreasing the amount of effort devoted to the task, acting on or changing the comparison other, or terminating the relationship.

In other words, a person is motivated to maintain the same balance between their contributions and rewards as that experienced by salient comparison person or persons.

Research way back in the 1960s and 1970s provided some support for equity theory (e.g. Pritchard, 1969), especially in laboratory-based studies where the key constructs of the theory could be controlled and measured. However, perhaps unsurprisingly, the predictions of equity theory are less often supported by research when people receive more than their share as opposed to when they receive less (Mowday, 1991). In other words, we are more likely to do something in response to feeling under-rewarded than over-rewarded. Furthermore, rather like need theories, equity theory is vague about exactly what people will do when they are dissatisfied. They might adopt any or all of the equity restoration devices listed above, and they might choose any of a number of comparison others. Equity theory is not good at specifying which restoration devices and which comparison others will be used (Greenberg, 2001). Perhaps, then, equity theory is better at providing a retrospective account of a person's motivation and behaviour than it is at predicting those things.

Like the other motivation theories discussed so far, equity theory has been researched less in recent years than in earlier ones. Nevertheless, it is still the subject of some work. It is also still frequently taught, perhaps partly because it provokes a lot of discussion about whether people really care about fairness when they are being over-rewarded. Bolino and Turnley (2008) have presented an interesting analysis of the cross-cultural applicability of equity theory. Pointing out that it originated in the US, they use cross-cultural theory to generate propositions about how equity theory might manifest differently in different parts of the world. For example, they suggest that in collectivist cultures people are likely to choose a group (e.g. people in my occupation) as their comparison other, whereas people in individualistic cultures are more likely to choose individuals (e.g. that person who started here at the same time as me).

Key Learning Point

The equity theory of motivation asserts that people are motivated by the fairness of the rewards they receive relative to the contributions they make, in comparison with other people.

Equity theory has been broadened into theories of organisational justice from the late 1980s onwards (*see*, for example, Cropanzano *et al.*, 2001; Greenberg and Colquitt, 2005). These theories focus on perceptions of fairness in the workplace. They have become very popular and widely researched, perhaps because organisational downsizing, etc. has brought issues of fairness to the fore. Equity theory refers mainly to what is called *distributive justice*: that is, whether people believe they have received (or will receive) fair rewards. However, this is only one kind of justice. There are debates about how many different kinds of workplace justice can be identified (*see* Colquitt *et al.*, 2001), but most work psychologists would say there are at least two more. *Procedural justice* reflects whether people believe that the procedures used in an organisation to allocate rewards are fair. *Interactional justice* refers to whether people believe they are treated in an appropriate manner by others at work, especially authority figures. The three forms of justice are depicted in Table 8.3.

If people believe that they are poorly paid relative to people doing similar jobs in other organisations, they may perceive distributive injustice. If at the same time they think their employing organisation is making available as much money for pay as possible, and operating fair systems to distribute them, then they may perceive procedural justice. If their bosses discuss pay openly and courteously, they may perceive interactional justice. Their satisfaction with pay would probably be low, but their commitment to their employer might well be high (McFarlin and Sweeney, 1992; Olkkonen and Lipponen, 2006).

Key Learning Point

The role of fairness and justice in motivation is becoming more prominent, and concerns a person's perceptions of the fairness of (i) who gets what, (ii) the systems used to decide who gets what and (iii) the courtesy and openness of interpersonal behaviour.

Table 8.3	Three forms of justice at work		
Distributive justice (appropriateness of outcomes)	**Procedural justice (appropriateness of the allocation process)**	**Interactional justice (appropriateness of the treatment received)**	
Appropriateness can be judged in various ways: *Equity* (as in equity theory) means that employee outcomes depend on their contributions. Alternatives include *equality* (everyone gets the same reward) and *need* (people get what they require)	This is said to depend on a number of factors: *Lack of bias* for or against any individual or group, i.e. consistent process. *Accuracy of information* used to make decisions. *Representation* for all stakeholders. *Correction* of errors or injustices via appeal or review procedure. *Ethical* codes of conduct are followed.	This has two components, which are sometimes considered two separate forms of justice. *Interpersonal* refers to the extent to which people are treated with dignity, courtesy and respect. *Informational* concerns the extent to which relevant information is shared with employees.	

Source: Adapted with permission from Cropanzano *et al.* (2007), p. 36.

Ideas about workplace justice have now been prominent for long enough to attract some close scrutiny. Helpful reviews of this field have been offered by Colquitt *et al.* (2005) and Fortin (2008). From the perspective of motivation, it is important to ask whether justice affects the direction, effort and persistence of work behaviour, and if so why? Starting with why, some people argue that justice is a moral virtue in itself, requiring no further justification other than to point out that it upholds human dignity. An alternative perspective is that being treated fairly signals that you personally are a valued member of a community, thus validating your personal and social identity. A more instrumental interpretation is that fairness enables you to control and predict what will happen to you in the future.

A lot of evidence indicates that the three forms of justice are associated with motivation and performance among other outcomes (*see* for example Folger and Cropanzano, 1998). As usual in work psychology, the number of studies in which it is clearly demonstrated that justice precedes motivation/performance rather than vice versa is limited. Even so, the evidence for the effects of justice is strong. Also, the presence of one form of justice can at least partially offset the negative effects of the lack of another form (Cropanzano *et al.*, 2007). For example, if your annual performance review does not lead to the bonus you feel you deserve (distributive injustice), if you perceive the review process as meeting the criteria for procedural justice shown in Table 8.3, your motivation will be less (or not at all) adversely affected than if you also thought the process was unjust. Another plus would be if you were given the chance to state your views (interactional justice). In fact, there is some long-established evidence that this chance to have a say seems to help even when it cannot make a difference to the outcome (Folger *et al.*, 1979). On the other hand, if people feel that in the past they have been repeatedly asked for their views and then ignored, being asked again can be more demotivating than not being asked, because it seems to be a sham and therefore a violation of interactional (and possibly procedural) justice (Folger, 1977).

STOP TO CONSIDER

From your experience of the workplace, to what extent do you think that people care about justice as a general concept, as opposed to (i) justice for themselves only and; (ii) maximising their gains? On what evidence is your answer based?

One important consequence when people in an organisation feel they have been treated justly is that they will be more willing to be 'good citizens' at work (*see* for example Liden *et al.*, 2003). Since the early 1990s, psychologists have shown a lot of interest in what have become known as organisational citizenship behaviours (OCBs) (*see* for example Moorman, 1991). This partly reflects a realisation that successful work organisations need people who help each other out in addition to doing the core tasks of their jobs well. OCBs are an interesting area for scholars of motivation, because OCBs are usually thought to be discretionary – that is, a person has choice over whether they perform them. OCBs include the following:

■ *Altruism*: helping another person with a work task or problem.

■ *Conscientiousness*: going well beyond minimum role requirements.

■ *Civic virtue*: participation and involvement in the life of the organisation.

■ *Courtesy*: preventing interpersonal problems through polite and considerate behaviour.

■ *Sportsmanship*: willingness to tolerate less than ideal circumstances without complaining.

There is some reason to question whether it is appropriate to consider OCBs 'extras', over and above the job. Research by Kam *et al.* (1999) suggested that to a considerable extent bank employees across four countries felt that the five OCBs listed above were indeed part of their job. Their supervisors thought so even more! There were some differences between countries, though. Courtesy and sportsmanship were expected to a greater extent in Japan and Hong Kong than in the United States and Australia. Another common assumption about OCBs is that they enhance organisational performance. This can be questioned. Perhaps OCBs simply distract people from doing their own jobs properly. However, Podsakoff *et al.* (2009) have found that OCBs have beneficial effects on organisational performance indicators, so the fear appears to be unjustified (*see* also Chapter 6).

Key Learning Point

The motivation to perform 'good citizen' behaviours is currently a topic of considerable interest to psychologists. This motivation is enhanced by a sense of justice.

Cropanzano *et al.* (2007) offer some helpful though not particularly novel suggestions to managers about how to use insights from justice theory in managing people. For example, they highlight the importance of giving people every opportunity to show what they can do during selection and promotion processes. It is probably important both practically and morally that justice is implemented because it is valued, and not simply as a manipulation to increase employee compliance:

> Organizational justice allows managers to make tough decisions more smoothly . . . power will be used in accordance with normative principles that reflect the dignity of all involved. This is sound business advice. *It is also the right thing to do.*
>
> *(Cropanzano et al., 2007, p. 45, italics in original)*

It is important not to get too starry-eyed about justice. At any given time, even in the best-run workplaces, there will always be some people who think something is unfair. That is partly because, although people often distinguish between what is good for them and what is fair, there is some overlap between outcome favourability and distributive justice (Fortin, 2008). In other words, we tend to be more tolerant of being over-rewarded than under-rewarded. Also, the various forms of justice do tend to go together. In the performance review example above, if we do not get the outcome we think we deserve (i.e. distributive injustice), we will probably explain it in terms of something wrong with the system (i.e. procedural injustice). Finally, just as in the case of equity theory, how much justice matters and how it is interpreted may vary quite a lot between cultures (Li and Cropanzano, 2009).

Key Learning Point

Perceived justice has significant consequences for people's work motivation and performance.

Goal-setting theory: how can I achieve my aims?

The theory

This approach to motivation was pioneered in the United States by Ed Locke and his associates, starting in the 1960s and continuing with increasing strength and sophistication ever since – so much so, that by the 1990s, well over half the research on motivation published in leading academic journals reported tests, extensions or refinements of goal-setting theory.

As Locke *et al.* (1981, p. 126) put it, 'A goal is what an individual is trying to accomplish; it is the object or aim of an action. The concept is similar in meaning to the concepts of purpose and intent.' Locke drew on both academic writing on intention (Ryan, 1970) and the much more practical 'management by objectives' literature in formulating his ideas. Figure 8.3 represents goal-setting theory, and provides the key concepts for this section.

The most fundamental proposition of goal-setting theory is that in most circumstances goals that are difficult but not impossible, and that are expressed in terms of

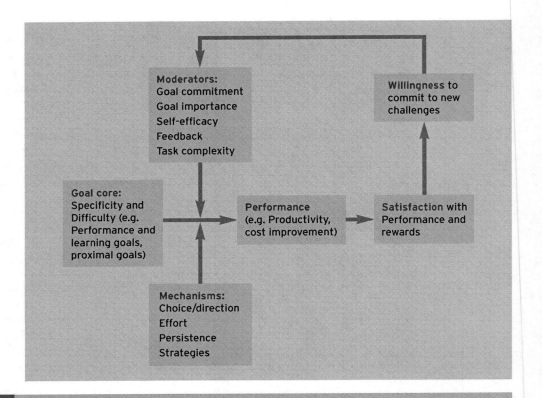

| Figure 8.3 | Essential elements of goal setting cycle |

a clearly defined performance level, produce higher levels of performance than other kinds of goals, or an absence of goals. In particular, goals of this kind produce better performance than vague 'do your best' goals. Difficult and specific goals have this effect by focusing a person's attention on the task, increasing the amount of effort they put into it, increasing the length of time they keep trying, and encouraging the person to develop strategies for goal achievement. These fundamental ideas of goal-setting theory have of course found expression in popular management practice, particularly in the form of so-called 'SMART' – specific, measureable, agreed, realistic and time-based – goals (see for example http://www.projectsmart.co.uk/).

Over the years it has been recognised that the goal-setting process can't always be quite that simple, for two main reasons. First, people and circumstances vary, sometimes in ways which affect the goal-setting process. Second, although the words and ideas in goal-setting theory are clear enough, applying them to any work situation is more complex than it initially seems. This is not a weakness of the theory, it's just how life is!

Some of these complexities have been incorporated into the goal-setting framework, and are shown as 'Moderators' in Figure 8.3. *Goal commitment* and *goal importance* both signal that the effect of goals on behaviour and performance is likely to be much greater if the goals matter greatly to a person than if they do not. Goal commitment can be defined as an unwillingness to abandon or lower the goal (Wright *et al.*, 1994). *Self-efficacy* reflects the point from expectancy theory that a person's belief that they are capable, or can become capable, of performing the necessary behaviours is an important component of motivation. There is good evidence that self-efficacy affects the level of difficulty of goals a person will be willing to feel committed to (Wooford *et al.*, 1992), which shows that these moderators inter-relate. It also seems to be the case that people with high self-efficacy are better than those with low self-efficacy at developing new strategies in response to failure or difficulty (Latham and Pinder, 2005). The provision of *feedback* on progress towards the goal enables a person to refine their strategies. *Task complexity* matters because a task that a person perceives as complex (that is unfamiliar, multifaceted and not easily achievable) may require learning goals rather than performance goals. Put another way, it might be better to set goals about learning the nature of the task (e.g. find five different ways in which the quality of the production process can be monitored) rather than achieving a specific level of performance (e.g. make sure that the production process produces no more than 1 per cent substandard product). This reflects research which showed that on complex tasks with which people are not familiar, setting performance goals hinders their learning of the best strategies, because they are too focused on the outcome itself, and not enough on figuring out the best way to achieve it (e.g. Kanfer and Ackerman, 1989). In general, it seems that goal-setting has greater effects on performance for simple tasks than complex ones (Wood *et al.*, 1987), but nevertheless, the beneficial effect of goal-setting on complex tasks is still well worth having.

Whilst a person might well derive some intrinsic satisfaction from successful task completion, attaching tangible rewards such as a cash bonus to that achievement will substantially increase the satisfaction, and consequently willingness to take on new challenges, perhaps even more difficult than before. Locke and Latham (1990) reported that the impact of monetary reward for performance occurs either through raising goal level, or through increasing commitment to a goal – so long as the amount of money on offer is considered significant, and not tied to goals perceived as impossible. In turn, willingness to take on new challenges can affect how committed the person is to a new goal, and of course over time successful performance is also likely to influence a person's sense of self-efficacy (Bandura, 1997), hence the feedback loop in Figure 8.3.

Key Learning Point

The setting of performance goals that are specific and difficult (but not impossible), and to which the person feels committed, is likely to improve their work performance. This is especially the case if the person receives feedback on progress, and rewards for successful performance.

What does research say about goal-setting? Many of the main features of the theory are now well-established, having been researched thoroughly (some would say exhaustively) in the 1970s to 1990s. Reviews by Locke and Latham (1990) and Mento *et al.* (1987) arrived at a number of conclusions, most of which fully or substantially supported goal-setting theory. Locke *et al.* (1981) reported that in goal-setting field experiments, the median improvement in work performance produced by goal-setting was 16 per cent. More recently, Locke and Latham (2002, p. 8) concluded that:

With goal-setting theory, specific difficult goals have been shown to increase performance on well over 100 different tasks involving more than 40,000 participants in at least eight countries working in laboratory, simulation and field settings. The dependent variables have included quantity, quality, time spent, costs, job behavior measures, and more. The time spans have ranged from one minute to 25 years. The effects are applicable not only to the individual but also to groups, organizational units, and entire organizations. The effects have been found using experimental, quasi-experimental, and correlational designs. Effects have been obtained whether the goals are assigned, self-set, or set participatively. In short, goal-setting is among the most valid and practical theories of employee motivation in organizational psychology.

It might be argued that Locke's enthusiasm could be partly because goal-setting theory has been a large part of his life's work, and he is therefore very motivated to see it positively. However, that would be too cynical. The evidence is more or less as he says it is, and in recent years he has shown a lot of interest in examining the less well-established areas of goal-setting and integrating it with other traditions in applied psychology, especially social cognition and self-regulation (see below).

Key Learning Point

Goal-setting theory is strongly supported by research.

Some issues around goal-setting

Locke (2000, p. 409) proposed that one way in which goals work is by unlocking or mobilising existing knowledge and skills that are relevant to the task in hand: 'It is a virtual axiom that human action is a consequence of . . . knowledge (including skill and ability) and desire'. This is a reminder of the point made near the start of third chapter that motivation does not provide a complete explanation of performance. Of course, if a person simply does not have the necessary knowledge or skill, and cannot easily acquire it, then the goal-setting process is unlikely to be successful, at least in the short-term. Therefore it could be argued that knowledge/ability should be added to Figure 8.3, even though it is partially reflected in self-efficacy, which concerns a person's beliefs about whether they have the necessary ability for the task at hand.

Key Learning Point

The impact of difficult and specific goals on a person's work performance occurs through the focusing of their strategies and intentions, and the mobilisation of their knowledge and ability.

As noted above, the notion of goal commitment has become very important in goal-setting theory. It is argued that if individuals do not feel commitment to a goal they will not exert effort in pursuit of it – even a difficult and specific one. Commitment is construed as more than simple acceptance of a goal. On the other hand, perhaps the notion of commitment is just another word for motivation – if I am committed to a goal, then that could be another way of saying I am motivated to achieve it. This means that a key focus, perhaps *the* key focus, of goal-setting theory should be how to foster goal commitment.

At one time it was argued that the best way to ensure goal commitment is to allow people to participate in discussions about what goals to set (e.g. Erez, 1986). Subsequently, however, some research suggests that often participation is not necessary. Its prime function seems to be information exchange, which can be achieved by dialogue between the person assigning a goal and the person expected to achieve it, and also by explanation of the reasons for the goals by the goal assigner. This might be the case where trust and respect are high, but that is not always the case at work. In any case, where a task is complex the goal assigner may find it difficult to specify a challenging but attainable goal without participation from those who are to try to achieve it (Haslam *et al.*, 2009).

Despite the clarity of goal-setting theory, it is not necessarily simple to implement in the workplace. In most organisations there are multiple goals to be achieved. For whole organisations, and for individuals and groups within them, there may be some conflict between goals. Achievement of one may be at the cost of another. For example, achievement of cost reductions in staff costs may be at the expense of quality of customer service. So when a manager is given goals to reduce costs by 10 per cent and to increase customer service by a similar amount, each goal on its own may be achievable but in combination they are not. This may well negate the positive effect of goal-setting. Also, in a turbulent environment, an organisation's goals and priorities may need to change at short notice. In this circumstance, and also where the tasks are inherently complex and relatively long-term (like writing this chapter!), there may be a particularly strong need to break down long-term goals into short-term (in Figure 8.3, 'proximal') ones such as 'write 3000 words that sum up the basic facts and issues in goal-setting in a scholarly but accessible way' (*see* also Fried and Slowik, 2004).

There are also other complications in applying goal-setting. These apply equally to any issue to do with managing performance, and as noted earlier are not a sign that goal-setting theory is 'wrong'. Effective goal-setting requires accurate assessment of whether a task is complex in the perception of the individual doing it, and what level of performance is difficult but not impossible for that person. If the person has a very low level of self-efficacy, it may be difficult to persuade them that even a moderate level of performance is attainable. Sometimes it takes time and trouble to provide feedback, and to link rewards reliably with performance. In this respect there are important dilemmas such as what reward, if any, to use if a person just misses a goal, or if circumstances change part-way through the process, making the goal either easier or harder to achieve. Locke and Latham (2004) offer an interesting analysis of these issues. Shaw (2004) provides a practical illustration of how goals can readily become vague aspirations rather than clear performance targets, and how this problem was addressed at Microsoft.

Key Learning Point

Although goal-setting theory is well-specified and uses well-defined concepts, successful implementation in the workplace still requires skill and sensitivity.

Exercise 8.3   Goal-setting in a car repair shop

Giovanni Russo was dissatisfied with the performance of the mechanics at his car repair workshop. He did not keep detailed records, but in his opinion too many customers brought their cars back after repair or servicing, complaining they were still not right. Others found that their cars were not ready by the agreed time. The garage had recently become the local dealer for one of the smaller car manufacturers. The mechanics had been relatively unfamiliar with cars of that make, and were still often unsure how to carry out certain repairs without frequently checking the workshop manual. Giovanni decided to introduce performance targets for the mechanics as a group. He told them that complaints and delays must be 'substantially reduced', and to sweeten the pill he immediately increased the group's pay by 8 per cent. The increase would continue as long as performance improved to what he regarded as a satisfactory extent. He promised to let the mechanics know each month whether he regarded their collective performance as satisfactory.

Suggested exercise

Use goal-setting theory and research to decide whether Giovanni Russo's attempt at goal-setting is likely to succeed.

STOP AND CONSIDER

Consider the extent to which you use goal-setting to manage and improve your own work performance. Could you use it more, or better? What special issues arise when goal-setting is used on oneself, rather than being administered by someone else?

Goals and self-regulation

Goal-setting could be criticised in its early days for being a technology rather than a theory. It successfully described how goals focus behaviour, without really addressing why or through what processes goals influenced behaviour. Starting in the 1980s, developments within the goal-setting tradition and outside it have helped progress on these issues.

Other motivation theories can also be integrated with goal-setting in order to explain further how people choose, change and implement strategies for achieving and reviewing goals (Kanfer, 1992). Social learning and social cognitive theories of *self-regulation* suggest some processes through which people do these things. Bandura (1986) argued that goals provide a person with a cognitive representation (or 'image') of the outcomes they desire. Depending on the gap between goal and the current position, the person experiences *self-reactions*. These include emotions (e.g. dissatisfaction) and self-efficacy expectations (that is, perceptions of one's ability to achieve the goal), as well as individual differences in the kind of 'self-talk' engaged in. For example, Bandura (2001) pointed out that some people respond to setbacks with thoughts that help them try again in a better way, whereas others tend to think of themselves as incapable of changing things for the better. These reactions, together with other factors, affect the level and direction of a person's future effort as well as their self-concept. For example, suppose a student is attempting to achieve the difficult task of writing a good essay in one evening's work, but by midnight only half the essay has been written. The student's self-efficacy expectations are likely to be reduced somewhat, especially if they were high to begin with. However, if self-efficacy is still fairly high, and so is dissatisfaction, the student is likely to persist until the essay is finished. If their self-efficacy has dropped a lot, or was low to start with, the student may give up even if dissatisfied with the lack of progress.

Other work relevant to the processes involved in goal-setting has been reported by Dweck (1986). She developed a theory of motivation and learning which distinguishes between *learning goal orientation* and *performance goal orientation*. Farr *et al.* (1993, p. 195) described these as follows:

> When approaching a task from a learning goal perspective, the individual's main objective is to increase his or her level of competence on a given task . . . Alternatively, when a task is approached from a performance goal orientation, individuals are primarily concerned with demonstrating their competency either to themselves or to others via their present level of task performance.

Farr *et al.* (1993) argued that people who adopt a performance goal orientation will tend to be more fearful of failure, less willing to take on difficult goals, and less receptive and able to respond constructively to feedback than those who adopt a learning goal orientation. In short, Farr and his colleagues suggested that goal-setting as a theory may be more applicable to, and useful for, learning goal-oriented people than performance goal-oriented ones. They also believed that in the long run, learning goal orientation is more likely to produce high performance and competence than performance goal orientation. They suggest that there is an increasing and ironic tendency in work organisations for goals to be set which are defined in terms of performance relative to other people, thus encouraging performance goal orientation rather than learning goal orientation.

There is quite a lot of evidence that the processes outlined in goal-setting theory do indeed apply more strongly to people with a learning goal orientation than those with a performance goal orientation (e.g. VandeWalle *et al.*, 2001). However, although goal orientations were originally conceived as a fairly constant feature of a person, akin to a personality characteristic, this has been questioned (DeShon and Gillespie, 2005). It seems that a learning goal orientation is quite easily induced in a given situation, even in those who score high on measures of dispositional performance goal orientation (Seijts and Latham, 2001).

Recently there has been increasing interest in possible subconscious influences on goal-setting processes. This is partly because goal-setting theory has placed high emphasis on conscious self-regulation and reasoning, possibly at the expense of the unconscious (Latham, 2007, Chapter 9). For example, it seems that a person's goal and/or motivation can be influenced by briefly seeing (a few hours earlier) a photograph showing someone winning a race, even though the person was not aware of the connection (Shantz and Latham, 2009).

Goal-setting theory has become increasingly integrated with social cognitive theories of self-regulation, and therefore more embedded in mainstream psychology

Self-concept and individual differences in motivation

Many of the most recent approaches to motivation have focused on how our sense of who we are, i.e. our self-concepts, personalities and values, influence the direction, effort and persistence of our behaviour (Leonard et al., 1999). To some extent this is reflected in research on the role of self-efficacy and goal orientation in goal-setting described earlier in this chapter.

However, some work in this area draws on other areas of social psychology, particularly self-categorisation and social identity (Turner and Onorato, 1999; Haslam, 2004). For example, it is proposed that a person does not have just one self-concept (i.e. set of perceptions about their own nature), but many. One distinction is between *personal identity*, which represents how we see ourselves relative to others in the same social groups, and *social identity*, which is those aspects of self-concept we think we have in common with others in the same group, and which differentiate us from members of other groups (*see also* Chapter 13). We have many different personal and social identities, depending on which social group is most salient to us at any given time. Furthermore, we are motivated to behave in ways that are consistent with our identity, or perhaps in some cases our ideal self – i.e. how we would *like* to be. In a work context this might mean that if our social identity as (for example) a member of the marketing department is most salient, then we will be motivated to perform behaviours that support the value of marketing and perhaps our marketing colleagues. On the other hand, if our personal identity as an ambitious young manager is most salient, we are more likely to pursue behaviours that we see as being in our own interest, such as concentrating on our own work or making ourselves look good in front of the boss in case there is a promotion opportunity on the horizon (Haslam et al., 2000; Van Knippenberg, 2000).

Leonard et al. (1999) suggested that our identities are composed of three elements. Traits are broad tendencies to react in certain ways. Competencies are perceptions of one's skills, abilities, talents and knowledge. Values are beliefs about desirable ways of being and/or patterns of behaviour that transcend specific situations. It is difficult to predict which of these three aspects of self will motivate behaviour at any given time. Leonard et al. proposed that various psychological processes involving the processing of information and integrating it with our sense of self lead to the following types of motivation:

- **Intrinsic process motivation:** the pursuit of activities because they are fun, whether or not they help in goal attainment.

- **Extrinsic/instrumental motivation:** the pursuit of individual or group goals because they lead to rewards other than satisfaction, especially material ones.

- **External self-concept:** the pursuit of success in order to gain affirmation from others for a social identity as a member of a successful group, or a personal identity as a competent person.

- **Internal self-concept:** the pursuit of success in order that the individual is able to feel competent, irrespective of what others might think of them.

- **Goal internalisation:** the pursuit of goal-achievement for its own sake, because it is valued by the individual.

Key Learning Point

People are motivated to act in accordance with their self-concepts and identities. Different aspects of these are salient (and therefore influence their behaviour) in different situations.

Exercise 8.4   Self and identity in motivation

Magnus Johannson was the captain of what he considered to be the best fishing crew in the Baltic Sea. Again and again his boat, *The Seagull*, brought back the highest quantity and quality catch of all the trawlers he knew about – and all the catches conformed perfectly to European Union regulations. In a very difficult era for all fishing fleets, he considered this to be a major achievement, and he valued the fact that his crew and other crews recognised it. He felt his particular talent was sensing where the best shoals of fish were likely to be, given currents and weather conditions. This was rarely the same place two days running, and sometimes Magnus's hunches proved more reliable than the ship's technical gadgets. Often his intuition about it differed from some members of his crew, but they had learned that Magnus was usually right. Indeed, it had become a standing joke on *The Seagull* that there was no point arguing with him. That was one of the things he liked best about his crew. They could laugh and joke but they still respected their captain and worked hard partly out of loyalty to him. Other crews did not seem to have that same mix of light-heartedness and purpose, as far as he could see. But Magnus sometimes felt concerned that many people with great reputations eventually fail, and he feared that a day might come when he was no longer able to find the fish or command the respect of his crew.

Suggested exercise

Which elements of the motivation themes described in the section 'self-concept and individual differences in motivation' do you think help us understand Magnus Johannson's work motivation?

Intrinsic motivation, extrinsic motivation and pay

Studies have found that when asked what motivates them at work the majority of people give answers such as variety, responsibility, recognition for achievements, interesting work and job challenge rather than pay or working conditions (e.g. Herzberg, 1966). In fact Herzberg's work has been influential in steering managers towards altering people's jobs rather than pay regimes in order to increase motivation. We discuss that view of motivation later in this chapter. It relates closely to a broad distinction between *intrinsic motivation* and *extrinsic motivation* (see also the Leonard *et al.*, 1999, analysis described above), which is often used in discussions about motivation. Ryan and Deci (2000, p. 56) defined intrinsic motivation as 'the doing of an activity for its inherent satisfactions . . . a person is moved to act for the fun or challenge entailed rather than because of external prods, pressures, or rewards'. In contrast, extrinsic motivation 'pertains whenever an activity is done in order to obtain some separable outcome' (Ryan and Deci, 2000, p. 60).

Essentially then, Herzberg argued that intrinsic motivation is more reliable and powerful than extrinsic motivation as a way of influencing behaviour at work. Intrinsic motivation has clear links with Maslow's esteem and self-actualisation needs. Some research in the 1970s suggested that high pay actually undermined intrinsic motivation by focusing a person's attention on extrinsic rewards (Deci and Ryan, 1980). More recently, however, it appears that pay can enhance intrinsic motivation, or at least not damage it, if the level of pay provides a person with information about their competencies. Damage to intrinsic motivation occurs only if the person perceives extrinsic rewards as an attempt to control their behaviour rather than to provide information about it (Deci *et al.*, 1999). The extent to which we perceive ourselves to have autonomy in pursuing extrinsic rewards, and in the way we go about it, can make a big difference. This insight has led to a more differentiated view of extrinsic motivation, which was much-needed for the analysis of work motivation. Most of us would not spend as much time doing the activities in our job if we were not paid for doing them, so extrinsic motivation must be relevant to the work context. Different forms of extrinsic motivation identified by Ryan and Deci (2000) are, in decreasing degrees of 'extrinsicness':

- *External regulation*: a person performs behaviour in order to satisfy an external demand, and experiences this as externally controlled and not what they would do by choice.

- *Introjected regulation*: similar to external regulation, except that the person has internalised the external demand enough for it to matter to their sense of self-esteem.

- *Identification*: a person accepts an external demand or reward as being of personal importance, and therefore also uses self-regulation in order to perform the required behaviours.

- *Integrated regulation*: similar to identification, but the person not only accepts external rewards or requirements as important, but also as an expression of self.

Key Learning Point

The distinction between intrinsic and extrinsic motivation is important conceptually, but in practice it is blurred, and it is important not to see intrinsic motivation as somehow morally superior to extrinsic.

The most obvious extrinsic reward is of course pay. In the case of external regulation, a person might do the work required simply because they need the pay to live. If it was a case of introjected regulation, then the person would also feel that what they earned was to some extent a reflection of their personal worth in the organisation and/or society. Identification would mean that the person viewed themself as someone who cared quite a lot about money (and would therefore work for it), whilst in the case of integrated regulation, money earned would be a central part of the person's self-concept and getting it would be an absolute necessity to retain not only a way of life but also a self-image.

Herzberg (1966) and others tend to argue that pay is not a key motivator at work, though it is acknowledged that this conclusion depends on some basic level of pay being provided in order to meet basic needs. What do the theories of motivation discussed in this chapter say about pay as a motivator? For Maslow, pay would be a motivator only for people functioning at the lower levels of the hierarchy of needs. Advocates of need for achievement point to the fact that pay and other material rewards often signal that a person is successful. So from this perspective pay is a motivator if and when it indicates that the person has succeeded in their work tasks. In expectancy theory, pay will be an effective motivator to the extent that it is desired by the person, *and* they can identify behaviours that will lead to high payment, *and* they feel capable of performing those behaviours. Igalens and Roussel (1999) reported data from a large sample of French workers which suggested that the valence of pay was much greater if good performance was rewarded by increases in salary rather than a bonus. Even then, this depended on people being able to see a connection between their efforts and successful performance. Locke and Latham (2002) provide a useful analysis of the advantages and disadvantages of different ways of achieving this connection.

From the perspective of organisational justice, people will be concerned with whether their pay is a fair reward relative to the rewards received by others. They will also want to see fair procedures for allocating pay. A common problem for performance-related pay is that these procedures are often *not* seen as fair. Bloom (1999) studied the pay of North American baseball players over the years 1985 and 1993 and found that the more equal the pay of the different players in the team, the better individuals and teams performed. This suggests that the pay of others matters as well as our own, and that having a small number of highly paid 'superstars' is not a good move.

Goal-setting theory normally involves goals that are defined in terms of a person's behaviour and/or accomplishments, not pay. Nevertheless, if there is a very clear and direct link between a person's accomplishments and pay, then specific, difficult goals defined in terms of earnings may be motivating. On the other hand, when pay is an indicator of how well a person is doing *compared with others*, we can expect it to encourage a performance goal orientation rather than a learning goal orientation. As noted above, this might be seen as a 'bad thing'.

Rynes et al. (2004) have argued forcefully that the importance of pay as a motivator is often underestimated by human resource managers. This is partly because of the work of Herzberg and Maslow, and partly because other research (e.g. Jurgensen, 1978) has asked people what motivates them at work and consistently found that pay is reported to be less important than many other things, such as job challenge, interesting work and opportunities for promotion. Rynes *et al.* argue that people's behaviour suggests that pay is more important to them than they say it is. Perhaps people do not realise the reasons for their own behaviour, or perhaps they do but are embarrassed to admit that pay matters a lot. Rynes *et al.* argue on the basis of some past research that carefully designed performance-related pay schemes can be shown to enhance performance very effectively, and that people's decisions about which job to take are often made on the basis of pay level. The importance of pay is due to its being what in behaviourist terms is called a 'generalised reinforcer'. As a Beatles song long ago pointed out, money cannot buy love, but it can buy a lot of other things, and people can use it in ways that suit them. This might include non-acquisitive purposes such as giving it away to good causes, using it to pay other people to do things you don't want to do yourself (such as home maintenance), or accessing desired leisure activities (such as joining a sports club).

Key Learning Point

Financial rewards tend to enhance performance, especially when they are seen as fair and providing accurate feedback about how well the person is doing.

Exercise 8.5   Is pay any use as an incentive?

However good the pay, it doesn't buy results

In a classic case of vanishing returns, in attempting to construct 'better incentives' and 'closer links between pay and performance', companies are expending more and more effort on trying to get right something that cannot, and should not, be done in the first place.

The catch-22 - the fatal flaw with all numerical targets and quotas - is that to be understood and acted on, incentives must be simple. But if they are that simple, in any organisation with objectives more multidimensional than a whelk stall, they are simplistic: inadequate to carry the information necessary for the accomplishment of other goals. It's impossible to specify a simple target for a complex organisation.

Simple incentives make clever companies stupid, like the banks, zapping even the instinct for self-preservation. But complex ones turn them into hotbeds of confusion, envy, fear and loathing, which is no better. Why should some people get bonuses and others not? Why is yours bigger than mine? In any organisation made up of multiple teams and interdependencies, calculating reliable attributions of responsibility for gain or loss is like counting angels on a pinhead. And trying to do it years later, with possible clawbacks depending on it, is a mathematical and legal nightmare.   ▶

Financial incentives lead to inequality in rewards - d'uh, that's what they're supposed to do. For jockeys, loggers and orange pickers that seems to result in higher performance. But it's death to the co-operation and teamwork on which overall organisational performance depends. From sports teams and university departments to publicly quoted companies, the greater the pay inequalities the worse the results, whether in terms of collaboration, productivity, financial performance or product quality. The moral of the story is that companies should be very careful what they choose to pay for - because that's what they'll get, and nothing else.

Source: Adapted from an article by Simon Caulkin, The Observer, 22 February 2009.

Suggested exercise

To what extent does the material in this chapter on goal-setting and pay as motivators support Simon Caulkin's argument?

Motivation through job redesign

Much of the discussion so far in this chapter has suggested that motivation is a property of the person. An alternative view is that motivation (or lack of it) is inherent in the nature of jobs. This viewpoint means that we need to look less closely at the person and more closely at what it is about work that can make it motivating.

Job simplification and job enrichment

Early recommendations for how to design jobs focused on efficiency and cost reduction rather than motivation. This usually meant minimising skill requirements of jobs, maximising management control and minimising the time required to perform a task. This may appear to make good sense, especially against economic criteria. Unskilled or semi-skilled labour costs less than skilled labour, and productivity is enhanced if tasks are done quickly. However, as we shall see, jobs designed in this way frequently have human costs, and perhaps economic ones too.

This 'traditional' approach to job design stems from a philosophy called 'scientific management', or 'Taylorism', after its creator, F.W. Taylor. Taylor (1911) formulated his ideas in the United States in the early twentieth century. As a machine-shop foreman, he felt that workers consistently underproduced, and that the way to prevent this was to:

- systematically (or 'scientifically') compile information about the work tasks required;

- remove workers' discretion and control over their own activities;

- simplify tasks as much as possible;

■   specify standard procedures and times for task completion;

■   use financial (and *only* financial) incentives;

■   by the above methods, ensure that workers could not deceive managers, or hide from them.

This of course bears a strong resemblance to the 'theory X' view of human nature (described earlier in this chapter). Observers agree that jobs in many, perhaps most, organisations are implicitly or explicitly based on Taylorism. Some argue that call centres are the most recent kind of organisation to exhibit Taylorism in a strong form (e.g. Bain *et al.*, 2002).

Key Learning Point

Scientific management, also known as Taylorism, emphasises standardised methods and minimisation of costs in the design of work.

Taylorism might make for a well-ordered world, but is it a happy and productive one? As long ago as the 1960s, a number of studies seemed to show that work organised along scientific management principles was associated with negative attitudes towards the job, as well as poor mental and/or physical health (e.g. Kornhauser, 1965; Turner and Lawrence, 1965). It was also often assumed that poor productivity would accompany such outcomes, and that simplified work actually *caused* poor mental health, motivation and satisfaction, rather than the reverse causal direction.

These studies of simplified work led to considerable concern about what came to be called *quality of working life* (QWL). Several theoretical perspectives were brought to bear on QWL. One was *job enrichment* – a concept developed through the work of Herzberg (1966) (see also the previous section of this chapter). Herzberg proposed a basic distinction between *hygiene factors* and *motivators*. Hygiene factors included pay, conditions of employment, the work environment and other features extrinsic to the work activities themselves. Motivators included job challenge, recognition and skill use – that is, features appealing to growth needs. On the basis of his data, Herzberg proposed that hygiene factors could not cause satisfaction, but that dissatisfaction could result if they were not present. On the other hand, motivators led to satisfaction: their absence produced not dissatisfaction, but a lack of satisfaction. Although Herzberg's data and conclusions can be criticised on several grounds, his recommendation that motivation and/or satisfaction can be enhanced by increasing skill use, job challenge, etc. is consistent with much subsequent work.

Another relevant theoretical tradition is *socio-technical systems* (Cherns, 1976, 1987; Heller, 1989). Arising from studies in the immediate post-1945 years, socio-technical theory emphasises the need to integrate technology and social structures in the workplace. Too often, technology is introduced with scant regard for existing friendship patterns, work groups and status differentials. Socio-technical theory attempts to rectify this, but it also makes wider propositions. For example, it states that job activities should be specified only in so far as necessary to establish the boundaries of that job. It also emphasises that boundaries should be drawn so that they do not impede transmission of information and learning, and that disruptions to work processes should be dealt with at source wherever possible, rather than by managers further removed from the situation. Such principles may seem self-evident, but close examination of many organisations will demonstrate that they are not adhered to. Socio-technical job design therefore emphasises autonomy, decision-making and the avoidance of subordinating people to machines.

Whatever their exact theoretical origin, until the early twenty-first century most attempts to redesign jobs centred on increasing one or more of the following (Wall, 1982):

- *variety* (of tasks or skills);

- *autonomy* (freedom to choose work methods, scheduling and occasionally goals);

- *completeness* (extent to which the job produces an identifiable end result which the person can point to).

This may be attempted in one or more of the following ways:

- *Job rotation*: people rotate through a small set of different (but usually similar) jobs. Rotation is frequent (e.g. each week). It can increase variety.

- *Horizontal job enlargement*: additional tasks are included in a person's job. They are usually similar to tasks already carried out. This too can increase variety.

- *Vertical job enlargement*: additional decision-making responsibilities and/or higher-level challenging tasks are included in the job. This increases autonomy, variety and possibly completeness. An increasingly commonly used term for this is *empowerment*: a person does not necessarily achieve an increase in formal status, but they are given more freedom to take decisions and implement them according to the needs of the situation at the time (Wang and Lee, 2009).

- *Semi-autonomous work groups*: similar to vertical job enlargement, but at the level of the group rather than the individual. In other words, a group of people is assigned a task and allowed to organise itself to accomplish it. Semi-autonomous workgroups have been introduced in some car factories.

- *Self-managing teams*: more often composed of managers and professionals than semi-autonomous work groups, these teams are often given considerable freedom to accomplish a group task, and perhaps even to define the task in the first place.

Key Learning Point

Job redesign can take a variety of forms and arise for many reasons (see Figure 8.4), but it has normally involved an attempt to increase the amount of variety, autonomy and/or completeness inherent in the work of one or more people.

Interest in job redesign has been stimulated in more recent years by concerns about the quality of products and services, and the needs for innovation and customer responsiveness. It is argued that well-motivated staff are particularly

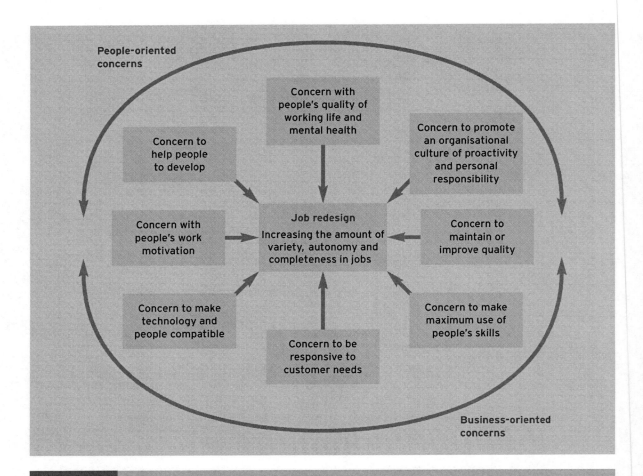

| Figure 8.4 | Concerns leading to job redesign |

important for the delivery of outcomes like these (e.g. Shipton *et al.*, 2006). In other words, job redesign is part of hard-headed business strategy rather than (or as well as) a philanthropic concern with the quality of working life. At the same time, cost-cutting and efficiency are also important for organisational competitiveness, so there is much attention to practices such as the use of new technology and so-called 'just in time' and 'lean' production methods. These may not be consistent with the creation of motivating jobs, though they can have benefits for organisational productivity (Birdi *et al.*, 2008; de Treville and Antonakis, 2006).

The question of whether it is possible to design jobs that are both efficient and motivating has been investigated by Morgeson and Campion (2002). They conducted a detailed analysis of a set of jobs in one part of a pharmaceutical company and then redesigned some of them to include more 'scientific management' efficiency-based elements, some to include more variety and autonomy, and some to include more of both. They found that it was possible to increase both elements at the same time, and that this produced some small benefits for efficiency and satisfaction.

The job characteristics model

The *job characteristics model* (JCM) of Hackman and Oldham (1976, 1980) has been very influential. It is depicted in Figure 8.5, which shows that Hackman and Oldham identified five core job characteristics:

1 *Skill variety* (SV): the extent to which the job requires a range of skills.

2 *Task identity* (TI): the extent to which the job produces a whole, identifiable outcome.

3 *Task significance* (TS): the extent to which the job has an impact on other people, either inside or outside the organisation.

4 *Autonomy* (Au): the extent to which the job allows the job holder to exercise choice and discretion in their work.

5 *Feedback from job* (Fb): the extent to which the job itself (as opposed to other people) provides information on how well the job holder is performing.

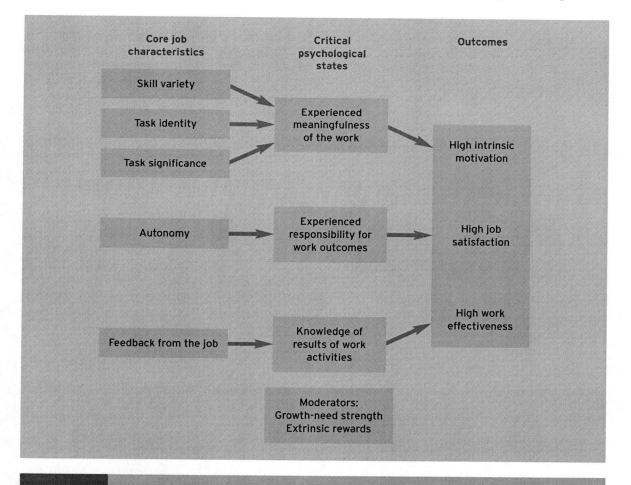

Figure 8.5	Hackman and Oldham's job characteristics model

Source: Adapted from J.R. Hackman and G.R. Oldham (1980), *Work Redesign*
© 1980. Reprinted by permission of Pearson Education, Inc., Upper Saddle River, NJ.

The core job characteristics are said to produce 'critical psychological states'. The first three core job characteristics are believed to influence *experienced meaningfulness of the work*. Autonomy affects *experienced responsibility for outcomes of the work*, and feedback from the job impacts on *knowledge of the actual results of the work activities*. Collectively, the critical psychological states are believed to influence three outcomes: motivation, satisfaction and work performance. This whole process is said to be moderated by several factors (*see* Figure 8.5). The most often investigated of these is growth-need strength. This refers to the importance to the individual of Maslow's growth needs (*see* earlier in this chapter). The model is said to apply more strongly to people with high growth needs than to those with low ones.

Key Learning Point

The job characteristics model specifies five features of jobs that tend to make them intrinsically motivating and satisfying.

The JCM provoked a huge amount of research, especially in the United States. This is not surprising, since it provides specific hypotheses about exactly which job characteristics matter, how they affect people's psychological states, what outcomes they produce, and which individual differences affect the whole process. Also, Hackman and Oldham produced a questionnaire called the Job Diagnostic Survey (JDS) which assesses the constructs shown in Figure 8.5. The JDS is completed by job holders.

A number of helpful observations about the JCM were made in review articles (see, for examples, Fried and Ferris, 1987; Kelly, 1993). In summary, the job characteristics identified by Hackman and Oldham did indeed usually correlate with motivation and satisfaction, though not so clearly with the performance of individuals or organisations. However, there were few studies in which attempts were made to *change* jobs so that they had more of the core job characteristics (which is, after all, the whole point of job redesign). So the correlations between job characteristics and motivation and satisfaction may not have reflected a *causal* relationship. There was also quite a lot of doubt about whether the effects on attitudes and behaviour of each core job characteristic were mediated by the critical psychological states specified by Hackman and Oldham. Indeed, in general the core job characteristics seemed to have more effect on people's attitudes to their work than on their work performance. It was also recognised that additional job characteristics may matter. Warr (1987) suggested availability of money, physical security, interpersonal contact and valued social position as likely contenders. More recently, yet more job characteristics have been identified. These are discussed a little later in this chapter.

Exercise 8.6   Bicycle assembly at Wheelspin

The Wheelspin bicycle company produces a range of bicycles for adults and children. At their factory, already-manufactured components are painted and assembled. Assembly is carried out on assembly lines which move at constant speeds. The factory manager decides which line will assemble which bicycle. Each member of staff has a specific part or parts which they screw, weld or otherwise fix onto the ▶

basic frame at a specified point on the assembly line. They carry out the same tasks about 80 times a day. Staff are recruited to a specific job: they generally remain on the same assembly line and deal with the same parts. Once every two or three months, the model being assembled changes, but generally the assembly tasks required are more or less constant. Noise levels are low enough to allow staff to chat to immediate neighbours as they work. Work quality is assessed at the end of the production line, where performance of the assembled bicycle is examined by quality control staff.

Suggested exercise

Examine the characteristics of the assembly jobs at Wheelspin. How might those characteristics be changed?

Ambrose and Kulik (1999) pointed out that research interest in the JCM decreased very markedly from about the mid-1990s. They argued that this may be appropriate, since it is now quite well understood. Nevertheless, the JCM has stood empirical testing reasonably well, especially considering the relatively large number of connections between specific variables it proposes. Even the more recent reviews acknowledge that the JCM specifies much that is important about jobs and job redesign (Parker and Wall, 1998; Humphrey *et al.*, 2007), despite a clear need to broaden the range of job characteristics beyond those specified in it.

Although the JCM is much less dominant than it used to be, it is still the basis of quite a lot of new thinking about work design. For example, Pierce *et al.* (2009) argue that the core job characteristics tend to foster a sense of *psychological ownership* for the person doing the job. The person feels psychological ownership because they have a sense of control over the job, know its 'ins and outs' very well, and find that it helps to shape a clear and positive sense of identity. Pierce *et al.* (2009) argue therefore that a sense of psychological ownership (rather than for example experienced meaningfulness of work, *see* Figure 8.5) is the key mediating variable between core job characteristics and outcomes. Like Hackman and Oldham, Pierce *et al.* list motivation, satisfaction and performance amongst the outcomes. However, they also suggest that there could be some negative outcomes as well, such as uncooperative territorial behaviours ('this is my job, don't you interfere') as a result of psychological ownership. The JCM also continues to be the foundation of some empirical research on job design (e.g. Millette and Gagne, 2008; DeVaro *et al.*, 2007).

More recent analyses of the nature of jobs

The need for employees to be responsive to customers and be willing to change and learn is said to be much greater now than it used to be. So is the need to acquire new information rapidly and share it with others who can use it. Some argue that it is better to use the term 'work', because the word 'job' implies a fixed and stable set of duties. Such constancy is rarer than it used to be. This is partly because of the pace of change in the workplace, and partly because people are often encouraged to engage in 'job crafting' (Wrzesniewski and Dutton, 2001), i.e. emphasise some parts of the job at the expense of others in order to maximise their contribution and their fit with their organisation.

Although it was quickly recognised that the JCM's list of job characteristics was not wide-ranging enough (especially given the context described in the previous paragraph), it took some time for well-developed alternative analyses to appear. The leaders in this respect are Fred Morgeson and Stephen Humphrey in the USA (Morgeson and Humphrey, 2006; Humphrey *et al.*, 2007). They argued that work redesign theory and practice needs to take into account all aspects of jobs in order to provide a sound basis for maintaining and improving the motivation, satisfaction and performance of individuals and organisations. Specifically, they make the case that:

- Whilst the JCM focuses mainly on the nature of tasks, it is also necessary to consider the *knowledge* requirements. For example, does a person's work require a deep specialist knowledge of an area? Does it require problem-solving, and are there a lot of factors to consider simultaneously? Also, whilst the JCM characteristic skill variety is important, so is task variety, and the two are not the same.

- Work is not only about tasks and knowledge. It is, for most people, also an intensely *social* activity. Therefore, a complete analysis of the nature of a person's work must include factors like the extent to which they receive social support and feedback from others, and have work which requires interaction and interdependence with others.

- The *context* in which work is carried out is also likely to be important. For example, is a person's workplace well-designed ergonomically (*see* Chapter 9)? What are the working conditions like in terms of noise, hazards etc.?

Humphrey *et al.* (2007) have reported a meta-analysis of studies that have tested the statistical relationships of work characteristics with motivation, performance and other outcomes. To the extent that they were able, they used the set of work characteristics developed by Morgeson and Humphrey (2006) for their analysis. Table 8.4 shows some of their results.

Note first of all that there are a lot of empty cells in the table, meaning that as yet there is no evidence about the associations of some of the work characteristics with outcomes. Second, note that the five JCM core job characteristics (autonomy, skill variety, task identity, task significance and feedback from the job) are all quite strongly associated with motivation, job satisfaction and organisational commitment, but not with performance (with the partial exception of autonomy). Again this illustrates the fact that motivation and performance are not always as closely connected as one might think – other factors matter too. Third, the strong relationships between the information processing and job complexity on the one hand and satisfaction on the other suggest that these two knowledge components may also be significant for motivation. Fourth, there is clear evidence that social factors are related to motivation and (even more) to satisfaction and commitment. Hence it seems that we do indeed need to move beyond the core job characteristics in order to understand how work influences motivation and other outcomes.

Key Learning Point

The core job characteristics, knowledge requirements and social features of jobs are associated with motivation. Improvements in job performance do not necessarily occur as a direct consequence of changes in job characteristics, even if motivation and/or satisfaction do improve.

	Work motivation	Work satisfaction	Work performance	Organisational commitment
Task characteristics				
Autonomy	0.27	0.37	0.14	0.30
Task variety		0.35	−0.03	
Task significance	0.30	0.31		0.34
Task identity	0.17	0.23	0.05	0.18
Feedback from job	0.29	0.33	0.09	0.29
Knowledge requirements				
Information processing		0.31		
Job complexity		0.32	−0.06	
Skill variety	0.30	0.32	−0.03	0.23
Social factors				
Interdependence	0.21	0.23		0.34
Feedback from others	0.22	0.32		
Social support	0.11	0.41		0.56
Interaction outside organisation		0.05		
Work context				
Physical demands		−0.15		
Work conditions		0.20		

Adapted with permission of American Psychological Association from Humphrey *et al.* (2007), pp. 1342–3.

STOP TO CONSIDER

What are the practical and theoretical implications if work redesign affects motivation but not performance?

Of course, these statistical associations do not prove that the work characteristics cause the so-called outcomes. Also, even if there is a causal relationship, it is not clear how it works, or whether it does so more strongly for some people than for others. As noted above, Pierce *et al.* (2009) suggest that at least some work characteristics create a sense of psychological ownership which in turn leads to the outcomes. Fried *et al.* (2007) use career theory (see Chapter 15) and suggest that some work characteristics matter more at some career stages than others. For example, they hypothesise that in their later career people become more concerned about task significance because at that stage making a positive contribution that benefits others matters a great deal to them. Of course, Hackman and Oldham also thought that their JCM would apply to some people more strongly than others – for example, those high in 'growth need strength' were expected to respond more favourably to the core job characteristics than those not so high.

Making a positive contribution that benefits others has also been the basis of some other recent thinking about work design. Arguing for the importance of social as well as task factors, Grant (2007) uses the term 'relational job design' to reflect this emphasis. Grant proposes that an important part of work motivation is, or can be, the motivation 'to make a prosocial difference' – in other words, to do things that benefit other people. In order to increase this form of motivation, Grant advocates the design of work to include frequent and in-depth contact with beneficiaries, and the opportunity to find out a lot about them. This, he says, will increase the person's perceptions of their impact on beneficiaries, and also foster a sense of commitment to them. These factors will then affect motivation to make a prosocial difference. Grant acknowledges that the notion of impact on beneficiaries overlaps with the JCM core job characteristic of task significance, but argues that his analysis is much more specific about (i) the social aspects of it and (ii) the implications for how relationships at work can and should be designed just as tasks are.

Exercise 8.7   Communication and motivation

When Alfred Josefsen, managing director of Irma, first arrived at the Copenhagen-based grocery chain, the workforce was anything but happy. Employee motivation was low and staff members were frequently leaving to go to work for other companies. 'It was a big crisis and, for the first couple of years we had to do a huge turnaround,' says Mr Josefsen.

Today, the company appears regularly on listings of best workplace awards, both in Denmark and overseas. In this year's 100 Best Workplaces in Europe, the company wins a special award for best practices in internal communication. Some 93 per cent of the company's surveyed employees believe Irma's management team is approachable ▶

and easy to talk to, while 83 per cent agree that management always informs them about corporate developments.

Mr Josefsen describes the process that was needed to get the company from its low point to this position. 'The first thing that was important was to decentralise the company and put much more decision making back to the hands of store managers,' he explains. The idea was to have each store operating more like a local grocery, competing with stores around the corner. The new approach – along with efforts to make internal communication much more informal – delivered results within a remarkably short time. 'In half a year, the atmosphere in the company was much more positive,' says Mr Josefsen.

Irma started life in 1886 as a small basement shop in Copenhagen that stocked dairy products. Today, it focuses on quality foods, pioneering the removal of trans-fats, additives and colourings from its products. It puts a large amount of organic produce on its shelves. Irma now has more than 1,700 employees working in 70 supermarkets and administrative offices. Many of them have received a visit from the managing director. Mr Josefsen likes to wander about in the company's head office and he also visits the stores themselves to talk to shop assistants and customers. It is not only Mr Josefsen who can be found in the aisles. Senior managers, too, pay regular trips to the stores and may even work in them for a day or two as 'interns'.

Cross-divisional meetings and regular workshops allow staff to come together in a professional capacity, as well as more informally at social events. At 'Strategy Days', hundreds of store-level employees get together for three days to share ideas. Mr Josefsen is frequently present at such events. 'I often walk to the side and see what's going on and usually all the people are communicating to each other very loudly,' he says. 'It's great to hear people speaking like that.'

However, perhaps the most powerful weapon in the company's communications armoury has been a short e-mail from Mr Josefsen that goes out regularly to all staff. In it, he uses personal experiences as a way of conveying key business messages.

Six years ago, when we were having problems, I wrote a little letter and e-mailed it to the stores [he says]. This weekly letter was read by everyone in the company. They liked to hear from the managing director. When I figured out that, with one little e-mail, I could communicate with everyone, I realised that this was a fantastic tool.

I try to be visible and in contact with people so they know that the managing director is working hard for the future of the company. My approach is value management, and you have to be in contact with people if you want to show what you're doing and that you have direction.

Source: Adapted from 'Irma: Grocery's idea bears fruit', *The Financial Times*, 18 May 2006 (Murray, S.), copyright © Sarah Murray. With permission.

Suggested exercises

1   Communication is not often talked about in motivation theory as a technique to increase motivation. Do you think Mr Josefsen's innovative ways of communicating with employees helped motivation in this case, and if so how?

2   What aspects of people's job characteristics in Irma might have been affected by the way Mr Josefsen led the company?

Twenty-first century work design

Although an expanded view of work characteristics is certainly important, an even more radical perspective is needed in order to guide the design of work in twenty-first century workplaces. Parker *et al.* (2001) have provided a careful analysis of this, and offer the following observations. Some of these observations reflect points that have already been made in this chapter, whilst others are new:

- In an era when many jobs are less clearly defined and less closely supervised than they were, it is inappropriate to assume that jobs have characteristics that remain fixed until someone tries to redesign them.

- There are more features of jobs that affect attitudinal and behavioural outcomes. In fact, those features probably always did matter; it is just that they are more obvious now. These include the extent to which the job is compatible with home commitments, and the various cognitive demands it makes (for example, problem-solving, vigilance). Another is whether the job requires so-called emotional labour – that is, the display of positive or negative emotion in order to, for example, empathise with customers.

- The processes by which jobs affect people may well not be confined to motivational ones, as assumed by traditional job redesign theories. Other processes may include the extent to which a speedy response to events is possible, and also whether employees are able to use their local knowledge to solve problems as and when they arise.

- The outcomes of job redesign should be evaluated at individual, group and organisational levels. As well as motivation, satisfaction and profitability, relevant outcomes might include creativity, innovation, customer satisfaction, accident rates, absence and turnover. Regarding creativity, Elsbach and Hargadon (2006) have argued that, at least for busy professionals, a spell of 'mindless' work during a day may help creativity because it gives them space to think. This interesting suggestion highlights the possibility that it may not be desirable for people to have 'enriched' work all day every day.

- A much greater range of factors than those suggested in the JCM may affect the impact of job characteristics (and changes in them) on outcomes. These include the extent to which tasks within an organisation are interdependent, and the extent to which the organisation is operating in an ambiguous and/or rapidly changing environment.

- Clearer thinking is needed about when it is best to redesign jobs at the individual level, and when at the group level. Factors such as task interdependence (see above) will probably be important here.

These points are encapsulated in Figure 8.6, which is adapted from Parker *et al.* (2001). It demonstrates how much expansion on the older models of job redesign might be required. It also suggests how difficult it might be to conduct research that includes all the relevant factors, and to provide managers with straightforward, easy to understand advice about what jobs in their organisations should look like.

Although the words used are not always the same, the model shown in Figure 8.6 encompasses many of the management techniques and terminology that have been used to try to improve individual and organisational outcomes. A good example is

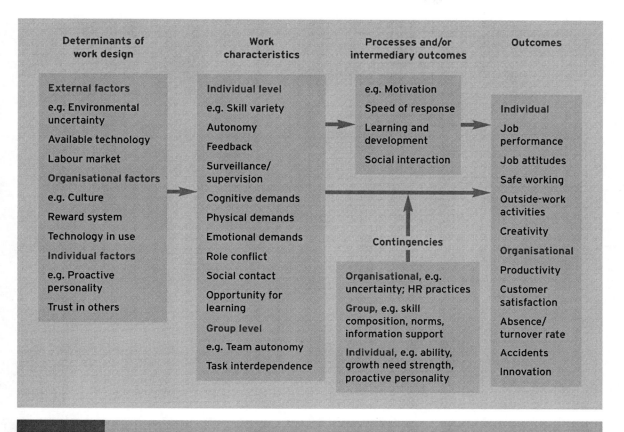

Determinants of work design	Work characteristics	Processes and/or intermediary outcomes	Outcomes
External factors	**Individual level**	e.g. Motivation	
e.g. Environmental uncertainty	e.g. Skill variety	Speed of response	**Individual**
Available technology	Autonomy	Learning and development	Job performance
Labour market	Feedback	Social interaction	Job attitudes
Organisational factors	Surveillance/ supervision		Safe working
e.g. Culture	Cognitive demands		Outside-work activities
Reward system	Physical demands		Creativity
Technology in use	Emotional demands	**Contingencies**	**Organisational**
Individual factors	Role conflict		Productivity
e.g. Proactive personality	Social contact	Organisational, e.g. uncertainty; HR practices	Customer satisfaction
Trust in others	Opportunity for learning	Group, e.g. skill composition, norms, information support	Absence/ turnover rate
	Group level	Individual, e.g. ability, growth need strength, proactive personality	Accidents
	e.g. Team autonomy		Innovation
	Task interdependence		

Figure 8.6   An elaborated model of work design
Source: Adapted, with permission, from Parker *et al.* (2001).

empowerment (Wilkinson, 1998), which refers to attempts to transfer more responsibility and scope for decision-making to people at low levels in an organisation. As Wall *et al.* (2002) have pointed out, empowerment often means increases in job control, performance monitoring, cognitive demands and possibly role conflict and social contact. It is likely to be embraced most wholeheartedly by people with a proactive personality, and perhaps have most impact in conditions of environmental uncertainty, where it is more likely that local quick decisions will be needed. Another recent management trend is towards 'high involvement work practices', which cover a mixture of human resource initiatives such as teamwork, participation in decision-making and suggestion schemes (Mohr and Zoghi, 2008). Using these practices may well have the effect of altering job characteristics (for example, feedback, task complexity and interdependence) but not explicitly under the label of work/job redesign.

Clegg and Spencer (2007) offer a new analysis of the process of work redesign that reinforces many of the arguments made by Parker *et al.* (2001). This is shown in Figure 8.7. In particular, they stress that individuals often have scope to change the nature of their work for themselves, especially if they are perceived as good and trustworthy performers. Also, they agree with Parker *et al.* (2001) that motivation may not be the only mechanism by which work characteristics affect outcomes.

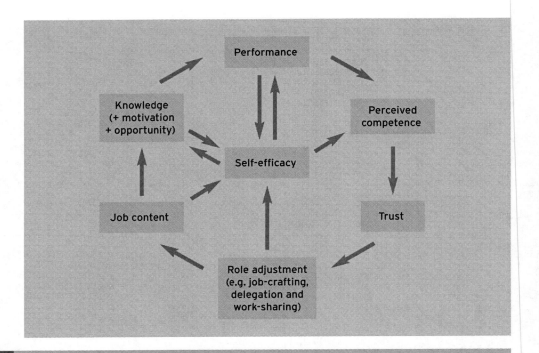

| Figure 8.7 | **A new model of the process of job design**
Source: Reproduced with permission from Clegg and Spencer (2007), p. 324. |

They suggest that the opportunity to acquire new knowledge and experience may also be relevant consequences of work redesign, especially for performance.

Clegg and Spencer (2007) also go beyond Parker *et al.* (2001) in at least two ways. First, they see self-efficacy as a crucial element of the work redesign process. It is either a cause or a consequence (or both) of every element in the process except trust. For example, self-efficacy can be enhanced by changes to job content, and this self-efficacy in itself can improve performance through sheer self-belief (not through motivation, knowledge or anything else). In this respect, Clegg and Spencer are reflecting trends in the goal-setting literature, where self-efficacy is also increasingly seen as a key variable (Locke and Latham, 2002). Second, and unlike Figure 8.6, the process is circular. In Figure 8.6, the arrows are going one way only. In Clegg and Spencer's opinion, it is better to depict the process as circular, feeding on itself, as shown in Figure 8.7. This makes sense, because although it is customary to see motivation, performance, etc. as outcomes at the end of a process, they are highly likely to have their own consequences. These 'outcomes' are therefore *not* the end of a process. Instead, they are part of something ongoing. For example, a consequence of improved work performance is likely to be greater perceived competence, which in turn will increase the trust in a person and give them more scope to make more changes to their job – and so on. One implication of this is that intervention can occur at any point in the process, and may not directly involve the alteration of job characteristics. For example, a well-designed piece of skills training could increase performance, which in turn would increase perceived competence and trust, which could then lead to changes in job content through job crafting.

Integration of motivation theories

There is nowadays general agreement that whilst some motivation theories get more support from research than others, (i) nearly all of them have something to offer, and (ii) in many respects they are compatible, or at least not contradictory. As Latham and Pinder (2005, p. 507) put it:

> the antagonisms among theorists that existed throughout much of the twentieth century have either disappeared or have been minimized. Much of the energy expended on theory destruction has been replaced by theory construction aimed at building upon what is already known.

To illustrate this point, Steel and Konig (2006) have proposed temporal motivation theory (TMT), which is designed to integrate a number of theories (some covered in this chapter and some not), including some from behavioural economics. Locke and Latham (2004) attempt a similar job, mostly using theories covered in this chapter. An adaptation of their model is shown in Figure 8.8.

Locke and Latham argue that most of the links in their model have at least some research to support them, and some of the links have a great deal of research support. It would take an ambitious programme of research to test the entire model, but if the field is to make progress then such endeavours will be necessary. Some aspects

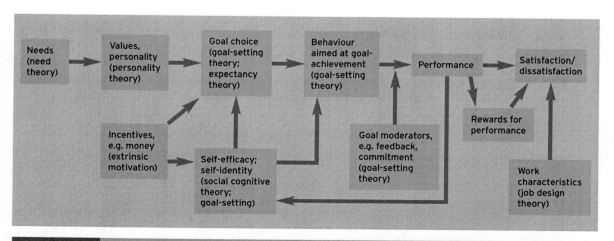

Figure 8.8   **An integrated model of work motivation**
Source: Adapted with permission from Locke and Latham (2004), p. 390.

of their model can be queried. For example, work characteristics are portrayed as affecting satisfaction but not motivation or performance. There is also a surprising lack of feedback loops – one might expect performance, rewards or satisfaction to affect goal choice and goal behaviour as well as self-efficacy. However, it is always possible to question some elements of a model as complex as this. The real challenges are to test it, improve it and use it in work settings.

Summary

Work motivation is a wide-ranging topic of considerable practical and theoretical importance. It concerns the direction, intensity and persistence of work behaviour. Some psychologists view motivation as a product of innate human needs. Others see it as a calculation based on the question 'how can I maximise my gains?' Still others take the view that we are motivated to achieve what we perceive as a fair outcome relative to that experienced by other people. Perhaps the most effective approach to motivation is goal-setting. It is based on the premise that intentions shape actions. If work goals (e.g. target levels of performance) are specific and difficult, and if they are accompanied by feedback on how well one is doing, work performance is usually enhanced. There are some circumstances, however, in which goal-setting in terms of levels of performance is less effective, especially if the task is novel and complex. The most recent analyses of motivation focus on how people allocate their cognitive resources such as attention, thinking and problem-solving to tasks, and how their self-concepts and identities influence their thought processes and are changed by their behaviour. There is also increasing interest in differences between people regarding how and why they are motivated. Another approach that has enjoyed some success is viewing motivation as something that is elicited by the right kinds of task. Here motivation is positioned as a property of the job, not the person. So the task for managers is to make jobs more motivating, not people more motivated. Early versions identified the extent to which jobs had variety and autonomy as being crucial for motivation. More recent theory and practice have broadened the range of work characteristics to include knowledge acquisition and use, the nature and extent of social interactions, and the physical conditions in which work takes place, as well as their impact on a wider range of outcomes for individual and organisation. Overall, motivation theories have done quite a good job of advancing our understanding of behaviour at work. But it is sometimes difficult to be sure about which theory is most helpful in any individual case. Recently, there are signs that an overall theory may be developed which encompasses ideas from many of the existing ones.

Closing Case Study   An unmotivated building inspector

Nobody at Kirraton Council planning department knew what to do about Simon Lucas. Simon was a building inspector. It was his job to approve proposals for small alterations to buildings (such as extensions and loft conversions) which did ▶

not need formal planning permission, and to check that the building work carried out was consistent with the approved plans. The trouble was, he didn't – at least, not often and not quickly. There had been a number of complaints about delays in approval of plans that were Simon's responsibility (each incoming application was assigned to one of the building inspectors for them to deal with independently). He did not seem to keep up to date with the frequent changes in building regulations, which meant that he sometimes made decisions that contradicted them. This had led to some appeals by builders and homeowners, and on three occasions the council had been forced to change its decision.

This was embarrassing and costly, and it was Simon Lucas's fault. He only rarely carried out site inspections, and even more rarely spoke directly with applicants or local residents who could be affected by a planning application. This meant that some of the less scrupulous builders got away with unauthorised changes to plans, and others who genuinely wanted his advice did not get it. This damaged the council's reputation and also increased the changes of a structurally unsound building being constructed.

However, it was difficult to point to specific rules that Simon Lucas was breaking. Council guidance was vague: plans should be dealt with 'within a few weeks'; site inspections conducted 'as and when necessary', and decisions made 'within the spirit', not the letter, of some of the less vital regulations. In any case, it wasn't always clear which of the regulations, if any, could be treated as less vital.

Simon's boss, Katherine Walker, decided that she would check his records and unobtrusively observe him at work – it was an open-plan office, so this was feasible. She discovered that Simon was 26, and had qualified as a building inspector two years earlier. Simon had been recruited by Katherine's predecessor, apparently partly because Simon had 'come up the hard way'. Rather than attending college full time to obtain the necessary qualifications, he had worked for several years as an architect's draughtsman and attended college night classes. In fact, he had been almost the last person to qualify in that way. The building inspectors' professional institute had subsequently decided that part-time study could not develop the necessary skills and knowledge for work as a qualified building inspector. Katherine knew it was true that the part-time route was often seen as 'second class'. She heard it said that this had prevented Simon from getting a job in another area of the country where he very much wanted to live. Few senior building inspectors held the view of Katherine's predecessor that Simon's route into the profession was superior to full-time study. Simon was certainly sensitive about it himself. He frequently mentioned how difficult it had been to combine study with work, but at the same time also remarked that he did not know enough about some things because his training had been 'too basic'.

Katherine observed that Simon often seemed not to be doing very much. He sat at his desk doodling quite a lot. He sometimes had to phone people more than once because he had forgotten to check something the first time. He seemed to have difficulty finding things on his shelves and desk. Sometimes he would give up after only a short and not very systematic search. He also sometimes jumped from one task to another without finishing any of them. As far as she could tell, his home life was not a particular problem. Simon was married, apparently happily, and seemed to participate in many social and leisure activities judging from his lunchtime conversations, not to mention his phone calls to squash clubs, camp sites, etc. during work time! He was especially keen on long-distance walking, and could often be seen at lunchtime reading outdoor magazines and carefully planning his walking club's next expedition. He joked to Katherine that he should have her surname because it described what he liked most.

Simon's job was relatively secure. Ultimately he could be dismissed if he demonstrated continuing incompetence, but he had successfully completed his probationary period (Katherine wasn't sure how). Because Kirraton Council covered only a small area, and because Simon's job was a specialist one, he could not be moved to another town or department. Building inspectors' pay depended on age and length of service, with slightly higher rates for those with a relevant college degree. Outstanding performance could only be rewarded with promotion, and this was extremely unlikely for anyone with less than 10 years' service. Katherine established that Simon would like promotion because of the extra money it would bring rather than the status, but he correctly perceived that he had virtually no chance of achieving it. Apart from the fact he had been at Kirraton for a relatively short time, he thought he was not scoring very well on Katherine's recently implemented building inspector performance criteria of no lost appeals, high client satisfaction, at least 15 complete projects per month, and acknowledgement of receipt of plans within four working days. This was bad for him, and also bad for the department as a whole because it affected its overall performance statistics.

The other four building inspectors were quite a close-knit group of building sciences graduates who had worked together for several years before Simon's arrival. Simon didn't really see himself as a member of the group, preferring instead to emphasise how he, unlike them, was 'on the same wavelength' as local people. He had found it hard to establish a relationship with them, and now it was even harder because they felt his apparently poor performance reflected badly on them all. They did not involve him much in their activities, nor did they appear to respect him. Simon was afraid that the others thought he wasn't doing his job properly and Katherine suspected that secretly he agreed with them. Katherine knew something had to be done, but what, and how?

Suggested exercises

1   Review the motivation theories discussed in this chapter. How would each one describe and explain the problems with Simon Lucas's motivation?

2   To what extent does each theory provide guidance to Katherine Walker about what she should do? What actions would they recommend?

3   Apply concepts from the job redesign literature to Simon's job. Do they explain why he is not motivated?

Test your learning

Short-answer questions

1 Describe the key features of the theory X and theory Y 'common-sense' views of motivation.

2 Suggest three ways in which Maslow's hierarchy of needs theory might helpfully be amended.

3 List five features of the 'self-actualising' person.

4 What are the components of the motivation to manage?

5 Define valence, instrumentality and expectancy. According to Vroom, how do they combine to determine motivation?

6 Name and define three kinds of perceived justice at work.

7 Draw a simple diagram that shows the key elements of goal-setting.

8 What are the key differences between performance goal orientation and learning goal orientation?

9 Name and define the five types of motivation suggested by Leonard *et al.* (1999).

10 Name and define four types of motivation that vary along the extrinsic–intrinsic continuum.

11 Draw a diagram which represents the main features of the job characteristics model (JCM).

12 Suggest three limitations of the JCM as a framework for job redesign.

13 Describe five characteristics of jobs not in the JCM that have been identified as being important in work redesign.

14 Briefly outline two ways in which Clegg and Spencer's (2007) model of work redesign is different from earlier ones.

Suggested assignments

1 Examine the usefulness of need theories in understanding and predicting behaviour at work.

2 In what ways, if any, do academic theories of motivation improve upon so-called 'common sense'?

3 It is often claimed that goal-setting is a theory of motivation which works. Examine whether it works better in some circumstances than others.

4 Examine the extent to which theories of motivation have or have not taken into account people's conscious sense of their own identity.

5   When and how is pay a motivator?

6   Discuss this statement: 'The job characteristics model was a useful start as a guide to how to redesign jobs, but it was no more than a start'.

7   To what extent does Locke and Latham's (2004) attempt to provide an integrated theory of motivation do justice to the earlier theories?

Relevant websites

There are very many sites which describe training courses in motivational techniques (for managing self or others) and provide very brief accounts of some well-known motivation theories, usually the oldest and most straightforward ones. Here are a few examples:

http://www.bizhelp24.com/personal_development/motivation_theory_importance.shtml is part of a managers' self-help site. This particular item gives prominence to Herzberg's theory. It also encourages managers to take on responsibility for the motivation of the people who work for them.

A site with a lot of interesting material, including an original article by Maslow, is http://www.themanager.org/Knowledgebase/HR/Motivation.htm. This is another managers' self-help resource site.

http://changingminds.org/explanations/theories/a_motivation.htm gives an index of different theories of motivation. Clicking on a theory brings you a little more information about it.

An easy-to-understand account of the key concepts and practical uses of goal-setting can be found at http://www.mindtools.com/pages/article/newHTE_87.htm.

 For further self-test material and relevant, annotated weblinks please visit the website at **www.pearsoned.co.uk/workpsych**

Suggested further reading

Full details for all references are given in the list at the end of this book.

1   Maureen Ambrose and Carol Kulik (1999) provide a good account of how various motivation theories have developed (and in some cases emerged) in recent years. It is quite a technical article, but worth the effort of reading carefully, because it presents both the fundamentals of theories and the details of how they are being extended and tested.

2   Gary Latham's book *Work Motivation* published in 2007 by Sage presents an historical, theoretical and practical analysis of work motivation. If this chapter has interested you, then Latham's book will be a real treat.

3   Ed Locke and Gary Latham's 2004 article attempts to specify an integrated theory of motivation. It is quite heavy going but well-written nevertheless, and a good way of expanding both your knowledge of theories and your understanding of how they might fit together.

Chapter 9

Managing marketing

Aim

To explain the benefits that all organisations gain if they give a prominent role to marketing, and how they can organise the activity.

Objectives

By the end of your work on this chapter you should be able to outline the concepts below in your own terms and:

1 Compare and contrast marketing with alternative organisational orientations

2 Describe the benefits to any organisation of adopting a marketing orientation

3 Explain why marketing is an information-intensive activity

4 Identify the responsibilities of the marketing manager

5 Explain market segmentation and the practice of selecting a target market

6 Describe the components of the marketing mix

7 Explain what is meant by product positioning

Key terms

This chapter introduces the following ideas:

marketing
marketing orientation
consumer
consumer centred
marketing environment
marketing information system
market segmentation
target market
marketing mix
product life cycle

*Each is a term defined within the text, as well as
in the Glossary at the end of the book.*

Manchester United FC www.manutd.com

With over 50 million fans across the globe, Manchester United Football Club (MU) is one of the best-known soccer clubs. Founded in 1878, it rose to prominence in the early 1950s. Since then the club has never been out of the sports headlines, hiring a series of almost legendary managers (including Sir Matt Busby and Sir Alex Ferguson) and buying or developing world-recognised players (including David Beckham, Ruud van Nistelrooy and Wayne Rooney).

In May 2005 the club was taken over in a £790 million bid by American sports tycoon Malcolm Glazer in a deal that was heavily financed by debt. The 2006 annual turnover was £173 million, generated from a wide range of football-related businesses (gate and TV revenues, sports clothes, etc.) and brand-related activities (MUTV, mobiles, travel, finance). Manchester United Football Club is only a part of worldwide operations: the holding company (Manchester United) owns MU, Manchester United Catering (Agency Company) and Manchester United Interactive. MUTV, the club's official channel, is a joint venture between Manchester United, Granada and BSkyB.

The club's ambition is to be the most successful team in football. Its business strategy is to do this by having the football and commercial operations work hand in hand, both in existing and new domestic markets and in the potential markets represented by the club's global fan base, especially Asia. The marketing strategy is built on maintaining success on the field and leveraging global brand awareness through new products and partnered services designed to appeal to MU's worldwide fans. A substantial partner is Nike, whose development and marketing channels are used to generate new value from the MU trademarks (for example, replica kits) by supplying the millions of MU fans in the United Kingdom and Asia.

PA Photos: Kin Cheung/AP.

MU attempts to control and develop its own routes to market for media rights (for example, MUTV), thereby exploiting the club's own performance and reputation rather than relying on the collective appeal of competition football. The management believes this enhances the ability to deliver branded services to customers anywhere in the world. They rely strongly on IT-based CRM (customer relationship management) technology to convert fans into customers.

Source: Based on material from Butterworth Heinemann Case 0181, *Manchester United and British Soccer: Beautiful Game, Brutal Industry*; 'Can football be saved?', *Business Week*, 19 July 2004; published Manchester United material.

Case questions 9.1

- Consider the marketing implications of MU's activities. What is it offering to customers?
- What groups would MU see as competitors? Are they simply other successful football clubs?
- How might MU improve its marketing?

Activity 9.1   Describing marketing

Before reading this chapter, write some notes on what you understand 'marketing' to be.

Think of some recent purchases, and consider the different ways in which you came across marketing before, during or after your purchase.

Keep your notes safe as you will use them again at the end of the chapter.

9.1   Introduction

Manchester United is very successful in raising awareness and reputation amongst fans and other customer groups. Its strategy revolves around the loyalty and trust that customers have in the club and the MU brand. There is a question as to what product or service customers think they are getting when they purchase an MU product. Different groups of consumers attribute differing benefits to the MU brand. An MU football fan might buy a season ticket to fulfil a psychological need to be part of a group with a common purpose, while a person with no interest in football might use an MU mobile phone because they trust the product, based on the MU reputation.

How should MU management manage the brand in these complex and sometimes unrelated markets? Might it be in the interests of the PLC to position the brand away from direct success on the football field, as that success cannot be guaranteed and the brand could be contaminated by a disaster (such as demotion from the Premier League)? How should MU promote itself? Standard advertising campaigns – based on the product's advantages over the competitor's offerings – are inappropriate.

Manchester United depends on good **marketing**. Originally conceived as a local football team to keep working men occupied and interested on Saturday afternoons, it is now a worldwide business managed by trained business managers rather than by retired football players. MU marketing managers are aware that they are satisfying psychological needs: when fans buy replica MU football jerseys as T-shirts, they are not keeping themselves warm and dry – they are making indirect statements about their personality. In a highly differentiated market such as this, buyers are not as price sensitive as they are in commodity markets. A football shirt which costs less than £2 to make and deliver can sell for up to £40.

All organisations face the challenge of understanding what customers want, and ensuring that they can meet those expectations. Managers of profitable firms of any size will usually attribute much of their success to marketing; marketing is often closely tied to the business strategy. IKEA, the Swedish furniture retailer, has found and refined a formula that appeals to its target market. In 40 years it has grown from a single store to a business with over 230 outlets in 35 countries. Virgin Direct, the financial services joint venture with Norwich Union, has become a major player. Successful not-for-profit organisations such as Oxfam and the Royal Society for the Protection of Birds also demonstrate the benefits of understanding a market and communicating with it effectively. All organisations need to give value for money, and so need to be aware of their customers, sensitive to changing needs and organised to deliver those needs.

The chapter opens by considering a marketing orientation, identifying the benefits of the concept to all organisations, and how they can make it the focus of their activities. It then discusses the management of marketing information and the roles of marketing management. It concludes with an explanation of the marketing mix and brand management.

Marketing is a management process that identifies, anticipates and supplies consumer requirements efficiently and effectively.

9.2   What is marketing?

People often confuse marketing with a range of sales techniques such as:

- glossy brochures;
- the latest promotional offer at a supermarket;
- sponsorship of popular television programmes by branded products, such as Toyota's relationship with Channel 4's weekend youth programming;
- endorsement of products or services by celebrity names, such as Gary Lineker (broadcaster and former England football captain) advertising Walker's crisps, or Gordon Ramsay (three-star Michelin chef and TV presenter) promoting Victoria Wine;
- e-mail messages from companies promoting travel offers or new books.

These techniques illustrate the way in which marketers try to sell products or services – but there is more to marketing than promotion. All definitions of marketing emphasise the need to identify and satisfy customer requirements. Kotler and Keller (2006) define it as 'a social and managerial process by which individuals and groups obtain what they need and want through creating and exchanging products and value with others'. Peter Drucker (1999a) places the activity even more firmly at the centre of business:

> Because the purpose of business is to create and keep customers, it has only two central functions – marketing and innovation. The basic function of marketing is to attract and retain customers at a profit.

These definitions imply that marketing refers both to a marketing function within the organisation and to a more deeply embedded marketing orientation that shapes other activities of the organisation. The former view that the marketing was done by marketing people is not suitable for today's competitive environment. As David Packard, co-founder of Hewlett-Packard, said: 'Marketing is too important to be left to the marketing department', i.e. the entire organisation should be marketing the company, from the company receptionist as 'Director of First Impressions' to the chief executive as 'Director of Shareholder Interests'.

Consumer marketing and industrial marketing

There are two categories of organisational marketing: (a) consumer marketing, which concerns creating and delivering products to satisfy consumers, and (b) industrial or business-to-business (B2B) marketing, which aims to satisfy the needs of businesses. The marketing concept is similar for both but this chapter is mainly concerned with consumer marketing.

A marketing orientation

Most commercial organisations have a marketing function – usually a group of people who focus on activities such as market research, competitor analysis, product strategy or promotion. Those which recognise the full significance of marketing incorporate it deeply in the organisation, adopting not only a marketing function but a **marketing orientation**. They concentrate their activities on the market and the **consumer**, being '**consumer centred**' or 'consumer driven'.

Levi have positioned themselves as a successful manufacturer of fashion clothing by making marketing a central organisational activity. With products like Levi's jeans, they

Marketing orientation is an organisational orientation that believes success is most effectively achieved by satisfying consumer demands.

Consumers are individuals, households, organisations, institutions, resellers and governments that purchase the products offered by other organisations.

Consumer-centred organisation is focused upon, and structured around, identifying and satisfying the demands of its consumers.

respond to the changing needs, wants and demands of consumers by investing in product development and marketing communications. They watch the customers to see how their clothes are worn: studies like this resulted in the popular hipster jeans, when marketers noticed that female jeans wearers were pulling the jeans down on their hips and responded with a line of products cut this way.

Charities such as Oxfam (**www.oxfam.co.uk**), Greenpeace (**www.greenpeace.com**) and Médecins sans Frontières (**www.msf.org**) pay attention to the interests of their supporters. As well as promoting established lines of work, they survey their donors to ensure an acceptable match between the charity's campaigns and the issues that matter to those who donate the funds. Adopting a customer-focused orientation enables them to continue achieving their goals (Kottasz, 2004).

---

management in practice Financial services become consumer centred

Prior to the 1980s, bank and financial service providers were not noted for their customer friendliness. Customers regarded them as organisations that almost had to be persuaded to carry out their core business, such as providing a loan. Today's financial services industry is an aggressive and competitive market. Faced with intense competition, encouraged by deregulation and the demutualisation of many building societies, most high street retail banks adopted a more consumer-centred approach. Rather than having to be persuaded to make loans, they trumpet the advantages of taking out a loan with them and listen to the (often changing) needs of their consumers. By investing in new products and widening access to their services through telephone and Internet banking, organisations such as the Co-operative Bank (**www.co-operativebank.co.uk**) have successfully responded to the new business and marketing environment and the competition that comes with it.

---

management in practice Marketing and the voluntary sector

Many staff and volunteers in charities are still uncomfortable with the idea that they are in marketing – preferring to see themselves as helpers or carers. Yet as Keaveney and Kaufmann (2001) say:

> donors, local authorities, opinion formers, the media, all have the choice of whether or not to support a particular charity. They also, through exercising that choice ... can change parts of what the charity does. They make up the markets within which the charity operates. Without knowledge and understanding of those markets, the charity, quite simply, will fail. This does not mean charities operate in a value-free vacuum; rather that by knowing themselves and their mission, and by knowing the markets they exist to serve or work in, charities can match their activities to external needs and make sure that they achieve as much as possible for their beneficiaries. (p. 2)

Source: Keaveney and Kaufmann (2001).

Alternative orientations

Table 9.1 summarises these alternative orientations.

Table 9.1

Alternative
organisational
orientations

Organisational orientation	Focus	Benefit	Disadvantage
Product	Product features	High-quality products	Research may not have identified demand for the product and it may not sell
Production	Production	Low costs	Costs determine price and production, not consumer demands. Production may not match consumer demand
Sales	Turnover and shifting product	Sales targets met; good for cash flow in the short term	High-pressure sales techniques may meet current targets but lose future ones if users find product unsatisfactory
Marketing	Continually on consumers and consumer demands	Product offering determined by consumer demands; organisational goals achieved	Initial investment in becoming consumer centred

Source: Based on Lancaster *et al.* (2002); Dibb *et al.* (2006); Jobber (2007).

Product orientation

Organisations operating with a product orientation focus on their technological strengths and expertise. They stress the products and product features that these strengths allow them to make. They pay less attention to the demands of the market and can often find themselves in a position similar to that of the De Lorean car:

> This stainless steel car was built in Northern Ireland with government grants and Lotus expertise. Targeted for the American market, it received free publicity from its appearance in the film *Back to the Future*. When the manufacturers introduced the car to the market they found that there was no demand. Nobody wanted to buy the car. (*Car Magazine*, supplement, April 1997)

While a product orientation is focused on products for which there may or may not be demand, a marketing orientation is focused on identifying consumer demands for particular products.

Production orientation

The production orientation holds that consumers will buy products that are highly available and low cost. Therefore, an organisation operating under the production orientation uses production efficiency and cost of materials to determine the quantity and price of goods to be produced. The production orientation focuses on efficiency and costs; it is relevant when the market has high growth prospects and the firm can benefit from economies of scale.

Sales or selling orientation

An organisation operating under the sales orientation aims to shift as much of a product as it can as quickly as possible. Levitt (1960) provides a clear understanding of the differences between selling and marketing philosophies:

Selling focuses on the needs of the seller; marketing on the needs of the buyer. Selling is a pre-occupation with the seller's need to convert his product into cash; marketing with the idea of satisfying the needs of the consumer by means of the product and the whole cluster of things associated with creating, delivering and finally consuming it.

As Kotler and Keller (2006) point out, the selling concept is typically practised with *unsought* goods, those that consumers do not normally think of buying, such as encyclopedias.

Marketing orientation

Putting the consumer at the beginning rather than the end of the production–consumption cycle enables organisations to discover what consumers want. They can then decide how best to use the strengths of the organisation to *return* to the marketplace with a product for which a demand exists. They use market information about demand and the price that consumers are prepared to pay to determine how much to produce and what production costs must be to offer a price acceptable to consumers. While the sales orientation focuses on shifting products, the marketing orientation focuses on satisfying consumers and building mutually satisfying relationships. To paraphrase Kotler and Keller (2006), the marketing concept takes an *outside-in* perspective rather than the *inside-out* perspective of the selling concept.

Satisfying latent need

Taking the marketing approach means meeting the consumers' needs. In some instances, consumers will not be aware of the usefulness or value of a product which they do not know about or that has not been brought to market. Demand that is waiting to happen is called latent demand. Examples of widely used products that satisfy a formerly latent demand include mobile phones, electric toothbrushes and organic foodstuffs.

Activity 9.2   Identifying consumers

A marketing orientation suggests that organisational success is best achieved by focusing on the consumer. Identify each of the following organisations' consumers and suggest the benefits that a focus on their consumers will bring to each organisation: Microsoft, easyJet (www.easyjet.com), Sainsbury's (www.sainsburys.co.uk), and Cancer Research UK (www.cancerresearchuk.org).

Benefits of a marketing orientation

Marketers assert that the most effective way of achieving organisational objectives is through consumer satisfaction. Organisations with a marketing philosophy still have to assess product features, efficient levels of production and sales targets (see the study by Shaw *et al.*, 2004 of the relationship between marketers and engineers in German and UK organisations), but decisions about these matters are not the focus of organisational activities. Instead, consumer demands determine product development, levels of production and sales targets.

Adopting a marketing orientation ensures that the whole organisation commits to achieving organisational goals by *continually* satisfying consumer demands. Aware of this objective and their potential contribution, functional areas cooperate and coordinate their activities towards a common goal – for a recent comparative study of two fashion retailers, see Newman and Patel (2004). Organisations such as Manchester United, Linn Products (see Chapter 8) and Sony Ericsson anticipate changing demands and are able to develop new products to meet them.

Apple   www.apple.com/uk

management in practice

With its share price tripling in 2004, doubling in 2005, and up 16 per cent in 2006, Apple is doing well. There appear to be two main drivers of its current success. First, the success of its iPod, which has sold over 90 million units since 2001: second, the revival of its personal computer business with the success of its laptops and desktops. Apple demonstrates a marketing orientation by continually satisfying customer demands.

The iPod is now in its fifth generation and has been improved every year since release, becoming smaller and more powerful. There are now different iPods to meet personal requirements: Shuffle, for those who seek the smallest and lightest music player; Nano, for those looking for style; and the main iPod, which has huge memory capacity (up to 80G) and can carry photos and video. Combined with this is the Apple Online Music Store that allows consumers to buy music legally online as opposed to illegal file sharing; as well as free iTunes that allow both Mac and PC users to control and play their music from their computer.

Apple has successfully responded to consumer demands for a seamless digital music experience before its rivals, giving it very high market share (up to 80 per cent of the UK market alone).

Sources: Company website; www.macobserver.com.

By identifying and monitoring consumer demands, marketing-oriented organisations are able to respond to these demands and ensure that the products they offer satisfy consumers. Above all else, the adoption of the marketing orientation offers stability in the marketplace (Figure 9.1).

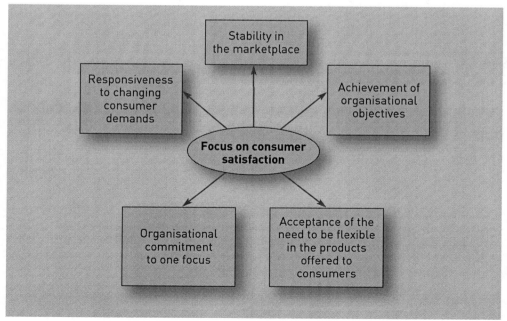

Figure 9.1

Benefits of marketing as an organisational orientation

This concept has been extended to include network marketing, which recognises a web of interdependencies between firms. While relationship marketing depends on managing relationships with customers, network marketing recognises that meeting their needs depends on a wider range of stakeholders – such as raw materials suppliers or delivery companies. Manchester United is an example of multiple stakeholders and relationship marketing combining to create network marketing.

---

key ideas   **Transactional marketing and relationship marketing**

Gronroos (2000) distinguishes between transactional marketing and relationship marketing. To ensure a stable position many organisations have replaced their focus on transactions (exchange of value, e.g. a purchase) with one that seeks to develop long-term relationships with their consumers. They argue that a focus on one-off transactions encourages organisations to concentrate on short-term profit maximisation and to pay less attention to their long-term position. Organisations that move towards a relational focus have a better understanding of consumer needs. They concentrate on developing a 'long-term, continuous series of transactions' that help them maintain stability in the market and achieve their objectives in the long term.

Others (such as Zolkiewski, 2004) argue that relationship marketing is not suitable for all organisations, and that not all long-term relationships are as beneficial or necessary as advocates of this approach claim.

---

management in practice   **Ted Baker**   www.tedbaker.co.uk

One of the fast-growing 'lifestyle' brands in the United Kingdom, Ted Baker offers stylish men's and women's wear and accessories. To build relations with its customers the company has heavily promoted its store card, offering discounts on purchases and invitations to evening events launching its new collections. Enjoying rapid growth since its formation in 1987 as a specialist shirt shop in Glasgow, the strategy appears to be working: it now has outlets all over the United Kingdom and has expanded into over ten countries. By keeping in touch with customers, their preferences and where they live, the firm is able to tailor its offerings more exactly. It also encourages them to be part of the Ted 'family' through regular events.

Source: Company website; other sources.

9.3   What types of organisation can use marketing?

The benefits offered by the marketing orientation apply to all types of organisations, including charities, churches and sports teams. Writing about the Health Service, Moutinho (1995) states:

> the present day marketing concept views marketing as a social process ... [to identify] consumer needs and satisfy them through integrated marketing activities ... Marketing thinking will lead to a better understanding of the needs of different client segments; to a more careful shaping and launching of new services; to a pruning of weak services; to more flexible pricing approaches; and to higher levels of patient satisfaction.

Some health care organisations now apply marketing to a broader set of problems by asking questions such as:

- Where should we locate a clinic or an ambulatory care unit?
- How can we estimate whether a new service will draw enough patients?
- What should we do with a maternity wing that is only 20 per cent occupied?
- How can we attract more consumers to preventive care services such as annual medical check-ups and cancer-screening programmes?

Church marketing www.churchmarketing.com

management in practice

Started in 1993, John Manlove's Church Marketing consultancy aims to offer churches a clear mission, vision, values and strategy statement. The company uses its experience in advertising and transfers many of the terms used in marketing to one not associated with business terms. On brand development for example, JMCM offers to 'bring essential information and ideas to the task of translating the church's identity and direction into a visual brand for the church's communication media'.

Source: Company website.

Activity 9.3 Evaluating market research

- What kind of information would a firm involved in church marketing seek to obtain? How would it go about doing this and what are the cost implications?
- Can you identify another social care organisation that could use market research to assist it?

Organisations with social or charitable aims are beginning to take a marketing orientation, including those raising awareness of the dangers of smoking, increasing charitable donations and promoting the benefits of an active lifestyle. Not-for-profit organisations focus on understanding the opinions, perceptions and attitudes of people whose opinions, attitudes or behaviours they want to change, or whose support they seek.

Andreasen and Kotler (2002) have expressed the not-for-profit transaction in terms of *favourable exchange*, where one party (the marketing organisation) can induce behaviour changes in another (equivalent to the consumer) by working on the assumption that people behave in ways that they believe will leave them better off than the alternatives. The authors believe that in attempting to understand consumer behaviour it is critical to differentiate between the exchange as a process and the exchange as an outcome. The latter is simply a transaction. The management of the exchange *process* is marketing.

A marketing orientation helps the homeless

management in practice

The Big Issue was established to tackle the problem of homelessness in a progressive and entrepreneurial manner. Rather than campaigning to raise funding and donations that could be used to address homelessness, *The Big Issue* sought to challenge conventions. By adopting a marketing orientation *The Big Issue* has successfully approached the challenge of homelessness in a novel and unique manner: by developing a new product, a street magazine that homeless vendors sell to the public, *The Big Issue* has addressed several objectives. Vendors earn money from the magazines they ▶

sell, which highlights the extent of homelessness; the public purchase an informative magazine and also support a social cause. Using the Andreasen and Kotler model, managing the exchange process is the main task. The newspaper sale transaction is almost incidental in terms of the consumer benefits. The exchange process in contrast is to be a complex mix of a desire to reduce homelessness, a desire to help the individual vendor, assuaging of guilt at the position of someone worse off, or even the reduction of mild fear at perceived aggressive selling.

9.4   Creating a marketing orientation

Michaels warned back in 1982 that: 'No one person, system, or technique will make a company marketing orientated' and stresses that a marketing orientation cannot be achieved overnight (Michaels, 1982). Advising on the implementation of a marketing orientation, he emphasises the following requirements:

- **Investment by top management** Before marketing can be instilled throughout the whole organisation, senior managers must commit themselves to the marketing orientation or other managers will not implement the necessary changes.
- **Injection of outside talent** Managements that successfully implement a marketing orientation have brought in new personnel. These have helped to educate other staff about the possible benefits of the new orientation.
- **A clear sense of direction** As with any change, it is essential that management takes a planned approach to its implementation. It must set objectives and timescales to guide the introduction.

Kotler and Keller (2006) continue to stress the importance of structuring the organisation to focus on the consumer. Managers need to educate themselves and their staff about the idea and how it may support long-lasting success in the marketplace. This applies to all levels and functions who must share a common commitment if they are to work together in the interests of the consumers. Without the support of top management, the focus on consumer satisfaction advocated by the marketing orientation will not become the guiding orientation for organisational decisions.

Manchester United – the case continues   CASE STUDY
www.manutd.com

One of the challenges facing Manchester United is the best organisational marketing structure to design and the internal culture to induce in managing its huge operation. At corporate level, the Glazer family owns football-related and non-football-related businesses and is involved with various joint ventures in TV, financial services and mobile phones. At business and product levels, management have to deal directly with their target segments. Promotional campaigns for individual products have to be sensitive to the image of sister MU products. Hoarding adverts of a noisy football crowd having a good time will be exciting to other potential fans but could be off-putting for someone who has to produce their MU credit card at local stores.

Preserving the perceived value of the brand is also important: the replica jersey product manager will not want stores such as Tesco to sell them at a discount. This raises important questions of channel management and relationship with suppliers whose strategy might be more cost focused than differentiated. In 2006

MU signed a record deal for £56 million over four years with the American Investment Group (AIG) to be their shirt sponsor. This represents a substantial increase from their previous £9 million a year tie-in with Vodafone, who were able to withdraw from their contract with MU after the Glazer takeover.

The structure of the organisation may have to change to allow all departments to become focused on and work together for the achievement of consumer satisfaction. Compare Figures 9.2 and 9.3. Figure 9.2 shows marketing as an important function within

Source: Adapted from Kotler (2003).

Figure 9.2
Marketing as an important function

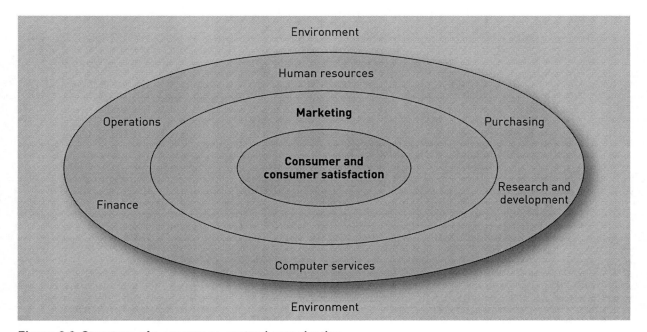

Figure 9.3 Structure of a consumer-centred organisation
Source: Adapted from Kotler (2003).

the organisation and Figure 9.3 is the structure required if an organisation is to become consumer centred. Such restructuring includes developing systems and procedures to collect, analyse and distribute data about the changing demands of consumers. It also requires that achieving organisational objectives through consumer satisfaction becomes the basis of decisions. An important area of organisational study is the management of the boundaries between marketing and the other functional areas, due to differences in culture. Tension can arise, for example, between the R&D team and the marketing team when new products need to be rapidly modified at concept stage to meet changing customer demands. Shortened product life cycles are a feature of today's markets, which exacerbates internal tensions and highlights the need for a flexible structure and a communicative culture.

9.5   Managing the marketing function

The effective implementation of a marketing orientation requires that marketing has the central position displayed in Figure 9.3. The continual satisfaction of changing consumer demands relies upon distributing information about these throughout the organisation. For this reason, marketing professionals claim that marketing requires a central position, in which the marketing department links the consumer and the enterprise. It monitors changes in consumer demands and alerts other people to changes in the environment that may require a response. It is the responsibility of marketing to research the marketplace and decide which consumer demands the organisation can satisfy most effectively. That decision, and the marketing tools to use, are the responsibility of the marketing manager.

In common with other functional area managers, the marketing manager gathers information to plan direction, creates a marketing organisation, leads staff and other players and controls the activity by evaluating results and taking corrective action. Figure 9.4 outlines these activities.

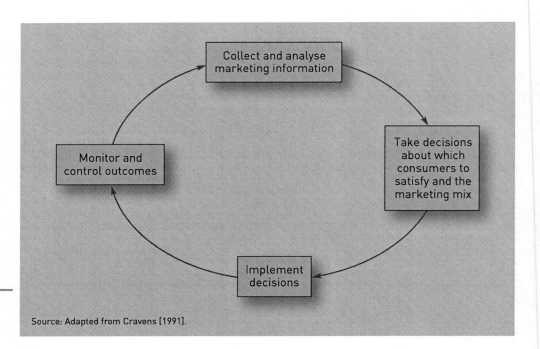

Figure 9.4

The marketing management process

Source: Adapted from Cravens [1991].

The figure shows that the marketing function is responsible for (a) identifying those consumers whose demands the organisation can satisfy most effectively, and (b) selecting the marketing mix that will satisfy consumer demands and succeed in achieving organisational objectives.

Case questions 9.2

- What customer demands were Manchester United seeking to satisfy at the time of the case study?
- What other demands does the business have to satisfy?
- What marketing tools are mentioned in the case?
- What management structure do you think would suit (a) the Glazers and (b) the football club?

In order to take these decisions, managers need information about consumer demands, competitor strategies and changes in the **marketing environment** (Armstrong and Kotler, 2006) that are likely to impact upon consumer demands. The marketing environment contains micro and macro components. The micro-environment is that part of an organisation's marketing environment to which it is close and within which it directly operates. Each organisation will have a micro-environment unique and specific to it; as shown in Figure 9.5, it comprises the stakeholders with which the organisation regularly interacts, including employees, suppliers, distributors, consumers, competitors and publics such as pressure groups and the general public. All organisations, including small and medium-sized enterprises, have some control over changes in their micro-environment and the likely impact these will have upon their marketing activities.

The macro component of an organisation's marketing environment is more remote and will be similar for all those in the same industry. Organisations have little direct influence over their macro-environment, which consists of the PESTEL factors outlined in Chapter 3 – repeated in Figure 9.6.

The **marketing environment** consists of the actors and forces outside marketing that affect the marketing manager's ability to develop and maintain successful relationships with its target consumers.

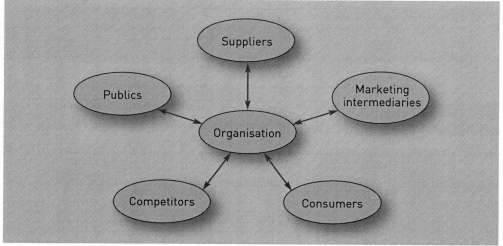

Figure 9.5

The micro-environment

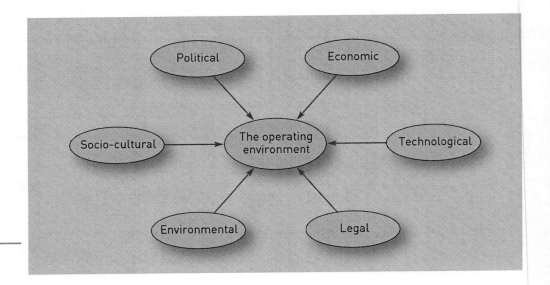

Figure 9.6

The macro-environment

Such frameworks are useful in identifying whether changes in the environment will have a positive or negative impact on the marketing activities of an organisation. This is because they can be useful in identifying both the *opportunities present in the environment*, such as those presented to multimedia organisations by developments in e-commerce, as well as *threats*, such as the impact of a natural disaster on a country's tourism industry.

Providing environmental information regularly makes marketing an *information-intensive activity*. Information about the marketing environment is used to assist the marketing manager in taking decisions about consumers' preferred products and distribution outlets. Other functional areas will also use marketing information – such as manufacturing to estimate production requirements, and finance to estimate the working capital needed to support a higher demand.

9.6   Marketing as an information-intensive activity

A **marketing information system** is the systematic process for the collection, analysis and distribution of marketing information.

To monitor and anticipate changes in the marketing environment, marketing-oriented organisations use systematic procedures for collecting and analysing information about that environment. This is often called the **marketing information system**.

Marketing information systems

To keep in touch, marketing managers need a marketing information system to provide accurate and up-to-date information. They need to have systematic processes to collect, analyse and distribute information about the marketing environment throughout the organisation. Cannon (1996) defines such a system as:

> The organised arrangement of people, machines and procedures set up to ensure that all relevant and usable information required by marketing management reaches them at a time and in a form to help them with effective decision making.

Figure 9.7 details the typical component parts of such a system.

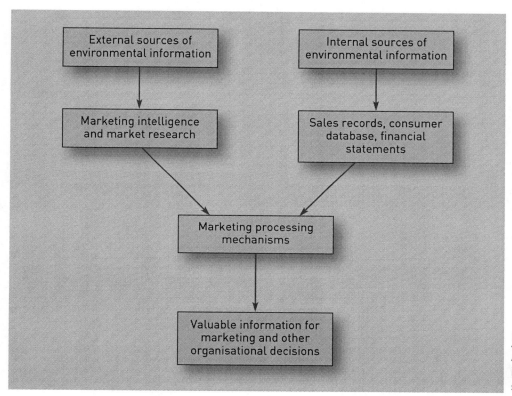

Figure 9.7

A marketing information system

A marketing information system contains internal and external sources of data and mechanisms to analyse and interpret the data. As Chapter 12 explains, data is not the same as information. Data in itself has no meaning. A company may discover that in December 2004, 59 per cent of a sample of people were aware of their product. In itself that has no value – but it does become useful information if it can be compared with similar data from earlier or later periods or with competing products. Management may then see a trend, and be able to decide if it needs to act. Table 9.2 summarises the main sources of marketing information.

Table 9.2

Sources of marketing information

Source	Description and examples
Internal records	Size and regularity of orders, cost of each level of production, customer complaints, quality statistics
Marketing intelligence	Data on micro- and macro-environments. Usually secondary data from newspapers, trade associations and industry reports. Informal sources from staff or customers are also valuable guides to, for example, competitor plans
Market research	Involves five stages: 1 specifying information required (how many people with X income, living in place Y, are aware of product Z?) 2 developing hypotheses (is awareness higher or lower in area B where the product has been advertised than in C?) 3 collecting quantitative or qualitative data to refute or confirm 4 analysing the data and 5 presenting the results

management in practice   Information on food shopping habits

All major supermarkets have for a long time monitored activity at point of sale so that they can order supplies close to when they will be needed. Loyalty cards keep a record of the frequency, value and type of food shopping bought by individuals, and small incentives reward customers for their store loyalty. Marketing departments use (a) the application form information (address, income bracket, family size, etc.) and (b) the regular information about buying patterns. This helps them to manage their inventory and their marketing communications, such as on sales promotions. There is more information on Tesco in the Part 6 case.

Figure 9.8 shows the processes involved in a market research project.

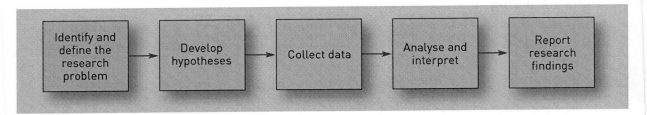

Figure 9.8 The market research process

Case question 9.3

● Suppose that Manchester United is approached by a snack food company wishing to manufacture 'Man U' breakfast bars for children and young people to have as snacks or in school lunch boxes. What type of market research would you recommend using?

9.7 Understanding the consumer – buyer behaviour

The marketing information system provides information on the marketing environment. The results of market research projects indicate solutions to precise marketing questions. Organisations with a marketing orientation also want to understand how customers decide to buy something.

Buyer behaviour research (Howard and Sheth, 1969; Engel *et al.*, 1978) has identified that consumers work through the series of decisions shown in Figure 9.9.

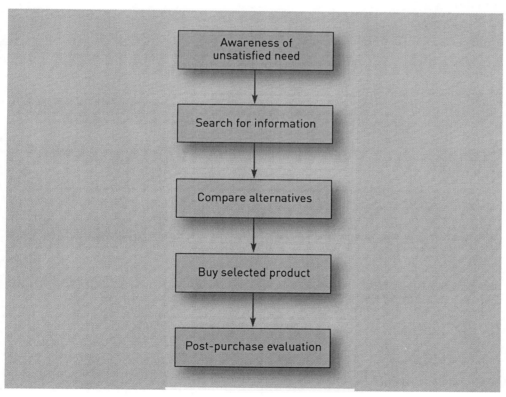

Figure 9.9

A model of consumer buying behaviour

Awareness of unsatisfied need

Consumers become aware of a need that they want to satisfy in two ways. The first is self-discovery. Stomach rumbles or a dry throat are physical signals that you are hungry and thirsty and need to satisfy these feelings. Consumers also become aware of an unsatisfied need by receiving some marketing communication from an organisation. For example, until 3M made you aware of 'Post-It pads' did you identify the need to have a small piece of paper on which you could write messages and stick to a surface? This is an example of latent need referred to earlier.

Theories of human motivation described in Chapter 15 give marketing managers guidance on the needs of potential customers. They use this to ensure that the product or service is helping consumers satisfy a need – for status, recognition, a sense of achievement and so on.

Search for information

Aware of a need, consumers search for information that will help them decide which product to buy. Many sources provide this information – personal experience is one powerful source; that of family and friends is another. A third source of information is from organisations providing products that may satisfy the need – by advertisements and other promotional activities. The information source at this stage in the buying process has great influence on the purchase decision. The poor service to a friend at a restaurant will usually dissuade a potential customer.

Activity 9.6 Reflecting on consumer information

Select from one of the following expensive products: a DVD player, a mountain bike, a round-the-world air ticket. For your selected product describe the type of information you would want before deciding which brand to buy, and why. Which of your information categories do you think would be useful for the marketing manager of that product?

The time spent on this stage of the consumer buying process depends on the type of product that consumers believe will satisfy their identified need. Buying some products is more risky than others, and customers usually seek more information on them to reduce the risk. The degree of risk depends on factors such as expense, effect on self-image and knowledge of the product. Self-image (or 'psychological closeness') is very important in some purchases such as a car or fashion clothing – or in whether to give to charity (Kottasz, 2004).

Compare alternatives

The more information a consumer has collected, the longer he or she will spend comparing different products against set criteria. For a new television, the main criteria may be brand name, surround sound, Internet access, wide screen and a reasonable price. Note that for a television, psychological closeness is less likely to be a factor. Marketing managers will take that into account in designing product ranges and variants.

Buy selected product

Having compared the alternatives and decided which will best satisfy their need, the customer makes the purchase. Even at this stage of the process other factors may intrude –

out of stock, a price cut on an alternative, or the advice of the salesperson may influence decisions. Note that the way a purchase is financed is a product feature, e.g. no-interest loans to purchase the product.

A football game is not a tangible product. A regular and significant intangible purchase by a Manchester United football fan is the £23–£38 ticket to see a home game at Old Trafford or £10 on a pay-per-view TV basis. There is no guarantee of satisfaction and no exchange or refund. No promotional advertising is needed and the ticket demand is relatively 'inelastic', i.e. prices can increase without sales volumes necessarily falling.

An important question for a marketing manager is 'How does a fan reach the decision to buy this experience and how is value measured?' The buyer behaviour framework described above can help: domestic UK fans are typically lifelong, acquiring perceptions of and loyalty to the club at school or in the home. Influencers would include peers and older pupils. Although football was formerly male dominated, young females are an increasing part of the market. Most fans travel in groups of two or more, so this is a segment attribute that can be managed in raising awareness and favourability. Publicity photos can depict fans celebrating or commiserating together and the whole emphasis of attending a football match can be positioned away from 'did we win?' to 'did we have a good time?' This approach is one of MU's declared marketing strategies.

Post-purchase evaluation

The final stage of the buying process is when the customer compares pre-purchase expectations with post-purchase reality. If expectation matches reality then the consumer is more likely to buy in the future. At this stage, consumer communications can affect future decisions. The quality of after-sales service might convince the car purchaser whether he or she made the right decision or not.

When thinking about the post-experience evaluation, marketing managers should be aware of the potential difference between how consumers think (rationally) about their product and how they feel (emotionally) about it. It is possible, for example, for football fans to think rationally that the home game they just saw was very poor but still to retain great affection and warmth for the experience and the team. This apparent dichotomy can be turned to advantage when planning promotional campaigns.

Internal and external influences shape the decisions consumers make at each stage. Table 9.3 describes these, and Figure 9.10 illustrates them.

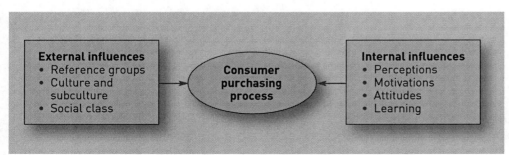

Figure 9.10

Influences on buyer behaviour

Table 9.3 Internal and external influences on buying behaviour

Influence	Description	Example
Internal influences **Perception**	How people collect and interpret information	Affects reaction to advertisements – images, colours, words. See Chapter 16 on communication
Motivation	Internal forces that shape purchasing decisions to satisfy need	Marketers design products to meet needs. Insurers remind people of dangers against which a policy will protect them. See Chapter 15
Attitudes	Opinions and points of view that people have of other people and institutions	Marketers design products to conform. Attitudes against testing cosmetics on animals led firms to stop this practice. Similarly for environmental issues
Learning	How people learn affects what they know about a product, and hence their purchasing decisions	Marketers help people to 'learn' to associate a product with unique colours or images – such as Coke with red and white, and Nike with its 'Swoosh' symbol
External influences **Reference groups**	Other people with whom the consumer identifies	Marketers establish the reference groups of their consumers, and allude to them in promotions – e.g. sponsoring athletes in return for product endorsement
Culture	The culture to which a consumer belongs affects their values and behaviour	Subcultures associated with music or cars influence buying behaviour – which marketers use in positioning products for those markets
Social class	People identify with a class based on income, education, where they live, and so on.	Purchase decisions confirm and reaffirm the class to which people belong, or to which they aspire. Marketers use this information in promotional material

key ideas   Needs, wants and demands

A marketing orientation implies that to satisfy the consumer it is necessary to identify the products for which there is *demand* and to understand the *needs* and *wants* which the product will satisfy for the consumer. Marketers distinguish between needs, wants and demands as follows:

- **Needs** These are the core feelings that consumers 'need' to satisfy; for example, thirst is a physical requirement that needs to be satisfied.
- **Wants** These are the preferences that individual consumers have about the ways in which they 'want' to satisfy the needs that they share in common with others. Consumers will want different liquids to satisfy the thirst that makes them need a drink.
- **Demands** The money that individual consumers have determines the types of drink they are able to buy. An individual who needs a drink may want to buy a Red Bull energy drink. The money in their wallet determines that their demand (their actual purchasing power) is for an own-label soft drink.

To satisfy consumers, marketers need to understand their needs, wants and demands. If they define demand too narrowly they may be unable to satisfy consumers.

9.8   Taking marketing decisions

The marketing manager now has information about the marketing environment, possible opportunities and threats, and the buying behaviour of consumers. The next stage is to decide which demands to satisfy and how to do this. The first decision is about market segmentation and targeting. The second is about choosing the correct mix of marketing tools to position products and make them attractive to consumers (Figure 9.11).

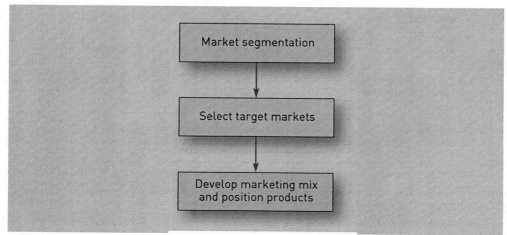

Figure 9.11
Taking marketing decisions

Segmenting markets

Organisations are increasingly using **market segmentation** strategies to satisfy the different needs that exist within the marketplace. Airlines offer consumers the choice of flying first class, business class or economy class. Notice that although the basic product attribute (transport from A to B) is the same for all passengers in the plane, the total offering is not: premium passengers pay for a premium service. Universities offer degrees by full-time, part-time and distance learning study. Athletic shoe companies offer shoes specifically for running, aerobics, tennis and squash as well as 'cross' trainers for the needs of all these sports.

Market segmentation is the process of dividing markets comprising the heterogeneous needs of many consumers into segments comprising the homogeneous needs of smaller groups.

Segmentation is based on the fact that consumers have different needs: it is more efficient for management to treat them as homogeneous groups, for the purposes of communication, advertising and so forth. The personal computer market consists of all the individuals who need a personal computer. Within that market people with similar needs can be grouped into distinct segments: travellers needing a laptop form one distinct segment; parents wanting a low-cost personal computer with Internet connection to help their children learn form another. Segmentation is very efficient when allocating the promotional budget. For example, note the number of beer sponsors involved with sports such as rugby, where both industries are targeting the same demographic profile, namely young men aged 18–35.

Segmenting the personal computer market (and any other market) relies on identifying the variables that distinguish consumers with similar needs, as follows:

● **Demography** The easiest way to segment a consumer market is by using demographic variables such as age, gender and education level. Magazine companies use gender and age variables to ensure that within their portfolio they have magazine titles which

Segmenting markets in the public sector

The idea of segmentation is highly relevant to managers providing public services, such as further and higher education, school meals and leisure centres. They need to know who uses the services, who might use them and how provision relates to demand. To understand these questions, public sector providers need to understand the needs and behaviours of current and potential users. A particular feature of the public sector is that services meet two types of demand (Chapman and Cowdell, 1998, pp. 122–126):

- non-discretionary demand – services that satisfy community demands which everyone needs, such as refuse collection, basic health care and street lighting;
- discretionary demand – services that people can choose to use, such as leisure and cultural services or public transport.

Market segmentation techniques apply equally to both – providers need to understand the needs of users and purchasers if they are to create value with the resources they use.

Source: Chapman and Cowdell (1998).

will suit the needs of females as well as males and those of different ages. Local authorities use information on age and family structures to help decide the distribution of facilities in their area.

- **Geography** This segmentation variable is commonly used by organisations competing in a global market. By segmenting markets by country, organisations such as HSBC (hsbc.com) have been able to 'think global but act local'. While maintaining uniform global standards of service and hygiene, the company competes differently in each country by varying the menu available to suit local tastes.
- **Socioeconomic** Segmentation on the basis of socioeconomic variables – such as income, social class and lifestyle. Lifestyle segmentation includes identifying groups of consumers who share similar values about the way in which they wish to live.

When segmenting consumer markets, marketers typically use a mix of these variables to provide an accurate profile of distinct groups. The magazine *Marie Claire*, for example, uses age, gender, education, lifestyle and social class to attract a readership of educated, independently minded women between the ages of 25 and 35, in income brackets ABC1.

Activity 9.7   **Identifying market segments**

- What market segments have the following identified: Swatch, Amazon.com, Borders Books?
- What marketing management benefits do you think their segmentation strategies offer?

A **target market** is the segment of the market selected by the organisation as the focus of its activities.

Having segmented a market using the variables described above, marketers have to decide which of those segments to select as **target markets** – those to be the focus for their activities. Marketing managers usually select target markets that meet the following three criteria:

- contain demands that the resources of the organisation can satisfy
- are large enough to provide a financial return
- have growth potential.

Ultimately, segments selected as target markets are those that offer the greatest potential for achieving management goals.

In 2005 Manchester United launched a Chinese website and appointed china.com as their official partner. Two hundred million Chinese regularly watch the team on TV. MU saw this as an opportunity for mail order sales to China and the rest of south-east Asia. As well as watching the games on TV, Asian fans frequently place bets on the outcome.

Source: Company website.

Case question 9.4

- What segmentation criteria would you have recommended for MU in this burgeoning sector?

9.9   Using the marketing mix

The final decision facing the marketing manager is the selection of the combination of price, product, promotion and place. This is known as the **marketing mix**.

The **marketing mix** is the mix of decisions about product features, prices, communications and distribution of products used by the marketing manager to position products competitively within the minds of consumers.

The marketing mix

key ideas

The marketing mix comprises four levers that marketing managers can control. The mix *positions* products in the market in a way that makes them attractive to the target consumers. The **position** that a product has within a market reflects consumer opinions of that product and the comparisons that they make between it and competing products. The aim is to position products *within the minds of consumers* as more attractive, and better able to satisfy their demands, than competing products.

To position products effectively, the marketing manager develops a coordinated marketing mix. Kotler and Keller (2006) define an organisation's marketing mix as 'a set of tools that work together to affect the marketplace'. The marketing mix has traditionally been presented as consisting of the so-called 4 Ps: product, price, promotion and place.

However, Gronroos (2000) points out that

> during the last two decades marketing researchers have increasingly found that the list of 4 Ps is too restrictive and more ... variables have been suggested ... such as people, processes and physical evidence. (pp. 240–241)

He suggests that adding further categories (see, for example, Judd 2003) is a symptom of the weakness of the marketing mix approach, although it may still be useful in certain types of market such as consumer packaged goods. The main problem with the approach, in Gronroos's view, is that it restricts marketing to a limited number of decision areas, and leads to the neglect of many aspects of what he calls the 'customer relationship life cycle' (pp. 242–243).

Marketing mix – product

Decisions about which products to develop will establish the range of goods and services an organisation offers. Some are physical products; others intangible personal services. Most are a mixture of the two. Note that the product can include non-core items such as packaging, after-sales service, maintenance and insurance.

management in practice

Swatch   www.swatch.com

The development and introduction of Swatch is a classic example of marketing techniques being used by a traditional industry to launch a new product. Faced with competition from low-cost producers SMH, an established Swiss watchmaker (brands included Longines and Omega) urgently needed a new product line. Its engineers developed a radically new product that was much cheaper to make than traditional models. The company worked closely with advertising agencies in the United States on product positioning and advertising strategy. In addition to the name 'Swatch', a snappy contraction of 'Swiss' and 'watch', this research generated the idea of downplaying the product's practical benefits and positioning it as a 'fashion accessory that happens to tell the time'. Swatch would be a second or third watch used to adapt to different situations without replacing the traditional 'status symbol' watch.

Swatch continues to reposition itself through new products and collections, and sponsorship of the Olympic Games as official timekeeper. Revenue was up 12 per cent in 2006 with sales exceeding $5 billion for the first time.

Source: Based on 'Swatch', Case No. 589-005-1, INSEAD-Cedep, Fontainebleau; and company website.

The extent to which offerings are tangible or intangible affects how marketing staff deal with them. Services present marketing with particular challenges because of their characteristics of perishability, intangibility, heterogeneity and inseparability.

Perishability

Perishable services cannot be held in stock for even the shortest amount of time. If a plane flies with empty seats these cannot be stored for another flight – empty seats are permanently lost sales.

Intangibility

Intangible services present the marketing manager with the greatest challenge. They cannot usually be viewed, touched or tried before their purchase. One way for consumers to 'try before buying' is to be given leaflets with attractive information on the service benefits: the financial services industry relies on information packs about features and benefits of mortgages, insurance policies and bank accounts. Consumers also have little information on which to assess the product benefits relative to their demands. A common source of service information is reference groups: organisations such as health clubs encourage existing members to invite friends and family to their fitness clubs for trial membership.

Heterogeneity and inseparability

Services are labour intensive. They rely on the skills, competences and experiences of the people who provide them, and this creates particular challenges for the marketing manager. *Heterogeneity* refers to variations in what in principle should be an identical service each time it is provided, e.g. a pedicure. *Inseparability* refers to a product or service that is consumed as it is produced, e.g. a haircut. Service providers and consumers will meet for some amount of time. For a doctor's appointment, it is necessary to meet with the doctor to discuss your health.

Organisations operating through branch systems such as banks or fast-food restaurants have to overcome the hazards of inseparability and heterogeneity to ensure consistent delivery standards. Both service providers and consumers have personalities, opinions and values that make them unique. This can create differences in the levels of service and standards that consumers experience when buying services. Organisations such as Pizza Hut and UCI cinemas try to minimise differences by providing staff with company uniforms, decorating premises in a similar way and setting firm guidelines for the way staff deliver the service.

Consumer products (both goods and services) can be classified as convenience, shopping, speciality or unsought products. Each poses a different marketing challenge, which Table 9.4 summarises.

Type of product	Examples	Marketing challenge
Convenience	Regular purchases, low price – bread, milk, magazines	Widely available, and easy to switch brands. Managers counter this by heavy advertising or distinct packaging of the brand
Shopping	Relatively expensive, infrequent purchase – washing machines, televisions, clothes	Brand name, product features, design and price are important and managers will spend time searching for best mix. Managers spend heavily on advertising and on training sales staff
Speciality	Less frequent, often luxury purchases – cars, diamond rings, houses	Consumers need much information. Sales staff vital to a sale – management invest heavily in them, and in protecting image of product by restricting outlets. Also focused advertising and distinctive packaging
Unsought	Consumers need to buy, but don't get much pleasure from – insurance, a car exhaust	Managers need to make customers aware that they supply this need, and distinct product features

Table 9.4

Market challenges by type of product using the marketing mix

The **product life cycle** suggests that products pass through the stages of introduction, growth, maturity and decline.

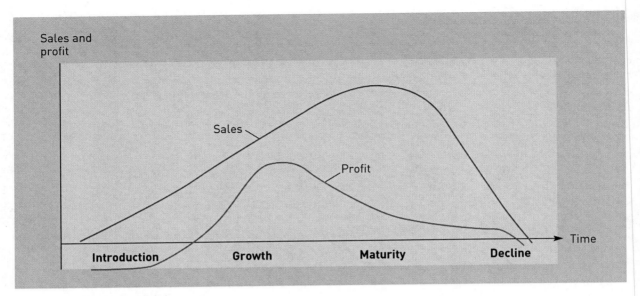

Figure 9.12 The product life cycle

Introduction

This is the stage at which products enter the marketplace. Profits are negative because sales from the early adopters have not reached the level needed to pay back investment in researching and developing the product. Few consumers are aware of – and therefore interested in – buying the product and few organisations are involved in producing and distributing it. The aim of the marketing manager at this stage is to invest in marketing communication and make as many potential consumers as possible aware of the product's entry into the marketplace.

Growth

At this stage consumers have become aware of and started buying the product. Sales rise quickly and profits peak. As people buy the product, more consumers become aware of it and the high profit levels attract new competitors into the industry. The aim of the marketing manager at this stage is to fight off existing competitors and new entrants. This can be done by (a) encouraging consumer loyalty, (b) distributing the product as widely as is demanded by consumers, and (c) cutting selling prices: production costs fall as total units increase, due to the learning curve effect. Competitors arriving later have not had time to cut costs so may baulk at entering the market.

Maturity

With profits peaking during the growth stage, profit and sales start to plateau and then decline towards the end of this stage. By this stage in a product's life cycle many consumers are aware of and have bought the product and there are many organisations competing for a decreasing amount of consumer demand for the product. The aim of the marketing manager is to fight competition by reducing the price of the product or by differentiating it by, for example, altering its packaging and design. Swatch continues to add value to its product in the later stages of its product life cycle with items such as the Infinity Concept watch launched in early 2007.

At this stage product differentiation can successfully reposition products to an earlier stage in their life cycle. It is also important that the marketing manager begins to consider ideas for replacement products and to select ideas for research and development.

Decline

In the decline phase, there is little consumer demand and all competing organisations are considering removing the product from the marketplace. It is important that, by this stage, the marketing manager has a new product ready to enter the marketplace and replace the product that is being removed. Certain rarity products can still generate profits in the decline phase, e.g. spare parts for old cars.

An awareness of the stage which a product is at in its life cycle can assist the marketing manager in deciding upon the course of marketing action to take. For example, aware that a product is at the maturity stage, the marketing manager might decide to reposition the product by changing the packaging or image created by the branding of the product. Consider the repositioning of Lucozade. Traditionally marketed as a health drink for older people, product modifications together with new packaging and celebrity endorsement have successfully repositioned Lucozade as a youth sports drink (www.lucozade.com).

Lynx/Axe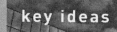

key ideas

Lynx (known as Axe throughout the rest of the world) has been a phenomenon since its launch it 1983. Much of its success is down to its iconic and award-winning advertising which has helped the brand gain 75 per cent market penetration of the 15–24-year-old male segment in the United Kingdom. However, Lynx faces a challenge: how to stay fresh and stylish, and avoid the fate of previous brand leaders in this category such as Brut – which is no longer produced.

The firm must continue to recruit a new customer base of 15–19-year-olds, but also constantly strive to improve its product offering. Lynx's method is clever yet straightforward: the advertising themes have followed UK male culture as it has evolved into the twenty-first century; and the weakest selling of six varieties of deodorant is removed and replaced every year. Thus the brand remains up to date and relevant to consumers, and allows the firm to charge a significant price premium. While Lynx has probably reached the maturity stage of the product life cycle, its focus on brand equity is preventing it moving into the decline stage.

Sources: www.unilever.co.uk/ourbrands/personalcare/lynx.asp; published sources.

Activity 9.8   Using the product life cycle

State the stage that you believe each of the following products to be in and comment on how long, in years, you believe their life cycle to be: drawing pins, iPods, umbrellas, hand soap.

Activity 9.8 shows that some products do not have a limited lifespan and other products can be repositioned to an earlier stage. Despite these criticisms, the product life cycle offers the marketing manager a useful aid to many product decisions.

Marketing mix – price

Price is the value placed upon the goods, services and ideas exchanged between organisations and consumers. For most products, price is measured with money, though consumers do not identify all the purchases they make as having a 'price': for example, accessing BBC television programmes is the cost of a television licence, and the price of street lighting and cleaning is the council tax that individual households are responsible for paying. Not-for-profit marketing can involve a time price (volunteering to work in a charity shop) or a psychological price for behaviour change (government campaigns to discourage drink driving).

In selecting the price that will position a product competitively within consumers' minds, the marketing manager must be aware of the image that consumers have of the product. Consumers have expected price ranges for certain types of product. In particular, for safety products, products for children, those associated with health or connected to their self-image, consumers have a *minimum* price they expect to pay. If the price is below this, consumers will not purchase the product because they perceive such products as being of inferior quality or lower value.

The price charged must also cover the costs of producing, distributing and promoting products. It must provide the organisation with an acceptable profit yet leave an acceptable margin for distributors and retailers.

Marketing mix – promotion

Properly referred to as marketing communications, this element of the marketing mix involves taking decisions about the information that will encourage consumers to buy a product or change attitudes and behaviours in some way. Organisations can communicate with their target markets in many ways. Packaging can provide information, a company logo may transmit a particular message, and sponsoring a football team or a concert indicates an organisation's values and attitudes. The most frequent modes of encouraging consumers to buy products include advertising, sales promotions, personal selling and publicity.

- *Advertising* is the form of communication commonly selected when an organisation wishes to transmit a message to a large audience. It is impersonal, as it does not involve direct communication between an organisation and a potential consumer. Advertising is effective in creating awareness of the offering but is less effective in persuading consumers to buy. It is, however, a cost-effective method of communicating with potential consumers in a mass market.
- Organisations typically use *sales promotions* to encourage consumers who are considering a product to take the next step and buy it. Both McDonald's and Burger King

management in practice   **A Department of Trade and Industry (DTI) advertising campaign**

The UK government launched an online campaign to promote its new Consumer Direct telephone, online and e-mail information service for consumers. Consumer Direct provides advice on consumer protection issues, including what rights consumers have or how to get redress for faulty goods. Run in partnership with local authorities and existing services, including Trading Standards, there are 11 contact centres across the United Kingdom.

Source: *Marketing Week*, 9 September 2004; www.consumerdirect.gov.uk.

frequently offer special promotions to encourage consumers to buy their brand. Companies also use promotions to encourage repeat buys and to encourage consumers to try out new products of which advertising has made them aware.

- Marketing departments use *personal selling* when consumers require first-hand information before making a purchase. It is particularly useful for infrequently purchased products such as DVD players and cars – and in industrial marketing. Personal selling is a direct transfer of product information to potential consumers: it is able to respond to questions that consumers might have and to explain complicated or technical product features. Personal selling requires that managers train salespeople properly, especially on specific product features. It is useful for expensive or technically sophisticated products.

- *Publicity* or PR (public relations) is effective in supporting a positive image of the organisation. It involves building good working relationships with the media and using them to promote a positive image of the organisation. The aim is to ensure that positive events of media interest (such as launching a new product) are fully reported, and that negative ones do as little damage as possible.

Marketing mix – place

'Place' refers to decisions about the ways in which products can be most effectively distributed to the final consumer, either directly or through intermediaries. Decisions about marketing channels concentrate on whether the distribution of products should be owned by the producing organisation or whether products should be distributed by external parties. These decisions depend on the products involved and the costs of distribution. If product quality and image are vital to market positioning then the organisation must maintain control over distribution.

Protecting the brand

management in practice

Paul Mitchell hair products maintain the image of quality that consumers attach to the name by detailing on the product packaging that authenticity cannot be guaranteed unless purchased from a Paul Mitchell approved outlet. Similarly, brands such as Calvin Klein, Nike and Clarins have expressed concerns about the distribution of their products through such stores as Tesco and Superdrug, which they believe detract from rather than add to the value of their branded products.

Distributor cost is a consideration in channel management. Having identified the price at which consumers demand to buy particular products, the costs involved in distributing products in-house relative to external providers must be considered.

A third channel decision is whether to make purchase of products available electronically through the Internet. This decision has been embraced by organisations such as easyJet, amazon.com and lastminute.com. Such organisations have decided to use electronic channels of distribution as a differentiation tool, on the grounds that consumers prefer online convenience and see this as a product feature. For many organisations electronic product distribution is a complementary channel used, for example, to widen product access to geographically remote markets. The major supermarkets and retailers all have busy websites, often offering discounts over store prices. This market channel also allows easy gathering of data for relationship marketing.

In developing a marketing mix that will place products competitively within the minds of consumers the marketing manager must be aware that changes in one element will create changes in other areas. For example, if the price of a product is reduced, consumer perceptions of the product might change. Creating an effective marketing mix with which to position products relies upon integration and coordination of each element.

management in practice   **Maintaining consistency**

In positioning their products as **value for money,** organisations ensure that each part of the marketing mix supports and reinforces this image. This means that products must not be highly differentiated, prices should be low, and promotion messages should stress the low price and value for money. The stores in which products are distributed should be simple in design. This avoids sending a message that the costs of creating a smart place in which to buy products will be reflected in the prices. A good example is the Asda supermarket (www.asda.co.uk).

9.10 Current themes and issues

Performance

The chapter has presented the benefits to organisations of adopting a marketing orientation, in the sense of incorporating marketing deeply into all of its activities. A marketing orientation requires that the whole organisation commits to achieving organisational goals by *continually* satisfying consumer demands. Aware of this objective and of their contribution towards it, different areas within the organisation are able to cooperate and coordinate their activities.

The challenge in moving to this position lies in the nature of the organisational changes that will be required. Chapter 13 examines this, including the view that organisations must change radically and relentlessly. Managers are advised that to survive they must continually review their missions and objectives, their processes, their structures and cultures, their relations with suppliers, and with their employees. 'Change or perish' is the rationale of those who propose unrelenting change. While the arguments may sometimes be valid, the counter-view is that disruptive change is costly, and does not necessarily improve performance, as excessive change may lead to initiative overload, change-related chaos and employee cynicism.

Responsibility

The adoption of a marketing orientation can clearly bring significant benefits to the commercial or other success of organisations. Commentators have also been critical of marketing. They argue that marketing manipulates consumer choices and encourages materialism and over-consumption. Food manufacturers have faced criticism for promoting the sale of foods with a high fat and sugar content, thus contributing to obesity: in response to such criticism, Mars announced in 2007 that it would stop advertising aimed at children under the age of 12. Chapter 5 (Corporate responsibility) also includes ideas relevant to marketing, such as the influence of ethical consumers, the success of the Fairtrade brand, and of individual products such as Café Direct, which promise producers a fair return.

Naomi Klein's *No Logo: Taking Aim at the Brand Bullies*

Klein (2000) presents a powerful argument against the growing dominance of some global brands in consumer markets, and how many use advertising to exploit impressionable teenagers. She argues that companies such as Microsoft, Gap and Starbucks now present themselves as purveyors of lifestyles, images and dreams rather than products. In doing so they harm both the cultures in which they operate and the workers they employ. She also reports a growing backlash by ethical shareholders, human rights activists and McUnion organisers demanding a citizen-centred alternative to the rule of the brands.

However, not everyone agrees that Klein is correct. She is accused of overstating her case, and brand advocates point out the many positives brands have for consumers, manufacturers and retailers. What is not in dispute, however, is that companies are now facing up to social and ethical responsibility as never before.

The debate on marketing's role within society will continue to run. Those concerned with environmental and public health issues will criticise organisations they perceive to be damaging the environment or knowingly causing harm to people's health. Others argue that adopting a marketing orientation in itself is not an ethical issue, as long as it is used to inform consumers and widen their choice. Responsible marketers do not advocate that consumers should be tricked into making purchases. Nevertheless it is a fact that some people use marketing concepts to sell pornography, traffic drugs and invade privacy.

Internationalisation

If you travel to another country, you immediately see many familiar consumer products or services – things that epitomise the idea that global brands are steadily displacing local products. In several industries identical products (Canon cameras, Sony Walkman, Famous Grouse whisky) are sold across the globe without modification. This trend was observed by Theodore Levitt (1983), a professor at Harvard Business School, who argued that advances in communications technology were increasingly inspiring consumers around the world to want the same things. Companies should become 'global' by standardising the production, distribution and marketing of their products across all countries. Sameness meant efficiency and would be more profitable than difference. From economies of scale would flow competitive advantage.

Levitt's argument soon influenced practice and many consumer companies, such as Coca-Cola and Marlborough, began promoting themselves as identical global brands, with standard practices and a centralised management structure.

By the end of the 1990s, managers began to change their approach. Customers were finding that new local brands offered better value and, as producers adopted western methods, good quality. Global brands, offering standard products regardless of local tastes, lost market share. So rather than 'going global' they began to 'go local': Starbucks varies its menu to suit local tastes; Nestlé has about 200 varieties of its instant coffee; and MTV varies programming to suit different countries and regions.

Activity 9.9   Revising your definition

- Having completed this chapter, how would you define marketing?
- Compare this definition with the one that you were asked to make in Activity 9.1 and comment on any changes.

Summary

1 Compare and contrast marketing with alternative organisational orientations

- Adopting a marketing orientation makes the customer the centre of attention and is different from product, production and sales philosophies. It becomes a guiding orientation for the whole organisation. If management wishes a marketing orientation to pervade the organisation, all activities are focused on meeting customer needs. Activity is monitored and controlled to ensure that work is done in a way which meets the needs of customers.

- Implementing the approach involves precise targeting of defined market segments. It also implies restructuring to ensure that the whole organisation focuses on the customer, with organisation-wide information systems to handle marketing data.

2 Describe the benefits to any organisation of adopting a marketing orientation

- A marketing orientation implies that in major business decisions management hears a consumer perspective, through mechanisms for involving the relevant players. A firm with a consumer-centred marketing orientation focuses all activities on meeting consumer needs and is organised with that in mind.

3 Explain why marketing is an information-intensive activity

- To meet consumer needs effectively, marketing is an information-intensive activity. A major element in marketing is the management of communications, i.e. ensuring that information about external developments and customer needs is gathered, processed and transferred around the organisation. Consumers also have to be informed of the offerings and their benefits.

4 Identify the responsibilities of the marketing manager

- The primacy of marketing can create organisational tension with other professional groups within the firm, whose status and position may be threatened by the primacy. Other departments are, however, expected to support and be committed to the central position of marketing.

5 Explain market segmentation and the practice of selecting a target market

- Greater consumer understanding enables a company to segment the market in various ways, and to target certain segments in the hope of meeting their distinctive needs.

6 Describe the components of the marketing mix

- The chapter then outlined the components of the marketing mix – product, price, promotion and place – that a company can use to position its offerings to consumers.

7 Explain what is meant by product positioning

- Marketing places particular emphasis on keeping in touch with external (micro and macro) developments that affect customers' needs and the organisation's objectives.

Review questions

1 What advantages does the marketing orientation have over each of the following organisational philosophies: production, product and sales?

2 Outline the benefits that the marketing orientation can offer each of the following organisations: a global brand, a football team, a university, a charity, a small firm and a high street retailer.

3 What are the key responsibilities of the marketing manager?

4 In what way is an organisation's micro-environment different from its macro-environment? Comment on which of these organisations' marketing environments have the greatest impact upon their marketing activities: LivingWell health clubs (www.livingwell.com), McDonald's (www.mcdonalds.com), your local library.

5 Outline various sources of marketing information and compare and contrast alternative ways of collecting and analysing information about an organisation's market environment.

6 Describe the process of buying decisions involved and identify the factors that might influence the purchase of a new car, a soft drink, a present for a friend's 30th birthday, a new clothes outfit for work.

7 What are the advantages of market segmentation and what are the variables upon which consumer markets are commonly segmented?

8 How are target markets identified and what is meant by product positioning?

9 What position does each of the following have in the marketplace and what mix of marketing tools has each used to achieve this position: Asda supermarkets (www.asda.co.uk), Tango soft drinks (www.tango.co.uk), Save the Children Fund (www.savethechildren.org.uk), Surf washing powder (www.surf.co.uk)?

Concluding critical reflection

Think about the ways in which your company, or one with which you are familiar, manages marketing. Review the material in the chapter, and perhaps visit some of the websites identified. Then make notes on these questions:

- What examples of the marketing issues discussed in this chapter struck you as being relevant to practice in your company?

- Considering the people you normally work with, what **assumptions** about the nature of the business and its customers appear to guide their approach – a production, sales or marketing orientation? How does this affect the way the business operates?

- What factors such as the history or current **context** of the company appear to influence this? Does the current approach appear to be right for the company in its context – or would a different view of the context lead to a different approach? What would the implications for people in the company be of a distinctive marketing orientation?

- Has there been any pressure to adopt a more customer-focused approach, perhaps based on evidence about similar organisations? If you could find evidence about such **alternatives**, how ▶

may it affect company practice? What would be the obstacles to a greater emphasis on marketing?

● The chapter has stressed the benefits of a marketing orientation, and of understanding customer needs in ever greater detail. What **limitations** can you identify in this philosophy, or others within the chapter? Are people only to be valued in their roles as consumers? How valid might ideas on marketing be in other cultures? What, if any, limitations can you now identify in the way an organisation with which you are familiar approaches marketing?

Further reading

Armstrong, G. and Kotler, P. (2006), *Marketing: An introduction* (8th edn), Financial Times/Prentice Hall, Harlow.

Provides a detailed introduction to marketing.

Baker, M. (2002), *The Marketing Book* (5th edn), Butterworth/Heinemann, London.

Contains an excellent selection of classic marketing articles.

Gronroos, C. (2000), *Service Management and Marketing: A customer relationship management approach*, 2nd edn, Wiley, Chichester.

Highly recommended to students wishing to read more about services marketing from one of Europe's leading writers on marketing.

Jobber, D. (2007), *Principles and Practices of Marketing* (5th edn), McGraw-Hill, London.

The most popular European-centred marketing textbook.

Judd, V.C. (2003), 'Achieving customer orientation using people power – the 5th P', *European Journal of Marketing*, vol. 37, no. 10, pp. 1301–1313.

Examines how employees can have a powerful influence on the value the organisation delivers to customers – and complements the '4Ps' outlined in the chapter.

Kottasz, R. (2004), 'How should charitable organisations motivate young professionals to give philanthropically?', *International Journal of Non-Profit and Voluntary Sector Marketing*, vol. 9, no. 1, pp. 9–27.

An example of how research can uncover consumers' motives – in this case finding that wealthy young men were more likely to be motivated to give to charities if they received some social benefits in return – such as invitations to black tie dinners, and being associated with a well-known charity.

Kotler, P. and Keller, K. (2006), *Marketing Management* (12th edn), Financial Times/Prentice Hall, Harlow.

The biggest selling marketing textbook worldwide, aimed at MBA or honours undergraduate level.

Mellahi, K., Jackson, P. and Sparks, L. (2002), 'An exploratory study into failure in successful organizations: the case of Marks and Spencer', *British Journal of Management*, vol. 13, no. 1, pp. 15–29.

Detailed empirical research into the deep-rooted internal problems that led to the difficulties which the company experienced in the late 1990s.

Newman, A.J and Patel, D. (2004), 'The marketing directions of two fashion retailers', *European Journal of Marketing*, vol. 38, no. 7, pp. 770–789.

Fascinating comparison of the recent performance of Topshop and Gap, relating the variation to their success (or not) in developing a marketing orientation throughout the business.

Schor, J.B. (2004), *Born to Buy: The commercialized child and the new consumer culture*, Scribner, New York.

A revealing account of the ploys some marketers use to sell products to children – turning them, she argues, into miniature consumption machines.

Weblinks

These websites have appeared in the chapter:

www.manutd.com
www.oxfam.co.uk
www.greenpeace.com
www.msf.org
www.co-operativebank.co.uk
www.easyjet.com
www.sainsburys.co.uk
www.churchmarketing.com
www.cancerresearchuk.org
www.apple.com
www.macobserver.com
www.ryanair.com
www.diesel.com
www.hsbc.com
www.swatch.com
www.lucozade.com
www.consumerdirect.gov.uk
www.livingwell.com
www.lynxeffect.co.uk
www.asda.co.uk
www.mcdonalds.com
www.tango.co.uk
www.savethechildren.org.uk
www.surf.co.uk

Visit two of the sites in the list (or that of another organisation in which you have an interest).

● What markets are they in? How have they segmented the market?

● What information can you find about their position in their respective markets, and what marketing challenges do they face?

● Gather information from media websites (such as www.ft.com) that relate to the organisations you have chosen. What stories can you find that relate to the marketing decisions they have made, and what the outcomes have been?

Annotated weblinks, multiple choice questions and other useful resources can be found on www.pearsoned.co.uk/boddy

CHAPTER 13

Groups, teams and teamwork

After studying this chapter, you should be able to:

1 outline the main features of the 'groupthink' model of group decision-making, and suggest two ways in which it may not be entirely accurate;

2 define group polarisation and explain why it occurs;

3 explain why relations between groups at work depend partly on individuals' sense of personal identity;

4 define stereotypes and specify two reasons why they can affect relations between groups at work;

5 describe the incidence of teamwork in Europe;

6 summarise how teams function;

7 explain the stages of team development;

8 describe the importance of team roles and a popular team role typology;

9 explain the ways in which the diversity within a team can affect team functioning;

10 explain some of the factors that influence team performance.

Opening Case Study   Playing the game

Team-building used to be about going to the pub on a Friday evening and helping your colleagues into a taxi when they'd had one drink too many. Gone are those days. Even team-building through paintballing is old news. These days nothing less than an African safari, hot air ballooning or sailing on the high seas will do, it seems.

The team is now the norm at work. Office life is no longer the atomised existence it once was. 'Teams have become a way of organising work,' says Rob Briner, organisational psychologist at Birkbeck College, London.

> The problem is that these teams are normally very artificial. One of the defining characteristics of a team is that you have to be interdependent, but that's rarely true of workplace teams. Part of the reason for recent interest in team-building is that these teams often aren't actually working properly.

As team-building has become the buzz word of HR departments, training providers have proliferated and their offerings diversified. Prices vary from £50 per person for a half-day activity up to several thousand pounds for week-long team-building activities overseas.

Team activities centre on forcing people into new situations. 'Getting people out of the mould and out of the existing hierarchy that they're used to is crucial,' says Alan Kiff, managing director of Campfire Adventures, which runs safaris in South Africa and dog-sledding in Finland. During week-long trips, activities include guiding a blindfold driver through an obstacle course using whistles, and doing a treasure hunt around a safari park.

Get to know your fellow workers in challenging and unfamiliar situations. Then you'll all work together better – that's the theory. But experts dispute this assumption. 'There is no strong evidence that team cohesion aids team effec-tiveness,' says Michael West, professor of organisational psychology and director of research at Aston University. 'People assume they work more effectively if they like the people they're with, but may simply conspire to do less work, spend longer ensuring they don't fall out, or even decide they don't like each other.'

The blame may lie with client companies and not the training providers, says Neil Russell, managing director of Eos Yacht Charters. 'Some companies really want to build a team in a genuine sense, but these are few and far between.' Many managers remain cynical about skills training and development, he says. 'People are much more into developing technical knowledge rather than teamworking skills.'

Team-building events are big business these days. And while doubts remain about the exact nature of their benefits, training providers and clients insist that they bond staff, build company loyalty and help break down barriers.

Source: Adapted from an article by Rosie Blau, 30 May 2002. 'Playing the Game (team building)', People Management, *Vol. 8(II) pp. 38-9.*

Introduction

The opening case study shows that teams and groups are a fashionable topic in the workplace, and allegedly a fashionable way of organising workers. However, the case study also shows that there is some scepticism about whether teams are necessarily a good way of organising work, and about whether team-building in exotic ways succeeds in enhancing team effectiveness.

In this chapter, the prevalence and impact of teamworking are examined, and some of the important psychological processes that occur in teams are identified. These include an examination of how creativity and innovation develop in teams, and the role of diversity in team membership. Teams can be argued to be a special case of groups, and this means that the research on groups can be very useful in helping us to understand teams. How we perceive and behave towards members of our own group and members of other groups has, for a very long time, been of great interest to social psychologists. Some of the key themes of that work are included in this chapter because they help us to develop a stronger understanding of how teams in organisations (*see also the prevalence of teamwork* later in this chapter).

Group decision-making

Groups versus individuals

Although many people are very cynical about the value of meetings and committees, the fact is that work tends to involve a lot of them. In work organisations most major decisions (and many lesser ones) are made by groups of people, and not by individuals. Hence the study of groups has attracted a lot of interest, an increasing proportion of which is from organisational psychologists (Guzzo and Dickson, 1996). There are some clear potential benefits of group decision-making. If handled in the right way, a decision made by a group can evoke greater commitment to it than one made by an individual: this is because more people feel a sense of involvement in the decision. On the other hand, group decisions usually consume more time (and more money) than individual ones: therefore, the enhanced quality of the decisions they make need to justify the extra costs. One often-asked question is whether individual or group decisions are superior (Davis, 1992).

One view is that 'many heads are better than one': this school of thought argues that, in groups, people can correct each other's mistakes and build on each other's ideas. An opposing view is that 'too many cooks spoil the broth', which argues that problems of communication and rivalry between group members more than cancel out any potential advantage of the increased total available knowledge, skills, abilities and other competencies.

In fact, research has shown that it is not possible to generalise about whether individuals or groups are universally better. It depends, to a large extent, on the abilities and training of the individuals and groups and on the kind of task being tackled (Hill, 1982). Examining the different activities that groups engage in allows us to better identify what it is that makes groups effective.

McGrath (1984) identified eight different types of task that groups can face. Four of these directly concern group decision-making. These are:

1 generating plans (e.g. how many new employees to hire to support expansion);

2 generating ideas (e.g. ideas for new products to help grow the business);

3 solving problems that have 'correct answers' (i.e. where the answer can be identified with a degree of certainty, for example the costs of hiring a new member of staff);

4 identifying issues that do not have a 'correct answer' at the time the decision is made (i.e. where there is considerable uncertainty over the answer, for example identifying exact levels of staff turnover in five years time).

The second and third of these provide the best opportunities for comparing group and individual performance, and these are examined in more detail below.

Brainstorming, for example, is a technique for generating ideas with which many readers will already be familiar. It was originally advocated by Osborn (1957), who argued individuals can think up twice as many ideas in a group as they could on their own, but only if those in the group agree that:

■ the more ideas they think of the better; and

■ members will be encouraged to produce even bizarre ideas, and not be ridiculed for them.

However, even if these conditions are met, groups are not always more effective than individuals during brainstorming. Some research has indicated that lone individuals who are encouraged to think of as many ideas as possible generate more ideas per individual than do groups (e.g. Lamm and Trommsdorf, 1973). A number of possible explanations have been suggested for this phenomenon. These include *evaluation apprehension*, where a person feels afraid of what others will think, despite the brainstorming instructions, and *free-riding*, where group members feel that other group members will do the work for them.

Diehl and Stroebe (1987) devised experiments to test different explanations, but their results supported a third explanation: *production blocking*. Simply, only one person at a time in a group can talk about their ideas, and in the meantime other members may forget or suppress theirs. Nevertheless, there is also clear evidence that exposure to the ideas of other people enhances creativity, especially if people are exposed to a diverse group of others (Paulus, 2000).

Taken together, the research indicates that the best brainstorming is achieved by exposing individuals to a diverse group of others, but without incurring production blocking or other negative group effects. Advances in information and communication technology can help here, by transmitting information between group members in a clear and impersonal way (e.g. Valacich *et al.*, 1994; *see also* Chapter 10 for an fuller examination of these issues). For example, it seems that groups linked by computer can produce more ideas than those meeting face-to-face, and also have greater equality of participation (Hollingshead and McGrath, 1995). However, such groups also tend to make more extreme decisions and have some hostile communications. There is more about virtual teams in Chapter 10.

Psychologists have conducted a number of experiments comparing individual and group performance on *problems with correct answers*. For example Vollrath *et al.* (1989) found that groups of people working together recognised and recalled information better than individuals. However, McGrath (1984) pointed out that there are different types of correct answers: group problem-solving processes appear to vary according to the extent to which the correct answer can be shown to be correct. This concept of 'correctness' is best explained by example.

One type of correct answer is found in 'Eureka' tasks – when the correct answer is mentioned, everyone suddenly sees that it must be right (e.g. when the group is tasked with identifying a factual answer such as the previous 12 months' production volumes). However, there are also problems where the answer can be proved correct using logic, even though its correctness is not necessarily obvious at first sight (e.g. the costs of borrowing large sums of money to take over a competitor organisation). Then there are problems where the correct (or best) answer can only be defined by experts, but whose wisdom may be challenged by a lay person (e.g. the environmental impact of an organisation's production processes).

The second type of problem is often used to investigate the complexities of group decision-making processes. One task often used in research, is the so-called 'horse-trading task'. In this task a person buys a horse for £60 and sells it for £70. Then they buy it back for £80 and again sell it for £90. How much money does the person make in the horse-trading business? Many people say £10, but the correct answer is £20 though strictly this assumes that the person does not have to borrow the extra £10 to buy back the horse, and it ignores the opportunity cost of using the £10 in that way rather than another.

Early research using problems of this kind (e.g. Maier and Solem, 1952) produced several important findings. First, lower-status group members had less influence on the group decision than higher-status ones, even when the lower-status people were correct. Second, even when at least one person in the group knew the correct answer, the group decision was by no means always correct. Third, group discussion made people more confident that the group's consensus decision was correct: unfortunately the discussion did not make a correct decision more likely! For problems like the horse-trading one, it typically needs two correct people, not one, to convince the rest of the group. Put another way, on average *the group is as good as its second-best member*. This could be taken to mean that, for solving problems with correct answers, groups are on average better than individuals, but inferior to the *best* individuals.

Key Learning Point

Key Learning Point

For problems with demonstrably correct answers, groups are (on average) as good as their second-best member. However, groups can do better or worse than this average depending on their membership and process.

However, conclusions of this kind cannot easily be generalised. In organisations, many groups are dealing with uncertainties. Many decisions made in organisations do not have a provable correct answer, or even an answer that well-qualified experts can agree on. More importantly, although organisations might find it interesting to understand how groups make decisions, they are likely to be more concerned with how they can be improved. Improving group decision-making when the group is faced with real-life issues is the focus of the next section of this chapter: it has been the subject of much popular and academic debate.

Group deficiencies and overcoming them

Some social scientists have concentrated on identifying the context within which groups are more likely to perform well (e.g. Larson and LaFasto, 1989). They point out necessities such as having group members who are knowledgeable about the problem faced; having a clearly defined and inspiring goal (*see* Locke's goal-setting theory in Chapter 8); having group members who are committed to solving the problem in the best possible way; and support and recognition from important people outside the group. Other work has attempted to identify the roles that group members should adopt in order to function effectively together. Perhaps the most influential has been Belbin (1981, 1993a), who identified the various roles required in an effective team (this work is covered in detail later in this chapter). Other observers of groups have concentrated more on procedural factors (e.g. Rees and Porter, 2001). Procedural factors include the practices of the chairperson in facilitating discussion and summing it up, ensuring that everyone has their say and that only one person speaks at a time, and making sure that votes (if taken) are conducted only when all points of view have been aired, and with clearly defined options, so that group members know what they are voting for and against.

Social psychologists have noted many features of the group decision-making process that can impair decision quality. Many of these underlie the practical suggestions already mentioned in this section that are designed to help groups avoid such pitfalls. Hoffman and Maier (1961) noted a tendency to adopt 'minimally acceptable solutions', especially where the decision task is complex. Instead of seeking the best possible solution, group members often settle on the first suggested solution that everyone considers 'good enough'. In certain circumstances this might be an advantage (e.g. in a situation where a quick, workable decision is required), but on most occasions it is probably not a good idea. Hackman (1990) pointed out that groups rarely discuss what strategy they should adopt in tackling a decision-making task (i.e. how they should go about it), but that when they do, they tend to perform better. Simply telling groups to discuss their strategy before they tackle the problem itself is usually not enough: discussion of the group's strategy has to be treated as a separate task if it is to be taken seriously and have an impact.

Motivational losses in groups can also be a problem. Experimental research has consistently shown that as the number of people in a group increases, the effort and/or performance of each one often decreases: this is the so-called *social loafing* effect (e.g. Latane *et al.*, 1979). On the other hand, this motivational loss can be avoided if individuals in the group feel that their contribution can be identified as their own, *and* that their contribution makes a significant difference to the group's performance (Williams *et al.*, 1981; Kerr and Bruun, 1983). Hence a group leader would be well advised to ensure that each group member can see the connection between the efforts of individuals and group performance (both for each individual themselves and so that they can see the contribution of other group members). Interestingly, culture may play an important role in group motivation. There is some evidence that social loafing does not occur in collectivist societies. Earley (1989) found evidence of social loafing amongst American management trainees in a management task set in a laboratory, but not amongst trainees from the People's Republic of China (even in the identical task). In collective societies, a person's sense of shared responsibility with others (in contrast with individualistic Western cultures) may explain this difference. Moreover, Erez and Somech (1996) found that differences in individualism–collectivism even within one country (Israel) made a difference to the social loafing effect (with those closest to the individualism end of the continuum being most prone to social loafing). This is a another example of the culturally specific nature of some phenomena in applied psychology.

However, social loafing appears only to occur when groups lack specific goals. As Erez and Somech pointed out, most groups in the workplace have members who: know each other, communicate with each other, have team goals that matter to them and contribute to the team in a way that means that individual performance can be identified. So social loafing may not be as widespread in the real world as it is in laboratory-based experiments: it may be the exception, not the rule, even in individualistic cultures.

Key Learning Point

Group members tend to reduce their efforts as group size increases, at least in individualistic cultures. This problem can, however, be overcome by setting teams specific goals and making team members accountable for their actions.

Another problem with group work concerns how a group reacts when things start to go wrong. It seems that groups may be even more likely than individuals to escalate their commitment to a decision (i.e. to stick to it), even if it does not seem to be working out well (Whyte, 1993). This can occur even if the majority of group members start off with the view that they will not invest any further resources in the initial decision. This essentially risky decision of the group (i.e. to persevere with a course of action even in the face of negative feedback about it) may be even more marked if the decision they are required to make is about avoiding losses rather than achieving gains. As noted earlier in this chapter, most people are more inclined to accept the risk of a big loss in the hope of avoiding a moderate loss (than they are to risk losing a moderate profit in pursuit of a big profit).

Groupthink

Janis (1972, 1982a,b) arrived at some disturbing conclusions about how some real-life policy-making groups can make extremely poor decisions that have serious repercussions around the world. He analysed the major foreign policy errors of various governments at various times in history. One of these was the 'Bay of Pigs' fiasco in the early 1960s. Fidel Castro had recently taken power in Cuba. As a response, the new US administration under President John F. Kennedy launched an 'invasion' of Cuba by 1400 Cuban exiles, who landed at the Bay of Pigs. Within two days they were surrounded by 20,000 Cuban troops, and those not killed were ransomed back to the United States at a cost of $53 million in aid.

Janis argued that this outcome was not just bad luck for the United States. Instead, such an outcome could and should have been anticipated. He suggested that in this and other fiascos, various group processes could be seen, which collectively he called *groupthink*.

According to Janis, groupthink occurs when group members' motivation for unanimity and agreement (i.e. consensus) overrides their motivation to evaluate carefully the risks and benefits of alternative decisions. This usually occurs in 'cohesive' groups, i.e. those where group members are friendly with each other, and respect each other's opinions. In such groups disagreement is construed (usually unconsciously) as a withdrawal of friendship and respect, rather than as a useful critical insight. When this is combined with (i) a group leader known (or believed) to have a position or opinion on the issues under discussion, (ii) an absence of clear group procedures for discussion and decision-making, and (iii) a difficult set of circumstances (e.g. time pressure, or high-stakes decision-making), then the group members tend to seek agreement. This leads to groupthink as shown in Figure 13.1. The symptoms can be summarised as follows:

- *Overestimation of the group's power and morality*: in groupthink, group members tend have positive opinions of each other and these are not challenged.

- *Closed-mindedness*: this can be seen through group members' efforts to downplay warnings and to stereotype other groups as inferior to their own.

- *Pressures towards uniformity*: this manifests itself through the suppression of private doubts, leading to an illusion of unanimity and the development of 'mindguards' to shield group members (especially the leader) from uncomfortable information.

Key Learning Point

Groupthink is a set of malfunctioning group processes that occur when group members are more concerned (although they may not realise it) to achieve unanimity and agreement than they are to find the best available solution to a problem or situation.

Janis (1982b) has argued that certain measures can be taken to avoid groupthink. These include:

- establishing impartial leadership (so that group members are not tempted simply to follow the leader);

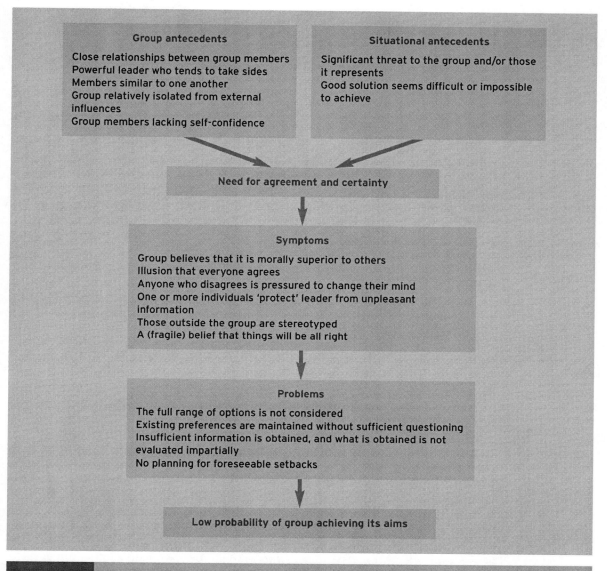

Group antecedents

Close relationships between group members
Powerful leader who tends to take sides
Members similar to one another
Group relatively isolated from external
influences
Group members lacking self-confidence

Situational antecedents

Significant threat to the group and/or those
it represents
Good solution seems difficult or impossible
to achieve

Need for agreement and certainty

Symptoms

Group believes that it is morally superior to others
Illusion that everyone agrees
Anyone who disagrees is pressured to change their mind
One or more individuals 'protect' leader from unpleasant
information
Those outside the group are stereotyped
A (fragile) belief that things will be all right

Problems

The full range of options is not considered
Existing preferences are maintained without sufficient questioning
Insufficient information is obtained, and what is obtained is not
evaluated impartially
No planning for foreseeable setbacks

Low probability of group achieving its aims

| Figure 13.1 | The Janis groupthink model |

- instructing each person in the group to give high priority to airing doubts and objections;

- having subject matter experts in attendance to raise doubts about the group's discussions and decision-making;

- including 'second chance' meetings where members express their doubts about a previously made, but not yet implemented, decision.

An overarching theme of these interventions is that groupthink can be minimised if there is a known 'group norm' that disagreeing with another group member does *not* signal disrespect or unfriendliness towards them.

It is possible for groups to use formal procedures to combat groupthink, even though these may mean that group discussion and decision-making takes more time, and may require more effort on the part of the group members.

Intuitively appealing as it is, Janis's work has not gone unchallenged. It has been argued that the groupthink syndrome is really simply a collection of separate phenomena that do not co-occur as neatly as Janis claims, and that these phenomena have already been separately investigated by other social scientists (Aldag and Fuller, 1993). Whyte (1989) argued that so-called groupthink is not itself a unitary phenomenon. Instead, it is a product of groups being inclined to accept risk when they perceive that losses are at stake, and of group polarisation (*see below*). In addition, Janis obtained much of his information from published retrospective accounts, which some argue may be inaccurate (i.e. what is published is not always what actually happened) and/or incomplete.

Aldag and Fuller (1993) have pointed out that some research has found that group cohesiveness actually helps open discussion of ideas (rather than inhibiting it as Janis has argued). In fact, when Mullen and Copper (1994) reviewed 66 tests of the relationship between group cohesiveness and group performance, they found that cohesiveness was, on average, a significant (though not large) aid to performance, especially when groups were small. They also found that successful group performance tended to foster cohesiveness more than cohesiveness fostered performance. This is not surprising: if we think of cohesiveness as a combination of interpersonal attraction, commitment to the task and group pride, we would reasonably expect all of these to increase when the group succeeds in its tasks.

It is worth noting that studies which have failed to replicate groupthink have been laboratory-based studies of groups that do not have the history implied by some of the antecedents listed in Figure 13.1. Park (2000) reviewed 28 tests of the groupthink model published between 1974 and 1998. Eleven of these tests were experiments using students, while most of the others were case studies of real-life events. Nine of the experiments produced partial support for the groupthink model, two produced no support and none was fully or almost fully supportive. The case studies did better: seven supported all, or nearly all, of the model, three offered partial support and three offered little or no support.

The greater support from case studies might be because the experiments were artificial situations (i.e. without the historical antecedents needed for groupthink to occur) or because data from case studies are inherently more ambiguous and open to interpretation in line with the groupthink theory. In another experiment, Park (2000) tested all the relationships between variables proposed by the groupthink model by collecting data from 64 groups of 4 students. Park found partial support for the groupthink model. Some of the key findings were:

- high group cohesiveness was associated with more symptoms of groupthink than low group cohesiveness;

- groups with members who had (on average) high self-esteem showed more symptoms of groupthink than where members had (on average) low self-esteem;

- group members' feelings of invulnerability and morality were associated with fewer symptoms of defective decision-making;

■ when the group discussion contained an incomplete survey of alternative solutions they tended to make poor-quality decisions.

You might find it helpful to refer back to Figure 13.1 and think about which of these findings are as Janis predicted, and which are not. For example, the groupthink model has little to say about the influence of individual differences such as self-esteem.

Although it has been an influential model, by no means all research into group decision-making has been designed to test the groupthink model. However, much of it has investigated phenomena similar to those identified by Janis. For example, Schulz-Hardt *et al.* (2002) found that groups of managers who had similar points of view even before they met tended to seek yet more information that supported their existing view. However, when there was genuine disagreement in initial points of view this led to the group carrying out a much more balanced search for information in their discussions. The presence of people instructed to be a 'devil's advocate' (i.e. to argue the opposite view of the group's preference whatever their own private opinion) also had some effect in reducing a group's preference for information that agreed with their initial opinions. These findings support Janis's ideas that groups where the members agree are prone to restricting their information search and that appointing a devil's advocate may go some way towards correcting that.

All of the criticisms of groupthink have some force. Nevertheless, Janis provided rich case studies which illustrate the many potential problems in group decision-making. There is now lots of well-designed research that dispels any comforting belief we might have that really important group decisions are always made rationally.

Exercise 13.1   Your experiences of group decision-making

Try to recall a time when you participated in a group that had to make a decision (for example, to choose between alternative courses of action). Bring to mind as much as you can about what happened, and then consider the following questions. If you can do so with someone else who was there, so much the better.

Suggested exercises

1   How cohesive was the group, and what consequences do you think that had for (i) the way the group went about its task and (ii) how you felt about participating?

2   Do you think the group members were (i) excited about the possibility of accomplishing something really worthwhile or (ii) fearful about making a mistake? Either way, how did that affect the discussion the group had and the decision the group made?

3   If there was a leader of the group, to what extent were they admired and trusted by the other members? What was the impact of this on how the group conducted itself?

4   To what extent were alternative options carefully considered? Think about why.

5   Finally, was the eventual decision actually implemented? Why (or why not)? Did the decision work out well, and if not, could that have been foreseen?

6   Consider how well (or not) your observations match the theory and research discussed in this chapter so far.

The groupthink model appears not to be entirely accurate, but it includes many ideas that have had a big impact on subsequent research on groups and teams.

Group polarisation

One often-voiced criticism of groups is that they arrive at compromise decisions. However, it seems that groups tend to make more extreme decisions than we might expect given the initial preferences of group members (Bettenhausen, 1991). This has most often been demonstrated with respect to risk. If the initial tendency of the majority of group members is to adopt a moderately risky decision, the eventual group decision is usually more risky than that. Conversely, somewhat cautious initial preferences of group members translate to even more cautious eventual group decisions. This is known as polarisation.

Using systematic research, psychologists have reduced eleven possible explanations for group polarisation down to two (Isenberg, 1986). The *social comparison* explanation is that we like to present ourselves in a socially desirable way, so we try to be like other group members, *only more so*. The *persuasive argumentation* explanation is that information consistent with the views held by the majority will dominate the group discussion, and (so long as that information is correct and novel) have powerful persuasive effects. Both explanations are valid, though the latter seems to exert a stronger effect. Polarisation is not in itself inherently good or bad. However, in order to benefit from group decision-making, group members need to ensure that they share all relevant information and ideas (this means that all arguments rejecting the initially favoured point of view are heard). Group members also need to avoid social conformity (one of the phenomena that Janis observed as so damaging to group decision-making). Chen *et al.* (2002) have shown that using a quantitative decision aid (e.g. a questionnaire) can reduce the impact of overly biased persuasive arguments on group members, albeit only slightly.

Contrary to popular opinion, groups often produce more extreme decisions, and fewer compromises, than do individuals working on their own.

Minority influence

Research has shown that minorities within groups only rarely convert the majority to their point of view. But how can they maximise their chances? Many people say that they should first gain the acceptance of the majority by conforming wherever possible, and *then* stick out for their own point of view on a carefully chosen crucial issue. However, research carried out by Moscovici and colleagues suggests otherwise

(Moscovici and Mugny, 1983; Moscovici, 1985). They found that, if it is to exert influence, a minority needs to *disagree* consistently with the majority, including on issues other than the one that is of particular importance to the minority group. They demonstrated that minorities do not exert influence by being liked or being seen as reasonable, but by being perceived as consistent, independent and confident. Consistent with this, Van Hiel and Mervielde (2001) found that group members believe that being *assertive and consistent is an effective strategy for minorities*, while being *agreeable is a better strategy for majority groups* than it is for minorities. If we think back to the previous section concerning group polarisation, we see that a minority can effectively limit the extent of group polarisation by expressing many arguments that oppose the majority point of view.

Much debate has centred on why and how minorities in groups exert influence (e.g. Nemeth, 1986; Smith *et al.*, 1996; McLeod *et al.*, 1997). The predominant view is that minorities and majorities exert influence in different ways. Nemeth (1986) suggested that majorities encourage convergent, shallow and narrow thinking. However, consistent exposure to minority viewpoints stimulates deeper and wider consideration of alternative perspectives. Nemeth (1986, p. 28) concluded from experimental data that:

> Those exposed to minority viewpoints . . . are more original, they use a greater variety of strategies, they detect novel solutions, and importantly, they detect correct solutions. Furthermore, this beneficial effect occurs even when the minority viewpoints are wrong.

This emphasises again that in order to reach good-quality decisions, groups need to encourage different points of view, not suppress them.

Key Learning Point

Minority views may be irritating for some group members, but their expression typically leads to better group functioning, even if they are incorrect.

Wood *et al.* (1994) reviewed 143 studies of minority influence, and found that minorities do indeed have some capacity to change the opinions of people who hear their message. This effect is even stronger if recipients of the message are not required to publicly acknowledge their change of opinion to the minority. Opinion change is also much greater on issues indirectly related to the message than it is on those directly related to it. Indeed, although the opinion of the majority usually has more effect than that of the minority, the minority exert greater influence on issues only indirectly related to the message. Ng and Van Dyne (2001) have found in an experimental study with students, that group members who (i) value collectivist beliefs (i.e. act according to social norms that emphasise interpersonal harmony) and (ii) do *not* value individualist beliefs (i.e. *do not* focus on personal goals and perspectives) are less influenced than others by minority views. This means that they tend to be more influenced by the majority, thus impairing their decision-making. Ng and Van Dyne also found that when a one-person minority happens to be the leader of the group, they have more influence than when the one-person minority is not the leader.

A soft drink product decision

Rudi Lerner was managing director of a medium-size soft drinks company. His father had founded and then managed the business for nearly 30 years before handing over to his son four years ago. Rudi felt he knew much more about the business than his colleagues on the top management team. They agreed about that, and they liked and respected their boss as well as each other. They usually went out of their way to avoid contradicting him. On the rare occasions they did so, they received a friendly but firm reminder from the chairman that he had been in the business much longer than they had. That was true, but the team membership had not changed for five years now, so nobody was exactly ignorant. However, it was hard to argue - after all, the company had been successful relative to its competitors over the years. Rudi attributed this to frequent takeovers of competitors by people from outside the business. He rarely commissioned market research, relying instead on his 'gut feeling' and extensive prior experience. Now a new challenge faced the company: should it go into the low-calorie 'diet' drinks market, and if so, with what products? The demand for diet drinks was recent but might be here to stay.

Suggested exercise

How likely is it that Rudi and the rest of the management team will make a good decision about entering the 'diet' market? Explain your answer.

STOP TO CONSIDER

At this point in the chapter, think about how much the material you have read so far tells us about decision-making among groups of employees. Having read the sections on group-think, polarisation and minority influence how well can we explain decision-making in work-groups using this body of knowledge? What are the issues that this literature has tackled successfully? What issues has it tackled less successfully? Also, consider the key question: under what circumstances do groups tend to make better decisions than individuals making decisions on their own?

Relations between groups at work

So far we have examined what goes on within groups that are attempting to generate ideas and/or solve problems. Another important perspective is what happens *between* groups at work (see also Chapter 10). Most workplaces are composed of a large number of overlapping groups – for example different departments, committees, occupations, locations, project teams or hierarchical levels. Some of these groups have responsibilities for making and/or implementing decisions (e.g. the management board), while others are defined simply in terms of members having something in common (e.g. accountants). Work organisations need groups to cooperate and relate well to each other, both for organisational effectiveness and for the well-being of people within them.

It is widely thought that our need for a clear and positive personal identity leads us, on occasions, to define ourselves in terms of our group membership(s): we evaluate those groups we are in positively (and, in particular, more positively than other groups that we are not in). So in effect we use the groups we belong to, to give ourselves a positive sense of who we are. These are the fundamental ideas behind social identity theory (Tajfel and Turner, 1979) and self-categorisation theory (Turner, 1999). These ideas have been applied to help us understand how groups work together in organisations.

A review of the inter-group literature by Hewstone *et al.* (2002) makes the following points:

■ Usually we tend to favour the group(s) we belong to (termed the 'in-group') more than we disparage out-groups, and this often happens without us even realising it.

■ Successful inter-group bias enhances self-esteem, as predicted by social identity theory. Some have also predicted that when people's self-esteem is low or threatened, they will be even keener to evaluate their in-group positively. However, there is much less evidence for this.

■ Groups of high status and numerical superiority tend to show more in-group bias than those of low status and low membership numbers. However, such dominant groups may show generosity to out-group members when they see the status gap as being very wide. Low-status groups show high in-group bias when they have a chance of closing the gap and/or see their low status as unfair.

■ Various methods have been tried to reduce in-group bias, on the assumption that this will improve relations between different groups. The methods include teaching people to suppress their biases; inducing them to behave positively towards out-groups so that they infer from their own behaviour that they must have a positive attitude; increasing people's knowledge about out-group members (so that they are seen as individuals more than group members); finding superordinate groups (for example, defining a group as everyone in the company) which allow people to re-categorise from out-group members to in-group members.

■ In some situations, and some cultures, people tend to define themselves in terms of their group memberships. In others they do so more in terms of their characteristics as an individual (Ellemers *et al.*, 2002). So the nature and extent of in-group bias may change almost minute by minute.

Key Learning Point

Relations between groups at work are affected, often negatively, by group members' wishes to see themselves in a more positive light than members of other groups. This is a major challenge for organisations who wish to reap maximum benefits from having a diverse workforce.

An issue closely related to group membership concerns stereotypes. Stereotypes are generalised beliefs about the characteristics, attributes and behaviours of members of certain groups (Hilton and Von Hippel, 1996, p. 240). Groups can be defined on any number of criteria. Obvious possibilities are race, sex, occupation and age, but research suggests that most people do not have broad stereotypes (e.g. of all women, or all men, or all old people). Stereotypes tend to be based on rather more specific groups such as old men or old white women (Stangor *et al.*, 1992). Some stereotypes held by a person refer to quite specific groups, as in the following hypothetical examples:

- 'Employee representatives are usually people who express the most militant views.'

- 'Most nurses are caring and conscientious.'

- 'Managers in this company never tell the truth.'

- 'Accountants are always more stimulating to talk to than anybody else in the company.'

- 'Production managers usually speak their mind.'

Clearly, then, stereotypes vary in their favourability. They also differ in their extremity. The third and fourth above do not allow for any exceptions, but the others do because they refer to 'most' rather than 'all'. Often stereotypes have some validity, in the sense that *on average* members of one group differ from members of another group. On average, senior managers may be more intelligent in some respects than building site labourers. But there is equally certainly a large overlap – some building site labourers are more intelligent than some senior managers. In fact, one of the problems with stereotypes is that they lead to the overestimation of the differences between groups (Krueger, 1991).

Stereotypes of groups can develop from very limited information about them – perhaps confined to what we see on television. For example, our stereotypes about police officers may be heavily influenced by the latest television crime drama (in reality, police work is likely to be very different). Other stereotypes can arise when a generalisation is true of a very few people in one group and practically none in another group. Suppose for a moment that 1 in 500 trade union officials are members of revolutionary left-wing political groups, compared with 1 in 3000 of the general population. Would you then expect that a trade union official you were about to meet for the first time would be a revolutionary left-winger? Clearly not, the chances of this are very small. While it is more probable that they hold such views than someone who is not a trade union official, it is still not very likely. In this example, it would be inaccurate then to define trade union officials by their membership of such political groups.

Perhaps most of us like to think that we are free of stereotypes. If so, we are probably fooling ourselves. At a university where two of the authors were employed, a small number of students came each year from Norway. One of us (who shall remain nameless!) was slightly surprised that many of these students were *not* blond and tall – this was the stereotype they had of Scandinavians.

Some of the causes and consequences of stereotypes are shown in Figure 13.2, and discussion of the role of stereotypes in assessing people at work appears in Chapter 6. Devine (1989) argues that we cannot avoid starting out with stereotypes.

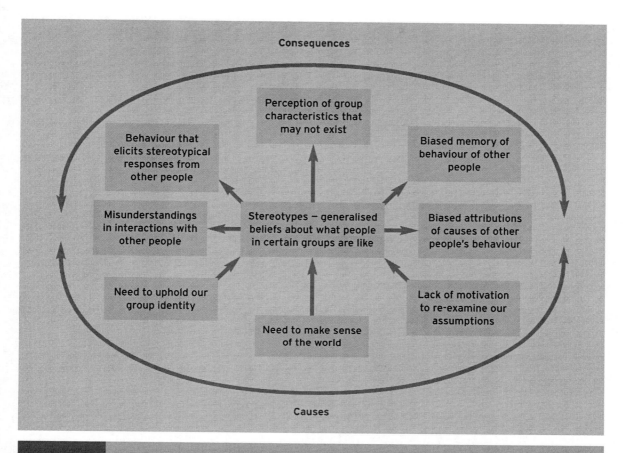

Figure 13.2   **Some causes and consequences of stereotypes**

The difference between prejudiced and non-prejudiced individuals is that the latter *deliberately inhibit the automatically activated* stereotype and replace it with more open-minded thoughts (Devine, 1989, p. 15):

> [This] can be likened to the breaking of a bad habit . . . The individual must (a) initially decide to stop the old behavior; (b) remember the resolution, and (c) try repeatedly and decide repeatedly to eliminate the habit before the habit can be eliminated.

Other work has shown that simply instructing people to try to suppress stereotypic thoughts can actually be counterproductive. Ironically, this type of instruction itself leads people to be more conscious of the stereotype they are trying to suppress (Bodenhausen and Macrae, 1996). As Devine implied, what matters seems to be a personal commitment to changing one's perception or behaviour. Often this will involve changing one's assumptions about why a particular person is the kind of person they are – for example, by thinking about whether someone has a powerful position in an organisation because of their talent, drive and determination, rather than because they have been lucky.

There is no doubt that these theories from social psychology can help us better understand inter-group biases in the workplace. However, what goes on within groups (i.e. intra-group variables) also plays an important role in determining behaviour. As Hewstone *et al.* (2002, p. 594) acknowledge:

> It would be a mistake, however, to consider ethnic and religious mass murder as a simple extension of intergroup bias . . . Real-world intergroup relations owe at least as much of their character to intra-group variables such as self-esteem, in-group identification . . . and group threat.

In the following sections we will consider how research carried out within workplaces has helped us to better understand teams and groups in the context of functioning organisations.

Teams in the twenty-first century workplace

The team/group distinction

Much of the previous section focused on the effectiveness of groups, mainly focusing on how they make decisions. Although very useful, a large percentage of this research has been carried out away from the organisational setting, with a focus on basic group processes. Clearly, there are other things that need to be considered when such processes take place in functioning organisations. In this section we look at how teams function from a broader perspective. You will also find relevant material in other sections of the book (e.g. Chapter 14, on leadership, has a lot to say about how to manage teams, as do the sections in Chapter 10 that deal with new methods of working and communication). Teams are increasingly common in organisations as functional boundaries break down and work is increasingly based on projects requiring input from people with different knowledge, skills, abilities and experience. The words team and group are often used interchangeably and in some cases this distinction is unimportant, but for organisational research purposes it is important to define the things being studied and teams are no exception.

A *workgroup* is characterised by being made up of individuals who:

- see themselves and are seen by others as a social entity, or unit;
- are interdependent, i.e. they rely on each other because of the tasks they perform;
- are embedded in one or more larger social systems (such as the organisation they work in);

■ perform tasks that affect others such as co-workers or customers (Guzzo and Dickson, 1996, p. 308).

Teams are different in the extent to which (i) members are interdependent (in teams levels of interdependency are very high) and (ii) the team as a whole (rather than the individuals in it) has performance goals (Sundstrom *et al.,* 1990). As Mohrman *et al.* (1995, p. 39) have put it, a team is 'a group of individuals who work together to produce products or deliver services for which they are mutually accountable'. Hackman (2002) suggested that true teams are characterised by four essential features:

1 Interdependence – team members are dependent upon each other to get things done, and the team members are not simply acting under the direction of a supervisor.

2 Membership boundaries – team members know who is part of the team (everyone knows who else carries some of the responsibility for getting things done).

3 Authority – a defined and bounded authority so that the team can manage what it does without excessive interference from, or reference to, others outside of the team. Teams are often defined according to their degree of decision-making authority (e.g. self-managing teams, semi-autonomous work groups).

4 Stability – a relatively stable membership for the lifetime of the team.

So, compared to a group, the composition of a team is relatively stable (although this stability may only last for a short period of time) and the people within it depend upon each other to achieve shared goals with the authority to act within defined boundaries. This is in contrast to assemblies of individuals (groups) where individuals rather than teams have work goals and there is much less close cooperation and interdependence. An example of a group would be all of the students studying the same course, attending the same lectures. An example of a team would be hospital employees (e.g. surgeons, anaesthetists, nurses) working together on a regular basis in an operating theatre environment. In the following sections we examine the advantages of teams (in terms of both how they benefit organisations and the individuals within them).

The prevalence of teamwork

Morita (2001) suggested that teamworking has two distinct origins. The first grew out of concern for the quality of working life in Europe (especially during the 1960s and 1970s). Teamworking was thought to provide people with more satisfying work than either working alone or in a group. The second origin was an interest in the perceived advantages of Japanese management styles, with their emphasis on multifunctional employees, loyalty to the collective and collective responsibility for the quality and quantity of work (all features of work that are important in teams). We can supplement these origins with an increased interest in the characteristics of the high-performance workplace (HPWP). Teamwork is one of several practices usually associated with the HPWP (also known as the high-commitment workplace because work practices aim to instil high levels of employee commitment). High-performance practices are implemented in an attempt to get stronger levels of employee engagement and involvement in the way that work is designed as a way of reaching higher than average levels of performance. Alongside teamwork, HPWP practices include extensive training and development, multiskilling for flexibility and performance-related pay.

So, how widespread is teamwork? The answer depends of course on how teamworking is defined, who is asked about it, and exactly how the question is asked. Perhaps the most informative analysis has been provided by Benders *et al.* (2001). Senior managers in nearly 6000 organisations in ten European countries were asked to describe the extent to which people in the largest occupational group in their workplace worked in *teams which had the authority to make their own decisions in each of the following eight areas*:

1   allocation of work;

2   scheduling of work;

3   quality of work;

4   timekeeping;

5   attendance and absence control;

6   job rotation;

7   coordination of work with other internal groups;

8   improving work processes.

Benders *et al.* decided that, in order to qualify as a 'group-based workplace' – somewhat confusingly, this means lots of employees working in teams:

■   at least four of the eight decision areas should be assigned to teams; *and*

■   at least 70 per cent of core employees should work in such groups (i.e. teams).

Only 217 workplaces (about 4 per cent of the total) met both criteria. In fact, only 1404 (24 per cent) of the workplaces assigned *any* of the eight decision areas to teams. Country by country, the 24 per cent were distributed as shown in Table 13.1.

Table 13.1	The incidence of teamworking in ten European countries	
	Percentage with at least one decision area assigned to teams	Percentage of workplaces 'team-based'
Sweden	44	11
Netherlands	38	5
France	27	5
UK	27	5
Germany	26	4
Denmark	24	3
Ireland	22	3
Italy	22	1
Portugal	6	0
Spain	4	0

Source: Adapted from Benders *et al.* (2001).

Sweden's place at the top of this table is unsurprising given its tradition of participative democracy, sociotechnical work design (*see* Chapter 8), and high-profile examples demonstrating the success of teamworking – for example Volvo. However, it is surprising that this did not spill over the border to Denmark. The low incidence of teamwork in the southern European countries is consistent with evidence that these cultures tend to emphasise status and hierarchy. Regarding which decisions teams made for themselves, improving work processes and scheduling were the most common, and job rotation, attendance and absence control the least common. Benders *et al.* note that 'headline' figures from studies of teamwork in the United States are higher than in Europe (e.g. Gittleman *et al.*, 1998, 32 per cent of workplaces using teamwork). However, on closer inspection it appears that this is partly because of differences in sampling methods and the way that questions were asked. If anything teamwork is more prevalent in Europe than in the United States. This is supported by more recent work (Blasi and Kruse, 2006; p. 572) which found that the level of adoption of self-managing teams in the 1990s was 'rather modest'.

Key Learning Point

In spite of a lot of enthusiasm for teamwork, true teamwork seems to be more the exception than the rule.

However, perhaps the stringent criteria used to identify teams underestimates the extent of organisations' efforts to implement team working. The latest (2004) Workplace Employment Relations Survey (WERS) – a very large survey of UK workplaces – shows that teamwork is the most common of the HPWP practices to be implemented (Kersley *et al.*, 2005). Almost three-quarters (72 per cent) of UK workplaces reported 'at least some of their core employees in formally designated teams'. This was very similar to the proportion in the previous 1998 WERS survey. There is some evidence of a public/private sector difference as 88 per cent of public sector workplaces claimed to be involved in teamwork compared to 68 per cent of private sector workplaces. While the WERS reported teams having a reasonable levels of responsibility for specific products and services and deciding how they can organise work, only a minority of workplaces (6 per cent) had the authority to decide who the team leader would be. Thus, organisations appear to retain a high level of control over team leader appointments.

These two large surveys suggest that UK managers report high levels if left to define teamwork for themselves: the extent of *real or true teamwork* seems considerably less. However, Scarbrough and Kinnie (2003) advise against the use of an objective definition of teamworking because the many different configurations of teamworking reflect the different work and organisational contexts in which it is attempted. Influences upon the extent of teamworking include, but are not limited to, the industrial relations context, methods of management control, the size of the organisation, the production technologies used and the extent to which they allow teamworking, the imperative for change to teamworking and the focus on teamwork in the supply chain. Given that all organisations need to exert control over employees to some extent, teamwork can be seen as a way of getting employees to control themselves while they continue to work within a framework set out by management.

How do teams work?

The input-process-output model

The classic starting point for looking at team functioning is the Input–Process–Output (I–P–O) model (McGrath, 1964). This recognises that for a given team, in a particular context, there are characteristics which can be seen as inputs that influence how the team performs (processes) and thus the final outputs. Inputs include team size, team-member diversity, structure and whether there are individual or group rewards for hitting targets. Other important input variables include the nature of the task(s) to be completed (e.g. physical or intellectual tasks, or both) and the organisational context the team is embedded in.

The interactions among the various inputs influence team processes. These include how cohesive team members feel, how well they communicate with each other and with stakeholders outside the team, how well they make decisions and how effectively team leadership occurs. Communication is influenced by the spontaneity and openness present at team meetings and may be enhanced if facilitating roles are shared rather than confined to a designated leader. While team leaders are usually appointed by the organisation this does not prevent other team members from taking leadership roles – perhaps when their specialist knowledge or personal skills can be leveraged. Another key process is decision-making (discussed earlier in this chapter) which requires the team to focus on a problem or task and deconstruct the problem/task into its components for analysis.

Naturally, outputs vary depending upon what the team exists to do. A management team could be focusing on objective, measurable targets such as income growth or cost reduction. It may also focus on introducing changes to systems or improving the efficiency of processes. Product development or customer service teams will have more clearly defined targets (e.g. to reduce the number of customer complaints filed against members of the team).

Key Learning Point

A simple model of how teams function is

Inputs → Processes → Outputs

However, the I–P–O model falls short of fully describing the complex nature of teams when they are embedded in organisational settings. It also says little about the way that teams change and evolve over time. Criticisms of the I–P–O model (Ilgen *et al.*, 2005) are:

- Many factors that influence the conversion of inputs to outputs are not processes but 'emergent cognitive or affective states' (Ilgen *et al.*, 2005, p. 520), i.e. how the team members think or feel about the problem is important, and not just the mechanics of what the team does.

- The I–P–O model implies linear paths throughout even though there are many feedback loops present. For instance, analysis of performance outputs after some intervention is an input to subsequent team processes and cognitive states and hence an input to performance at time 2.

- Relationships between the main effects in the model (e.g. the effect of team size on cohesion) are not linear as there are complex interactions between inputs and process. For example, changes in the size of the team may have an impact on how cohesive the team is. There may also be interactions between different processes, if, say, the appointment, or emergence, of a new team leader could influence the openness of team meetings.

Beyond the I-P-O model

Kozlowski and Ilgen (2006) point out that the I–P–O model was not offered as a causal model but as a way of organising the research literature that had looked at different aspects of teams. It has, however, come to be seen as a useful working model. Ilgen and colleagues go beyond the I–P–O model by proposing an 'input-mediator-output-input' (IMOI) model. Processes have been replaced by mediators to capture a wider range of variables than processes alone: mediators encompass a whole range of factors within and outside of the team that influence what the team does and the results of its efforts. The addition of 'input' to the end of the model captures the influence of feedback (i.e. the teams results being known and used to influence how it goes about its work). Removal of the hyphens in IMOI is more than just stylistic: it deliberately signifies that causal paths are more likely to be non-linear than linear.

Ilgen *et al.* (2005) propose three main stages in team functioning. The early stages of team development they called *forming*, and are described by inputs and mediators (IM). The next stage they called *functioning* which captures mediators and outputs (MO). This is followed by a *finishing* stage which captures outputs and inputs (OI). These stages are summarised below.

Forming

Forming requires three activities: trusting, planning and structuring. Trusting is about team members, collectively, believing they have the wherewithal to be effective. It also requires that team members trust each other's intentions and motives: we can all think of how we guard ourselves in the presence of people that we do not trust, particularly when they have some power over us. Guarded contributions tend to impede team performance and so a climate of psychological safety is needed.

Planning involves gathering and using information. Communication needs to be open and information needs to be shared freely (and not only when people feel under pressure to do so). With information gathered the next step is to turn it into a strategy. This calls for goals to be articulated and shared.

Structuring represents the shared mental models held by team members. The concept of mental models has helped to advance team research: they describe how people see the interrelationships that exist and who is responsible for particular outcomes. Where the mental models of team members are different, then teamwork will be compromised by differing views about how the task should be achieved (and there may be some differences about what the task actually is). Where mental models are similar then coordination is more efficient. Structuring also involves setting up a 'transactive memory': during this team members need to become aware of what is known within the team and of who knows what.

Functioning

Functioning involves *bonding, adapting and learning*. Bonding extends beyond trusting each other to reflect a genuine desire among team members to work together. It reflects concepts which have already been mentioned in this chapter including cohesion, commitment and social integration. The extent of bonding can be influenced by the diversity within the team. However, the basis of the diversity matters; personality diversity may be counterproductive if, for example, members differ widely on agreeableness (i.e. there are some people who really like a good argument, and others who will do anything they can to avoid one!). The ability to manage conflict is therefore an important aspect of team bonding.

Adapting covers two distinct concepts; the ability of a team to recognise when conditions change from being routine to being novel (and to respond when they do) and the ability to share workload among the team through mutually supporting behaviour.

Learning relates to changes in the body of knowledge that a team draws upon. One aspect of this is learning from minority and/or dissenting team members (*see also* Minority influence above). A minority in this context means people having minority views ('the lone voices'). At extremes, views that do not fit with the dominant paradigm can be suppressed to the point that the person holding them is isolated and treated as if they do not understand how complex the problem is (*see also* Groupthink above). However, teams need to hear minority opinions as they can challenge comfortable thinking. Likewise teams need to learn from the 'best' member in the team. This is not necessarily the same person all the time, but as the team's needs change so may the most knowledgeable person on a particular topic.

Finishing

This phase of decline and winding-up of a team is not well understood and we currently know very little about what happens in the end game.

Key Learning Point

In reality, there are many feedback loops operating in teams. The complexity of interactions between inputs, processes, cognitive states and outputs is very difficult to model and test.

What is teamwork?

The I–P–O and IMOI models describe how teams tackle tasks, i.e. they are descriptive. However, they are not designed to provide a detailed explanation of what effective teams do differently when compared to ineffective teams, i.e. they do not really tell us what good teamwork is. The phrase 'we need good teamwork' is so often heard in organisations that it is important we understand what good and bad teamwork are and how to identify them! Two recent studies help us to answer this question. Hoegl and Gemuenden (2001) developed a theoretical model of the quality of teamwork (and an accompanying Teamwork Quality questionnaire) comprising six dimensions:

1   Communication: good communication is frequent, spontaneous, direct between team members and open.

2   Coordination: good coordination means that there is a shared understanding of who is doing what, for whom and when.

3   Balanced contributions from members: all team members are able to input what they know.

4 Mutual support: there is collaboration and cooperation (not competition) over tasks.

5 Effort: whatever the level of effort required, it is important that team members know it and accept it.

6 Cohesion: this concerns the desire of team members to work together to stay together.

Senior and Swailes (2007) asked members of management teams to discuss examples of poor-, average- and high-performing teams in order to identify the key differences between teams performing at the three different level. Using repertory grid analysis of data they developed a seven-dimensional model of teamwork (and a Teamwork Survey that can be used to measure these seven dimensions in other teams). The seven dimensions that appeared to be linked to team performance were:

1 team purpose: goal clarity and acceptance by members;

2 team organisation: allocation of roles, responsibilities and a structure for operating;

3 leadership: the presence of appropriate leadership style and leader support for members;

4 team climate: openness, professionalism, morale, respect for differences;

5 interpersonal relations: care and support, healthy rapport, honesty and liking;

6 team communications: constructive handling of conflict, frequency of contact, coordinated communications;

7 team composition: the mix of personality and abilities and continuity of membership.

An eighth dimension reflecting the team's interaction with the wider organisation was added. This was based on previous research which shows how the impact of team is mediated by wider organisational factors such as respect for the team within the organisation, support for the team's development and the alignment of the team's objectives with organisational goals.

These models of teamwork are useful because they help us to better understand not just what teams do, but how their activities are linked to their success (or failure). They help us to understand the links between inputs, mediators and outputs. For example, measures of teamwork might help to explain why a diverse team fails to achieve its goals. Such measures can also be used in team development interventions in order to diagnose problems with team functioning (e.g. by getting people to reflect (in a structured way) on their own team and how it functions).

Putting together a good team: selecting people for teams

Knowledge, skills and abilities

Stevens and Campion (1994) argued that there is a set of individual-level competencies that influence a person's performance in teams and thus the overall team performance. Teamwork competencies, or knowledge, skills and attributes (KSAs), were proposed that covered two main areas: interpersonal knowledge and self-management. Interpersonal knowledge relates to the team member's competence when relating to others and responding to their emotions to in order to release their ideas and to maximise team members' contributions to problem-solving. More specifically, this includes:

- Conflict resolution: a person's ability to recognise it, to discourage it and where possible to use disagreement positively, e.g. by finding a constructive way forward.

- Collaborative problem-solving skills: a person's skills which are used to overcome barriers and enable the team to use the resources of all members.

- Communication skills: which include listening without evaluating, communicating openly, awareness of non-verbal cues, and the ability to engage in social conversations.

Self-management KSAs relate more to the goal-setting and the distribution of tasks within the team. More specifically, this includes:

- the team member's ability to set realistic and relevant goals for themselves, team members and for the team collectively; and

- the team member's ability to allocate work within the team to maximise the usage of the particular mix of personal skills and technical knowledge available.

Thus it follows that when selecting for teams, the extent to which potential team members already possess these KSAs needs to be considered. Fortunately, specific tests of these KSAs have been developed. The Teamwork KSA Test (Stevens and Campion, 1999) is a 35-item questionnaire embodying the KSAs listed above. However, research has shown that it had virtually the same power to predict team-related outcomes as general aptitude tests (and therefore added little extra). However, if we think of our own experience of teamwork we may remember work colleagues with potentially valuable contributions that were suppressed by their shyness, or of the dominant but not so bright colleague whose bold assertions steer the team to its final destination (a very frustrating state of affairs!). This line of thinking led Miller (2001) to point out that it is not enough for team members to possess teamwork KSAs: it is the ability to put them into practice that really matters. Although the evidence is mixed, tests such as the Teamwork KSA Test show some potential to predict individual team member behaviour and thus predict individual level effectiveness in teams (McClough and Rogelberg, 2003). Such KSAs may, therefore, be a necessary, not sufficient, requirement for effective individual performance in a team.

Team roles

Another concept of interest to teamwork theory and to the practical questions about selecting people for teams and team development programmes is that of team roles. Although several typologies of team roles exist, Meredith Belbin (1981, 1993a) developed a model that has been particularly influential and which is still widely used by organisations. He observed teams in action and concluded that that teams made up of the brightest people did not necessarily produce the best outcomes. This led him to develop a theory of team roles: he argued that a key factor behind effective teams is the presence in the team of set people who each perform

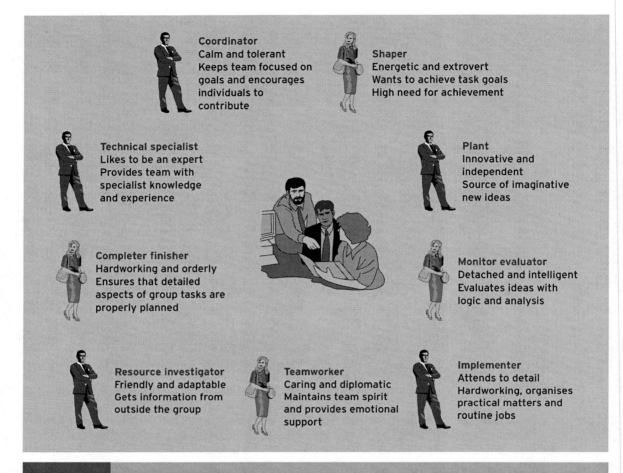

| Figure 13.3 | Belbin's nine team roles |

specified team roles. He argued that people taking different roles needed to be appropriately combined in a team in order to achieve high performance. He identified nine roles that team members need to fulfil if the team is to be successful. These are shown in Figure 13.3.

Of course, not all teams contain nine people, each of whom takes one role. Each of us, according to the theory, has one or two preferred roles and one or two roles that we are capable of doing if no one else in the team does them better. Hence, four or five people can possess all nine roles predicted by theory. Most individuals are capable of playing more than one role and it is clear from Figure 13.3 that there are some roles that each of us would find it very difficult to fill effectively.

Key Learning Point

In theory, team members need to pool a range of different competences in order to optimise performance. However, empirical evidence for this hypothesis is limited.

Belbin developed a Team Role Self-Perception Inventory (TRSPI) and an Observer Assessment Sheet (OAS) to help identify a person's role preferences. The TRSPI gives a person's self-assessment of their role profile and should be used in conjunction with predictions from two or three others who know them, e.g. a supervisor and a colleague, via the OAS. The combined results should then be used for team development purposes. In practice, however, most situations usually only use the TRSPI, which curtails the amount of information used in development discussions.

The main value of the Inventory is to raise awareness and to provide a vocabulary with which people at work can appreciate the characteristics and strengths of others and thus talk about their teams and their roles in them. As such, it has an important developmental role.

The TRSPI, however, has attracted some rather critical psychometric evaluations that cast doubt on the reliability of the nine scales and the differences between them: this in turn cast doubt on its ability to measure stable aspects of personality. Rather, it appears that people can take on a number of different roles in a team situation. Furnham *et al.* (1993) led the charge against it but it is important to see Belbin's response to get both sides of the argument (Belbin, 1993b). Other critical assessments include Fisher *et al.* (2001) who questioned its lack of convergent and discriminant validity, i.e. that team roles did not show consistently high positive correlations with other similar constructs, or show consistently low correlations with different constructs. Anderson and Sleap (2004) questioned whether there are gender differences in the ways people respond to the Belbin questionnaire – e.g. women score significantly higher on the 'teamworker' scale. Some studies of the TRPSI have looked at reliability in different and arguably more appropriate ways, and are more supportive of its basic properties (e.g. Swailes and Aritzeta, 2006).

Key Learning Point

Team members can usually adopt two or three different roles and should appreciate the value of all the roles needed.

Virtual teams

Most of the research on teams has focused on people working in close proximity to each other, either in an organisational setting or in experimental research designs. However, as organisational structures have changed so too has the nature of teamwork in some organisations. Globalisation backed by information and communication technologies (ICT) has led to the evolution of virtual teams. These have members who are typically distributed throughout different locations and rely heavily on ICT to share information and to conference. Chapter 10 gives some details on how technology impacts on the way such teams communicate.

To what extent, say, six people in six different countries are a team is of course debatable. However, if we suspend that concern then there are some interesting questions touching on how virtual teams operate and how the competences needed for success differ, if at all, to conventional teamwork KSAs.

In relation to the competences needed, Hertel and colleagues (2006) built upon the framework of Stevens and Campion (1999) and others by proposing an additional group of competences; 'telecooperation-related KSAs'. They were conceptualised as:

- Self-management skills which are required in situations where control by a supervisor and other team members is reduced by physical separation. They include the ability to self-organise, persistence towards targets, motivation to learn in new contexts and creativity.

- Interpersonal trust: the need for this is amplified in the absence of close relationships and when the scope to intervene and help the work of a team member who is falling behind is restricted.

- Intercultural KSAs: these relate to sensitivity in dealing with other team members likely to have come from different social, educational and cultural backgrounds, a situation more likely in geographically distributed teams.

Hertel *et al.* (2006) developed a 39-item Virtual Team Competency Inventory which they argue can assist the selection of people for roles in virtual teams.

Teams: a view from the inside

Influences on members' attitudes

What does teamworking do for members' work attitudes and performance? Allen and Hecht (2004) provide an interesting counter to the thrust of much of the literature on teams. They claim that 'current beliefs in the effectiveness of teams are out of proportion to the evidence regarding their effectiveness' (p. 454). They go on to say that this state exists because teams make people more satisfied at work and raise confidence. These psychological benefits are important and are good reasons in themselves for organisations to continue using teamwork as a way or organising. However, it is useful to ask what is the evidence for these enhanced psychological states?

Rasmussen and Jeppesen (2006) reviewed 55 studies and found that teamwork generally does associate with psychological variables such as cohesion, organisational commitment and job satisfaction, although this is not always the case. Team type and size had no influence on the likelihood of the implementation of teamwork having a successful outcome. Van Mierlo *et al.* (2005) found that only job satisfaction was consistently related to self-managing teamwork.

Harley (2001) points out that on one hand there are the job redesign enthusiasts who argue that teamwork increases the amount of control people have over their work. On the other hand theorists from the 'critical management' school maintain that teamworking leads to more work and less discretion for individuals, with senior managers effectively allowing pressure and scrutiny from other team members to substitute for formal supervisory control.

Harley analysed data from the 1998 British Workplace Employee Relations Survey looking at the level of discretion (autonomy), commitment, satisfaction, stress and relations with managers. He found no significant differences between people in a team or not in a team. Harley (2001, p. 737) concluded that 'team membership does not matter much' adding:

> The results leave [both] positive and critical accounts of teamwork looking rather for-lorn. While teamwork does not, according to this analysis, herald a transformation of work in which employees regain the discretion denied to them by Taylorist work organisation, nor does it appear to involve reductions in discretion and hence increased work intensification.

A possible explanation for this finding is that a large proportion of the people supposedly in teams were not really in a *true* team at all, although Harley rejects this idea. His preferred explanations are:

- that teams are managerially driven (i.e. implemented in order to raise perform-ance) and therefore higher levels of psychological well-being and satisfaction do not necessarily occur alongside improvements in performance; or

- that teams are so widely used that their formal implementation makes little dif-ference to the hierarchical managerial structures already found in the organisa-tion. Therefore, on many occasions, implementing teamwork has little impact on member attitudes and behaviour.

Visions of teamwork

Some case-study based work also suggests that teamwork may have multiple and complex meanings – a team in one organisation might look very different from a team in another. This makes the overall impact of teams difficult to discern. For example, Procter and Currie (2002) studied a local branch of the United Kingdom's tax col-lection system, Her Majesty's Revenue and Customs. It had reduced its layers of management during the 1990s and reorganised work so that tasks were allocated to teams rather than individuals. There was a general belief that teamwork was partly intended by management to elicit more workless resources. Procter and Currie note (2002, p. 304) that in some ways teamworking had meant little substantive change in job design, but that its impact was felt in other ways:

> The range of work is little changed; employees exercise little in the way of new skills; they appear reluctant to adopt responsibility for the work of others; and the perform-ance management system operates on the basis of individual performance. Nonethe-less, teamworking appears to work in the Inland Revenue. It does so by having a team rather than an individual allocation of work, and by encouraging individual identity with the team target.

Steijn (2001) points out that one reason why some studies find little or no im-pact of teamworking may be that non-teamworkers in fact comprise two very dif-ferent groups. One group is people who work in mundane jobs with low skill requirements and little discretion. The other is professional or craft workers who exercise both skill and discretion in pursuing their individualised un-teamlike work (i.e. their job provides for them to use skills and makes decisions, without needing to work in a team). In a survey of 800 Dutch workers, Steijn found that the mun-dane jobs are less pleasant for the people who do them than both professional/craft work and for those involved in teamwork. In terms of how pleasant the jobs were, professional/craft work and those done in teams differed little from each other.

A sophisticated analysis of some aspects of teamwork has been offered by Griffin *et al.* (2001). Like many others, they suggested that the introduction of teamwork reduces the role of supervisors and that this can be a difficult transition for those involved. Griffin and colleagues obtained data from nearly 5000 employees in 48 manufacturing companies in the United Kingdom, and also made their own assessments of the extent to which each company had introduced teamworking. As they hypothesised, employees' job satisfaction was influenced by the extent to which they felt their supervisors supported them, but (again as hypothesised), this effect was smaller in companies which used teamwork a lot than in those which made little use of it. In other words, teamworking does indeed reduce (but not eliminate) the impact of supervisors on their employees' job attitudes.

Overall then, the use of teamworking seemed to lead to a small reduction in job satisfaction but this was an outcome of two conflicting forces: on the one hand teamwork reduced the amount of supervisor support employees experienced, and this in turn eroded job satisfaction. On the other hand, teamwork also led to more enriched jobs (e.g. multiskilling, responsibility) which tended to increase job satisfaction. These two opposite effects occurring together may be another reason why Harley (2001) among others found little or no overall impact of teamwork on people's job attitudes. It can also be that implementing teamwork increases the autonomy of the team, while at the same time reducing the autonomy of some of the individual team members.

Key Learning Point

Teamworking appears to have a complex association with work attitudes. This is partly because the introduction of teamworking may leave some work practices unchanged, improve others and also have a negative impact on some aspects of job design. It is also partly because people who do not work in teams have many different kinds of job – some of which already contain the beneficial features of job design that teamworking may introduce.

Another important issue concerns the way people describe a team using images and concepts. This is likely to indicate quite a lot about, for example, what they expect from a team leader (*see also* Chapter 14) and their other colleagues within the team. Such images are also likely to vary somewhat between cultures. Gibson and Zellmer-Bruhn (2002) present an analysis of how employees in pharmaceutical firms in Europe, South East Asia, Latin America and the United States talk about teams. They invoke the concept of metaphor, which they define (p. 102) as 'mechanisms by which we understand our experiences. We use metaphors whenever we think of one experience in terms of another. They help us to comprehend abstract concepts and perform abstract reasoning.'

From a careful analysis of how people talked about teams, Gibson and Zellmer-Bruhn identified five types of teamwork metaphor:

1   Sports metaphor: engage in specific tasks with clear objectives and performance measurement; members have clear roles; interaction between team members is largely confined to task-related matters; relatively little hierarchy; focus on winning and losing.

2   Military metaphor: similar to sports in that the team also engages in tasks with limited scope and clear objectives, but these teams have a clear and indisputable hierarchy; the focus of the metaphor is on life, death, survival and battle.

3   Family metaphor: these teams engage in broad-ranging tasks and interact across most domains of life; they have a relatively low emphasis on goals; clear roles (e.g. 'brothers' and 'sisters') and hierarchy ('father', 'mother').

4   Community metaphor: like families, communities are broad in the scope of interactions between members. However, roles are quite informal and ambiguous; goals sometimes quite ambiguous and the team quite amorphous.

5   Associates: these teams limited activity, with interactions only in the professional domain; little hierarchy; roles may be clear but can change; ties between group members quite loose.

Where a team leader holds a teamwork metaphor that differs from those held by other team members, problems are likely to arise. For example, if the leader tends to construe a team as a sports team but the others see it more like a community, the members may feel confused or alienated by their leader's concern with meeting targets and restricting interaction to the task. Managers need to be aware of the team members' metaphor in order to manage their team effectively.

Different countries tend to exhibit somewhat different cultures (*see also* Chapter 1). This has implications for multinational companies where managers are assigned to countries other than their own, and where teams are often made up of people of various nationalities. For example, as Gibson and Zellmer-Bruhn (2002) point out, Latin American countries tend to emphasise both collectivism and status differentials, which would tend to imply a *family team metaphor*. If a leader is from a highly individualist and low power distance culture such as the United States, they may find it easier to think in terms of a sports team metaphor or the associates metaphor.

Factors influencing team performance

Teams have tasks to do and, at a simple level, team performance is simply the extent to which a task is achieved, but the extent of task achievement does not tell us anything about how the team itself performed at team level. For instance, a team aiming to improve road safety in a region may be judged by the number of accidents, injuries and fatalities on certain roads over time. While these are good indicators of road safety, even if improvements do occur those statistics do not tell us anything about team-level performance, e.g. whether the team atmosphere fostered creativity and innovation, or whether it used all of the information available to it to tackle the problem. A significant thrust of team research is about understanding the links between teamwork and team outputs. Indeed, it is important to be clear about whether team performance is being used to describe *within-team processes* or the achievement of *objective output measures*.

With that caveat in mind, researchers have devoted considerable time and effort to understanding the factors that influence team performance and the conditions under which their influence occurs. There are too many to consider all of them here, so a selection of key factors is summarised below.

Stage of team development

Teams are not fully functional from the start: anyone who follows a sports team can see that they usually need time to reach their full potential. Over time there may be changes in personnel, and the team may change in terms of how team members approach their tasks and relate to each other. One early analysis (Tuckman, 1965) suggested that teams tend to go through a series of stages in their development:

1 *Forming*: this is the stage when a team first forms, when there is typically ambiguity and confusion. The members may not have chosen to work with each other. They may be guarded, superficial and impersonal in communication and unclear about the task.

2 *Storming*: this can be a difficult stage when there is conflict between team members and some rebellion against the task as assigned. There may be jockeying for positions of power and frustration at a lack of progress in the task.

3 *Norming*: in this stage it is important that open communication between team members is established. A start is made on confronting the task in hand, and generally accepted procedures and patterns of communication are established.

4 *Performing*: having established how it is going to function, the group is now free to devote its full attention to achieving its goals. If the earlier stages have been tackled satisfactorily, the group should now be close and supportive, open and trusting, resourceful and effective.

Most teams have a limited life, so it is probably appropriate to add another stage that could be called *disbanding*. It would be important for team members to analyse their own performance and that of the group, to learn from the experience, agree whether to stay in touch and if so what that might achieve.

Understanding where a team is in terms of these stages of development might help us to understand team processes. However, not everyone agrees that these stages are either an accurate description or a desirable sequence. Teams composed of people who are accustomed to working in a certain way may jump straight to the norming stage. The members may already know each other. Even if they do not, they may be able quickly to establish satisfactory ways of interacting without conflict. In any case, many teams are required to perform right from the start, so they need to bypass the earlier stages, at least partially. West (1994, p. 98) has argued that key tasks in team start-up concern the establishment of team goals and individual tasks that are both meaningful and challenging, as well as setting up procedures for performance monitoring and review.

Key Learning Point

Some teams go through stages in their development, but many need to achieve high performance straight away, with these stages being very short-lived, or absent altogether.

Team climate

West (2002) argued that teams at work are often required both to think of new ideas and to implement them. He refers to the former as creativity and the latter as innovation and these can be seen as performance outcomes. Creativity is encouraged by diversity of perspectives in the group, coupled with participation of all members, feelings of respect for each other and expectations that it is acceptable to argue constructively with each other. These factors also help innovation. However, pressures from the environment have the opposite effect. These pressures can include uncertainty (e.g. about market conditions), probably by increasing team members' anxiety and consuming their cognitive resources. On the other hand, they may also encourage innovation because this involves action and active problem-solving to improve a possibly difficult situation.

Because of the potential pay-off from creativity and innovation (i.e. better products, services and systems) both are highly prized by organisations. In light of the widespread use of work teams and the use of teams to deliver innovative solutions, Anderson and West (1998) developed a way of measuring the climate for innovation through a Team Climate Inventory (TCI). The theoretical basis of this is a four-factor model of the drivers of work group innovation. These are:

1   Vision – this embraces the idea that clearly defined objectives lead to behaviour focused on achieving the objectives. It is broadly defined and spans the extent to which the vision is understood, valued and shared by team members.

2   Participative safety – this embraces the idea that the team climate is conducive to raising and challenging ideas and information, and to making decisions without prejudice from others. For example, if a team member felt that another would bad-mouth them to their boss then the climate for innovation would be compromised.

3   Task orientation – this concerns staying focused on the task by allocating responsibility and by evaluating and changing performance in light of progress towards agreed targets.

4   Support for innovation – the best ideas will struggle if team members do not feel that there is a genuine willingness in the workplace to change things. To be convincing, support needs to be visible (*enacted*) and not just *articulated* (for instance, by managers outside the team).

This theoretical model of is the basis of the 86-item TCI. It can be used in surveys of organisational climate, as a diagnostic tool to help understand team effectiveness and at team development events as a way of helping team members to discuss issues touching upon innovation in their own work contexts.

Team-building

Team-building and development are widely practised by organisations from junior levels of new recruits to the most senior levels of top management. This happens because organisations assume that team development is an antecedent of better team performance. Team-building is carried out on the assumption that optimal team performance occurs some time into the lifetime of a team: team development and team-building interventions are designed to move teams more quickly towards the latter stages of development. Therefore such interventions address, among other things:

- the respect for team members, their views and distinctive skills;

- team members' confidence to raise and to challenge views or information;

- the clarity of the teams' goals and priorities;

- the allocation of work within the team and relationships with others outside the team.

We may ask, given the considerable costs of conducting it, whether there is any evidence that team-building actually has any impact on team performance. In some respects, this is a question for individual organisations to answer. If an employer is convinced that in their particular context their investments are being repaid then that is enough for them. Salas *et al.* (1999) carried out a meta-analysis of team-building research. Their main findings were:

- Overall there was a non-significant effect of team-building on team performance. The effect was non-significant for objective measures of performance but a weak positive effect was found when subjective performance measures were used.

- The only component of team-building that had a significant effect was role clarification such that the more role clarification was a part of team-building the stronger the effect on performance.

- The effects of team-building on performance decreased as team size increased. Hence it may be more beneficial in smaller teams than larger teams.

- Shorter team-building interventions were more effective than longer ones.

In common with other meta-analyses the study aggregated different studies with different definitions of teams, different research settings and different measures of performance, all against a backdrop of diverse ways of attempting team-building with different development targets. This means that the findings do not necessarily apply to all team-building interventions, but they do represent interesting trends in the previous research.

Key Learning Point

This meta-analysis indicates that if team-building is attempted it is best focused on role clarification in small groups, but the final decision rests with organisations who must make their own judgements.

Team diversity

The importance of role diversity in teams and the need for effective teams to have people with differing outlooks and strengths is now generally accepted. The problem is, of course, that we may devalue characteristics we happen not to possess ourselves. While diversity in terms of occupational or organisational roles is common in teams, diversity in terms of gender, nationality, ethnicity, age or personality is perhaps less often considered. It is also difficult to manage effectively, because team members may have quite different values and expectations of how to behave. So although teams with diverse members have the *potential* to be highly effective because of the varied outlooks they possess, they often fail to achieve that potential (Kandola, 1995). Maznevski (1994) and Paulus (2000) have argued that teams need integration, and that this is more difficult to achieve as they become more diverse. Integration relies on a number of factors:

- a social reality shared by group members;
- the ability to 'decentre' – that is, see things from others' points of view;
- the motivation to communicate;
- the ability to negotiate and agree on norms of behaviour within the team;
- the ability to identify the true causes of any difficulties that arise (e.g. not blaming people for things that are not their fault);
- self-confidence of all group members.

These are good guidelines for any team, but are harder to achieve in a diverse one. Teams with diverse members must be especially careful to establish integration. How to get the best out of team member diversity has, in recent years, attracted increasing research attention. This is for good reasons. As Shaw and Barrett-Power (1998, p. 1307) have put it: 'Diversity is an increasingly important factor in organisational life as organisations worldwide become more diverse in terms of the gender, race, ethnicity, age, national origin, and other personal characteristics of their members.' This quote illustrates the fact there are many different aspects to diversity. Pelled *et al.* (1999), for example, refer to diversity in occupational backgrounds of team members, as well as diversity of race, age and tenure in the employing organisation. They suggest that functional diversity tends to lead to task-related conflict (that is, disagreement between group members about preferred solutions and methods) and that this (as long as it is handled well) helps group performance. On the other hand, diversity in race and tenure tends to lead to emotional conflict between group members, and this can undermine group performance. Jehn *et al.* (1999, p. 742) point out that 'No theory suggests that a workgroup's diversity on outward personal characteristics such as race and gender should have benefits except to the extent that diversity creates other diversity in the workgroup, such as diversity of information or perspective.'

Consistent with this assertion, Jehn *et al.* found that, among a sample of 545 employees, *informational diversity* in teams was associated with good group performance. Social *category diversity* (in the form of age and gender) made people more satisfied with their team, while *value diversity* (defined as disagreement about what the team's goals should be) tended to produce more relationship conflict within the team, and to undermine slightly the performance of the team.

Key Learning Point

There are different dimensions of diversity in teams, and each has different implications for team processes and team outputs.

A feature of society (in developed countries at least) is one of fast-changing demographics resulting in a workforce that is much more diverse (e.g. with an increasing proportion of the workforce being women, or coming from cultures or ethnic groups that have traditionally made up a very small proportion of the workforce). Work teams are often assembled by selecting a mix of individuals according to their specialist knowledge with little regard for the behaviour that they typically display. Over and above the mix of knowledge, skills and abilities that this produces, does team member diversity *in itself* have an influence on team performance? Homogeneous and heterogeneous teams may function differently through different social relations. A team of white males in their 30s is likely to function differently from a team of ethnically mixed women of different ages. Of course, as well as differences in these easily observable features, diversity also includes personality differences, team role variety, leadership skills and technical knowledge.

The theoretical background (Tziner, 1985) draws on alternative theories from social psychology. Similarity theory says that groups and teams comprising people with similar characteristics will be the most productive. This is because of the mutual attraction held by people of similar demographics, e.g. working class women relating more closely to each other than they would relate to middle class men, but the key question is: even if ties are stronger does this translate into higher performance at team level?

The alternative view says that where diverse backgrounds are combined the resulting tension will be constructive in terms of team outputs (e.g. more decision alternatives will be considered). However, equity theory describes how people adjust their inputs, up or down, to situations depending on their perceptions of their own rewards and the rewards given to others. In a team setting, individuals may lower their contribution if they see another team member as having more status due to their greater expertise or higher position in the organisation. Hence, in some circumstances heterogeneous teams could be less effective due to an unhelpful focusing on interpersonal differences.

Bowers *et al.* (2003) provide a meta-analysis which showed that, overall, the combined effects of team composition on performance were insignificant. This result took into account heterogeneity in terms of ability, sex, personality and their influence upon the quality, quantity and accuracy of team outputs. Some differences were found in that homogeneous teams performed better when task difficulty is low and heterogeneous teams performed better when task difficulty is high. So once again, we see small meta-analytic effects: it is important to be aware that these findings should not negate the view that in particular organisational contexts the diversity/performance link can be positive and quite strong (e.g. Fay *et al.*, 2006).

Key Learning Point

Research on diversity and team performance has shown some strong effects in individual studies but meta-analysis results show weak links. This may be because when the results of various studies are combined, the strong effects of diversity in some studies are offset by weak effects in other studies.

Exercise 13.3   Roles and diversity in a team

Recall your experience of working in a group or team that you used for Exercise 13.1. This time, consider the following questions:

Suggested exercises

1   How diverse were the team members in terms of (for example) age, sex, ethnic or religious affiliation, outlook, personality, past experience, social class? What consequences did the diversity (or lack of it) have for how the team went about its task, and for the final decision?

2   From the descriptions of Belbin's nine team roles above, which do you think were most often displayed by team members? Consider whether this was helpful or not, and whether more (or less) of certain roles would have been helpful.

Cognitive ability

One of the reasons why Meredith Belbin felt moved to create the TRSPI was that, as a management trainer at the time, he noticed that teams comprising the most intelligent students did not necessarily perform better than other teams of more mixed abilities. His explanation for this drew upon the presence or absence of team roles as we have seen. While general intelligence is now thought to be a good predictor of performance in a job at individual level (because higher intelligence leads to better analysis and decision-making) it does not follow that high cognitive ability at individual level translates directly into high performance at team level.

A meta-analysis of cognitive ability and team performance (Devine and Phillips, 2001) found that intelligence of team members was positively correlated with team performance for a range of tasks. However, the relationship was much weaker in real work settings than it was in experimental (laboratory) conditions. Their key finding was that the average cognitive ability of team members explained just 8.6 per cent of variance in team performance. This means that 91.4 per cent (rather a lot!) is explained by other variables than the intelligence of team members. This finding gives some support to the rather intuitive conclusions that Belbin drew from his observations over 30 years ago.

Devine and Phillips (2001) identified a number of factors that might impact on the intelligence–performance relationship. Much stronger association between intelligence and performance may be found with complex tasks: when the team needs to be good at physical work (e.g. assembly or maintenance tasks) the association could be lower than when the task is more about planning and problem-solving. In addition, over time, the association between intelligence and performance diminishes as team members get more experience of what the task needs in order for it to be done successfully. Thus, intelligence may be more influential at the start of a team's life cycle than in the mature stage. Overall, where tasks are relatively straightforward, familiar to the team and largely behavioural, intelligence and team performance are not strongly linked. Where team tasks are more complex and intellectual, then intelligence may be a much stronger predictor of performance.

This is another good example that illustrates the importance of organisational setting and context in explaining relationships among variables.

Personality in teams

Peeters and colleagues (2006) examined how team composition in terms of personality is related to performance. They hypothesised that performance agreeableness, conscientiousness, emotional stability and openness to experience would be positively associated with performance because they impact on achieving results (and, therefore, that extroversion is not related to performance). The Big Five personality dimensions were measured by the average scores in the team across all members on each dimension.

Meta-analysis showed that there was as predicted no correlation with extroversion. The expected correlation with agreeableness was found and this is presumed to derive from 'interpersonal facilitation' within the team. Conscientiousness, which has been found to correlate with individual level performance, was correlated with team performance. Contrary to predictions, there were no correlations between emotional stability or openness and performance. The type of team moderated the relationships such that positive links between agreeableness and conscientiousness and performance were only found in work teams and not in the student teams often studied by researchers. Peeters *et al.* suggest that high agreeableness and conscientiousness are viable criteria to use in the selection of team members.

Participation in decision-making in organisations

Guzzo and Dickson (1996) have pointed out that improved group performance does not guarantee improved organisational performance. It depends on the appropriateness of what the group is being asked to do, and how well the efforts of different groups are coordinated. Macy and Izumi (1993) found that organisational financial performance improves most when a range of change initiatives (*see* Chapter 16) are used, such as organisational structure, technology and human resource management techniques, but team development interventions were among the more effective of those initiatives. So group interventions do appear to be useful in the wider organisational context.

Decisions in organisations can be divided into various types, and each decision has various phases (Mintzberg *et al.*, 1976; Heller and Misumi, 1987). Therefore, when we look at applying team research in its wider organisational context we need to consider the type of decision-making that teams are involved in, and at which phases of the decision-making process they have some involvement. As regards the types of decision, there are (i) operational decisions (usually with short-term effects and of a routine nature); (ii) tactical decisions (usually with medium-term effects and of non-routine nature but not going so far as reviewing the organisation's goals); and (iii) strategic decisions (usually with long-term effects and concerning the organisation's goals). In line with leadership research (*see* Chapter 14), it is also possible to distinguish between people-oriented and task-oriented decisions within each type. The phases of decision-making include (i) start-up, when it is realised that a decision is required; (ii) development, when options are searched for and considered; (iii) finalisation, when a decision is confirmed; and (iv) implementation, when the finalised decision is put into operation or fails (Heller *et al.*, 1988).

Much attention has been focused on who in organisations really makes decisions, and how their influence is distributed across the decision types and phases described above (e.g. Mintzberg, 1983; Heller *et al.*, 1988; Vandenberg *et al.*, 1999). The concept of *power* is frequently invoked. Power concerns the ability of an individual or group to ensure that another individual or group complies with its wishes. Power can be derived from a number of sources, including the ability to reward and/or punish, the extent to which a person or group is seen as expert and the amount of prestige or good reputation that is enjoyed by a person or group. These sources of power are distinct, though they tend to go together (Finkelstein, 1992). Especially if they are in short supply, individuals and groups often use *organisational politics* to maximise their chances of getting their way. Politics consists of tactics such as enlisting the support of others, controlling access to information and creating indebtedness by doing people favours for which reciprocation is expected. In extreme forms politics can also involve more deceitful activities such as spreading rumours. In general, however, the effectiveness and morality of power and politics depend on their intended goals. The distinction between the two goals of self-aggrandisement and organisational effectiveness is often blurred. After all, most of us probably construe ourselves as playing important and legitimate roles in our work organisations, and it is easy to jump from there to a belief that what is good for us must therefore also be good for the organisation.

Several large studies over the years have explored the question of who participates in organisational decisions. Heller *et al.* (1988), for example, conducted a detailed longitudinal study of seven organisations in three countries (the Netherlands, the United Kingdom and the former Yugoslavia). Not surprisingly, they found that most decision-making power was generally exercised by top management. The lower levels and works councils typically were merely informed or at best consulted. The distribution of power did, however, vary considerably between organisations and also somewhat between countries, with Yugoslavia (as it then was) generally having the most participation by people at low organisational levels, and the United Kingdom least. There was also some variation between types and phases of decision-making.

Top management was most influential in strategic decisions. Within tactical decisions, workers had quite high influence at the start-up phase of people-oriented decisions but little thereafter. This led to frustration. For tactical task-oriented decisions, they had much influence in the finalisation phase. This was often less frustrating, since the right of management to initiate decisions of this kind was rarely challenged (i.e. high legitimate power).

Senior managers are often tempted to make decisions in quite an autocratic way, involving only a few senior colleagues with little or no consultation. This is not necessarily because those managers have autocratic personalities. In fast-moving environments it may be necessary to make decisions quickly, and the participation of a large number of people slows things down. However, Ashmos *et al.* (2002) have argued for a simple management rule: use participative styles of decision-making. Although this can be time-consuming and confusing, it has a number of well-documented benefits, including:

- using the skills and knowledge available in the organisation;

- developing people's sense of involvement in the organisation;

- increasing information flow and contacts among members of the organisation;

- making decisions that reflect the real (and changing) nature of the organisation's environment.

Ashmos *et al.* argue that most organisations tend to have complex systems of rules and procedures that ensure that organisational decisions are predictable and standardised. The use of established procedures tends to eliminate real participation by organisational members. If the simple rule 'use participation' is followed, decisions are made and actions taken in less predictable and comfortable ways, but they are better suited to the specific situation. Ashmos *et al.'s* ideas are summarised in Figure 13.4. They are consistent with the proposition in the Vroom–Yetton theory of leadership (*see* Chapter 14) that participative methods are appropriate in most situations.

Key Learning Point

The amount and type of workforce participation in organisational decision-making vary between countries, between types of decision, and between phases of the decision-making processs.

Finally, examinations of strategic decision-making by senior management have been undertaken (e.g. Forbes and Milliken, 1999). Some interesting findings have emerged. For example, Papadakis and Barwise (2002) have examined strategic decisions in medium and large Greek companies. They were interested in how comprehensive and rational the decision-making process was, how hierarchically decentralised it was, how much lateral communication occurred and how political it was. They found that the personalities and other characteristics of the chief executive officer and top management team had relatively limited impact on how decisions were made. Instead, the extent to which the decision would have an impact on the firm seemed to matter. Encouragingly perhaps, higher impact was associated

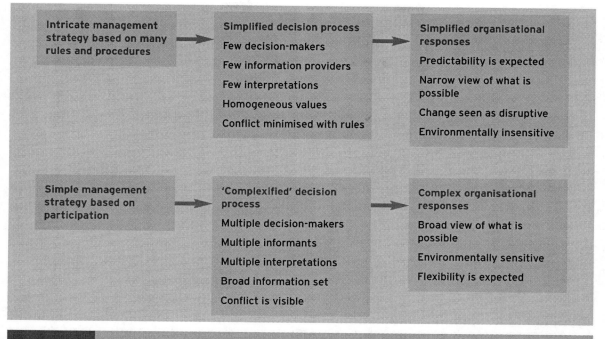

| Intricate management strategy based on many rules and procedures | Simplified decision process
Few decision-makers
Few information providers
Few interpretations
Homogeneous values
Conflict minimised with rules | Simplified organisational responses
Predictability is expected
Narrow view of what is possible
Change seen as disruptive
Environmentally insensitive |
| Simple management strategy based on participation | 'Complexified' decision process
Multiple decision-makers
Multiple informants
Multiple interpretations
Broad information set
Conflict is visible | Complex organisational responses
Broad view of what is possible
Environmentally sensitive
Flexibility is expected |

Figure 13.4   **Participation in organisational decision-making**
Source: Adapted from Ashmos *et al.* (2002), 'What a mess! Participation as a simple managerial rule to 'complexify' organizations'. *Journal of Management Studies*, 39(2), pp. 189–206, Blackwell Publishing Ltd.

with a more comprehensive process with more decentralisation (i.e. the involvement of a range of different people) and communication.

Dean and Sharfman (1996) used multiple in-depth interviews with senior managers involved in decision-making to investigate the process and outcomes of 52 strategic decisions in 24 companies. The most common types of strategic decision concerned organisational restructuring, the launch of a new product and organisational change. Their findings are summarised in Figure 13.5. The procedural rationality of the decision-making process (that is, the extent to which relevant information was sought, obtained and evaluated) had a significant impact on decision effectiveness, particularly when the business environment was changeable, requiring careful monitoring of trends. Even more important was the thoroughness and care with which the decision was implemented. This is an important reminder that managers cannot afford simply to make decisions – the decisions must be followed through. However, not everything is under decision-makers' control. The favourability of the business and industrial environment also had an impact on decision effectiveness. Political behaviour by those involved was bad for decision effectiveness. So, behaviour such as disguising one's own opinions, and complex and distracting negotiations between factions of the decision-making group, should not be accepted as an inevitable part of organisational life. They impair organisational performance, though of course they may serve the interests of individuals or subgroups.

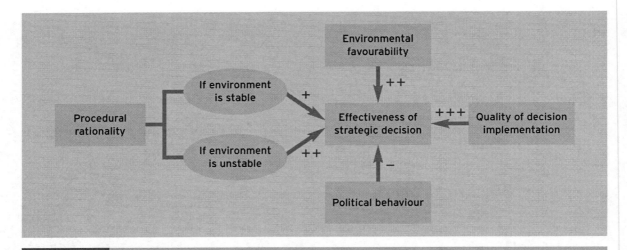

Key Learning Point

Taking care over decision-making and implementation processes really does make a difference to organisational effectiveness.

There are also plenty of demonstrations that the biases in individual decision-making described early in this chapter occur in strategic decision-making. For example, Hodgkinson *et al.* (1999) demonstrated the tendency for people to be *risk averse* when potential gains are highlighted, but *risk-seeking* when potential losses are highlighted (this is the so-called framing bias). In two experiments Hodgkinson and colleagues asked students and bank managers to consider what they would do about a business strategy decision, where the same possible profits were described in one of two ways: either in terms of cash (highlighting the positive) or relative to a target (highlighting the negative). Negative framing led people to favour decisions that had a *low probability of a big profit and a high probability of no profit* over decisions that had a *high probability of moderate profit and a low probability of no profit*. However, this tendency was virtually eliminated if people were asked to draw a diagram representing their thinking about factors relevant to the decision (causal mapping) before making it. This leads to the optimistic conclusion that by engaging in careful thought processes we can overcome more instinctive biases in our reasoning.

There is no particular reason to believe that groups of top managers responsible for strategic decisions will behave differently from other groups. This is reinforced by Forbes and Milliken's (1999) theoretical analysis of the behaviour of company boards of directors. They make a number of propositions that are very consistent with more general theorising about groups and teams, particularly concerning the impacts of team cohesiveness and diversity. For example, they suggest that board members feeling a sense of cohesiveness is a good thing up to a point, but that too much cohesiveness impairs decision-making. This is a similar prediction to that made by Janis in his groupthink model discussed earlier in this chapter. Also, Forbes and Milliken predict that cognitive conflict (i.e. disagreements about the best solutions to problems) will increase the board's effectiveness, but reduce its cohesiveness. This is closely in line with the findings of Jehn *et al.* (1999) also noted earlier in this chapter.

Key Learning Point

Analyses of strategic decisions in organisations support the findings and perspectives of much other research on groups and teams.

STOP TO CONSIDER

Participation in decision-making is often seen as one of the major benefits of implementing teamwork. Now that you have read about participation, consider the benefits and risks of increasing levels of participation in decision-making. As you read more of this book you might also want to consider how other bodies of research help us to understand why participation might be important and beneficial. In particular think about what theories of motivation (Chapter 8), work stress (Chapter 12) and leadership (Chapter 14) tell us about the possible risks and benefits of participation in decision-making.

Topics for future research

Given the vastness of the teams literature there are many avenues where further research could increase our knowledge of them. Paris *et al.* (2000) point to the need to know more about how teams acquire knowledge and information and act on it. How do individual members contribute to information processing and the building of shared mental models? They also highlight the need to develop better ways of assessing teamwork as a way of understanding more about how teamwork affects team outputs (i.e. how the processes that take place in teams impact upon the performance of an organisation).

Guzzo and Dickson (1996) suggest that with increasing use of distributed teams better understandings of how information and communication technologies influence teamwork and team performance in virtual teams are needed. They also call for research into finding team development strategies that make a difference to effectiveness and for more studies of teams in their natural work settings, e.g. the workplace rather than artificial teams (often students) in artificial settings. This would give a better understanding of the influence of contextual variables such as the performance culture and reward practices.

We also suggest that if teamwork is to increase there is a need for a much better understanding of the social conditions and relations in the workplace that lead to the formation and functioning of real teams.

Summary

Decisions by individuals and groups are influenced by many psychological phenomena. Groups are usually more effective than the average individual but less so than the best individual in decision-making tasks. Groups can make terrible decisions, especially if characterised by problems such as the 'groupthink' syndrome. However, the research evidence about the 'typical' effectiveness of groups should not be viewed as the best that groups can do. Possible ways in which groups and teams can improve include more consideration in advance of the problem-solving strategy they wish to adopt, a clear expectation that members should challenge each other, and an understanding that such challenges do not signal hostility or disrespect. When such conditions exist, diversity within groups can have important benefits.

The extent to which employees are part of real teams seems to be relatively low overall although it does vary from country to country. The processes that occur in teams are very complex with continuous cycles of feedback and adjustment occurring rather than a simple linear pathway. Teams pass through a life cycle that involves forming, mature functioning and then winding-down. Models of teamwork emphasise the importance of factors such as goal clarity, balanced sharing of duties, open communication, good interpersonal relationships and the ability to manage conflict. Questionnaires exist to assess a person's propensity to fit with these constructs and can be used for team selection. The concept that effective teams require a balance of different team roles is popular and is the basis of much of the team development that organisations carry out.

Many organisations rely on teamwork and use it to fuel creativity and innovation in the workplace. Aside of questions about whether teams actually perform better than individuals do, the evidence that being in teams leads to higher levels of job-related attitudes (such as job satisfaction) is patchy. A long list can be made of the variables that have been used to predict team performance. They include: stage of development; climate inside the team; extent of team-building; diversity in terms of team roles, personality and gender among others; and cognitive ability.

The nature of decision-making tasks, their importance and their subject matter all have implications for the way they are handled. The amount and type of employee participation in making decisions vary widely and the ways that decisions are made and implemented do link to organisational effectiveness.

Closing Case Study   To expand or not to expand?

The management team of the Fastsave retail chain store company had a decision to make. Should they build a new store in Danesville, a medium-sized town in which the company owned a suitable patch of land? Fastsave was doing quite well, and had more than enough financial resources to make the necessary investment in a town that did not currently have a major supermarket. On the other hand, there were two existing large superstores within 25 kilometres. It was agreed that there was no significant danger of substantial losses: the question was more whether the time and effort involved in expansion would be worth the return.

The management team consisted of the general manager (GM), finance manager (FM), marketing manager (MM), operations manager (OM), personnel manager (PM) and company secretary (CS). Each member of the team had been supplied with reports on the demographic make-up of the town, a market research survey, detailed costings of building the store and the likely attitude of the local council planning authority.

Group members were accustomed to working together and there was rivalry (at present friendly) among them about which of them if any would succeed GM when she retired in about three years. At the outset of the meeting, GM made it clear that she would act as an impartial chairperson, and not reveal her own opinions until the end. In the past, however, she had usually been cautious about business expansions. The following extract is representative of the group's deliberations:

FM: I suspect the time is not right. We are currently upgrading six other stores, and to start a completely new one would run the risk of spreading our resources too thin. In purely financial terms we can do it, but would we do a good job?

OM: Yes, we've certainly got our hands full at present. In fact, I would be in favour of reviewing two of our already-planned store upgradings because I'm not sure they are really worth it either. Generally we're doing all right as we are – let's consolidate our position.

MM: I can't believe I'm hearing this! According to our market research report, the population of Danesville wants its own big supermarket, and what's more the 45+ age group particularly likes our emphasis on low price rather than super de luxe quality.

CS: Come on, as usual you're taking an approach which could possibly pay off but could land us in trouble . . .

MM: Like what?

CS: Well, there has been a lot of housing development in Danesville, and the local council is under pressure to preserve what it sees as the charm of the town. It would be very bad public relations to be perceived as undermining that. And having a planning application refused wouldn't be much better.

FM: That's right, and being seen as an intruder would probably reduce sales too.

PM: I can't comment on that last point, but as a general principle we should not stand still. Our competitors might overtake us. If resources are spread too thin, we can recruit more staff: we have the money, and experience suggests that the labour force in the region has the necessary skills. ▶

FM: You've had a rush of blood to the head, haven't you? You're normally telling us how difficult it is to manage expansion of staff numbers. I must say I share the concern about a couple of our existing upgrading plans, let alone building an entirely new store. Do those stores really need refitting yet? They are doing all right.

CS: I notice that Danesville has an increasingly young, mobile population these days. In spite of the market research report, will they really be interested in a local store, especially with our position in the market?

MM: They can be made to be. Anyway, who says that a Danesville store should not go slightly more upmarket? Tesco seem to manage to have both upmarket and downmarket stores.

OM: Well yes, but I don't think we are big enough to be that versatile . . .

Suggested exercises

1   Examine this case study from the following perspectives:
     a.   the likely attitude to risk
     b.   group polarisation
     c.   minority influence.
2   Given this examination, what do you think the group is likely to decide? What is your evaluation of that decision?

Test your learning

Short-answer questions

1   What is groupthink?

2   What are the differences between a workgroup and a work team?

3   Summarise the I–P–O model of team functioning.

4   Suggest three possible negative consequences of stereotypes in the workplace.

5   What strategies should minorities in groups use in order to maximise their chances of influencing a group decision?

6   What is group polarisation and why does it happen?

7   List the team roles identified by Belbin and explain why they are needed for team effectiveness.

8   Briefly outline three reasons why groups sometimes make poor decisions.

Suggested assignments

1 Discuss the proposition that Janis's groupthink model adequately accounts for failures in group decision-making.

2 What gains can organisations make by organising their employees into teams? What are the risks for organisations who do this?

3 Examine the potential benefits and problems of diversity in teams.

4 To what extent is true teamwork become a normal feature of working life?

Relevant websites

A simple Google search for 'teamwork' or 'team development' leads you to many consultants' websites. They are interesting as they show how practitioners approach the topic.

The International Society for Performance Improvement, as its name suggests, is concerned with promoting techniques that will raise performance levels of individuals and organisations. It carries articles that relate to specific topics including one on virtual teams which is at http://www.pignc-ispi.com/articles/cbt-epss/virtualteam.htm.

Information about team roles and samples of the team role instruments are at http://www.belbin.com. Various documents relating to how psychometric tests can be used in team development can be found at http://www.shl.com/whatwedo/shlreports/pages/teamdevelopmentreports.aspx. The Improvement and Development Agency has a report on the composition and effectiveness of top management teams on its website at http://www.idea.gov.uk/idk/aio/5028661.

 For further self-test material and relevant, annotated weblinks please visit the website for this book at **www.pearsoned.co.uk/workpsych**

Suggested further reading

Full details for all references are given in the list at the end of this book.

1 Michael West's chapter entitled 'The human team: Basic motivations and innovations' in volume 2 of the 2001 *Handbook of Industrial Work and Organisational Psychology* gives an up-to-date and scholarly but accessible review of many team processes and outcomes.

2   R. Meredith Belbin's book *Beyond the Team* (published in 2000) is a good example of a genre that attempts to use everyday language to help people understand how to make teams work.

3   Chris Brotherton's 2003 chapter on the psychology and industrial relations in the book *Understanding Work and Employment* provides a personal and wide-ranging analysis of the field.

4   Steve Kozlowski and Daniel Ilgen provide a full review of team effectiveness in their paper in *Psychological Science in the Public Interest,* 2006.

Chapter 13

Managing change and innovation

Aim

To outline theories of change in organisations and show how these relate to practice.

Objectives

By the end of your work on this chapter you should be able to outline the concepts below in your own terms and:

1 Explain the meaning of organisational change and give examples

2 Explain what the links between change and context imply for those managing a change

3 Compare life cycle, emergent, participative and political theories of change

4 Evaluate systematically the possible sources of resistance to change

5 Explain the meanings of organisational development and the learning organisation

6 Illustrate the factors believed to support innovation.

Key terms

This chapter introduces the following ideas:

external context

perceived performance gap

performance imperatives

organisational change

interaction model

receptive contexts

non-receptive contexts

life cycle

emergent model

participative model

political model

counterimplementation

organisation development

sensitivity training

process consultation

survey feedback

creativity

innovation

idea champions

Each is a term defined within the text, as well as in the Glossary at the end of the book.

Vodafone/Ericsson www.vodafone.com, www.ericsson.com   CASE STUDY

In 2007 Vodafone offered mobile services to subscribers in 28 countries and was the world's largest mobile network operator, with about one-quarter of the market. Ericsson was the world's largest supplier of mobile network infrastructure, and Vodafone its largest customer. Vodafone has achieved its strong market position partly by internal growth and by acquiring other operators – such as AirTouch (USA) in 1998 and Mannesmann (Germany) in 2000. Many of these acquisitions also had shareholdings in other mobile operators, meaning that in some countries Vodafone operates through partially rather than wholly owned subsidiaries.

As demand for mobile services grew, Vodafone extended the network on a country-by-country basis, with local management teams running the business. They usually ordered network equipment from Ericsson, negotiating terms with Ericsson staff in their country. Although Vodafone's in-country managers communicated with their counterparts in other countries, Vodafone did not attempt to coordinate the way they operated. Ericsson operated in a more centralised fashion, though with some scope for local managers to establish terms of business that reflected their market or competitive environment.

This had the following consequences:

- Terms and conditions for purchasing network equipment varied between countries.
- Communication between the two companies in each country was direct, through meetings, telephones, letters, fax and e-mail.
- Communication about Ericsson products between Vodafone operators in different countries was *ad hoc*.
- Sharing of product information between Ericsson and Vodafone was in-country, mainly through written documents.
- Ordering and order tracking was done by local systems in each country.
- Configuration of network equipment varied between countries, as did service and support arrangements.

Before the merger with AirTouch, Vodafone management had begun to assess what synergies it could gain from the merger, especially in the supply of network equipment. The company expected to make big savings if it could aggregate its worldwide requirements for net-

© Vodafone 2007.

work equipment, and source this from common global suppliers. The later acquisition of Mannesmann increased the scope for synergy – and claims about the potential savings in this area were made to shareholders and the financial markets.

Vodafone therefore began a project with Ericsson to develop new ways of managing the relationship. The intention was to find ways of aggregating Vodafone's global requirements so that the companies would manage their relationship in a unified way. They realised that managing a change of this scale would raise difficult issues about the:

- degree of planning to undertake
- scale and value of the synergies from a new global relationship
- attitudes of those managing Vodafone operations in the various countries
- resources that would be needed to manage the change.

Source: Based on material from Ibbott and O'Keefe (2004).

Case questions 13.1

- How may the structure of Vodafone's in-country operations affect the project?
- Will a new global relationship mean a more centralised or a more decentralised company?
- Should the two companies put significant resources into planning the change in advance?

13.1 Introduction

The manager whom Vodafone appointed to manage this change faces a problem that is familiar to many managers. The chief executive has put him in charge of implementing a major change that will affect many people, some of whom will be uneasy about how it will affect them. Changing from a country to a global structure will have implications for the way they run the business in their country, and change their relationship with their main equipment supplier.

Managers initiate or experience change so regularly that in many organisations change is seen as the normal state of affairs, interrupted by occasional periods of relative stability. In the most innovative areas of the economy some senior managers see one of their primary tasks as being to challenge current practices, hoping to foster a climate of exploration and innovation. They want people to see change as the norm – merely one further intervention in a continuing flow of events rather than something that will be followed by a return to stability. At BP, for example, the challenge to successive senior managers has been to continue transforming the business from a relatively small (for that industry), diversified business into the world's second-largest oil company. Mergers, such as that between Chrysler (USA) and Daimler (Germany), are usually followed by internal changes. Small businesses make radical changes too – as when Hindle Power, an engineering company with 30 employees, faced the loss of a valuable distribution contract unless it changed the way it worked. It embarked on a radical programme of change that returned the company to profit, and grew the business (*People Management*, 3 February 2000, p. 52).

The external environment described in Chapter 3 is the main source of change. The evolving PESTEL factors change what people expect of a business – which may encourage managers to alter their strategy or operations. Research by the Institute of Personnel and Development (IPD) into 151 large organisations found that major reasons for change were a need to create closer customer relationships, significant financial pressure to improve performance, or intensifying competition (IPD, 1999). Anecdotal evidence is that while most managers accept the need for change, many are critical of the way their organisations introduce it. Managers still experience great difficulty in implementing major organisational changes successfully.

This chapter presents theories about the nature of change in organisations. It begins by explaining current external pressures for change, and how these prompt internal change to one or more elements of the organisation. The chapter then outlines a model that shows how change depends on the interaction between the external and internal environments of the organisation. It then presents four complementary perspectives on

Activity 13.1   Recording a major change

From discussion with colleagues or managers, identify a major attempt at change in an organisation. Make notes on the following questions and use them as a point of reference throughout the chapter.

- What was the change?
- Why did management introduce it?
- What were the objectives?
- How did management plan and implement it?
- How well did it meet the objectives?
- What lessons have those involved taken from the experience?

how people try to manage that interaction, each with different management implications. Further sections deal with diagnosing the characteristics of a change, managing resistance, skills and structures, and organisation development.

13.2   Initiating change

Chapter 1 introduced the idea that managers work within a context that shapes what they do, and which they may also change. This chapter explains the interactive nature of that process, and Figure 13.1 illustrates the themes it will cover. A particular episode of change begins when enough people perceive a gap between desired and actual performance – usually because the internal context of the organisation is unable to meet the external demands upon it. Using their implicit or explicit theory of change, they initiate a project to change one or more aspects of the internal context in the hope of closing the performance gap. The outcomes of the change effort will be affected by practical issues of design and implementation – but whatever the outcomes they will in turn affect the subsequent shape of the external and internal contexts, providing the starting point for future changes.

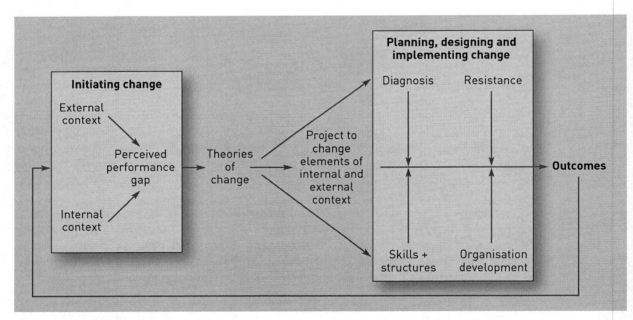

Figure 13.1 A model of the change process

The external context

Chapter 3 described the **external context** of business and successive chapters have illustrated the changes taking place, such as internationalisation, information technology and expectations about corporate responsibility. Together with deregulation and the privatisation of former state businesses these are transforming the competitive landscape in which firms operate. They face competition from unexpected quarters, threatening their prosperity or even their survival. Managers at British Airways and KLM have had to respond to the pressure of new competition from low-cost airlines such as Ryanair and

The **external context** consists of elements beyond the organisation such as competitors, or the wider PESTEL factors.

easyJet. Established banks face competition from new entrants such as retailers (Sainsbury's) or conglomerates (Virgin) offering financial services. The growth of the Internet has enabled companies offering high-value/low-weight products to open new distribution channels and invade previously protected markets.

---

management in practice   Successful change at GKN   www.gknplc.com

GKN is a leading global supplier to automotive, aerospace and off-highway manufacturers, employing 40,000 people in GKN companies and joint ventures. It was created by a series of mergers at the start of the twentieth century, creating Guest, Keen and Nettlefolds – then one of the largest manufacturing businesses in the world. It was involved in iron and coal mining, steel production and finished products such as nuts, bolts and fasteners.

Its present form reflects a small number of successful decisions made in the 1980s. The first was to abandon any thought of re-entering the steel industry (its interests there had been nationalised in the 1960s), and to focus instead on seeking growth in the motor components business. This decision was shaped by a piece of luck, in that in 1966 it had bought a UK engineering company and in doing so acquired a share in a German business which had worldwide patents for a unique constant velocity joint system for powering front-wheel drive cars.

A second decision was to cut back sharply on non-vehicle activities, into which the group had diversified in the 1970s. At that time unrelated diversification was a popular management strategy, but it soon became clear that unrelated businesses were best run independently: GKN soon disposed of most of that portfolio.

The third decision was to purchase Westland Helicopters – mainly because it gave GKN entry into the rapidly growing business of manufacturing aerospace components, which complemented the automotive business (Westland was sold in 2004).

In his book *Change Without Pain* Abrahamson (2004) identifies GKN as one of the most successful companies at managing significant strategic changes – not by disposing of skills, but by recombining them in ways that create even greater value – see Section 13.9 for more on Abrahamson's ideas.

Sources: *Financial Times*, 6 January 2004, 28 February 2007; *Independent*, 15 March 2007; company website.

These forces have collectively meant a shift of economic power from producers to consumers, many of whom now enjoy greater quality, choice and value. Managers wishing to retain customers need continually to seek new ways of adding value to resources if they are to retain their market position. Unless they do so they will experience a widening performance gap.

Perceived performance gap

A **perceived performance gap** arises when people believe that the actual performance of a unit or business is out of line with the level they desire. If those responsible for transforming resources into outputs do so in a way that does not meet customer expectations, there is a performance gap. Cumulatively this will lead to other performance gaps emerging – such as revenue from sales being below the level needed to secure further resources. If uncorrected this will eventually cause the business to fail.

In the current business climate, two aspects of performance dominate discussion – what Prastacos *et al.* (2002) call '**performance imperatives**': the need for flexibility and the need for innovation. In a very uncertain business world the scope for long-term

A **perceived performance gap** *arises when people believe that the actual performance of a unit or business is out of line with the level they desire.*

Performance imperatives *are aspects of performance that are especially important for an organisation to do well, such as flexibility and innovation.*

planning is seriously limited. Successful businesses are likely to be those that develop a high degree of strategic and organisational flexibility, while also (Volberda, 1997) maintaining efficient and stable processes. This apparent paradox (combining flexibility and stability) reflects the fact that while companies need to respond rapidly they also need to respond efficiently. This usually depends on having developed a degree of stability and predictability in the way they transform resources into goods and services.

The other imperative identified by Prastacos *et al.* (2002) is innovation:

> to generate a variety of successful new products or services (embedding technological innovation), and to continuously innovate in all aspects of the business (p. 58).

In many areas of business, customers expect a constant flow of new products, embodying the latest scientific and technological developments: companies that fail to meet these expectations will experience a performance gap. Selling, say, an advanced mobile phone profitably depends not only on the quality of the applied research which goes into a better screen display, but also on turning that research into a desirable product *and* delivering the devices at a price which customers will pay. This depends on the organisation – the internal context of management.

The internal context

Chapter 1 introduced the internal context (Figure 1.3, repeated here as Figure 13.2) as the set of elements within an organisation that shape behaviour. Change begins to happen when sufficient influential people believe, for example, that outdated technology or a confusing structure is causing a performance gap, by inhibiting flexibility or innovation. They notice external or internal events and interpret them as threatening the performance that influential stakeholders expect. This interpretation, and their implicit theory of change, encourages them to propose a change to one or more aspects of the organisation, shown in Figure 13.2.

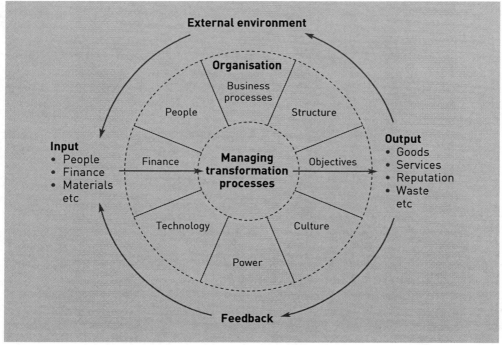

Figure 13.2

Elements of the internal context of management

They then have to persuade enough other people that the matter is serious enough to earn a place on the management agenda. People in some organisations are open to proposals for change, others tend to ignore them – BP faced new competitive pressures throughout the 1980s, but it was only around 1990 that sufficient senior people took the threats seriously enough to initiate a period of rapid change.

People initiate organisational change for reasons other than a conscious awareness of a performance gap – fashion, empire building or a powerful player's personal whim can all play a part. Employees or trade unions can propose changes in the way things are done to improve working conditions. The need for change is subjective – what some see as urgent others will leave until later. People can affect that process by managing external information – magnifying customer complaints to make the case for change, or minimising them if they wish to avoid change.

Whatever the underlying motivations, **organisational change** is an attempt to change one or more of the elements shown in Figure 13.2. Table 13.1 illustrates specific types of change that people initiate under each element, including some which appear elsewhere in this book.

> **Organisational change** is a deliberate attempt to improve organisational performance by changing one or more aspects of the organisation, such as its technology, structure or business processes.

Table 13.1

Examples of change in each element of the organisation

Element	Example of change to this element
Objectives	Developing a new product or service Changing the overall mission or direction Oticon's new strategic objectives as a service business (Chapter 10 Case)
Technology	Building a new factory Creating a website on the Internet Pensco implementing a new computer system (see Section 13.4)
Business processes	Improving the way maintenance and repair services are delivered Redesigning systems to handle the flow of cash and funds Benetton's new system for passing goods to retailers (Chapter 20 Case)
Financial resources	A set of changes, such as closing a facility, to reduce costs New financial reporting requirements to ensure consistency The Royal Bank of Scotland reducing costs after the NatWest merger (Part 4 Case)
Structure	Reallocating functions and responsibilities between departments Redesigning work to increase empowerment Vodafone/Ericsson moving to a global structure (Chapter 13 Case)
People	Designing a training programme to enhance skills Changing the tasks of staff to offer a new service IKEA's policies to encourage high staff commitment (Chapter 15 Case)
Culture	Unifying the culture between two or more merged businesses Encouraging greater emphasis on quality and reliability GSK creating a more entrepreneurial research culture (Chapter 10)
Power	An empowerment programme giving greater authority to junior staff Centralising decisions to increase the control of HQ over operations

It is rare for any significant change to consist of only one element. The systemic nature of organisations means that a change in any of these areas is likely to have implications for others. When Tesco introduced its Internet shopping service alongside its established retail business the company needed to create a website (technology). In addition, managers needed to decide issues of structure and people (would it be part of the existing store business or a separate business unit with its own premises and staff?) and about business processes (how exactly would an order on the website be converted to a box of groceries delivered to the customer's door?). They had to manage these ripples initiated by the main decision. Managers who ignore these consequential changes achieve less than they expect.

Once they have perceived a need for change, those promoting it then use their implicit or explicit theory of change (Sections 13.3 and 13.4) to set up and implement change (Sections 13.5–13.8) in the relevant organisational unit. How well people manage the steps in this process determines the effect on the performance gap, which in turn feeds back to the context.

Case questions 13.2

Identify the possible ripple effects that may need to be managed in the Vodafone/Ericsson change, using the elements in Figure 13.2 as a guide.

- How may the move to a global relationship affect the structure area?
- What implications may that change have for other elements?
- Which of these are likely to cause most difficulty?

These begin to form the management agenda for this project. If possible compare your answers with others on the course, to see how many *alternative* possibilities you have identified.

13.3   The interaction of context and change

How managers implement change depends on their theory about its nature. This section presents an 'interaction model', a theory of how a change interacts with its context. The following section outlines four complementary perspectives on managing that interaction.

> The **interaction model** is a theory of change that stresses the continuing interaction between the internal and external contexts of an organisation, making the outcomes of change hard to predict.

People introduce change to alter the context

Management attempts to change elements of its context to encourage behaviours that close the performance gap. Vodafone wanted to change the context within which it worked with Ericsson. By moving from country relationships with Ericsson to a more unified global structure, management hoped to create a structure that enabled people in both companies to reduce the cost to Vodafone of expanding the network. When Tesco introduced online shopping management needed (at least) to change technology, structure, people and business processes to enable staff to deliver the new service. When people plan and implement a change they are creating new 'rules' (Walsham, 1993) that they hope will guide the behaviour of people involved in the activity.

People do not necessarily accept the new arrangements without question, or without adapting them in some way: in doing so they make further changes to the context. As people begin to work in new circumstances – with a new technology or a new structure – they make small adjustments to the original plan. As they use a new information system or website they decide which aspects to ignore, use or adapt.

As people become used to working with the new system their behaviours become routine and taken for granted. They become part of the context that staff have created informally. These new contextual elements may add to, or replace, the context that those formally responsible for planning the change created. These informally created aspects of the context may or may not support the original intentions of those who initiated the project. The interaction between people and context continues into the future.

Sun Microsystems and a supplier www.sun.com

Boddy *et al.* (2000) studied Sun Microsystems and one of their suppliers as they moved towards a more cooperative supply chain relationship. Managers in both companies introduced changes to the context of work – technology, processes and roles. These were designed to create a context that encouraged more cooperation, and closer interpersonal links, between people in the two companies. For example, the supplier's sales coordinator:

> There is a close relationship with my opposite number in Sun. We speak several times a day, and he tries to give me as much information as he possibly can.

Sun staff echoed this:

> What makes them different is that you're talking to them daily . . . The relationships are a bit different – it is a bit closer than an ordinary supplier where you don't have that bond. Dealings are more direct. People are becoming more open with each other.

Both groups came to appreciate the other's requirements and tried to make things easier for them. Sun staff learned about the supplier, and vice versa. Both spoke of 'harmonising expectations'.

Source: Boddy *et al.* (2000).

The context affects the ability to change

While people managing a project aim to change the context, the context within which they work will itself help or hinder that attempt. All of the elements of Figure 13.2 will be present as the project begins, and some of these will influence how people react. Managers who occupy influential positions in an existing structure will review a proposal to change it from the perspective of their careers, as well as of the organisation. At Tesco the existing technology (stores, distribution systems, information systems) and business processes would influence managers' decisions about how to implement the Internet shopping strategy.

The prevailing culture (Chapter 3) – shared values, ideals and beliefs – influences how people view change. Members are likely to welcome a project that they believe fits their culture or subculture, and to resist one that threatens it.

Culture and change at a European bank

While teaching a course to managers at a European bank, the author invited members to identify which of the four cultural types identified in Chapter 2 best described their unit within the bank. They were then asked to describe the reaction of these units to an Internet banking venture that the company was introducing.

Course members observed that colleagues in a unit that had an internal process culture (routine back-office data processing) were hostile to the Internet venture. They appeared to be 'stuck with their own systems', which were so large and interlinked that any change was threatening. Staff in new business areas of the company (open systems) were much more positive, seeing the Internet as a way towards new business opportunities.

Source: Data collected by the author.

Culture is a powerful influence on the success or failure of innovation – see Jones *et al.* (2005) for evidence of how it affected the acceptance of a new computer system. Some cultures support change: a manager in Sun Microsystems commented on that fast-moving business:

> A very dynamic organisation, it's incredibly fast and the change thing is just a constant that you live with. They really promote flexibility and adaptability in their employees. Change is just a constant, there's change happening all of the time and people have become very acclimatised to that, it's part of the job. The attitude to change, certainly within the organisation, is very positive at the moment.

At Sun (and many other companies such as Google or eBay) the culture encourages change, while elsewhere it encourages caution. Cultural beliefs are hard to change, yet shape how people respond:

> Managers learn to be guided by these beliefs because they have worked successfully in the past (Lorsch, 1986, p. 97).

Receptive contexts are those where features of the organisation (such as culture or technology) appear likely to help change.

Non-receptive contexts are those where the combined effects of features of the organisation (such as culture or technology) appear likely to hinder change.

Receptive and non-receptive contexts

key ideas

Pettigrew *et al.* (1992) sought to explain why managers in some organisations were able to introduce change successfully, while others in the same sector (the UK National Health Service) found it very hard to move away from established practices. Their comparative research programme identified the influence of context on ability to change: **receptive contexts** are those where features of the context 'seem to be favourably associated with forward movement. On the other hand, in **non-receptive contexts** there is a configuration of features that may be associated with blocks on change' (p. 268).

Their research identified seven such contextual factors, which provide a linked set of conditions that are likely to provide the energy around change. These are:

1 quality and coherence of policy
2 availability of key people leading change
3 long-term environmental pressure – intensity and scale
4 a supportive organisational culture
5 effective managerial–clinical relations
6 cooperative interorganisational networks
7 the fit between the district's change agenda and its locale.

While some of these factors are specific to the health sector, they can easily be adapted to other settings. Together these factors give a widely applicable model of how the context affects ability to change.

Source: Pettigrew *et al.* (1992).

The distribution of power also affects receptiveness to change. Change threatens the status quo, and is likely to be resisted by stakeholders who benefit from the prevailing arrangements. Innovation depends on those behind the change developing political will and expertise that they can only attempt within the prevailing pattern of power.

The context has a history, and several levels

The present context is the result of past decisions and events: Balogun *et al.* (2005) show how internal change agents adapted practice to suit aspects of their context, such as the degree of local autonomy, senior management preferences, rewards systems and financial reporting systems. Management implements change against a background of previous events that shaped the context. The promoter of a major project in a multinational experienced this in his colleagues' attitudes:

> They were a little sceptical and wary of whether it was actually going to enhance our processes. Major pan-European redesign work had been attempted in the past and had failed miserably. The solutions had not been appropriate and had not been accepted by the divisions. Europe-wide programmes therefore had a bad name. (Boddy, 2002, p. 38)

Beliefs about the future also affect how people react. Optimists are more open to change than those who feel threatened and vulnerable.

Vodafone/Ericsson – the case continues
www.vodafone.com, www.ericsson.com

CASE STUDY

Vodafone conducted business in each country in partnership with other operators, with Vodafone often having a minority shareholding in the company. For example, in the United Kingdom it owned 100 per cent of the equity, in Germany 99 per cent and in Australia 91 per cent. In The Netherlands, Portugal and Spain this fell to 70, 50 and 22 per cent respectively.

This meant that

considerable political skill and discussion was required to handle the attitudes of the various operating companies with regard to Ericsson's local in-country operations. Some countries had acquired very favourable terms and conditions that would not necessarily be matched by the global agreements, while others had key skills that would now be 'given up' to the global effort.

Source: Ibbott and O'Keefe (2004), p. 226.

The context represented by Figure 13.2 occurs at (say) operating, divisional and corporate levels. People at any of these will be acting to change their context – which may help or hinder those managing change elsewhere. A project at one level may depend on decisions at another about resources, as this manager leading an oil refinery project discovered:

> One of the main drawbacks was that commissioning staff could have been supplemented by skilled professionals from within the company, but this was denied to me as project manager. This threw a heavy strain and responsibility on myself and my assistant. It put me in a position of high stress, as I knew that the future of the company rested upon the successful outcome of this project. One disappointment (and, I believe, a significant factor in the project) was that just before commissioning, the manager of the pilot plant development team was transferred to another job. He had been promised to me at the project inception, and I had designed him into the working operation. (Boddy, 2002, pp. 38–39)

Acting to change an element at one level will have effects at this and other levels, and elements may change independently. The manager's job is to create a coherent context that encourages desired behaviour, by using their preferred model of change.

Activity 13.2   Critical reflection on reactions to context

- What aspects of the contemporary context, shown in Figure 13.2, have had most effect on a project you are familiar with?
- How have historical factors affected people's reactions?
- Were the effects positive or negative for the project?
- To what extent is the context receptive or non-receptive to change?

Case questions 13.3

- How may the existing context of Vodafone and Ericsson affect how in-country managers react to the proposed change?
- How may that affect the way the project leader manages the change?

13.4 Four models of change

There are four complementary models of change, each with different implications for managers – life cycle, emergent, participative and political.

Life cycle models

Much advice given to those responsible for managing projects uses the idea of the project life cycle. Projects go through successive stages, and results depend on managing each one in an orderly and controlled way. The labels vary, but common themes are:

1 Define objectives.
2 Allocate responsibilities.
3 Fix deadlines and milestones.
4 Set budgets.
5 Monitor and control.

> Life cycle models of change are those that view change as an activity which follows a logical, orderly sequence of activities that can be planned in advance.

This approach (sometimes called a 'rational–linear' approach) reflects the idea that a change can be broken down into smaller tasks, and that these can be done in some preferred, if overlapping, sequence. It predicts that people can make reasonably accurate estimates of the time required to complete each task and when it will be feasible to start work on later ones. People can use tools such as bar charts (sometimes called Gantt charts after the American industrial engineer Henry Gantt, who worked with Frederick Taylor), to show all the tasks required for a project, and their likely duration. These help to visualise the work required and to plan the likely sequence of events – as illustrated in Figure 13.3.

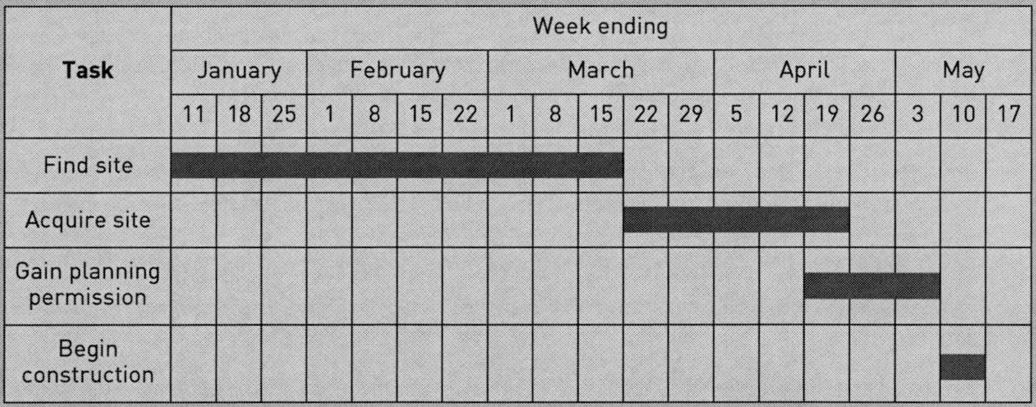

Task	Week ending																	
	January			February				March					April				May	
	11	18	25	1	8	15	22	1	8	15	22	29	5	12	19	26	3	10	17
Find site	██	██	██	██	██	██	██	██											
Acquire site									██	██	██	██							
Gain planning permission														██	██	██			
Begin construction																		██	

Figure 13.3 A simple bar chart

In the life cycle model successfully managing change depends on specifying these elements at the start and then monitoring them tightly to ensure the project stays on target. Ineffective implementation is due to managers failing to do this. Figure 13.4 shows the stages of a manufacturing project (Lock, 2003). He advises project managers to ensure that the stages are passed through in turn, 'until the project arrives back to the customer as a completed work package'. He emphasises the iterative, cyclical nature of the method:

> Clockwise rotation around the cycle only reveals the main stream. Within this flow many small tributaries, cross-currents and even whirlpools are generated before the project is finished (p. 26).

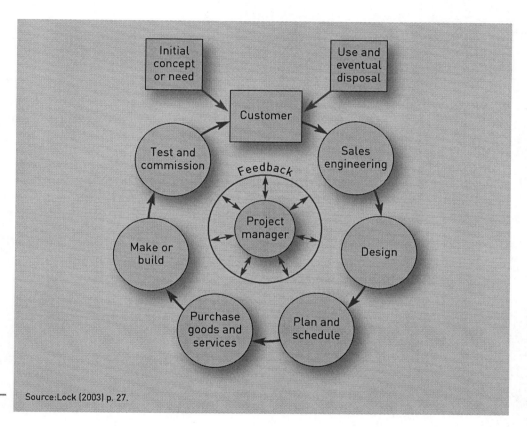

Figure 13.4

A project life cycle

Source:Lock (2003) p. 27.

Many books on project management, such as Woodward (1997) and Lock (2003), present advice on tools for each stage of the life cycle. Those advising on IS changes usually take a similar approach, recommending a variety of 'system development life cycle' approaches (Chaffey, 2003). For some changes the life cycle gives valuable guidance. It is not necessarily sufficient in itself, since people may not be able at the start to specify the end point of the change – or the tasks which will lead to that. In uncertain conditions it may make little sense to plan the outcomes in too much detail. It may be wiser to set the general direction, and adapt the target to suit new conditions that develop during the change. Those managing such change need an additional theory to cope with emergent change.

Activity 13.3 Critical reflection on the project life cycle

You may be able to gain some insight into the project life cycle by using it on a practical task. For example:

- If you have a piece of work to do that is connected with your studies, such as an assignment or project, sketch out the steps to be followed by adapting Figure 13.4; alternatively do the same for some domestic, social or management project.
- If you work in an organisation, try to find examples of projects that use this approach, and ask those involved when the method is most useful, and when least useful.
- Make notes summarising how the life cycle approach helps, and when it is most likely to be useful.

Emergent models

In Chapter 8 (Section 8.6) Barthélemy (2006) offers an insight into the strategy process at IKEA (Chapter 15 case), showing how many of its strategies have emerged from chance events or external conditions, rather than from a formal planning process. Evidence such as this led Quinn (1980) and Mintzberg (1994a, 1994b) to see strategy as an *emergent* or adaptive process. These ideas apply to change projects as much as they do to strategy. Projects are the means through which organisations deliver strategy. They take place in the same volatile, uncertain environment in which the organisation operates. People with different interests and priorities influence the means and ends of a project. So while the planning techniques associated with the life cycle approach can help, their value will be limited if the change is closer to the **emergent model**.

Emergent models of change emphasise that in uncertain conditions a project will be affected by unknown factors, and that planning has little effect on the outcome.

Vodafone/Ericsson – the case continues

CASE STUDY

www.vodafone.com, www.ericsson.com

The globalisation strategy was developed and implemented through the Global Supply Chain Management (GSCM) forum that first met in 1999. Initially it was attended by representatives from both companies in those countries where Vodafone had a majority shareholding in the local operating company, though membership gradually expanded to include most countries in which Vodafone operated. The initial meeting resolved that all joint activities should be conducted in an open and transparent way: 'It would be a process of learning through experience; there would be no requirement to produce plans that formed a rigid basis of change control' (Ibbott and O'Keefe, 2004, p. 224).

The members believed that a planned project approach would not have worked, as it was important to be able to cope with rapid change.

Both the end point and direction were uncertain, and fundamental process changes had to be agreed within and between companies. The acquisition of Mannesmann of Germany, unplanned at the start of the transformation, provided an opportunity for further benefits (p. 229).

The forum also recognised that the two sides would benefit in different ways, but there was no attempt to plan how to share the benefits – either party would retain whatever benefits they secured. Vodafone's equity-based structure in the different countries meant that those leading the project had to sell the concept of the global endeavour to the management teams of each entity. Ericsson's more unified structure of wholly owned subsidiaries gave them less scope for resisting proposals.

GSCM meetings set up several work streams that would move the relationship towards global collaboration. The leadership of each work stream was assigned to one or other of the participating countries. The teams leading them had to secure resources for the project from within their country operations, working as they saw fit. Examples of work streams were:

- creating a global price book for all products bought from Ericsson (UK team)
- agreeing a standard base station design (UK team)
- agreeing a common procedure for software design and testing (Australia)
- developing a computer-based information system linking the parties for information sharing – initially called groupware (The Netherlands).

While the groupware project was at first intended to support communications between the teams working on the globalisation project, it later evolved into a system through which both parties conducted routine transactions – such as ordering products. The simple communication system emerged, without any formal plan, into a system for handling all orders from Vodafone to Ericsson that had a global price.

Source: Ibbott and O'Keefe (2004).

Boddy *et al.* (2000) show how this emergent process occurred when Sun Microsystems began the partnering project described earlier. Sun's initial intention was to secure a UK source for the bulky plastic enclosures that contain their products, while the supplier was seeking ways to widen its customer base. There were few discussions about a long-term plan. As Sun became more confident of its supplier's ability it gave them more complex work. Both gained from this emerging relationship. They acknowledge that at first they did not foresee the amount and type of business they would eventually be undertaking. A sales coordinator:

> It's something we've learnt by being with Sun – we didn't imagine that at the time. Also at the time we wouldn't have imagined we would be dealing with America the way we do now – it was far beyond our thoughts. (Boddy *et al.*, 2000, p. 1010)

Mintzberg's point is that managers should not expect rigid adherence to 'the plan'. Some departure from it is inevitable, due to unforeseeable changes in the external environment, the emergence of new opportunities, and other unanticipated events. A flexible approach to change is one which recognises that

> the real world inevitably involves some thinking ahead of time as well as some adaptation en route (Mintzberg, 1994a, p. 24).

Case questions 13.4

- Were those leading the change taking a life cycle or an emergent view?
- Which of those views does the evidence of later events seem to support?

Participative models

The **participative model** is the belief that if people are able to take part in planning a change they will be more willing to accept and implement the change.

Those advocating **participative models** stress the benefits of personal involvement in, and contribution to, events and outcomes. The underlying belief is that if people can say 'I helped to build this', they will be more willing to live and work with it, whatever it is. It is also possible that since participation allows a wider range of views to be expressed the outcome will be of higher quality than if it takes account of a limited range of views. Empirical support for this was provided by the study by Ketokivi and Castañer (2004), cited in Chapter 6 (Section 6.4). They found that when employees participated in planning strategic change, they were more likely to view the issues from the perspective of the organisation, rather than their own position or function. Participation can be good for the organisation, as well as the individual.

Enid Mumford and participation

key ideas

A leading advocate and practitioner of participative approaches to change was Edith Mumford, who applied the principles of socio-technical systems in her work. This theory was outlined in Chapter 2 (Section 2.7) and is based on the idea that an organisation has both technical and social components. Mumford and her colleagues focused on change based on the introduction of computer systems, noting that IS development projects typically overemphasised the technical, and underestimated the social aspects. She sought, through the development of the ETHICS method (Mumford and Weir, 1979), to enable developers to give adequate attention to both. Advocates claimed that this approach would lead to systems that not only worked (from a technical perspective) but were also more attractive from a human point of view, enhancing motivation and job satisfaction.

The approach required a high degree of participation by users in the design, to ensure as much compatibility with the social system in which the technology would be set. This participative approach typically involved people in decisions about the design of the system, and in making decisions within a work team about its operation. Reflecting on the limited acceptance of participative systems in recent years, she concludes that a major barrier has been that of the cultural context. With many organisations retaining a hierarchical form, those in higher positions are frequently reluctant to give up power to the degree implied by participative approaches to change (Mumford, 1997, 2006).

Source: Mumford (1997, 2006).

Staff participation in planning the CGU merger

management in practice

One of the UK's biggest mergers in 1998 was that of Commercial Union and General Accident to form CGU. The merger involved many changes, and management decided to involve employees in planning these, mainly through three large meetings of hundreds of staff, nominated by their colleagues:

1 Two hundred staff conducted a culture survey of the two companies. They were paired, one from each company, and escorted each other into the other's company, where they used a set format to build a culture map – how the firms were similar and how they differed.

2 Five hundred managers and technical specialists attended a two-day conference to work in teams on the results of the culture survey and other data. Their task was to form a view about what would make CGU the 'best place to work'. Video cameras captured the action and displayed it overhead on giant television screens around the hall, giving the two days the feel of a vibrant sporting event. Amongst the priorities the delegates agreed were clear boundaries of authority, freedom to take decisions within those boundaries, clear expectations, feedback, access to opportunity, and support for development.

3 Eighty people attended a four-day structured design workshop. Their task was to start designing a new organisation to meet the needs of shareholders, customers, employees and business partners. They produced a design that included principles of access (ensuring all would have easy entrance to their new offices), size of business units (30 to 50 people), and size of teams (between 10 and 12).

▶

Tony Clarry commented:

The roll-out in the 51 locations so far has been smooth, which we attribute to the degree of commitment to the integration teams and to the conscientiousness of our people. Of course, there has been pain ... but involving people in decision making continues to be at the heart of what we do. We believe our approach has proved the value of real consultation.

Source: Based on an article by Tony Clarry, who led the integration of the two companies, in *People Management*, 2 September 1999.

While the approach is consistent with democratic values, it is not free. It takes time and effort, and may raise unrealistic expectations. It may be inappropriate when:

- there is already agreement on how to proceed;
- the scope for change is limited, because of decisions made elsewhere;
- those taking part in the exercise have little knowledge of the topic;
- decisions are needed urgently to meet deadlines set elsewhere;
- management has decided what to do and will do so whatever views people express;
- there is fundamental disagreement and inflexible opposition to a change.

Participative approaches assume that a sensitive approach by reasonable people will result in the willing acceptance and implementation of change. Other situations contain conflicts that participation alone cannot solve.

Activity 13.4   Critical reflection on participation

Have you been involved in, or affected by, a change in your work or studies?

If so

- What evidence was there that those managing the change agreed with the participative approach?
- In what way, if any, were you able to participate?
- How did that affect your reaction to the change?

If not:

- Identify three advantages and three disadvantages for the project manager in adopting a participative approach.
- Suggest how managers should decide when to use the approach.

Political models

The models described so far offer little guidance where a change challenges established interests, or where powerful players have opposing views. Change often involves people from several levels and functions who will pull in different directions, pursuing personal as well as organisational goals:

Strategic processes of change are ... widely accepted as multi-level activities and not just as the province of a ... single general manager. Outcomes of decisions are no longer assumed to be a product of rational ... debates but are also shaped by the interests and commitments of individuals and groups, forces of bureaucratic momentum, and the manipulation of the structural context around decisions and changes. (Whipp *et al.*, 1988, p. 51)

Several analyses of organisational change emphasise a **political model** (Pettigrew, 1985, 1987; Pfeffer, 1992a; Pinto, 1998; Buchanan and Badham, 1999). Pettigrew (1985) was an early advocate of the view that change requires political as well as rational (life cycle) skills. Successful change managers create a climate in which people accept the change as legitimate – often by manipulating apparently rational information to build support for their ideas.

Political models reflect the view that organisations are made up of groups with separate interests, goals and values, and that these affect how they respond to change.

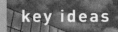

Tom Burns on politics and language

key ideas

Tom Burns (1961) observed that political behaviour in the organisation is invariably concealed or made acceptable by subtle shifts in the language that people use:

> Normally, either side in any conflict called political by observers claims to speak in the interests of the corporation as a whole. In fact, the only recognised, indeed feasible, way of advancing political interests is to present them in terms of improved welfare or efficiency, as contributing to the organisation's capacity to meet its task and to prosper. In managerial and academic, as in other legislatures, both sides to any debate claim to speak in the interests of the community as a whole; this is the only permissible mode of expression. (p. 260)

Pfeffer (1992a) also argues that power is essential to get things done, since decisions in themselves change nothing. It is only when someone implements them that anyone notices a difference. He proposes that projects require more than people able to solve technical problems. Projects frequently threaten the status quo: people who have done well in the past are likely to resist them. Innovators also need to ensure the project is on the agenda, and that senior managers support and resource it. Innovators also need to develop a political will, and to build and use their power. Buchanan and Badham (1999) consider why political behaviour occurs, and conclude that:

> Its roots lie in personal ambition, in organisation structures that create roles and departments which compete with each other, and in major decisions that cannot be resolved by reason and logic alone but which rely on the values and preferences of the key actors.
>
> Power politics and change are inextricably linked. Change creates uncertainty and ambiguity. People wonder how their jobs will change, how their workload will be affected, how their relationships with colleagues will be damaged or enhanced. (p. 11)

Reasonable people may disagree about means and ends, and fight for the action they prefer. This implies that successful project managers understand that their job requires more than technical competence, and are able and willing to engage in political actions.

Henry Kissinger on politics in politics

key ideas

In another work Pfeffer (1992b) quotes Henry Kissinger:

> Before I served as a consultant to Kennedy, I had believed, like most academics, that the process of decision-making was largely intellectual and all one had to do was to walk into the President's office and convince him of the correctness of one's view. This perspective I soon realised is as dangerously immature as it is widely held. (p. 31)

Source: Pfeffer (1992b).

Politics and change in the public sector

These views of change as a fluid process find support in a contemporary account of project management in the public sector, based on research amongst a group of managers implementing major change projects:

> The powerful influence of the political process on organisational and cultural change is transparent for local authorities, but this may also be relevant in other non-elected organisations. Competing values and interests between different stakeholders are often less overt but none the less powerful factors championing or blocking processes of change.

Source: Hartley *et al.* (1997) p. 71.

The political perspective recognises the messy realities of organisational life. Major changes will be technically complex and challenge established interests. These will pull in different directions and pursue personal as well as organisational goals. To manage these tensions managers need political skills as well as those implied by life cycle, emergent and participative perspectives.

They need to be sensitive to the power and influence of key individuals, aware of how the change may alter those, and able to negotiate and sell ideas to indifferent or sceptical colleagues. They may have to filter information to change perceptions, and do things that make the change seem legitimate within the organisation.

Political action in hospital re-engineering

Managers in a hospital responded to a persistent performance gap (especially unacceptably long waiting times) by 're-engineering' the way patients moved through and between the different clinical areas. This included creating multi-functional teams responsible for all aspects of the flow of the patient through a clinic, rather than dealing with narrow functional tasks. The programme was successful, but was also controversial. One of those leading the change recalled:

> I don't like to use the word manipulate, but ... you do need to manipulate people. It's about playing the game. I remember being accosted by a very cross consultant who had heard something about one of the changes and he really wasn't very happy with it. And it was about how am I going to deal with this now? And it is about being able to think quickly. So I put it over to him in a way that he then accepted, and he was quite happy with. And it wasn't a lie and it wasn't totally the truth. But he was happy with it and it has gone on.

Source: Buchanan (2001), p. 13.

Pensco

Pensco was a life insurance business. Changes to legislation brought new opportunities in the market for personal and group pensions, and also more competition. The board appointed a new general manager who began to change the organisation towards a market-led, sales-maximising approach. He recruited a colleague from his previous company as head of information systems (IS), who had a reputation as an autocratic and aggressive manager. Changing the pensions products depended on new IS to process the new business.

> The actuarial department (AD) proposed some new pension products. Staff in sales and marketing (S&M) interpreted the market differently, were dismissive of the AD proposals, and actively lobbied for their alternative ideas. S&M also believed that the IS department had
>
> > too much power in the organisation ... We are working to change that. S&M should drive the organisation ... But I can't get away from the view that IS still dictate what the company can and can't do. (Knights and Murray, 1994, p. 187)
>
> For their part, IS had trouble identifying the business requirements – partly because of unresolved conflicts between AD and S&M over the product range. The head of IS was seen to be seeking favour with the general manager by accepting all requests for systems developments – which staff were unable to deliver.
>
> The company presented the project as a success. The authors of the case reported different views from the clerical staff who were processing new proposals (without adequate IS support). As a team leader commented:
>
> > They [the managers] don't have a grasp of what's going on. They just want the figures. They don't appreciate our problems. I wish they'd acknowledge there is one. (p. 162).
>
> Source: Based on Knights and Murray (1994).

These perspectives (life cycle, emergent, participative and political) are complementary in that successful large-scale change, such as that at Vodafone/Ericsson, is likely to require elements of each. Table 13.2 illustrates how each perspective links to management practice.

Perspective	Themes	Example of management practices
Life cycle	Rational, linear, single agreed aim, technical focus	Measurable objectives; planning and control devices such as Gantt charts and critical path analysis
Emergent	Objectives change as learning occurs during the project, and new possibilities appear	Open to new ideas about scope and direction, and willing to add new resources if needed
Participative	Ownership, commitment, shared goals, people focus	Inviting ideas and comments on proposals, ensuring agreement before action, seeking consensus
Political	Oppositional, influence, conflicting goals, power focus	Building allies and coalitions, securing support from powerful players, managing information

Table 13.2

Perspectives on change and examples of management practice

13.5   Driving and restraining forces – Kurt Lewin

Lewin (1947) observed that any social system is in a state of temporary equilibrium. Driving forces are trying to change the situation in directions they favour. Restraining forces push the other way to prevent change, or to move it in another direction. This equilibrium 'can be changed either by adding forces in the desired direction, or by diminishing the opposing forces' (p. 26). Figure 13.5 illustrates the idea: see Burnes (2004) for an appraisal of the influence and continued relevance of Lewin's ideas.

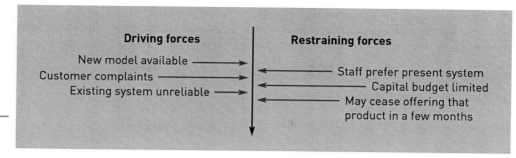

Figure 13.5

Driving and restraining forces

Driving forces encourage change from the present position. They encourage people and groups to give up past practice and to act in ways that support the change. They take many forms – such as a newly available technology, an inadequate business process or the support of a powerful player. Conversely factors such as the already-installed technology, shortage of finance, the opposition of powerful players or the company culture can be restraining forces. In many small companies, managers are said to be so absorbed in day-to-day matters that they are unable to put time and energy into major changes that would help the business to grow. They become committed to maintaining existing practice.

Those advocating a change can, in Lewin's terms, 'add forces in the desired direction' by stressing the advantages of the change, emphasising the threat from competitors or making the benefits seem more attractive. Mr Yun Jong-yon, chief executive of Samsung Electronics, was credited with transforming the company from a struggling producer of cheap electronics into one of the world's best-performing and most respected IT companies. He explained part of his approach:

> I'm the chaos-maker. I have tried to encourage a sense of crisis to drive change. We instilled in management a sense that we could go bankrupt any day. (*Financial Times*, 13 March 2003, p. 15)

Alternatively they can seek to 'diminish the opposing forces' by showing that the problems will not be as great as people fear, or pointing out that difficulties will be temporary.

Lewin observed that while increasing the driving forces could produce change in the desired direction, it could also increase tension amongst those 'forced' to change. The change may then be short-lived, or offset by the negative effects of the tension. Since these secondary effects may go against the interests of those promoting change, he suggested that trying to reduce the forces restraining change is usually the wiser route. The Management in Practice feature shows an alternative view – namely that increasing the driving forces can also work.

---

management in practice   The power of the visual image

Kotter and Cohen (2002) give several examples of the use of dramatic visual images to overcome inertia. In one case, showing a video of an angry customer to employees sparked a sense of urgency that helped to overcome long-standing resistance to improving the product. Another explains how a taskforce handling poor investment planning made a light-hearted video with spoof characters who mimicked the damaging behaviour of senior executives. The video apparently shocked the executives into changing their behaviour. Kotter believes that the main reason why change efforts of any size fail is that there is not a great enough sense of urgency about the need to change – and that visual shocks can help break that barrier.

Source: Kotter and Cohen (2002).

External events can trigger and drive change: new competition, a change in legislation, the activities of a pressure group, a chance conversation. Information from any of these sources can trigger change. People with sufficient power can use these and countless other external signs to justify a proposal.

In the same way, forces within the organisation – changing management priorities, the availability of funds, opposition from groups who see their privileges threatened – can drive change, or restrain it. The degree and direction of change in an organisation reflect the shifting balance and direction of the driving and restraining forces.

13.6   Forms and sources of resistance to change

Most managers are expected to implement change in the context in which they work. In doing so they use their power to influence others to act in a particular way. Chapter 14 outlines theories of power and influence, so this and the following sections examine just three aspects of this activity – understanding resistance to change, using front-stage and back-stage tactics, and supporting individual activity with formal structures.

Much of the management literature presents resistance to change in pejorative terms as something to be overcome, but this discussion takes a more neutral stance. There is anecdotal evidence of managers introducing change to further personal interests – to build a reputation or extend departmental influence. Since organisations comprise political and career systems as well as working systems, this is inevitable. Even when people intend to support organisational interests they may misinterpret the situation and propose misguided changes.

For all these reasons people at all levels will sometimes resist change, either as a threat to their interests or because they believe it will damage the organisation. Many change programmes fade from view – unless someone is able to make the change stick by creating a favourable context (Roberto and Levesque, 2005).

Forms of resistance

Overt and public resistance is often unnecessary. There are many other ways in which those opposed to a change can delay it, including:

- making no effort to learn
- using older systems whenever possible
- not attending meetings to discuss the project
- excessive fault finding and criticism
- deliberate misuse
- saying it has been tried before and did not work then
- protracted discussion and requests for more information
- linking the issue with pay or other industrial relations matters
- not releasing staff for training.

These delaying tactics come from anywhere in the organisation – they are as likely to come from managers who see a change as a threat to their interests as they are to come from more junior staff. Change creates winners and losers, and potential losers are apt to engage in what Keen (1981) termed the tactics of **counterimplementation**.

Counterimplementation refers to attempts to block change without displaying overt opposition.

key ideas   Peter Keen on counterimplementation

Keen (1981) suggested that overt resistance to change is often risky, and may not in practice be necessary. He identified several ways in which those wanting to block a change can do so – even while appearing to support it. They include such tactics as:

- **Divert resources** Split the budget across other projects; give key staff other priorities and allocate them to other assignments; arrange for equipment to be moved or shared.
- **Exploit inertia** Suggest that everyone wait until a key player has taken action or read the report or made an appropriate response; suggest that the results from some other project should be monitored and assessed first.
- **Keep goals vague and complex** It is harder to initiate appropriate action in pursuit of aims that are multidimensional and specified in generalised, grandiose or abstract terms.
- **Encourage and exploit lack of organisational awareness** Insist that 'we can deal with the people issues later', knowing that these will delay or kill the project.
- **'Great idea – let's do it properly'** And let's bring in representatives from this function and that section, until we have so many different views and conflicting interests that it will take for ever to sort them out.
- **Dissipate energies** Have people conduct surveys, collect data, prepare analyses, write reports, make overseas trips, hold special meetings ...
- **Reduce the champion's influence and credibility** Spread damaging rumours, particularly amongst the champion's friends and supporters.
- **Keep a low profile** It is not effective openly to declare resistance to change because that gives those driving change a clear target.

Source: Based on Keen (1981).

Activity 13.5   Critical reflection on resistance

Discuss with someone who has tried to introduce change in an organisation what evidence there was of resistance.

- Which of the forms listed by Keen (in Key Ideas above) were in evidence?
- Can they identify any other forms?

Then consider these questions:

- Have you ever resisted a proposed change?
- What form did your resistance take?

Sources of resistance

Kotter and Schlesinger (1979) identified that sources of resistance included self-interest, misunderstanding and lack of trust: 'people also resist change when they do not understand its implications and perceive that it might cost them much more than they will gain' (p. 108). Employees assess the situation differently from their managers and may see more costs than benefits for both themselves and the company. Recardo (1991) made similar points from a study of new manufacturing systems. Change requires learning and exposure to uncertainty, insecurity and new social interactions, yet communication about the changes is often poor. Additional factors that Recardo identified as causing resistance were reward systems that did not reward the desired behaviour and a poor fit between the change and the existing culture.

These views can be enlarged by using the elements of the organisation shown in Figure 13.2. People can base their resistance on any of these contextual elements, as shown in Table 13.3.

Element	Source of resistance	
Objectives	Lack of clarity or understanding of objectives, or disagreement with those proposed	
People	Change may threaten important values, preferences, skills, needs and interests	
Technology	May be poorly designed, hard to use, incompatible with existing equipment, or require more work than is worthwhile	
Business processes	As for technology, and may require unwelcome changes to the way people deal with colleagues and customers	
Financial resources	Scepticism about whether the change will be financially worthwhile, or less so than other competing changes; lack of money	
Structure	New reporting relationships or means of control may disrupt working relationships and patterns of authority	
Culture	People likely to resist a change that challenges core values and beliefs, especially if they have worked well before	
Power	If change affects ownership of and access to information, those who see they will lose autonomy will resist	

Table 13.3

Sources of resistance to change

In addition to these substantive or content reasons for resisting change, people may also resist because of the way others manage the change. They object to the process of change, irrespective of the specific change being made. Change is disturbing, and people are likely to resist if they do not feel they have been able to participate in discussions about the form it should take.

13.7 Organisation development

Organisation development (OD) is a comprehensive and widely used approach to managing change. It embodies a clear set of values about people and work, many of which relate to ideas on organisation culture (Chapter 3), human resource management (Chapter 11), and work design (Chapter 15).

A common theme in managing is how to balance the needs of the individual with the behaviour required for high organisational performance. OD practitioners believe that

> with appropriate interventions based on social scientific understanding, the conflicting interests of organizations and their members can be diagnosed and reconciled. (Huczynski and Buchanan, 2007, p. 560)

Practitioners use OD to resolve conflicts within a single business unit or for the organisation as a whole, aiming for both individual development and organisational effectiveness. They try to achieve these mutually supporting goals through deliberate and systematic interventions, using knowledge from the social and behavioural sciences.

Robbins (2001, p. 553) outlines the values that underlie most OD activities:

● The individual should be treated with respect and dignity.
● The organisation climate should be characterised by trust, openness and support.

Organisation development is a systematic process in which applied behavioural science principles and practices are introduced with the goal of increasing individual and organisational performance.

- Hierarchical authority and control are de-emphasised.
- Problems and conflicts should be confronted, not disguised or avoided.
- People affected by change should be involved in its implementation.

Some practitioners believe that this agenda is worth pursuing in its own right, though others stress that implementing practices based on these values will make a business more efficient and effective.

A common theme in OD is that bureaucracy is an obstacle to performance, and that an organisation in which staff have more freedom and flexibility in the way they work will also show a better financial performance. Table 13.4 summarises how OD practitioners tackle these problems in both private and public sector organisations (Bate, 2000).

Table 13.4

Bureaucratic diseases and OD cures

Bureaucratic disease	Symptoms	OD cures
Rigid functional boundaries	Conflict between sections, poor communications	Team building, job rotation, structural change
Fixed hierarchies	Frustration, boredom, narrow specialist thinking	Training, job enrichment, career development
Information only flows down	Lack of innovation, minor problems escalate	Process consultation, management development
Routine jobs, tight control	Boredom, absenteeism, conflict with supervisors	Job enrichment, job rotation, supervisory training

Source: Buchanan and Huczynski (2007), p. 563.

Common OD techniques are listed below, and more detail on each is contained in Huczynski and Buchanan (2007, pp. 568–572).

Sensitivity training is a technique for enhancing self-awareness and changing behaviour through unstructured group discussion.

Process consultation is an OD intervention in which an external consultant facilitates improvements in an organisation's diagnostic, conceptual and action planning skills.

Survey feedback is an OD intervention in which the results of an opinion survey are fed back to respondents to trigger problem solving on the issues the survey identifies.

- **Sensitivity training** Conducted in small groups, the aim of **sensitivity training** is to allow participants to discuss themselves, to observe and discuss how the members interact with each other and to exchange feedback on each other. The intention is that through such discussions participants become more sensitive to their behaviour, the effects they have on others, and how others see and relate to them.
- **Changing structure** OD projects often include efforts to decentralise organisations by giving more decision-making power to local units, or changing the horizontal structure of the organisation through business process redesign. Structural changes signify which areas of the organisation are becoming more significant, and which are in decline.
- **Process consultation** A consultant undertakes **process consultation** to help members of the organisation to develop a clearer insight into the problems facing the organisation, as distinct from an external consultant doing the analysis. It is consistent with core OD values that people are ultimately responsible for their development.
- **Survey feedback** This refers to the technique of conducting a survey of employee attitudes, and providing managers or supervisors with anonymous analyses of the results – hence the term **survey feedback**. Respondents may be invited to suggest themes or questions to include in the survey, and to take part in group discussions of the results.
- **Team building** Attempts to develop more effective teams using a wide variety of methods, such as that developed by Meredith Belbin (1993) in which members identify the distinctive team roles they play, and how different combinations affect performance (Chapter 17).

- **Intergroup development** This helps overcome the boundaries which can arise between groups that are expected to work together. Functional boundaries and diverse experiences lead groups to develop a strong internal identity – and possibly strong negative feelings towards other groups. Intergroup development helps to break down assumptions, and encourage more cooperative working across boundaries.
- **Grid organisation development** This is an application of Blake and Mouton's (1979) managerial grid, described in Chapter 14. The grid assumes that leadership styles vary on two dimensions – concern for production and concern for people. Managers can be assessed on the extent to which they are high, medium or low on each dimension. The prescription is that ideally they should be high on both, and the technique is intended to help managers reflect on their style, and move closer to the ideal type.

13.8   Stimulating innovation

An increasingly common aspect of managers' jobs is the pressure to stimulate innovation in the areas for which they are responsible. This covers being innovative in creating new products and services, and in the processes that deliver them. Some organisations have developed a reputation for being better able than others at sensing and satisfying consumer trends.

Lorne and Agnes Campbell and TravelCo

management in practice

TravelCo is an entrepreneurial travel company that specialises in delivering customised, luxurious holidays to US visitors interested in Scottish heritage. Employees must follow highly specified routines and systems in matters such as ticketing and scheduling: this is essential to ensure error-free reservations and other arrangements for their customers. However the same employees must be able to devise creative solutions to meet customers' individual requirements for their visit to Scotland – from where their ancestors often came. The company encourages employees to think laterally and creatively for this aspect of the work.

It does this by allowing them wide decision-making powers to come up with imaginative holiday ideas. An example was a US customer who wanted his itinerary to include an opportunity to meet some of his Clan Campbell ancestors. His guide, Abigail Forbes, was able to arrange for him to lunch with Lorne and Agnes Campbell, her 80-something grandparents in the ancient Scottish town of Inverary – which delighted the visitor as an imaginative and innovative way of achieving exactly what he wanted.

Source: Private communication.

Creativity and innovation

Creativity refers to the ability to combine ideas in a new way, or to make unusual associations between ideas. This helps people and organisations to generate imaginative ideas or ways of working: but that in itself does not ensure added value. That only comes when people turn the creative process into products or services that meet a demand, which they can meet profitably. In the public sector **innovation** is reflected in new ways of delivering services (such as the growing provision of online services); in the charities sector it could be a new way of raising funds, such as the RED brand associated with leading pop stars, which devotes a proportion of its profits to designated charities.

Creativity is the ability to combine ideas in a unique way, or to make unusual associations between ideas.

Innovation is the process of taking a creative idea and turning it into a useful product, service or method of operation.

Stimulating innovation

The systems model introduced in Chapter 1 helps to understand how organisations can become more innovative. Figure 13.6 shows that getting the desired outputs (more innovative products or work methods) depends on both the inputs and the transformation of those inputs.

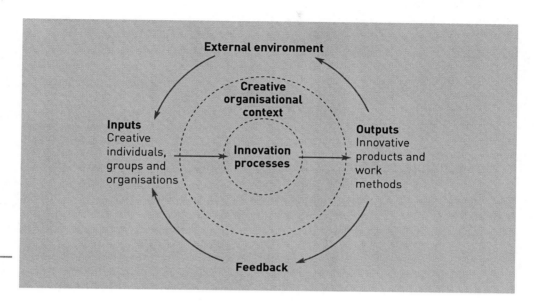

Figure 13.6

Systems view of innovation

Inputs include having creative people and groups who are able to generate novel ideas and methods, but creative people can only sustain their creativity in a favourable context. Figure 13.7 shows three significant elements of that context – cultures, HR policies and structures.

Cultures for innovation

Innovative organisations tend to have cultures that encourage experimentation, reward success and accept that some failures are inevitable – a source of learning rather than shame. Robbins and Coulter (2005, p. 329) suggest that an innovative culture is likely to have these features:

- *Acceptance of ambiguity* Too much emphasis on objective analysis and detailed planning constrains creativity.
- *Tolerance of the impractical* Individuals who offer impractical, even foolish, answers to speculative questions are not ridiculed. What at first seems impractical may lead to innovative solutions.
- *Low external controls* Rules, regulations and procedures are kept to a minimum.
- *Tolerance of risk* Employees are encouraged to experiment without fear of the consequence if they fail. Mistakes become opportunities for learning.
- *Tolerance of conflict* Diversity of opinions is encouraged. Harmony and agreement between people and sub-units is not taken as a sign of high performance.
- *Focus on end rather than means* Goals are clear, but individuals choose how to achieve them.
- *Open system focus* People are encouraged to monitor the business environment and to be ready to respond to change as it occurs.

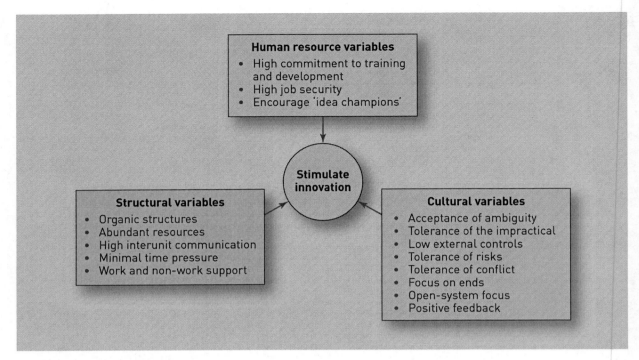

Figure 13.7 Innovation variables

- *Positive feedback* Managers provide positive feedback, encouragement and support so employees feel their creativity will receive attention.

HR policies for innovation

Innovative organisations actively promote the training and development of their members so that their knowledge remains current, offer job security to overcome the fear of making mistakes, and encourage people to become 'champions of change'. Such **idea champions** actively and enthusiastically support new ideas, build support, overcome resistance, and ensure that ideas are implemented. Idea champions tend to have similar personalities – high self-confidence, persistence, energy and a tendency to take risks. They also inspire and energise others with their vision of the potential of an innovation, and through their strong personal commitment to its success. They also need to be good at gaining the support of others – especially those at more senior levels of the organisation – which helps them overcome doubts elsewhere.

Idea champions are individuals who actively and enthusiastically support new ideas, build support, overcome resistance, and ensure that ideas are implemented.

Structures for innovation

Research into innovation has identified structural factors that encourage it, such as having an organic structure, encouraging horizontal communication, encouraging people to contribute ideas outside their loosely designed roles, having abundant resources, and frequent communication between units. Organic structures help because they have little formality, work in a decentralised way and encourage people to apply skills and knowledge to a wide range of tasks: this creates an atmosphere of cross-fertilisation and adaptability that in turn fosters innovation. Abundant resources help since they enable managers to purchase required expertise that may have developed in other companies, and also enables them to take risks by investing in new projects without too much anxiety that failure will damage the business. Frequent communication between units fosters the exchange of ideas and information, which can in turn stimulate combinations of knowledge, or its application, in unusual ways. Finally, there is evidence that when an organisation's structure provides explicit support for creativity from work and non-work activities, an employee's creativity is enhanced. Support includes encouragement, open communication, readiness to listen and useful feedback.

13.9   Current themes and issues

Performance

In a business world characterised by uncertainty and change, many advocate that organisations must change radically and relentlessly (see for example Foster and Kaplan, 2000). Managers are advised that to survive they must continually review all aspects of the way they do business. 'Change or perish' is the rationale of those who propose unrelenting change, who assume: 'that people naturally resist change and that leaders should destroy or cast aside the old ways in order to create a spanking new future' (Abrahamson, 2004). While the arguments may sometimes be valid, such as where an over-protected organisation suddenly faces new competition, disruptive change is costly, and does not necessarily improve performance (Barnet and Freeman, 2001).

Abrahamson (2004) identifies three symptoms of organisations suffering from excessive change – initiative overload, change related chaos and employee cynicism.

Initiative overload

An organisation in which managers become convinced of the need for radical change is likely to require more change than even they anticipate. Figure 13.2 reflects the systemic nature of organisations – a change in one area is likely to require complementary changes in others. An investment in IS may lead to further changes affecting, say, structures, people and business processes. They may or may not succeed – and if they fail then further changes follow. People experience 'initiative overload' and become dispirited and disinterested in whatever is proposed. Someone attempting to introduce a change in one area of a large business observed:

> There are so many changes taking place, they are more or less numb, and this is simply another change which they are just going to have to take on board. The result is that they are somewhat passive and neutral, and when I ask what their requirements might be, the response is usually 'you tell me'. (Boddy, 2002, p. 38)

Change related chaos

Major change inevitably means a period of overlap between old arrangements and the new, during which time there will be more than the usual scope for chaos. Abrahamson (2004) quotes the example of a bank that changed its cheque processing systems. Managers closed the previous system one Friday, opening the new one the following Monday. Things began to go badly wrong, as paper accumulated at all points in the system, which eventually collapsed:

> Why did the change fail so spectacularly? Because ... the new processes had not been fully tested and implemented. In the end, it became apparent to everyone that the change process had wreaked such chaos that it was almost destined to fail. (p. 17)

Employee cynicism

A succession of initiatives leading to change related chaos makes staff anxious and inse-cure. Communication failure will make this worse, leading to progressive alienation and dissatisfaction. Abrahamson (2004) refers to one senior banker he interviewed soon after a merger of the bank with a rival who told him that she was the only person left of the 60 people who had worked in her unit.

An alternative approach – change without pain?

Having taken a critical view of 'creative destruction', Abrahamson (2004) develops an alternative approach based on what he calls recombination. This takes the view that change will be a great deal less painful if managers take more time to analyse the positive aspects of the existing elements in the organisation. Taking these as the starting point, and basing change as far as possible on small adaptations to familiar arrangements will be much more acceptable to staff, and likely to produce better performance improve-ments than the radical alternatives.

Responsibility

The biggest challenge facing those implementing major change is that stakeholders will take different views of an organisation's problems, and will have varying degrees of com-mitment to changes intended to deal with them. Chapter 3 also quoted research by Nutt (2002) that half of the changes he studied produced poor results – in large part because decision makers failed to attend to interests and information held by key stakeholders.

An important step in influencing stakeholders is to assess their relative power and interest (Eden and Ackerman, 1998), which can be prepared to analyse the relative posi-tion of the stakeholders in an issue or project on two dimensions:

- their interest in the issue or activity being proposed, and
- their power to influence the outcomes of the issue or activity.

Those with both a high level of interest in the issue and high power to influence the out-come are the key players whom the organisation must seek to satisfy. Conversely those with low interest and power may require only minimal attention to ensure their acquies-cence in a proposal.

A dilemma facing anyone with responsibility for implementing a change is how much attention they pay to different stakeholders. An instrumental approach would be to put most time and effort into meeting the needs of powerful stakeholders, as these are the ones who could cause most trouble if their needs are unmet. An alternative view would suggest that a responsible approach would take more account of the interests of those with less evident power – such as the disadvantaged, inarticulate or under-represented communities. Considerations of enlightened self-interest, as discussed in Chapter 5, could lead to a different approach to change management than one that only looked after the interests of the powerful.

International

The growing internationalisation of business has implications for the way international or global firms manage change. The issue here reflects one of the central themes within Chapter 4, namely the balance between a unified, global approach seeking to establish a common identity across all operations, or an approach that adapts the way the company operates to local conditions. Managers of local business units will have local priorities, and are likely to be unreceptive to change that the centre, or even another unit, appears to be imposing. The issues managers can face is illustrated by the experience of one who tried to introduce a new order processing system that would require compatible changes across seven European plants: see the Management in Practice feature.

management in practice   A Europe-wide change project

An individual needs to go out on a limb with an idea and be able to articulate that idea to a wider audience before they can get any interest, support and investment to go forward. In our company where the products and the business plan change very quickly it is enormously difficult to get people to focus on what is important rather than on what is urgent. We have seven sites all at different stages of development. We have in some way to make sure that each of them is positioned both in terms of resources, energy and commitment to support an integrated European programme. It is because we have a business which is fairly complex and so diverse that we have adopted the approach that basically says – generate a common level of understanding of what needs to be done, then allow each area to specify their unique requirements within this overall framework. It also allows each individual location to move at their own pace as long as they don't get too far out of line.

The team member from Valbonne wrote to me two weeks ago indicating that he's now been asked to do another European programme. Therefore because his particular group in Valbonne are very short of resources he will not be able to support this team. From my point of view as a programme manager that is totally unacceptable as his plant is a very big part of the order-fulfilment process. So without a representative from there any solution that we devise will only be partially successful.

Source: Boddy (2002), p. 172.

In this case, the manager was able to secure support for his role from European senior management, and was able to exert some influence over the individual plants. However, that influence was limited, meaning that the change introduced was less comprehensive, and less integrated, than would have been possible with a more centrally controlled structure. This balancing act faces all companies operating internationally.

Summary

1 **Explain the meaning of organisational change and give examples**
   - Organisational change refers to deliberate attempts to change one or more elements of the internal environment, such as technology or structure. Change in one element usually stimulates change in other areas.

2 **Explain what the links between change and context imply for those managing a change**
   - A change programme is an attempt to change one or more aspects of the internal context, which then provides the context of future actions. The prevailing context can itself help or hinder change efforts.

3 **Compare life cycle, emergent, participative and political theories of change**
   - Life cycle: change projects can be planned, monitored and controlled towards achieving their objectives.

- Emergent: reflecting the uncertainties of the environment, change is hard to plan in detail, but emerges incrementally from events and actions.

- Participative: successful change depends on human commitment, which is best obtained by involving participants in planning and implementation.

- Political: change threatens some of those affected, who will use their power to block progress, or to direct the change in ways that suit local objectives.

4 **Evaluate systematically the possible sources of resistance to change**

- Reasons can be assessed using the internal context model, as each element (objectives, people, power, etc.) is a potential source of resistance. Analysing these indicates potential ways of overcoming resistance.

- The force field analysis model allows players to identify the forces driving and restraining a change, and implies that reducing the restraining forces will help change more than increasing the driving forces.

5 **Explain the meaning of organisational development and the learning organisation**

- OD refers to a set of techniques that practitioners use to reconcile the conflicting interests of people and organisations, both to satisfy human needs and to improve organisational performance. Typical values include treating individuals with respect, a trusting, open and supportive climate, flat rather than hierarchical structures, confronting conflict, and involving those affected by change in implementation.

6 **Illustrate the factors believed to support innovation:**

- Structural – organic form, abundant resources, high communication between units, and work and non-work support;

- Cultural – acceptance of ambiguity, low external controls, tolerance of risks, open systems focus, and positive feedback;

- Human resource policies – high commitment to training and development, high job security, and creative people.

Review questions

1 What does the term 'performance gap' mean, and what is its significance for change?

2 Explain what is meant by the inner context of management, and give examples of attempts to change one or more elements.

3 What are the implications for management of the systemic nature of major change?

4 Review the change that you identified in Activity 13.1 and compare its critical dimensions (Table 13.1) with those at the Royal Bank of Scotland.

5 Can managers alter the receptiveness of an organisation to change? Would doing so be an example of an interaction approach?

6 Outline the life cycle perspective on change and explain when it is most likely to be useful.

7 How does it differ from the 'emergent' perspective?

8 What are the distinctive characteristics of a participative approach, and when is it likely to be least successful?

▶

9 What skills are used by those employing a political model?

10 Is resistance to change necessarily something to be overcome? How would you advise someone to resist a change to which he or she was opposed?

11 What are likely to be the benefits and disadvantages of using an OD approach to a major change project?

12 To what extent does the evidence from Google (Chapter 12) support the innovation theory implied by Figure 13.7?

Concluding critical reflection

Think about the way people handle major change in your company, or one with which you are familiar. Review the material in the chapter, and perhaps visit some of the websites identified. Then make notes on these questions:

- What examples of the themes discussed in this chapter are currently relevant to your company? What performance imperatives are dominant, and to what extent do people see a performance gap? What perspective do people have on the change process – life cycle, emergent, participative or political?

- In implementing change, what **assumptions** about the nature of change in organisations appear to guide the approach? Is one perspective dominant, or do people typically use several methods in combination?

- What factors in the **context** of the company appear to shape your approach to managing change – is your organisation seen as being receptive or non-receptive to change, for example, and what lies behind that?

- Has there been any serious attempt to find **alternative** ways to manage major change in your organisation – for example by comparing your methods systematically with those of other companies, or with the theories set out here?

- Does the approach typically used generally work? If not, do managers recognise the **limitations** of their approach, and question their assumptions?

Further reading

Pettigrew, A.M. and Whipp, R. (1991), *Managing Change for Competitive Success*, Blackwell, Oxford.

Pettigrew, A., Ferlie, E. and McKee, L. (1992), *Shaping Strategic Change*, Sage, London.

Both of these books provide detailed, long-term analyses of major changes – the first in four commercial businesses and the second in several units within the UK National Health Service. The theoretical approach of these works has informed the development of this chapter, emphasising the interaction of change and context. Although the cases are old, they still provide useful empirical insights into the task of managing change.

Lock, D. (2003), *Project Management* (8th edn), Gower, Aldershot.

An excellent source of information on conventional project management techniques.

Buchanan, D. and Badham, R. (1999), *Power, Politics and Organizational Change: Winning the turf game*, Sage, London.

A modern approach to politics in organisations, offering a theoretical and practical guide, based on extensive primary research.

Balogun, J., Gleadle, P., Hailey, V.H. and Willmott, H. (2005), 'Managing change across boundaries: boundary-shaking practices', *British Journal of Management,* vol. 16, no. 4, pp. 261–278.

An empirical study of the practices that change agents used to introduce major boundary-shaking changes in large companies, and how the context shaped their use. Many insights into practice in this valuable research.

Roberto, M.A. and Levesque, L.C. (2005), 'The art of making change initiatives stick', *MIT Sloan Management Review*, vol. 46, no. 4, pp. 53–60.

Another empirical study, this time in a single organisation, of how the context affected the willingness of people to change, and how senior managers needed to create a supportive context.

Weblinks

These websites have appeared in this and other chapters:

www.vodafone.com
www.ericsson.com
ww.gknplc.com
www.sun.com
www.siemens.com
www.ikea.com

Visit two of the business sites in the list, and navigate to the pages dealing with corporate news, investor relations or 'our company'.

● What signs of major changes taking place in the organisation can you find?
● Does the site give you a sense of an organisation that is receptive or non-receptive to change?
● What kind of environment are they likely to be working in, and how may that affect their approach to change?

Annotated weblinks, multiple choice questions and other useful resources can be found on www.pearsoned.co.uk/boddy